THE
INSIDERS'®
GUIDE
TO

Yellowstone

THE INSIDERS' GUIDE® TO

TO

Yellowstone

by
Candace Burns
and
Jo Deurbrouck

Insiders' Publishing Inc.

Co-published by:
Post Register
333 Northgate Mile
Idaho Falls, ID 83401
(208) 522-1800

Published by:
Insiders' Publishing Inc.
105 Budleigh St.
P.O. Box 2057
Manteo, NC 27954
(919) 473-6100
www.insiders.com

Sales and Marketing:
Falcon Distribution Services
P.O. Box 1718
Helena, MT 59624
(800) 582-2665
www.falconguide.com

•

FIRST EDITION
1st printing

•

Copyright ©1998
by The Post Register

•

Printed in the United States
of America

•

Publications from The Insiders' Guide® series are
available at special discounts for bulk purchases
for sales promotions, premiums or fundraisings.
Special editions, including personalized covers,
can be created in large quantities for special
needs. For more information, please write to
Insiders' Publishing Inc., P.O. Box 2057, Manteo,
NC 27954, or call (919) 473-6100 Ext. 241.

ISBN 1-57380-054-6

Post Register

President and Publisher
Jerry Brady

Managing Editor
Dean Miller

Advertising Manager
David Gilchrist

Account Executive
Linda Grant

Insiders' Publishing Inc.

Publisher/Editor-in-Chief
Beth P. Storie

President/General Manager
Michael McOwen

Creative Services Director
Giles MacMillan

Art Director
David Haynes

Managing Editor
Dave McCarter

Project Editor
Eileen Myers

Project Artist
Bart Smith

Preface

Yellowstone. For you, perhaps, the word evokes a picture of bears, Old Faithful and mountains. For those who call this region home, the word conjures a wealth of images almost too chaotic and lovely to hold onto. Yellowstone is the name of a park, but the word also names a region that sprawls out from that park in all directions, encompassing an area the size of Maine. Yellowstone and Grand Teton parks contain only 14 percent of the wild and near-wild lands comprising Greater Yellowstone. The region holds pieces of Montana, Wyoming and Idaho, parts of seven national forests and three wildlife refuges, along with 3.3 million acres of private land. Nearly one-third is protected wilderness.

For many who live here, the 3 million tourists who visit Yellowstone and Grand Teton parks annually make these places anomalous in Greater Yellowstone. This is not a region of crowds and traffic jams. It's a region of wildness. That's why this book doesn't stop at the parks' borders: We want you to know the real Yellowstone country. It's so much more than Yogi Bear.

Scraping its skies are peaks in the Beartooth Mountains, the Gallatins and Madisons, Centennials and Lionheads. Then there are the Tetons, Salt Rivers, Gros Ventre and Wyoming ranges, Wind Rivers and Absarokas. The Grand Teton is the second-highest mountain in Yellowstone country at 13,770 feet, but dozens of peaks soar to more than 12,000 feet. Beneath these peaks are broad swaths of open valley and tight, forested canyons. Waterfalls froth the many rivers, including the Snake, Green and Yellowstone. These rivers' trickling headwaters begin within a few miles of each other on the Yellowstone Plateau, destined for the Pacific and the gulfs of California and Mexico.

Along river valleys are the towns: quiet agricultural communities like Ashton, Idaho, and booming tourist meccas like West Yellowstone, Montana, and Cody and Jackson, Wyoming. There are also the towns caught awkwardly between: neither the backwater mountain villages they were nor yet the tourist-serving communities they're becoming. We even have cities such as Idaho Falls and Billings, where many of the inhabitants have come seeking a balance between the benefits of civilization and the aching loveliness of wild vistas they can almost see from their backyards.

As our communities grow, we find ourselves constantly defining what it means to be Westerners. Part of what tourism in this region does is glorify and revel in the Western myth. We do it in our art, our cuisine, our dress and our architecture.

It's great fun, this pioneer, cowboy and mountain man thing, but it's also serious business: What we glorify, if it ever truly existed, can't last. We caretake the remnants of a larger-than-life time in this nation's history. Surviving, and sometimes thriving, in the shadow of human growth are the wilder inhabitants of this region. Grizzly bears, black bears and wolves, the largest elk herds and trumpeter swan populations in the lower 48, moose and bison and bald eagles. In fact, nearly all of the species that ambled, flew or swam in Greater Yellowstone 300 years ago can still be found here. No place else in the lower 48 can say that.

Mysteriously percolating beneath it all is a sea of magma. Where you live, molten rock is probably more than 90 miles deep; here it's less than 40. In places, bubbles of magma reach to within 4 miles of the ground we walk on. This is what creates the estimated 10,000 thermal features in Yellowstone Park, including its signature steamworks display, Old Faithful. Most geysers are little things that spit and sputter, but six in Yellowstone Park erupt 100 feet or higher on a predictable basis. Old Faithful erupts every 45 to 90 minutes. Steamboat Geyser may not erupt for decades, but when it does it can spew water 380 feet into the air. The rest of Yellowstone's thermal features are steaming pools, hissing fumaroles, bubbling mud pots and warm seeps. Many of these are colored in rainbow hues, courtesy of algae, bacteria and hot-springs mites which have adapted themselves to live where you could not set foot. Yellowstone Park boasts the last relatively intact large geothermal basin in the world not commercially developed — and therefore relatively undamaged — by humans. In winter, the warmth of the thermal basins shelters oases of plant life. Winters in Yellowstone country are harsh. Temperatures can reach 65 below zero, and snow depths of 6 feet or more are common. Yet delicate mosses, grasses and even flowers grow pocketed in the steamy warmth of geyser basins and hot springs.

Come explore. But before you do, consider Yellowstone Lake — a fine metaphor for our hope, as you visit our home, that you'll come to appreciate the complexities and drama of Yellowstone's ecosystem. Clear, sparkly and ringed by lodgepole pine, the largest mountain lake in the lower 48 is lovely to view and to photograph. If that's all you did, you would be enriched. But what if you knew what scientists recently discovered: This 330-foot-deep pool of ice-clear water hides a bubble of molten rock just a mile beneath its floor? What if you knew that myriad underwater geysers and steam vents turn the lake's watery depths into a hell of constant mudslides and temperatures that vary hundreds of degrees within a few yards? What if you knew that tiny creatures have adapted to live in that hell? Or what if you caught a Mackinaw trout out of those clear waters and learned that the fish you're holding has a bounty on its head? Mistakenly planted in these drainages years ago, voracious Mackinaws threaten the survival of native cutthroat trout. Anglers who catch these fish are asked to kill them and bring the heads to the rangers, who are collecting data on Mackinaw colonization of these waters.

We wrote this book because we treasure the Greater Yellowstone region. It's flamboyantly Western and determinedly wild; it's huge and lovely and yet so poorly understood. And to the degree that it's not understood, it's at risk. Look hard, and Yellowstone country's size and grandeur won't disguise from you the fact that it's fragile. Fragile places need to be understood. We wrote because we want you to begin to understand this place; we believe that as you do, you will come to treasure it too. To endure in this shrinking world, fragile places must be treasured. Please, dive deep.

About the Authors

Candace Burns

Candace Burns was raised in Washington, Idaho and Montana, with a brief stop in St. Paul, Minnesota. Ask her where she grew up, though, and she'll say, "Salmon, Idaho," where she has lived and worked for the past 22 years. An award-winning journalist, she has been the central Idaho correspondent to the Idaho Falls *Post-Register* for 10 years. She also has written for *The Christian Science Monitor*, *High Country News* and numerous Northwest publications. She has driven through blizzards, climbed high mountain peaks, tracked wolves, ridden the range and shot the rapids of the Salmon River looking for the people and places that best tell the story of Idaho's wild heart.

Candace currently writes from her home in Salmon. Since moving to town, she has owned and operated a preschool and served as the central Idaho stringer for an Idaho Falls television station. When she can break away from writing deadlines, she works as an assistant midwife.

A single mother for 19 years, Candace has one daughter, Syringa, a dog, a cat and a rambling yard. Now living in an empty nest, she has watched the isolated ranching, logging and mining community grow from a wild frontier town into a bustling but tamer recreation destination. She has a passion for children, gardening, camping, crumbling log cabins, one-room schoolhouses, hiking, backpacking, dancing, exploring and listening to old-timers tell tales of the Old West.

Jo Deurbrouck

Jo's earliest memories are flavored with the tang of pine and sage. Her parents supplied this gift, but with it came a misconception: The family did so much weekend camping, hiking, fishing and rockhounding that their middle child decided the world consisted of glorious wilderness, interrupted — very occasionally — by farms or a town.

In central Washington state 30 years ago, this was an understandable error.

It wasn't until the family drove south and east to their new home in Oklahoma City that the 10-year-old discovered the truth. Inevitably, drawn by mountains and memories, an older Jo began wandering back. She thought she would return to her native Washington. But a decade ago Jo wandered into the Northern Rockies of Idaho, a region where even today her childhood picture seems almost accurate. She doesn't plan to leave.

Jo currently resides in Idaho Falls, on the edge of Greater Yellowstone. She and husband, Barry, ski, kayak, climb and hike some of the loveliest wildlands in the nation, much of it barely a shout from their door. From the sage-covered hilltop behind their old farmhouse Jo can count eight mountain ranges.

Like many Northern Rockies residents, Jo works as a guide. Every summer she pilots raft-loads of curious visitors down Idaho's world-class whitewater rivers. In winter she stokes the woodstove and sits down at the computer to write.

Acknowledgments

Candace Burns

Researching and writing this book was fun — a little like hunting for and then collecting Easter eggs. I couldn't have found them by myself, though. It was the people of Greater Yellowstone — the stranger at the lunch counter next to me, the garrulous motel clerk, the helpful waitress and the busy shop owner — who steered me toward the information that I needed, and more.

Wherever I went by phone or by car, individuals gladly shared their passion for the roles they play in Greater Yellowstone communities. To those often anonymous individuals, I give thanks not only for valuable information but for taking time out from their busy lives to answer endless questions and to share their stories. Included in the long list of those who helped with this book are individuals at Chambers of Commerce throughout Greater Yellowstone. Special thanks go out to Claudia Wade, Paul Hoffman and Kim Wimmler, models of Western hospitality at the Cody Chamber of Commerce. And thanks to Marge McCoy at the Gardiner Chamber of Commerce who never once groaned when she heard, "Hi, Marge, this is Candace Burns," at the other end of the line. Thanks to Viki Eggers at the West Yellowstone Chamber of Commerce for her sense of humor and her well-organized office. And thanks to those at Chambers in Bozeman, Livingston, Red Lodge and Cooke City for their help.

Countless individuals with the National Park Service answered my endless questions. Thanks, especially to Sheryl Matthews and Anita Varley. And thanks to Stephanie Anderson of Amfac Parks and Resorts.

To other authors who have gone before us, I extend my gratitude. Among them are Aubrey Haines, T. Scott Bryan, Mark C. Marschall, George Wuerthner, Seymour L. Fishbein and Lee Whittlesey.

Thanks to Bob Richard of Grub Steak Expeditions for a delightful day touring Grand Teton and Yellowstone parks, and to his wife, Mel, for her easy hospitality.

To Eileen Myers, project editor, thank you for your steady patience and calm approach under pressure from the West and the East.

Special thanks go to coauthor Jo Deurbrouck for her constant sense of humor and her keen ability to zero in on a problem, then dissect, bisect and reassemble it into order. Her writing and insight have been a delight, her determination and enthusiasm an inspiration.

To Dean Miller, my mentor and managing editor of the Idaho Falls *Post Register*, I extend gratitude for nurturing the writer in me and for making me believe that I could write this book — a piece at a time. He said I would cuss him, and I did.

To my parents, Jim Burns and Kinnie Thrall, who taught me at an early age the value of the written word. To my friend Pam Dahle who didn't give up on me when I dropped out of her life for weeks at a time.

To my friend and greatest supporter, Pat Marcuson, I give a special thanks. Pat put me back together when stress scattered me to the winds. He filled my woodbox, helped weed my garden, mowed my lawn and cooked meals while I kept the midnight burning. More than that, he waited patiently for *The Insider's Guide*® *to Greater Yellowstone* to vacate the front seat of my life.

Jo Deurbrouck

Researching this book involved months of bothering busy people with my endless questions. The process taught me that I live in a place where folks give away their stories and their time graciously, simply because a stranger asked. So, although there are far too many to list, I need first to thank all the business people, store clerks, Realtors, bookstore owners, waiters, newspeople, passersby, community leaders, gas station attendants, cowboys, concierges, ranchers and computer programmers of Greater Yellowstone who wanted to help us get this thing right. You people make me proud to say I live here.

Much of what's best in this book came from other authors. The books that taught me the most are included in our Resources section both as a way of saying thanks and because I hope others will also find them useful. Thanks is also owed the many journalists and feature writers whose ideas probably ended up somewhere in here without my even knowing it.

At the risk of overlooking some, special thanks go to Karen Connelly and Jesse O'Connor of the Jackson Hole Chamber of Commerce; to many helpful and informative people at the Wyoming Information Center in Jackson; to the knowledgeable folks at Idaho Falls' Eastern Idaho Visitor Information Center; various members of the Island Park Chamber of Commerce; the vastly helpful Rexburg Chamber of Commerce; Dean Miller of the *Post Register* for being a good coach and a better cheerleader; the *Post Register's* Bill Hathaway for deft advice and feedback; *Post Register* Photo Editor Monte LaOrange for making this book look good; Ed Brashier of Harriman State Park; Jeff Cleeland of the Grand Teton Lodge Company; Rob Van Kirk of the Henry's Fork Foundation; U.S. Forest Service and National Park Service personnel too numerous to name; Marv Hoyt of the Greater Yellowstone Coalition; authors Jerry Painter and Tony Huegel; Jan Phillips of Grand Targhee Ski and Summer Resort; several Insiders' Publishing staff members, including but not limited to editors Dan DeGregory and Eileen Myers; Marilynne Manguba, who passes along useful material; Bob and Arlene Deurbrouck for that whirlwind, weeklong Yellowstone journey; Candace Burns for teaching good lessons without even seeming to try — I'd love to learn those classy ways.

And, in a sentence all to himself, thanks to Barry Rabin for endless support and more kinds of assistance than would fit the allotted space.

Photo Acknowledgment

Many thanks to *Post Register* Photo Editor Monte LaOrange for his tireless pursuit of images to illustrate this book. Working with the paper's resident Yellowstonologist, Robert Bower, and with the paper's other shooters, he came up with a hundred pictures worth a thousand words.

DEAN MILLER
Managing Editor

Maybe you're hoping to hear a wolf howl. City lights have lost their luster and you'd like to rest your eyes on things beautiful and wild for a few days.

There's a lot of country out here. By picking up this book, you've saved yourself hours of digging through libraries, brochures and maps or wandering around looking for that Yellowstone moment.

The Post Register couldn't be more proud of this book, which represents the best of travel writing: educational, up-to-date and a time-saving partner to first-time and repeat visitors. Our authors, both highly competent outdoorswomen, have done the digging for you, criss-crossing the region by car, on foot and on horseback, by snowmobile, bicycle, skis, kayak, snowshoes and canoe.

Coordinating projects like this is our specialty. The Brady family's newspaper has spent more than 100 years chronicling life in and around America's oldest national park and winning awards for journalism on wildlife, recreation and resource issues. This time, we were proud to partner with Insiders' Publishing Inc., the experts in travel information.

So, if you'd like to spend a day or two on horseback, on a snowmobile or on skis, wading a trout stream or rafting through whitewater, you're headed the right direction.

And about that wolf howl: get your imagination going by visiting the Yellowstone section of our Internet homepage at www.idahonews.com. Click on the paw print and close your eyes. You'll get the picture.

Happy trails!

Dean Miller

P.S. We'll be updating this book regularly, so let us hear from you. Drop us a line at Insiders' Publishing Inc., P.O. Box 2057, Manteo, NC 27954. Or visit our web site at www.insiders.com., where you will find a response form on the site.

Table of Contents

Directory of Maps

Greater Yellowstone

Yellowstone National Park

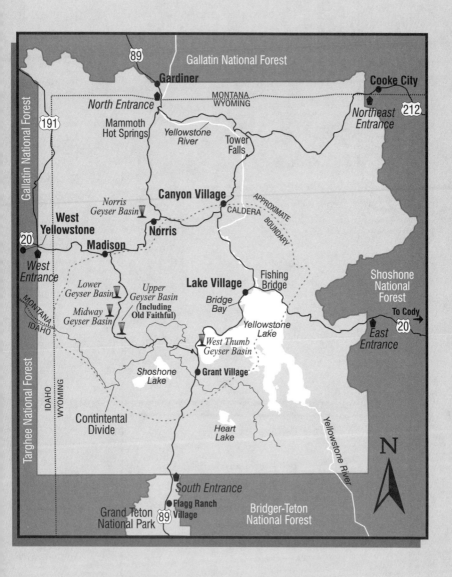

Grand Teton National Park

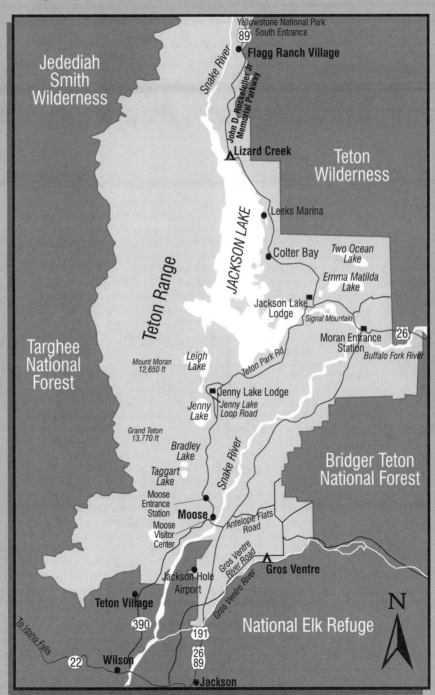

How to Use This Book

Yellowstone National Park is the heart of this book because it's the heart of Greater Yellowstone, a loosely defined area that surrounds the Park. It's a region often defined like a dot-to-dot picture by its perimeter towns: Jackson, Lander, Dubois and Cody, Wyoming; Red Lodge, Livingston, Bozeman and Ennis, Montana; and Island Park, Ashton, Rexburg and Idaho Falls, Idaho. In this book, we have excluded both Lander and Dubois, Wyoming, simply because we had to rein it in somehow.

Inside the Greater Yellowstone outline is an area about the size of Maine. It includes two national parks, parts of three states, seven national forests, 10 counties, three national wildlife refuges and five state parks. In the Area Overview, History and Our Natural World chapters, we tell you about the land and its inhabitants — both wild and civilized. We urge you to read these three chapters first so you know more about us when you arrive. Being better informed can also help you decide which places you'd like to visit. In ambiance and philosophy, Jackson is planets apart from Cooke City, as West Yellowstone is from Cody. Reading these chapters first will add an extra dimension when you start checking out the Nightlife, Restaurants and Shopping chapters, for example.

Although we know most visitors to this region are headed for the national parks and Jackson, we also know there are as many fun things to do and neat places to stay outside the parks as inside them. That's why we've included at least a few sights and accommodations even for towns at the very edge of Greater Yellowstone. So remember, in each chapter we start with the big three: Yellowstone

Park and its entrance communities (West Yellowstone, Gardiner and Cooke City), Grand Teton Park and then Jackson Hole. Then we move to the farthest reaches of Greater Yellowstone and work our way back in, touching the highlights first in eastern Idaho, then in southwestern Montana and last in northwestern Wyoming.

Beneath each geographical heading for the outlying areas, we have listed entries as you approach the national parks and Jackson from the perimeter. Under Eastern Idaho, we start farthest out with the Idaho Falls area, which includes Ririe and Rigby. Moving east and north on U.S. Highway 20, we cover the Rexburg area next, including nearby St. Anthony, then Ashton and Island Park. A second route into Jackson takes you from Idaho Falls east on U.S. Highway 26, with a possible turn onto Idaho Highway 31 and Idaho Highway 33. So after Island Park we cover Swan Valley, which lies along the South Fork of the Snake River (here we include Alpine, Wyoming, technically above Swan Valley), then Teton Valley, which includes the towns of Driggs, Victor and Tetonia, Idaho, and Alta, Wyoming.

Because four different routes lead from the Montana perimeter of Greater Yellowstone into Yellowstone Park, we have listed Southwestern Montana entries in a particular pattern. First we start in Bozeman and follow U.S. Highway 191 through the Gallatin Canyon and past Big Sky to the Park. Next we follow U.S. Highway 89 from Livingston through Emigrant to Gardiner. The third route takes you along U.S. Highway 287 from Ennis to Cameron past Hebgen Lake to West Yellowstone. Finally, we begin at Red Lodge and follow U.S. Highway

212 over the Beartooth Highway to Cooke City. In some chapters, such as Shopping, where there are only a few entries listed under Southwestern Montana, they are arranged alphabetically. In chapters like Campgrounds and RV Parks, Restaurants, and Hotels, Motels and Cabins, entries will be alphabetized by areas within Southwestern Montana.

In Northwestern Wyoming, organizing information is easy, since U.S. Highway 20 is (almost) the only road with services and accommodations leading from Cody into the Park. There is one exception: In the Camping and RV Parks chapter, you'll find a couple of Forest Service campgrounds listed on Wyo. Highway 296, sometimes referred to in this book as the Chief Joseph Highway.

In some chapters we list the geographical areas under special headings. For example, the Annual Events chapter is broken into months. Under each month you'll find events listed in the same order of geographical location. In the Shopping chapter, we have included six kinds of stores. Under each heading, the stores are grouped according to their geographic location. And in Kidstuff, you'll find an A-to-Z list of fun things to see and do geared to the younger set.

Throughout this book we remind you that Greater Yellowstone has three area codes: 307 in Wyoming and all of Grand Teton and Yellowstone national parks, 208 in Idaho and 406 in Montana.

In each chapter, we whisper a few Insider's Tips, and in some chapters we've included Close-ups — stories about people, places, events and animals we think rate closer inspection, such as dude ranches and the Cody Nite Rodeo.

The broad scope of this book means that we're probably the only travel guide you'll need while you explore Greater Yellowstone, whether you're looking for wildlife in a geyser basin in Yellowstone Park or looking for a motel off I-15 in Idaho Falls' spud fields. We're pretty proud of that. We hope you'll take this book to bed with you, carry it in your car, read it on the plane, study it by flashlight in your sleeping bag, mark it and dog-ear it until it resembles a well-used telephone directory. And we hope the information in this book will lead you to a rich and memorable visit to Greater Yellowstone.

We'll be updating this guide annually, and we want to hear from you if we've missed something you think absolutely must be included in this book. Drop us a line at Insiders' Publishing Inc., P.O. Box 2057, Manteo, NC 27954. Or visit *The Insiders' Guide®* to *Greater Yellowstone* at www.insiders.com/yellowstone, where you'll find a comment form on the site.

Yellowstone National
Park came with no
instructions, no rules,
no budget, no official
name and no ideas
about what a national
park should be.

History

In 1997, Yellowstone National Park celebrated 125 years of "the best idea America ever had."

But when Nathaniel P. Langford, the Park's first superintendent, was handed the reins of Yellowstone in 1872, he might well have asked, "What's the big idea?" Like a rare diamond, Yellowstone was cut out of the wilderness to be preserved and protected for the "benefit and enjoyment of the people." The Park came with no instructions, no rules, no budget, no official name and no ideas about what a national park should be. Park officials, politicians and conservationists have been struggling ever since to define and redefine Yellowstone National Park. If history has taught managers one thing, it's that wild land, corralled only by legal boundaries, defies static definition and management.

Take the subterranean world where the fiery innards of the earth bubble and steam, a constant reminder of the intense pressure and subsequent volcanic eruption that created the Yellowstone caldera 600,000 years ago. It's also a constant reminder to Park managers that at any minute it could once again erupt and end their worries forever. Mother Nature offers more subtle dilemmas. Take the Opal Terrace at Mammoth Hot Springs. This gleaming white travertine terrace grows a foot a year. Officials didn't bat an eye in 1947 when it began to take over a tennis court. Today, though, it threatens a historic house designed in 1908 by famous Park architect Robert Reamer. They have bought time by erecting a berm between house and terrace.

While the world seething below ground has confounded managers, above ground the Park has grown bigger than its 2.2 million acres. Once a distant and little-seen place, the Park has in the era of mass media become the very visible political, economic and ecological engine that drives Greater Yellowstone. Elk, bison, wolves and grizzlies, all brought back from the edge of extinction in this region, now spill out of the Park onto national forest and private lands. Elk eat ranchers' hay and range grass outside the Park, while wolves and grizzlies kill livestock. Bison tear down fences and carry brucellosis, a disease that causes cattle to abort. At the same time, elk that leave the Park each fall bring thousands of hunters and millions of dollars to Greater Yellowstone communities in Idaho, Wyoming and Montana. These same communities depend on Park visitors who increasingly come to watch wildlife in the Park. From the outside, development creeps into wildlife habitat, and threatens to interrupt or degrade the ecosystem.

If Yellowstone is the engine that drives Greater Yellowstone, and the sprawling neighbor whose pets roam into others' backyards, it is also an ideological battleground. Some believed this gem's greatest beauty lay in its undisturbed ruggedness. Others saw opportunity swimming in the blue waters of hot springs. In the 1870s and 1880s, railroads and concessionaires fought to build empires in the Park. In the 1920s, irrigators in Wyoming, Montana and Idaho campaigned to raid Yellowstone Park waters with plans to dam the Yellowstone River as well as rivers in the Park's southwestern corner. Philosophical and political camps courted Congress like suitors vying for the hand of a maiden princess. Each time, Park defenders narrowly won the battles.

Yellowstone Park's little neighbor, Grand Teton National Park, is no less a study in the science of ecology married to the realities of politics. Because Teton Park was pieced together, some call it a bastardized version of a national park. Within its boundaries, Grand Teton not only allows livestock grazing, but it also contains dude ranches, a commercial airport and a major highway. It is also the only national park that allows elk hunting. Within the boundary of this 310,000-acre park are 103 private tracts of land. Jackson Lake, the largest in Grand Teton, was dammed in the early 1900s to supply irrigation water to eastern Idaho farmers. In the 1980s the lake was emptied and the dam raised to hold more water. Grand Teton also allows water-skiing and rafting on some of its waters.

Today, Grand Teton is still dealing with issues — often controversial — born of its patchwork past. For example, a proposed expansion of the Jackson Airport, which exists on land leased to the county by Grand Teton Park, more fits the needs of Jackson business people than the best interests of a national park. Even without expansion, noise and traffic at the airport, which existed before the Park was formed, is an intrusion into the Park. Each year that passes, private inholdings become more valuable and less attainable by the Park Service. Development on those properties threatens to mar the Park's landscape.

All but one of the grazing leases extended to leaseholders when Grand Teton Park added valley land to its boundaries in 1950 would have been terminated in 1997. But the leases were extended by the Park superintendent because of open space concerns. Their home ranches and hay lands lie on the edge of Jackson and provide a pastoral landscape uninterrupted by buildings — a vanishing commodity in the midst of rampant development. Without summer range to graze their cattle, the ranch operations would no longer be profitable. If these ranchers sell their land, homes would likely sprout amidst the ranchlands.

While theorists struggled with grand ideas, front-line Yellowstone managers struggled with a paradox: how to impose some kind of civilized order to protect the primitive value of the Park. With no budget and no laws to back them, civilian superintendents were hardpressed. When Army troops brought order in 1886, they paved the way for a whole new set of battles: the fight to protect lands outside the Park from development. They won the first round in 1891 with the formation of the forest reserves. In 1897, they scored more points when the reserves became national forests. In 1864, they won further protection of many forest lands through the Wilderness Act. In January of 1988, the Forest Service announced a moratorium on all logging and road-building across 33 million acres of national forest not at the time protected from commercial activity, saying managers needed a "sort of time out" to assess which lands need to be protected for recreation and which set aside for logging and other uses. But as conservationists march against environmentally unfriendly development on public lands, homes and fences push into Greater Yellowstone's valleys and canyons like chicks tucked under the wings of a mother hen.

Each generation's advances have made their mark of the Park. Consider this: It's possible to sit at a family dinner with some kin who toured the Park on horseback, some who were in the first cars to ply its roads and others who first "visited" the Park via the internet. Changeless as Old Faithful may be, our experience of it has changed rapidly. Earlier in the century, bicyclists and car owners clamored outside the gates for admittance to the Park. In 1915, when automobiles finally drove through Yellowstone Park gates, they carried 51,895 visitors — more than twice as many as the year before. More visitors brought bigger management problems, and the battle to balance public pleasure with wilderness protection — always a dilemma — began in earnest.

With no formula for finding that balance, Yellowstone became a laboratory in which managers learned by trial and error. Officials are still grappling with how best to prevent visitors from loving the wilderness to death. Because it is a rare protected and almost complete ecosystem, the Park has also become a laboratory for learning about wildlife, wildfire, wilderness and ecosystem management.

Finally, Yellowstone is a land of inspiration. Artists have tried to capture it in paintings, sketches and photographs. And writers have filled the pages of more than 8,000 books about it. Studying the multi-hued Grand Canyon at sunset, or gazing at geysers through the foggy mists of winter, inspires awe. Everywhere you turn in the Park is a blessed reminder that this mysterious place is truly wild, uncontrollable and full of surprises.

Our history of Yellowstone Park begins with the white man's first glimpses of this remarkable land. Long before white men penetrated its mountains, though, other humans roamed this land. More than 1,500 archaeological sites tell us humans have passed through Yellowstone country for at least 10,000 years. Those Paleo Indians eventually led to the Native American tribes found in the region by early explorers. By the time Meriwether Lewis and William Clark made their expedition in 1805, the Shoshone-Bannock, the Crow and the Blackfeet tribes inhabited different areas of Greater Yellowstone. In addition, the Nez Perce, Gros Ventre and Arapahoes regularly traveled through it. A band of Shoshone called Sheepeaters were the only Native Americans to call today's Yellowstone Park home — and then only during the summer.

Trappers and Miners and Discovery

Isolated from civilization, and protected naturally by the rugged mountains that ringed it, the Yellowstone Plateau remained pretty much a mystery to Euro-Americans into the 1860s. By then word of its fantastic spouting geysers and fuming hot springs had trickled eastward. But descriptions of the rumbling earth beneath its scorched crust, and the sulphurous gases billowing from below, were received with the same skepticism as modern day reports of UFO sightings.

Word of the mysterious country may first have reached Washington, D.C., in 1805, the same year that Lewis and Clark led their expedition up the Missouri River north of Greater Yellowstone. President Thomas Jefferson received a cryptic note from the governor of the newly purchased Louisiana Territory. It told of a volcano on the "Yellow Stone River." Officially named by Lewis and Clark that same year, the Yellowstone River was apparently first given its moniker by 18th-century French trappers referring to the golden sandstone cliffs of the river's lower course. On Lewis and Clark's return trip in 1806, the Expedition split up and Clark set out to find the headwaters of the Yellowstone River. He never made it. Instead, he crossed through the beaver-rich Gallatin Valley near present-day Bozeman, then over into Trail Creek near Livingston. From there he and his men built canoes and traveled down the Yellowstone to the Missouri River, missing the Mammoth Terraces by only 50 miles.

John Colter, a veteran of the Lewis and Clark Expedition, is credited by many historians as being the first white man to enter Yellowstone. The winter of 1807-08, Colter made an epic 500-mile trip from the Bighorn River to the Shoshone River near present-day Cody, down to the Wind River and west into Jackson Hole. From there, he apparently crossed into Teton Valley, then headed up onto the Yellowstone Plateau and back over what was later named Colter Pass into the Bighorn Basin. A map drawn by Colter in 1808, pinpoints a "Hot Spring Brimstone." But Colter and other trappers who followed were often uneducated and held little influence with anyone other than their fellow mountain men. Later mountain men like Jim Bridger, an accomplished storyteller (with little else to do, spinning yarns became an art around trapper campfires), probably didn't help the Yellowstone cause any. Bridger had a penchant for fantastic embellishment.

If folks back east weren't heeding stories about eerie geysers, they did listen closely to tales of a country crawling with beaver. By the 1820s, large brigades of trappers had worked their way into Yellowstone country. In 1818, a brigade led by Donald MacKenzie found its way to the headwaters of the Snake River. In 1822, William Ashley, who popularized the mountain man rendezvous, led 100 men west. After wintering at the mouth of the Yellowstone River, many of them headed south through the Bighorn Basin, then into Jackson Hole. Among Ashley's men were notables like Bridger, Jedediah Smith, Thomas Fitzpatrick, William Sublette and David Jackson, who wintered in "the Hole." From then on it was called Jackson's Hole.

Canadian, American and English fur trading companies vied with one another for beaver pelts made precious by European hat fashions. Competition among trappers was fierce, so fierce that some vowed to trap areas into "deserts," leaving no beaver for their competitors. Far from fashionable themselves, the trappers sought mostly adventure and a bit of money. The pelts were worth as much as $6 apiece. But the price of adventure was higher. Living by their wits, they fought the elements and unfriendly Indians. To improve their odds of survival, they traveled in groups, often bringing along Indian wives, children, friends and relatives. It's no wonder they looked forward each year to the rendezvous, which began in 1825. At this annual event all of the mountain men and Indians gathered with their pelts at a prearranged spot where they traded their furs for another year's supplies. For a week or more mountain men and Native Americans celebrated. They drank, caroused, feasted, swapped stories and ran horse races.

The gatherings, held on the Green River and in Pierre's Hole (present-day Driggs, Idaho), weren't always peaceful. One year, 200 mountain men joined with 200 lodges of Nez Perce, Flathead, Shoshone and Bannock Indians in Pierre's Hole. While they were waiting for the supply train to arrive, a band of Blackfeet rode into camp. A battle, triggered by old quarrels, ensued. Twenty-three men were killed during the fight.

While towns, mountains, wildernesses and rivers have been named after these early trappers, it may be Osborne Russell who left behind the greatest legacy. A farm boy from Maine, Russell was one of the few literate trappers. His journals, published as *Journals of a Trapper*, in 1955, describe the country and give rare insights into a trapper's life from 1834 to 1843. Russell came to Yellowstone country with the Columbia River Fishing and Trading Company led by Nathaniel Wyeth. Wyeth, a Boston ice merchant, led 40 men with freighting goods to a rendezvous on Ham's Fork of the Green River. When he arrived, he found another supplier had beaten him there. Stuck with wagons full of unmarketable goods, Wyeth continued on and established Fort Hall, site of the Shoshone-Bannock Indian Reservation south of Blackfoot, Idaho.

About the time beaver were disappearing, wagonloads of settlers took up their epic migration along the Oregon Trail to the south. The discovery of gold in California brought even more people, who eventually fanned out into Washington, Idaho and Montana. Looking for their own motherlode, they scoured the streams of the Rockies. Here and there prospectors hit pay dirt outside the present-day Park. To the north in Virginia City, Montana, miners found gold — lots of it — in 1863. Three years later, they found another strike to the west at Leesburg, Idaho. In 1870, two years before Yellowstone would become the nation's first national park, Bart Henderson and four partners staked their claims to a strike in Cooke City.

Providence protected the heart of Yellowstone country from gold discoveries. Like trapping brigades hunting beaver, disillusioned miners came from the California and Colorado gold fields. Southerners and Easterners came to escape economic depression and the aftermath of the Civil War. A few penetrated the mountains that surrounded the Yellowstone Plateau. Walter DeLacy and his 41-man prospecting party followed the Snake River from Jackson hole, searching for gold at the river's headwaters. They found only steaming holes, yawning river canyons and thundering waterfalls. Disappointed, they moved on.

Some folks gave up looking for gold and found a way to earn a living by supplying miners with food, firewood, lumber and other necessities. A few ranched and raised beef or raised garden produce. Others milked cows and supplied dairy products. Still others did laundry or ran hotels, saloons and stores. In 1868, the Bottler Brothers took up the first homestead in the Yellowstone Valley across from a small strike at Emigrant Gulch. To the west of the Park at Henrys Lake, Gilman Sawtelle established a ranch at Staley's Springs. Distance seemed to be no object. He made a booming business of spearing trout from the lake, packing them in ice then hauling them by wagon over Raynolds Pass to Virginia City where he sold them to miners. A handful of men built toll bridges, like the one built in 1870 by Collins Baronett across the Yellowstone River near Lamar Junction. Baronett charged Cooke City miners $1 per man or mule to cross his bridge. To the west, Matt Taylor built a toll bridge across the Snake River at Eagle Rock (present-day Idaho Falls) in 1863. Much later, in 1894, Bill Menor built a ferry crossing on the Snake River near Moose in Jackson Hole. For those who wanted to stay, there were plenty of ways to eke out a living.

The track of the Oregon Short Line (Union Pacific) reached Yellowstone Park's western gateway in 1908 and brought visitors to the Park for 60 years.

The Explorers

Inch by inch, word of Yellowstone crawled eastward across the plains and rivers. And one by one, exploratory expeditions turned back before they had reached the plateau. The U.S. Corps of Topographical Engineers failed in two attempts during the 1850s. Capt. William F. Raynolds of the corps traveled the southern and western outskirts of today's Yellowstone Park in 1859, looking for a route over the rugged mountains. By the time he reached today's Targhee Pass, inclement weather and a tight schedule forced Raynolds to forego the exploration and instead head north to the Three Forks of the Missouri River. In 1865, Father Francis Kuppens trekked into Yellowstone with a band of Piegan Indians. Impressed with the country, he told Acting Territorial Governor Thomas Meagher about it in such glowing terms that he organized an expedition in 1867. But Meagher drowned at Mammoth Hot Springs and the expedition was abandoned.

The heart of Yellowstone seemed to defy discovery until 1869, when David E. Folsom, Charles W. Cook and William Peterson headed out from Bozeman on July 12. After crossing into the Yellowstone Valley, they followed the river to present-day Tower Junction where they forded the Yellowstone River. They explored the Grand Canyon and the Falls, Yellowstone Lake and West Thumb, and the "Valley of Death," as they called the geyser basins along the Firehole River.

That winter, Folsom worked in Helena for Henry D. Washburn, surveyor general for the Montana Territory. Intrigued by Folsom's stories, Washburn was itching to explore the fantastic country the next summer. Under military escort, he and a collection of men left Bozeman and followed Folsom's trail. Nathaniel Langford, a newly appointed agent for Jay Cooke of the Northern Pacific Railroad, was among the party. History suggests that it was Langford who promoted the expedition. Cooke, curious to know more about Yellowstone country, may even have helped finance it. The party's troubles began after they scouted the landscape from the top of present-day Mt. Washburn, then chose to follow the east side of Yellowstone Lake. They ran into tree thickets, bogs, uncrossable rivers and unstable ground before stumbling onto Old Faithful just as it was erupting. Along the way, they had literally lost one of their party, Truman C. Everts. Everts, whom his rescuers at first mistook for a wounded bear, was found crawling up a hillside 27 days after his disappearance. His diet of thistle roots had reduced him to a skeletal shadow. The balls of his frostbitten feet were worn to the bone, and he had burned his thigh in a hot spring.

The story of the Washburn expedition swept through newspapers across the country, but it was Langford who, through a series of lectures in the East, stirred up real interest in Yellowstone. Ferdinand V. Hayden, head of the U.S. Geological Survey of the Territories, was the next explorer to catch Yellowstone fever. Hayden pulled enough Congressional strings to secure $40,000 for a full-blown expedition that included topographers, scientists, artists Thomas Moran and Henry Elliott and photographer William H. Jackson. (Moran's colorful watercolors and Jackson's collection of more than 400 photographs helped sway congressional minds when it came to a vote for the first national park.)

Traveling by train on the Central Pacific and Union Pacific railroads in mid-May of 1871, Hayden set up a rendezvous camp in Ogden, Utah. On June 11, the party rode north to Fort Hall, then on to Bozeman where they were joined at the last minute by another expedition led by Capt. John W. Barlow of the Army Corps of Engineers. The two parties spent just over a month in what is now Yellowstone Park.

No one is certain who first suggested the idea of a national park. Legend has it that the idea was first voiced among the Washburn party while camped near what is now Madison Junction. It is clear that it was Hayden who first publicly pressed for a national park that would preserve a piece of the frontier for everyone. When Hayden returned to his Washington, D.C., of-

Yellowstone Fires of 1988

Talk to residents in communities surrounding Yellowstone Park and many of them still smolder at the mention of the fires of 1988. Fueled by nearly 200 years worth of dead and fallen trees and fanned by high winds, there was no stopping the fires that stormed like an angry army across Yellowstone Park. Thousands of people and countless planes, helicopters, bulldozers and tanker trucks tried. The federal government spent $120 million in the attempt. Despite those efforts, 13 major fires and countless smaller ones burned 1.4 million acres in Yellowstone Park and adjacent Forest Service lands from mid-June until mid-October. One million of those acres were within the Park. In the end it was Mother Nature herself who put out the fires she had mostly started with lightning strikes. Snowfall finally doused the flames firefighters had vainly battled all summer.

While three of the fires were caused by humans, the rest were started by lightning. What caught everyone by surprise is the fact that a fire of any kind would normally never find enough dry fuel to burn into a fire of dangerous size. From 1972 until 1988, 235 naturally caused fires occurred in the Park. With no attempts to suppress them, they charred an average of only 240 acres each. Until 1988, the largest fire in the Park had been 18,000 acres. The largest fire since 1972, when a let-burn policy was instituted in the Park, had been 7,600 acres. Buried each winter under an average of 4 feet of snow that melt slowly with the coming of warm weather, the Park is usually too wet to burn in summer. Rains supplement the melting snow.

In their wake, the blazes left much of the Park's forest lands denuded and its meadows charred. All around was devastation, yet when spring came Mother Nature showed her amazing powers of regeneration. Amidst the blackened logs that littered the landscape, bright green spears of grass poked up through the ground. Wildflowers followed. As people watched for other signs of hope, they weren't disappointed. Tiny lodgepole seedlings sprouted by the gazillions. Without the fire the seeds would have stayed locked up inside the cones, unable to sprout. Lodgepole cones need the heat

— continued on next page

of fire to make them open so that the seeds can do their job. At the same time fire was opening the cones, it was also sweeping away all the clutter on the ground, creating an open space where the seedlings like to grow.

Subalpine fir had grown up underneath the towering lodgepoles, creating an understory too shady for lodgepole seedling growth. The firs, though, made perfect fuel for the fire. Flames climbed them as if they were tinder-dry matches. When the fire "crowned" in their tops, burning embers blew ahead of the fire, landed in forests sometimes more than a mile away and started new fires. As the lodgepoles grow and rub branches, the lower ones will self-prune so that future fires can't climb up their trunks.

In the meantime, the former forest lands, now opened to light, are providing more feed for rodents, birds and larger mammals. Since the fires of '88, there have been other interesting surprises. For example, aspen groves, which normally regenerate from underground suckers,

A firefighter sprays down the roof of the Old Faithful Inn.

sprouted by the trillions. They also sprouted from seeds. During the fires people feared wildlife populations would be devastated. But a post-fire count turned up only about 350 animals burned by fire. That winter, though, about 8,000 elk died, not so much because their winter forage was burned, but because the drought had prevented its growth.

Ten years after the devastating fires, scientists are still watching the Park to learn more about fire and its role in the ecosystem. It has become a laboratory for watching natural processes at work. As they struggle with the adverse effects of 100 years of fire suppression in national forests throughout the Rockies, they hope that Yellowstone's story will give them clues about how to handle fire outside the Park.

---

fice, he found a letter from Jay Cooke encouraging him to recommend to Congress that Yellowstone be declared a public park. Cooke foresaw Yellowstone as a tourist destination that would attract visitors from around the world. Their vehicle would be his train. Armed with Moran's colorful paintings and the best of Jackson's photographs, Hayden had no trouble pushing the Park through Congress. On March 1, 1872, President Ulysses S. Grant signed the as-yet-unnamed park into being.

Railroads

Full of wonders so incredible that newspapermen refused to publish early accounts of it for fear of being called liars, Yellowstone be-

came a magnet for explorers and exploiters alike. From the north, east, south and west, railroads raced to lay their tracks to Yellowstone's boundaries — inside them if they could. First came the Northern Pacific.

Delayed for a decade by an economic depression, it was 1882 before sweaty crews pounded the last spike in the rails that led to Livingston, Montana. Besides being a teeming support town for Northern Pacific's cross-country railroad, Livingston became the gateway to Yellowstone National Park. From that budding railroad town, the tracks turned south and stopped 3 miles short of the Park boundary at Cinnabar. A cantankerous miner, who refused to relinquish claims blocking the railroad's path, prevented it from going all the way to Gardiner.

Finally, in 1903 the Northern Pacific rolled into Gardiner. That same year, President Teddy Roosevelt dedicated the monumental 50-foot-high Roosevelt Arch at Gardiner's Park entrance.

While the tracks stopped at the Park's boundary, the railroad's power did not. Well-connected to Washington, D.C., officials of the Northern Pacific had enough political clout to seat and unseat Park superintendents like Langford and Philetus W. Norris. But they couldn't accomplish their greatest desire: to ram those railroad tracks right through the Park. For more than a decade, Northern Pacific officials fought, fussed and finagled to get the job done, but Yellowstone Park supporters like Sen. George Graham Vest of Missouri blocked their path. The congressional battle over the rails was costly. It prevented other Park bills from passing — bills that would have granted more money and better management to the Park.

While the Northern Pacific fought Park supporters in one arena, in another the railroad was one of the Park's greatest allies. The Northern Pacific and later railroads advertised the scenic wonders and brought America to its first national park. Those who came fell in love with Yellowstone and returned home among its growing throng of supporters.

Until 1901, when the Burlington Northern reached Cody at the East Entrance, and 1908 when the Oregon Short Line pulled into West Yellowstone, the Northern Pacific hauled almost all tourists who came from the east. Prior to the Oregon Short Line, those who came from the south had to ride the Union Pacific to Corinne, Utah, then travel a long, bumpy road by stage-coach to Bozeman or Virginia City, Montana.

From there, they traveled over the wagon road used by Sawtelle at Henrys Lake. In 1927, well after rail travel had declined, the Chicago, Milwaukee and St. Paul Railroad built a 40-mile line to Gallatin Gateway, where it erected the huge and very grand Gallatin Gateway Inn. (See both our Restaurants and Hotels, Motels and Cabins chapters for more information on this restored inn.) The Chicago and Northwestern Railroad served Lander, Wyoming, 150 miles southeast of Yellowstone Park, after the advent of the automobile. From Lander, tour buses took visitors to the Tetons and to Yellowstone Park.

The affordable Ford, carrying families, tents and supplies, eventually put a dent in railroad profits — so much so that by World War II some began to call it quits. The Oregon Short Line held on until 1959.

Taking Care of Tourists in the Wilderness

By the time the Northern Pacific reached Cinnabar, the National Hotel at Mammoth was unfinished but ready to receive guests. As the Park's road system grew under the supervision of the Army Corps of Engineers, the Northern Pacific began to sell its customers a "coupon" package for touring the Park. While in the Park, coupon holders could stay at hotels and ride on stages owned by concessionaires that were Northern Pacific affiliates. After a night at the National Hotel, they would pile into a caravan of four-horse, 11-passenger stagecoaches spaced 500 feet apart to help reduce the dust. Packed into the stagecoaches for the day, passengers were at

Jackson may have been the first and the only town in the nation to have an all-woman government. It included a sheriff, the town clerk and the town's health officer. When Mayor Grace Miller and her four-woman council took over in 1920, they found the city coffers held only $200. Careful examination of the books showed overdue taxes and fines. The first night of their administration, they sent out notices to delinquent citizens then followed up with door-to-door visits. Within two weeks, they had collected $2,000, which they immediately applied to community improvements. They upgraded the town water ditch, installed culverts at ditch crossings, cleaned up the town, established an official dump site, beautified the cemetery and built a road to it.

the mercy of the drivers, most of whom were creative cussers as well as inveterate storytellers. A few were drunks to boot. The stagecoach rides were not only bumpy, dusty and crowded, but also dangerous, with frequent runaways, occasional wrecks and at least four holdups.

If you happen to be staying overnight in a Park hotel or cabin, take a look around. Compared to some of the accommodations early visitors endured, your room is not as primitive as you might think. Until 1891 when the modern Fountain Hotel was built, tourists spent the first night at the Firehole Hotel where the tiny rooms held two beds and had canvas walls. At other places visitors slept like sardines on the plank floors of primitive hotels with broken windows. The Fountain, on the other hand, slept 350 guests, had steam heat and electric lights and used hot spring water for baths. The Lake and Canyon hotels, two other lavishly grand hotels built from 1889 to 1891, were also regular stops. The Canyon, which measured a mile around its base, burned in 1959. Old Faithful, the queen of Park hotels with its giant Douglas fir and rock construction, didn't rise from the wilderness floor until 1903. For six glorious days, couponers explored, gawked, dined, danced and bumped through the wilderness before returning to Mammoth and then the train terminal.

In addition to the geysers, there was another attraction. By the 1880s, bears had come out of the forest to feed at hotel dumps. Each evening, spectators gathered on benches to watch as hotel keepers fed them garbage. A mounted ranger gave lectures to the crowds while the bears ate garbage. All but one of the hotel shows stopped in the 1920s after a big black bear chased a little black bear through the rickety wire fence and into the grandstand.

In 1893, William Wallace Wylie, a school superintendent from Bozeman, was granted a two-year permit to operate tent camps in Yellowstone Park. The candy-striped tents, Wylie's hallmark, were staffed by enthusiastic young college students and teachers. The hotels, on the other hand, were staffed by gruff, rough, rude employees openly hostile to guests. Neat as a pin, Wylie's camps had sleeping tents clustered around huge kitchen, dining and reception tents. Abhorred by other concessionaires, Wylie offered a seven-day tour for $35, while the Yellowstone Park Association charged $50 for six days. His employees also interpreted Park features and held evening campfires, the predecessors of today's ranger-naturalist campfire programs. Another group of travelers, contemptuously called "sagebrushers," came from neighboring states in their own horse-drawn wagons and bypassed hotels and tent camps altogether. They came equipped with everything they needed to camp out.

Order in the Park

From 1872 to 1886, civilian superintendents struggled to maintain order with no budget or laws to back them. Poachers blatantly killed elk by the thousands, while would-be concessionaires squatted at major attractions. Visitors hacked away at geysers and hauled the pieces home in satchels. They carted off whole petrified trees and skinny-dipped in hot springs. They stuffed geysers with logs, rocks, handkerchiefs, clothes, everything — then sat back and watched them blow. Why wouldn't they? There was nobody there to tell them otherwise. Nathaniel Langford, who was superintendent from 1872 until 1877, made three quick trips to the Park and wrote one report during his tenure.

His successor, Philetus W. Norris, served until 1882. An energetic pioneer-scientist, he managed to get enough money from Congress to build the Norris Road to the geyser basins. He also collected crates of geological and biological specimens, which he shipped to the Smithsonian. Three more civilians served from 1882 until 1886, but apathy and avarice combined to create lawlessness so scandalous that Congress refused to fund the Park in 1886. Fortunately, two years earlier Sen. George Graham Vest of Missouri had won passage of the Civil Sundry Appropriations Bill, which allowed the Secretary of the Interior to request military assistance in protecting the Park.

The military's presence brought almost immediate order to the Park. Even without the enforcement provisions of the Lacey Act of 1894, the soldiers doggedly pursued poachers using secret telegraph codes and informers to catch up with them. By the 1890s they operated from a network of 19 outposts supplemented with 15 snowshoe cabins for winter patrols. Prior to the Lacey Act, all soldiers could do was confiscate a poacher's possessions and evict him from the

Park, which they did with relish. They also found ways to keep poachers in the guardhouse for weeks or months. The Lacey Act, promoted by an outdoor journalist who witnessed the capture of a notorious bison poacher, made it a federal offense to break Park laws. It called for stiff fines and lengthy imprisonment for serious violations.

In 1916, when the National Park Service was established, Gardiner residents pulled enough political strings to keep the 450-soldier post at Mammoth for two more years. The much smaller 50-ranger staff couldn't compensate for the loss of that many soldiers. Since alcohol wasn't allowed at Fort Yellowstone, soldiers trekked 5 miles to Gardiner to tie one on. There they also found brothels and venereal disease.

When the Park Service finally took over, many of the soldiers, selected for their woodsmanship and their sense of pride in the Park, became rangers. By the 1930s, there were about 71 rangers. Twenty-nine of them worked year-round, while the rest were seasonals with a long list of summer duties similar to those of today. They checked cars at the entrance gates, patrolled popular areas on foot or horseback and highways by motorcycle, they fought forest fires, investigated accidents, administered first aid, took care of problem bears, checked campgrounds and did paperwork. During the off-season, full-time rangers caught up on maintenance, worked the buffalo herd, put up hay for horses, bison and elk, patrolled the Park's perimeter and killed predators like the wolf and coyote. In winter, they manned outposts and patrolled the Park on skis.

Horace Albright, Park superintendent from 1919 to 1929 (a period when visitation jumped from 62,000 to 260,000), cracked down on lawbreakers including bootleggers and speeders. He also began an official interpretive branch of rangers. And he built a strong alliance with concessionaires who, he said, provided the services that the Park's poor funding could not. The relationship between the Park and concessionaires was one of mutual dependence. As long as the concessionaires paid their 4 percent to the Park, Albright didn't care how much they made.

The Car Paves the Way for Millions

Car owners honked their horns at Park gates for four years before getting the green light. In 1915, when the gates opened, more than 50,000 mostly middle-class Americans flooded into Yellowstone Park. Unlike the upper class who had ridden the rails in style with trunks full of clothes for dinner and dancing, these working people loaded their aunts, uncles, brothers, cousins and children into Fords and packed for fun. They strapped tents, washtubs, pots, pans, chairs and bedding to their cars, tucked a few extra tires and some gasoline into the trunk, and headed west on the Yellowstone Highway. In 1911, just one year after Henry Ford put motorized wheels under America's appetite for adventure, a "pathfinder crew" from the Minnesota Automobile Association scouted out a practical route from St. Paul to Bozeman. Pieced together with two-rut rural and county roads, the road roughly followed today's Interstates 90 and 94. Plate-sized orange circles painted on rocks, barns, logs and fenceposts marked the route. That same year, another crew blazed a route from Yellowstone to Glacier National Park in northern Montana.

Inside the Park, stagecoach drivers and transportation concessionaires cussed the coughing, sputtering, lurching contraptions, saying they'd not only scare the horses but they'd also be the ruination of Yellowstone. Transportation through the Park was big business for three companies: the Yellowstone and Monida of West

---

INSIDERS' TIP

Western novelist Owen Wister, author of *The Virginian*, first came to Jackson Hole in 1887 as a big-game hunter and returned for years after that. Many of his characters are said to have been fashioned after Jackson Hole oldtimers.

Yellowstone, the Cody-Sylvan Pass Stagecoach Company of Pahaska Tepee and The Yellowstone Transportation Company out of Gardiner. Together they owned three six-horse, 29-passenger Concords or "Tally-hos"; 165 four-horse 10-passenger Concords; 79 two-horse surreys; 14 formation wagons; 129 mountain spring wagons; and 1,372 horses. Besides a crew of colorful stagecoach drivers, the companies employed herd tenders, blacksmiths, wagon painters and washers, and freighters to haul hay and grain for the horses. Each company's fleet of stagecoaches was identified by a different color: red, brown and yellow.

Cars not only drove all the horses and stagecoaches off Park roads, but they also forced the restructuring of Yellowstone concessionaires. In the fall of 1916, National Park Service Director Stephen T. Mather called the concessionaires to Washington, D.C. The reorganization forced concessionaires to make major investments just when World War I was keeping Americans closer to home. The Yellowstone Park Transportation Company, suddenly designated as the sole Park transportation concessionaire, had to spend $427,000 to buy 116 motor buses. Frank J. Haynes, owner of several hotels and other businesses, had to sell them all and become the photographic concessionaire. The Yellowstone Park Hotel Company became the sole hotel concessionaire, while Wylie Permanent Camps merged with Shaw and Powell. Because cars could carry visitors much farther in a day, several of the motels, tent camps and lunch stations were torn down.

Concessionaires

Let's take a minute to talk about concessionaires. While they reaped big benefits as co-conductors of the region's economic engine, national events more than once took the steam from their smokestacks. From 1900 to 1929, concessionaire profits were high — in some cases outrageously high. But the intermission between the Great Depression and the lean years of World War II wasn't long enough to offset losses. Gas and tire rationing, combined with the scar-

city of men, dried visitor numbers to a trickle. In 1943, only 64,000 visitors toured the Park, the lowest number since 1919, and down from 561,000 in 1941.

Concessionaires boarded up their facilities and left them to weather the harsh elements of Yellowstone during the war years. Already crying for repairs and upgrades before the war, they were fairly screaming for attention by 1946 when 815,000 war-weary Americans swarmed into the Park. The Park's chief concessionaire, The Yellowstone Park Company, wasn't prepared and the owners, strapped for cash, were reluctant to spend money on improvements. Complaints filtered into congressional offices, newspapers and public meetings about the poor service, bad food, wretched housing and overpriced accommodations in the Park. Wyoming state officials were so concerned about the deplorable state of the region's economic engine that in 1955 they made a bid to buy out the Park's chief concessionaire.

Operating in a crisis mode, the National Park Service set out to deal with its biggest dilemma since the creation of Yellowstone Park — the rising flood of humanity. In 1955, the Park Service outlined a 10-year plan for updating Park facilities and called it Mission 66. Roads, restrooms, campgrounds and vandalism threatened to crumble under the strain of the increased use. The Park and concessionaires would share the cost of construction and renovations to concession facilities. A period of growth and construction followed. Power and telephone lines were updated, and an FM radio communication system was installed. Permanent and seasonal housing was improved and expanded for the growing staff. And a grade school and clinic were built at Mammoth.

Meanwhile, the Yellowstone Park Company searched desperately for a buyer. In 1966 they found one: a conglomerate calling itself General Host. Concession facilities and service spiraled downward for the next decade. In fact, conditions at Park hotels and restaurants owned by General Host were so wretched and drew so many complaints that in 1976 the Interior Department began an indepth study of the Park's concessions. The results prompted the government to cancel

Greater Yellowstone Benchmarks

Research by Teri Anderson of the Idaho Falls Post Register

1807 — John Colter explores the area that will eventually become Yellowstone National Park.

1852 — Jim Bridger's *Tall Tales* is published for the first time. He was in the area in the 1830s.

1869 — Cook-Folsom-Peterson Expedition of 1869 enters the Park, seeing geysers and hot pools. The three men return to Montana territory with tales that many doubted.

1870 — Gen. Henry Washburn and Nathaniel Langford, who later became the first superintendent of the Park, are among the members of the official exploration party.

1870 — Old Faithful is discovered and named.

March 1, 1872 — President Ulysses S. Grant signs National Park Act, which creates Yellowstone National Park. It is the first national park in the world.

1877 — The Nez Perce Indians, led by Chief Joseph, pass through Yellowstone during a retreat after they were routed in a series of summer battles, losing 300. The retreat is later hailed as a masterful military move.

1883 — Chester A. Arthur becomes first U.S. President to visit the Park.

1886 — The U.S. Army takes over the Park's administration.

1888 — Excelsior Geyser, which erupted up to 300 feet in height, ceases major eruptions.

1894 — Lacey Act is passed to "protect the birds and animals in Yellowstone National Park, and to punish crimes in said park." The act led to the end of hunting, with heavy penalties for poaching game in Yellowstone.

1900 — About 9,000 people visit the Park this year.

1901 to 1953 — The world's largest trout hatchery operates on the shores of Yellowstone Lake.

1902 — Park officials count only 22 bison.

1903 — President Theodore Roosevelt dedicates the Roosevelt Arch on Aug. 24.

Close-up

1904 — Old Faithful Inn, the world's largest log hostelry, opens.

1907 — The first recorded attack by grizzly bear in Yellowstone occurs when a visitor chases a cub up a tree.

1915 — First automobiles are officially allowed to enter Yellowstone.

1915 — Charles Hamilton acquires Klamer's Store.

1916 — President Woodrow Wilson signs Act of Congress on Aug. 25 creating the National Park Service as a bureau of the Department of the Interior. Shortly thereafter, civilian superintendents are appointed, replacing the Park's military overseers.

1932 — Pelican control practices come to a halt in the Park. Hundreds of eggs were removed, and scores of young pelicans are killed between 1924 and 1932.

1934 — National Park Service completes the Park's Golden Gate Bridge.

1941 — Park officials end feeding shows. The shows, during which the bears were fed garbage, began as a way to entertain visitors during the days when the Army controlled the Park.

*1946 — Park officials feed hay to bison for the last time.

1948 — More than 1 million visitors come to the Park for the first time.

— continued on next page

Photo: Courtesy Robert Bower

This 1910 Haynes postcard shows Park visitors watching bears as hotel employees dump the day's garbage. At one time, bleachers were even built for viewing. Park dumps were closed during the 1960s, and bears had a difficult time, resulting in conflicts among bears as they sought food elsewhere.

1950 — Park officials remove debris from Morning Glory Pool. Among the debris is $90 in coins, towels and clothes and 100 handkerchiefs.

1958 — Lake hatchery is closed. Stocking is stopped.

1959 — Earthquake causes considerable damage, including a rock slide at Golden Gate Bridge. The quake's epicenter is at Hebgen Lake, Montana.

1959 — Canyon Hotel closes.

1965 — For the first time, the number of Park visitors exceeds 2 million.

1988 — Fires sweep the Park.

1997 — Yellowstone turns 125 with an average of 30,000 to 40,000 visitors each day of the summer.

General Host's franchise in 1979. Despite the fact that the company failed to invest $10 million in its facilities, General Host sold its holdings to the U.S. government for $19 million — a profit of nearly $13 million.

Trans World Corporation took over the company and operated as TWA Services on a two-year trial basis. The company did such a good job that it was granted a 30-year lease. In the 1980s, a 10-year restoration project brought the Lake Hotel back to life. And new accommodations, including a lodge at Grant Village, were built. Today, Amfac Parks and Resorts owns those concessions.

Wildlife, Wildfire and Wilderness Management Changes Definition

At the same time that Park managers grappled with ways to manage millions of visitors more closely, they began to realize that less management was in order for the wild pieces of Yellowstone. In 1958, they quit stocking the Park's lakes and streams with fish. Since 1890, folks in federal fisheries agencies had stocked lakes with exotic fish while robbing native spawning beds to stock other streams across the country. In the 1970s, state managers outside the Park followed the new trend toward natural fisheries. They also popularized and instituted catch-and-release fishing. Park managers today are committed to the animals that feed on fish — their needs come before those of visiting anglers.

Bear management also changed. By 1941, when the Park officials ended the last of the organized feeding shows, the bears had become more than a nuisance. They hung out on roads and held visitors up for tidbits of food. They lurked around campgrounds, broke into kitchens and tore apart cars looking for food. Like spoiled children with a big bite, they were quick to express their displeasure with uncooperative visitors. While feeding shows were officially stopped, visitors who knew where and when to look could find Park dumps crawling with black bears and grizzlies.

Finally, in the 1960s, rangers figured out how to get rid of the visitors' favorite attraction. They cleaned up and closed the dumps. They removed and relocated the most aggressive bears and shooed the rest off to fend for themselves in the wild. For decades, critics showered Park managers with acrimony. But, the bears not only survived, they thrived. Now managers grapple with ways to keep humans from bothering bears.

Elk, killed by the thousands each winter when poachers ruled Yellowstone, quickly multiplied under Park protection. In the 1950s studies determined that the Park's northern range could support 5,000 elk without being overgrazed. Today about 18,000 graze the same range, and overgrazing debates rage among managers. Without natural predators, managers have been hard-pressed to find socially acceptable ways of checking the herd's growth. They've trapped and relocated more than 5,000, shot nearly 9,000 and used hunting seasons outside Park boundaries to try to control the rest. None of the methods is popular.

In the 1940s, bison, which now number about 2,200, were released from their display pens, weaned from their winter ration of supplemental hay and turned loose to roam in the Park. At the turn of the century, bison numbers had dwindled to an alarming 25. Managers rounded them up, brought in breeding stock and began raising buffalo like cattle. Park employees raised hay in the Lamar Valley and fed it to the bison. They castrated all but a few of the males and kept some of the craggy creatures penned for display.

These days you'll see bison wandering at will. In winter, especially severe winters, they migrate out of the Park. Because they carry brucellosis, a venereal disease that causes cattle to abort, Montana passed a law in 1995 that allows the State Department of Livestock to capture and slaughter buffalo that leave the Park. During the winter of 1995-96, 433 bison were destroyed. The following winter more than 1,000 were killed outside the Park. Another estimated 500 died during that exceptionally severe winter. The bison wars aren't likely to subside soon.

The same year that Montanans began shooting stray buffalo, the U.S. Fish and Wildlife Service put wolves back into the ecosystem. They hope the predators, which numbered about 100 in the fall of 1997, will multiply enough to keep elk and bison numbers pared. Ranchers, who fought wolf reintroduction with a vengeance, aren't so anxious for their recovery. Wolves were exterminated early in the century by Park man-

INSIDERS' TIP

In August of 1877, Nez Perce Chief Joseph led his people through Yellowstone Park during a desperate attempt to reach the Canadian border. U.S. Army troops dogged his trail as Chief Joseph led 800 men, women and children and 2,000 horses on a 1,500-mile flight that included 18 engagements and four major battles. At his surrender 40 miles from the Canadian border on October 4, Joseph made his famous speech, "Hear me, my chiefs! I am tired. My heart is sick and sad. From where the sun now stands I will fight no more forever." Officers were so impressed by Chief Joseph's military tactics that they were taught to officers in training.

Photo: Robert Bower

Keefer Island sits in the middle of the Snake River in downtown Idaho Falls — a piece of history essentially untouched by time.

agers in order to protect elk and bison as well as livestock outside the Park. Like their prey, wolves wander out of Yellowstone Park, easily moving 50 miles in a day. Already some have tangled with livestock. Park managers fought more than 20 years to bring back the wolf.

Even fire was set free. In 1972, Park managers implemented a "let-burn" policy for naturally caused fires. They suspected that the forest's health depended on fire to clean and prune it. That policy caused a firestorm of criticism in 1988 when 13 major fires and countless smaller ones swept through Yellowstone Park, leaving half of it burned to a crisp. Out of the blackened rubble rose some of this century's greatest lessons in the miraculous mysteries of Mother Nature. Ten years after the fire, scientists are still watching carefully and learning from the process of regrowth in Yellowstone.

The Battle for Grand Teton National Park

As early as 1882, Gen. Phillip Sheridan proposed a Greater Yellowstone — expansion of Yellowstone Park to protect the winter range of its wildlife in general and its elk in particular. That Greater Yellowstone movement, which first was

manifested in the formation of forest reserves in 1891, eventually grew into today's national forest system. To the south, it ended in the piecemeal creation of the controversial Grand Teton National Park. The process took 33 years (from 1917 to 1950) to complete, although several small parcels have been added to the Park since 1950.

Though first conceived by Sheridan and proposed by Congress in the 1880s, the Greater Yellowstone movement didn't take off until 1917 when a 1,200-square-mile addition to Yellowstone Park was proposed to the south. The addition, which encompassed lands already publicly held by the Forest Service, would have followed more natural boundaries: the Absaroka Range ridge to the Buffalo Fork of the Snake River, then west, south of Jackson, Leigh and Jenny lakes. In 1918, the expansion looked like it would pass Congress. But I.H. Larom, a recent graduate of Princeton University and a dude rancher near Cody, got wind of the movement and spurred the Wyoming Legislature into opposing the bill. For the next decade, efforts to expand Yellowstone were bound up in political knots tied mostly by livestock interests who used parts of the area for grazing. Wyoming officials were also concerned about turning National Forest lands over to the Park Service. A percentage of the receipts from grazing fees on forest lands helped pay for the operation of local schools.

In 1928, Sen. Gerald P. Nye apparently took Congress by surprise when he introduced a bill, not for the expansion of Yellowstone Park but for the creation of a whole new park: Grand Teton National Park. The new park would encompass only the beautiful Teton Mountains, too steep and high for use by livestock interests. The bill passed and was signed into law on February 26, 1929. It was a beginning.

John D. Rockefeller Jr. was one person who wanted to see the whole area protected from commercial development. To that end, he formed the Snake River Land Company and bought up 35,000 acres ($2 million worth) of private bottom lands to donate to Grand Teton Park. What history books won't tell you, but local Jackson historians will, is that it was a group of local citizens that roped Rockefeller into the land purchases. According to local historians, Horace Albright, then former superintendent of Yellowstone Park and retired director of the National Park Service, met with two ranchers, a banker and two others on July 26, 1936, in the Maude Noble Cabin at Menor's Ferry. The ranchers had learned that taking in dudes was more profitable than raising livestock in this high-elevation country. They saw that rampant and sloppy development could destroy the landscape of the pastoral life that high-paying Easterners sought on their dude ranches. Farsighted, they aimed to turn "the Hole' into a living museum of ranching and recreation. In addition to preserving the mountains and lakes, these ranchers wanted to protect their view of the Tetons.

Rockefeller bought the land between 1927 and 1943, but congressional and local opposition prevented Rockefeller from transferring the land to public ownership until 1949. Impatient with the stalemate, Rockefeller forced the issue by threatening in 1943 to sell the land on the open market. President Franklin Roosevelt made a decision: He set aside the 221,000-acre Jackson Hole National Monument by presidential decree.

Roosevelt's move began a whole new war. First, Congress passed a bill abolishing the monument, but Roosevelt vetoed it. Next, the state of Wyoming sued the Grand Teton National Park superintendent — and lost. Then Congress cut funding for the monument's maintenance. Finally, in 1950, all parties reached a compromise: The federal government would reimburse Teton County for taxes lost through the transfers from private to federal ownership. (Nearly 97 percent of Teton County is in federal ownership.) Livestock grazing in Grand Teton would be allowed for the lifetime of the existing leaseholders' heirs. Other existing uses would be allowed to continue. That same year, the Jackson Hole Monument was incorporated into Grand Teton Park.

Jackson Hole, first settled in earnest by Mormons in the 1880s, was populated with tenacious farmers and ranchers clinging to their hard-won high-elevation land. By 1909, the town of Jackson claimed 200 residents, while the Jackson Hole population neared 1,500 inhabitants who picked up their mail at nine different post offices. By 1990, Jackson's permanent population had reached about 4,500, and the economy was based almost solely on recreation in nearby Grand Teton Park.

As in Yellowstone Park, Grand Teton struggles to control burgeoning elk and bison populations. A bunch of 16 bison owned by Lawrence Rockefeller on his ranch near Moran grew to 380 and now roams the Park. Rockefeller's fences couldn't contain them. By the spring of 1998, authorities expect their numbers to exceed 400 — the limit determined by Park officials. Elk numbers are also growing and an in-Park hunt each fall is failing to stabilize the population.

The Greater Yellowstone Ecosystem — And Beyond

Like a tiny seed that falls on fertile ground, the concept of a Greater Yellowstone Ecosystem was planted while Yellowstone Park was still in its infancy. In the past 15 years it has grown so much that it's difficult to determine just when it sprouted into an idea big enough to be studied and named. Maybe it was Frank Craighead in his 1979 book, *Track of the Grizzly*, who defined it. If it was Craighead, there were plenty of people who watered and fertilized the idea until it mushroomed into a way of thinking, a way of seeing Yellowstone National Park and its surrounding lands.

In 1983, when the Greater Yellowstone Coalition formed at the Teton Science School in Jackson, the concept, when spoken and promoted, was a dirty word. Now it rolls off unlikely tongues throughout the ecosystem and has been adopted by federal and state agencies. The Greater Yellowstone Coalition, a conservation organization headquartered in Bozeman, is one of the most successful environmental organizations in the country. The coalition leads the fight to protect the ecosystem, monitoring, studying, coordinating and agitating for change every step of the way.

As technology and affluence allows man to creep ever closer to the Park with ever more destructive tools, patrolling Yellowstone's legal boundaries is no longer enough. Just outside the Park's boundaries, development threatens the ecosystem's waters and the Park's thermal features. In 1990, for example, the Church Universal and Triumphant, a religious group headquartered near Gardiner, wanted to tap a geothermal feature on their land. Concerned because thermal areas in the United States and other countries have been ruined by outside tampering with connected systems, authorities studied the problem and determined that geothermal tapping outside the Park could damage those inside it.

A proposed open pit gold mine near Cooke City was blocked in 1996 by President Clinton. Other development is crowding the Park: oil and gas drilling, logging, mining, water and hydroelectric projects promoted by the National Energy Act of 1978, recreational resort and home developments and poaching.

Within the Park boundaries, authorities have their own problems. Since 1965, winter use of Yellowstone Park has increased so dramatically that thousands of snowmobiles clutter the Park and pollute the air on some days. Conservation groups have sued the Park, which is working on an environmental impact statement to study and remedy the problems. The solutions won't come

easily. West Yellowstone, the Snowmobile Capital of the World, would fall into instant and serious economic depression if snowmobiles were banned from the Park.

For years, the Park Service has been studying ways to minimize traffic and control crowds on the Park's dilapidated highways. The only seeming alternatives — limiting numbers or using buses — are unpopular. Other infrastructure, like the sewage system at Old Faithful, is decaying. In the meantime, federal budgets are declining.

Pine beetle epidemics that have invaded lodgepole stands in the Park are now deemed good for the ecosystem and are no longer combatted with insecticides. But exotic weeds invading the Park are a different story. And while fish are no longer planted, cutthroat-destroying lake trout that have invaded Yellowstone Lake are caught and killed whenever possible.

Managing this 18 million-acre system, divided into three states, seven national forests, two national parks, three wildlife refuges, countless counties and even more towns, is the possibly impossible challenge of the future. In order to do so, each agency and people in general may somehow have to embrace a definition full of compromises that moves toward the wild center while maintaining communities and economies on the edges.

Since Yellowstone was first discovered, its challenges have always been about managing people — inside and outside the parks — and protecting the Park. Much of that management has been dependent upon ever-changing politics often fanned by journalistic pens. That's as true today as it was when Nathaniel Langford was named the Park's first superintendent in 1872 and instructed to promote and preserve America's best idea. As national park managers and other residents of Greater Yellowstone look to the future, history will someday tell how successfully all grasped the idea of Yellowstone National Park — the wild heart of Greater Yellowstone.

Like your grandmother's handmade quilt, Greater Yellowstone consists of both pattern and piece.

Area Overview

Like your grandmother's handmade quilt, Greater Yellowstone consists of both pattern and piece. For many residents, the pieces — especially theirs — are easier to see. But look more closely: The pattern that connects us is rich indeed.

First, there are the pieces. Greater Yellowstone overlays parts of three politically and culturally distinct states: Montana, Wyoming and Idaho. Within each state exist politically and culturally distinct groups, most of whom rely on the land for their living or their lifestyle. In many cases, what would assist one group in its efforts to make a living — for instance, diverting water from the Snake River to irrigate farmland — interferes with the livelihood or lifestyle of other groups, such as fishing guides and recreational boaters who feel they would be better served by an untapped, undammed river. And vice versa.

But state and economic pieces are only the beginning. Our region centers on two national parks, which are in turn buffered by parts of seven national forests. No one agency oversees these entities — each is managed independently and for different ends. National parks, for instance, are managed primarily for preservation of their special qualities and for visitor enjoyment. National forests are supposed to balance interests that range from recreation and timber to ranching and mining. Within each national forest are several ranger districts; each may strive for that balance in a different way. Then there are the Bureau of Land Management, which oversees some federal rangelands, and the Bureau of Reclamation, which has jurisdiction over some water-use issues associated with dams it built here. The U.S. Fish and Wildlife Service has partial jurisdiction, too. Each state also has a fish and game agency and a state parks supervisory agency. And that's just for starters.

Like we said, pieces are easy to see. What about the pattern? It exists, of course, within the pieces themselves. Every dividing issue contains a thread of connection.

Dividing and Connecting

Yellowstone National Park, in particular, both separates us and defines us as a region. First, there are physical barriers. The Park is nearly ringed by mountain ranges. Northeast of the Park boundary lie the Beartooth Mountains, with 29 peaks above 10,000 feet. The eastern border is walled by the Absarokas. The Madisons, Centennials and Lionheads lie off the Park's west boundary like coral reefs guarding a tropical atoll. Yellowstone's southern reaches are squeezed between the Teton Range to the southwest and the lower Absarokas to the southeast. This limits southern access to the valley through which the Snake River exits, a valley whose walls pinch inhospitably together about 60 miles from the south border of Yellowstone. Access from the east is possible only by navigating mountain passes. The broad Yellowstone Valley sweeps north out of the Park through Gardiner, marking what was once the only easy way into the Park.

While in our time Yellowstone's rugged mountain encirclement is a recreational plus, not long ago it was a formidable barrier. Communities on opposite sides of the Yellowstone Plateau and its near bracelet of mountains might as well have been worlds apart rather than a mere 70 or 80 miles. This isolation has tended to foster independence and a proud individuality in Yellowstone communities.

But Yellowstone National Park predated nearly all the communities that surround it. Its existence has cut many towns from whole cloth and shaped the basic weave of others. For instance, Gardiner is not a booming tourist town, partly because once the railroads quit operation, its northern location was out of the way. Gardiner came into being because someone had to supply those who ran the Park from Mammoth, including army troops and the Park Service. Gradually, Gardiner residents came to rely on employment with the Park Service and concessionaires. So Gardiner never got too excited about tourist dollars. On the other hand, West Yellowstone was, from day one, a tourist staging area for expeditions into the Park. The main railroad stop was here. Cody and Jackson have historically been staging areas for the Parks as well. For them, this has meant a prosperity otherwise unlikely — a prosperity not shared, in general, by nearby communities.

Then there's Idaho's Teton Valley. Rugged mountains block direct routes between Teton Valley and Yellowstone Park. This made the valley a backwater; tourists who were focused on reaching Yellowstone and Grand Teton national Parks moved past the ranching communities here without stopping to notice that this valley was richly beautiful in its own right. Only in recent decades have recreational property sales and tourist services begun to flourish here as nearby visitor-oriented areas became crowded.

Through this region flow 17 rivers, including the Yellowstone, Snake, Madison, Gallatin, Clarks Fork, Henry's Fork and Salt. All carry the most precious cargo in the arid West, the water that allows communities to grow, ranchers to run cattle and farmers to irrigate fields.

Most of these rivers have carved valleys through otherwise inhospitably rugged country. So, to a striking degree, where our rivers go, so go our roads. And before the roads came the railroads, which needed to follow rivers both for the paths they had carved and for access to the water that ran railroad steam engines. River valleys allowed a gradual weaving together of the human pieces of this region. And, of course, where road and rail made supply and commerce possible, towns sprang up, each connected to the others by the threads of transport that created them in the first place.

But rivers are also barriers, channeling and limiting travel routes and seeming to carve our region into pieces. Idaho Falls, on the southwestern edge of Greater Yellowstone, is so located in large part because an enterprising 19th-century entrepreneur built first a ferry and then a bridge at one of the Snake River's few possible fording spots, charging travelers a toll to cross. In lovely Swan Valley, near Idaho Falls, the South Fork of the Snake and the rugged terrain on its west bank have created a string of tiny communities on the east side with uninhabited wilderness a stone's throw across the river.

Climate is a barrier as well. At one time, this region's long, snowy winters fell between neighboring communities like thick white curtains. Mountain passes became impassable or nearly so. For instance, in the early days of automobiles, the one-day motor trip between Jackson and Victor, less than 30 miles apart but on opposite sides of 8,200-foot-tall Teton Pass, sometimes became a two-day ordeal. Old photos show teams of horses dragging slipping vehicles up sharp inclines between impossibly high walls of snow.

But the climatological challenges that separate us also pull us together, even today. When Teton Pass closes, both Jackson, Wyoming, and Idaho's Teton Valley feel the pinch. People stuck on either side find willing help from locals who have been stuck a few times themselves. When the Snake River and her tributaries flooded with snowmelt in the spring of 1997, communities up and down the river corridor reached out to each other, often offering assistance they were only too likely to need themselves if the water continued to rise.

The Big Pieces: State Lines

Greater Yellowstone communities are connected and know it, but residents tend to focus on differences more than connections. Added to that tendency are the very real physical, economic and cultural distances between our communities. All this makes larger identities, like those that fall along state lines in other areas, as hard to see as the pattern on a quilt

UNCONVENTIONAL.

wrapped around your own shoulders. Residents of Yellowstone country find their sense of place in their town or valley or county more than in their state. This community identity means Idaho, Montana and Wyoming are better defined by internal contradictions than by any kind of unity. Nevertheless, we're going to take a shot at rough sketches of those big pieces.

Eastern Idaho

As every successful Idaho politician knows, this is a state held together, if it's held together at all, by a fierce belief in individual freedom, in each person's and each community's right to do exactly what they please, thank you. In eastern Idaho, that breaks locals into three main camps.

There are the descendants of Mormon homesteaders who cleared sage and irrigated the desert and who still feel an intense but not always careful ownership of the land they were born to. Theirs are mostly the valley towns, such as Rexburg and Rigby, where agriculture can, with hard work, be made to pay.

In more mountainous areas like Island Park live descendants of mountain men and hardscrabble ranchers, remembering the old days and living precariously off the tourist trade. They work as hunting and fishing guides; they're horse packers and shop keepers. Some have become developers, subdividing their own or their neighbors' ranches. In larger towns like Idaho Falls, these children and grandchildren of farmers and pioneers have become urbanized, but that doesn't mean the school teacher you meet in the grocery store line doesn't drive out to the old homestead on weekends to check on the cattle. Rural roots run deep here.

Then there are the newcomers, often former urbanites. In eastern Idaho, they're drawn by recreational opportunities and high-tech jobs spawned by the national laboratory near Idaho Falls. Others are modem cowboys — professionals who once worked in big office buildings in big cities, but who can now jack into the whole wide world even from tiny Driggs, Idaho. Logging, mining, agriculture and ranching have been traditional Idaho occupations, but more and more Yellowstone country Idahoans see their future in tourism and natural resource conservation. The loudest voices in favor of conservation tend to be these newcomers, frantic to preserve the basis for the rural clean living that drew them here.

Most eastern Idaho communities are not cleanly of one school or another. Instead they struggle to draw a single identity from conflicting factions. A few towns are so homogenous they seem not to need struggle. Mormon communities have neatly gridded streets that reflect their underlying, neatly planned and executed reality. On the other hand some communities, like Driggs, seem better defined by their internal differences than by any solidarity between the cowboy-hatted descendants of Mormon homesteaders and the folks Teton Valley old timers call "move-ins." Move-ins are the mountain-loving lifestyle seekers and well-heeled recreational property owners who populate the valley in ever-increasing numbers and make up the third recognizable camp of eastern Idaho residents. Many in this group are older, retired or retiring. The spare time they have to devote to issues that matter to them, as well as their often substantial financial resources, make their voices loud in proportion to their numbers. They too tend to be conservation-minded.

Idaho as a whole is a state that cheerfully embraces contradiction: Idahoans vote Republican in large part because we love to hate government and government regulation. Yet 64 percent of Idaho is federal land. We live in its constant shadow. To a striking degree, it feeds us. Much of the state's ranching and agriculture are accomplished through federal subsidies in the form of cheap power, cheap water and cheap public grazing. The descendants of homesteaders and miners owe the land their grandfathers ceded them to homesteading laws that passed out parcels to anyone who could claim and hold them.

Then there's this: Idaho is a poor state, with an average annual income ranked 44th in the nation. Yet the state's birthrate is high — ninth in the United States. Or this: Historically the state has seen itself as heavily reliant on agriculture for its livelihood, yet only 15 percent of Idaho's land is agricultural. One of the most on-target books on Idaho politics says it all right on the title page. The book's called *Paradox Politics: People and Power in Idaho.*

Southwestern Montana and Northwestern Wyoming

In some ways, Montana and Wyoming are similar to Idaho. Both are largely rural and sparsely populated. Both have been settled by the descendants of trappers, miners, cattlemen and homesteaders. For nearly a century they lived unnoticed in the land that nobody wanted. Suddenly it has become the land that everybody wants.

All three states are so close to their frontier roots that here and there you'll find some folks who still haul their water, live without electricity or telephones and heat their homes with wood stoves. Even those natives who now plug into the Internet remember the days when rural economies were supplemented with "making do" and "doing without." Back then, the closest thing to recreation for many of them was packing a picnic for a day of gathering the winter's wood in the mountains.

Like Idahoans, Wyoming and Montana residents share their states with the federal government. Forty-nine percent of Wyoming's lands are under federal ownership, while 28 percent of Montana is federal. Tally the federal lands in Wyoming's and Montana's shares of Greater Yellowstone, and the number rises to more than 50 percent.

As in Idaho, each community has been shaped by the region's topography. Gardiner, Montana, sits in a narrow canyon on the edge

Idaho's state gemstone is the star garnet, a translucent red stone that reveals a ghostly pattern of rays at some angles.

Photo: Randy Hayes/Post Register

A recent deep snow pack in the Teton Mountain Range exceeded a 30-year high as copious amounts of moisture fed the growing levels.

of Yellowstone Park, while the county seat at Livingston enjoys a wider space connected to the Paradise Valley. Pinched off from the valley where ranches and agriculture prop up local economies, Gardiner's residents have always had to turn to mining and the Park for employment. Livingston not only has its own diverse economy, but also is close enough to Bozeman for residents to commute. East of Gardiner, the Beartooth Mountains cut off Cooke City from the east. Cooke City's children are educated in a one-room schoolhouse; residents live cheaply here only because the trip to "town" (Livingston, Billings or Cody) is so long they seldom go anyplace where they can spend their money. Cody residents, isolated from the rest of Wyoming by the Big Horn Mountains, party in Red Lodge and do business in Billings.

The states share other similarities, such as a flood of Southerners moving in after the Civil War. From there, though, their roots stray. While eastern Idaho was mainly Mormon, Montana was dominated by the Irish Catholics who worked the mines in Butte and Anaconda. Butte miners gave birth to the labor movement in the West when they struck back at their employers, the heavy-handed Copper Kings who dominated Montana politics and publications until the 1950s.

The states' politics differ, too. Idaho and Wyoming have traditionally been Republican states. Until recently, Montana has been Democratic.

And while Montanans gave birth to the labor movement, Wyoming suffragettes were on the forefront of women's rights. In 1869 — about a half-century before the 19th amendment was added to the U.S. Constitution giving women the right to vote — William Bright introduced the bill in Wyoming. Bright's wife, Julia, supported women's suffrage. The first woman in the nation to cast her vote was 70-year-old Louisa A. Swain on September 6, 1870, in Laramie, Wyoming. Not bad for a state whose logo is a cowboy riding a bucking bronc.

Montana is a state divided into west and east, mountains and plains. In the western third, the towering Rockies hide immense chunks of wilderness softened by trees and separated by valleys. Tumbling out of the mountains and winding their way through the valleys are rivers and streams — 32,000 miles of them — flowing either to the Pacific or Atlantic oceans. The Yellowstone River, which begins in the heart of the Park, slips through Montana's mountains then veers off into the plains until it joins the Missouri River.

Montana's 147,138 square miles hold nine national forests and 3,331,881 acres of wilderness.

Wyoming ranks 50th in population with 481,000 people. That's 4.5 residents for every square mile. Like Montana, Wyoming is divided into west and east, mountains and plains. Included in its boundaries are most of Yellowstone National Park, Grand Teton National Park, five national forests and millions of acres of Bureau of Land Management lands. What eastern Wyoming lacks in precipitation, it makes up for in rich oil and gas reserves resting below the sagebrush-covered landscape. Three-quarters of the state records an average precipitation of less than 16 inches. Pockets like the Bighorn Basin, where Cody is, average less than 8 inches.

When it comes to education, Wyoming walks away from its neighbors. In 1997, 89 percent of Wyoming's residents were high-school graduates — fifth in the country. Idaho ranked 13th with 86 percent, and Montana ranked 19th with 85 percent. In 1994, Wyoming ranked second in the nation when it came to per capita expenditure on education. Montana ranked 35th, and Idaho ranked 41st that same year.

Blurring State Lines

The crowning contradiction of our three states is also our crowning glory: our two lovely, tourist-flooded national parks. Yellowstone National Park lies in all three, but we claim our respective pieces with awkward shrugs.

There are more traffic jams on a typical summer day in Yellowstone than there are in a month in Idaho Falls, Greater Yellowstone's largest community at 50,000 inhabitants. More than 3 million visitors flood through the Parks each year. That's more than the combined populations of Idaho, Montana and Wyoming. Dornan's, a little grocery store in Grand Teton National Park, stocks plum pudding and other luxury tidbits you couldn't find at the largest supermarket in Rexburg, Idaho, population

14,000. Yet barely a stone's throw from those crowded summer roads and tourist services is more of the wilderness that, for most of us, is the well-loved signature of this region.

As we've argued, the easy way to account for the strongly individual character of this region's communities is by pointing at the landscape. But we've also tried to show that a compelling argument can be made in the opposite direction as well: If we are ever to be a single, coherent region, it will be because of that landscape, because of our struggle with and affection for the lands that surround us.

In fact, it could be argued that we aren't nearly as different from each other as we like to think. Because one way or another, we're all about the land. We want to play in it, work in it, control it, make it feed us, take care of it. Most of us can't help but love it. So let's ignore the pieces now and find the pattern.

The Regional Pattern: A Greater Yellowstone

Yellowstone Park's borders were established in 1872, at a time when surrounding lands were virtually uninhabited. The wonders that awed many who saw them into desiring their preservation were geologic. They were geysers and hot springs, spectacular waterfalls and the Grand Canyon of the Yellowstone. The plentiful wildlife was of secondary interest. Today few residents of the area value Yellowstone Park simply for its strange and lovely landscape. Many of us see our region as an organic whole, a Greater Yellowstone centered around the nation's first national park. The idea is a century old, but only recently has it begun to take firm hold.

In the late 19th century, Yellowstone National Park was patrolled first by soldiers and then, after the creation of the National Park Service, by rangers. But protective rules were few and vague, and the protectors' numbers small. The nation had never promised to preserve such a vast chunk of land before. Nobody was quite sure how to go about it. And anyway, the vast teeming forests seemed too large to damage, a generous gift to later generations — or an irritating waste of good resources, depending on how you looked at things. Back then most locals hated the idea of declaring off-limits such rich resources so near their back doors.

Only 10 years after its creation, the truth had become obvious: Yellowstone needed help. Poachers were killing off the Park's elk and bison at an impressive rate. By 1902, 25 bison made up the nation's only remaining wild herd. Vandalism of the Park's natural wonders by passers-through and tourists was rampant.

Civil War General Philip Sheridan, traveling through the Park in 1882, saw the mayhem and was horrified. Poaching and vandalism were only part of the problem. Already ranches and homesteads were encroaching on neighboring wildlands necessary to the survival of Yellowstone's wildlife. Elk and bison summered on the Park's Yellowstone Plateau, but they had to drop to more hospitable elevations to survive the harsh winters. Sheridan proposed extending the borders of Yellowstone to the east and south. This action would have pulled wildlife migration routes and low elevation wintering areas under the Park's protection.

Enlarging Park boundaries would also have hampered poachers, whose operations were most profitable in winter, when the animals were outside the Park wallowing in shoulder-deep snow, helpless to escape the hunters' guns. Stories from Yellowstone travelers of this period tell of bison and elk carcasses littering the land. Bison were stripped of their hides, but elk died simply for their ivories, residual tusks that had become coveted symbols of a fraternal organization now known as the Elks Lodge. Yellowstone National Park was big, but it wasn't big enough to preserve Yellowstone's wildlife. Sheridan's call to action was a bit before its time, but eventually the concerns he raised became the hottest topic in the region.

The first attempts to address this issue in the late 1800s led to the formation of the National Forest system, which surrounded Yellowstone with public lands that would otherwise have been homesteaded and developed. Other attempts to pull critical areas under the Yellowstone umbrella eventually resulted in creation of Grand Teton National Park and the adjacent National Elk Refuge.

A Unified Whole

Wildlife protection, as much as anything, finally taught us that Yellowstone National Park couldn't be treated as separate from the rest of the region. As elk and bison herds began to regain numbers, winters found them once again heading up the Yellowstone Valley to Gardiner and down the Snake River into Jackson Hole. Only now those areas were ranch and farm land. These animals competed with cattle for winter forage, ate farmers' hay and broke down fences. They still do. Today in Gardiner, you fence your trees if you want to keep them alive. In Jackson Hole, you fence your haystacks. At one time it was more serious. Ranchers barely eking an existence could be starved out by the additional demands of hungry elk. For these locals, there was no escaping the basic connection between Yellowstone country, its wildlife and its people. These ranchers fed starving elk in winter not only out of kindness but in order to survive themselves.

More recent lessons are even more complicated. One in Montana revolves around a disease, brucellosis, carried by Yellowstone bison and elk. Most experts believe the illness won't jump from Yellowstone wildlife to Montana cattle. But the state's ranchers can't forget the tremendous cost they will bear if it does. Brucellosis makes cattle abort their fetuses; western Montana's ranch economy is based on "cow-calf" operations that produce a yearly crop of calves, which can't be sold if Montana loses its certification as a brucellosis-free state. Another sticky issue has been the reintroduction of wolves to Yellowstone National Park. Wolves don't know Park boundaries either, and as they leave the Park in search of prey (occasionally in the form of livestock), conflict dogs their trail.

It was around 1979 that the phrase "Greater Yellowstone Ecosystem" first appeared in print, a new name to help us talk about our region as a quilted whole as well as a wad of political pieces. Frank Craighead is credited with coining the term in his book *Track of the Grizzly*. The Craighead brothers conducted bear research in Yellowstone Park, and for Frank, the Greater Yellowstone Ecosystem equated roughly with the ranges of Yellowstone grizzlies. This would have made Greater Yellowstone about twice the size of the Park itself, or about 4.5 million acres.

The idea of an organic whole — a Greater Yellowstone defined by its rivers, mountains and wildlife rather than by political boundaries — caught like brush fire. Now we have organizations like the Greater Yellowstone Coalition and the Yellowstone Hotspot Association, which promote, each in its own way, a picture of our region as an inescapable whole instead of three states, two national parks, seven national forests, miscellaneous private lands and human communities.

The transition has not been easy and is by no means complete. As you travel Yellowstone country, most of the communities you'll pass are struggling to hang on to traditional extractive economies — logging, ranching and mining — while trying to face this new ethic of ecosystem interdependence. Tourism has been one critical answer, but tourism's impact on communities is not always positive. Many old ranching families in Jackson, for instance, bemoan the good old days when their sleepy little town supplied few jobs but lots of peace and quiet. Others point out that although Jackson has plenty of jobs in tourist service industries, most don't pay well, particularly in relation to the glitzy town's high cost of living.

Desirability aside, tourism isn't always an answer. In many towns with less desirable locations or with access difficulties, the only jobs available are those that make it difficult to worry about the intricate interlocking of ecosystems. If your weekly paycheck is signed by the owner of a sawmill, you may question how much timber we should be pulling from the lodgepole forests, especially when you notice how

the creek outside of town runs brown when it once ran clear. But how can you vote to stop logging in the mountains behind your house? That's voting yourself out of food on the table.

To complicate matters, the survival of this sprawling region depends on an even larger interdependence. Salmon, which bring tourist dollars and which once provided a booming fishing industry here, must travel down the Snake River through four states, then out into the Pacific Ocean. This means Idaho fisheries are impacted by Washington coast sea lions and, much more importantly, by federal dams hundreds of miles beyond the state's borders. For many residents, the pattern rapidly grows too big, too complicated, too hard to care too much about.

The Ecosystem

An ecosystem is an area that functions as a self-contained unit. The Greater Yellowstone Coalition is our region's most effective proponent of a more unified approach to living and working in Yellowstone country. They believe it's possible to draw a line around "the contiguous mountainous region in and around Yellowstone National Park," roughly 18 million acres, and treat that area as a self-contained, organic whole.

Most residents of Greater Yellowstone buy into that idea to some degree. It's hard not to. A glance at a map shows us that our political boundaries ignore the natural ones of mountain range and river valley. We understand that brucellosis-bearing bison killed in wintertime Montana after they wander outside the protection of Yellowstone Park didn't know they crossed a state line. They were merely following the biological imperative to feed themselves and survive the harsh winter. Greater Yellowstone residents do not, however, agree on what should be done about the fact that political and ecological boundaries make liars

Greater Yellowstone encompasses the intersection of three wild Western states: Idaho, the most populous with more than 1 million people; Montana, with around 850,000; and Wyoming, the ninth-largest in the nation geographically, with only 476,000 residents.

of each other. The arguments run through our newspapers and enliven talk at our bars; they make or break political careers. The future of our region will draw its shape largely from how — indeed, whether — we can resolve this complex issue.

Climate

If the human climate around here sometimes seems a little raucous and fragmented, it only mirrors a larger pattern. In Greater Yellowstone, a single local forecast tells you little about the weather across the region.

Two major influences create the weather variations of our region. Most of our weather patterns originate in the warm, moist air of the Pacific Northwest. But as the air stream sweeps across the mountain ranges of Washington and Idaho, it loses much of its moisture. This makes our climate cool and dry. In winter, arctic air masses often sag down from Canada bringing clear weather and bone-aching cold.

In general, western Yellowstone has the higher winter precipitation and milder temperatures brought by Pacific Northwest weather patterns. The eastern side of our region gets cooler, drier weather. There, January can bite with the arctic fierceness of a Great Plains winter.

Mountain Weather

For each 1,000-foot elevation gain, expect temperatures to drop an average of 3.5 degrees. This can mean that rainfall on a November day in Idaho Falls is a blizzard on nearby Pine Creek Pass. Our dry air undergoes greater temperature fluctuation than moister air would, since water cools and heats more slowly than air. The temperature difference between midday and midnight can be as much as 50 degrees, and the difference between sunshine and a small cloud obscuring the sun can make you pull on a jacket, even in summer.

Two other weather anomalies of mountain regions are inversions and orographic effects. Inversions happen as cold air drains downslope to pool in the valleys. These cold-air pools can become trapped beneath a layer of warmer air. Inversion is why West Yellowstone is often the coldest spot in the nation in winter. It's also why towns such as Jackson have to breathe their own woodsmoke and car exhaust for prolonged periods every winter: Trapped beneath a warm air blanket that acts much like a ceiling, pollutants can't escape as they do in summer.

The second mountain-induced weathermaker is responsible for significantly higher precipitation in Yellowstone country towns that tuck up to the feet of mountains, especially on their west-facing slopes. Air climbing over a mountain range cools. Because cool air can't hold as much moisture as warmer air, suspended water vapor forms into droplets. This creates orographic effects such as the bright puffy clouds that form over mountains. Valleys in the east side of mountain ranges are often dry and sunny while rain or snow falls just over yonder.

A third weather effect of our landscape is wind. River corridors, mountain passes and wide-open valleys can whip up surprisingly forceful winds. Livingston, Montana, is known for its gusty weather. Average wind speeds in that town are 21 mph. Idaho Falls on the upper Snake River Plain is more likely to experience winter road closures from drifting snow than from snow depths. We've seen drifts form so quickly on wind-scoured Antelope Flats near Idaho Falls that even following 500 yards behind a snow plow made for precarious travel.

What all this should mean to a smart mountain visitor is this: Dress in layers and plan for weather variation as the day progresses or as you travel. Rain and wind protection are a must here. And even in summer you'll want to carry something warm for evenings or unexpected clouds. If you're driving, don't expect the weather to be the same when you get out of the car as it was where you climbed in, especially if you're going to move from one elevation to another or from one mountain valley to another.

The Best Time to Come

That depends on you.

Spring brings snowmelt and mud to our mountain towns and early green to our valley communities. You'll start to see wildflowers down low in June. Our rivers usually run big and muddy from late May through July. All this means that in early summer, the fishing isn't generally too hot, the mosquitos are swarming, and the high country is not easily accessible due to slow snowmelt and swollen, difficult creek crossings. However, the weather is pleasantly cool, and lower-elevation wildflower meadows can be breathtaking.

Summer in the high country is short; it usually runs from mid-July through mid-August. Our biggest tourist crowds show up then, as does our most stable, warm weather (don't take stable to mean it can't snow anywhere in Yellowstone country anytime, though, because it can — it just doesn't stick around long in summer). The wildflowers burst out in the higher elevations. Down low, farmers' markets begin to fill with local produce. First frost can come as early as late August. Recreational gardeners watch the news every evening for frost warnings after about the first week of September.

Fall means stable high-pressure systems, bringing cool days bracketed by chilly nights. Aspens and cottonwoods begin to glow gold as early as September at higher elevations; down low they turn by late October. Lower valleys are still enjoying fall weather as the mountain towns slip into winter. This means that if you stay low, you enjoy shirt-sleeve weather and the sight of lovely snow-dusted peaks silhouetted against brilliant blue skies. Up in Grand Teton and Yellowstone parks, fall usually means sweater weather until the sun sets. Then it gets cold. Most of Yellowstone country tucks under its snow blanket by late November or early December, with the most consistently snowy weather sweeping through in January and February. The coldest months are December through February; you'll enjoy the best skiing from mid-January through late March or early April.

The Communities
Entrance Communities
West Yellowstone, Montana

Since 1908, when the Union Pacific Railroad's Oregon Short Line chugged up to the Yellowstone Park border, West Yellowstone has had one purpose: to serve Yellowstone Park tourists. Now a booming year-round mecca for tourists and recreationists, "West," as the 1,000 residents like to call their town, has been shaped by four dominant forces: Yellowstone Park, the national forests that surround it, the climate and snowmobiles.

Until the mid-1960s, when the snowmobile came screaming into the picture, West was a "100-day town" that rose to frenetic activity each summer, then fell into quiet seclusion when winter blew in 6 feet or more of snow. The town's population swelled and shrank with the seasons. These days, cross-country skiers and snowmobilers add four months of bustling winter business to the town's economy.

In November, the town belongs to the quiet swish of champion cross-country ski and biathlete teams in training. From Christmas until mid-March, though, snow-machines rule. On a winter's morning, you might hear thousands of snowmobiles idling (there are 1,600 rental snow-machines in West — enough to match every motel room) before they blast off into Yellowstone Park. Or they can drive straight from their motel rooms to more than 1,000 miles of groomed trails that lead into the national forest lands bordering West Yellowstone's city limits (see our Winter Sports chapter).

INSIDERS' TIP

In 1922 a Rigby boy showed his high school chemistry teacher a design for transmitting pictures electronically. His name was Philo T. Farnsworth, and at least around here, he's credited with being the father of modern television. A fellow graduate of Rigby High School was well-known writer Vardis Fisher, author of *The Mountain Man*.

Come March, locals are left alone to await the spring thaw. Some escape to a much-needed vacation. Others sweep the dust off their store counters, fatten up their inventories and prepare to make hay while the sun shines. In West Yellowstone, the sun always shines brightest from Memorial Day until Labor Day. The 2 million visitors that pass through West Yellowstone on their way to and from the Park also fish, hike, bike and backpack in the Park and on surrounding forest lands.

While some locals cuss the commotion created by snowmobiles, it was their advent that dragged West Yellowstone from an unorganized frontier community into the well-ordered town it now is. Snow machines forced the town fathers to incorporate in the late 1960s so that the vehicles could navigate city streets. The new business and increased prosperity doubled the town's population and brought a high school to town. Parents no longer had to send their teenage children to board in Bozeman. About the same time, newcomers steered the town toward a sewer system to replace existing cesspools. In the early '80s, city fathers passed a 3 percent city tax — the first community tax in the state — to improve and build infrastructure.

Ironically, the very public lands that have turned West Yellowstone into a recreation mecca now squeeze the town's bulging boundaries. West Yellowstone sprang up amidst National Forest lands. To establish property for the growing town, the Madison National Forest (now Gallatin National Forest) set aside 26 1-acre blocks to be used for the 500-acre townsite. Land is scarce. And, now that West Yellowstone has dressed up, the rush for recreational homesites is on. Property prices have skyrocketed, and housing is growing scarce and expensive. Huge businesses like the IMAX Theater, the Grizzly Discovery Center (see our Attractions chapter), giant RV parks and new motels have been built on the year-round economy. Once a town too poor to live in, West Yellowstone is quickly becoming a town too expensive to live in.

The Public land policies — and particularly those in the Park — will determine West Yellowstone's future. Officials are concerned about pollution from snowmobiles and winter disturbance to wildlife. There is talk of dramatically curtailing snowmobiling, and murmurings persist about limiting Park visitor numbers. If the town's population once rose and fell with the seasons, West Yellowstone's fortune has always followed the Park's visitation. Townsfolk pay close attention to each new Park superintendent, knowing that the policy he sets can make them or break them.

Gardiner, Montana

Ten years ago we might have told you Gardiner was a town that refused to be tamed by the prospect of tourist dollars. Still unincorporated — it's the residents' way of saying "No thank you" to conformity and regulation — Gardiner has only recently begun to make an obvious bid for tourist trade. Towering new motels have risen to replace aging cabins popular with Europeans but disdained by most Americans. Behind the modern structures you'll see remnants of the frontier border town that is going, going, almost gone. You'll see simple homes and dirt streets — reminders that the 1,000 or so residents of this blue-collar town have relied more on serving the Park and its concessionaires than on catering to the tourists who visit it.

Gardiner began as a supply town and stopping-off place for Yellowstone Park visitors in 1872, when the Park was created. In 1883, when the Northern Pacific Railroad pushed its Park Branch Line as far as Cinnabar 3 miles away, Gardiner got another economic boost. It also got its share of ruffians who followed the rails hoping for work. Three years later, when Army troops took over management of the Park at Mammoth, the number of saloons and brothels in Gardiner took a big leap. In 1903, when the Park Branch Line finally rolled into town (a cantankerous miner held claims that blocked its path for 17 years), Gardiner burst into bloom. Stagecoaches, wagons, and outfitters with horses hustled to meet train-loads of visitors with trunkloads of clothes.

Once the grand entrance (a huge stone arch stands as a reminder) for tourists traveling to Yellowstone Park via the railroad, the northern Park entrance at Gardiner now ranks fourth in visitor numbers. It is the Park's only year-round entrance. Just 5 miles from Mammoth, where permanent Park employees live all year, Gardiner is home to the warehouses of Amfac Resorts, the Park's main concessionaire. Five miles to the northeast is Jardine, the site of a gold mine that has teased the town with a century of boom and bust. Down the canyon, a few ranches add a tiny trickle to the local economy. Farther down the canyon is Livingston, the county seat and a growing center for writers, artists and actors. Between lies the Paradise Valley, where ranchers are quietly giving way to retirees and wealthy urban refugees including actors such as Peter Fonda and Dennis Quaid. To the south is Yellowstone Park, the capricious benefactor that Gardiner residents love-hate.

The relationship between Mammoth and Gardiner runs deeper than that of employer and employee. Mammoth high schoolers attend classes in Gardiner. And Gardiner parents take their children to the doctor at the Mammoth Clinic. In winter, elk and bison from the burgeoning Park herds (they're the biggest in the nation), flow out of the Park to their winter range in and around Gardiner, where it's only a mile high and the ground is often bare. Some wander through town and down the Yellowstone River Canyon. Others stay on summer and winter, mercilessly pruning ornamental trees and shrubs. Living with the elk is a part of living with Park policy. Some residents like having an elk peer through their picture windows and others don't. They're good for business, bad for gardens.

Like West Yellowstone and Cooke City, Gardiner is hemmed in by public lands. You'll find river rafting and fishing on the Yellowstone River that cuts through town. And you'll find hiking in and out of the Park. In the fall, you'll also find hunting, especially a late hunt used to thin the Park's elk herd.

Cooke City and Silver Gate, Montana

Before Yellowstone became a national park, miners had already dug into the hillsides and discovered gold in Shoofly, today's Cooke City, at the Park's northeast entrance. If those miners had had their way, the Northern Pacific Railroad would have laid its tracks from Gardiner across the Park to Cooke City. They

didn't, though. And when the mines finally closed in the 1950s, Cooke City withered to fewer than 20 year-round residents. The rest catered to tourists during the summer and moved elsewhere to work for the winter.

The town sits at 7,600 feet, where snow buries it, locking winter residents in. To the east the 11,000-foot Beartooth Highway to Red Lodge and Billings closes mid-October. About November 1, crews clearing the Chief Joseph Highway to Cody (Wyo. Highway 296), stop plowing at the Montana state line about 10 miles east of Cooke City. The 50-mile road to Gardiner is plowed all winter.

Like West Yellowstone, snowmobiles have shot winter life into Cooke City. (In 1997 a counter outside town tallied 45,000 snowmobiles.) These days, motels and a few cafes stay open through the winter. During the summer, Cooke City's population grows from 80 to about 300, and Main Street is crowded with cars and people. Off Main Street, cabins and log houses cling helter-skelter to the hillside.

The New World Mine looms in limbo on the mountain above town. A proposed open-pit gold mine that was temporarily halted by President Clinton would change Cooke City — and possibly the Park — forever. The president and Congress are working on a land swap with mine owners.

In addition to snowmobiling and cross-country skiing, Cooke City is a mecca for hikers, backpackers and hunters. You'll find a few mountain bikers. In the fall, it's also a good place to see bears. And any time of year, wolves can be spotted in the Lamar Valley in the northeast corner of the Park. Reintroduced to the Park in 1995, the wolves have become a growing tourist attraction and have produced a noticeable trickle of fall wolf-watching visitors who stop into Cooke City for a bite to eat.

Silver Gate, which is actually the town closest to Yellowstone Park's northern entrance, is much smaller than Cooke City. It has mostly motels and a cafe for services. The town was laid out in the 1930s with covenants that dictated a rustic theme. Few folks here stay through the winter. They go to Cooke City 3 miles east for gas, grub and gab.

Cooke City is what some locals like to call a "dog" town. It has so few full-time residents (about 80) they can be easily tracked by not-

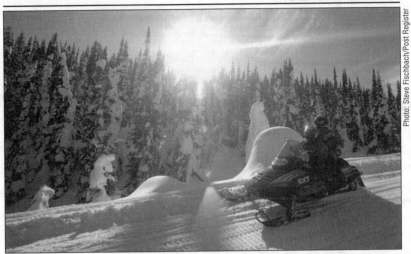

Photo: Steve Fischbach/Post Register

Yellowstone country is a snowmobilers' paradise throughout winter.

ing the whereabouts of their dogs. You'll know Old Joe is at the Miner's Saloon when you see his dog lying outside the door.

Jackson Hole, Wyoming

If you find yourself in Jackson, Wyoming, you may discover an overwhelming, previously unsuspected desire to own a cowboy hat or a fringed leather jacket. Luckily, you're in cowboy consumer heaven. Jackson has come up with more uniquely Western ways for you to spend your money than you probably knew existed. It's all here, from fine Western art galleries to fine dining restaurants that feature wild game. You'll discover shops selling antler chandeliers, shearling jackets and everything in between. And the Million Dollar Cowboy Bar here will serve you in the saddle — literally. All the bar stools are *saddles*.

But locals are quick to point out that the tourist Jackson is not the only Jackson. That rawhide glitz overlays a real Wyoming town in a valley peopled by folks who wave at each other from behind the wheels of their pickups, whose grandparents moved here before the days of RVs, bed and breakfast inns and quad chair lifts. Tourist activity also tends to obscure

the other group that calls the Hole home: the Gore-Tex-clad hardbodies drawn by nearly endless opportunities for extreme outdoor sports, as well as the pleasures and benefits of what local historian Jesse O'Connor calls "mountain living." If Jackson locals look fit and healthy to you, it's because they are.

What's really fun about Jackson is that it's all three of these at once. If you want to see the quiet Jackson, the little town in the big valley surrounded by mountains and the wind-swept state of Wyoming, come in spring or fall. Winter is a bit tougher, but you might catch a glimpse if you stay away from Teton Village. Between Memorial Day and Labor Day, you will see only the Jackson that belongs to endorphin worshipers, tourists and the exuberant myth of the West. But don't be fooled. They exist within each other all the time.

Jackson, so close to the wild bounty of the Tetons, was once a town of trappers, outlaws and poachers. Determined homesteaders eked a bare living, irrigating hayfields with the waters of the Snake and Gros Ventre rivers, running cattle on the fertile valley floor and trying to raise a few crops before the inevitable early freeze. From the beginning, Jackson seemed to know it had to become a tourist town or flounder. Now it's the bustling county seat of Teton County, Wyoming.

Jackson's population is around 6,000, just under half that of the county itself. In summer, the steady flow of tourists and short term residents swamps the locals into invisibility.

Most of the county is filled by Jackson Hole, a 48-mile-long, 20-mile-wide valley that encompasses much of Grand Teton National Park and extends nearly as far south as Hoback Junction. Jackson takes its name from this, the largest high-mountain valley in the lower 48.

Other communities in Teton County, Wyoming, none of which are incorporated, include Wilson, at the foot of Teton Pass, and Teton Village, less a town than a cluster of ski-centered services at the base of Jackson Hole Mountain Resort. In or at the edges of Grand Teton National Park are the tiny communities of Moose, Kelly and Moran. Alta and Grand Targhee Ski and Summer Resort are also in Teton County, although mountain barriers mean that the towns closest to them are in Idaho, not Wyoming.

Jackson has some of the lowest unemployment in the state (around 2.3 percent in 1997) to complement its service-oriented economy. The government provides jobs, too, since supervisory headquarters for the Bridger-Teton National Forest are located here, as well as a district office of Wyoming Game and Fish. National Park Service jobs number in the hundreds in summer, and Park concessionaires account for more than a thousand.

Unfortunately housing is the priciest in the state. Median rent in 1992 was more than $600 per month; a typical price for a single-family home is currently around $290,000.

Recreational opportunities in the area are almost limitless, but tend to focus on downhill skiing at Jackson Hole and Grand Targhee, backcountry skiing and snowboarding on Teton Pass, mountain biking, hiking and technical mountaineering in the Tetons, wildlife watching, and rafting, kayaking, canoeing and fishing on the upper Snake and tributaries.

Surrounding Areas

Eastern Idaho

"A lot of state, this Idaho, that I didn't know about," former Idaho resident Ernest Hemingway once said.

Most Idahoans could say the same thing. After all, their home contains nearly 84,000 square miles, but only 1.2 million people. The last state to be "discovered" by Euro-Americans boasts nearly 16,000 miles of fishable streams and rivers, more than 2,000 natural lakes, 11 national forests and five wilderness areas. Idaho contains more wilderness than any state except Alaska, more forest lands (more than 40 percent of Idaho is national forest) and more running water and whitewater. Not bad for a state best-known as the home of a lowly tuber, the potato.

Idaho Falls, Idaho, Area

Greater Yellowstone's largest community, population 50,000, is also its least tourism-dependent. Situated on the broad Snake River Plain some 90 miles from Jackson, its mountains are all low-horizon mirages. Agriculture thrives in the rich volcanic soil left behind eons ago as the hotspot now underlying Yellowstone National Park wandered east across the Snake River Plain. Canal systems bring the plentiful water of the Snake to fields of potatoes and grain. Idaho Falls is also a retail hub for the approximately 200,000 people of the upper Snake River Valley.

The biggest single factor in the local economy, though, is the INEEL, the Idaho National Engineering and Environmental Laboratory. In its heyday, the INEEL employed more than 10,000 people in mostly engineering and technical professions. Although it was recently downsized, the facility still accounts for some 38 percent of all jobs in Bonneville County. The laboratory has been responsible for an

INSIDERS' TIP

You have almost certainly eaten Idaho potatoes many times: J.R. Simplot, Idaho's "Potato King" and one of the state's two richest men, supplies McDonald's restaurants with more than half the french fries the fast-food giant serves.

unusually high standard of living for county residents — not long ago the highest in the state — and for the dramatic influx of masses of well-educated recreation hounds who chose to pursue their technical careers here because outdoor play opportunities are unrivaled at other technical sites.

The Mormon church and "the site," as locals call the INEEL, make Bonneville County home to two nearly unconnected communities. Sixty percent of county residents are Mormon, mostly descended from homesteading pioneers. These folks tend to value the community and feel a strong sense of ownership of the land. Many are still tied to parcels claimed by their ancestors under homesteading laws. Then there are the techies, thrilled just to be able to play here and, since they've already arrived, begrudging the next influx for the impact it will have on their beloved skiing, fishing, hiking and mountain biking opportunities. "Community" for many of these imports means co-workers and perhaps the next-door neighbors. For others, it's the people they ski with.

Idaho Falls is surrounded by satellite communities that are even more strongly Mormon and rooted in agri-business — towns like Iona, Ammon, Ucon, Rigby and Ririe. Time spent in these communities is like a peek into the area's past. In little Iona, street names like Rockwood, Steele and Olsen document the original homesteaders — and the contents of the listings in the current phone book.

Recreation in this area generally involves a drive to Teton Valley or Swan Valley, to Island Park or Jackson or Yellowstone. Within a 90-minute drive in various directions lie world-class fly fishing, great powder skiing at Grand Targhee Ski and Summer Resort and nearly endless hiking and cross-country skiing. There is snowmobiling, especially at the snow-machine meccas of Island Park and West Yellowstone, mountain biking in the Big Holes and the only backcountry entrance to Yellowstone National Park, at Bechler, near Ashton. Hunting season brings locals out after elk, mule deer, antelope and moose. The area also boasts golf courses and tennis courts, racquetball facilities, miniature golf and a rock climbing gym.

Rexburg, Idaho, Area

It's hard to imagine a more wholesome

town. The streets run ruler-straight through a clean, old-fashioned downtown district. Pretty trees shade frame houses. Lawns are green. Ricks College, wholly owned by the Mormon church and named for one of the town's founding fathers, occupies a scenic hill above Rexburg. Irrigated farmland stretches away in all directions. In 1994, Rexburg had no reported cases of murder, no robberies, two cases of arson and 40 burglaries in a county with a population of 23,000.

Rexburg comes by this well-scrubbed existence honestly. First, it was settled by Mormons in 1883. The church believed that ideal communities could be created to foster the best in communal support, and Rexburg, like many eastern Idaho towns, was one of its experiments. Second, disaster struck in 1976 when Teton Dam burst at its seams. Ironically, part of the shiny-penny look of the town can be credited to the tragedy that nearly washed it away. On June 5, the newly completed Teton Dam collapsed; millions of cubic yards of it mixed up in 80 billion gallons of water rampaged down the valley. The flood claimed lives, destroyed homes and stripped topsoil. It caused $800 million in damage. Folks in Rexburg still break their town's history into two pieces: "before the flood" and "after the flood." There aren't many buildings in the lower areas of Rexburg that haven't had some substantial attention paid them since 1976. Many had to be completely rebuilt. (From 1960 to 1969, about 700 new houses were built in Madison County, but between 1970 and 1979, the decade of the flood, the number soared to four times that many.) So the town of Rexburg is pretty both by design and by disaster.

Like Idaho Falls, Rexburg is near spectacular outdoor recreation in the Big Holes, the Tetons, the St. Anthony Dunes area and Island Park. But Rexburg itself is not a mountain mecca. It does, however, put on a pretty good party every year for the International Folk Dance Festival in July (see our Annual Events chapter).

Near Rexburg, but actually a county seat in its own right, is sleepy little St. Anthony, population 3,800. It's a town easily overlooked unless you're from there — or unless you've ever been to the traditional Free Fishermen's Breakfast on Memorial Day Weekend. Or unless you know about the anomalous sand dunes 12 miles west of town that are the winter home of 2,500 elk and the summer playground of four-wheelers and dirt bikers (see our Attractions chapter). St. Anthony is bisected by the world-class trout waters of the Henry's Fork of the Snake River.

Ashton, Idaho, Area

Ashton is Fremont County's second-largest town, with around 1,100 inhabitants. This little burg, the sidewalks of which always seem to have just been rolled up, clings to the top of the Upper Snake River Plain just before you climb onto the Yellowstone Plateau.

Despite its altitude-pinched growing season of about 86 days, Ashton is farm country. The self-proclaimed seed-potato capital of the world has produced certified seed stock for nearly 100 years. Many of the 42 area potato farmers are third- and fourth-generation seed-potato growers. As is true farther down the valley, farmers enjoy a productive combination of rich volcanic soil (naturally low in pathogens) and low humidity coupled with plentiful supplies of irrigation water.

Although farming is arguably the mainstay in Ashton now, tourism was her impetus. A railroad spur ran from here to West Yellowstone, for decades shuttling tourists intent on reaching the nation's first national park. Tourism is still important here — but unreliable. One striking fact about Fremont County is that residents don't leave home. Between 1990 and 1994, less than 1 percent of the population emigrated. Perhaps their unique location keeps residents home: Fremont County borders both Wyoming and Montana and, because it's practically next door to Yellowstone, gets credit as Idaho's gateway to that national park.

Nearly 29 square miles of the county are water, and almost 60 percent of the land area is federally owned. At Aspen Acres, Ashton's aspen-studded golf course, an occasional plodding bear obstacle reminds local golfers that they may live in settled farmland, but they abut wild, wild country.

Other recreational opportunities are as close as the 25-mile-long Mesa Falls Scenic Byway, which begins right outside of town and provides hiking, sightseeing and fishing opportunities. Nearby Bechler is Yellowstone National Park's only backcountry entrance (until recently it was also the Park's only free entrance, but a couple years ago the Park Service began to charge the hikers and horsepackers who access the Park at Bechler). A short whitewater stretch on the Fall River, runnable only in spring, is a favorite of local kayakers and rafters.

Island Park, Idaho

We've heard three stories about how this town was named. One is that a local railroad-tie camp in the 1920s happened to be nearly surrounded by streams: Tom Creek, Split Creek, Chick Creek, Little Warm River and the Buffalo River. The result was nearly an island. A second story says that in the late 1890s, the local stop for the Yellowstone stage was a natural clearing in the midst of heavy forest, and that a tiny village grew up around the stage stop, an island of park among the trees. And early resident Charles Pond explains that the town was named for the stands of timber that ride like islands on the sage-dotted plain.

However the town got its pretty name, Island Park didn't need its moniker to make it unusual. This is a town with a 33-mile-long main street and fewer than 250 year-round residents. It's also a town contained entirely within the world's largest known caldera. A caldera is a collapsed lava dome. A similar structure exists in nearby Yellowstone National Park. Island Park's caldera is about 2 million years old and roughly 18 miles wide by 33 miles long. Even if you know it's there, evidence of the massive feature is hard to see. Geologists say that Sawtelle Peak, nearly 10,000 feet tall, is a section of what was once the caldera rim.

INSIDERS' TIP

Two-thirds of Idaho's approximately 10,000 Native Americans live on the state's five reservations.

This irrigation system hydrates a potato field west of Idaho Falls, Idaho, helping to grow one of the state's agricultural staples.

The 1860s saw the first settlement here as trappers moved in to harvest the area's fur-bearers. But it wasn't until Yellowstone became a national park in 1872 that the area began to boom. At first, stage lines ran through Island Park into Yellowstone. A railroad line was completed in 1908.

Tourism is still the underpinning of Island Park's economy. Away from U.S. Highway 20 you can find the crumbling remains of former working cattle ranches and along the highway corridor see clearcuts from the not-too-distant days of heavy logging. Most apparent, though, will be the regular clusters of tourist services. Businesses along U.S. 20 are waiting to feed you, rent you the toys you need to play in their playground, guide you to the best hunting and fishing, put you up for the night or the summer, or sell you your dream cabin. Don't look for a lot of retail here, though. Nobody's here to shop. These days, Island Park

is eastern Idaho's outdoor playground. Idaho Falls residents who own recreational cabins most likely own them here, plus there's a huge contingent from Salt Lake City. Rexburg and St. Anthony families headed out for weekend camping trips are likely to be coming this way. Island Park Reservoir, dammed into existence in 1938, is a favorite with local powerboaters. It boasts five boat launch sites.

In winter Idaho snowmobilers deluge the area's 200 miles of groomed snowmobile trails. These trails connect with Lionhead and West Yellowstone trails to make a total of more than 1,000 miles of groomed snowmobile heaven. The area is laced with more than 40 miles of groomed cross-country ski trails, including trails in lovely 16,000-acre Harriman State Park, winter home of moose and hundreds of trumpeter swans.

Much more than locally famous, though, is the fishing. Henry's Lake is 8 square miles of clear, cold mountain water, practically jumping with landlocked kokanee salmon, rainbow, cutthroat and a natural hybrid locals call cuttbow. About half of the Henry's Lake fishery are natural spawners. The occasional 30-incher surprises no one. The Henry's Fork of the Snake, home to rainbow, brook trout and cutthroat, is world-class fly-fishing water. In fishing season, waders are almost obligatory attire for the well-dressed Island Park visitor.

Swan Valley, Idaho

Swan Valley is, in many ways, kin to Island Park. The valley and its largest town are named for the lovely and endangered trumpeter swans who frequent the area. The South Fork of the Snake, yet another of eastern Idaho's premier fly-fishing rivers, runs the valley's length. The river is lined with cottonwoods, overflown by bald eagles, paralleled by highway and punctuated by little towns. Little Swan Valley has about 150 residents; Irwin just up the road has about 110. Farther south, the even-tinier town of Palisades doesn't exist for some map makers, but its residents know where they live.

Many locals are Mormons — the local Mormon temple is the largest structure in the valley. They've made their livings as ranchers, but, following an east Idaho trend, more and more of the area's support comes from tourist dollars. Anglers floating the South Fork, boaters headed up to 20-mile-long Palisades Reservoir and tourists looking for a pretty route to Teton Valley or Jackson all drop a few bucks here and there. Right now the area still lacks the tourist facilities that would make it a destination. Area accommodations are sparse, limited mostly to RV spots, cabins and a couple small roadside motels. The only luxury accommodations in the valley are at an elegant little fishing lodge at Palisades Creek.

The area has a few restaurants, and we dare you to find an afternoon's worth of shopping in the valley. In fact, the most complete cluster of tourist services in the valley isn't in

what locals consider to be Swan Valley at all: They're at the head of Palisades Reservoir in Alpine, Wyoming. What Swan Valley has in undisputed plenty is the lovely, trout-filled Snake, a long green swath of fertile range edged on both sides with nearly unroaded mountains, spectacular hiking up the side drainages and wildlife-watching opportunities along the river corridor. We suspect that in the none-to-distant future, locals will remember the quiet Swan Valley of today with nostalgia.

Teton Valley, Idaho

Teton Valley, often called Teton Basin by residents, once went by a different name, Pierre's Hole. "Hole" is the name trappers gave to a high valley surrounded by mountains: the former Pierre's Hole is a 20-mile-long valley ringed by the Big Holes to the west, the spectacular Tetons to the east and the Snake River range to the south. To the north, the valley gradually widens as it carries the trout-filled Teton River toward its meeting with the equally trout-filled Henry's Fork of the Snake.

The name Pierre's Hole is the only remnant of the wild, mountain-man days of the early 1800s in this valley, when the area was home to trappers and Indians. Gone is the raucous annual mountain-man rendezvous where trappers traded their winter's furs for supplies and a good party. Teton Valley's next wave of inhabitants were determined Mormon ranchers who arrived in the 1880s, first in Driggs (now the Teton County seat), then in Victor, Tetonia and nearly a dozen tiny communities that exist today only in locals' memories. Valley towns like Sam, Judkins, Clementsville and Bates aren't even dots on maps anymore. And all that's left of little Cedron is a tiny rangeland cemetery.

Teton County residents have made their living from ranching and some agriculture, (mostly seed potatoes, which can tolerate the short growing season). But tourism and real-estate development are supplanting traditional employment.

INSIDERS' TIP

Sandhill cranes, blessed (or perhaps cursed) with a call that resembles the working of unoiled machinery, fly into Teton Valley as many as 17,000 strong each September to stage their journey south.

Teton Valley grew more than 50 percent between 1990 and 1996, bumping local population to more than 5,000. Although growth has been substantial and steady since the early '70s, the latest jumps are striking. New home construction has also jumped: Between 1985 and 1990, about 150 new homes were built. But between 1990 and 1994, more than 400 went up. That's a whole lot in a once-sleepy area.

One of the things that fuels the local tourist and recreational housing boom is Grand Targhee Ski and Summer Resort, up winding Ski Hill Road and over the border in Wyoming. Grand Targhee was a homegrown ski hill, built with the help of grants to create jobs for locals. It boasts spectacular powder and striking views of the Grand from the top of lovely but perhaps unimaginatively named Fred's Mountain. Now the ski hill is owned by a corporation that owns several resorts; it's likely that under new leadership Grand Targhee will become more a destination resort and less a locals' hill.

Another impetus for rapid growth and tourist interest is that booming Jackson is literally "over the hill," as Jackson commuters say. Barely 22 miles — but several thousand feet of elevation gain and loss on Teton Pass — separates Victor from Jackson. And as the cost of housing in Jackson has become more and more expensive, Teton Valley has become more attractive to less well-heeled Jacksonites.

Teton Valley in general and Driggs in particular have the reputation of being "granola" heaven. Around here a granola is a health-food-munching, late-'90s version of the '60s hippie. Besides the descendants of Mormon ranchers, the most influential group in the valley may be these folks. They are artists, craftsmen, writers, construction workers and restaurant owners. They are fiercely protective of the little mountain valley they've adopted.

Locals say that one of the things all valley residents share, though, no matter how they make a living or how many generations their families can claim here, is concern for the environment and this region on the cusp of irrevocable change. All this concern about change means that residents of the valley keep a close eye on their elected officials. The elections of November 1996 resulted in an 86-percent voter turnout and the turnover of every single local office.

Outside of politics, recreational opportunities include skiing, especially at Grand Targhee and in the backcountry reachable from Teton Pass. Snowmobilers frequent nearby Pine Creek Pass. Fishing on the Teton River is first-class. Hiking, mountain biking and camping opportunities abound.

Southwestern Montana

Bozeman, Montana

Bozeman is a cowtown with big growing pains — such big pains that three candidates promoting planned growth ousted incumbent pro-growth commissioners in the 1997 election. From 1990 to 1995, Bozeman's population grew nearly 4 percent per year. Traffic is so congested at times that cars wear bumper stickers that read, "So you came here to be in a hurry?"

Established in 1864, this hub of the arts was named after trailblazer John Bozeman, who promoted his route that led from the Oregon Trail to the Montana gold fields in Virginia City, Montana. The fertile Gallatin Valley became a supply source for miners, ranchers, and Yellowstone Park expeditions. But it wasn't until the 1900s, when the Milwaukee Railroad built a cross-country line with a spur leading to Gallatin Gateway for Yellowstone Park tourists, that Bozeman joined other towns as a "Yellowstone Connection."

Today, Gallatin Field Airport is a main connection to Yellowstone. It's also an important link to the outside world. Each Monday morning, traffic carrying air commuters flows toward the airport.

Home of Montana State University, Bozeman has mushroomed into 28,000 full-time residents with an average personal income of about $20,000 — about the same as those who live in Cody, Wyoming. Bozeman offers a wide array of recreation opportunities, including the Bridger Bowl Ski Area to the north and Big Sky Ski Area to the south. The city also is near a rainbow of blue-ribbon trout streams and millions of acres of national forest and wilderness lands. Additionally, Yellowstone Park is just 90 miles to the south of the Gallatin Valley. In town, businessmen ski around Lindley Park during lunch or jog on the old railroad bed. Evenings, they may attend a performance of the Bozeman Symphony Orchestra or a play at the Emerson Cultural Center. This combination of amenities has attracted a growing number of newcomers who want to protect their backyard — Greater Yellowstone — from destruction.

Headquartered in Bozeman is the Greater Yellowstone Coalition, a group that has led the conservation charge since 1983. Today, they are scrambling to keep tabs on subdivisions and development in the Greater Yellowstone. And they're looking for ways to maintain wide open spaces and wildlife habitat, by keeping ranchers in business and slowing subdivision.

Separated from Yellowstone Park by 93 miles, Bozeman is the seat of Gallatin County, population 50,000. It is also the epicenter from which development is seeping into some of the wild parts of Greater Yellowstone.

Big Sky, Montana

Big Sky was once a ranch tucked into a quiet draw of lush alpine meadows in the Madison Mountain Range. Now, towering condominiums and a thousand second homes cluster in "villages" with street names such as Little Coyote and Ouzel Falls. During summer, they stand like restless teenagers looking for something to do. Banners in mini-commercial centers advertise condo rentals. The Chamber of Commerce operates on an answering machine.

People come to Big Sky to play. Summer or winter, the Gallatin Canyon is a recreation destination lined with Forest Service campgrounds and a rich offering of hiking and biking trails. Groups of horseback riders file out through the sagebrush beside the river. Others play golf or tennis in the Big Sky complex. Come winter, they trade their horses and bikes for skis and snowmobiles. And the snow-laden meadows hum with people playing.

Unincorporated as a town and run by a board of directors, Big Sky Ski and Summer Resort is former newscaster Chet Huntley's dream. When the resort opened in 1974, the celebration turned into a memorial service for Huntley, who had just died of lung cancer. Back then those who followed Huntley's dream

lived in tents because there was no place else to live. Now, summer employees live in tents because they can't afford to rent condos.

In the narrow canyon below, the Gallatin River runs like a ribbon from Yellowstone Park. Before Big Sky came about, a few dude ranches and stage stops clung to the blue-ribbon trout stream, hoping to snag those driving the road to Yellowstone. Now they cater to both Yellowstone and Big Sky visitors, while their young children go to the two-room schoolhouse (K through 8) beside U.S. Highway 191. Teenagers commute to Bozeman for high school.

In the past six years, Big Sky has doubled its runs and lift capacity to accommodate 18,000 skiers per hour. From the ski hill to the Meadow Village, Big Sky is a bustling hub of winter activity aimed at the dedicated sports enthusiast — but not shoppers. Skilled shoppers would be bored in a few minutes here. Big Sky is one of eight ski areas slated for expansion or construction in Greater Yellowstone.

Livingston, Montana

Just months after the Northern Pacific Railroad rolled into town in 1882, Livingston had sprung into a full-blown town boasting six hotels and restaurants, four stores, five feed stables, two butcher shops, two liquor stores, a lumber yard and 30 saloons. Livingston has since found much of its fortune in the rails (and rivers) that run through it, despite the fact that automobiles coupled with cheap gas and a booming post-World War II economy dried up passenger rail service to the Park, and eventually to Livingston. Always a headquarters for repairing ailing locomotives, the town today hosts the Livingston Rebuild Center, where locomotive engines from around the world are repaired.

Downtown, you'll find things looking pretty much the same as they did before World War II. It's not an accident. Influenced by a thriving community of internationally famous writers, artists and actors, residents have made it a point to preserve their downtown heritage. (In 1997, when the U.S. Postal Service tried to move the Livingston post office from downtown, it took only four days for 1,500 citizens to sign a petition, contact their Congressmen and stop the move.)

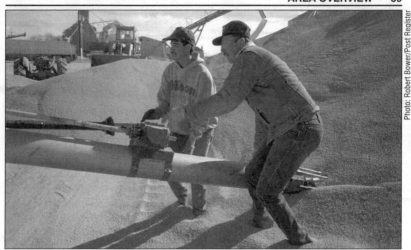

Photo: Robert Bower/Post Register

Eastern Idaho is one of the nation's leading wheat-growing regions.
The loose volcanic soil and abundance of irrigation water make
the dry and warm climate ideal for grain crops.

Livingston is so well-kept, in fact, that more than one movie has been set in and around Livingston. In the summer of 1997, both Robert Redford's *The Horse Whisperer* and Dennis Quaid's *Everything That Rises* were shot in the Livingston area. Parts of Redford's *A River Runs Through It* were also shot here.

Home of the Federation of Flyfishers, Livingston is a town quietly melding the Old and the New West into its vision of paradise. On a summer's evening, you might find folks from every social strata sipping wine, tasting hors d'oeuvres and viewing art in one of three summer gallery walks. Afterwards, those same people might adjourn to the Stockman Bar for a steak in a small restaurant at the back of the bar. Or you might find some of them gathering down the street at the Livingston Bar and Grille, owned by Russell Chatham, an internationally known Western impressionist painter who calls Livingston home. Around the corner is the Cowboy Connection, a small shop that sells the old West cowboy memorabilia. See our Restaurants and Shopping chapters for more about these.

Livingston, population 7,500, has an economy based on Montana Rail Link, the Livingston Rebuild Center, agriculture, a lumber mill, fly tying, outfitting, guiding and tourism. The number of motel rooms, though, is a clue that tourism doesn't rank as high as in, say, Cody. Livingston offers 600 beds, while Cody, just slightly bigger than Livingston, claims more than 1,300 beds within its city limits.

Red Lodge, Montana

The poverty of the past is now the pride of this town. Because residents lacked the money to fix up or raze old buildings, most of Red Lodge's downtown has been put on the National Register of Historic Places. When the coal mines shut down in the 1940s, Red Lodge suffered through decades of bleak existence before building a tourism-based economy. Planners started with Red Lodge Mountain Ski Area and added recreation options to their menu. The town is now a playground for Billings and Cody residents.

In turn, Red Lodge residents go to Billings, 50 miles away, for their supplies. Red Lodge's only hardware store closed its doors in 1997, the same year that one of two grocery stores in town called it quits. Folks go to Cody and Billings for fun.

A tight-knit community with houses huddled shoulder to shoulder like men trying to block out the cold, Red Lodge, population 2,000, sits between the Beartooth and the Pryor mountains. The mile-high town still holds the charm of bygone days when coal mining was the economic mainstay. Red Lodge sprang up in the 1880s after the discovery of coal, a commodity badly needed by copper smelters in Anaconda and Butte, Montana, and by the Northern Pacific Railroad for its coal-fired locomotives. Hundreds of European miners moved into Red Lodge, each nationality carving out an ethnic neighborhood: Little Italy, Finn Town, and separate sections for the Scots, Irish, English, Welsh, German, Scandinavian and Slavic populations. When most of the mines closed in the 1930s, some residents took up bootlegging during Prohibition. Their moonshine, which they labeled "syrup," was so good it was marketed as far away as Chicago and San Francisco.

Today, the ethnic lines have blurred, and the average per capita personal income of Carbon County's 8,000 residents is about $17,000. The division these days stands between "old-timers" who have weathered tough times, and "newcomers" who have brought their money and new ways with them. On one side of the town's main street, mountain-biking, climbing, hiking recreationists hang out at a local coffee bar where they pay $2.50 for a cup of cappuccino. Across the street, retired cowboys drink 50¢-a-cup java at the coffee shop. One group eats exotic pasta dishes. The other eats chicken-fried steak.

To the south is the Beartooth Highway, which leads over a 11,000-foot summit to Yellowstone Park. Charles Kuralt once called it the most beautiful drive in America (and nobody in Red Lodge will let you forget it). Depending on the winter, it is closed from October 15 until June 1. In the summer, though, the Beartooth Mountains are a paradise of hiking, backpacking and fishing. And Red Lodge residents are doing their darnedest to capitalize on them.

Northwestern Wyoming

Cody, Wyoming

The banner above the entrance to the Cody High School says it all: "Make Dust or Eat Dust." Cody residents have been making dust since the 1880s when Col. William F. "Buffalo Bill" Cody rode into the Big Horn Basin and decided to call it home. He had a vision, and Cody is it: A thriving tourist destination with a diverse economy.

Renowned as a hunter, guide and scout for the army during the Indian wars, Cody became an international showman who took the West to the East. On the road, he nurtured his vision, sent his money home and built his dream. In 1902, he bankrolled the construction of the Irma Hotel, the same year the North Fork Road from town to the east entrance of Yellowstone Park was completed. That same year the Burlington Northern (induced by Buffalo Bill himself) laid tracks to Cody. To accommodate guests, he built two lodges along the North Fork Road. Then he hired guides to take guests into the Park.

Cody's link to the Park had been established. But that wasn't enough for Buffalo Bill's town. Next he helped convince President Teddy Roosevelt to form a Bureau of Reclamation that would build dams and reservoirs to irrigate arid Western lands. In 1910, the Buffalo Bill Dam (the highest in the world at the time) blocked the North Fork of the Shoshone River and brought life to the dry lands of the Big Horn Basin — and to Cody's dream of a prosperous community.

Liquid gold — rich oil and gas deposits — in the Oregon Basin has since greased the wheels of progress. Like Buffalo Bill, oil and gas patriarchs sank money into their town, funding facilities and infrastructure. Today, Cody is a town more than comfortable with its history. Residents have capitalized on their founder's name and adopted his showy style, using both to celebrate their Western lifestyle through well-organized and widely marketed annual events. The Cody Nite Rodeo, begun 60 years ago as a tourist attraction, is today's version of Cody's Wild West Show (see our Spectator Sports chapter). The Buffalo Bill Historical Center (see our Attractions chapter for more information) a 237,000-square-foot museum that attracts 250,000 visitors each year, is the hub of the community. Downtown offers world class shopping and dining.

Despite Cody's population of only 8,600, its Yellowstone Regional Airport offers daily direct flights from Denver and Salt Lake City at competitive fares (see our Getting Around chapter).

A vigorous chamber of commerce (founded in 1900) is the engine that drives the town. As Cody had envisioned, his town has a diverse economy based on agriculture, oil and mining, tourism, a gypsum plant, timber and healthcare as well as federal and state employment. Marathon Oil is the major private employer with about 300 workers. The per capita personal income of Park County's 25,000-plus residents is $19,426, about the same as residents of Gallatin County in Montana but considerably higher than in Carbon, Park and Madison counties in Montana.

Far from Yellowstone Park and its migrating herds (it's 53 miles), Cody's economic welfare lies largely in the policies of nearby public lands including the Park and National Forest and Bureau of Land Management lands. Merchants can — and will — easily measure their losses caused by four recent years of road construction on the east entrance road. Construction on the highway outside the Park will continue at least through 1998. In addition, 82 percent of Park County is public land, and 50 percent of the county lies in wilderness, unreachable except on horseback or by foot. The town's growing recreation economy relies on these lands for hiking, bicycling, hunting, fishing, camping, rafting, snowmobiling and skiing. Its resource extraction industries also rely on public land policy.

Getting Around

If a river runs through it, chances are so does a highway. Take a look at the map and see the logic. Like rivers that follow the path of least resistance, so do the highways and byways of Greater Yellowstone follow the valleys until, blocked by the towering mountains, they must climb the most obvious pass over and through them.

Now, look at the map again. Even those who fly into the five regional airports in Yellowstone country must drive or ride the roads leading into its heart. From airports and interstates, from the east and the west, the north and the south, 3 million visitors stream into Yellowstone and Grand Teton parks each year. Compared to major metropolitan areas, the airports are simple get-in-and-get-out facilities. There isn't one in which you couldn't holler (if you dare) from one end to the other. While some of these airports are on the outer fringe of Greater Yellowstone, none is more than 90 minutes from the national parks.

Once you leave the airports and the interstates, the highways are just as simple. Two-lane, uncluttered ribbons of asphalt, they connect the residents of Greater Yellowstone to each other, and they'll lead you to this land of wonders. The avenues for getting there are many. Yellowstone Park has five entrances and 10 roads leading to those entrances. A sixth entrance deadends at a campground in the Park. Grand Teton has three entrances with five roads leading to them. In this chapter, we will give you a peek at the different routes.

By Car

You're anxious to get into the Parks, but there is so much to see and do outside them, too. Watch the dark purple majesty as the sun sets on the Madison Mountain Range. Park and picnic at the base of Emigrant Peak in the Paradise Valley near Pray, Montana. Hear the crickets chirping and the soothing sound of

water, then climb into your car and keep on driving. Slowly. You're on vacation. If you're lucky, in spring or fall you'll run into a cattle drive moving like a mirage up the highway. Cowboys aren't much on warning you about the hazards ahead, so be alert. Fresh splats of green manure smearing the highway mean livestock ahead. Break out your cameras and camcorders and capture those cowboys hunkered on their horses against the cold wind. With any luck, those bovine won't be heading the same direction as you. If they are, you've just gotta creep along, maybe bang the side of your car with your hand — please don't honk your horn — and wait for those dogies to break away to the side. (Be sure to record that sea of hide-covered steaks bobbing ahead of your car hood.)

While cattle drives and cowboys are getting scarce these days, the area has other more common hazards to watch for along the way. From dusk 'til dawn, expect wildlife of all kinds to appear out of nowhere. Since most highways follow river bottoms, it follows that critters cross highways to tank up on the rivers' waters. If you see a sign that reads "rolling rocks," pay attention, especially after a rain or during snow melt. We came around a corner in a blizzard one night and bumped into a house-size boulder blocking the road. Usually, though, you'll find smaller rocks, the kind that can flatten a tire or empty your oil pan.

Since we're warning you about the thrills of driving to this region, a few words about mountain driving. If you've never driven in the mountains before, a few of the passes in Greater Yellowstone can be downright terrifying. Take Beartooth Pass, for example. Almost daily during the summer, an RV or auto full of vacationers starts up the Beartooth Highway (U.S. Highway 212) then turns around and heads back down, afraid to tackle the top. Steep, winding, narrow and without guard rails in some places, it's easy to see where you'll land (way down there) if you go over the edge. For those of you in a hurry, we recommend patience. Beartooth Highway demands attention and commands respect. All around are scenic vistas that make heads turn and necks crane. Everywhere people are pulling off and on the road. For you who are afraid, we say "buck up." Vehicles rarely go over the edge, and the view on top is worth the adrenaline: alpine meadows and lakes and snowbanks so deep the brave and the slightly crazy ski the headwalls on the Fourth of July. Speaking of snow, it can fall any time of year on the 11,000-foot-high Beartooth Highway, which closes each year from October 1 until the end of May.

www.insiders.com

See this and many other Insiders' Guide® destinations online — in their entirety.

Visit us today!

Winter Driving

There are a few things you need to know about getting around Yellowstone country between November 1 and mid-April to late May. The Gardiner to Cooke City road is the only Yellowstone Park road open through the winter. Other winter travel through the Park is limited to snowmobiles or snowshoeing and cross-country skiing (see our Wintersports chapter). Inside Grand Teton Park, U.S. Highway 26/89/191 is plowed all winter. Outside the Parks, the Beartooth Highway (U.S. Highway 212) is the only one that closes for the winter. Teton Pass between Targhee and Jackson (Wyo. Highway 22/33) is sometimes closed temporarily because of avalanches. In eastern Idaho, roads can close in an instant due to ground blizzards, which occur when the wind whips existing snow into a swirling white mass that obliterates the road before you. Some passes, like the Chief Joseph Highway (Wyo. Highway 296), are plowed all winter, but blowing snow can quickly close them. Later in this section we have listed phone numbers in Idaho, Wyoming and Montana you can call for daily reports on winter road conditions and closures.

In the valleys you might find different hazards. Knee-deep snow, willows made lacy with hoarfrost and steamy fog rising from the icy waters of the Gallatin River create the perfect picture of a winter wonderland — and a recipe for icy roads. Slow down and drive carefully. Many winter travelers opt to take shuttles from the airport to their recreation destination of choice. In West Yellowstone, the snowmobile capital of the world, only a few streets are reserved for cars only. The rest are shared with snow sleds. A car can be a pain to navigate. At Big Sky, Teton Valley and Targhee, many of the condos are at the base of the ski hill, so who needs a car?

If you plan to drive multiple days and over long distances, we recommend packing at least a small survival kit that includes warm clothing, winter boots, matches, a candle, a small cooking pot, some emergency food, water and a blanket. Winter traffic can be pretty sparse. If you venture out at night and run into car troubles, it could be a long time before help arrives. Be prepared to sit it out in comfort.

Highways and Byways

Three routes lead to West Yellowstone, the most popular entrance to our first national park. Two of them lead south from Interstate 90, the east-to-west highway running across Montana. The third leads from Interstate 15, which comes up through Salt Lake City, Utah, passing near Idaho Falls on its way north.

U.S. Highway 191, the most popular northern route to Yellowstone Park, heads up the Gallatin Canyon through Big Sky to West Yellowstone. To get to U.S. 191, take I-90 Exit 306 onto Montana Highway 85. A few miles down the road, Mont. 85 turns into U.S. 191. Besides taking you to Big Sky, this road winds beside the Gallatin River, providing good fishing and lots of campgrounds.

U.S. Highway 287 also takes you south through wide open spaces then into the Madison Valley and up through the Madison River Canyon, past Quake and Hebgen lakes (see our Attractions chapter), then into West Yellowstone. Getting to U.S. 287 depends on which way you're headed on I-90. From the east, take Exit 274 at Three Forks then head southwest on Mont. Highway 2 for 11 miles until you come to the U.S. 287 junction. From the west, it's I-90 Exit 256. Follow Mont. Highway 2 for 13 miles then turn south at the U.S. 287 junction. If you're bound for West Yellowstone via Henry's Lake, turn south onto Mont. Highway 87 about a half-mile past the Wade Lake turnoff on U.S. 287. This 16-mile stretch of road bypasses Quake and Hebgen lakes and meets up with U.S. Highway 20. West Yellowstone is 13 miles east of the U.S. 20 junction.

U.S. Highway 20 takes you from Idaho Falls up the Snake River Plain through pin-neat Rexburg and sleepy Ashton. Just outside Ashton, decide if you're in a hurry or if you want maximum scenery. For scenery, catch the Mesa Falls Scenic Byway (it hooks up with U.S. 20 just below Island Park). On the byway you can camp, fish in the Warm River, hike and visit Upper and Lower Mesa Falls. Be warned that this road is narrow and winding, with lodgepole forest creeping nearly to pavement's edge. Nor is it all paved. The direct route stays with U.S. 20, running alongside the blue-ribbon trout fishing of the Henry's Fork, to and through Island Park. You'll pass Henry's and Hebgen lakes, then wind down from the plateau and over the Montana border into West Yellowstone. Watch for the "Bison Crossing" sign for a one-of-a-kind photo opportunity.

From the Park entrance at West Yellowstone, drive 14 miles to Madison Junction, where you must decide if you'll be driving the Park's upper or lower loops or just passing through. Each option offers its own mysteries and rewards, so we recommend both if you have time.

If you exit the Park going south, you'll take the John D. Rockefeller Jr. Memorial Parkway for just under 8 miles before you reenter national park, this time Grand Teton National Park. The parkway is also called U.S. Highway 89/287/191 — we're a bit short on roads here, so we like to give each one plenty of names. Fifty miles farther south (the same road is now called U.S. 26/89/191) you will have left Grand Teton Park and entered cowboy playland at Jackson. We hope you take the time to drive the Teton Park Road — folks call it the inside road — which loops past glacier-

formed Jenny and Leigh lakes, close beneath the spectacular Grand Tetons. This sidetrip is 25 miles long and only open during the snow-free months. U.S. 89 through Grand Teton National Park is plowed to Flagg Ranch all winter.

In both national parks, you'll find other side roads to explore and many pullouts guaranteed to add hours (days, if you're smart) to travel times. See our Attractions chapter and recreational chapters to help you plan your driving.

Two popular routes bring you to the tourist mecca of Jackson from Idaho Falls, which lies 91 miles to the west. In both cases, take U.S. Highway 26 up the South Fork of the Snake River and through Swan Valley. The South Fork flows quietly through this broad, cottonwood-swathed valley, providing more of the premier trout fishing the region is known for. Now you can take Idaho Highway 31 over scenic Pine Creek Pass and into Teton Valley, pick up Idaho Highway 33 and climb up and over Teton Pass. Make sure you stop at the top of the pass to enjoy the view down into Jackson Hole (a hole is a valley, so Jackson Hole is the whole valley, and Jackson is the valley's largest town). Your road becomes Wyoming Highway 22 as you descend the steep grade. Be warned that this is mountain driving at its steepest and most winding. The signs warn of a 10 percent grade, but some folks around here suspect it's steeper. Take your time. Be patient with slower vehicles.

Let's say you want to avoid Teton Pass, either because you don't like heights or because it's snowing and you want to stay low. In that case, from Swan Valley continue up the South Fork of the Snake on U.S. Highway 26 past Palisades Dam and drive along the more than 20-mile-long Palisades Reservoir. Turn with the highway at Alpine, Wyoming, and head up the upper Snake River Canyon (a.k.a. the Grand Canyon of the Snake) into Hoback Junction 13 miles south of Jackson. Several national forest campgrounds can be found after you pass Alpine.

If you're approaching Yellowstone country from the east, you can take U.S. Highway 26/287 from Dubois over Togwotee Pass into Grand Teton Park at Moran Junction. This takes you through Buffalo Valley and along the Buffalo Fork River. You won't see many people, but you're almost sure to see wildlife along this road. Around Hatchet, before you enter the Park at Moran, look for inexpensive national forest campgrounds.

You can also leave Cody on U.S. Highway 16/14/20, which takes you through the East Entrance of Yellowstone Park. This route takes you down Buffalo Bill Cody's old highway along the North Fork of the Shoshone River. Parts of U.S. 16/14/20 are scheduled for construction during the summer of 1998, but you'll find a nice stretch of new highway once you get into the Park. You'll also find lots of campgrounds along the North Fork, and about a dozen lodges and ranches that welcome drop-in dinner guests and overnighters.

U.S. Highway 212, one of the loveliest summer routes to Yellowstone Park, leaves I-90 16 miles west of Billings. It passes through Red Lodge 53 miles to the south. From Red Lodge, it climbs over 11,000-foot-high Beartooth Pass, dubbed by the late Charles Kuralt the most scenic drive in America. Be aware, if you've never driven in the mountains before, the Beartooth Highway can be scary. You can run into snow or slush on the road even in midsummer; the route closes each winter. On the backside you pass through Cooke City to enter Yellowstone Park at Silver Gate, the northeast entrance.

To get to Yellowstone Park's north and original entrance at Gardiner, head south from I-90 on U.S. Highway 89 at Livingston. This route will take you up the open Yellowstone Valley, through Emigrant (don't blink or you'll miss it) and on to Gardiner. The fishing is good here, but campgrounds aren't as plentiful as they are along the other northern routes.

Driving in the Parks

Yellowstone National Park

You've heard about Yellowstone, you've read about Yellowstone, and now you're here. Read your map. If it says the distance from Mammoth to Norris is 21 miles, count on it taking nearly an hour to drive. The speed limit in the Park is 45 mph, but the average speed is 33 miles per hour. There are only 12 safe places to pass, so slow down.

And prepare to bump, bounce and brake your way across the 350 miles of roads in the Park. Since roads were first built here in the 1880s, crews have fought to keep up with the disastrous effects of harsh winters, heavy use, and insufficient funds. Expect road construction delays. And expect narrow, bumpy, potholed roads in parts of the Park. Fortunately, recent years of construction have transformed some of the roads into smooth thoroughfares with actual shoulders. The biggest obstacle to smooth sailing, though, will be you and other drivers. We have seen traffic backed up for a mile while drivers stop in the middle of the road to photograph a bison by the road. "Bear jams" are worse. People park on the road and leave their cars, creating regular traffic knots. To complicate things, you (we do it, too) will try to navigate the knot while craning your neck to see what all the fuss is about. It's all a part of the Park experience. Laugh and enjoy it.

If you look in the rear-view mirror and see a long line of vehicles behind you, pull over and let them pass. Those who live in the communities surrounding the Park have to use Park roads to get from one place to another. While they love to watch wildlife too, they're very often traveling through on business, not vacation. If you

---

INSIDERS' TIP

You're getting off your plane at Idaho Falls Municipal Airport, and in front of you is an expectant, festive gathering of 10 or 20 or more. The near-daily event you're probably witnessing is a Mormon missionary's homecoming. Devout young Mormons leave home for two years to promote their religion around the world. Homecomings are proud and happy, often involving banners and balloons. One family last year even greeted its young returning missionary with a five-piece band.

hit the west or north entrances at about 8 AM, you'll find yourself waiting in line as cars creep through their turns at the gate. You have 14 miles before you have to decide which way to turn. If you want to race through the Park with barely a stop (we don't recommend it), the 142-mile Grand Loop takes you past almost every major attraction in Yellowstone. Even splitting your visit into a day each on the Upper Loop and the Lower Loop roads can be grueling because you'll want to hike, explore and simply stare. (See our Parks and Forests chapter for more information on the Loop roads.) We leave the planning and the decision-making to you. Happy Trails.

Grand Teton National Park

In Grand Teton Park, driving is easier. Planners started the Park in 1929 and didn't acquire most of its land until 1950. This means Park roads are highways first and scenic attractions second, unlike Grand Teton's older sister to the north. What locals call the outside road, U.S. Highway 89, carries a 55-mph speed limit until you pass through a Park entrance. This isn't Yellowstone Park: You can drive quite a ways inside Park boundaries without passing through an entrance station.

On Teton Park Road, which Park employees call the inside road, and on U.S. Highway 89 after you pass through an entrance station, speed limits drop to 45 mph, and generally you can expect to be able to go that fast. The tiniest loop road, Jenny Lake Loop, is also the only narrow, slow road of any significance. Wildlife and scenic wonders don't create the same kinds of congestion in Teton Park that they do in Yellowstone, either: Pullouts have been well-placed to coincide with the most likely places to sight wildlife or to "oooh" and "aaah" at the Tetons. So the most important consideration in this Park is not how slowly you must go, but how slowly you *should* go. It's often possible in Grand Teton Park to drive much faster than you ought to if you care about wildlife, which regularly cross roads to get to food and water. Slow down. And watch for the rubber-neckers. Mount Moran rising behind Jackson Lake, trumpeter swans gracefully sweeping onto the glassy surface of the Snake River Oxbow, a field of brilliant wildflowers — they do pull folks' attention from the dotted yellow lines.

Road and Travel Information

In Yellowstone Park, tune your radio to 1610 AM wherever you see the roadside signs. You will hear recorded safety messages and general Park information.

In Montana, call (800) 226-ROAD or (406) 444-6339 for statewide information. For the Bozeman area, call 586-1313; for the Billings area, call (406) 252-2806.

In Wyoming around Cody, call (307) 587-9966.

In eastern Idaho from November through March, call (208) 745-7278 for a 24-hour recorded message. For a real person, call (208) 745-7781.

Highway patrol emergency numbers in Greater Yellowstone are: (800) 442-9090 in Wyoming, (208) 587-9966 in Idaho and (406) 444-7000 in Montana.

By Air

International Airports

Salt Lake International Airport and Logan International Airport in Billings, Montana, are the two international airports serving our region. Salt Lake, with its high volume of flights, often has the cheapest rates around. Both airports are served by major carriers and six car-rental companies.

A shuttle operates between **Salt Lake International**, (801) 565-2400, and several eastern Idaho communities. Rexburg-based SLASH (Salt Lake Airport Shuttle Hop), (800) 359-6826, makes two runs per day in winter and three in summer at a one-way cost of less than $40. Another bus shuttle runs you up to Jackson Hole Airport and back. Jackson Hole Express, (800) 652-9510, operates several times per week for a one-way cost of less than $50.

If you're driving, the fastest, easiest route from the Salt Lake City airport into Yellowstone country is to head north on I-15. You'll be in Idaho Falls in 3½ hours if the weather's good. In winter get a road report, since drifting snow closes the interstate periodically. Alternatively, you can take the sce-

Yellowstone Country's Backcountry Byways

The following passage was supplied by Tony Huegel, author of Idaho Byways: Backcountry Drives for the Whole Family. *He is also the author of similar guides for California, Utah and Colorado.*

Traffic congestion may be the single most common complaint about visiting Yellowstone National Park and its environs. Without even realizing it, you can end up gazing not so much at natural wonders as at the rear ends of lumbering RVs, tour buses and countless cars — unless you know where to find Yellowstone country's quiet and scenic, though sometimes rough, unpaved backways. Two easy dirt roads inside the park allow motorized travelers to get a feel for old Yellowstone. Both historic byways are one-way, single-lane "auto trails" that let you escape the park's often-crowded paved roads. They parallel paved primary roads, providing alluring alternatives without major detours. A bit rocky here and there, they are closed after rain and snow storms. They offer fine mountain-biking opportunities. RVs and trailers are not permitted.

The 7-mile Blacktail Plateau Road, open June through September, begins west of Phantom Lake, on the south side of the Grand Loop Road midway between Mammoth Hot Springs and Tower Junction. It follows the approximate route of the old Bannock Indian Trail of the mid-1800s. As it ascends Blacktail Deer Plateau and passes south of Crescent Hill, the views include the Gallatin Range, Electric Peak, Sepulcher Mountain, Bunsen Peak and Antler Peak. Wildflowers bloom through June and July. Soon it passes through a mosaic of burned and unburned forests, reminders of the fires of 1988. It reconnects with the Grand Loop Road just west of the petrified tree turnoff.

High on the west rim of Gardner Canyon, the Old Gardiner Road courses for 5 miles between Mammoth Hot Springs and the park's north entrance station, near Gardiner, Montana. It is open May through October. The 1880s stagecoach and wagon route

— continued on next page

Photo: Jo Deurbrouck

A sign on the highway between Island Park, Idaho, and West Yellowstone, Montana, is a Greater Yellowstone feature.

crosses sagebrush tableland, providing panoramic views of the Gallatin Range, Gardiner and Mammoth and the traffic inching through the river canyon below. In spring and fall watch for pronghorn, elk, bison, mule deer, perhaps even bighorn sheep. The entrance to the Old Gardiner Road is a bit tricky to find. In Mammoth, go behind the hotel and to the right of Chittenden House. Go left at the stop sign, then immediately right. You'll see the sign.

Outside Yellowstone Park, more byways await. Just east of Cooke City, outside the park's northeast entrance, angle north from the famous Beartooth Highway at the sign for Daisy Pass. This generally easy 10-mile 4x4 loop, which can be snowy and muddy into July, will take you through glaciated Rocky Mountain scenery and over Daisy and Lulu passes, both about 9,700 feet. Below Lulu Pass you'll go down a gulch that would be the site of the hotly debated New World gold mine. You'll pass the Goose Lake Jeep Trail, a rough 4x4 and hiking trail to the Absaroka-Beartooth Wilderness. Then you'll ford Fisher Creek on the way back to the highway.

Another route begins in the John D. Rockefeller Jr. Memorial Parkway, between Grand Teton and Yellowstone. The occasionally rough Reclamation Road, a.k.a. Grassy Lake Road, runs 48 miles through aspen and lodgepole pine to Ashton, Idaho, from Flagg Ranch, Wyoming, coming out at U.S. Highway 89/191/287.

Put some effort into getting off the beaten path, and traffic won't be among your Yellowstone country memories.

nic route, exiting I-15 at Brigham City and heading up U.S. Highway 89 to Montpelier. At Montpelier take U.S. Highway 30 to Soda Springs, then Idaho Highway 34 to Freedom and then north on U.S. Highway 89 to Alpine, Wyoming. This will bring you to the Snake River Canyon, a short, scenic drive from Jackson Hole. The scenic route is not recommended for winter travel, but it takes you past the Wellsvilles, America's steepest mountain range, scenic Bear and Gray lakes and Blackfoot Reservoir. Plan on doubling your travel time if you choose this route.

At **Logan International Airport**, you'll find four car rentals and two taxi services. We recommend calling ahead to reserve rental cars, especially during the summer. You can call **Avis** at (406) 252-8007, **Budget** at (406) 259-4162, **Hertz** at (406) 248-9151 and **National** at (406) 252-7626. Taxis are usually waiting curbside at the airport for incoming passengers. If for any reason you do need to call a taxi, though, call City Cab at (406) 252-8700 or Yellow Cab at (406) 245-3033.

Powder River Tours operates a daily shuttle between Cody, Wyoming, and Billings. **Phidippides** out of Cody and **Red Lodge Shuttle** out of Red Lodge both operate reservation shuttles from Billings to their communi-

ties. For more information about all these shuttles, see the entries below under "When You Don't Need a Car."

From Billings, you head west 16 miles on I-90, then turn south on U.S. Highway 212. This route will take you through Red Lodge, Montana, over the Beartooth Pass to Cooke City, Montana, then into the Park. It takes about four hours to drive from Logan International to Yellowstone Park.

Regional Airports

West Yellowstone Airport
Airport Road, West Yellowstone, Mont.
• **(406) 646-7631**

Built in 1965, this high-elevation airport (6,642 feet) is open only during the summer months. During the summer, though, it's a hopping place serving numerous private planes and one commercial airline, SkyWest, which has three flights a day. Doris's Cantina, a Mexican restaurant in the airport, serves an array of Tex-Mex food good enough to entice West Yellowstone residents to drive the 3 miles from town (see our Restaurants chapter). Pilots can sleep overnight at an on-site campground. At the airport, you will find two rental car companies: Budget at (406) 646-7735 and Avis at (406) 646-7635. Grayline Tours of Yellowstone has a regular airport shuttle that in 1997 met flights for a round-trip fee of $22.50. Some of the hotels and motels in West Yellowstone also have courtesy phones at the airport.

Idaho Falls Municipal Airport
2140 N. Skyline Dr., Idaho Falls, Idaho
• **(208) 529-1221**

Idaho Falls Municipal Airport opened for business in 1929 with a 1,500-foot runway and one carrier called National Park Airways. But Idaho Falls has grown up, and so has its airport. A second runway was built. Since 1953, there have been three extensions of the longer of the two. In 1997, both runways underwent extensive refinishing. Now the airport regularly accommodates jets as large as Boeing 737s, but can land planes as large as 747s. Air Force One, a 747, has touched down here twice. Idaho Falls Municipal Airport now hosts more than 5,000 flights a year.

The big months for travel through the airport are July and August. April is the slowest month. Carriers are Delta, Delta's partner SkyWest, and Horizon, which partners with Alaska Airlines and Northwest. Flights are routed through Salt Lake City or Boise, so your first flight out or last flight in is always a short hop. Automobile rental companies at the airport are Avis, (800) 831-2847; Budget, (800) 527-0700; Hertz, (800) 654-3131; and National, (800) 227-7368. No shuttle service is available here; the only taxi service in town is Easy-Way Taxi and Delivery, (208) 525-8344.

Jackson Hole Airport
1250 E. Airport Rd., Jackson, Wyo.
• **(307) 733-7682**

This little airport has one terminal but six commercial carriers. Delta, SkyWest, American, United, Horizon and Mountain West all bring folks into Jackson Hole. Of these, Delta, with a major hub in nearby Salt Lake City, is by far the most active. You'll deplane from the 737, 757 or smaller propeller-driven plane onto the tarmac; the first thing you'll see is the raw, jagged skyline of the Tetons. Airport staff say it's tough tearing disembarking passengers away from that vista and moving them into the terminal. Jackson Hole Airport is the only commercial airport in the country located inside a national park. The airport is 9 miles north of Jackson. You're probably renting a car, but if you're not, Alltrans Inc., (307) 733-3135, meets every flight, 365 days a year. They'll take you to any hotel or condo in Teton County. A round-trip transfer to Jackson costs just less than $20. You can also call Buckboard Cab, (307) 733-1112. Car rental companies at Jackson Hole Airport are Alamo, (800) 327-9633; Avis, (800) 831-2847; Budget, (800) 527-0700; and Hertz, (800) 654-3131.

Gallatin Field Airport
No. 6 Gallatin Field, Belgrade, Mont.
• **(406) 388-8321**

It's confusing. Commonly referred to as the Bozeman airport, the Gallatin Field Airport is really in Belgrade, 8 miles north of Bozeman. When you land at the airport, if you rent a car, the most direct route to Yellowstone Park bypasses Bozeman. This 70,000-square-foot airport has been remodeled several times since it was built in 1942, and passenger service has grown accordingly. Delta, Northwest, Horizon and SkyWest all fly into Gallatin Field, which served 196,378 passengers in 1996. Northwest, the first airline to fly into Gallatin Field in 1947, has been serving the Bozeman area for 51 years. At Gallatin Field you'll find a restaurant and lounge upstairs, as well as a gift store downstairs.

To reserve a rental car at the airport, call Avis at (406) 388-6414, Hertz at (406) 388-6939, Budget at (406) 388-4091 and National at (406) 388-6694. A shuttle service, 4x4 Stage, provides year-round transportation from Gallatin Field to Big Sky, West Yellowstone and Mammoth Hot Springs. (See the entry below for more information.) City Taxi Inc., (406)586-2341, pro-

INSIDERS' TIP

If you want to wander around Jackson for a few hours in summer, don't waste your time cruising for parking spaces on the streets. Head for the free municipal parking lot on N. Cache, only two blocks from town square.

This powder-hound snowmobiler gets all he bargained for.

vides transportation from the airport to Bozeman as well as to outlying areas.

Yellowstone Regional Airport
3001 Tuggleby Dr., Cody, Wyo.
• **(307) 587-5096**

Of the 12 airports in Wyoming, the Yellowstone Regional Airport is the third-busiest in the state, with five daily flights to Denver and Salt Lake City. Despite the fact that it is a small regional airport, airfares on United Express and SkyWest flights to Cody are only $20 to $40 more than those to Billings, Montana's, Logan International Airport. In 1997, the 12,000-square-foot Yellowstone Regional Airport served nearly 60,000 passengers with just two gates and no concourses. You'll find a gift shop and a cafe in the airport that serves breakfast, lunch and dinner from 5 AM until 8 PM during the summer and from 5 AM until 7 PM during the winter.

Three rental car companies have offices in the airport. To reserve a car and find out more about drop-off fees (they can be very high, especially during the summer), call Hertz at (307) 587-2914, Avis at (307) 587-5792 and Thrifty at (307) 587-8855. Phidippides, an airport transportation messenger service, offers taxi services to and from the airport as well as custom transportation to Yellowstone Park. (See our heading below for more information.)

When You Don't Need a Car

Most visitors to Yellowstone country prefer to either drive their cars or rent at a regional airport. Others, like foreign visitors or winter travelers, want to leave the driving to someone else. If you're one of those people who quivers at the thought of navigating a mountain pass or nearly passes out when you see a road covered with black ice and blowing snow, you're not alone. Several bus companies and shuttle services in Greater

Yellowstone will pick you up at the airport and drive you straight to Yellowstone and Grand Teton parks or to entrance communities surrounding the Parks. Some of these same companies will take you for tours through the Parks and explain things you couldn't learn otherwise. To learn more about these services, read on.

Yellowstone National Park and West Yellowstone, Montana

Amfac Parks and Resorts Sightseeing Tours
Mammoth Hot Springs, Yellowstone National Park • (307) 344-7311

Some people traveling through the Parks without their own vehicle use Yellowstone Park Tour buses to get around. These tours depart from the Old Faithful Inn, Grant Village, Lake Hotel, Fishing Bridge RV Park, Canyon Lodge, Gardiner and Mammoth Hot Springs each day from mid-May through September 1. They follow three routes through Yellowstone Park and cost from $19.50 to $29.50 per person, depending on the tour and the pickup point. (Refer to our Attractions chapter for more information).

Grayline Tours of Yellowstone
633 Madison Ave., West Yellowstone, Mont. • Summer (406) 646-9374 or (800) 523-3102, winter (800) 733-2304

Grayline Tours of Yellowstone, a franchise of the national line, runs a shuttle between the West Yellowstone Airport and local hotels and motels. Grayline also operates tours of West Yellowstone and Big Sky that pick up passengers at some motels, hotels and campgrounds. Led by 25-year veteran driver Dennis Paterson,

Grayline's fleet of five driver/guides is trained to answer your questions. Courteous, enthusiastic and patient, these drivers can teach you in a day what you might never figure out on your own. Besides being tutored by Paterson (and by a series of audio tapes he has produced), new and experienced drivers have access to a huge library on Yellowstone. Grayline offers five trips, including ones that will take you through the Upper Loop, the Lower Loop (see our Area Overview chapter for more on the Loops), Quake Lake and Virginia City (see our Parks and Forests chapter) and Grand Teton Park; you can also take a Wildlife Safari. For more information on any of these tours or the shuttle service, we suggest that you call Grayline at the above number.

A tour of the Upper or Lower Loops will cost you $36 from West Yellowstone. A round-trip shuttle from the West Yellowstone airport to your hotel cost $22.50 in 1997.

Grand Teton National Park and Jackson Hole

Grand Teton Lodge Company
Jackson Lake Lodge, U.S. Hwy. 89 • (307) 543-2811

Grand Teton Lodge Company operates tours in the Park's original tour buses (spiffed up a bit, of course), dating back to the '40s and '50s. The fanciest of the three, The Bullet, seats 20 in plush reclining seats. The company also offers daily shuttles in summer from Jackson to Jackson Lake Lodge in the Park and between Colter Bay Village and Jackson Lake Lodge. The half-day Grand Teton Park tour starts at Jackson Lake Lodge and heads north and then south on the Park loop. It stops at Signal Mountain Lodge, Jenny Lake, Menor's Ferry, Chapel of the Transfiguration and other scenic and his-

---

INSIDERS' TIP

In Rexburg and other Mormon communities, streets are laid out Salt Lake City-style. A typical address would read like this: 253 E. 400 N. To decipher this, just remember that addresses on a given street are derived from that street's "name." In other words, 253 is on a street labeled 400, which is east and north of the center of town. There will also be a 253 W. 400 S.

toric stops. These tours cost $18, a bargain for the chance to gawk without having to watch where you're going. One-day trips begin at Jackson Lake Lodge, head north out of Grand Teton National Park and travel Yellowstone Park's lower loop, stopping for a picnic lunch and various Yellowstone attractions before heading back down past Flagg Ranch and finishing at the lodge. These trips cost around $40 and include lunch. Robert Reed guides most of these trips; he's been at it for seven years and gets rave reviews. Tours are available mid-May to mid-October.

National Park Tours/Gray Line of Jackson Hole Inc.

1680 Martin Ln., Jackson, Wyo.
• (307) 733 4325, (800) 443-6133

Your tour guide stands at the front of the bus in a cowboy hat. If he's like most Gray Line guides, he's been around these parts for more than 10 years. He's been trained at locally famous Teton Science School in geology, history and ecology. He may even be Jack Starks, former superintendent of Grand Teton National Park. Your bus is plush: a 31-passenger vehicle with tinted windows, heating and air conditioning and a television in front so you can watch videos on fire ecology and Yellowstone history. Your seat reclines. Gray Line picks up at all hotels and condos in Jackson Hole, including those in Teton Village. Your tour may take you into Grand Teton National Park and include a scenic boat ride across Jenny Lake ($38 plus your Park entrance fee). Or you may travel through Grand Teton National Park to Yellowstone Park, spin around Yellowstone's lower loop, stopping for lunch at Old Faithful, and return to Jackson in about 10 hours ($41 plus Park entrance fee, lunch not included). Both trips involve stops at scenic and historic

Getting off the pavement in Greater Yellowstone.

attractions. National Park Tours/Gray Line also offers year-round custom tours and charters throughout the Intermountain Rockies. Park tours are available May 1 to October 1.

A Personal Guide Service

No credit cards • 320 Bar Y Rd.,
Jackson, Wyo. • (307) 733-6312

There are no buses here and no alternative to your car. What Art Davis and Larry Rieser do is hop in your vehicle and guide you to the best sights. Trips are catered to your interests and built to fit your schedule. Rieser has lived in Jackson Hole for 24 years. He came here to ski but fell in love and stayed. Both men are ski instructors. This company started after Rieser, now in his 60s and guiding Snake River float trips for Barker-Ewing, decided the boats had gotten too heavy to haul up on a trailer. He

---

INSIDERS' TIP

If you're traveling through Idaho Falls, be sure to stop by the innovative Eastern Idaho Visitor Information Center, 505 Lindsay Boulevard, (208) 523-1010. Those smart folks bundled the Chamber of Commerce, the local visitors bureau, the Bureau of Land Management and Forest Service under one roof. The center has a vast array of brochures, pamphlets and books, several interpretive displays and extensive files for those who want more detailed information about almost anything Idaho-related.

worked for a local bus tour company one year but didn't feel that he was getting to know his guests. A Personal Guide Service is now 6 years old. Davis and Rieser operate about 200 trips every summer May through October. Half-day trips in Grand Teton National Park run around $125. Daytrips up to Yellowstone run $175.

Jackson's Hole Adventure
P.O. Box 2407, Jackson, WY 83001
• **(307) 654-7849, (800) 392-3165**

This is another quiet option: L.E. Schoenhals operates small, customized tours in her 1992 winterized Chevy van (with sunroof and tinted windows). You'll be one of six passengers. Schoenhals will almost certainly be your guide. Schoenhals has lived in Jackson Hole for nearly 20 years. A member of the Jackson Hole Historical Society, her main interest is pioneer history, but she can also show you great places for photos, teach you about the geology of the region and explain bear conservation issues in the Parks. Schoenhals conducts about 200 tours per year. All start at your hotel. In summer you pay $48 plus the Park entrance fee. The destination is Grand Teton Park. A boxed picnic lunch at Jackson Lake is the high point of the trip for many. In winter, the trip is more elaborate. You pay $72 for a driving tour around Jackson Hole, a stop at the spectacular National Museum of Wildlife Art and a sleighride out onto the National Elk Refuge where nearly 10,000 elk winter. There's no Park entrance fee because you never enter the Park.

Southwestern Montana

4x4 Stage
1765 Alaska Blvd. S., Belgrade, Mont.
• **(406) 388-6404**

Based at the Gallatin Field Airport north of Bozeman, 4x4 Stage shuttled about 14,000 people last year from the airport to Big Sky or to Yellowstone Park. During the winter, when travelers are heading to Yellowstone country to play in the snow, 4x4 runs four to six shuttles each day to West Yellowstone, seven trips to Big Sky and one to Mammoth Hot Springs. In the summer, when tourists feel more comfortable bringing their own vehicles, 4x4 cuts back the shuttles to two daily runs to West Yellowstone and one tour a day through Yellowstone Park. In addition, 4x4 Stage offers reservation tours from Bozeman through Yellowstone.

Red Lodge Shuttle
P.O. Box 635, Red Lodge, MT
• **(406) 446-2257, (888) 446-2191**

Red Lodge Shuttle provides by-reservation door-to-door service between Red Lodge and the airports in Billings and Cody. If driving the Beartooth Highway to get to a trailhead or Cooke City freaks you out, call Red Lodge Shuttle. Owners Mike Rick and Nancy Immel will drop you off at trailheads in the area, including those across Beartooth Highway near Cooke City. During the winter they provide a shuttle service from the town of Red Lodge to the Red Lodge Ski Area.

Northeastern Wyoming

Phidippides
P.O. Box 24, Wapiti, WY
• **(307) 899-1851, (307) 527-6789**

Frank Alvaro, a retired sheriff's deputy from California, will transport you, your lost luggage, packages, messages, you-name-it, from the Cody airport (and Cody) to almost anyplace in the region. If you want to celebrate your 50th wedding anniversary at Old Faithful, he or one of his drivers will pick you up at the airport and take you to Old Faithful, then return a few days later to bring you back. Alvaro, who has been running his service for four years, will deliver you to a trailhead anywhere in Yellowstone

INSIDERS' TIP

Bypass crowds at the south end of Grand Teton National Park by taking the back way in: scenic Wyo. Highway 390, also known as the Moose-Wilson Road. No trailers or RVs are allowed on the narrow stretch between the Park boundary and the visitor center in Moose.

country, take you to the Billings airport and deliver lost luggage in the middle of the night. He and his drivers, who keep a fleet of four Suburbans and a 15-passenger van on the road, carry backpacks, fishing poles and sleeping bags with them because they never know where they'll end up for the night. Alvaro charges $35.95 for a trip to Billings and $1 a mile for trips into Yellowstone or Grand Teton parks.

Powder River Tours
1700 E. Hwy. 51, Gillette, Wyo.
• **(307) 527-6316, (800) 442-3682**

Powder River offers a daily run from Cody to Billings. In addition, from the end of May until the end of September, Powder River features a daylong tour from Cody through Yellowstone Park's Lower Loop. The tours leave Cody at 7:30 AM and return at 7 PM. When you make your reservations, you can arrange to be picked up at your motel or campground. In 1997, the tour cost $49 plus tax and a $10 Park entrance fee per person. For more specific information about the Powder River tours from Cody, call (307) 527-6316.

As you plan your trip,
remember that although
Greater Yellowstone is
an area of low population
and seasonal solitude,
in summer we
are full up.

Hotels, Motels and Cabins

Innkeepers and hotel staff in Jackson, Wyoming, tell of desperate phone calls originating as far north as Old Faithful Inn in Yellowstone Park 97 miles away, from travelers in search of a roof to sleep under. As you plan your trip, remember that although Greater Yellowstone is an area of low population and seasonal solitude, in summer we are full up. To the gills. Even good campsites aren't easy to find at the last moment. In general, this becomes truer the closer you get to Yellowstone Park, Jackson and Grand Teton Park.

So the word to the wise is: Make your reservations early — very early if you are planning to stay in a prime location (say, Old Faithful Inn) or at a prime time (say, July 4 or New Year's).

Yellowstone country is full of unique accommodations options. Included elsewhere in this book are chapters on camping, guest ranches, resorts and lodges and on bed and breakfast inns. What you'll find in this chapter is a selection of the more interesting and pleasant hotel, motel and cabin accommodations available in our region.

We've tried to cover the range of available prices and styles from posh to simple-and-clean to ultra-rustic. It would be impossible to include all the choices in our region, so we've gathered together places we feel will meet your needs and then some. If you know of an establishment that should be included and isn't, we'd love to hear about it.

Most hotels and motels and many cabins are available year round. If an establishment closes for one or more seasons, we've pointed that out. We also let you know if a business does not accept credit cards. Following are a few notes on amenities.

•Especially at higher elevations, rooms may lack air conditioning; we don't address that fact in their entries though, since heat is more likely to be useful during our chilly nights. Our cabins and hotel/motel rooms are all heated.

•Unless noted, expect that hotel and motel rooms have cable or satellite TV and phones.

•You may also expect private baths in all listed options, unless noted.

• If kitchenettes are available, we let you know.

•With almost no exceptions, the establishments we've selected offer wheelchair-accessible and nonsmoking rooms.

• Many provide complimentary shuttles from nearby airports. Establishments close to ski areas generally either have free shuttles to the lifts or know about convenient, low-cost transportation.

• Most do not accept pets, and those that do prefer not to advertise the fact.

• Most establishments told us they could accommodate a variety of group sizes, but some are more flexible than others, of course. If these issues concern you, ask when you make your reservation.

www.insiders.com

See this and many other **Insiders' Guide®** destinations online — in their entirety.

Visit us today!

so that accommodations in Yellowstone Park and its gate communities come first. Next is Grand Teton Park and Jackson Hole. Surrounding areas in Idaho, Montana and Wyoming come next, in that order.

Finally, we offer a section on hostels, those traveler-friendly places that offer the basic overnight amenities without taking a big bite out of your budget.

If you don't find what you're looking for here, you may be looking for something in our other accommodations chapters. Many lodges and guest ranches, for instance, accept drop-in overnight traffic if they have room. For about the cost of a nicer motel, you can stay the night on a ranch. Check out those chapters for more information.

Oh, and a final word about "rustic charm." Around here, that phrase gets attached to everything from falling-down cabins with no electricity to high-end hotels that happen to have log walls and Native American patterns on their plush down comforters. If your prospective host says the establishment has rustic charm, ask what that means. It could mean no private bathroom. Or no heat.

Price Code

To help you determine an accommodation that suits your budget, we have included a dollar-sign code in each listing representing that establishment's lowest price range for a two-person stay in the most expensive season. For most hotels and motels, this is summer; around ski areas it's winter. Most establishments offer a variety of room styles with rates that spiral up from the listed range.

$	$25 to $49
$$	$50 to $75
$$$	$76 to $100
$$$$	$101 and more

Please note that pricing information was provided by the establishments and can vary during holidays and other events. Also note that in Jackson and Grand Teton Park, many accommodations have prices that top our scale and break through the other side. So $$$$ in Jackson can mean a room priced at anywhere from $101 to — no kidding — $450.

Many establishments offer at least three sets of rates: summer, winter and shoulder (fall and spring) with shoulder rates being generally the lowest. This makes travel in fall and spring a real bargain, with savings of more than half off in many areas. In general, the closer you get to Grand Teton and Yellowstone parks, the more pronounced the shoulder savings.

As in most chapters, entries are organized

Yellowstone National Park

Inside the Park

Before you make reservations for your stay in the Park, there are a few things you ought to know. First of all, the Park is not a city. That means several things. Some of the accommodations, like the cabins at Roosevelt, may seem downright primitive to you. They're heated with woodstoves (easy-light logs are supplied), and they don't have bathrooms. This means you'll have to share a communal bathhouse with other folks in camp. We hope this information won't discourage you from staying in the cabins. If you look at them from a historic perspective and realize that some folks in Yellowstone country still live in cabins with no running water or electricity, you may be able to appreciate the charm.

Many of the rooms at the Old Faithful Inn, built at the turn of the century, also won't have private bathrooms. But we think the charm and privilege of being able to stay in this old inn far outweigh the inconvenience. A couple other things you won't find in your rooms are telephones and TVs. In fact, there's only one TV available to the public in the whole Park, and that's in the lounge at the Mammoth Dining Room.

Also, don't expect neatly manicured lawns with bright flowers planted here and there. This is the Park, where wild grass grows up to your porch and wild animals may walk right up to your door. In fact, in the fall of 1997, a bull elk in rut refused to let cabin dwellers at Mammoth out of their rooms until he was chased off. Rut is the breeding season, and all that testosterone sometimes goes to a bull's head, making him belligerent. You may also wake up to find a bison standing in front of your porch. Please remember that even though these animals may look slow, sleepy and pettable, they can be very quick and dangerous.

In Yellowstone Park, you'll find 2,500 rooms, including 1,232 cabins. Two of the hotels listed below — Mammoth and the Old Faithful Snow Lodge — are open during the winter from mid-December until about the first week in March. The rest are open only during the summer months. A new log Snow Lodge, built around the old Snow Lodge at Old Faithful, should be ready for the 1998 summer season.

All these facilities are operated by the Park's chief concessionaire, Amfac Parks and Resorts. For reservations at all Park hotels and cabins, call Amfac Reservations at (307) 344-7311.

Canyon Lodge and Cabins

$ • Canyon Village, Yellowstone National Park • (307) 344-7311

Built in the 1950s and '60s, the Canyon Lodge offers some standard hotel-type rooms as well as fourplex "cabins." All cabins have private bathrooms. Cascade Lodge (smaller than and separate from the main lodge), is the Park's newest lodging facility, built in 1993. It offers 30 hotel-style rooms in a country setting. At the main lodge, you'll find an activities desk in the lobby, as well as restrooms, a lounge, a gift shop and several dining options. Canyon Village is a hopping-off spot for Park visitors, so expect lots of traffic and plenty of people in the village itself. The community has a visitor information center along with a Hamilton General Store, a U.S. Post Office and a photo shop.

Grant Village

$$ • Grant Village, Yellowstone National Park • (307) 344-7311

Completed in 1984, Grant Village is one of Yellowstone's newest lodging facilities. In six two-story complexes that house 50 rooms each at the southern tip of Yellowstone Lake (see our Natural Attractions chapter), you'll find regular motel-style rooms with private bathrooms with showers. They're a welcome relief if you've just spent days camping on the road. Nearby, you'll find two restaurants, a lounge, a gift shop and a laundry facility. Grant Village is one of the pickup spots for the Yellowstone Park Tour bus.

Lake Lodge Cabins

$ • Lake Village, Yellowstone National Park • (307) 344-7311

The Lake Lodge offers a rustic alternative to the elegance of the grand Lake Hotel. Inside the lodge, just off the huge lobby lounge with open beams and a wood floor, you'll find a cafeteria and a gift shop. Lake Lodge offers both Western and Frontier Cabins, all with private baths. Built in the traditional bar-

---

INSIDERS' TIP

If you like saving money on your stay in Jackson Hole, book accommodations out at Teton Village for the summer. The "hottest" months here are during ski season, so you can expect bargains when temperatures rise. In winter, stay in Jackson and grab a shuttle to Jackson Hole Mountain Resort to save big bucks on a motel bill. Many Jackson motels charge as little as half their summer rate in winter.

rack style of the 1950s and '60s, these cabins offer a comfortable stay on the shores of Yellowstone Lake. Slip out of bed early in the morning, get a cup of coffee at the cafeteria, stroll to the shores of Yellowstone Lake and watch morning flood the water. You'll find laundry facilities nearby. And the Bridge Bay Marina, where you can take a scenic cruise, a guided fishing trip or rent a boat, is just a hop, skip and a jump away. (For more information on Bridge Bay Marina, read our Attractions chapter.)

Lake Yellowstone Hotel and Cabins
$$ • Lake Village, Yellowstone National Park • (307) 344-7311

Glide into the Lake Hotel, admire the blue-tile fireplace and the sweeping staircase, then head straight for the long, elegant sunroom. Find yourself the most comfortable wicker chair facing the best view of Yellowstone Lake, sit down and gaze into the distance. Evenings, you can do your gazing to the tunes of a piano player. Anytime, you can sip mint juleps.

Built in 1891 by the Northern Pacific Railroad, the Lake Hotel was treated to reconstructive surgery in the 1920s by architect Robert Reamer (he designed the Old Faithful Inn) who transformed the shoebox-shaped hotel into its current elegant state. The sunroom was his idea. So was the dining room, another grand space with Bordeaux tablecloths and plenty of windows facing the lake. This hotel, which now houses 194 guest rooms, underwent a 10-year restoration project in the 1980s in which new rooms were added. The old rooms are spacious and high-ceilinged with bathrooms, and the new rooms follow suit. The cabins (there are 102 of them), are painted a creamy yellow; they all have private bathrooms.

Mammoth Hot Springs Hotel and Cabins
$$ • Mammoth, Yellowstone National Park • (307) 344-7311

This year-round hotel, built in 1911 and finished in 1937, hints of the days when trips to Yellowstone were mostly limited to the wealthy. The hotel and an annex behind it offer a total of 150 rooms and suites. During the summer, the annex rooms are used as a managers' dorm, but they are open to the public during the winter months. In addition to the hotel rooms, the complex has 126 cabins with and without private baths (communal facilities with toilets and showers are available). In 1997, the cabins rented for $69 and $38 respectively. Clustered behind the Mammoth dining room and lodge, these cabins are spacious, light and airy despite their 1930s vintage.

Just 5 miles from Yellowstone's North Entrance, the Mammoth Hotel is at the heart of the Park's headquarters and right across the street from the Albright Visitor Center. You'll find fine dining at the Mammoth dining room (see our Restaurants chapter) and a comfortable lounge adjacent to it. At the other end of the building is a fast-food outlet. You can stock up on groceries and camping supplies at the Hamilton Store in Mammoth. If it's a tour of the Park you'd like, Yellowstone Park Tours will pick you up at the door.

Old Faithful Inn
$ • Old Faithful, Yellowstone National Park • (307) 344-7311

Sit on the outside balcony and sip a Bloody Mary or slurp an ice cream cone while you wait for Old Faithful to erupt right in front of the inn. Or lounge on one of the inside balconies and read a good book, write a letter or just watch people. The crown jewel of Yellowstone Park lodging, the Old Faithful Inn is worth a visit (and a tour) even if you don't stay overnight. Built of massive Douglas fir logs with a huge lobby that opens to the crow's nest 85 feet above, the inn is a testimony to the determination and ingenuity of the workmen who built it in 1904. At the center of the lobby is a 14-foot-square, four-sided chimney with eight fireplaces. It's made of 500 tons of rhyolite stone. A hand-forged wrought-iron clock clings to the massive chimney and still keeps perfect time.

When the hotel opened, it had 146 rooms and was equipped with running water, electricity and steam heat. Today, the 75 remaining original rooms are much the same as they were at the turn of the century — small and dimly lit with a dangling bulb; the only thing missing is the chamber pot. You'll find restrooms and showers down the hall and two "bath" rooms with claw-legged tubs for guests who choose to soak. In the newer wing, 250 larger, brighter rooms each have private bathrooms. Several of the older balcony rooms, which are larger and overlook the geyser basin in front of the inn, are so sought-after they're reserved two years in advance. In all, the inn has 325 rooms ranging from small with no private bath that rent for $47 to large suites for $305.

Besides the grand formal dining room, the Old Faithful Inn houses a fast-food outlet, an ice cream counter, an espresso cart, a lounge and a gift shop. Nearby, you'll find a gas station and general store. The Park's tour buses pick up passengers at the inn.

Old Faithful Lodge Cabins
$ • Old Faithful, Yellowstone National Park • (307) 344-7311

Opposite the Old Faithful Inn, on the other side of its namesake geyser, the Old Faithful Lodge is the Park's modern-day answer to accommodating hordes of tourists. Inside the lodge itself, you'll find a gift shop and several dining options including a cafeteria, two snack shops and an espresso cart in the lounge. The 132 "cabins" at Old Faithful Lodge are barrack-like structures built in the '50s and '60s and range in price from $25 to $41, depending on whether or not they have private bathrooms.

Old Faithful Snow Lodge and Cabins
$ • Old Faithful, Yellowstone National Park • (307) 344-7311

In summer, this year-round lodge is overshadowed by the Old Faithful Inn. During winter, though, the Old Faithful Snow Lodge is the happenin' hub of Yellowstone's winter wonderland and a welcome sight at the end of the snowmobile trail. The lodge itself offers 31 rooms, while 38 cabins offer more private ac-

commodations. The lodge has a family restaurant and a gift shop. A nearby snack shop is open summer and winter.

Roosevelt Lodge Cabins
$ • Yellowstone National Park
• (307) 344-7311

Step into the Old West and turn-of-the-century living at the Roosevelt Lodge Cabins. Ease into one of those lodgepole rocking chairs lining the Lodge's sprawling porch, tip back your hat, prop those feet up on the porch railing and survey the landscape before you. Named after President Teddy Roosevelt, who liked to camp where the lodge now stands, the Roosevelt Lodge was built in 1908. Inside, you'll find a large lodgepole family-style dining room. Outside you'll find an array of cabins ranging from $27 to $69, depending on their amenities. The Roughrider and Rustic cabins have woodburning stoves, and the Economy cabins have a toilet and a sink, but no shower. A few Frontier cabins come equipped with a shower and toilet. Communal bathrooms and showers are scattered throughout the cabin area.

The Roosevelt Corral offers guided horseback riding, stagecoach rides and chuckwagon dinner cookouts. (For more information, see our Other Recreation chapter.) If you're planning to stay in the area, it's best to make reservations well in advance for the activities at the Roosevelt Lodge.

Entrance Communities

West Yellowstone, Montana

Alpine Motel
$$ • 120 Madison Ave., West Yellowstone, Mont. • (406) 646-7544

After 41 years of same-family ownership, the Alpine was bought in 1997 by the owners of the Chinatown Cafe next door. This motel is

---

INSIDERS' TIP

Where is Kelly? This tiny community just outside Grand Teton National Park is marked on maps but no longer exists. Founded in 1907, the town was wiped out by the 1927 flooding of the Gros Ventre River.

small with only 12 units, all with two queen-size beds. They are very clean, cheerful, spacious, conveniently located and reasonably priced. The Alpine is open from May through October.

Best Western Cross-Winds Motor Inn

$$$ • 201 Firehole Ave., West Yellowstone, Mont. • (406) 646-9557, (800) 528-1234

There's no fuss and no muss at this compact 70-unit motel within easy walking distance of every major attraction in West Yellowstone. The rooms, decorated in darker colors that suggest sprawling and lounging are expected here, are spacious and comfortable. The Cross-Winds offers rooms with single and double queen-size beds, as well as a few king suites. A few rooms have microwaves and refrigerators.

Evenings, you can swim or soak away the day in the Cross-Winds' indoor pool and spa. Mornings, you can stroll to the motel lobby,

snack on complimentary rolls and sip hot coffee. Then walk your dog or swing your child at the West Yellowstone Town Park across the street. If it's snowmobiles you're after, the Cross-Winds can arrange rentals for you on-site or ahead of time, through an arrangement with Yellowstone Adventures (see our Winter Sports chapter).

Best Western Executive Inn

$$$ • 236 Dunraven, West Yellowstone, Mont. • (406) 646-7681, (800) 528-1234

Situated around a courtyard and a deliciously inviting swimming pool, this two-story, 83-room motel spells affordable fun, summer or winter. The rooms, cheerfully decorated with varying themes of mauve, blue or sage carpet and matching floral bedspreads, are spacious and clean. The Executive offers a variety of room sizes and combinations including family suites and some with fireplaces. A few on the back side of the main floor have doors that open to the alley — perfect for private parking, even better for driving your snowmobile right up to the door. A dining room off the main lobby offers breakfast and dinner, including an all-you-can-eat buffet for both meals. The Executive will arrange snowmobile packages for guests wanting to sled during the winter months. You'll find a playground across the street at the Town Park.

Brandin' Iron Motel and RV Park
$$ • 201 Canyon St., West Yellowstone, Mont. • (406) 646-9411, (800) 217-4613

Park your car and head out on foot (or snowmobile, if it's winter time.) The Brandin' Iron is right smack-dab in the middle of the action. Cross one street and you're in the West Yellowstone Town Park. Cross kitty-corner and you're at Kentucky Fried Chicken. Cross the other way, head down the block and you're at Bud Lilly's Trout Shop (see our Shopping chapter). Owned by Ventures West, the out-of-Park division of the Hamilton Stores, Yellowstone Park, the Brandin' Iron has 87 spacious and recently redecorated rooms. Each room comes with a telephone and other amenities, including a clock radio and a refrigerator. Mornings you'll find coffee in the lobby. Winter mornings you're apt to find a fire crackling in the lobby fireplace.

The Brandin' Iron offers snowmobile packages for winter guests. You'll also find outdoor plug-ins (for car heaters) and two hot tubs in which to soothe those sore muscles. A 16-unit RV park behind the motel is open during the summer. Spaces rent for $23.50 per night.

Dude Motor Inn
$$ • 3 Madison Ave., West Yellowstone, Mont. • (406) 646-7301

When he was the governor of California, Ronald Reagan once stayed here while attending a governor's conference in West. The face of the Dude Motor Inn has since changed, but its location on Boundary Street, which borders Yellowstone Park, has not. Simple, clean and on a back street, the Dude is still only a block off Main Street. After a day in the Park, bypass the Main Street traffic and slip into the Dude. In winter, cruise up to the Dude on your snow machine, dude. Bring your own machine or reserve one from the rental fleet provided by owners Dean and Leila Seely. The Dude has 25 rooms and 60 snowmobiles.

The Hibernation Station
$$$ • 212 Gray Wolf Ave., West Yellowstone, Mont. • (406) 646-4200, (800) 580-3557

Chances are you won't want to get out of bed once you sleep between the country-fresh sheets topped with a goose-down comforter at the Hibernation Station. Come to think of it, maybe that's why the owners called this collection of picture-perfect (inside and out) log cabins the Hibernation Station. Built with big, fire-killed Douglas fir logs, each cabin is designed and decorated differently. Each has at least one tapestry-covered wall and hand-hewn log furniture. Each has some carpet, accented with tile or slate or wood floors. Some have fireplaces, a few have kitchenettes, a couple have spas and fireplaces. All 26 cabins are unique — no cookie-cutter cabins here. And all (except for an upstairs-downstairs duplex) are one-room, one-bath units approximately 16-foot-by-22-foot.

Now entering its third season of operation, the Hibernation Station is still evolving, which means you'll see signs of construction around the complex. The owners have, so far, built 10 cabins each year, and they plan to keep on going until they have 55. At the south edge of town, the Hibernation Station is within easy walking distance of the Grizzly Discovery Center and the IMAX Theater (see our Attractions chapter). Snowmobiles are welcome. You park right outside your cabin door, and Yellowstone's West Entrance is just a couple of blocks away.

Kelly Inn West Yellowstone
$$$ • 104 S. Canyon Ave., West Yellowstone, Mont. • (406) 646-4544, (800) 259-4672

New with a rustic theme that includes chainsaw-carved bears, raccoons and a cougar hanging from posts, peeking in windows and crouched on rooftops, the three-story Kelly Inn houses 78 spacious rooms. Plush carpet, wallpaper and curtains that accent both make these rooms soothing. Most are standards with two queen-size beds. You'll also find several deluxe rooms with either two kings or two queen-sze beds with a sofa-sleeper, a refrigerator and a microwave. A few Jacuzzi suites are outfitted with a king-size bed and sofa-sleeper, as well as a microwave, sink, refrigerator and wet bar. Rooms on the ground floor have both interior and exterior doors, which means snowmobilers can drive their sleds right up to the outside door. After donning their swimsuits, they can exit through the interior door and head for the Kelly Inn's indoor swimming pool, one of the largest in West Yellowstone. Mauve tile surrounds the pool, while tables and chairs invite poolside relaxation and conversation. You can soak in the sauna and whirlpool in the pool room. A continental breakfast is served each morning in the lobby. The Kelly Inn opened its doors in January 1996. It is across the street from the National Geographic IMAX Theater and within easy walking distance of downtown restaurants.

The Madison Hotel

$ • 139 Yellowstone Ave., West Yellowstone, Mont. • (406) 646-7745

He was a stagecoach driver and she worked at a restaurant. They married, bought a piece of ground in West Yellowstone, put up a tent hotel and then began building the Madison Hotel in 1912. Years later, owners Roxy and Dolly Bartlett were entertaining Clark Gable and other movie stars at their grand hotel. Today, the Madison Hotel is not so grand and not for those who must have amenities. It is for those who have a fascination with the olden days and love surprises. Step through the creaking latch-door and into the old pine lobby and you'll see what we mean. Straight ahead is the original log staircase. If you shut your eyes for an instant, you might be able to see a turn-of-the-century tourist floating down the stairs to lounge in the lobby and read the news. Upstairs, you'll find an assortment of rooms with pine beds, antique dressers, an old-fashioned sink and an antique wooden medicine cabinet. The sheets are snow white and soft. The walls, not exactly soundproof, are plain, unplaned planks. You'll find showers and restrooms down the hall. The Madison has a large gift shop and 17 newer motel rooms (with private baths) in back. We recommend the older rooms for those with an adventuresome spirit.

Roundup Motel

$$ • 3 Madison Ave., West Yellowstone, Mont. • (406) 646-7301

Owners Dean and Leila Seely have virtually rebuilt the Roundup. The older, one-story brick motel has been replaced by a two-story structure with 34 spacious and functional rooms. But the old neon sign featuring a miniskirted cowgirl twirling two lariats still stands above the office. (It serves as office for both the Dude Motor Inn across the street and the Roundup.) Like the Dude, the Roundup looks across the street into Yellowstone Park. The Roundup shares a snowmobile fleet with the Dude Motel.

Stage Coach Inn

$$$ • 209 Madison Ave., West Yellowstone, Mont. • (406) 646-7381, (800) 842-2882

Step into yesteryear at the Stage Coach Inn, where the lodgepole staircase and mezzanine rail remain as reminders of simpler frontier times in West Yellowstone. Built in 1948, the Stagecoach has since had several face lifts. But the best of the old building remains in the lobby, and the updated exterior still resembles the old Stage Coach Inn featured in photos throughout the inn's halls. Decorated in soothing sandstone tones with a wildlife motif, the inn's 80 rooms are simply appointed.

You'll find a friendly, helpful staff and a spacious knotty-pine-paneled lobby with a concierge desk where someone can meet your every need. You'll also find a coffee shop and a dining room. And we hope you packed your dancing duds because, get this, the Stage Coach has an upstairs and a downstairs bar, each with a dance floor (see our Nightlife chapter). The underground garage has spaces for 24 vehicles on a first-come, first-served basis. The outside lamp poles also have plug-ins for car heaters.

Three Bear Lodge and Restaurant

$$ • 217 Yellowstone Ave., West Yellowstone, Mont. • (406) 646-7353, (800) 646-7353

You know the feeling. You've been in and out of the car all day. You've stopped to watch wildlife, walked through geyser basins, woven your way through traffic, waited for Old Faithful to erupt and wrangled with hot, tired kids. Now you want a place to park your car and rest your weary carcass. If you've had one of those days, you're in luck at the Three Bears Lodge. Drive right out of the West Entrance, go straight for two blocks and park your car. Head for your room and sink into a comfortable chair. Or put on your swim suit and head for the heated pool. Ahhh. Now, you might be ready to think about dinner. You won't have to think too hard, though. Right next door is the Three Bears Restaurant, a casual restaurant that serves good food in a cozy atmosphere. (For more information, see our Restaurants chapter.)

The Three Bears Lodge, a West Yellowstone favorite since 1948, has 75 up-to-date, cheerful rooms that range from a basic single (queen-size bed) to an executive suite with a king-size bed and a spa. The Three Bear Lodge has a 120-snowmobile rental fleet for winter guests. The Lodge also rents snowmobile clothing and offers a guide service, including snowcoach tours of the Park.

Wagon Wheel Campgrounds and Cabins

$$, no credit cards • 408 Gibbon Ave., West Yellowstone, Mont.
• (406) 646-7872

The Wagon Wheel boasts eight well-maintained, spotless cabins in a cute and cozy RV park/campground shaded by mature trees. The cabins, made of logs and decorated in different themes, were built in the 1940s. They range from a honeymoon cabin with one queen-size bed to a two-story, three-bedroom cabin that sleeps seven or eight. Some have kitchenettes. The Wagon Wheel closes for the winter. For more information about the Wagon Wheel, see our Campgrounds and RV Parks chapter.

West Yellowstone Conference Hotel Holiday Inn SunSpree Resort

$$$$ • 315 Yellowstone Ave., West Yellowstone, Mont. • (406) 646-7365, (800) 646-7365

The list of amenities at this new hotel is longer even than the name itself. Besides the indoor pool, spa, sauna and exercise room just off the lobby, you'll find a refrigerator, a microwave, a coffee maker and a hair dryer in each of the 123 rooms. Built in 1994, the West Yellowstone Conference Hotel Holiday Inn SunSpree Resort (we like to say this mouthful) is a popular convention center that also caters to families. That's why you'll find the latest Nintendo games in each room, too. The activities desk in the lobby is for everyone. There, someone can help you arrange bike rentals, tours, rafting, horseback riding or a day of guided fishing. In winter, you'll want to rent one of the hotel's 200 snowmobiles or reserve a ride in a snowcoach.

For you conventiongoers who insist upon mixing work with your play, the Holiday Inn has 10,000 square feet of meeting space. Savor microbrews at the Iron Horse Saloon, then eat elk, buffalo or beefalo (a cross between beef and buffalo) at the Oregon Short Line Restaurant on the premises. Adults and children alike will delight in a stroll through the Oregon Short Line 1903, a beautifully restored VIP railroad car adjacent to the restaurant and saloon. (For more information, see our Attractions chapter.)

Gardiner, Montana

Absaroka Lodge

$$$ • U.S. Hwy. 89 at Yellowstone River Bridge, Gardiner, Mont.
• (406) 848-7414, (800) 755-7414

Before or after a day in Yellowstone, sit on your private balcony overlooking the Yellowstone River below and the Park beyond. If it's one of the kitchen suites you're in (they cost only $10 more than the regular rooms with two queen-size beds), put dinner in the oven and let it cook while you contemplate. Brand-new and well-maintained, the Absaroka Lodge has 41 clean, comfortable, carpeted rooms with private baths and plenty of space

---

INSIDERS' TIP

Why do they call it Jackson Hole? In fur trapper lingo, a hole was a valley. Jackson Hole was named after trapper David E. Jackson. If you want to do it like the locals, call the town Jackson and the valley Jackson Hole.

Cedar siding and indoor murals by local artists —part of the
charm of accommodations in Greater Yellowstone.

to sprawl. All but two of the rooms have two queen-size beds.

There is a lawn in front of the Lodge with park benches overlooking the river and the town of Gardiner. The lodge owners will gladly help you map out a day in or out of the Park, and they can arrange guided fishing or rafting trips. The Absaroka Lodge is within easy walking distance of dining and shopping in Gardiner.

Hillcrest Cottages
$$ • U.S. Hwy. 89, Gardiner, Mont.
• (406) 848-7353, (800) 970-7353

These cute little cottages are perched on a side street just off U.S. Highway 89 on the north side of the Yellowstone River in Gardiner. Newly refurbished, each of the 12 units has either a small kitchenette or a full kitchen. Rooms range from one- to five-bed cottages, the biggest sleeping up to eight people. Sit on your cabin steps and sip coffee in the morning or a cocktail at night. Or stroll down the back street and peek behind the scenes of Gardiner. If you must, walk downtown and sample Gardiner's nightlife. Clean and simple, the Hillcrest's charm lies in the friendly, homey atmosphere provided by owners Art and Annie Bent, who will loan you cooking utensils if you

have forgotten to bring your own. The Hillcrest Cottages have been in the Bent family for 25 years.

Maiden Basin Inn
$$$ • 4 Maiden Basin Rd., Gardiner, Mont.
• (406) 848-7080, (800) 624-3364

We weren't sure where to put this unique inn, which sits back from Mont. Highway 89, 5 miles north of Gardiner overlooking the Yellowstone Valley. Maiden Basin Inn caters to families and offers seven cabins, five of which include full kitchens or kitchenettes. They rent by the night or week and range from a spacious studio with a kitchenette to the Yellowstone Suite with a private deck and whirlpool bath, a full kitchen and panoramic views. One cabin without a kitchen is wheelchair-accessible. A continental breakfast is available to all guests. Winter rates are lower.

Yellowstone River Motel
$$ • 14 Park St., Gardiner, Mont.
• (406) 848-7303

Hidden behind the Amfac warehouse in Gardiner, the Yellowstone River Motel is a combination of functional Western and old-fashioned rooms. An older wing has spacious, newly carpeted rooms with knotty pine or plaster walls. Although these rooms do not have air conditioning, windows on either side of the room provide plenty of cross-ventilation for the cool mountain air in the evenings. (Some chilly nights you won't want to leave your windows open.) Rooms 109, 110 and 111 open onto an older patio overlooking the Yellowstone River. Watch otter play in the river or elk hang out in front of your room. The newer rooms are more spacious and air-conditioned. The Yellowstone River Motel has 40 units and is open from mid-April until Halloween.

Yellowstone Village Inn
$$$ • U.S. Hwy. 89, Gardiner, Mont.
• (406) 848-7417, (800) 228-8158

The sign here says: "Elk Stay Free." So do children younger than 12. If you've been to Gardiner before, you'll know what the sign means. From late fall through spring the elk move into town, nibbling on anything that isn't protected by a very tall fence. Built in 1992, the Yellowstone Village Inn has 43 rooms, including three family condos and one suite. Most rooms, though, have either one or two queen-size beds. The Inn also offers a complimentary continental breakfast and provides a guest laundry on the premises.

For recreation, in addition to an indoor pool and sauna, the Village Inn arranges horseback rides with a local outfitter. Mornings, you'll find free coffee in the lobby. On cold mornings, you'll find a fire crackling in the lobby fireplace. Summer evenings, you'll want to treat yourselves to a chuckwagon dinner theater at Montana Blues, located in a barn-like building in front of the Village Inn. (For more information, see our Nightlife chapter.)

Silver Gate and Cooke City, Montana

Alpine Motel
$$ • U.S. Hwy. 212, Cooke City, Mont.
• (406) 838-2262

Make your reservations as early as possible at this popular 25-unit motel in snow country. Right across the street from the Miner's Saloon and right in the middle of town, the Alpine has sparkling clean rooms ranging from singles to suites with kitchens. Most of the rooms, though, are singles or doubles with queen-size beds. You'll find newer rooms in a two-story complex built in 1993. The Alpine is open year round.

High Country Motel
$ • U.S. Hwy. 212, Cooke City, Mont.
• (406) 838-2272

Winter or summer, the High Country offers cabins and motel rooms to weary travelers and wayward snowmobilers. Whatever the season, the High Country is right in the middle of the action. In summer, High Country's 15 units fill fast (often months ahead of time between mid-June and mid-August), so be sure to call ahead. You'll find an assortment of carpeted, wood-paneled rooms with either one queen-size or two double beds. From Christmas to New Year's and on President's Day weekend, the units are booked almost a year in advance.

Soda Butte Lodge
$$ • U.S. Hwy. 212, Cooke City, Mont.
• (406) 838-2251

Last fall when a black bear decided to take a bath in the creek below Soda Butte Lodge, guests eating in the Lodge's restaurant left the table and crowded to the picture windows in the adjacent bar. While bears don't walk past the picture windows often, wildlife watching from the Soda Butte Lodge is a popular pastime. The lodge has an indoor pool and hot tub and 32 rooms ranging from those with a single double bed to king suites. Built in 1959, Soda Butte is simple and functional.

Guests gather in the Oar House Saloon (on the premises) to watch Monday Night Football and other sporting events. The Prospector, an on-site restaurant, serves three squares a day, including seafood, steaks and pasta dinners. Soda Butte, a hopping place during summer, winter and early spring, also offers snowmobile packages to guests. The lodge is open year round.

Grand Teton National Park

Jackson Lake Lodge, Jenny Lake Lodge, Colter Bay Village and Signal Mountain Lodge all offer cabin, hotel-style or motel-style accommodations inside the Park. Just north of Grand Teton Park is Flagg Ranch. Since these establishments also offer activities (generally at additional charge) and many visitors focus on a particular establishment's activities, you'll find them described in our Guest Ranches, Resorts and Lodges chapter. If money is a consideration, Colter Bay, Signal Mountain and Flagg Ranch are less expensive. Jackson Lake Lodge has more activities available among its horse corrals, bus tours, scenic floats and swimming pool. Lovely, rustic Jenny Lake Lodge is high-priced (and worth every dime).

Dornan's Spur Ranch Cabins
$$$$ • 10 Moose St., Teton Park Rd. at Moose Junction, Wyo. • (307) 733-2522

Dornan's is an institution around here. It's a bustling little complex of shopping and dining opportunities, plus 12 newer log cabins from which to enjoy them.

Few self-respecting outdoors enthusiasts drive past Moosely Seconds, a discounted gear store, without at least poking their heads in. Dornan's Deck looks over the sage-covered hills toward the Snake River and the Tetons. Climbers and hikers stop by after Park adventures for the obligatory microbrew and perhaps a pizza. Another option is Dornan's Chuckwagon, very nearly a perfect thing. It's a summer-only outdoor barbecue pit with picnic tables scattered about on the lawn. If it rains, folks head into the two huge teepees to eat. Dornan's Barbecue has been serving lunch and dinner here since 1948.

The cabins are part of the ambiance, too. Built in 1992, they're situated on a flat wildflower-speckled meadow below the busy commercial complex. This means that even though you have access to services, including a gas station, they don't impact you much. Neither will cars: You and other guests park up on the hill and walk down a short path to the cabins. Happily, these pretty log structures also are not lined up in tidy rows. They're scattered about the meadow much as the wildflowers are. Kitchens are completely equipped. The furniture is woven rawhide, and the walls are logs. Foot trails run between the cabins.

Other conveniences and amenities available at Dornan's include a well-stocked gro-

cery store, an amazing wine selection in the liquor store, a gift shop, sports equipment rentals including mountain bikes and canoes, whitewater float trips and a tackle shop from which you can arrange guided fishing trips.

Cabins and most retail facilities at Dornan's are open year round, but The Chuckwagon closes for winter.

Grand Teton Climbers Ranch
$ • Teton Park Rd. near Moose, Wyo.
• (307) 733-7271

Run by the American Alpine Club, this is bare-bones accommodations for climbers. The charge is $6 per person per night, but they'll take more if you can afford it. You get a bunk (bring your own mattress and sleeping bag) in a bare-walled cabin with a private bath, access to the roofed outdoor cooking area (bring your own stove) and to the small practice climbing wall studded with artificial handholds and footholds. The bulletin board on the office door provides weather reports and a place for you to advertise for a climbing partner if you're looking for one. There are no phones.

Hatchet Motel
$$$ • U.S. Hwy. 26 at Buffalo Valley, Wyo. • (307) 543-2413

OK, so these folks aren't really inside Grand Teton Park. They're 7 miles away, at the foot of Togwotee Pass. But the Hatchet is too nifty to ignore.

Hatchet Motel has 22 small log- and pine-paneled rooms with curtains that match the bedspreads, propane heat and no phones or TVs. The motel sits at the back of the property, so you can stand on the long, ranch-style porch and look toward the road past flowerpots, pine trees and grass. Then there's the cafe, which makes nearly all its menu items from scratch and loves to fry up rainbow trout for your breakfast.

Logs for the motel, which was built in 1954, are locally harvested lodgepole pine. They're also coped, which means each log was cut on a curve to fit the curve of the log beneath. This process is laborious and therefore generally not done.

At the Hatchet, you'll be 38 miles from Jackson and 33 miles from the south entrance into Yellowstone. Since there's nothing else at this wide spot in U.S. Highway 26 besides the motel and its little cafe, you'll also be blissfully secluded.

Hatchet Motel closes in mid-September and reopens in early June. The cafe serves breakfast, lunch and dinner in season.

Luton's Log Cabins

$$$$ • U.S. Hwy. 26 at Buffalo Valley, Wyo. • (307) 543-2489

Owner Joanne Luton suggests you bring a good book for the quiet evenings. Luton's offers no activities or TV distractions from the quiet loveliness of Buffalo Valley as it borders Grand Teton Park. There are no phones and no nearby neighbors on the valley floor.

Her nine duplex cabins are 6 years old and pleasantly designed with just enough smooth white wall to make the log and pine look magnificent. Each cabin has either one bedroom or two, plus a fully equipped kitchen, a private bath, a sitting area and a dining area. A covered porch runs the length of each cabin. Cabins were constructed from fire-killed logs from nearby forestlands. Out front, several small grassy areas are equipped with picnic tables. A volleyball court awaits the first serve.

Joanne is a third-generation Jackson native. The ranch on which these cabins sit has been in her family since the '40s. She says one of the most interesting winter activities for guests is watching cowboys on horseback struggle through deep valley snows to feed and tend their stock.

Luton's closes January through May.

Jackson Hole

Jackson, Wyoming, and Vicinity

49'er Inn

$$ • 330 W. Pearl, Jackson, Wyo. • (307) 733-7550

One good reason to stay at the 49'er is the indoor hot tub, where you can lounge in steamy comfort with 30 of your closest friends. (If you only have a few friends along, there's a conventional-size hot tub outside, too.) Even better are the fireplace rooms and suites, with their wood-burning or gas fireplaces. Amenities in the higher-priced rooms may also include refrigerators, wet bars, microwaves, coffee makers, hair dryers and more. A small fitness room is on premises.

The 49'er is a short stroll from Jackson's town square and just off Broadway, a main thoroughfare. It's owned by the same family that operates nearby Antler Motel.

The Alpenhof Lodge

$$$ • 3255 W. McCollister Dr., Teton Village, Wyo. • (307) 733-3242, (800) 732-3244

Established in 1965, the Alpenhof was the first lodge at Teton Village. It was built the same year the original ski lifts were installed. Rates are higher here in winter than in summer.

Recently remodeled, this hotel distinguishes itself by resisting the nearly universal Jackson impulse to go Western: The handmade furnishings are Bavarian. The cozy continental feel is complemented by fresh flowers scattered about, a nightly turn-down service, oversize outdoor pool (kept open in winter), a hot tub and sauna and on-call masseuses. Rooms range from extremely comfortable to downright decadent (the bathroom in the Edelweiss Room has a heated tile floor and a heated towel rack!), but all have down comforters, full baths and hair dryers. VCRs are available for rent.

Two restaurants are on premises. The Bistro is particularly pleasant. When weather allows, you can take advantage of lovely outdoor dining on a second story deck shaded by Englemann Spruce and Subalpine Fir. The Alpenhof Dining Room specializes in continental cuisine with a Western flair. Between the two, you're covered for breakfast, lunch and dinner.

Oh, did we mention that you can ski to the lifts?

Anglers Inn

$$$ • 265 Millward, Jackson, Wyo. • (307) 733-3682

Set on a quiet street that runs into sedate Flat Creek at the edge of town, Anglers Inn is still only a brisk five-minute walk from town square.

Recently remodeled, the 28 units of this popular motel feature locally made lodgepole pine furniture and pine accented walls. All rooms are outfitted with microwaves, refrigerators and ski racks with drip pads. Many are equipped with sitting areas.

Antler Motel
$$$ • 43 W. Pearl, Jackson, Wyo.
• (307) 733-2535

Good value for the money and only one block from Jackson's town square, the Antler Motel has 100 units ranging from cute but simple little cedar-paneled rooms with A-frame ceilings to suites with whirlpool tubs and fireplaces.

The Antler Motel belongs to Clarene and Creed Law, longtime residents of the Hole. Clarene, a Wyoming state legislator, began her innkeeping career in 1962 when her father offered his life savings, $10,000, to help her start a business. She built the Antler Motel.

Thirty-odd years later, it's obvious that dad's trust was well-placed. If you ask locals for a good, clean, inexpensive motel, odds are pretty good they'll point you toward one of Clarene's properties.

Each room at the Antler Motel is equipped with a winter plug-in for your car and a full bath. Twenty-four newly remodeled rooms feature log furniture. Don't forget to enjoy the hotel's sauna and hot tub before you tuck yourself into bed.

Best Western The Inn at Jackson Hole
$$$ • 3345 W. McCollister Dr., Teton Village, Wyo. • (307) 733-2311, (800) 842-7666

Of the 83 rooms in this hotel, the hands-down winners are the loft rooms. Five have king-size beds up a spiraling oak staircase with living and kitchen areas downstairs. The other five are for larger parties, with two queen-size beds downstairs and one king-size bed up in the loft. Many rooms (not just the loft rooms) have fireplaces, and the bellman not only brings your wood but also lights the match. Room decor is classy, simple and *not* Western, a surprise in cowboy-to-the-hilt Jackson Hole.

Other amenities here include ski lockers, an on-site ski tune shop, a pleasant outdoor deck and pool area with three hot tubs, a massage room with on-call masseuses, a small video arcade, laundry facilities and a restaurant named Jenny Leigh's which specializes in dishes prepared with unusual meats and wild game.

The Inn at Jackson Hole sits at the foot of Jackson Hole Mountain Resort's lifts, so rates are lower in summer than in winter. The hotel is also on a back route into Grand Teton National Park (it's a narrow road, so no trailers are allowed).

Best Western The Lodge at Jackson Hole
$$$$ • 80 S. Scott Ln., Jackson, Wyo. • (307) 739-9703, (800) 458-3866

Locals call it "that place where the bears are." It's as good a name as any for this newer upscale hotel festooned with 33 hand-carved creatures, mostly bears. They're all over it. Some peer in windows, others sprawl sleepily across rafters. They're the children of Afton, Wyoming, sculptor Jonathan LaBenne. Your children are gonna love them.

The building has 154 rooms on three floors. King rooms are particularly nice, with whirlpool tubs, gas fireplaces in the sitting areas, wet bars, room safes, microwaves, coffeepots and stocked fridges. The TV and VCR are demurely recessed in an armoire. Queen rooms are nearly as nice, although they don't have fireplaces and some don't have whirlpool tubs. The decor is Western .

Our two favorite places in The Lodge are 1) the main stairway out of the lobby, made from split logs; and 2) the pool! It's an indoor/outdoor deal with a huge glass door that pulls down to separate you from the snowy cold in winter. When the door's up in summer, the big pool is half outside. Inside, pool room walls are decorated with mountain murals. Outside, views from the deck are as pleasant as any in Jackson. You look up at Snow King, the in-town ski hill.

For families, another consideration is the on-site Fun Stop Arcade; your kids get free tokens when you check in.

Although there's no restaurant on premises, nearby Gunbarrel, China Town and Bleu Moon Diner all deliver room service.

Camp Creek Inn
$$ • U.S. Hwy. 189, near Hoback Junction, Wyo. • (307) 733-3099

Nine pleasant cabins look down a grassy slope to Camp Creek Inn's restaurant and bar (see our Restaurants chapter), with U.S. Highway 189 and the Hoback River beyond. Seven of nine are cute A-frames with porches. Inside, all are pine paneled with oversize windows, wall-to-wall carpet, lodgepole pine furniture and either one or two double beds.

Amenities include a small coffee maker, refrigerator and complimentary continental breakfast in summer. In winter, when many cabins are not accessible or are closed for the season, Camp Creek Inn's cabins are available and easily reached from regularly plowed U.S. 189.

The folks at Camp Creek Inn also do business as Camp Creek Outfitters. In summer they can take you on guided pack and fishing trips. During hunting season they'll help you bag your deer, elk, moose or bighorn sheep. They also maintain a tackle shop and a stocked casting pond on the property.

Cowboy Village Resort
$$$ • 120 S. Flat Creek Dr., Jackson, Wyo. • (307) 733-3121, (800) 962-4988

It's a cabin village right in the middle of Jackson. Each newer cabin has a covered porch, barbecue grill and picnic table. Most floor plans are generous with sitting areas, wall-to-wall carpeting, kitchenettes (dishes not provided) and full baths. Mini-blinds screen the oversize windows. You'll arrive to find mints on your dining table. Outside, the grounds are immaculate with razor-edged lawns dotted with young trees; flower baskets riot everywhere. For best enjoyment of the pretty landscaping, make sure you ask for a unit that doesn't face the grocery store that's conveniently nearby. Another bonus for visitors to the Cowboy Village Resort is that on-site babysitting services can be arranged.

Davy Jackson Inn

$$$$ • 85 Perry Ave., Jackson, Wyo.
• 739-2294, (800) 584-0532

Just like the delicate china cup from which you'll sip afternoon tea in the lobby, the Davy Jackson Inn is a one-of-a-kind. Your innkeeper, Kay Minns, added some special touches to the lace-and-flowers country inn she built in romping, leather-and-antler Jackson. Hallways are wide and ceilings are 10 feet high. Decorative molding tops doorways and windows.

Each of the inn's 11 rooms is unique, but all have down comforters, computer modem jacks and sitting areas. Most are equipped with an armoire to hide the television. Some have spas, some old-fashioned clawfoot tubs. Many are equipped with king-size beds decked with graceful lace canopies.

If your room doesn't have a spa, don't worry: A wood-decked hot tub waits outside.

A full country breakfast is included in your room price, so in the morning be sure you wander down to the cozy dining area to enjoy food that has been featured on PBS's *Country Inn Cooking*.

Elk Refuge Inn

$$$ • 1755 U.S. Hwy. 89, National Elk Refuge, Wyo. • (307) 733-3582,
(800) 544-3582

When you call to reserve one of this motel's 22 rooms, make sure you tell Craig and Elizabeth Harmening you want the second floor. Not only are these rooms furnished with sliding glass doors from which to watch the thousands of elk who winter on the valley floor at the National Elk Refuge, but you don't even have to walk up a flight of stairs: you drive around back where a higher parking lot lets you park at your door.

These upstairs rooms are large, with kitchenettes, high-slanted ceilings and chairs on the deck. They cost about a third more than the cinderblock-walled rooms downstairs, but it's money well-spent, especially in winter when rates become significantly lower than anything comparable in Jackson proper.

Elk Refuge Inn is located just 2 miles from Jackson's shops, restaurants and bars. The inn can put up your horse in the corral, or if you're here to hunt, let you hang your game on the meat pole behind the motel.

Flat Creek Motel

$$$ • 1935 N. U.S. Hwy. 89, National Elk Refuge, Wyo. • (307) 733-5276,
(800) 438-9338

The 72 newer rooms in this year-round motel feature refrigerators and microwaves. The facility also offers a laundry room, a hot tub and a sauna, a ski waxing area and horse corrals if you're traveling with a four-hooved friend. On the same property, you'll find a gas station and convenience store — very convenient since you're a couple miles beyond Jackson proper here.

Here and at the Elk Refuge Inn next door, the main attraction is across the highway on the National Elk Refuge. In winter (when Flat Creek Motel's rates drop by more than half, by the way) more than 8,000 elk gather and feed on the valley floor. So if you're coming to Jackson Hole between mid-October and May, reserve a room here and pack your binoculars.

The Golden Eagle Inn

$$ • 325 E. Broadway, Jackson, Wyo.
• (307) 733-2042

This older motel offers standard amenities, including a heated outdoor pool (not operative in winter). The 22 rooms are simply furnished but clean. The nifty thing about The Golden Eagle Inn is its location in a residential area several blocks from town square. You can enjoy the lower traffic volume and relative quiet and still get to your favorite restaurant or gallery in a couple minutes' walk.

The Golden Eagle, like many Jackson motels, offers truly fantastic shoulder season bargains: Prices drop by half in spring and fall.

Hoback River Resort

$$, $$$ for cabins • 1055 S. U.S. Hwy. 89, Hoback Junction, Wyo.
• (307) 733-5129

If you came to Jackson looking for quiet and learned, to your surprise, that thousands of other travelers did, too, you'll love this place. It won't surprise you, for instance, that your hosts, Kathy and Mike Shidner, escaped to this sweet spot from southern California nearly nine years ago.

Located at the confluence of the Hoback and Snake rivers on a high bench overlooking the Hoback, the resort has 12 large (450 square feet) motel rooms which access a pleasant deck through sliding glass doors, or for a bit more you can stay in one of the older cabins or pleasantly appointed newer cottages. Four small motel rooms are also available.

Four older cabins dating to the 1930s sit down on a low bench. Their grassy lawns dip straight into the river. They're equipped with grills, picnic tables and long, covered porches you can almost fish from.

All accommodations here are equipped with TVs but no phones. Those that have kitchens are furnished with necessary kitchen items. All have heating and private baths. Cabins are not available from October through May, but motel rooms are open all year.

The Shidners prefer to rent their cabins and cottages for a three-night minimum.

Hitching Post Lodge
$$$ • 460 E. Broadway, Jackson, Wyo.
• (307) 733-2606

Clustered behind a renovated cedar lodge built in the early 1900s are the motel-cabins of Hitching Post Lodge. Lodge amenities include a heated pool and hot tub (in summer only); rooms are outfitted with log and pine furniture, refrigerators and microwaves. Continental breakfast is served every morning except during the slow spring and fall months in a pleasantly renovated old log house which also holds the office and reception area.

This small motel complex is on a quiet residential street a few blocks' walk from town square. Or you can hop into your car and be in the National Elk Refuge before the engine warms up.

Hostel[x]
$ • 3315 McCollister Dr., Teton Village, Wyo. • (307) 733-3415

Let's say you're a skier or serious hiker or type-A sightseer, and you believe motel rooms are for sleeping in, not for using up your hard-earned fun tickets. Hostel[x] is for you.

Rooms are plywood with simple mattresses on wooden frames and a private bath. But you can watch TV or play backgammon in the fire-warmed lounge area, mess with your skis in the waxing room or play with your kids in

Pooh's Corner, the well-equipped playroom. Best of all, you can ski to the motel door: In summer you're nearly at the entrance to Grand Teton National Park.

Rates at this year-round motel are even more spectacular if you're a member of the American Youth Hostel Association or a comparable organization.

Inn on the Creek
$$$$ • 295 N. Millward, Jackson, Wyo.
• (307) 739-1565, (800) 669-9534

From the warm hardwood paneling to the recessed lighting and the artful disarray of the throw rugs, you'll love this inn as soon as you walk in the door. Rent one of our favorite rooms — casually luxurious with a whirlpool tub and a gas fire that lights at a touch to flicker through the tub's welcoming steam — and we can almost guarantee you'll be permanently hooked.

Staff say the inn is a favorite for honeymooners and couples on romantic getaways. Certainly Inn on the Creek is not a family inn, since none of the rooms are equipped with more than one queen-size bed.

The inn's back yard is a small but pleasant grassy bench that slips quickly into Flat Creek. An outdoor hot tub is tucked back there, too. All rooms are equipped with down comforters and pillows, robes and slippers; the TV and VCR are tucked graciously into an armoire. Staff slip in nightly to turn down your bed and leave a mint on your pillow.

Afternoon tea is served in the sitting room daily. Continental breakfast is delivered to your room, since the staff know from experience you don't want to leave, even for a cup of coffee, quite yet.

Mad Dog Ranch Cabins
$$$$ • Moose-Wilson Rd., Teton Village, Wyo. • (307) 733-3729, (800) 99CABIN

Mad Dog Ranch asks that you stay a minimum of three nights during most of the year, with higher minimum stays at Christmas. That won't be a problem, though.

You're gonna love the clean, light feeling of your cabin — high-ceilinged, paneled with pine and bright with light from the generous windows. At night you'll cozy up to the woodstove or picnic outside on your barbecue grill. Perhaps you'll soak in the outdoor hot tub before heading in for the night.

Each gray-painted cottage has two bedrooms, a fully equipped kitchen, wall to wall carpet and a long porch with a picnic table. If you're traveling with horses, these folks have a corral you can use. You're a 10-minute drive from Jackson Hole Mountain Resort and about the same distance from the dining, shopping and entertainment options of Jackson.

Nowlin Creek Inn

$$$$ • 660 E. Broadway, Jackson, Wyo.
• (307) 733-0882, (800) 533-0882

Mark and Susan Nowlin (pronounced with a "now," as in "now and then") run a fine bed and breakfast inn barely six blocks from Jackson's central square and literally a stone's throw from the National Elk Refuge (see our Bed and Breakfast Inns chapter). Behind their lovely new country house is your cabin, built in the 1920s by Mark's grandfather and furnished with a charming, low-key eccentricity.

The cabin is generously large, with two bedrooms, a full kitchen, a living room equipped with gas fire, a TV and a VCR, a cordless phone and a stereo. The laundry room and a large cold room off the front door are for storing your ski gear or mountain bikes. The yard is nearly private, screened from the inn with a high privacy fence. In the yard, a replica covered wagon waits for kids to come play on it. The yard also comes equipped with a gas grill and Mark's full-size wire sculpture of a horse grazing the lawn (both of your hosts are artists: Susan's work is stenciled on the walls).

The whimsically decorated living room is hung with a flamboyant crystal chandelier through which Jerome, a mule deer shot by Mark's dad, solemnly peers.

A three-night minimum stay is requested.

Old West Cabins

$$$ • 5750 S. Hwy. 89, Jackson, Wyo.
• (307) 733-0333

Six miles south of Jackson near Flat Creek and the Snake River sit two rows of cabins. They're near the highway, but below it, so you won't have headlights invading your sleep at night. The nicest cabins are the ones that face away from the complex toward Flat Creek and the South Elk Feeding Grounds.

Many of these rustic cabins were built in the 1930s, but they contain modern conveniences like wall-to-wall carpeting, kitchenettes, color cable TVs, phones and on-site coin-operated laundry facilities. Morning coffee is available.

Cabins rent by the night or by the season. They are various sizes, sleeping from two to six people. The grounds contain a corral for your horses and plenty of room for your kids to run and play. This is a great site for family reunions.

Ranch Inn Jackson Hole

$$$ • 45 E. Pearl, Jackson, Wyo.
• (307) 733-6363, (800) 348-5599

Ranch Inn is the closest motel to town square's restaurants, art galleries, clothing stores and bars. If you stay here, the action is barely a block away, and you won't have to hunt for parking. When it's time to shop, just walk out of your room.

This motel is relatively small, with only 57 rooms. But these folks still offer a range of choices. Standard rooms are just that: clean, no-frills accommodations with amenities such as free local phone calls, radio alarm clock and access to the motel's two hot tubs (one is indoors, the other out). Ranch Inn's nicest rooms have full kitchens, wood-burning fireplaces, private balconies, hair dryers and extra bathroom phones. Complimentary continental breakfast is served daily.

Red Lion Wyoming Inn of Jackson Hole

$$$$ • 930 W. Broadway, Jackson, Wyo.
• (307) 734-0035, (800) 844-0035

It's hard to walk in without admiring the massive bolted cedar beams in the entry and the oversized doors. Inside, the ponderous moose antler chandelier catches your eye. Throw rugs, Western art and leather chairs dress the lobby. A gas flame flickers quietly in the river-rock fireplace.

Wide hallways lead to guest rooms with cherry wood doors and entry ways. The 73 rooms are oversized and the bathrooms are spacious. You'll enjoy little extra touches like pullout makeup mirrors and hair dryers. All the standard amenities you would expect are complemented by coffeepots, desks and sitting areas. All are decorated with Western art. A few have fully equipped kitchens, some have spas, and 20 have fireplaces.

The facility offers continental breakfast, free guest laundry and same-day valet service. No smoking is allowed on the premises.

Trapper Inn
$$$ • 235 N. Cache, Jackson, Wyo.
• (307) 733-2648, (800) 341-8000

Most of the Trapper Inn's 54 rooms are standard motel fare, clean and comfortable. Nine older rooms are cozily pine paneled and pleasantly nonrectangular. In the newest of the three motel buildings are more luxurious rooms, some with fridges, microwaves and coffee makers and one with an in-room hot tub and wet bar.

The best reasons to stay here, though, aren't in your room. First, you're only a few minutes walk from town square. The second is Max, and the third could snap your head off. Fifty-nine year-old Jackson native Max Kudar is Trapper Inn's owner. His stories are worth the price of the room. The thing that could remove your head is a massive grizzly bear trap on the lobby wall, part of a fairly impressive collection of old traps and tools ranging from hay knives to husking gloves to one item Max hasn't been able to identify (want to take a shot at it?)

Twin Creek Cabins
$$$$, no credit cards • Twin Creek Ranch, National Elk Refuge, Wyo.
• (307) 733-3927

Susan Johansson and her family came here from Jackson in 1955; they've done a lot of things right ever since. The seven cabins Susan rents date to the '20s, when Twin Creek Ranch was a working ranch and these were working buildings. One was the entertaining house, one the bunkhouse, another a storage room. They've been renovated just enough:

You'll feel like you're on an old Jackson-area ranch (you are), and you'll find the furnishings old (and sometimes odd), but you'll lack no comfort. If you've never experienced the sleep-inducing radiant heat from a woodstove, you may even discover a brand-new kind of comfort. All cabins are fully furnished with linens, full kitchens and electric heat.

Nor, if you like quiet, will you be bored. The 9-acre property abutting the National Elk Refuge offers horseshoe pits, swing sets, a large sandbox and barbecue grills for a perfect Teton cookout. Some clear nights Susan gets out her telescopes and shows guests what all that clear mountain air can do for night-time visibility. A stocked casting pond is reserved for the kids.

Three cabins afford Teton views; the others, tucked into aspen groves, offer a feeling of green seclusion.

Johansson rents for a seven-day minimum. Her cabins are available May to September. The drive into Jackson takes about 10 minutes.

Wagon Wheel Motel
$$$ • 435 Cache, Jackson, Wyo.
• (307) 733-2357, (800) 323-9279

Wagon Wheel Village is pure Jackson: unabashedly commercial, Western to the hilt and solidly rooted in Hole history. You might stay here simply for the Village's motel: 97 units with modern amenities. The Wyoming Suites, housed in two-story log buildings at the back of the property with views of Flat Creek, are the newest and most pleasant of the accommodations here. The older rooms are, well, older.

But more likely you'll choose the Wagon Wheel for its quirky flavor. Current owner Barry Remington's grandfather won the money to buy the original nine cabins in a card game 54 years ago; you can still stay in eight of them. The place lights up like Christmas at night;

during the day, an army of totem poles, carved wooden Indians and bears outside the gift shop make the place tough to miss.

The Village Wheel, Wagon Wheel Village's funny little annual newspaper, makes great morning reading over coffee with tidbits like, "If you don't think this is up to *New York Times'* standards, just remember what you paid for it." And motel staff will tell you that the you-have-to-see-it-to-believe-it lobby is probably the most photographed motel lobby in the country (we believe it).

Or you'll choose this motel for convenience. The complex includes a coin-operated laundry, gift shop, cafe, saloon, liquor store, RV park (see our Campgrounds and RV Parks chapter), hot tub and a rafting company. The Wagon Wheel is situated directly across the street from the helpful folks at the Jackson Hole visitors center.

The Wort Hotel
$$$$ • Corner of Glenwood and Broadway, Jackson, Wyo.
• (307) 733-2190, (800) 322-2727

Back in 1915, homesteader Charles J. Wort bought four lots in Jackson and started telling folks about the luxury hotel he would build there. The town stopped laughing in 1941, when Charles' sons Jess and John did it. Today, The Wort is a historic landmark. It's also a AAA four-diamond hotel, one of only three lodging establishments with that distinction in the area (the others are Jenny Lake Lodge in Grand Teton National Park and the Rusty Parrot on Flat Creek in Jackson).

Each room is unique in appearance. Most beds have down comforters, many covered in a dramatic buffalo check that manages to look luxurious and down-home at the same time. Other rooms are papered in a print designed especially for the Wort that shouldn't look classy but does: It's a faint, vertical silhouette of barbed wire.

And 20 of the 60 rooms are decorated with blown-up prints of old-time Jackson and Jacksonites obtained from the local historical society. JJ's Silver Dollar Grill, the hotel's fine-dining, casual-dress restaurant, also displays these fun old photos. On display in the adjoining Silver Dollar Bar are exactly 2,032 uncirculated silver dollars embedded in the surface of

the bar (more on JJ's and the Silver Dollar Bar in our Restaurants and Nightlife chapters, respectively).

Enjoy complete room service, indoor hot tubs and a fitness room, along with all the expected amenities of a hotel. Oh, and there is Sam, that cute, floppy teddy bear sitting on your bed: If your kids fall in love with him, don't worry — The Wort can sell you a Sam of your own to take home.

Surrounding Areas

Eastern Idaho

Idaho Falls, Idaho

Best Western Driftwood Inn
$$ • 575 River Pky., Idaho Falls, Idaho
• (208) 523-2242, (800) 939-2242

The riverside location in town is perfect, and the price is fair. Best Western Driftwood has 74 rooms, 14 with kitchenettes. All rooms are equipped with microwaves, fridges and coffee makers; outside you can swim in the heated pool and enjoy pleasant landscaping with benches and tables. The Driftwood even supplies bicycles so you can pedal along the Snake River on paved paths just across the street.

A few special picks at the Driftwood include the four huge kitchenette units (one is a complete apartment), for a bit over $100 per night. The six rooms in The Overhang, which looks down onto the Snake River and its magnificent man-made falls, are particularly pleasant.

Blacksmith Inn
$$ • 227 N. 3900 E., Rigby, Idaho
• (208) 745-6208, (888) 745-6208

Ringed by huge cottonwoods, cedar-sided Blacksmith Inn presides over a swath of lawn and pretty flowerbeds. The building is made up of two cylinders with low, conical roofs, connected by more conventional architecture.

Inside, a large breakfast room holds several oak tables, and the adjacent sitting room, outfitted with overstuffed couches and Western tromp l'oeil artist Bev Doolittle's prints, practically begs you to stretch out and relax after your meal (a country breakfast is included in the price of your room).

Two of six guest rooms have private entrances. Among the niceties are alarm clocks, generous storage areas recessed into the walls and access to the first-floor or second-floor deck. All have large private bathrooms. All the beds are made up with handmade quilts; each room features a Western mural by a local artist. One wall of the Wildflower Room is a meadow scene spangled with flowers. The Cowboy Room has an idyllic camp scene by a mountain stream. Even the bed frames are handmade.

Cavanaughs on the Falls
$$$ • 475 River Pky., Idaho Falls, Idaho • (208) 523-8000, (800) 432-1005

Idaho Falls' trademark hotel and its oldest overlooks the dramatic man-made falls that *didn't* give the town its name (the name came first, then the falls). Luxury rooms are housed in the eight-story cylindrical Tower Building. Standard rooms, some small and some larger, wrap around the restaurant and large outdoor pool. If you reserve a luxury room, be sure to ask for a view of the Snake River and its falls: Private decks accessed by generous, floor-to-ceiling sliding glass doors beg to frame a river.

Amenities for standard rooms include coffee maker and a full complimentary breakfast in the dining room. Luxury rooms, besides having copious amounts of empty space, may also come equipped with refrigerators, sitting areas and more. The hotel also offers laundry facilities, conference rooms, a fitness room and an indoor hot tub, a dining room and lounge.

Evergreen Gables Motel
$ • 3130 S. Yellowstone Hwy., Idaho Falls, Idaho • (208) 522-5410

One of the few motels in town not associated with a big chain, Evergreen Gables offers budget accommodations with a homey touch. Owners Lamont and Vaunita Lewis have done most of the renovation themselves for the last 20 years. Daughter Kami manages day-to-day operation and lives on-site. As in most budget accommodations, furniture and buildings are older, but the only

amenity you might miss is air conditioning. Some units have kitchenettes.

Most of the motel's 26 rooms face each other across a courtyard and lawn shaded by mature trees, blocked from view of the road by the office. It feels a little like having your own yard. Perhaps that's why Evergreen Gables is so successful as a weekly and monthly rental facility: For little more than you'd pay for upscale accommodations downtown for one night, you can stay here for a week with a shady yard in which to relax every evening. The Lewises provide a couple gas grills for your family barbecue.

Motel West
$ • 1540 W. Broadway, Idaho Falls, Idaho • (208) 522-1112, (800) 582-1063

The furnishings are standard motel fare, clean and functional, but the price is good and the attached cafe, Home Town Kitchen, is a locals' favorite. (If you're a night owl, enjoy being a couple of blocks from Idaho Falls' 24-hour dining establishment, O'Brady's.)

Among the amenities are an indoor pool and hot tub, a laundry room and VCR and movie rental. Three spacious suites, rented mostly by locals celebrating anniversaries and other special events, have in-room whirlpool tubs. Rent one of these (they're cheaper than you might think) and you'll find a bottle of champagne, a basket of candy and other goodies waiting for you when you arrive.

Shilo Inn
$$$ • 780 Lindsay Blvd., Idaho Falls, Idaho • (208) 523-0088

When the Shilo opened in 1988, it instantly became the high-end favorite in town. This independently owned and operated 161-room hotel is one of the largest facilities in town. It has the largest convention facilities in Idaho Falls, which has attracted groups like the National Pyrotechnics Association and the International Flyfishers Conclave.

All rooms are oversize studio suites. Ten dollars over the base price buys you a view of the Snake River and its parklike shore — we suggest you pay it.

All rooms come with coffee makers, fridges, wet bars, microwaves, irons and ironing boards and 27-inch satellite TV/VCR combo. As a guest of the Shilo, you also get to use the 24-hour steam room, hot tub and sauna, the swimming pool and the fitness center with modern aerobic equipment. You can receive and send faxes at no charge; also free is a full breakfast buffet and a morning newspaper to read as you eat.

The folks at the Shilo can arrange vacation packages for you. In summer ask about fishing and whitewater packages; in winter try snowmobiling. Package travel usually takes you up to Island Park or over to Jackson. Neither is more than 100 minutes away in good weather.

One huge advantage to staying at the Shilo is that, because they cater more to business travelers than tourists, weekends tend to be slower than weekdays. When accommodations closer to the parks are full up, these folks often have rooms.

Rexburg, Idaho

Best Western Cottontree Inn
$$ • 450 W. 4 S., Rexburg, Idaho • (208) 356-4646
You'll love the lobby, with its angled glass walls and indoor garden.

With 100 rooms, this is the largest motel in town. It's also the only motel with an on-site restaurant, Frontier Pies. The Rexburg Chamber of Commerce rents space in the motel's conference center, so you can stroll over from your room to pick up handy information about the area.

Nearly half the rooms have refrigerators and microwaves; many have been recently renovated. Other thoughtful touches include irons and ironing boards.

Comfort Inn
$$ • 1513 W. Main, Rexburg, Idaho • (208) 359-1311
Conveniently located next to the second Rexburg exit from U.S. Highway 33, Comfort Inn is the newest motel in town. It has 52 standard rooms. If you're looking for a little more space, there are four studio suites with microwaves and fridges.

The facility includes an exercise room, hot tub and indoor swimming pool. Their complimentary continental breakfast will start your day right.

Days Inn
$ • 271 S. 200 W., Rexburg, Idaho • (208) 356-9222
These folks are right next to Mormon church-owned Ricks College; most of their guests are parents visiting their kids or tourists heading to the national parks. Days Inn bought the motel three years ago and completely remodeled the facility. All 43 rooms have standard amenities, some have microwaves and fridges for a few dollars more. In summer, enjoy the outdoor heated pool. Continental breakfast is free of charge.

Ashton, Idaho

Jessen's R.V. Park and Bed & Breakfast
$, no credit cards • 1146 S. 3400 E., Ashton, Idaho • (208) 652-3356
These pleasant little white frame cottages have TVs, propane heat, air conditioning, floral curtains and velvet-upholstered chairs. Each has its own bathroom. The grounds, however, are the real reason you come to Jessen's. Your cabin is equipped with a picnic table outside, but you'll probably spend more time in the slatted gazebo near the old white farmhouse. In late summer you can eat plums, apples and cherries right off the trees while the kids cool off in the irrigation canal that runs through the property.

Jessen's also has two bed and breakfast rooms upstairs in the farmhouse and an RV park on the premises, so invite your whole family for an outing. The bed and breakfast inn operates all year, but the RV park and cabins are only open May through November. Reservations are recommended. (For more information, please see our Bed and Breakfast Inns and our Campgrounds and RV Parks chapters.)

Log Cabin Motel
$ • 1001 E. Main, Ashton, Idaho • (208) 652-3956
Is it cabins or a motel? Neither. Both. The Log Cabin Motel is Ashton's niftiest accommodation and a great jump-off spot for adventures in the Bechler or Cave Falls areas of Yellowstone Park or Island Park, or the fine fishing waters of the Warm River.

Flowers hang from each cabin's roof. Hedges sprout near the doors. You can sit out front and enjoy the wildflower garden in the small complex's center, or if you rented one of two cabins that face away from the parking lot, you may contemplate an adjacent grain field.

Each cabin has cable TV, a heater and a full bath. Most of these cabins date back more than 64 years; they practically purr with quaint, old-fashioned simple comfort.

Owner Venis McCarthy closes up from November to April and often finds herself full up during the summer travel months. Log Cabin Motel also has a few RV sites behind the cabin complex. Some have full hookups.

Super 8
$ • 1370 U.S. Hwy. 20, Ashton, Idaho • (208) 652-7885

This motel, completed in 1997, has a couple pleasant extras. One is the lobby area, large and high ceilinged, made for lounging. It is warmed by a gas fire on one wall and lit by generous floor-to-ceiling windows on another. Lodgepole pine furniture lends a Western look.

Another nice touch is extra-large rooms: Several of the standard rooms are L-shaped and spacious. There are also three suites. A laundry room, a 24-hour convenience store and gift shop and a popular restaurant (see our Restaurants chapter) are also on-site.

Super 8 is the only large motel chain currently in the Ashton area and in fact is the only large motel chain for many miles in any direction. Perhaps because they're brand new and trying to attract attention, rates are substantially cheaper here than for rooms back down the road in Rexburg.

Island Park, Idaho

A word on Island Park accommodations: Many are cheaper in summer than in winter. They're booked for the big winter weekends — Presidents' Day, Christmas and New Year's — up to a year in advance. The reason? Well, it ain't skiing: Island Park is a snowmobile mecca. More than 200 miles of groomed snowmobile trails ply the immediate area; these trails connect with trails in the region to bring that total to around 1,000 miles. See our Winter Sports chapter for details.

Lakeside Lodge Bed "n" Breakfast
$$ • 3857 Lakeside Lodge Ln., Island Park, Idaho • (208) 558-7417

Enjoy breakfast in the main lodge building — it's more than 100 years old! — which houses a cafe, a bar and a tiny convenience store. You'll be well away from busy U.S. Highway 20 on Island Park Reservoir and conveniently near several boat ramps.

Your hosts, Bill and Pat Ashton, offer several breakfast options which are included in the price of your room, from continental breakfast to Belgian waffles. On Sunday, they serve an all-you-can-eat champagne brunch for a small additional charge.

The motel rooms have been recently remodeled; the look is clean and uncluttered. All rooms look out on the reservoir. The lodge rents movies for the in-room TV/VCR, and each room has a gas fireplace and two double beds with peeled pine headboards and Indian print bedspreads. All rooms have full baths, one with a whirlpool tub.

The lodge is open all year and requires reservations for guests. The cafe and bar are open to the general public. The cafe serves breakfast, lunch and dinner every day except Wednesdays, when it's closed. Sundays the cafe is closed for dinner.

Last Chance Lodge and Hyde Outfitters Inc.
$ • 3408 N. U.S. Hwy. 20, Last Chance in Island Park, Idaho • (208) 558-7068

Clean, no-frills hotel-style accommodations are available at Last Chance Lodge. The lodge sits across Highway 20 from the magnificent fly-fishing waters of the Henry's Fork and on the same property as Hyde Outfitters, one of the area's better-known guide services. Each room has a small TV but no phone. A few suites are available; these have kitchenettes and fireplaces.

At Hyde Outfitters, just outside your room, you anglers can shop for all of life's necessities: flies, leaders, waders, hats, etc. While you're here, make sure you treat yourself to a day of fishing with Hyde's local guides in drift boats, built in nearby Idaho Falls, that bear the Hyde name (see our Fishing and Hunting chapter).

Mack's Inn Resort

$ cabin, $$ motel • U.S. Hwy. 20, Mack's Inn at Island Park, Idaho • (208) 558-7272

Thirty-eight motel rooms in two pleasant locations make up the bulk of available accommodations at Mack's Inn. One cinderblock building faces the lovely Henry's Fork, which flows past, shallow and dimpled, 10 feet from your sliding glass doors. Some of these riverfront units have fireplaces and/or kitchens. The other building is tucked into the trees across the highway. These smaller rooms are simply appointed, some with fireplaces and all with private baths. You have no phone; you can rent a TV and VCR.

The 26 cabins are older, some as old as 70 years, and in varying degrees of repair. All have private baths; some have fireplaces or woodstoves, and some have kitchens (but you need to supply the utensils). Appointments are simple.

The buildings, including a store, a coin-operated laundry and an RV park (see our Campgrounds and RV Parks chapter) together sprawl across 17 acres. The property also has a volleyball court, firepits, a dinner theater (in summer), a log playground and boat rentals so you can enjoy the Henry's Fork or Big Springs area upstream (see our Attractions chapter for a must-do daytrip.)

Ponds Lodge

$ • 3757 N. U.S. Hwy. 20, Pond's Lodge in Island Park, Idaho • (208) 558-7221

This place is hard to beat for convenience and comfortable cabin accommodations. Island Park facilities tend to cluster together; this cluster is smaller than most, but still offers, under one roof, a small grocery store (fresh fruit, even!), a selection of wines by the bottle, fishing supplies, a gift shop, a restaurant that serves breakfast, lunch and dinner and the Buffalo River Saloon. Outside are RV hookups (see our Campgrounds and RV Parks chapter) and cabins.

The 18 cabins are set back from U.S. Highway 20 behind the lodge, so you won't feel like you're living in traffic. Choose from small, inexpensive units with a single queen-size bed, bath and tiny kitchenette, or step up to a unit with five queen-size beds, two baths and a full

kitchen unit with woodstove. Cabins do not have phones, TVs or kitchen utensils/dishes, but you can leave your bedding and linens at home. Walls are pine-paneled and floors are carpeted.

The huge lodge, built in 1935 by Charles and Myna Ponds, is also available for your use. It centers around a pleasant commons area with a massive woodstove and log-frame couches and chairs. The cafe has some outdoor seating, so it's another nice place to hang out. Or you can walk down to the Buffalo River, which runs almost right next to Ponds Lodge.

Behind the lodge is a huge, rough-walled building that practically begs you to stage a family reunion or a dance. It has a low stage on one wall and big doors that open to a grassy picnic area.

Sawtelle Mountain Resort

$$ • U.S. Hwy. 20 and Sawtelle Rd., Mack's Inn at Island Park, Idaho • (208) 558-9366, (800) 574-0404

These folks have the newest facility in Island Park, and in typical Island Park fashion, it's a somewhat bewildering cluster of accommodations and services. There are 36 standard motel rooms, plus a group facility called the Bunkhouse, which is one long room so large that you can watch TV at one end and not bother your friend's nap at the other.

The motel has comfortable standard rooms with and access to the two outdoor hot tubs. TV reception is via satellite.

There's also a gift shop, a small grocery and an RV park (see our Campgrounds and RV Parks chapter). Sawtelle also offers horseback riding, chuckwagon dinners and Tigershark personal watercraft for use on Island Park Reservoir. In winter they rent snowmobiles and offer snowmobile packages.

Swan Valley, Idaho, and Vicinity

Alpen Haus Hotel

$$ • U.S. Hwy. 26 at U.S. Hwy. 89, Alpine, Wyo. • (307) 654-7545, (800) 343-6755

You won't believe it: a quaint Austrian hotel on the Idaho/Wyoming border. Alpen Haus gets its continental look from the decorative paintings on the exterior walls of its two buildings, created by an Austrian friend of owners Clarence and Dorothy Reinhart.

Rooms are larger in Alpen Haus 1, the main hotel building, and all have balconies. Rooms in both buildings have private baths and down comforters. Some rooms enjoy fridges, hair dryers and full baths. The honeymoon suite promises inexpensive luxury with skylights, a king-size bed, a dry bar, a big-screen television and a living area with a pullout sofa. Let the staff know you're celebrating a wedding or anniversary and they'll have a bottle of champagne waiting for you.

Alpen Haus Hotel also has a gas station, a small grocery store, an ice cream parlor, a bar and restaurant, video rental, a Western clothing store, a laundry room and a hot tub.

Now, don't think you'll be in the middle of a massive tourist complex if you make your reservations here. Alpen Haus 1 and 2 together have only 55 rooms, yet the hotel is the hoppin'est thing in tiny Alpine.

Hansen-Silver Guest Ranch
$$$ • 956 Rainey Creek Rd., Swan Valley, Idaho • (208) 483-2305, (800) 277-9041

This is a working ranch which ran 250 yearlings in 1997 and operates a guest ranch in the summer months. But when the cabins aren't occupied by ranch guests and in winter after the guest ranch shuts down, they're available for drop-ins as motel-style accommodations. Choose between the duplex cabins with decks front and back and one white frame cottage. Cabins are furnished Western-style, but they're not rustic; walls are a clean white, the scent of eucalyptus perfumes the air, and furniture is modern. Each has a private bath and queen-size bed but no TV or phone.

Swan Valley has little in the way of accommodations, so these cabins are a real find for those who want to enjoy the superb trout fishing on the South Fork of the Snake. Hansen-Silver Guest Ranch is only a 15-minute drive from the Spring Creek boat ramp in Swan Valley. See our Resorts, Guest Ranches and Lodges chapter for more information.

Huskey's Resort
$ • 3781 Swan Valley Hwy., Palisades, Idaho • (208) 483-3581

Don't let the highway sign that says you're in Irwin fool you: Locals say Irwin starts nearly 5 miles down the road. And here in Palisades the best noncamping accommodations are in Randy and Wenda Huskey's newer little motel cabins. Each of the five units has television (no cable), a fridge and a private bathroom. The glossy pine-paneled walls are not overdecorated. What you're paying for are clean, simple accommodations. Outside, you have a picnic table for pleasant evening meals al fresco.

Huskey's is one-stop shopping for travelers. These folks also run an RV park (it's behind your cabin; see our Campgrounds and RV parks chapter for more), a convenience store, a cafe, a tackle shop, a liquor store and a gas station. There's even a drift boat and a 9.5-horse trolling rig available for rent if you want to fish the South Fork without a guide.

These folks close up their cabins and RV park from mid-October to early May.

The Nordic Inn
$$ • Colonial Ln. at U.S. Hwy. 89, Alpine, Wyo. • (307) 654-7556

The Nordic Inn was a hunting camp when the Clingers, a family of Wyoming natives, bought it in 1963. Now it's a clean, cozy 10-room motel. The outdoor hot tub is screened by a lush, piney-smelling mass of hops plants. Flower beds and boxes grace the building; a long lawn slopes out to the highway.

Most rooms have Pendleton blankets, pine wainscoting and bathrobes for you to use while you're here. All have full baths and TVs; none have phones.

Anne and Michael Clinger, mother and son, and their partner Brent Johnston live in a newer, columned Southern Colonial-style home behind the motel. They occasionally rent a 1,000-square-foot suite in their house to special guests.

The Nordic Inn is home to a tiny bar (decorated with memorabilia honoring Anne's late husband, Dallas Clinger, Wyoming's only World War II ace fighter pilot) and a small gift shop stocked with oddities Anne Clinger picks

up in her world travels. And it houses tiny, magnificent Brenthoven's Restaurant (see our Restaurants chapter).

These folks spend their winters in New Zealand, so the Nordic Inn closes up in mid-October and reopens in June. A round of special concert dinners are hosted at the house around Christmas. The entertainment is furnished by Johnston, a master concert pianist who has performed at Carnegie Hall. He's also the chef (check out our Annual Events chapter for details).

Teton Valley, Idaho

Beard Mountain Ranch
$$, no credit cards • P.O. Box 84, Tetonia, ID 83452 • No phone

Trixie and Carl Beard are Teton Valley natives. In fact, nearby Beard Mountain is named after a homesteading ancestor. The little cabin they rent year round is tucked far enough off the beaten path that you will almost imagine you've driven back in time to when the first Beards rode into Teton Valley.

The cabin is shag-carpeted and filled with boxy, older furniture. It has a kitchen, a three-quarter bath, linens, cooking utensils and a TV that receives five local stations. It will sleep four to six people, so when you are there, the greatest number of people you're likely to see outside the mirror is five. You won't even see the ranch residents unless you go looking because the cabin is situated at the end of a private gravel road.

If you do go looking, Trixie and husband Carl will be happy to arrange horseback riding, guided or unguided fishing, hunting and pack trips for you. Carl has been a guide in the area for 35 years.

Best Western Teton West
$$$ • 476 N. Main, Driggs, Idaho • (208) 354-2363, (800) 252-2363

If you want lodging with an indoor pool (kept warm enough for lounging, summer and winter) *and* a hot tub, this is the place. Out of the 40 rooms at Teton West, the best are in the newest part of the motel; they're larger and have windows looking west to the distant Big Hole Mountains. Also on-site are a guest laundry and a small conference facility.

Intermountain Lodge
$$ • 34 Ski Hill Rd., Driggs, Idaho • (208) 354-8153

The location couldn't be better: Intermountain Lodge is between Driggs and Grand Targhee Ski and Summer Resort, just outside the Targhee National Forest. The 4-acre property is screened from the highway by huge cottonwood trees. Lodging is in seven newer duplex cabins, each with a covered porch.

Amenities include a hot tub and laundry facility, plus kitchenettes in each log and pine-paneled room. The most popular rooms have queen-size log-framed bunkbeds. Managers Bob and Roberta Williams keep VCRs available for rent; they'll loan you movies from their own private collection for free. Unlike many cabin facilities in our area, Intermountain Lodge is open during the snowy months, too.

Pines Motel/Guest Haus
$ • 105 S. Main, Driggs, Idaho • (208) 354-2774, (800) 354-2778

Leaf through the hand-embroidered guest book at John and Nancy Nielson's little establishment and the words you'll see again and again are cute, cozy and friendly. We'd add one: eccentric. Antiques, mostly from the 1920s, furnish the paneled guest rooms. Many of the showers are paneled in knotty pine. Nancy sews the curtains and matching tasseled lampshades. She also hand-sewed most of the matching quilts. Some of these quilts are works of art; one set took her and her kids three months to stitch.

The six upstairs rooms are the nicest. Much of the building is an original two-story log cabin from the turn of the century, paneled over to match an addition built in the late 1930s. Some rooms face onto Main, motel-style. Others face an inside hallway. Most have private baths.

Pines Motel/Guest Haus is inexpensive. In fact it's so inexpensive that John sometimes jokes to surprised guests that he can charge extra if it would make them feel more comfortable. Don't be fooled by the price tag: This charming little hybrid of a hotel and bed and breakfast inn lacks few amenities. Its acre of lawn contains a large hot tub, a fireplace, a gas grill, a swingset, a tree house (fun!) and a couple hammocks. Lupine and columbine, poppies and iris surround the building. Huge willows and flowering crab apple shade the yard. Out back is a tree swing and a sandbox. Each room is scrupulously clean.

Pines' huge yard has for years been home to an antique show the first week of July. In 1997 the Nielsens expanded their casual event into the juried Rocky Mountain Arts Festival. Great idea, John and Nancy. We can't think of a better setting for strolling about in the sunshine looking at paintings and sculpture.

Super 8 Teton West

$$ • 133 N. Hwy. 33, Driggs, Idaho
• (208) 354-8888

This is the newest of the two lodging chains in Teton Valley. These folks have 22 spacious rooms, all with small refrigerators and microwaves. A guest laundry and an indoor hot tub are available; continental breakfast is served every morning in the lobby. Rooms on each of the two floors are accessed by a central hallway.

Teton Mountain View Lodge

$$ • 510 Egbert Ave., Tetonia, Idaho
• (208) 456-2741, (800) 625-2232

Two nice features make this motel stand out. The first is a design that made us wonder why all motels aren't made this way. You see, the windows in the main building don't face the walkways or the parking lot — they face the pasture behind the motel. You don't need to close the curtains because there's nothing back there but grass.

The other advantage to staying at Teton Mountain View is that these folks offer guided horseback riding from the property in summer and unguided snowmobiling in winter.

A hot tub is available; TV reception is via satellite.

Teton Ranch

$$$$, no credit cards • 227 E. 600 N., Tetonia, Idaho • (208) 456-2010

As you leave Highway 33, one of Teton Valley's few paved roads, you're going to know you've found your mountain retreat. In fact, you may have to pinch yourself to make sure you're awake: The setting is too idyllic and the prices too reasonable.

Your two "cabin" accommodations are really houses, fully furnished with Western motifs, log walls and hardwood floors. The main house is a two-story log home built in 1929. It has a rock fireplace and open-beam ceilings. Big windows invite the surrounding seclusion and scenery right into the house. In summer, up to 29 hummingbirds have been known to swarm the feeders dangling outside one window.

The smaller house is new, built in 1987. It has two decks and two bedrooms, each with private bath. A fireplace warms the cozy living room.

The grounds are surrounded with buck and rail fence, aspens and evergreens. The lawn is dotted with flowers, an herb garden and raspberry bushes. Enjoy a cookout on the propane grill — but bring your mosquito repellent in summer; there's a price to be paid for all that lush greenery!

Several paintings in the two houses are by neighbor Trixie Beard, Tetonia native. Trixie says her three favorite things to paint are the Tetons, the Tetons and mountains. You'll see what she means.

Teton Ranch rents its two lovely homes year round and provides a helpful on-site manager who lives in a small house on the grounds.

Trails End Motel

$ • 10 N. Main, Victor, Idaho
• (208) 787-2973 or 787-2771

These folks offer a hodgepodge of accommodations options: eight cabins, two motel rooms and a three-room apartment perfect for large families or groups. The nicest choices are the four newer cabins with log beds, log interiors and full baths. All rooms are furnished with microwaves and refrigerators.

A pleasant location adjoining City Park in downtown Victor finishes out the picture. Make sure you walk across the street to the Victor Emporium for a huckleberry shake after you check in. They're famous, and rightfully so (see our Restaurants chapter for more on Victor Emporium).

Northwestern Wyoming

Cody, Wyoming

Best Western Sunset Motor Inn
$$$ • 1601 Eighth St., Cody, Wyo.
• (307) 587-4265, (800) 624-2727

There is something unexpectedly serene about the 122 rooms, all ground-floor, at the Sunset Motor Inn. They ooze cool, soothing elegance from the creamy carpet tones to the plush bedspreads. Chances are the Sunset Motor Inn can accommodate your every need since they have about every room combination available. Most rooms have queen-size beds, although some are king suites and one comes equipped with three queen-size beds.

A slow stroll from the Buffalo Bill Historical Center (see our Attractions chapter) and downtown, the Sunset has a list of amenities to match the soothing interiors and its sprawling, manicured lawns. Choose between an indoor pool/spa and a sunny outdoor pool. You'll also find an exercise room, a guest laundry and a children's playground. The Sunset House Family Restaurant, adjacent to the motel, serves three squares a day, breakfast and dinner buffets and offers three different dining rooms with a total seating capacity of 210.

Bill Cody Ranch
$$$$ • 2604 Yellowstone Hwy, Cody, Wyo. • (307) 587-6271

Even though the Bill Cody Ranch gears its schedule toward multiple-day visits, they do hang out the vacancy sign when they have room for overnight guests. If you're in the area give them a call. Don't be surprised, though, if they're full. (For more information on this facility, see our chapter on Guest Ranches, Resorts and Lodges.)

Elephant Head Lodge
$$ • Yellowstone Hwy., Wapiti, Wyo. • (307) 587-3980

Every once in a while, you'll find that this heavenly spot outside Cody has a vacancy from a last-minute cancellation. It's worth calling to find out if you're in the area. (For more

about Elephant Head Lodge, see our Guest Ranches, Resorts and Lodges chapter.)

The Irma Hotel
$$ • 12th St. and Sheridan Ave., Cody, Wyo. • (307) 587-4221

Built in 1902 by Buffalo Bill Cody himself, The Irma Hotel is as much an attraction as an accommodation. In its heyday — heated by steam, lighted by gas, equipped with telephones in every room — the Irma was the hub of high living at the end of the Milwaukee Railroad spur. The hotel had an elegant bar, billiards, a telegraph office, a barber shop and baths. The dining room featured fresh produce, meat and dairy products from its own farm. And a livery stable sat ready to serve customers with every kind of rig and horse possible, including camp and pack outfitters to take guests hunting, fishing and sightseeing in Yellowstone Park.

Today, the Irma is a shadow of its former self. Enough signs of the frontier days remain, though, to make a stay at this landmark a special occasion. The rooms, mostly upstairs, range from the simple to the elegant with a combination of old and new. All have private baths, and you'll find an amazing list of sleeping combinations.

Downstairs, you'll find the Irma Restaurant, a giant dining room featuring a cherry wood bar presented to Bill Cody by the Queen of England. Adjacent to the restaurant is the Buffalo Bill Bar, a favorite watering hole for tourists and locals alike. Each summer evening, the Irma features re-enactments of bank robberies and shootouts on the front steps.

Rainbow Park Motel
$$ • 1136 17th St., Cody, Wyo. • (307) 587-6251, (800) 341-8000

This single-story, well-maintained, 40-unit brick motel wrapped U-shaped around the parking lot fills up fast. The prices are right, and the rooms are clean. The Rainbow, at the east end of Sheridan Avenue, Cody's main thoroughfare, has both regular rooms and ones with kitchenettes.

You'll find a small fenced, shaded playground on a grass island in the center of the parking lot. The grounds also have barbecu-

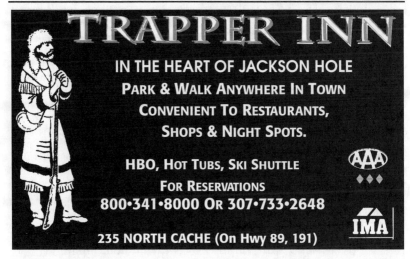

ing facilities. On the premises is the Cody Coffee Company, a cheery little place that serves a continental-style breakfast with a great cup of coffee as well as a simple lunch (see our Restaurants chapter).

Skyline Motor Inn
$$ • 1919 17th St., Cody, Wyo.
• (307) 587-4201, (800) 843-8809

Next to McDonald's, Burger King and Taco Bell at the east end of Cody, the Skyline prides itself on clean rooms — it has 56 units — and reasonable rates. The Skyline has an outdoor heated pool, a small playground and a sign that reads, "American Owned."

Southwestern Montana

Bozeman and Gallatin Gateway, Montana, and U.S. Highway 191

Best Western GranTree Inn
$$$ • 1325 N. Seventh Ave., Bozeman, Mont. • (406) 587-5261, (800) 624-5865

If you've landed late at the Gallatin Field airport and you don't mind heading a little bit off course from the most direct route to Yellowstone Park, the GranTree Inn is a good one-stop accommodation. At the Grantree, you'll find 103 rooms or suites from which to choose plus a restaurant, a lounge, a casino, an atrium, an indoor pool, a guest laundry and winter plug-ins. In addition to standard motel rooms, the GranTree offers executive suites, each with a sitting area and either a king-size bed or two queen-size beds. The bridal suite features a king-size bed and a hot tub. Other niceties include hair dryers, irons and ironing boards available at the office desk. You can also bask in the atrium or bake in one of the thermasol steam units. Children younger than 16 stay here free. And the motel offers a free airport shuttle service. The Grantree also offers banquet and meeting rooms.

Buck's T-4 Lodge
$$$ • U.S. Hwy. 191, Big Sky, Mont. • (406) 995-4111, (800) 822-4484

The first time we stopped at Buck's T-4, the place was teeming with people from three different parties (two wedding receptions and a reunion) going on at once. While Buck's isn't always so busy, it is a popular spot for parties of all kinds. Equipped with two restaurants, meeting and banquet facilities, a lounge, a game room, a gift shop and a liquor store, Buck's has the space and the staff to handle large parties or individual guests. You'll find 75 rooms ranging from standard to deluxe suites, as well as two giant hot tubs. Eight mini-suites are equipped with microwaves and refrigerators and can sleep two to four people each. Two larger suites have kitchenettes and can sleep four each.

Buck's T-4, situated on the Gallatin Canyon Road 48 miles north of West Yellowstone and 1 mile south of the Big Sky Resort area, has a country Western atmosphere with lots of lawn and landscaped garden nooks. You'll find snowmobile rentals on-site. The lodge also has a coin-operated laundry. Inquire about snowmobile and ski packages.

Cinnamon Lodge
$$ • U.S. Hwy. 191, Big Sky, Mont.
• (406) 995-4253

Casual and comfortable, the five cabins at the Cinnamon Lodge aren't for those who seek finely appointed accommodations. They are for those who like to kick back and enjoy the best of the Gallatin Canyon without dipping into their savings. Situated close to the banks of the Gallatin River, each cabin has a porch and fire grill facing the river. Decorated with an eclectic assortment of furniture and accessories, the cabins range from one room to two bedrooms with kitchenettes. The Lodge serves tasty Mexican (and American) food in an old-fashioned log dining room. A small bar just inside the lodge entrance is a favorite hangout for locals. In addition to the cabins and lodge, the Cinnamon Lodge has an RV Park. During the summer, horseback riding is available through a local outfitter.

Gallatin Gateway Inn
$$$ • U.S. Hwy. 191, Gallatin Gateway, Mont. • (406) 763-4672, (800) 676-3522

Once given up as a lost cause, the Gallatin Gateway Inn has risen from the rubble into its former glory as one of the grand railroad hotels of the Rocky Mountain West. Built in the late 1920s by the Chicago, Milwaukee and St. Paul Railway as a destination summer resort for Yellowstone Park visitors, the Inn echoes the tenor of the past. The only thing missing from the old days is the train and its tracks.

From the moment you walk into the 65-foot by 40-foot foyer with its 35-foot-high ceilings you'll feel like you've stepped back in time. Arching carved and stenciled beams of Polynesian mahogany, a checkered tile floor, an assortment of fig and palm trees and two dozen 15-foot-high Spanish-style arched windows create a light, airy elegance that invites travelers to bask in the grand

lounge off the foyer. A piano, silent during the day, comes to life at least one evening a week. The dining room beyond, with its double tablecloths and fresh flowers, offers award-winning fare to match its flair. The menu, which reflects the seasons, is a favorite with locals (see our Restaurants chapter).

The Gallatin Gateway Inn offers 35 refurbished rooms ranging from a room for two with either a king- or queen-size bed to suites with a king-size bed and a sitting room. The price spread between a standard rate and a suite rate is slim. In addition, the inn has a swimming pool, hot tub, tennis court and casting pond. Be sure to ask about naturalist-guided tours into Yellowstone, as well as fly fishing guides and whitewater raft trips.

Livingston, Montana

Murray Hotel
$$ • 201 W. Park, Livingston, Mont.
• (406) 222-1350

The rooms and halls of this hotel in the heart of downtown Livingston ooze old times and understated class. Built in 1905 and recently refurbished, the Murray is still a favorite haunt of visiting movie stars and directors following in the footsteps of film director Sam Peckinpah who called the Murray "home." The lobby, which has an old-fashioned tile floor and comfortably sedate furniture, is a good place to watch the world go by. Who knows who you might see? Such notables as actor Matt Dillon and TV personality Barbara Walters have graced the place.

Except for two rooms, all accommodations offer private baths. All have either one or two queen-size beds.

In case you get tired of people watching, stroll into the Murray Lounge and tip a few with the locals, or wander into the Winchester Cafe, where you'll find breakfast, lunch and dinner served with style. The Murray is a must for anyone who likes to rub shoulders with the Old West.

Paradise Inn
$$ • Park Rd. and Rogers Ln., Livingston, Mont. • (406) 222-6320, (800) 437-6291

An indoor pool, an on-site restaurant and lounge and 43 ground-floor rooms make the Paradise Inn a convenient stage stop on your way to Yellowstone Park. Except for one room with a king-size bed, all rooms at the Paradise have either one or two queen-size beds. Thirty rooms have two outside doors. From every room, you can walk to the restaurant without going outside. In case you forgot your hair dryer or your iron, check at the office.

Arranged in your basic horseshoe shape, the Paradise is just west of U.S. Highway 89 and easily accessible from Interstate 90. Just take Exit 333, then turn north on U.S. 89 until you see the Paradise Valley sign.

Yellowstone Inn
$$$ • 1515 E. Park St., Livingston, Mont.
• (406) 222-6110, (800) 826-1214.

The Yellowstone Inn came to life in 1997, when partners Paul Grossman and Tim Barnes took over the 100-room hotel/motel/convention center. Both Barnes and Grossman are former longtime managers of Chico Hot Springs. (See our Resorts, Guest Ranches and Lodges chapter for more information). Barnes and Grossman are also among the owners of Uncle Looie's, a popular Livingston restaurant with Italian cuisine (see our Restaurants chapter).

Besides remodeling every room and suite, Barnes and Grossman have changed the name of the in-house restaurant from Buffalo Bill's Restaurant and Saloon to The Inn. They have also changed the menu and hired a new chef who turns out consistently good food. An indoor, atrium-like pool, where you can dine poolside, is a favorite for wedding receptions and other gala events like the "Evening of the Stars," a fundraising dinner theater sponsored each spring by the Livingston Chamber of Commerce.

The inn offers shuttles to and from the Bozeman Airport as well as shuttles to Bridger Bowl Ski Area in the winter. If you know ahead of time what you want to do while you're in Livingston, the staff can make arrangements for you before your arrival.

Virginia City and Ennis, Montana, and U.S. Highway 287

El Western Motel
$$ • U.S. Hwy. 287, Ennis, Mont.
• (406) 682-4217

If you have no other reason to go to Ennis,

a stay in the cabins at the El Western may be enough. Situated on 13 lush acres east of Ennis near the Madison River, the El Western offers 28 immaculate cabins accented with mature trees, shrubs and perennial flower gardens. Using a combination of individual log cabins and duplex cabins, the El Western has an array of sleeping cabins and kitchenettes in a setting so peaceful that you won't want to leave. Almost all have paintings of wildlife scenes on the exteriors and a Western motif on the inside.

In case you get a case of cabin fever and have to go to town, Ennis is just a couple miles away — walk, ride your bike or go in the car. We recommend heading for the river with your fishing pole instead. The El Western is open from mid-April until mid-October.

Fairweather Inn
$ • Main St., Virginia City, Mont.
• (406) 843-5331

Stroll down the boardwalk in Virginia City and duck into the Fairweather Inn, a well-preserved Victorian-era hotel that hints of its past lives as a butcher shop, a saloon and several different hotels. Step up to the registration desk and check yourself into a room right in the heart of the Old West. From the Fairweather, which was restored and re-opened in 1946, you can walk across the street to the Bale of Hay Saloon or the Wells Fargo Cafe. Take your time, though, there's plenty to see and experience in Virginia City, the only privately restored historic town in the nation. (See our Attractions chapters for more information.) Simply appointed in Victorian decor, the rooms at the Fairweather come with or without private baths.

Madison River Cabins and RV
$ • 1403 U.S. Hwy. 287, Cameron, Mont.
• (406) 682-4890

Resurrected from the edge of extinction, these conveniently located cabins have had reconstructive surgery inside and out. Arranged in a tidy little horseshoe, with redwood porches, a gravel driveway and islands of mature lilac bushes, the Madison River Cabins are cozy and country-style inside. The original 10 cabins range from compact one-bedrooms to a three-bedroom with a large living room and a standard-sized kitchen. All have private baths. Two newer log cabins overlooking the Madison River offer privacy, down-home Western comfort and plenty of space to accommodate six for only $115 per night.

Madison River Cabins also has nine RV spaces as well as sparkling clean restrooms and a laundry. The Crazy Lady Outpost, a grand log building surrounded by a sea of lush grass, has a combination gift, grocery and fly shop. The cabins are clean, the property tidy and the landscaping expansive. The owners have planted 80 trees and loads of lawn. Just a couple of stone's throws away is the Grizzly Bar and Grill, a lively local hangout with great steaks and burgers and a fun-loving crowd (see our Restaurants chapter).

Rainbow Valley Motel
$$ • U.S. Hwy. 287, Ennis, Mont.
• (406) 682-4264, (800) 452-8254

What other motel do you know that has a horse corral for its guests' horses? You'll feel like you're walking up to someone's ranch house when you stay at this tidy log motel surrounded by acres of lawn. Each room, paneled with knotty pine and decorated to look like an individual cabin, has its own private patio. Some have kitchens, a few have two bedrooms, and all are within hollering distance of the Madison River. Other nice touches include a heated pool, a guest laundry and a barbecue picnic area. Rainbow Valley also has a three-bedroom, two-bath cabin that has its own deck with a spectacular view. This inviting motel has a good reputation and lots of repeat guests, so make your reservations early.

West Fork Cabin Camp
$ • 1487 U.S. Hwy. 287 N., Cameron, Mont. • (406) 682-4802

There is nothing fancy about the 10 housekeeping cabins at the West Fork Camp, They're just clean, comfortable and very popular with anglers, families and hunters. Cabins range from those with one double bed to a couple that can accommodate four or five. Every cabin has a fully equipped kitchen, but you won't find telephones or TVs in your room — they interfere with the experience, says owner Gary

Evans. If you must watch a football game, you can join the other guests in the lounge.

Located on the west side of the Madison River at the West Fork bridge, West Fork Camp Cabins is a laid-back place that includes a convenience store, a fly shop and a guide service, a 24-unit RV park, laundry facilities, a shower house and raft rentals.

RV spaces — they're pull-through with full hookups — rent for $15 by the night, $100 by the week and $300 for a month. Evans says it's common for people to park their RVs for at least a week at the camp, which is in the heart of blue-ribbon trout fishing. It is also close to Yellowstone Park to the south and Virginia City and Lewis and Clark Caverns to the north (see our Attractions chapter). West Fork Camp is open from early April through November.

Red Lodge, Montana

The Pollard
$$$ • 2 N. Broadway, Red Lodge, Mont.
• (406) 446-0001, (800) POLLARD

If the brass rails leading into the Pollard Hotel say "posh" to you, you've read them right. Stroll to the hotel's History Room (just inside the entrance to the right) and you'll see what we mean. Sink into a deep leather chair and reach for something to read. Chances are it'll be something like *On the Road with Charles Kuralt* or *Farm Boy* by Archie Lieberman, or the *New York Times FAX*. Later, you can fidget and stand in line with the other guests anxious to get their hands on today's *Wall Street Journal*. (It arrives, same-day service, at 2 PM each day.)

Built in 1893 as the Spofford Hotel, it became the Pollard in 1900 when Mr. and Mrs. Thomas Pollard took over and added 25 rooms to the existing 35. Through the years politicians, movie stars, copper kings, mountain men and notables of the day Buffalo Bill Cody and Calamity Jane graced the halls of the Pollard, a landmark among grand Rocky Mountain hotels. In 1991 the Hotel Company of Red Lodge bought The Pollard and immediately began renovating the rooms. The owners replaced all the windows, ceilings, carpets, furniture, draperies and linens. And they added an exercise room, two racquetball courts and a ski storage room.

Most rooms have one queen-size bed. If that's all you'll need, ask about a deluxe queen with a hot tub and a balcony overlooking the gallery. (Six rooms have balconies.) Rooms are decorated with antiques, and you'll find hairdryers and telephones in the bathroom, along with two bathrobes.

The dining room offers fine dining with understated elegance. Breakfasts are included in the price of your room. Ask about the adventure trips offered by The Pollard. They include fly fishing, horseback riding, rock climbing and river rafting, as well as a scenic flight over Yellowstone Park.

Yodeler Motel

$ • 601 S. Broadway Ave., Red Lodge, Mont. • (406) 446-1435

Sneak in the back door of your room at the Yodeler, then saunter out the front door. Easy access makes this chalet-looking motel a dream to drop into. And, speaking of dreaming, the Yodeler prides itself on its brand-new Mattress Mill beds made in nearby Bozeman and designed for all-night comfort. Another new feature: a new phone system with high-speed data ports for those of you who must bring your business along. Ground floor rooms are spacious with front and back doors. Downstairs rooms are half-basement units with large daylight windows.

Hostels

The Bunkhouse

$ • 215 N. Cache, Jackson, Wyo. • (307) 733-3668

It's not a motel, it's a hostel, and the rate is a mere $15 per person per night. You get a bunkbed, a locker, linens, soap and shampoo. You also get the use of a large lounge with phone, TV with HBO, sinks and a utility area with microwave and refrigerator. Your bunk, one of 25, is semiprivate. The entire facility is about 5,000 square feet and equipped with men's and women's showers and a gear room. The Bunkhouse is in the basement of the moderately priced brick-red Anvil Motel near town square. No alcohol is permitted.

Montana International Backpackers Hostel

$ • 405 W. Olive St., Bozeman, Mont. • (406) 586-4659, (800) 364-6242

Eight years ago, Jim Marshall bought a Victorian-era home in Bozeman and turned it into a 14-bunk hostel. Today, the hostel is heavily used during the summer, mostly by foreigners accustomed to the hosteling concept. Two of the bedrooms have been converted to bunk rooms. Visitors have access to two bathrooms, a kitchen and a living room. The cost is $10 per person. During the winter, overnight skiers stay at this hostel. Ask about the Yellowstone Hostel Express, a shuttle service that treats travelers (there must be four passengers to put together a shuttle) to an overnight, round-trip tour through Yellowstone Park to Cooke City and back to Bozeman.

West Yellowstone International Hostel

$ • 139 W. Yellowstone Ave., West Yellowstone, Montana • (406) 646-7745

The historic Madison Hotel offers hostel rates of $18 per person per night to anybody belonging to a hostel organization. (For more information, refer to the Madison Hotel entry earlier in this chapter.)

Yellowstone Yurt Hostel

$ • W. Broadway St., Cooke City, Montana • (800) 364-6242

Perched at the edge of Broadway Street, one block north of U.S. Highway 212, the Yellowstone Yurt Hostel is a semi-primitive facility that offers an alternative to Forest Service campgrounds or more expensive motels. The Yurt, owned by Jim Marshall, has six bunks (bring your own sleeping bag) and a wood stove. The $10 overnight fee entitles you to the use of a shower and a toilet on the premises. The hostel also has a primitive outside kitchen equipped with a Coleman stove. Backcountry recreationists come here summer and winter. Marshall also owns the Montana International Backpackers Hostel in Bozeman.

One of the charms of bed and breakfast inns is that amenities and policies vary. Some of our favorites are graciously upscale; others offer a relaxed, casual home environment.

Bed and Breakfast Inns

The most memorable vacation moments are those when, by plan or happy accident, the traveler gets invited inside — into locals' homes, dreams or favorite places.

Like this book, bed and breakfast inns are a way to get inside. Meet the innkeepers — people who moved here a decade ago because they fell hopelessly in love with our mountains — as well as those whose families have carved their livelihoods from the Northern Rockies for generations. Share your morning meals with other travelers, some with stories and travel suggestions to share with you, and others dying to hear your stories and suggestions.

This is definitely not an all-inclusive list, and we love learning about new and wonderful places: Please tell us about your favorite Yellowstone-region inn if you don't find it described here.

All the bed and breakfast inns we single out are unique. Your innkeepers often masterminded their construction. They decorated their inn and landscaped its surrounding property — and they live in it. It's their vision of hospitality and comfort that you will experience. Relax and enjoy. You're invited inside.

One of the charms of bed and breakfast inns is that amenities and policies vary. Some of our favorites are graciously upscale; others offer a relaxed, casual home environment. Some may seem familiar, like childhood visits to grandma's house or your cousin Mary's. Others offer lifestyles you've never experienced.

What your hosts have in common is an interest in the region you've come to see and a wealth of information that will help you plan your vacation. Most provide maps, brochures and books to help you plan excursions. Some will arrange your entire itinerary and even make your reservations at restaurants and for various activities. A few loan snowshoes, water bottles or other equipment to make excursions more comfortable.

Policies differ regarding reservations, deposits and cancellations as well as children and pets. In our opinion, the best bed and breakfast inns for children often are those in which children live; you'll find several listed here. Generally, pets aren't welcome at bed and breakfast inns. Many inns are nonsmoking. In addition, many innkeepers are happy to arrange your transportation from nearby airports with advance notice. Discuss these issues when you call.

Reservations often are required and always are preferred. Most inns have cancellation policies that require you to provide generous advance notice before you change your plans. Some require minimum stays of two or more nights. Please inquire about these policies too.

For the heavy travel months of July and August, the most popular inns will be booked by the preceding late winter. Some vacationers book next year's stay before they leave their inn of choice this year, particularly if they have a favorite room they want to enjoy again.

This does not mean it isn't sometimes worthwhile to drop in or attempt a reservation on short notice: Innkeepers in Yellowstone Country work within a fairly short busy season. If they get a cancellation, they're generally happy to accommodate you.

Most inns are open year round and accept major credit cards. We note exceptions for you.

Price Code

The average nightly rate for two adults during the peak summer season is indicated by the following dollar-sign ($) chart. Please note that many bed and breakfast inns offer a range of rooms at a range of prices. Larger rooms and rooms with more spectacular views, private decks or private entrances generally cost more than the price we indicate.

$	Less than $85
$$	$85 to $115
$$$	$116 to $150
$$$$	$151 and more

Yellowstone National Park

Entrance Communities

West Yellowstone, Montana

Sportsman's High Bed and Breakfast
$$ • 750 Deer St., West Yellowstone, Mont. • (406) 646-7865

Imagine sleeping under the softest floral chintz, then rising to pen a letter as the morning sun creeps across the floor. Something outside catches your eye. It's a fat doe with her new fawn, standing for a moment among the aspen trees outside your window. All of this — and more — is real at the Mountain High Bed and Breakfast where owners Diana and Gary Baxter have carved their niche in paradise. Eight miles from Yellowstone Park, Sportsman's High is also minutes away from several blue-ribbon trout streams and lakes. Just out the front door are trails for hiking, mountain biking, horseback riding, cross country skiing, and hundreds of miles of groomed snowmobile trails. In each of the five rooms at Sportsman's High, guests will find plumped feather pillows, country-fresh decor, robes, cheery bath amenities, a hair dryer, an antique desk and an assortment of guide and

information books. The Bear Cabin, a one-room log cabin, offers extra privacy and charm. Diana serves a hearty breakfast at a 12-foot-long harvest table. There is a cozy upstairs sitting room for guests.

Gardiner, Montana

Slip and Slide Bed and Breakfast
$$, no credit cards • U.S. Hwy. 89, 11 miles north of Gardiner, Mont.
• (406) 848-7648

Don't let the name slip you up. This bed and breakfast is named after the Slip and Slide drainage in which the inn sits, off the highway and away from the bustle. Owners Franklin and Susan Rigler are newcomers to the bed and breakfast business, but they're old hands at hospitality. A third-generation rancher, Franklin is a hunting and fishing guide. For an extra fee, he will pack you into the mountains so you can fish away from the crowds. The Riglers also will share Insiders tips on where to go and what to do. They offer three rooms and two shared baths on the first floor of their house. In addition to a large living room with a bar, refrigerator and range top, guests can walk right out the door and enjoy the view (Electric Peak will be staring you in the face). If you're in the mood to cook up a steak, there's a barbecue on the patio. There are also laundry facilities. Susan serves up a ranch breakfast garnished with western hospitality. There are two private fishing ponds on the property.

The Yellowstone Inn
$ • Main St. and U.S. Hwy. 89, Gardiner, Mont. • (406) 848-7000

In the heart of Gardiner, this turn-of-the-century stone bed and breakfast is clean and country, but not cutesy-country. It is the closest bed and breakfast inn to the Park's north entrance, and the oldest operating one in Gardiner. Nine spacious, simply decorated rooms, divided between two buildings, offer a multitude of choices. On the third floor is the Yellowstone Suite. With two bedrooms, a bath and a sitting room, it is private and big enough to accommodate a family. Or get together a gang and reserve four bedrooms on the second floor. You'll have to share the three bathrooms all in a row, though. Breakfast — usually a hot country dish with muffins, cereal or yogurt — is cooked up in a huge kitchen and served in a communal dining room. This bed and breakfast fills up fast with folks frequenting the Park, so make your reservations well ahead of time.

Yellowstone Suites
$ • 506 Fourth St., Gardiner, Mont.
• (406) 848-7937

The bottom is made of river rock, and the top half is made of rock left over from the construction of the Roosevelt Arch, Yellowstone Park's first (and grandest) entrance, dedicated in 1903 by Theodore Roosevelt. Simple in design, this three-story home built in 1904 is a unique bed and breakfast. The second floor, which has two bedrooms with a shared bath and the dining room, opens at the back onto a porch and an "upstairs" yard. Owned by John and Anita Varley, both longtime Park employees, this bed and breakfast makes the perfect place to stay while snooping about Yellowstone Country. John and Anita currently staff a manager during the week, but on weekends they run the place. They are a wealth of information about Yellowstone Park. Bay windows, balconies, a veranda and a hot tub add to the airiness here. A third-floor suite offers privacy with a bath, window seat, nifty dormer, TV and kitchen.

Breakfast is a quasi-continental serve-yourself setup in a charming upstairs dining room.

Jackson Hole

Many of Jackson's best have banded together to make information gathering and reservations easy for you. Contact The Jackson Hole Bed and Breakfast Association, P.O. Box 6396, Jackson, WY 83002, (800) 542-2632, for a brochure or to ask about specific inns represented by the association. More than a dozen are represented.

Jackson, Wyoming

The Alpine House
$$ • 285 N. Glenwood, Jackson, Wyo.
• (307) 739-1570, (800) 753-1421

After you've wandered through this sunny, uncluttered inn — an easy stroll from Jackson's downtown shopping and entertainment possibilities — you won't wonder why The Alpine House was selected as one of *Country Inns'* top 10 affordable luxuries of 1996.

The seven guest rooms are upstairs, facing each other across a 2½-story open area that overlooks the dining and gathering areas downstairs. The warmth of exposed beams blends well with cool white walls, big windows and open space.

Rooms are not large, but each has a private bath, balcony and radiant floor heat (you'll love this feature when you step barefoot from bed on a chilly January morning). Two rooms have loft areas served by log ladders.

Breakfast is served buffet-style and enjoyed at several small tables scattered through the common area; so is afternoon tea. No television will draw your attention from the pleasant Scandinavian feel of your accommodations or the book you picked from the well-stocked adventure and recreational library.

Innkeepers Hans and Nancy Johnstone are both former Olympic athletes — Hans was a Nordic skier and Nancy, a biathlete — and both are deeply involved in local outdoor recreation. Hans currently works with Exxum Guides as a mountaineering and rock climbing guide. Their specialized knowledge of the area makes The Alpine House uniquely suited for the hard-core adventure traveler as well as being comfortable and upscale enough for the luxury vacationer.

Nowlin Creek Inn

$$$$ • 660 E. Broadway, Jackson, Wyo.
• (307) 733-0882, (800) 533-0882

Owners Susan and Mark Nowlin (that's NOW-lin, not NO-lin) may have the perfect location for an in-town inn. Easy to find on one of Jackson's main streets and only six blocks from the crowd-filled town square, Nowlin Creek Inn manages to feel like a quiet refuge.

Mark's great-grandfather homesteaded across the street in what is now the National Elk Refuge; he was the refuge's first superintendent. Nearby Nowlin Creek carries his name.

Mark and Susan are artists and former museum curators, and their special touch adds sparkle and eccentricity to every room in this large country house. Clean white walls prevent the many fine pieces of art from seeming cluttered. Offbeat chandeliers hang from vaulted ceilings. Stenciled ivy (Susan's handwork) twines across lacquered pine floors. And if you look closely, you'll notice that the win-

dow frames aren't really there: They're painted and stamped (also by Susan) onto the walls. Beyond the outdoor hot tub, a giant cowboy — once a sign on an old building downtown — waves a big welcome.

The two-story inn has five comfortable rooms, all set in corners of the house so they're flooded with light during the day and with crisp breezes at night. The Nowlins spoil you with evening snacks, plush robes and slippers to relax in, and a gourmet breakfast is served before you head out to explore Jackson or the Elk Refuge just outside the door.

The Nowlins also rent the cabin out back — built by Mark's grandfather in the 1920s and furnished with an even more exuberantly eccentric artists' touches. (See our Hotels, Motels and Cabins chapter.)

Twin Trees Bed & Breakfast

$$ • 575 S. Willow, Jackson, Wyo.
• (307) 739-9737

From the dining room window, winter guests at Twin Trees watch skiers *schuss* underneath the lifts at Snow King, the locals' ski area. On the Fourth of July, fireworks explode over the inn; in April, guests can sit on the comfortable porch and experience the roar and excitement of the World Championship Snowmobile Hillclimb.

Twin Trees is a gracious alternative to Jackson's downtown motels, but it's every bit as convenient. A 10-minute walk will take you to shopping and dining destinations. The bus for Teton Village, where world-class skiing awaits, picks up almost at the front door. And Snow King Resort — home to concerts, a convention center, ice rink and ski hill — is just across the street.

Innkeeper Pat Martin and her cats welcome you to an eclectically furnished house with three unique guest rooms. Down comforters and plush robes await in your small but cozy room. One room features a kimono hung on the wall and a vaguely Oriental decor. Another has an arched ceiling and cushioned window

---

INSIDERS' TIP

Most bed and breakfast inns have color brochures that show you what their establishments look like. Ask to have one sent to you before you book your room.

seat. On summer nights, the full moon arcs past this window and lights the whole room. The work of local artists adorns the living and dining areas downstairs.

Amenities include an enclosed outdoor hot tub with sliding screens (so it can be opened to the cool night air), television in the living area, a lovely yard with privacy fence and a long shaded porch. Rooms have private baths but no phones.

Pat prides herself on the care she gives to her guests' dietary needs. Breakfasts — plentiful, flexible and healthful — are enjoyed at a warmly polished walnut table while Pat bustles about in the kitchen on the other side of the breakfast bar, perhaps preparing her wonderful English fruit scones.

Wilson, Wyoming

Bentwood Bed & Breakfast
$$$$ • 4250 W. Raven Haven, Wilson, Wyo.• (307) 739-1411

Just outside Jackson, off the Village road, a 5,800-square-foot log home hides in a grove of cottonwoods. It's massive, but seems less so because of the gracious way it curves around the trees and flower beds at its main entrance. Bentwood is the kind of place that, if you do happen to glimpse it through the trees, you might covet. Perhaps you'd wonder what's behind the lace curtains that so sweetly soften its massive log presence.

Innkeepers Bill and Nell Fay would love to show you. Gracious hosts in a gracious house, the Fays offer five distinctively appointed rooms, all with private baths and balconies, gas fireplaces (operated by hand-held remote!), cable TV and telephone; most have Jacuzzis. One pretty room particularly well-suited for families features a sitting area, a queen-size Inglenook bed tucked into three walls and a loft equipped with three twin beds.

The main living area is spacious and open to the second floor. A 30-foot-high, river-rock fireplace anchors the room. Your hosts, whose quarters are one side of the house, run their inn with professional hospitality: They're there when you'd like them to be, but in general, the main areas of the house are yours. Make yourself at home in log luxury.

The Fays have been hosting travelers here for three years. They say their house is ideal for groups and conventions, which often reserve the entire house. The 3-acre property, ringed by cottonwoods, is ideal for cookouts and family get-togethers. But don't be surprised if you have wild guests: The family of great-horned owls that nests in the grove often stops in to see what's up.

Moose Meadows Bed & Breakfast
$ • 1225 Green Ln., Wilson, Wyo.
• (307) 733-9510

Moose Meadows is one of the most reasonably priced bed and breakfast inns in the area. It may also be the most laid back. Owner/innkeeper Juli James invites you to share her home and the family scene in her large, western-style house with its odd and entertaining mix of antiques, collectibles and huge elk mounts, moose antlers, mountain goats and longhorn skulls. Family pets roam the spacious house — and so should you and your children, insists the friendly innkeeper.

Juli also likes to share her enthusiasm for the western art collection hanging on the walls. You'll even eat from part of that collection: Her breakfast plates were crafted by well-known Montana artist Buckeye Blake.

The antiques that furnish much of the house and the four guest rooms belonged to Juli's grandmother. Other furnishings reflect Juli's travels and her family's accomplishments. Decorations from Africa and India are scattered about. Her father was once ambassador to India; a punched-steel sign on the Porch Room wall commemorates his stint as U.S. Attorney General. One daughter was the 1997 National High School Rodeo Girls' Cutting Champion. Championship belt buckles are displayed in the living room.

The house is conveniently located near Wyo. Highway 22 in a small subdivision in Wilson, so guests can reach Grand Teton Park without entering the bustle of Jackson. They can also enjoy views of the Tetons and of game-filled meadows through the house's large back and side windows or from the hot tub on the back deck. Two winters ago, a wounded cow moose took up residence on that deck. After a few weeks she moved into the nearby woods. The following summer she raised her calf nearby.

Breakfast is what Juli describes as a blend of Wyoming and English cuisine, featuring such items as elk sausage with "bubble and squeak." The meal is served on a big, round lazy Susan table in a dining room that features Teton views.

The Painted Porch Bed & Breakfast
$$$ • 3755 N. Moose-Wilson Rd., Wilson, Wyo. • (307) 733-1981

Maybe it's the white picket fence. Maybe it's because, in the land of log, Martha MacEachern's pretty inn is a white-shuttered, porch-railed farmhouse. Or maybe it's the aspens that whisper and hiss like restless water, hiding the vague traffic noises from the Village road nearby. For whatever reason, we walked through the front gate and onto the green painted porch of this inn with a sigh of pure pleasure.

The house was built in nearby Teton Valley in 1901 by a farming family. In 1967, it was partially dismantled and brought here through Teton Pass — you know, that 10 percent-plus grade your car labored over the other day before dropping into Jackson Hole?

But the hardest thing you'll do here is pick which of the four uniquely appointed rooms you prefer. Each room has a private bath (two offer Japanese soaking tubs), cable television and Ralph Lauren bed linens, towels and comforters. But they range in feel from nouveau cowboy to sweetly sunlit and feminine.

The spacious kitchen/dining room, where the ample country breakfasts are served, is one of the most pleasant rooms in the house, with its shiny white tile counters and long dining table with fancifully painted chairs. A mass of variously colored and shaped pillows rests on a bench seat beneath the large bay window. Hmmm, coffee here or out on the deck in the hammock? Another tough decision.

The Sassy Moose Inn
$$$ • 3859 Miles Rd., Wilson, Wyo. • (307) 733-1277, (800) 356-1277

Polly Kelley runs the bed and breakfast inn that her son Craig built five years ago on the Moose-Wilson Road (also called the Village road) between Jackson and Teton Village. Some of the nicer features Craig installed include an entrance hallway that allows guests to access rooms without passing through the common living and dining areas, and sound-damping in the walls so that one group may enjoy the television in the living area while you nap undisturbed in your room.

One suite is particularly well-suited to a larger group. It is upstairs and includes a sitting room and bedroom; it adjoins a loft area overlooking the house's main living space. The loft is furnished with a hide-a-bed. All rooms have private baths.

Polly leaves a bowl of fruit and sweets out for guests during the day. In the afternoon, she provides wine and other beverages; her guests often relax together over snacks and wine to recount the day's adventures. She describes her inn's feel as informal, relaxed and fun.

A Teton Tree House Bed & Breakfast
$$$ • 6175 Heck of a Hill Rd., Wilson, Wyo. • (307) 733-3233

In the stylish bed and breakfast scene in and around Jackson, you have to do something spectacular to stand out. A Teton Tree House does.

Innkeeper Denny Becker's fanciful four-story building clings like ivy to a steep hillside above Wilson. The gentle 92-stair hike from your car lands you in a place that seems a million miles away from busy Jackson (actually, it's only 8). From every window seat and every deck, you'll feel like you're enjoying the view from your very own tree-house retreat.

INSIDERS' TIP

Many bed and breakfast inns have nonrefundable deposits to cover cancellations after a certain date. This makes trip insurance a good idea. Many inns themselves can provide information about trip insurance, as can reservation centers and travel agents.

Photo: The Alpine House

The vaguely Scandinavian feel of this bed and breakfast's main living area is unusual in mostly log- and pine-paneled Jackson Hole.

Denny, a contractor, designed and built the hybrid post-and-beam structure. His specialty is staircases, so make sure you take special note of the curving staircase, the spiral staircase and what Denny calls the staggered staircase (it takes a bit of practice to navigate). He also built the lovely long oval dining table, where you'll enjoy breakfast while watching the finches, grosbeaks and nuthatches at the window feeders enjoying theirs.

The house has six rooms of various sizes and styles. Each has deck access. Most have private decks, and all have private baths. Denny provides a cordless phone for your convenience: Take it into any room you choose, or get really silly and make your calls from the hot tub on the main deck.

Breakfast is what Denny likes to call "full with low cholesterol:" homemade granola, lots of fresh fruit, exotic blended fruit drinks, breads

and muffins and hot whole-grain cereals, but no eggs and no meat.

Most guests at A Teton Tree House are couples; it's easy to see why. We can't imagine a more romantic setting for your weekend getaway, honeymoon or second honeymoon.

Denny is open for business year round, but he cautions that Heck of a Hill Road is not lightly named: In winter, four-wheel or front-wheel drive vehicles fare best on the well-maintained but steep, winding road.

The Wildflower Inn
$$$$ • 3725 Teton Village Rd., Wilson, Wyo. • (307) 733-4710

It's not just a name: During the summer, the driveway to Sherrie and Ken Jern's 8-year-old inn is lined with wildflowers. Color dances in the entry way and hugs the log walls of the house. Pots of bright blooms hang from the second-story deck. "Idyllic" is the word that keeps coming to mind.

The interior is just as pleasant — and as flower-filled. Cut flowers brighten the long table and bay window in the dining room. Sunshine streams in through the many windows, transforming the weight of log walls and a river-rock fireplace into warm, elegant comfort.

Log homes are a dime a dozen out here, but this house has special touches. For instance, instead of synthetic chinking between logs, the Jerns chinked with wood — more laborious and more attractive. Interior log-ends were allowed to extend into the rooms, sawed into pleasant curves. The roof beams are massive and exposed. Touches like these have won Wildflower Inn awards and recognition from publications such as *National Geographic Traveler* magazine and *Glamour*.

All five guest rooms are equipped with log beds, down comforters, private baths, pedestal sinks and pleasant views. Most have private decks. The inn is open year round. Reservations should be made as far in advance as possible: Many people book their summer accommodations at the Wildflower Inn in January or February.

Sherrie likes to help her guests leave early for their Teton adventures, so she's happy to pack a picnic breakfast. But our guess is you'll leave the wildlife for later so you can relax over Wildflower Inn's fine fare: all your favorite morning food enlivened with your host's gourmet twist. One guest favorite is the vegetable frittata — a deep-dish concoction of fresh veggies and Gruyère, Swiss and Parmesan cheeses. Mmm, to heck with hiking!

Surrounding Areas

Eastern Idaho

Rexburg Area

Porter House Bed & Breakfast
$ • 4232 W. 1000 N., Rexburg, Idaho
• (208) 356-6632

When we walked into Virginia and Craig Porter's home, the smell of fresh bread spread from the kitchen. Somehow, though, it seemed to stop at the door to a startlingly anomalous room. The step through that doorway transported us from a modern country farmhouse to a rustic hunting lodge.

The lodge room is festooned with bear skins and elk, deer and pronghorn antelope mounts. Log rafters span the high ceiling above a massive, river-rock fireplace. The room, in which you are encouraged to relax, is equipped with a TV, VCR and a small selection of movies.

Back in the very "unlodge-like" farmhouse, Virginia stenciled floral patterns on the walls of the guest rooms, most of which have private baths. One of the best features is that three guest rooms downstairs have connecting doors that create a wonderful three bedroom, two bath suite for families. The inn also has one guest room upstairs.

Also perfect for families is the expanse of landscaped lawn out front. The swing set and trampoline out back are there for the Porters' kids to play on, but you're welcome to join them.

The inn is close to Teton Lakes Golf Course and is only 10 minutes from U.S. Highway 20, near Rexburg.

Virginia would hate to have you drive out to her place and find it booked up, so she recommends reservations. However, unlike many bed and breakfast inns, Porter House requires no deposit and accepts drop-ins with ease.

Ashton, Idaho

Jessen's R.V. Park and Bed & Breakfast
$, no credit cards • 1146 S. 3400 E., Ashton, Idaho • (208) 652-3356

Velvet upholstery on the chairs, lace edging on the comforters and matching pillows, floral patterns everywhere: Jessen's small guest rooms are literally crammed with nostalgic comfort. One room contains a print of that famous painting in which Jesus knocks on the door to your heart. A massive wooden wardrobe occupies a corner. Both rooms have televisions. They share a bedroom-size bath outfitted with a claw-foot tub and an Exercycle.

The rest of the two-story farmhouse is filled with more velvet furniture, pictures of the

Jessens' large family and well-kept antiques. It's like a visit to grandma's house.

Neica and Jack Jessen, your hosts, have been here long enough to seem a part of the 10-acre property, with its wild rose bushes, fruit trees, white gazebo and massive black willow trees. The property also encompasses several guest cottages (breakfast is not included in this option) and an RV park and campground. These accommodations as well as the spacious grounds make Jessen's ideal for family reunions in which different members may prefer different levels of comfort. (See our Hotels, Motels and Cabins chapter and our Campgrounds and RV Parks chapter for more information.)

Stegelmeier Farmhouse Inn
$ • 1357 N. 4350 E., Ashton, Idaho • (208) 652-3363

If you'd like your bed and breakfast stay to include a healthy dose of local history, you are in the right place. Cathy Stegelmeier invites you into the 1912 farmhouse in which her father was born. Out the kitchen window you can see the spot where a sod cabin once stood. Her grandfather was born there. And she'd love to tell you how to find the remains of the dugout home built by her great-grandfather, a trapper and German immigrant named Otto Stegelmeier.

The two-story farmhouse was the first in the area to have an indoor bathroom: At that time it was a simple gravity feed to the tub.

Cathy and her family remodeled the old farmhouse in 1996-97 in order to open its doors to you, so while you'll enjoy her stories and the finely preserved family antiques, you won't lack for comfort or modern amenities. A large deck stretches behind the house, perfect for morning coffee. You'll eat breakfast in a pleasantly modern dining room connected to the kitchen by a bar. And each small but comfortable room has its own bathroom (Grandma's room is especially fun with its claw-foot tub and suspended shower curtain).

Teton Valley

Alta Lodge Bed & Breakfast
$ • 590 Targhee Town Rd., Tetonia, Idaho • (208) 353-2582

Teton climbing legend Paul Petzold once owned this property. The story goes that he traded climbing lessons for construction assistance, but the lodge he intended was never finished. When Bob and Judy Blair bought the place six years ago, they tore the half-built structure back down to its foundations and began again.

What the Blairs created was a four–guest-room inn, quiet and comfortable, with fantastic Teton views through the 25-foot-tall windows that are the house's eastern wall. The inn has the youthful landscaping of a new home in a spacious subdivision, but you won't care about that once you're inside.

The Blairs and daughter Susie offer quiet comfort, a hot tub and private baths in two of the four rooms. Downstairs in the basement is a big-screen satellite TV with VCR. The Blairs will join you in the living room for conversation. You can also make use of their well-stocked library.

The modern log home has lots of nice extra touches. A massive unpeeled lodgepole pine pillar anchors the vaulted ceiling. One large guest room, called the Grand Room, has windows on three sides and white carpets and walls for an airy, spacious feel.

Rooms do not have phones or TVs. The inn is 6 miles northeast of Driggs on a good dirt road that will barely slow your car.

Pines Motel-Guest Haus
$ • 105 S. Main, Driggs, Idaho • (208) 354-2774, (800) 354-2778

Bed and breakfast is an option at John and Nancy Neilson's friendly motel. Well, OK . . . it's not exactly a motel (but see our Hotels, Motels and Cabins chapter anyway). It's more like a . . . like a — OK, we give up. There's nothing quite like this delightful old building with its handmade matching quilts, lamp shades and curtains in each small, quaint room. Behind the motel you'll find an acre stretch of tree-shaded lawn; in front is Driggs's character-packed Main Street with its shops and eateries.

Many of the breakfast offerings are one-of-a-kind too: Pumpkin waffles get great reviews from guests, as does Blueberry Surprise (we won't ruin the surprise by telling you what it is, but we will say this may be your first chance to have ice cream for breakfast).

For Nancy, taking over the eight-room motel from her parents has meant coming home:

She lived in one of the upstairs rooms as a girl. John, who used to run a dairy near here (not fun in Teton Valley's harsh winters, he'll tell you), does all the renovation on the little motel that, the Neilsons explain, has always been a work-in-progress.

Pines Motel-Guest Haus is only a 20-minute drive from Grand Targhee, a ski area known for its amazing powder and lack of snow-making equipment (they don't need it).

Wilson Creekside Inn
$, no credit cards • Alta N. Rd., Alta, Wyo. • (307) 353-2409

We liked this inn before we even saw it: The drive toward the mouth of Teton Canyon, alongside Teton Creek, toward the Grand Teton is, well, Teton-ful. Then we saw the sprawling, 3-acre lawn surrounded by a white fence. A profusion of flowers marched around the sides of the house. A hot tub waited on the back deck.

It only got better inside. Each room is pleasantly and simply decorated to remind you of home. Bathrooms are shared. The upstairs rooms are particularly nice with their high ceilings and small private balconies.

Surprises are around every corner: a barbed-wire collection, family photos dating back generations, family heirlooms and antiques and the gift shop. Yes, that's right, the house contains a tiny room stuffed with handmade collectibles and gifts. Most of the crafts people represented here are family members and friends.

Another nice surprise comes when you learn that Janice (say it Ja-NEESE) will, on request, cheerfully prepare your evening meal as well as the full breakfast she offers in the mornings.

Church groups and large families will love the largest guest room, a converted garage. It contains nine pull-down bunk beds with space left over.

Janice's inn is only 5 miles from Grand Targhee, just inside the Wyoming border. Janice says that during the busy summer season a month's notice will probably be necessary to secure a room.

Southwestern Montana

Emigrant, Montana

4M Bed and Breakfast
$ • East River Rd., Emigrant, Mont. • (406) 333-4784

The view is spectacular and the organic garden is yours for the picking at the 4M Bed and Breakfast near Emigrant, owned by Phil and Ginger Keck. Pull a carrot, crunch on a radish, harvest some lettuce. (If you do, chances are Ginger will fix you up with a salad.) The two guest rooms are in a private wing with a shared bath (it has a quiet toilet). The Creek Side Room, with its sitting area and view of Six Mile Creek, is restful. The Mountain View Room, on the other hand, has a breathtaking view of Mount Emigrant and the Crazy Mountains.

Ginger is into health food and uses the bounty of her garden to concoct gourmet breakfasts. (If you're wondering about the funny-looking things in a jar on the table, they're flax seeds. You don't have to eat them, but it wouldn't hurt to try.) The inn also offers gold panning and "doorstep" fishing.

Ennis, Montana

9T9 Guest Ranch
99 Gravelly Range Rd., Ennis, Mont. • (406) 682-7659, (800) 484-5862, pin 7659

Owners Vaughan and Judy Herrick like to say they are "inconveniently located" 10 miles south of Ennis. Their place is worth the drive just for the view. They overlook building-free meadows, the Madison River — world-renowned for its trout fishing — and the towering Madison Mountain Range beyond. They have private access to the river, and Vaughan is a licensed fishing guide. He accommodates anglers with a place in the garage for them to hang waders and fly rods. Guests are welcome to use a fly-tying table

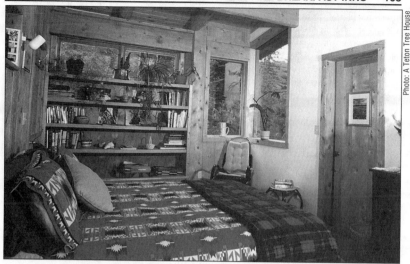

The view from the window seat of this bed and breakfast room is of the Gros Ventres and a distant mountain that the locals call the Sleeping Indian.

in the living room or watch wildlife through his spotting scope.

If you aren't into fishing, the drive is worth it just to experience the gracious and genuine welcome of this vibrant retired couple. Judy, a bubbly blond involved in her church and the community, is such a good cook that locals began requesting that she begin a Saturday night "restaurant." She applied for the license and now serves 12 people (by reservation only) at "Judy's Table" in her dining room during the winter months when local restaurants close. Her breakfasts will delight you. And their Wednesday night chuck wagon dinners are out of this world. Accommodations are simple, clean and country. A large living room downstairs (where the three bedrooms are located) is a comfortable refuge after a long day on the river.

Livingston, Montana

The Island
$$, no credit cards • 77 Island Dr., Livingston, Mont. • (406) 222-3788, (800) 438-3092

Location, location, location: It's secluded. It's five minutes from downtown Livingston.

And it's on an island. Owner Fran Eggar offers two bedrooms with a shared bath, three ponds with catch-and-release fishing, and 60 acres with lots of deer and a shy moose. Guests have access to the living and dining rooms as well as a sun room with refrigerator. A patio with a barbecue (feel free to use it) is off the sun room. Fran encourages relaxing and wandering about the island. She also has a three-bedroom, two-bath guest house at the end of the island road that rents for $1,000 weekly or $175 nightly.

Bozeman, Montana

Lindley House Bed and Breakfast
$$$ • 202 Lindley Pl., Bozeman, Mont. • (406) 587-8403, (800) 787-8404

Goldilocks would have had a hard time choosing just which of the eight rooms she liked best in this historic Victorian bed and breakfast inn. No matter which bed she tried, she would have found a piece of candy on the pillow. She also would have found fresh flowers, a carafe of purified water and gingerbread cookies awaiting her in each of the rooms. Owner Stephanie Volz spent three years restoring this four-story brick mansion, literally from the rafters down. Mature trees, an English flower garden, private nooks and crannies all add to the Lindley House experience. Afternoons, Volz offers her guests tea, coffee, wine or sherry in the parlor. And evenings, you'll find brandy and a snifter beside your bed. At breakfast you'll sit down to a three- or four-course meal with delicacies like fruit-stuffed French toast with chokecherry syrup; spinach and mushroom souffle topped with freshly grated cheese; or sourdough crepes wrapped around plump blueberries — all served on fine china and polished silver. You'll recognize the Lindley House by the antique bed filled with flowers on the front lawn, and by the sign out front that tells all about it.

The Lindley House, two blocks south of Main Street, is on the National Historic Register. Volz offers a range of rooms that includes a penthouse suite. She also has a massage therapist on call for her guests. She requires a two-night minimum stay.

Torch and Toes Bed and Breakfast
$ • 309 S. Third Ave., Bozeman, Mont.
• (406) 586-7285, (800) 446-2138

You'll find the Torch and Toes in Bozeman's historic Bon Ton District near downtown. Built in 1906, this two-story Queen Anne-style brick house has three guest rooms, a carriage house suite, and 2,000 different mouse traps collected during the innkeepers' travels. While the traps are displayed in the breakfast nook, other objets d'art are scattered throughout the house, adding charm and fancy to the inn's eclectic decor. Downstairs you'll find oak woodwork and maple floors. Upstairs you'll find carpet, cafe curtains across big windows, and a private bath in each room. The carriage house — a favorite among Torch and Toes guests — has a bedroom, bath and kitchen downstairs, with a sitting room, fireplace and futon sofa upstairs. It sleeps up to six people. All guests will find facilities for badminton, horseshoes, and a soak in the hot tub. Space for a game of English croquet is planned for this summer. Breakfasts are complete with fresh fruit, homemade sweet breads and entrees such as coddled eggs or omelets with a breakfast meat.

Red Lodge, Montana

Willows Inn
$ • 224 S. Platt, Red Lodge, Mont.
• (406) 446-3913

If you arrive at this charming Victorian inn after dark, you'll find proprietress Carolyn Boggio has left the lights on for you. The cheery white Christmas lights strung on the fence in front are just one of the thoughtful details she uses to make your stay at the Willows Inn unique. Beautifully restored inside and out, the Willows Inn says, "We care," from each perfectly appointed room to the English flower garden outside. Carolyn serves refreshments in the afternoon and offers a continental-plus breakfast that includes homemade Finnish pastries made by her mother-in-law, fresh fruit, hot and cold beverages and cheese.

The Willows Inn also offers two equally beautiful cottages year round. Adjacent to the inn, each cottage is bright, cozy and loaded with antiques. Equipped with kitchens and linens, these cottages each sleep six. They rent for $80 per night for two people (add $10 for each additional person and subtract 10 percent for stays of five days and longer).

Northwestern Wyoming

Buffalo Valley

The Inn at Buffalo Fork
$$$$ • 18200 U.S. Hwy. 287, east of Moran, Wyo. • (307) 543-2010

The Buffalo Valley is a broad, flat expanse of sage, grasses and moose willow. It takes its name from the Buffalo Fork, the fine fishing river that winds through it. Sandwiched between the Teton Wilderness to the north and Bridger-Teton National Forest to the south, both valley and river empty into Grand Teton National Park.

The 4-year-old Inn at Buffalo Fork sits on 6 acres of open valley, seemingly contemplating the distant granite masses of Mount Moran and the Grand Teton. In this remote valley with few inhabitants — and little traffic after the summer folks have come and gone — the inn frequently is visited by wildlife, especially moose. The Moran entrance to Grand Teton National Park is only 6 miles away.

Three of five guest rooms offer Teton views, as does the dining room. Flower beds and boxes enliven the exterior of the house. The inn is completely surrounded by a working cattle ranch, the Hatchet Ranch. In winter guests can watch the hands plow through deep snow on horseback to feed cattle.

Gene and Jeannie Ferrin are your innkeepers; he is a fly-fishing guide, and she is a former schoolteacher. Many of the inn's guests fish with Gene. He'll take them floating down the Snake River as it slips past his grandfather's old homestead, now part of Grand Teton National Park.

Cody, Wyoming

Buffalo Bill's Cody House
$$ • 101 Robertson St., Cody, Wyo.
• (307) 587-2528

Buffalo Bill Cody lived here. Heck, he built the place and would have died here if fate hadn't laid him down elsewhere. He'd be right proud, though, to be a part of this humming hub of creative Western hospitality. The flower and vegetable gardens are gorgeous. His daughter Irma's room is rosy and restful. And the breakfasts? They're downright out of sight. If it's Western, (mother) Nancy and (daughter) Julie Short will serve it. If it's exotic and their guests request it, they'll try it. Take the chocolate Belgian waffles. Julie (she's the cook) experimented all one summer until she had them down pat. Preparations for breakfast begin the day before. Guests who return from a long day of sightseeing may find the tummy-tugging smell of fresh-baked cinnamon rolls wafting across the huge living room and into the parlor. From photos on the walls in every room, Buffalo Bill watches it all. Nancy has collected Cody photos and info from the Buffalo Bill Historical Center. Better than that, she and her house were the hub of the 1996 Cody family reunion. Fifty-two Cody family descendants descended on Cody to discuss family business and rehash little-known details of Cody's life. Nancy heard it all.

Parson's Pillow
$$ • 1202 14th St., Cody, Wyo.
• (307) 587-2382, (800) 377-2348

Innkeepers Lee and Elly Larabee say, "It's OK to sleep in our church." But before you sleep, you'll want to peek around in every little nook and cranny that this converted church hides. In the steeple, you'll find a bathroom decorated cowboy-style with an oak-framed prairie tub and telephone-style shower head. In the Garden Room, you'll find relaxation and roses, greens and lattice, and a vintage pedestal tub tucked into a cozy corner. In each of the four rooms, you'll find a delightful armoire. Built in 1902 by Methodists (it was Cody's first church), the building has been completely restored and converted. The long, narrow church windows offer lots of light; lace adds a touch of grace; and the Larabees's thoughtful antique selection bespeaks style. A large parlor is always open to guests who want to lounge, read the morning paper, peruse the library, play the piano or the fiddle or, if you must, watch the evening news.

Breakfasts are abundant and delicious.

Windchimes Cottage
$$ • 1501 Beck Ave., Cody, Wyo.
• (307) 527-5310

Windchimes aren't the only soothing sound at this charming bed and breakfast in a quiet residential neighborhood one block off Cody's Main Street. The wind rustling in the leaves of the giant elm trees, and the birds singing in the secluded yard, are just what your doctor would order after a day of sightseeing, rafting, hiking or shopping. A native stone patio invites you to sit for a spell under the old apple tree and sip something cool and soothing to the soul. Owners Hardy and Sylvia Stucki have restored and remodeled this beautiful home using imagination and ingenuity. Each bedspread in the light, airy rooms is hand-quilted by Sylvia. The wallpaper and woodwork, combined with antiques and art, create a cheery space. Families will want to check on the new Jungle Bungalow, a suite in the Stucki's converted garage that is creatively and humorously conceived.

Meals are straight from the farm (read fresh) and served with a touch of elegance.

To experience what is unique to Yellowstone country you must stay at a guest ranch, a resort or a lodge — places that have made mountain surroundings and mountain recreation as integral to vacation lodging as the bathtub or the bed.

Resorts, Guest Ranches and Lodges

Folks in Yellowstone country feel connected to mountains. Partly, that's our heritage: Early settlers made their livings from wilderness bounty. They trapped, farmed with irrigation water diverted from the mighty Snake, grazed cattle in alpine meadows, mined the mountain's mineralized bones and harvested her trees. And from the earliest pioneering days, particularly around Yellowstone Park, locals served tourists drawn by the wilderness.

More recent imports also feel connected to mountains, no longer because we make our living from them — that's becoming less practical — but because we play in them. Folks who live here don't stay home on weekends. We ski, bike, hike, fish, climb, hunt, boat, snowmobile and golf. We still serve tourists, but today's visitors don't want simply to see mountains but also to play in them. So, although our region offers standard lodging options as well as more intimate bed and breakfast inns, that's not where you can experience what is unique to Yellowstone country. For that you must stay at a guest ranch, a resort or a lodge. These are the places that have made mountain surroundings and mountain recreation as integral to vacation lodging as the bathtub or the bed.

Resorts and Lodges

Resorts and lodges offer both a roof and activities. At most, you'll pay for recreation separately, à la carte. These folks often specialize; we've listed fishing lodges, ski resorts and even, for the more civilized, golf and tennis resorts. Some lodges also offer a range of options, say horseback riding, mountain biking, rafting, volleyball and fishing. Many lodges and resorts are home to restaurants; others simply plan to feed you as part of their service. What ties these diverse establishments together is that they make playing in Yellowstone country easy.

Guest Ranches

Hasn't every little kid wished to be a cowboy? Indulge that childhood whim here, where dude ranching is a time-honored tradition. At a guest ranch, you are not only invited to enjoy wilderness and wilderness recreation, you get to step back into the wild, wild West. Guest ranches offer accommodations, meals and activities, generally for one lump price. At most guest ranches you'll trail ride, enjoy cookouts and barbecues, go fishing and perhaps float a nearby river. Other activities can include swimming, volleyball, horseshoes, barn dances, cattle driving, riding lessons and gymkhanas (a series of competitive horseback games). You may head into town to see a rodeo, shop or go dancing.

Guest ranches vary in how long they ask you to stay (usually at least three days), how many activities they offer for their blanket price and how scheduled your days will be. Reading our descriptions of these guest ranches is a good start, but shop carefully.

Unlike resorts and lodges, guest ranches can be so isolated you can't just jump in your car and spend a day elsewhere. They also do more planning for you, so it's important that you like the plan. When shopping for a guest ranch, think first about what you want to do with your days, how comfortable you want to be (lodging can be luxurious or rustic, but don't expect in-room phones, alarm clocks, TVs or wall-to-wall carpet) and how many decisions you want made for you. If you have kids, do you expect help supervising them? Do you want riding lessons, or just someone to check the girth strap before you mount? Another thing you'll want to think about is how secluded you'd like to be. Some guest ranches are practically in town. Others are accessed by a half-day's drive on dirt roads through country where the chief inhabitants have more legs than you do.

Then make phone calls. Ask to see the schedule of activities: It may detail every hour of your vacation, or you may be told there isn't a schedule. Ask for names of satisfied customers you can call. Ask about the riding program. You'll probably spend part of every day on a horse, so this is perhaps the most important facet of the ranch operation to ask about. Also ask if the ranch is a member of the Dude Ranchers' Association. Some very fine guest ranches aren't members, but association members do submit to periodic inspection and abide by certain rules likely to increase your vacation enjoyment.

Remember that, since some of these places include everything in their rates and others charge you for each activity, establishments that appear more expensive can actually be very reasonable when you reach the bottom line. Also remember to factor in the fact that most lodges, guest ranches and resorts offer complimentary or inexpensive shuttles from the nearest airports.

Price Code

To help you choose your guest ranch, resort or lodge accommodations, we've provided a price symbol that represents the lowest high-season charge for a two-person, one-night stay. For guest ranches and most lodges, the high season is summer; for ski resorts, winter. Fishing lodges are generally busiest in late summer and fall.

$	$70 to $120
$$	$121 to $170
$$$	$171 to $220
$$$$	$221 and more

Yellowstone National Park

Entrance Communities

West Yellowstone, Montana

The Firehole Ranch
$$$$ • 11500 Hebgen Lake Rd., West Yellowstone, Mont. • (406) 646-7294

In Yellowstone country, when you have to drive 14 miles on a dirt road to get to a lodge, you just know that at the end of the trail you're going to find someplace special. That's just what we found at The Firehole Ranch. Surrounded by National Forest lands and situated in a lush meadow that leads right to the banks of Hebgen Lake, The Firehole Ranch is an angler's dream. While guests can opt for horseback riding, mountain biking, hiking or canoeing, most prefer to fish all day every day on every blue-ribbon stream in Yellowstone.

After a hearty gourmet breakfast in Firehole's cozy, 50-year-old lodge, you'll stroll to the lake — chances are you'll see a moose

---

INSIDERS' TIP

One way to learn more about individual dude ranches is to call the Dude Ranch Association. Its many members are voluntarily inspected. Call (970) 223-8440.

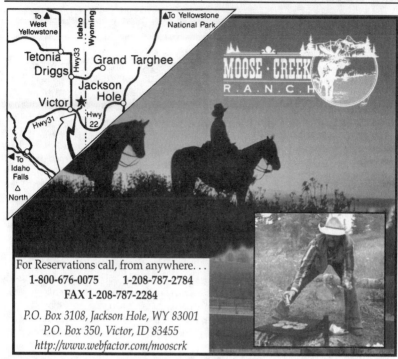

along the way — and ride a 30-foot pontoon boat to the other side where nine professional fishing guides wait to lead you and the 19 other guests to the fishing paradise of your choice. And, after a day of reeling 'em in, you can look forward to a cocktail hour in the lodge followed by a gourmet dinner cooked up by chef Bruno Georgeton. Georgeton works for broadcasting magnate Ted Turner when he is not at the Firehole Ranch.

Firehole accommodates 20 guests in 10 spacious, updated cabins complete with carpet, plush furniture, woodstoves, modern bathrooms and private decks. This dream ranch has a 100-percent occupancy rate and an 85-percent return rate. To secure reservations, it's best to call at least a year (and maybe more) ahead of time. Since prospective guests are required to pay a hefty deposit in January, you may be able to pick up someone else's cancellation for the coming season. The Firehole Ranch, open from the first week in June until the end of September, has a minimum four-night stay requirement, and stays must begin or end on a Saturday. Nightly rates include lodging, three meals, beverages, open bar and all ranch activities except guided fishing trips.

The Bar N Ranch

$$$ • Targhee Pass Hwy., 5 miles west of West Yellowstone, Mont., on U.S. Hwy. 20 • (406) 646-7121, (800) BIGSKYS

Inside, the Bar N Ranch lodge oozes luxury. Giant Douglas fir beams, solid-brass fixtures, a wide, sweeping split-log staircase and deep, cushy couches in the high-ceilinged living room of this brand-new lodge conjure up images of formal balls and black-tie dinners in days gone by. Don't dress up, though, because outside you'll find a relaxed ranch atmosphere.

The Bar N occupies a square mile of land, including 5 miles of frontage on the South Fork of the Madison River and four fishing ponds. Owned by the Kephart family of Philadelphia since the turn of the century, the Bar N Ranch is just 5 miles from Yellowstone National Park.

In 1997, the owners moved their guest quarters out of the old ranch house and into the 10,000-square-foot, three-story lodge. With eight rooms (including the Housedog's Hideaway, a third-floor apartment that sleeps up to 15) and four cabins, this is the perfect place for a corporate retreat, honeymoon or a family vacation.

Each room, named and decorated in honor of family members and former ranch employees, is uniquely decorated with mostly Montana antiques and art. Most have Jacuzzis, some have private balconies, and all have fireplaces. Meals (mostly country-style comfort food interspersed with an outside barbecue and weekly gourmet dining) are included in the room price.

Evenings, you'll dine to piano music and sing along around the fireplace after dinner. Also included in the room price are minimal ranch activities such as the use of rowboats, a paddleboat, inner tubes and a small sailboat. Self-guided fishing on the nearby river or in the ponds is also free. During the winter, the Bar N offers unlimited cross-country skiing and short dogsled rides on the ranch. No snowmobile rentals are available; you can either bring your own or travel in the ranch's mini-snowcoach (dubbed "Miss Kitty") 5 miles to West Yellowstone.

Grand Teton National Park

Grand Teton Lodge Company operates three lodge facilities in Grand Teton National Park: Jenny Lake Lodge, Colter Bay Village and Jackson Lake Lodge. The Park's largest concessionaire also operates tour buses, a golf course and more. From any of its three facilities you can book activities at any other. And don't worry about driving: The Grand Teton Lodge Company buses will get you where you need to go.

Jenny Lake Lodge
$$$$ • Teton Park Rd. at Jenny Lake • (307) 733-4647, (800) 628-9988

The exquisite fine dining and 37 cabins of Jenny Lake Lodge constitute perhaps the only place on earth to which the words elegant and rustic both apply. The original six buildings date to 1922, when Tony Grace homesteaded 160 acres in what was soon to become Grand Teton National Park.

Folks who know rave about Jenny Lake Lodge's culinary delights, which you'll definitely sample since your room rate includes both breakfast and dinner (see our Restaurants chapter). Others point out that Jenny Lake Lodge is the only luxury accommodation within Grand Teton Park that has managed to retain a secluded, rugged feel. It wasn't easy: When a steel support roof was added to reinforce the original lodge so it would safely hold winter snowloads, it had to be carefully concealed above the old log ceiling.

Your cabin has a private bath and distinctive quilts on the bed. If you don't like the log look, request one of the newer, smooth-walled cabins. You'll enjoy other thoughtful touches, such as those two umbrellas in the corner of your cabin. The main lodge has a small store and tiny lending library. The concierge can set you up with golf or tennis, whitewater and flatwater float trips on the Snake River, guided fishing, cruises of Jackson Lake and more. Horseback riding and bicycling are included in your daily rate. Despite the heavy price tag, Jenny Lake Lodge is wildly popular both for its accommodations and dining. Short-notice availability is rare. The lodge is open from the end of May to early October.

INSIDERS' TIP

Three seriously upscale fishing lodges in southeastern Idaho are Teton Valley Lodge, The Lodge at Palisades Creek and Henry's Fork Lodge. If your credit card is not maxed out and you want to stay in an idyllic setting, pampered to the hilt, while you fish under the direction of topnotch guides, give these folks a call.

Jackson Lake Lodge
$ • U.S. Hwy. 89 at Jackson Lake Junction • (307) 543-2811, (800) 628-9988

This huge complex sits on a bluff overlooking Jackson Lake. Some parts of the lodge complex offer a fine view of Mt. Moran, from this angle more spectacular than the Grand Teton herself. Nevertheless, staying here is not a wilderness experience. Forty-eight rooms occupy the blocky, mountainous main lodge building, which also contains various shops, two restaurants and a bar (see our Restaurants chapter).

The lounge, with its famous picture-window view of Moran, is built on a scale to rival the mountain itself. The twin fireplaces are impossibly massive: You could host a small wedding in each. Scattering out from the lodge are dozens of motel buildings — the "cottage" accommodations. Rooms are pleasantly shaded by spruce and fir, and many have log privacy walls at their entrances. Room service is available for breakfast only. In the evening, you can order a box lunch to carry with you on your adventures the next day.

Jackson Lake Lodge offers horseback riding, including breakfast and dinner rides (wranglers cook the meal over a fire) and trail rides of varying lengths. The lodge also hosts boat rides on Jackson Lake, Snake River float trips, bus tours of Grand Teton and Yellowstone parks and a lifeguarded swimming pool. Use of the pool is free to guests, but other activities are at additional charge. Accommodations are available from May 18 to October 15.

Colter Bay Village and Marina
$ • U.S. Hwy. 89 on east shore of Jackson Lake • (307) 543-2811, (800) 628-9988

Calling itself a "family resort," Colter Bay offers accommodations of every imaginable sort. You may stay in the Park Service campground, the RV park or the refurbished older log cabins that lie along roads stacking up the hill to the most interesting option of all: cabin tents. A cabin tent is canvas and log with a canvas roof and a concrete floor. Bunks pull out from the walls (you can rent sleeping bags and mattresses if you brought none of your own). Each has a covered outdoor cooking area for rainy-day dinners. The more conventional cabins are simply furnished, Western style. You also get use of a lounge cabin where you can meet other guests.

Many activities are available at Colter Bay, all at additional charge except for Park Service programs like visits to the Colter Bay Visitor Center, with its fine Native American art and craft museum, and the nightly campfire programs at the amphitheater in Colter Bay Campground. Colter Bay Village Corral offers breakfast and dinner rides as well as trail rides of varying lengths. Breakfast and scenic cruises on Jackson Lake originate from the marina daily, as do evening steak-fry cruises.

Other services at Colter Bay include a laundry, showers, snack bar, grocery store, gas station, fishing tackle, gift and clothing shops, a post office and two restaurants. Colter Bay opens near the end of May and closes the end of September.

Flagg Ranch Resort
$ • U.S. Hwy. 89 on John D. Rockefeller Jr. Memorial Pky. • (307) 543-2861, (800) 443-2311

Look up Flagg Ranch on the map and it appears to be nothing in the middle of nowhere. Perhaps that's why it's so popular. Situated on a narrow, 9-mile-long gooseneck between Yellowstone and Grand Teton parks, Flagg Ranch is a bustling tourist center with RV park, cabin and motel accommodations and a tempting array of activities — in the middle of nowhere. Motel rooms look across a grassy river frontage to the Snake River. They're in three two-story buildings connected by wooden boardwalks. Their glass doors open to a view of the river. Although rooms have no phones and no TVs, they are standard motel fare in every other way.

The nicest rooms here are in the duplex or four-plex cabins clustered into a cabin town. These newer log buildings have baseboard heat, full baths, coffee makers and phones. Their vaulted ceilings add to the impression of spaciousness. If you stay here, ask about the cabins that occupy a low ridge overlooking the Snake; they each have private decks with wooden rocking chairs and a bit more room.

Your activities choices include short whitewater trips in Flagg Canyon and longer scenic floats lower on the Snake. You can also trail ride in summer and snowmobile or ride the resort snowcoach into Yellowstone in winter. All involve additional charge. Other reasons to come to Flagg Ranch include: The Bears Den, a pleasant restaurant in the large, rustic-modern lodge building; a gift shop; and the entire Greater Yellowstone, in the middle of which this resort is uniquely and centrally located.

Signal Mountain Lodge

$ • Teton Park Rd. on south shore of Jackson Lake • (307) 733-5470

This is the only major lodge facility in Grand Teton Park not run by Grand Teton Lodge Company. The general feel is pleasant, a bit quieter than other communities in the Park. You have several accommodations options here. The lodge has several simply furnished log cabins, some with fireplaces. There are also motel rooms and lakefront apartments. Some of these have fireplaces, too. The lakefront apartments are spacious and newer, opening onto decks that face Jackson Lake.

The main lodge building has big windows and a large deck area facing the lake. A short walk from the lodge takes you to The Aspens dining room and the Coffee Shop, serving breakfast, lunch and dinner. Aspens Lounge is open daily noon to midnight. The house specialty is huckleberry Margaritas. We recommend you eat (or drink) on the deck if the weather is nice.

Also at Signal Mountain are a clothing store, a gift shop, a service station, a convenience store and a marina. The marina offers boat rentals, guest buoys and guided fishing trips. The lodge can also take you and your family on a 10-mile scenic float on the Snake River. These activities are all at additional charge. Signal Mountain Lodge is open from mid-May to mid-October.

Lost Creek Ranch

$$$$, no credit cards • U.S. Hwy. 89, 8 mi. north of Moose, Wyo. • (307) 733-3435

Western it may be, but rustic it ain't. Think along the lines of Club Med in Wyoming. From the nightly bed-linen turndowns to the bronze sculptures, antler chairs and antique-rifle collection in the main lodge, this guest ranch is topnotch. Forty staff members devote their time and attention to a maximum of 55 guests — ensuring personal, attentive service.

Cabins are plush, with views up into the Tetons and out over the sage-covered valley that backs the ranch. Two cards are left on your pillow each evening next to those mints: One tells you what sort of weather to expect tomorrow, and the other contains a historical tidbit about the area.

Lost Creek prides itself on the wide range of activities included in its fee, so you can pretty much leave that checkbook at home. Just head to the office and sign up for your float down the scenic Snake River, riding lessons, laundry service, van tour of Yellowstone Park and more. You'll pay for massages and facials, fishing trips, whitewater rafting trips, skeet shooting and babysitting.

Lost Creek has been a guest ranch since the late 1960s, but it was originally homesteaded in the 1920s. That's why it's here: Like several other ranches enclosed by Grand Teton Park, it's been here since before the idea of a Teton National Park gathered steam. The ranch is open from early June to mid-October.

Triangle X Ranch

$$$$, no credit cards • U.S. 89, 12 mi. north of Moose, Wyo. • (307) 733-2183

Only 25 miles from Jackson, Wyoming, at the edge of Grand Teton Park is the only dude ranch in this country under concession from the National Park Service. Other guest ranches in Grand Teton Park are actually on private lands called inholdings. Triangle X is sitting on your national park. The ranch is run by the Turner family; four generations ago they owned the land it sits on. Then they sold it to John D. Rockefeller Jr., who leased it back to them. This makes Triangle X one of the oldest guest ranches in the area — 68 years old. It's also one of the cheapest for groups of four or more, which attracts many families and returnees (last June the ranch was full up, but only one new family joined the fun).

Harold Turner says that Triangle X is a riding ranch. You want to be excited about horses and horseback riding if you're thinking of coming here. The ranch owns horses to suit all levels of riders; you'll ride the same horse every day, developing a relationship with your animal.

Included in your base price are meals (served family style in the lodge), rustic cabin lodging, horseback riding and other ranch activities. For an additional charge, you may enjoy wilderness pack trips, float trips, fishing and hunting trips and an inexpensive airport shuttle. If you call the Turners for more information, make sure you request that they send the fact- and photo-filled *Triangle X News*, a little annual newspaper for guests.

Buffalo Valley

Most of Buffalo Valley, through which U.S. Highway 26 and the Buffalo Fork River run, is not in Grand Teton Park. We've listed Buffalo Valley guest ranches with Park listings to show you how very close to one another they are. You get the same views and the same wildlife here as inside the east entrance gate at Moran a few miles away.

Heart 6 Guest Ranch

$$$$ • 16985 Buffalo Valley Rd., Moran, Wyo. • (307) 543-2477

They're only in their third year, but the folks at Heart 6 have a lot of well-thought-out plans for you. The ranch is planted on a hill overlooking the Buffalo Fork River and Buffalo Valley as it meanders down toward the Tetons. Fishing is good on the Buffalo; so is wildlife viewing along the willow flats. You'll show up on Monday in time for a welcome barbecue on the west deck. Your kids will play in the heated, above-ground pool. The ranch hires four kid counselors whose only job is to play with and supervise your children. This means kids learn more, take more hikes and get more time in the pool, while you take challenging wilderness trail rides or simply relax in your cabin.

The ranch is open year round. In summer they focus on riding, rafting and fishing mixed into a pleasant schedule of social events such as slide shows and cookouts. In fall the business is hunting; the ranch maintains hunting camps 17 and 35 miles into the Teton Wilderness. The upper camp is on the headwaters of the Yellowstone River. Starting in December, Heart 6 invites you snowmobiling: They

buy all new snowmobiles every year. They'll guide you on dayrides out of the ranch or take you on longer adventures into Yellowstone Park, Togwotee Pass and the Continental Divide Snowmobile Trail.

Amenities at Heart 6 include a hot tub, a comfortable lodge building with two dining rooms and a main lounge with an oversize fireplace and comfortable cabins and cabin/motel accommodations, each with a private bath and some with fireplaces or woodstoves. Cabins do not have phones or TVs. Rates include meals, lodging, riding and other ranch activities. Float trips are extra.

Minimum stays of three nights or six nights are the norm, but occasionally during fall, winter and spring, cabins may be rented by the night, with or without activities.

Diamond D

$$$$ • 22250 Buffalo Valley Rd.
• (307) 543-2479

Rod Doty was raised in windy, snowbound South Dakota, where he made his living as a farmer. But after a stint in the military, Doty vowed to hunt and fish for the rest of his life. He has. Diamond D, in lovely Buffalo Valley, is a guest ranch in summer, runs pack and hunting trips into nearby mountains in fall and in winter offers bed and breakfast accommodations to snowmobilers and cross-country skiers.

The ranch is small and the staff friendly. Dude ranch employees tend to be wanderers, but many of Diamond D's staff have been coming back every year for five, 10 and even 18 years. The ranch can accommodate up to 36 guests at once, but Doty likes to keep the number around 20.

The lodge is a pleasant building with a sunken sitting area cradling a woodstove and tall windows that practically invite the pretty valley surroundings in. From the kitchen wafts the aroma of fresh-baked bread, homemade cookies and other temptations. The newer duplex cabins are log or log-sided, with picnic tables on the lawn; many face the Tetons. Rooms have fridges and fireplaces. Furnishings are simple but comfortable. Included in the ranch price is an overnight pack trip, van tours of the area, guided horseback riding, Western riding lessons (Doty is particularly proud of his 4-H-style horse safety program for kids), and planned ranch activities such as hayrides and photography outings.

Turpin Meadows Ranch
$$$$ • East end, Buffalo Valley Rd.
• (307) 543-2496, (800) 743-2496

Turpin Meadows is a family-owned guest ranch at the top of lovely Buffalo Valley just outside Grand Teton Park. The staff are like family here, and after a couple days, owner LaRae Castagno promises, so are you. Also part of the family is Apache McClean (he's not Apache) who has been performing Indian dances at area guest ranches for 31 years; he found a permanent home when the Castagnos bought this old guest ranch five years ago. He lives in a little cabin on the property with his snakes (yes, they're real). On Monday nights another resident, Bill Staggs, dresses up in full mountain-man regalia, fox fur hat on his head, to demonstrate hatchet throwing and blackpowder shooting.

LaRae and husband Dale's three sons and their wives all work here, too. Says LaRae, "Those boys love the outdoors. Put 'em in a building and they'd knock out the walls." But Dale says the friendly atmosphere, cozy, rustic accommodations and lovely scenery aren't the real reasons you come to Turpin Meadows: He says it's the food. It's Western-style home cooking, served up buffet style. Steaks and ribs get rave reviews.

Eight older cabins, furnished simply and equipped with heat and full baths, face out onto the lovely meadow that gave the ranch its name. One luxuriously large cabin with two huge bedrooms, a living room and two bathrooms, once was visited, so legend has it, by radio personality Arthur Godfrey. The ranch also has four motel-style rooms that are clean, modern and simple. Their big glass doors face the grassy clearing around which other ranch buildings cluster.

Included in the fee are lodging, meals,

horses, scheduled ranch events such as the chuckwagon and a trip into Jackson to watch the rodeo, a Yellowstone Park van tour and transportation to and from Jackson Hole Airport. Turpin Meadows is open year round. Fall hunting trips are available, as are snowmobile rentals in winter with or without guides (most folks prefer to be guided so they end up in the prettiest places).

Jackson Hole

R Lazy S Ranch
$$$$, no credit cards • 7800 N. Moose-Wilson Rd., Teton Village, Wyo.
• (307) 733-2655

Each cabin faces the parklike clearing in the trees, and each backs into the aspens that ring the ranch. Porches and decks are equipped with flower boxes and hanging flower baskets. Cabins are comfortable, with private baths, fireplaces or woodstoves, coffee makers, carpeted floors with Indian weave throw rugs and Western decor.

When you arrive, you'll find a thoughtful bowl of snacks and fruit waiting in your cabin; fresh-cut flowers brighten your temporary log home. One hundred yards from the four newest cabins is the buck-and-rail fence that separates Teton National Forest from Grand Teton Park. A couple hundred yards down a dirt trail is a child's dream: a small swimming hole, filled with chilly water from nearby Lake Creek, a rope swing and a wooden raft beckoning. Parents can take the plunge off the diving platform or bask in the sun on the deck. Manager Claire McConaughy likes to keep her 45 guests busy. On Wednesdays the staff will take you into Jackson to enjoy the rodeo. Thursday is cookout night. Friday night talent shows are a particular favorite for many guests.

Rates include lodging, meals, riding and instruction, scenic boat rides and water-skiing on Jackson Lake and fishing in the ranch's

---

INSIDERS' TIP

If cost isn't an issue, the easy way into some of our more remote locations around Jackson Hole and Grand Teton Park is by charter plane; call Jackson Hole Aviation (800) 487-5387. Or you could go by helicopter; call Mountain Rotors at (307) 733-1633.

stocked pond. For an additional charge, you can take a guided fishing trip or a wilderness pack trip.

Gros Ventre River Ranch
$$$$, no credit cards • 18 Gros Ventre River Rd., near Kelly, Wyo. • (307) 733-4138

Cowboy-hatted, blue-jeaned Tina Weber and her husband, Karl, bought this ranch in 1988. Back then it was only four cabins in an idyllic location. Gros Ventre River Ranch is still an idyllic location — just outside Grand Teton Park's southeast boundary on the banks of the rollicking Gros Ventre River. Now it has corrals, four more cabins and a lovely new lodge building. The lodge has a dining room, two decks overlooking the river, a bar, a game room, a living room and a long, covered porch.

While we were there, a doe minced out onto the lawn below the dining deck, nibbled at the blossoms in the wildflower garden and danced off when she realized she was being observed. As Tina says, life is good here. Most of the cabins cluster around a grassy circle equipped with swing sets, hammocks and a fire ring. Older cabins are more rustic; the newest lodging is upscale. All have carpeting, electric heat, private baths and log furniture made by a local artisan. Some have private decks, brick-floor entryways, kitchenettes and washer/dryers. Most have woodstoves.

Two favorite nights for guests are those evenings when a local expert drives out to teach fly fishing in the ranch's stocked pond and Wednesdays, when a local cowboy poet with handlebar moustache and guitar recites Robert Service poems and sings cowboy songs. The staff bring out the ranch's brand and heat it in the fire so guests may brand their boots, belts and wallets.

The ranch can accommodate 34 guests. During the riding season, your rate includes lodging, meals, your horse and use of ranch facilities such as the game room with its big screen TV and VCR, Ping-Pong, pool tables and foosball. Although the guest ranch is open only May 1 through the end of October, the three new housekeeping cabins are available year round. Cross-country skiers will enjoy coming home to warm, modern comfort at the end of a winter trek. Snowmobile trips can be arranged at additional charge.

Red Rock Ranch
$$, no credit cards • Gros Ventre River Rd. past Crystal Creek • (307) 733-6288

Yellowstone country hosts all kinds of guest ranches. This is the kind that makes you forget the world you came from. You'll stay for a minimum of seven days at this small, family-owned cattle ranch in the heart of the Gros Ventre Mountains. Navigating the road in is slow and painful; once here you're likely to see nobody but the wranglers and the 29 other guests.

You stay in comfortable but rustic cabins; each has a private bath, a sitting room, a wood burning stove and a sun porch. Most are outfitted with twin beds. Your daily rides into the Bridger-Teton National Forest and Gros Ventre Wilderness are included in the price, as are meals and all other ranch activities. Kids enjoy playing volleyball and pickleball and competing in the weekly gymkhana. A counselor/wrangler arranges just-for-kids trail rides and even a kid version of an overnight camping trip into the mountains.

The ranch also has laundry facilities, a heated outdoor pool, a casting pond and a pleasantly rustic lodge building. Although relatively schedule-free, this remote guest ranch offers something exciting every day. Red Rock Ranch is open only in summer; winter access is a bit of a problem.

Trail Creek Ranch

$$$$, no credit cards • Old Pass Rd., Wilson, Wyo. • (307) 733-2610

Former Olympic skier Elizabeth Woolsey skied through the 300-acre, forested valley that is now Trail Creek Ranch five decades ago: It was love at first sight. Elizabeth's guest ranch began as a place where her many friends could get together and ride horses or ski. Although the ranch's famous owner recently died, this Western home away from home is alive and well.

Most of the fresh greens and herbs used in guests' meals are harvested from the ranch's garden, and the trout served on Friday nights once swam in the pond just behind the main ranch buildings. Kids enjoy the game room, with its bumper pool table and board games. Horseshoe pits are set up outside. For guests who are kids at heart, the ranch hosts a shindig (called a gymkhana) featuring horseback games and barrel racing. Besides the daily trail rides and riding instruction in the arena, fishing opportunities abound in Jackson Hole. Wranglers can arrange pack trips that loop past good fishing streams or set you up with a local fishing guide on the Snake, Teton or Green rivers. Canoes are available for guest use, as is a limited supply of fishing equipment.

The ranch hosts as many as 25 guests in summer and 14 in winter. If you're considering a visit, Trail Creek Ranch will cheerfully provide references, but don't be surprised if you are asked for yours. With its 40-percent return rate and a long tradition of patronage by friends and family, the ranch tries hard to protect its small, intimate style.

Spring Creek Resort

$ • 1800 Spirit Dance Rd., Jackson, Wyo. • (307) 733-8833, (800) 443-6139

Head out of Jackson toward Wilson and Teton Pass, then turn off on Spring Gulch Road: You'll immediately begin winding up into sage-covered hills. It feels like you're headed for wilderness — until you roll over the top of East Gros Ventre Butte and see the condos, neat lawns and houses of Spring Creek Resort.

This upscale resort sits on 1,000 acres of a wildlife preserve overlooking Flat Creek and Jackson Hole nearly 1,000 feet below. Enjoy the views on horseback. Swim in the pool, soak in the hot tub and play tennis. In winter, ski the resort's groomed Nordic trails. The concierge will competently and cheerfully book you into a staggering variety of other activities in the area. In fact, "cheerful" seems to be the staff motto: It's hard to sneak past a Spring Creek employee without receiving a smile and a pleasant nod.

Accommodations range from hotel rooms and condos to suites and homes that accommodate up to eight people. Prices range clear up to $1,200 per night. All are luxurious in a Southwestern/rustic sort of way and include fireplaces, refrigerators, remote-control cable TV and coffee makers. Some have fully equipped kitchens and washer/dryers. Convention facilities are available, as are various kinds of activities packages. Spring Creek is open year round.

Make sure you check out The Granary Restaurant while you're here: The only thing better than the food and the wine list is the view.

Rusty Parrot Lodge

$$ • 175 N. Jackson, Jackson, Wyo. • (307) 733-2000, (800) 458-2004

If we had to pick our three favorite upscale accommodations options in the Jackson/ Grand Tetons area, they'd be Jenny Lake Lodge, the Wort Hotel and the Rusty Parrot.

Jenny Lake Lodge made rustic-ness luxurious, the Wort is a classic with class, and Ron Harrison's Rusty Parrot just couldn't have been done any better. Perfect isn't a word to use lightly, so maybe we'd better explain. First, the lobby and dining room: Imagine white walls and hallways with adobe-style curved corners, accented with hand-turned log. Imagine emerald carpet and a river-rock fireplace where the flames never flicker out from October to May.

Upstairs in your room, imagine down comforters, handmade Mexican tile in the bathroom, woven willow screens on the closet doors and an outdoor hot tub on the tiled roof. A few rooms have in-room hot tubs; half are warmed by fireplaces (the staff lays the fire for you). If the word "rustic" came to mind when you imagined logs and fireplaces, kick it back out and let's talk breakfast. Chef Rich McLaughlin serves what he calls a Jackson breakfast every morning to guests from the Rusty Parrot's 32 rooms. You choose one of four hot entrees, each one innovative, creative and Western — like Russian eggs Benedict with smoked trout, or pork medallions in apple-spiced tomato cream sauce with fried eggs. If you're still hungry, fill up on the homemade granola and breads.

Last but not least, there's the staff. Ron tells us that, besides being professional and friendly, there's almost no request you can make that they can't accommodate.

Snow King Resort

$$$ • 400 E. Snow King Ave., Jackson, Wyo. • (307) 733-5200, (800) 522-5464

This is Jackson's in-town ski hill and resort (see our Winter Sports chapter). The resort was built in 1976 and recently renovated. Accommodations include condominiums and a hotel at the base of Rafferty Chairlift. Furnishings are Western, accented with pine and log. Stay in one of the 204 rooms in the seven-story hotel building and you'll have use of the year-round outdoor heated pool, sauna, two whirlpools and exercise room.

Not included in your room price but worth stopping by are the ice-skating rink, gift shops, The Atrium Cafe and Shady Lady Saloon. Other activities available on the premises in summer include mountain biking, miniature golf and an alpine slide. You can also buy a ticket up the lift in summer to access Panorama House, a restaurant that serves up a spectacular view.

Lone Eagle Resort

$ • U.S. Hwy. 89 near Hoback Junction, Wyo. • (307) 733-1090, (800) 321-3800

Drive under the totem pole arch and down a dirt road lined with buck-and-rail fence. Just after you cross the Hoback River on a narrow bridge, you'll enter civilization in the middle of wilderness: the RV and cabin resort of Lone Eagle. The grounds are immaculate, grassy and illuminated by electric lanterns at night. The resort has basketball and volleyball, an outdoor swimming pool, a laundry facility, hot tubs, a snack shop/convenience store, a gift shop and a casting pond. You could picnic on the sparkly clean floors of the tiled shower rooms.

Lone Eagle offers three-day and overnight visits. Each includes whitewater fun on the Snake River and meals prepared by the staff. There's even a barn dance with a live band some nights. Accommodations range from your own tent or RV to clean, simple, newer log cabins lined up on a bench overlooking the Hoback's tangle of willow flats. It's hard to imagine a better setting for a family resort. See our Campgrounds and RV Parks chapter, too.

Teton Pines Resort

$$$$ • 3450 N. Clubhouse Dr., Jackson, Wyo. • (307) 733-1005, (800) 238-2223

Smack in the middle of flamboyantly rustic, neon-Western Jackson Hole is an elegant little resort — only 22 guest rooms — with an award-winning, Arnold Palmer-designed golf course, indoor and outdoor tennis, 14 kilometers of groomed cross-country ski trails in winter, spacious accommodations and aspen-dotted landscaping. Many guests take advantage of the stocked casting pond below the clubhouse and engage the services of Jack Dennis, renowned fly fisherman, for a little brushing up or a brand-new hobby.

Teton Pines Resort is closer to Teton Village than to the town of Jackson, so your location is perfect for winter skiing, too. Your room rate buys reduced green fees and preferred golf starting times, access to tennis courts, the outdoor swimming pool and hot tub and the Athletic Club's Nautilus and free-weight equipment. Continental breakfast is served every morning in the clubhouse.

A full bar and fine-dining restaurant are also on the premises (for a tip on après ski at Teton Pines clubhouse, see our Nightlife chapter).

Jackson Hole Mountain Resort
Teton Village, Wyo. • (307) 733-2292

Jackson Hole Mountain Resort has no accommodations of its own. (Folks around here usually call it Jackson Hole, which can be confusing because that's the name of the valley, or Teton Village, which can be confusing because that's the name of a cluster of tourist facilities, of which Jackson Hole Mountain Resort is one.) What it does have in winter are two mountains' worth of skiing (more on this in our Winter Sports chapter) and dinner sleigh rides out to a remote cabin, for a four-course meal. You can also enjoy the 17-kilometer Nordic track or take a guided cross-country trek into Grand Teton and Yellowstone parks. In summer, enjoy horseback riding, aerial tram rides and a lineup of great music festivals and other events.

Spotted Horse Ranch
$$ • 12355 S. U.S. Hwy. 191, near Hoback Junction, Wyo. • (307) 733-2097

Most folks reserve their spots here six months in advance. Some book their next stay before checking out and heading home from their current visit. You'll see why when you drop down next to the Hoback River to find this cluster of cabins and corrals nestled on its bank. Spotted Horse Ranch has a unique combination of easy, paved-road access and a secluded atmosphere with rides originating right at the ranch.

Ten cabins, all pleasantly close to the Hoback, have river views from their porches; one guest room is in the lodge. Dining is

family-style. A hot tub and sauna cabin sit a stone's throw from the river. Other amenities include laundry facilities, a big-screen TV, a video library and a recreation room in the lodge and private baths in the cabins. Activities include river floating, Western dance lessons, a steak cookout across the river and excursions into nearby Jackson for the twice-weekly rodeo.

If you were looking for the perfect combination of dude ranch and fishing lodge, you may have found it here. Not only will guides take you to the best waters in the area, but especially in August, you can literally reel 'em in from your porch. The ranch is open June to October for one-week stays.

Darwin Ranch
$$$$, no credit cards • Union Pass Rd. near Darwin Peak, Wyo. • (307) 733-5588

The story goes like this: Homesteader Fred Darwin, a Rough Rider friend of Teddy Roosevelt, fell in love with lush upper Gros Ventre Valley. So, apparently by presidential decree, Teddy gave him 160 acres of it. Darwin Ranch sits on that original homestead completely surrounded by Teton National Forest, at an elevation of 8,200 feet. The nearest town, Pinedale, is 50 miles away over mostly dirt roads rough enough that you may want to charter a plane, hire a taxi or rent a car rather than put the wear and tear on your vehicle. The final 4-mile approach to the ranch is so rough that staff members drive out to meet you in a four-wheel-drive vehicle. If none of this has scared you off, you'd probably enjoy a stay in what may be the most remote guest ranch in Wyoming, so read on.

Rates cover everything but your transportation into and out of the ranch. You'll stay in rustic but modern cabins with private or shared bathrooms and electricity generated by nearby Kinky Creek or by propane. Meals are served family-style on a long trestle table in the log dining room. You may take packtrips (usually

Photo: Randy Hayes/Post Register

A wrangler watches a mare, colt and stallion inside the corral.

very small and intimate; you are asked to help with the chores), fly fish on the Gros Ventre or trail ride with guides or without.

Only 20 guests are invited at any one time. Believe it or not, the ranch is open year round, although summer is the busy time. In winter, activities shift to cross-country skiing, snowshoeing and snowmobiling.

Surrounding Areas

Eastern Idaho

Idaho Falls, Idaho

Granite Creek Guest Ranch
$$$$, no credit cards • Off Swan Valley Hwy., Ririe, Idaho • (208) 538-7140
Every guest ranch is different. That's why some vacationers sample a new one every year. But if you like things on the rustic side — small, informal and friendly — and if your idea of a ranch is a place where real cowboys live and work and where you can help them with their chores, you may decide to stop sampling here. Granite Creek's buildings were mostly built around the turn of the century with logs cut from ranch property. Electricity and plumbing (but no heat) have been added; your cabin will be rough but clean.

What we like best about Granite Creek is its cozy size. It has only four guest cabins, which can accommodate a total of 12 to 15 guests, so you'll get lots of personal attention and plenty of quiet. You also get to try your hand at activities most guest ranches can't provide: Learn to rope in the corral, help on a real cattle drive, feed the animals and help with other ranch chores. There's little in the way of a schedule here — another advantage of the small size. You decide what you want to experience, and the staff tries to make it happen.

The ranch likes to cater to families; kids love to canoe on the 5-acre, spring-fed pond. Everyone enjoys the homemade root beer. Meals are often cooked and served outside. No alcohol is allowed on the ranch, which is usually open from May to October, depending on weather.

Island Park, Idaho

Henry's Fork Lodge
$$$$ • Off U.S. Hwy. 20 near Island Park, Idaho • (208) 558-7953

Stroll across the back deck, a glass of complimentary wine in hand, and survey the Henry's Fork of the Snake below you. Remember with pleasure the 30 or more fish that rose to your fly today; anticipate the fine dinner being created in the cedar-paneled lodge at your back. You'll choose from several entrees — the menu changes daily — ranging from veal piccata to roast duck breast to Chilean sea bass. And they'll all be wonderful (see our Restaurants chapter). So will your rest this evening.

Henry's Fork Lodge is a topnotch fishing lodge that has spared few expenses when it comes to comfort and aesthetics. The lodge was designed by renowned architect Joseph Esherick and perches on the bank of the Henry's Fork. Local artist Mark Smith's fish imprints hang on the walls (yes, he really does make those lovely images by coating fish with paint and then pressing them onto paper) along with work by other outdoor and wildlife artists. The rough cedar paneling manages to look more warm than rustic.

Each of the 12 simply decorated rooms has a fireplace bricked with warm, tan sandstone; a large window in each room looks down on the river. All rooms have private baths. In the morning the lodge will pack you a sack lunch to take along on another day of blue-ribbon fishing. In fact, the only amenities not in easy reach are phones and television. They're available on request, explain staff members, but most people find little need of them. The fishing's just too good.

The lodge offers lodging/meal packages as well as packages that include guided fishing. The guide service is provided by local outfitters up the road at Last Chance; you're welcome to arrange your own fishing guide if you prefer or to fish without a guide. Transportation from Idaho Falls or West Yellowstone is also included in the base price. The lodge is open May 15 to October 15, depending on weather. A three-day stay is encouraged.

Jacobs' Island Park Ranch
$ • Off Kilgore Rd., Island Park, Idaho • (208) 662-5567, (800) 230-9530

For an unstructured ranch vacation, it's hard to beat Jacobs'. Your accommodations are one of three comfortable cabins on a forested ridge overlooking the main ranch buildings. Families and groups may elect to stay in the huge, two-story house with three bedrooms, a full kitchen, arched ceilings and two-story deck. All three cabins and the house are constructed of peeled logs and feature private baths, hot tubs, decks, woodstoves and lovely views. The owners thoughtfully positioned each cabin out of view of the others.

Friday and Saturday nights, you may choose to eat at The Barn, a massive structure that houses Jacobs' weekend barbecues (see our Nightlife chapter). There is no minimum stay at Jacobs' and no real schedule; the staff are happy to arrange trail rides, fishing excursions, boat tours, Jet Ski riding, hayrides, cattle drives and even babysitting, all at additional charge. Jacobs' is open winters, too, unlike most ranches. After the snow flies, guests cross-country ski or snowmobile on the 2,000-acre ranch.

Elk Creek Ranch
$, no credit cards • 3906 Loop Rd., Island Park, Idaho • (208) 558-7404

Eight rustic but comfortable cabins scatter around a 100-year-old lodge furnished with family antiques and mounts collected for a museum in England but never sent there (see our Restaurants chapter). Access is surprisingly easy, considering you feel like you're in your own private wilderness retreat. U.S. Highway 191 is out of sight in the trees but can be accessed by a quick drive down a good dirt road.

Included in the accommodations price are meals (including picnic lunches for anglers) and fishing (no license required) in the stocked private pond. Wildlife viewing is also a popular pastime: Trumpeter swans are regular visitors, as are elk, moose, osprey and sandhill cranes.

The cabins vary in size and age. All are log, most have fireplaces and deer mounts on the walls, all have bathrooms and living areas. Several offer pleasant views of the shallow lake beyond the lodge. Some have covered porches and porch swings. The serious angler won't be disappointed, either. A 10-minute drive takes you to the renowned fly-fishing waters of the Henry's Fork of the Snake. Other nearby streams beckon, too: the Buffalo, Madison, Firehole, Gibbons and Gallatin rivers. Managers Gary and VeAnn Merrill know the area and its fishing opportunities well. VeAnn has spent her summers here since she was a child. The ranch has been in the family for 49 years. Elk Creek Ranch is open May through October.

Island Park Village Resort

$ • N. Big Springs Loop Rd., Island Park, Idaho • (208) 558-7502, (800) 272-8824

It's like a mirage: Island Park Village Resort is a tennis and golf resort — in the middle of nowhere. Accommodations for nonowners consist of 66 condos, most privately owned and individually decorated in Western motifs, stacked about the manicured grounds. All condos have kitchens, woodburning fireplaces and cable TV. VCRs may be rented. At the clubhouse, guests have free access to the indoor pool, a sauna, two hot tubs, a racquetball court, tennis courts (clinics available) and, for a fee, the nine-hole golf course. Nearby are grocery and dining facilities. N. Big Springs Loop Road is off U.S. Highway 20.

Swan Valley

The Lodge at Palisades Creek

$$$$, no credit cards • 3720 Hwy. 26 east of Irwin, Idaho • (208) 483-2222

Anglers book their visits here a year in advance — and with good reason. Nowhere else in Swan Valley can you revel in such secluded, pleasantly upscale cabins or dine on delicacies like pheasant in boysenberry sauce from chef Bill Ryan's ever-changing menu. The main

lodge is a sunlit building where you can visit with other guests or enjoy a quiet drink. You'll float the adjacent South Fork of the Snake every day with the lodge's fishing guides, catching nearly as many big, beautiful trout as you dreamed about the night before. Other extra touches include a bottle of complimentary Idaho wine to celebrate your arrival and nightly linen turndowns.

A four-day minimum stay is requested between July 1 and September 1. The lodge's season runs from early June to mid-October. The base rate includes lodging, meals, your guide and his boat. For those in your party who don't fish, lower rates and scenic trips in the area can be arranged. It is also possible to arrange a guided fishing excursion with The Lodge at Palisades Creek even if you choose to stay elsewhere (see our Fishing and Hunting chapter for more on The Lodge's fishing services).

South Fork Lodge

$$ • 40 Conant Valley Loop, Swan Valley, Idaho • (208) 483-2112, (800) 483-2110

Welcome to fishing heaven. South Fork Lodge has a campground, a motel and an RV park, as well as Last Cast, a restaurant favored by locals (see our Restaurants chapter), but, let's face it: The real game in town is blue-ribbon fishing on the South Fork of the Snake River. The Snake winds past South Fork Lodge through cottonwood flats, literally jumping with trophy-size native cutthroats. Angling fanatic and Swan Valley native Spence Warner bought the lodge and its fishing business from his father in the early 1970s. At first he handled about 20 trips per season. Recently that number has been more like 750, most of them during fishing prime time on the South Fork — July through September, depending on weather.

Warner's fishing service and his beloved South Fork have twice been featured on television programs about the outdoors, the most recent, in 1996, hosted by fishing legend Curt Gowdy. Fishing packages include a variety of accommodations options, including RV sites with full hookups, a grassy pasture campground (showers and a fine view of the river at no additional charge) and comfortable rooms, some with river views, televisions or patios. Rates on motel rooms more than double during the fishing months of July, August and September.

South Fork Lodge is a great option for a family with one or two anglers as well as family members who'd rather eat a fly than learn to cast one. The Lodge arranges trail rides and cattle drives with nearby Granite Creek Ranch (see a previous write-up in this chapter about Granite Creek Ranch), and the long, grassy bench that holds both campground and RV park stretches clear to the river — a perfect playground for kids. Spence recommends fishing parties make guide and accommodations reservations well in advance. His office is open year round, although the restaurant, motel and campground close for the winter.

Hansen-Silver Guest Ranch
$$$$ • 956 Rainey Creek Rd., Swan Valley, Idaho • (208) 483-2305, (800) 277-9041

You might come for the cooking: Ranch-style meals cooked in Dutch ovens and on the barbecue grill, served outside when weather permits. Breads and soups are homemade, as are pasta, pies and pastries. You might come because this working family ranch is real Idaho: The Hansen family emigrated to the state in the late 1800s. Que Hansen owns the ranch, and Brett, his brother, is its manager.

Or you might come for the recreational opportunities. This family-owned guest ranch can accommodate those who want to trail ride and muse at the nightly campfire as well as those who enjoy sightseeing in Yellowstone or shopping in Jackson. Young children appreciate the expanse of lawn, the casting pond and the TV room. And the nearby blue-ribbon waters of the South Fork beg to be fished. The Hansens invite you to do as much or as little as you please in this unstructured setting. Unlike many guest ranches, there's no schedule of activities: The agenda is relaxation and fun, and the schedule is yours to create.

You may choose to stay anywhere between three and seven days. Accommodations are pleasantly upscale. The ranch has one duplex cabin with decks front and back, one white frame cottage and a barn. Our recommendation: Stay in the barn. The cabins offer pleasant privacy, but the 100-year-old barn, recently renovated by Brett Hansen and his father-in-law, Calvin Collins, features exposed beams from the original structure. The spacious rooms have pine furnishings. With their oddly undersize windows and extra nooks and crannies, they exude character. In two of the bathrooms, Brett and Calvin got creative and sawed holes into old vanity dressers, mounting the sinks into them. All rooms have private baths and queen-size beds but no TVs or phones.

The guest ranch operates late May to mid-September, but when they have space, the Hansens offer overnight accommodations with or without reservations year round. Swan Valley has little in the way of accommodations, so this is a real find for anglers. Hansen-Silver Guest Ranch is only a 15-minute drive from the Spring Creek boat ramp in Swan Valley.

Teton Valley

Grand Targhee Ski and Summer Resort
$ • Ski Hill Rd., Alta, Wyo. • (307) 353-2300, (800) 827-4433

There's more about Grand Targhee's famous powder shots in our Winter Sports chapter. Let's talk about the summer personality of this locally grown resort. First, your accommodations options: You can choose from standard rooms at Targhee Lodge, open-loft condos in Sioux Loft Condominiums or the deluxe fare in Teewinot Lodge. The unifying theme at Targhee is a Southwest feel; you see it in the rounded fireplaces that look like Pueblo bread ovens and in the softened corners of doorways.

INSIDERS' TIP

Whether you stay at Jackson Lake Lodge in Grand Teton Park or not, a stop at the main lodge building will not disappoint. The massive picture window view of Mount Moran is rightfully famous.

This adobe look complements nicely the Native American art on the walls and the Western furniture. Grand Targhee has won awards for the cozy design of its ski village.

Summer activities include mountain biking (rentals are available) for which you take the ski lift to the top and let gravity take its course (you only have down to go!), horseback riding (you can take Western- or English-style lessons), tennis, volleyball, horseshoes, miniature golf, swimming, hot tubbing, nature walking and working out at the small fitness center. You can also arrange for a massage or aromatherapy at the spa.

Several dining options are available, summer and winter. For locals, the biggest reasons to go to Targhee in summer are the two music festivals, both held in July (see our Annual Events chapter).

Except for use of the pool, exercise room and hot tubs, you'll pay extra for activities. In winter, Grand Targhee offers ski packages. Winter activities include snowshoe tours, dog sledding and sleigh-ride dinners for an additional fee and use of the swimming pool, hot tubs and spa, all included in your room price.

Teton Valley Lodge
$$$$, no credit cards • 379 Adams Rd., Driggs, Idaho • (208) 354-2386

Home of dry-fly fishing specialists since 1938, Teton Valley Lodge attracts the serious angler. The Teton River, Henry's Fork and Snake South Fork are well-suited for dry flies, and Teton Valley Lodge floats them all. Guides can also show you great wading areas on the Teton, Fall River and Henry's Fork. Stay a week and you won't fish the same river section twice. An average fishing day nets 60 fish per boat. The lodge record is 206.

Neither will you be roughing it. This upscale lodge charges top dollar with good reason: Prices are inclusive and cover meals, spacious cabin lodging, guide service, flies and leaders, transportation, soft drinks and beer. If you get back late from fishing and would like dinner served in your cabin, just ask. Cabins (OK, they look more like comfortable houses) face the Teton River across a well-kept strip of lawn. Some are smaller and appropriate for couples. Others can accommodate up to three couples comfortably and with relative privacy. All have four-poster beds and pine paneling. Most have living rooms, wet bars and woodstoves. All have covered porches from which to watch the river.

The lodge is open May through October, with a special "Cast and Blast" option that starts with the opening of grouse and duck seasons.

Moose Creek Ranch
$$$$ • 215 E. Moose Creek Rd., Victor, Idaho • (208) 787-2784, (800) 676-0075

As you walk away from the 4,500-square-foot main lodge on the planked boardwalk, you pass under a sign that says "Hurry back." Take our word for it: You'll want to. If there's such a thing as the guest ranch that has everything for a family vacation, Kelly Van Orden's Moose Creek Ranch is it.

A kid counselor is always around to entertain young'uns. The ranch prides itself on the "horse sense" training program which teaches guests not only how to ride, but also how to care for and stay safe around horses. You'll ride and care for the same horse all week. The grassy grounds house a playground, a generous indoor pool, a sauna, a hot tub, a picnic area, Ping-Pong tables, horseshoe pits and volleyball and basketball courts. Moose Creek meanders across ranch property, so although more famous fishing rivers — the Snake, Teton and Henry's Fork — are a moderate drive away, you always have the option of getting your line wet a short stroll from your cabin. Van Orden has been riding since he was a kid. He remembers a time when guest ranches catered mostly to families. That's the kind of traditional experience he and his family work to provide on the land Van Orden's dad bought in 1964.

Moose Creek Ranch is not a working ranch, which means it's all about you. For a change of pace, every fall for one week, Moose Creek Ranch hosts adults only. In winter the ranch, situated on the Western slope of the Tetons barely a stone's throw from the Jedediah Smith Wilderness, offers bed and breakfast accommodations to skiers and snow lovers.

Teton Teepee Lodge
$ summer, $$$$ winter • Ski Hill Rd., Alta, Wyo. • (307) 353-8176, (800) 353-8176

Fifteen minutes from powder heaven at Grand Targhee and 45 from the dramatic vertical rise of Jackson Hole Mountain Resort is the ultimate ski lodge. The Melehes brothers and their partner, Brent Palmer, promise to do everything for you but carve your turns. You pay a flat fee (a three-night minimum is requested), and your lift tickets, transportation, accommodations, all-you-can-eat breakfast, dinner and beverages are included.

In the evenings, relax around the huge fireplace, watch videos on the big-screen TV or warm your bones in the hot tub. Kids enjoy the game room and the un-hotel-like freedom to wander around the lodge and play. Teton Teepee even takes care of your social life during your ski vacation: The lodge's 18 rooms all open into the huge, teepee-like interior of the lodge. You'll meet everyone there in no time. And don't worry if the music and merriment don't sound fun to you tonight: Your room is equipped with not one but two doors to block out the noise.

For a real social experience, rent the dormitories downstairs. Each bunk bed is equipped with locker space and shower access. School and Scout groups love it. In summer Teton Teepee operates much like a hotel, although they love to host weddings, conferences and reunions. If you're visiting in summer, we recommend you take advantage of the lodge's bike rentals and maybe even participate in a guided bike trip. The staff will take care of your transportation and snacks and show you the prettiest rides (see our Other Recreation chapter).

Southwestern Montana

Bozeman, Montana

Mountain Sky Guest Ranch
$$$$ • P.O. Box 1128, Bozeman, Mont.
• (406) 587-1244, (800) 548-3392

Tennis, anyone? A quick swim in the pool? The menu of options at Mountain Sky is enough to keep even the most easily bored occupied: Ping-Pong, volleyball, softball, horseshoes, hiking, fishing, riding, dining, dancing — or nothing at all. From its sweeping lawns and graciously appointed rustic cabins to its gourmet meals and thoughtful staff, Mountain Sky is pure luxury carved into the Western landscape. An optional children's program, run by qualified staff, offers youngsters of all ages a diversity of activities, including crafts, nature walks, swimming, games and fishing in Mountain Sky's private trout pond.

Dining at Mountain Sky is an event all by itself. Whether it's poolside barbecues featuring steaks and chicken or seafood or an inside meal of gourmet continental cuisine, you won't want to be late for a meal. Breakfasts range from light to hearty, depending on your preference. Lunch, served outside buffet-style after the morning ride, may include homemade soups, pasta salads, pizza, enchiladas, stir-fries or a host of other Mountain Sky specialties.

For a special experience, Mountain Sky offers a rent-a-ranch program, in which your group can have Mountain Sky all to itself.

Big Sky, Montana

Big Sky Ski and Summer Resort
$$ • Mountain Village, Big Sky, Mont.
• (406) 995-5000, (800) 548-4486

The dream of now-deceased NBC news anchor Chet Huntley, Big Sky opened in March 1974. Today Big Sky offers quality, quantity, convenience and year-around recreation galore. In winter, it's skiing: 3,500 acres of terrain accessed by 15 lifts built to accommodate 18,000 skiers an hour! Big Sky has 4,180 total vertical feet of skiing (the most in the United States), one tram, three high-speed quads, one gondola, one quad chair, three triple chairs, three double chairs and three surface tows. The longest run, Liberty Bowl to Mountain Mall, is 6 miles. The steepest run, Castro's Shoulder, is 50 degrees. The average snowfall is 400 inches, and the average winter daytime temperature is 20 degrees.

Big Sky has 850 rooms — 4,000 pillows nightly — and is owned by Boyne USA Resorts. Snowmobilers will find hundreds of miles of trails, one of which leads to Yellowstone Park. And nearby Lone Mountain Guest Ranch has 65 kilometers of groomed cross-country ski trails. In summer, it's golf at an 18-hole, par 72 golf course, swimming at the Huntley Lodge and tennis club, rafting on the Gallatin River, hiking or biking in the backcountry, horseback riding, touring Yellowstone Park (it's just 18 miles south of Big Sky) and fishing blue-ribbon streams.

The Huntley Lodge and Shoshone Condominium Hotel, owned by the Big Sky Resort, have a combined 294 rooms. The Shoshone Condominiums feature loft and one-bedroom suites, while the adjoining lodge has 200 guest rooms.

Lone Mountain Ranch
$$$$ • Lone Mountain Rd., Big Sky, Mont. • (406) 995-4644, (800) 514-4644

While Lone Mountain is busiest these days from June through August, this oasis of Western hospitality began in the 1970s as a cross-country ski center. Today, its 65 kilometers of meticulously groomed trails are legendary among skiers nationwide. Also legendary is Lone Mountain's food served in a Western log dining lodge lit by handmade antler chandeliers and warmed by a floor-to-ceiling stone fireplace. In addition to in-season wild game, fresh trout, local beef and lamb, you can expect to find vegetarian dishes and home-baked breads, pastries and desserts. In summer, Lone Mountain features weekly outdoor barbecues with steaks, ribs and chicken. During the winter, a weekly trail buffet is served on a long table made of snow, much to the delight of guests.

Another winter favorite is an evening sleigh ride to the North Fork cabin where the staff will serve you a prime rib dinner cooked up on an old-fashioned wood cookstove. (Nonguests can sometimes squeeze into the dining room for dinner, but they must make reservations ahead of time. Breakfast and lunch for nonguests are on a walk-in basis.)

Lone Mountain employs a staff of naturalist guides to lead hiking, biking, fishing, horseback riding, and Yellowstone Park tours in both summer and winter. Winter tours, which feature both snowcoach and cross-country skiing, are open to nonguests. The cost for these tours is extra for guests. During the summer, Lone Mountain specializes in family groups (the ranch can accommodate 115), with a kid's program from June 15 to August 30. Youth activities, which change depending on their ages and interests, might include volleyball, adventure hikes, nature discovery hikes, llama hikes, horseback riding, overnight camp-outs and canoeing.

Lone Mountain has 23 cabins in varying sizes. None have TVs or telephones, and the ranch is smoke-free. Lone Mountain offers summer (and winter) fly fishing vacations, a discovery package that offers horseback riding and many naturalist-guided trips, and a winter cross-country ski package. All packages are for seven-night stays and include meals, lodging and transportation to and from the airport.

Rainbow Ranch Lodge
$$ • 5 miles south of the Big Sky, Mont., entrance on U.S. Hwy. 191 • (406) 995-4132, (800) 937-4132

Known in the 1920s as the Halfway Inn — it's midway between Bozeman and Yellowstone National Park — the newly renovated Rainbow Ranch Lodge offers travelers a taste of the New West with a twist of the Old. Twenty-one rooms, each with lodgepole beds, down comforters, heavy canvas curtains and deep, comfortable chairs and couches have decks overlooking the Gallatin River below.

The lodge itself, which is surrounded by beautiful landscaping, has a custom-made bar, a comfortable lounge and gourmet dining so popular with locals and guests from other ranches you'd better call ahead for a reservation if you plan to arrive around dinner time. Meals are not included in the room rates. For breakfast and lunch you'll have to go elsewhere. The Corral across the highway serves great food at a reasonable price.

If you're interested in horseback riding — there are trails galore in the Gallatin Canyon — Diamond K Outfitters operate from corrals at the Rainbow Ranch Lodge. They offer two-hour, half-day or all-day rides. They also offer Western horsemanship lessons, evening dinner rides and daylong backcountry fishing trips. Diamond K also offers overnight to six-day, full-service tent-camping pack trips into Yellowstone Park backcountry.

During the summer, the Gallatin Canyon offers hiking, mountain biking, golf, tennis, kayaking or river rafting. During the winter, if you can tear yourself away from the cozy fireplace in your room or the lounge, you can downhill ski at Big Sky Resort, cross-country ski in Gallatin National Forest or snowmobile right into the mountains.

Gallatin Gateway, Montana

320 Guest Ranch
$$$ • 205 Buffalo Horn Creek, Gallatin
Gateway, Mont. • (406) 995-4283,
(800) 243-0320

With 60 rooms, a dining room open to the public, a 200-person convention hall and a kaleidoscope of on-site activities, 320 Guest Ranch offers plenty of variety year around for anyone seeking a corporate convention or a Western vacation near Yellowstone Park. While many guest ranches require at least a four-night stay, you can hang your hat at the 320 for a minimum of two nights. Rooms and cabins range from a one-room duplex log cabin to a three-bedroom log home with a full-size kitchen, two bathrooms, beds for eight adults and plenty of floor space for kids and sleeping bags. By the way, children 12 and younger stay free at the 320 Guest Ranch.

The 320 offers several winter and summer packages. Winter packages, such as the two-day Get-A-Way, a four-day downhill or cross-country skiing or the seven-day Winter Dream, include such extras as ski-lift passes at Big Sky Resort, Yellowstone snowmobile excursions and some meals. In summer, you can choose from a four-night mini-vacation or the seven-night Western Dream package that includes a variety of horseback rides, the Chuckwagon BBQ, an all-day horseback fishing trip to an alpine lake and several meals. Meals are served in a Western dining room. If you pay by the night, it'll cost you extra for meals and ranch activities such as the Chuckwagon Dinner and Breakfast rides, the Camera Safari, horseback riding or guided fishing trips.

Wild Trout Outfitters (see our Fishing and Hunting chapter) operates a fly shop and outfitting service from a tiny, old log cabin on the premises. Included with your room, though, are horseshoes, volleyball, evening bonfires and hayrides. The 320 also has a small playground for children and a guest laundry located in one of the older log cabins.

A popular spot for snowmobilers, the 320 is just a few miles from the Buck Ridge snowmobile trail. And the area also has plenty of groomed cross-country ski trails.

The Covered Wagon Ranch
$$ • 34035 Gallatin Rd., Gallatin
Gateway, Mont. • (406) 995-4237

You won't find hot tubs or TVs at the Covered Wagon Ranch in the Gallatin Canyon. Established as a dude ranch in 1925 and owned until 1996 by the founding family, the Covered Wagon is one of the few remaining ranches where visitors can find the Old West alive and well. Families with toddlers will scoot their youngsters up to the table in the same highchair owner Vic Benson used as a boy. And they'll stay in cabins that, except for the addition of bathrooms, have changed little since the old days. That's because guests who have returned to the ranch year after year (The Covered Wagon has a 65-percent return rate) insist on the same simple charm and the genuine Western hospitality that they've come to count on through the years.

Hearty country meals are served family style — the ranch accommodates only 24 guests at a time — in a new lodge (until 1996, guests dined in two shifts in a smaller dining hall.) Evenings, children and adults alike gather 'round the campfire or in the game room, a separate building equipped with a piano, a foosball table, books, puzzles and board games. Horseback riding is the mainstay of the Covered Wagon experience. Guests are assigned a horse for the week; everyone has a favorite, and some longtime guests even buy horses to keep on the ranch. And they can ride for as long as they want on any number of trails. With no more than six guests assigned to a wrangler, you can choose which trail you want to ride.

If your knees start creaking after too many days in the saddle, you can put on your city duds and head for Bozeman, slip on your fishing vest and cast your line into the nearby streams or break out your camera and drive into Yellowstone Park, just a few miles away, for the day.

INSIDERS' TIP

Grand Teton Park is home to about 40 black bears — but most of them aren't black. Colors range from black to reddish-brown to blond.

Nine Quarter Circle Ranch

$$, no credit cards • 5000 Taylor Fork Rd., Gallatin Gateway, Mont.
• (406) 995-4276

Gather up your young'uns and head for the Nine Quarter Circle Ranch, where the Kelsey family has perfected the fine art of treating young and old alike to the Western experience. Located in a picture-perfect setting at 7,000 feet, the Nine Quarter Circle is surrounded by National Forest filled with breathtaking views, mountain meadows and alpine lakes.

Yes, there's riding, and lots of it, with 120 ranch-raised horses (the Kelseys raise Appaloosas) from which to choose. Four or five rides head into the mountains daily, each taking a trail tailored to a different ability level. When you get there, you might want to kiss your kids good-bye for a week. Between the Kiddie Wrangler, the Baby Sitter and a herd of kids to play with, chances are you'll only catch a glimpse of them now and then. Saturday morning you and the rest of the parents will drape yourselves over the corral fence and watch the kids take their turns in a gymkhana. Later that night you'll swing with them at the square dance in the hayloft of the ranch's old barn.

During the week there are also volleyball and softball games as well as an overnight pack trip. The log ranch buildings which stretch a half-mile from one end to the other were built with timber from the ranch. A big lodge with living and dining rooms plus a string of cabins built mostly to accommodate family groups will accommodate guests. Come fall, when the families head back home for school, anglers fly in to the ranch's 4,000-foot-long airstrip, soak in the still autumn air and fish to their heart's content.

The Nine Quarter Circle has been written up in more than 40 national publications, so make your reservations a year ahead of time — it's popular. The Kelseys require a reference exchange.

Yellowstone Valley Ranch

$$$$ • U.S. Hwy. 89, south of Livingston, Mont. • (406) 333-4787, (800) 626-3526

There is one thing that can tear a fisherman away from a hot blue-ribbon fly-fishing stream. That's the promise of a fabulous supper simmering on the stove in the ranch kitchen. Anglers will find both, and a lot more, at the Yellowstone Valley Ranch south of Livingston. Don't think "ranch" as in old and rustic. Think "ranch" as in comfortable and quietly elegant.

World-class trout fishing on privately leased and fish-for-fee spring creeks, is the calling card of this ranch overlooking the Yellowstone River and the Absaroka Mountains. In case you or your spouse are not into fishing, though, the Yellowstone Valley Ranch offers an alternative Outdoor Adventure package that includes horseback riding, mountain biking, naturalist-led hikes, guided tours of Yellowstone Park and introductory lessons in kayaking and canoeing. No matter what you choose to do each, at the end of it you'll find cocktails and dinner waiting at the lodge.

Unlike other fishing lodges and guest ranches, you can choose when you want to eat (as long as it's between 6:30 and 9:30 PM) and you can select from three entrees (seafood, pasta or beef based) cooked up by chef Dave Rees. Rees, who concocts new creations and old favorites depending on the season and his whim, came with the Yellowstone Valley Ranch when owners Steve and Taffy McGrath, and John and Nancy Boisvert bought it in 1993.

The Yellowstone Valley Ranch has 10 rooms, each with two queen beds and a private patio overlooking the river. The Ranch offers six-night, five-day packages that begin on Saturday and end on Friday. Included in the price are transportation to and from the airport, meals, lodging and guided fishing trips or the adventure trips mentioned above. Options are available for shorter stays. For children's rates, we recommend the same since the owners will negotiate rates depending on their ages and lodging arrangements.

Chico Hot Springs Lodge

$ • Pray, Mont. • (406) 333-4933, (800) HOT-WADA

Tucked into a nook of the Paradise Valley 30 miles north of Yellowstone Park, Chico Hot Springs has a reputation for excellence as far away as the East Coast and across the Atlantic. As famous as it is, Chico Hot Springs is an affordable paradise with accommodations options ranging from Victorian-themed rooms without baths to plush suites with custom-made hardwood furniture. Built at the turn of the century, Chico Hot Springs has been restored to its former glory and then some. Sweeping lawns and plump perennial gardens surround the sprawling Victorian-era hotel, which houses the Chico Inn (a world-famous restaurant featured in our Restaurants chapter), the hot spring pool, the Poolside Grill, a bar and an array of refurbished rooms in the Main Lodge (with or without private bathrooms) furnished with antiques collected by owners Mike and Eve Art.

The inn offers other accommodations (there are 90 in all) on the 150-acre property. The Lower Lodge, built in 1996, offers 16 plush, spacious units with custom-made Mission-style oak furniture. Units in the Lower Lodge range from upscale standard rooms to two bedroom suites with kitchens. The Upper Lodge, a modern motel on a hill overlooking the Main Lodge, looks like any other motel you might stay in. Chico also offers five log cottages furnished with log furniture. Fully-equipped condos and houses sleep from two to 20 guests. You won't find telephones or televisions in the rooms, but you will find an unusual landing strip if you want to fly in for a stay. After radioing ahead to the Lodge, pilots land on the secluded county road leading to Chico.

The Chico Inn is known for its exceptional food served in elegant Western style. The more casual Poolside Grille serves lunch and dinner. The Chico Saloon rocks with live bands on the weekends and is a comfortable place to hang out during the rest of the week. The bar caters to the Monday Night Football crowd with two big-screen TVs.

Besides its 104-degree hot spring pool, Chico offers horseback riding, fishing at a private lake, hiking, mountain biking, river rafting, cross-country skiing (you can rent skis here), dogsled tours, and massage therapy — all for extra fees. Chico Hot Springs also has a Children's Activity Program for kids ages

5 to 12. This program includes arts and crafts, gardening, noncompetitive sports, nature walks and educational games.

Northwestern Wyoming

Double Diamond X Ranch
$$$ • 3453 Southfork Rd., Cody, Wyo.
• (307) 527-6276, (800) 833-RANCH

You may come as a guest to Double Diamond X, but you'll leave as a friend. Staffed by a crew of friendly wranglers, cooks and housekeepers, the Double Diamond X offers a regular menu of Western guest ranch options, including a children's program designed to educate and entertain. An indoor swimming pool and spa, plus a recreation building and a cozy living room in the main lodge offer plenty of pleasant diversions. During the day, chances are you'll want to go for a horseback ride. Wranglers here work with guests young and old to make sure they're comfortable and capable before they head out of the arena and onto the trail.

The Double Diamond X books weeklong packages that include a chuckwagon cookout and a night trip to the Cody Nite Rodeo followed by a continental breakfast in your cabin the next morning. Another day you can go to the Buffalo Bill Historical Center, and any old day you can ride or fish from the ranch's private access to the South Fork of the Shoshone River below the ranch house. Thirty-four miles southwest of Cody, the Double Diamond X is surrounded by Forest Service land. All meals, served family style, are included in the package. The Double Diamond X also offers backcountry pack trips tailored to your needs.

Hidden Valley Ranch Resort
$$$ • 153 Hidden Valley Rd., Cody, Wyo.
• (307) 587-5090

Out of sight, out of mind — the name says it all. Tucked into a hidden valley (we hate to be redundant, but it's true), this ranch

Photo: Moose Creek Ranch

Family-style dining is what you're likely to find at dude ranches
and bed and breakfasts in Yellowstone country.

can make you forget about the rest of the world. To help you forget, Hidden Valley Ranch owners Duaine and Sheila Hagen have a hands-off policy when it comes to planned activities. Spontaneity and flexibility is their motto. One evening you might find yourself watching Duaine breaking a colt in the corral, the next you might be singing songs around the campfire. If it rains, maybe it's a good day for you to read (and rest your derriere), or troop off to town to shop or stroll around museums. If you like, lounge around the pool all day, or go whitewater rafting on the Shoshone River.

Whatever you do, remember you can go riding any time you want (once in the morning and again in the afternoon), and you've got 40 horses from which to choose. Duaine is also a licensed hunting outfitter who guides elk and deer hunts in the Absaroka Mountains. Meals, hearty ranch fare, are served buffet style in a large dining room adjoining a recreation room with Ping-Pong and pool tables.

Though the Hagens encourage mini- and full-week vacation packages, occasionally they do let people stay for just one night. If you stay just one night, chances are good that you'll want to linger.

Elephant Head Lodge
$ • 1120 WP Yellowstone Hwy., Wapiti, Wyo. • (307) 587-3980

Warning! The log cabins at this lodge 11 miles east of Yellowstone Park are so cozy you may not want to do anything but sit and soak in pure priceless peace. Each of the 10 cabins, which owners Phil and Joan Lamb modernized without sacrificing their Old West charm, is decorated differently. All, though, have thick, old-fashioned quilts and screened windows that you can throw open to enjoy the cool Rocky Mountain night air. One sleeps nine, another has a fireplace, and two have kitchenettes.

No matter how comfy you are, sooner or later hunger will drive you to the dining room, another log building just a hop, skip and a jump from yours. There you'll find a Franklin stove, five tables decked with red-checked tablecloths and home-cooked meals served with fresh-baked bread and homemade desserts. At dinner, Phil will be outside grilling ribeyes, filet mignons and New York strip steaks. Joan will be in the kitchen cooking up a storm.

While the owners welcome overnight guests, most visitors stay three to five days to do some horseback riding and to use the lodge as a base for touring Yellowstone Park and

Cody. The Elephant Head also offers hiking, rock climbing, antler-hunting nature walks, nightly movies in the old lodge living room, a recreation area for children and a small lounge for Mom and Dad.

The Elephant Head offers a European Plan in which guests pay a flat rate for their cabin, then pay extra for meals and activities. The American Plan package is good for guests who want to do a lot of horseback riding. In addition to your cabin, the package includes three meals a day and up to four hours a day of riding.

Bill Cody Ranch

$$ • 2604 Yellowstone Hwy., Cody, Wyo. • (307) 587-6271

Drive into the Bill Cody Ranch on a Wednesday evening about 5:30 and you're liable to find guests moseying down to dine at the chuckwagon cookout. You'll see elderly couples holding hands and young adults dressed in cowboy duds draped over lodgepole rails on the log lodge porch. In the thick of it all, John and Jamie Parsons, Wyoming natives and owners of the Bill Cody Ranch since 1996, are natural-born hosts dishing out a generous portion of cheerful Western hospitality.

At the ranch, horseback riding is the specialty. The Parsons employ eight wranglers, and John keeps his string of 70 horses on a rotating schedule so that each one stays fresh with plenty of time off. He offers two-hour, half-day and all-day rides into the Shoshone National Forest. A horse hand himself, Parsons these days most often rides the "Blue Horse" — an all-terrain vehicle with a saddle for a seat — back and forth to the corrals and to the post office down the road at Wapiti.

The Bill Cody Ranch offers nightly and packaged vacation rates that include meals and horseback riding. The ranch also offers regular trips to the Cody Nite Rodeo, and the Parsons can arrange for other services such as fishing guides. While you can probably get a room here at the last minute during the off season, we advise reservations during the summer months. The "No Vacancy" sign is becoming a regular sight each evening at the Bill Cody Ranch gate on the Yellowstone Highway.

The Bill Cody Ranch doesn't take credit cards for a reservation deposit, but they do accept credit cards once you're here.

UXU Ranch

$$$ • 1710 Yellowstone Hwy., Wapiti, Wyo. • (307) 587-2143

At the UXU, the attraction is the horses — and a lot more, such as water-skiing and windsurfing on Buffalo Bill Dam Reservoir, mountain biking or museum meandering in Cody, trap shooting in Cody or traveling to Yellowstone Park just 17 miles to the West. Take your pick. And, if you want to stay on the ranch, there's still plenty to please you: a pool table, a piano, porch swings, a horseshoe pit and a well-stocked honor bar. Or you may just want to sit on the lodge deck watching the horses graze in the lush meadow below.

UXU has a resident fishing guide for those who want to cast their line in the North Fork of the Shoshone or any Yellowstone river. For those who long to see the wilds of the backcountry, the UXU provides pack trips. Guests stay in 10 one- to three-bedroom cabins equipped with carpeting, remodeled bathrooms, brand-new mattresses, down comforters and private porches. A few have fireplaces. Meals at the UXU are among the best we found. The chef prepares two gourmet entrees each evening, and meals are served in the main lodge dining room with windows galore overlooking the meadow. Come September, the UXU offers cooking, photography and painting workshops.

The UXU has a four-night minimum stay.

INSIDERS' TIP

The reason you can stay in guest ranches and lodges on private land within Grand Teton National Park is because of the piece-meal way park lands were acquired. Yellowstone Park was created by one flourish of a pen, but much of Grand Teton Park was purchased over a period of years, mostly by John D. Rockefeller Jr., and then ceded back to the people.

Pahaska Tepee

$$ • 183-B1 Yellowstone Hwy., Cody, Wyo. • (307) 527-7701, (800) 628-7791

Located just outside the east entrance to Yellowstone National Park on U.S. Highway 14-16-20, Pahaska Tepee is the site of Buffalo Bill Cody's hunting lodge. Now a buzzing burg for visitors going to and from the Park, Pahaska is best-known these days as a winter recreation mecca. It is the only resort open all year serving snowmobilers and cross-country skiers. You can drive your snowmobile from your room and travel on groomed roads 110 miles through Yellowstone Park to West Yellowstone, Montana.

Pahaska has a fleet of snowmobiles for rent as well as suits and other equipment needed to brave the cold. Just a mile to the east, the Sleeping Giant Ski Area (see our Winter Sports chapter) offers 17 downhill trails. There are also several miles of groomed cross-country trails in the area. Pahaska, which has a gas station, a gift store, a restaurant and horseback riding (for an extra fee), houses guests in older A-frames and other buildings.

Allen's Diamond Four Ranch

$, no credit cards • P.O. Box 243, Lander, Wyo. • (307) 332-2995

There are few ranches left, even in Yellowstone country, that are beyond electricity, television and neighbors. Allen's Diamond Four Ranch at the edge of the Popo Agie Wilderness in the Wind River Mountains is one of them. You won't find fancy fare here. Just simple charm and log cabins with propane lights and woodstoves. At 9,200 feet, you may want to fire up that woodstove, sending a wisp of smoke winding through the dewy, damp woods, before heading to the lodge for breakfast. Stays include three meals a day, horseback riding, fishing, natural-history hikes and wildlife watching. Guests share a shower house. And, by the way, it's BYOB — Bring Your Own (sleeping) Bag. Children younger than 8 stay at a 50-percent discount.

Owners Jim and Mary Allen also offer an assortment of pack trips that leave from the ranch June through September. Guided pack trips ($175 per day per person) supply everything you need, including a camp cook. For half that much, you can outfit your own camp and let the Allens furnish the horses and the packtrain in and out of remote areas. (Early reservations are highly recommended for these drop camp trips.) The Allens also outfit and guide custom trips including hiking with pack horses, wilderness seminars, cross-Continental Divide tours as well as an Oregon Trail wagon trip and cattle drives. Spring and fall, the Allens offer a working-ranch experience in which you can help with such things as branding, roundup and general ranch work. They also have a hunting guide service in the fall (see the Fishing and Hunting chapter).

On your way to Yellowstone country, you'll find RV parks and campgrounds that range from simple mom-and-pop stops in and out of town to high-tech, asphalt-covered parking lots with amenities galore.

Campgrounds and RV Parks

Load up your gear, put the dog in the kennel, say goodbye to your neighbors, lock up your home and breathe a sigh of relief. You're headed for camping country where the possibilities are almost limitless. Hook up your TV, plug into a phone jack, play video games or dive into a pool at some of the more modern privately owned RV parks. Or ditch the crowd and pitch your tent at a quiet little Forest Service campground outside the Parks. Stake your claim to a site in one of Yellowstone Parks' reservation campgrounds. Or take your chances on finding a nook in the wildly popular Jenny Lake Campground. No matter what your pleasure, once you get to Yellowstone country, you'll find the camping spirit rising with the flames of an evening campfire and soaring with the osprey on their morning flights.

On your way to Yellowstone country, you'll find RV parks and campgrounds that range from simple mom-and-pop stops in and out of town to high-tech, asphalt-covered parking lots with amenities galore. Inside the Parks, you'll find big, busy campgrounds and smaller, cozy ones. Countless free and undesignated campsites are scattered throughout the public lands, but you'll have to leave the highway and head into the mountains to get to them. We recommend you stop at a local ranger district office for advice and a map (see the Parks and Forests chapter for the names, addresses and phone numbers).

In this chapter, we've listed numerous public and private campgrounds that, for one reason or another, make them special places to stay inside and outside the Parks. Some are reservation-only campgrounds while others on national forest lands have only a few reserveable sites in each campground.

Generally, you'll find Forest Service and Bureau of Land Management campgrounds are quite a bit less expensive than privately owned RV parks. You'll also find fewer amenities, though. Forest Service campgrounds often have full-time hosts who can answer your questions or sell you firewood. To pay fees, though, you place your money in an envelope and then pop it into a locked box. Rangers pick up the money each day.

Because the national parks are slightly different, we'll tell you what you'll find in each. And since you'll be in bear country, we'll first give you some special tips for camping with bruins. Finally, because none of us wants our backcountry (or front country) camping experience marred by the careless remains of others' campsites, we'll remind you of a few courtesies in the "Leave No Trace" land ethic.

Camping Information

Bear Safety

When you get off the plane at Cody's Yellowstone Regional Airport, you'll see your first bear sign — a giant grizzly paw print painted on the airport wall. Believe the signs and similar ones posted elsewhere in Yellowstone country campgrounds. Yellowstone has an estimated 200 grizzlies and 400 black bears. Read and heed the rules about food storage. They're there for your own and the bears' protection. It takes only one sweet can of Pepsi or a bag of buns for a grizzly or a black bear to put a campground on his list of regular nightly food stops.

Bears that hang around campgrounds looking for a handout become dangerous and demanding very quickly. That's when Park and Forest Service rangers have to step in. And they have only three options to take care of the problem bear. They can close the campground until the bear forgets about the reward (this may be years), they can trap and transport the bear to a location 100 miles away, or they can destroy the bear. Each year in Yellowstone Park, at least one bear has to be destroyed. In Grand Teton, the average is fewer than one bear destroyed each summer. Outside the Parks the number is much higher. In 1997, 19 grizzlies died in all of Greater Yellowstone. Ten deaths were caused by humans.

In the front country, store your food and other fragrant items like lip balm, sunscreen or shaving cream either in a bear-proof box or the trunk of your car. If you store your food inside your car, you may be surprised like the woman in Cooke City who awoke one morning to find that a bear had broken into her convertible and tried to pull her back seat through the window. In the backcountry, where you don't have a car, officials recommend hanging food at least 10 feet high in a tree. Yellowstone Park provides food storage poles at designated campsites, while Grand Teton offers detailed instructions about how to hang our food from a branch.

Park and Forest Service rangers also advise campers to cook at least 100 yards from their tent, to keep clothes with food odors outside the tent and to thoroughly wash cooking utensils away from your tent. In Yellowstone Park and some national forests, food storage regulations are strictly enforced by patrolling rangers. If you leave food out, they will confiscate it. At some campgrounds, you will find bear-proof storage boxes. Almost all campgrounds in and around the Parks have bear-proof garbage cans.

www.insiders.com

See this and many other **Insiders' Guide®** destinations online — in their entirety.

Visit us today!

For more information on bears, see the Close-up in our Fishing and Hunting chapter.

Leave No Trace

The explosion in the number of campers and other recreation enthusiasts has brought heavy use to some parts of Greater Yellowstone. To minimize the effects and, let's face it, the damage, public land management agencies promote a Leave No Trace ethic. We have included some of their tips for loving the lands of Greater Yellowstone.

• Use designated campsites whenever possible and camp at least 200 feet from streams, rivers, lakes, trails and meadows.

• Pick a campsite where the drainage will be good. Digging ditches or trenches around tents causes erosion and leaves scars.

• Use established campfire rings whenever possible. If you must build a campfire in a new site, dig out a divot of sod, build a small fire, then replace the sod before you leave. Build fires away from trees, shrubs, rocks and meadows. Fires built on top of a deep layer of pine needles can burn down into the rotting needles, smolder unnoticed for days, then erupt into a forest fire. Use only dead and down wood. When you're finished, make sure the fire is dead-out and scatter the ashes to naturalize the area.

• Plan to filter or boil all drinking water.

• Use a "cat-hole" to bury human waste. It should be at least 6 inches deep, 200 feet from your camp and at least 200 feet from any water source.

• Never bury your trash! Pack it in. Pack it out.

Reservations

For Yellowstone Park campsite reservations in all but the Fishing Bridge RV Park, call

---

INSIDERS' TIP

June and July are the mosquito months throughout most of Yellowstone country. Read the labels: The most effective repellants contain the most DEET.

(307) 344-7311. For the Fishing Bridge RV Park call Mistix Reservations at (800) 365-2267. For campground reservations in national forest campgrounds, contact the U.S. National Forest Reservation Center, P.O. Box 900, Cumberland, MD 21501-0900, (800) 280-2267. Grand Teton National Park has one reservation campground, at Colter Bay.

Price Code

The following ranges of nightly rates, indicated by a dollar-sign code in each write-up, are intended as a guideline for pricing your stay in Greater Yellowstone campgrounds and RV parks.

$	$4 to $9
$$	$10 to $16
$$$	$17 to $23
$$$$	$24 and more

Yellowstone National Park

Yellowstone Park offers 11 campgrounds and one RV park with a total of 2,145 campsites. Of the 12 sites, seven are operated on a first-come, first-served basis and require no reservations. The other five — Madison, Canyon Village, Grant Village, Bridge Bay and the Fishing Bridge RV Park — contain more than 1,700 spaces that may be reserved in advance by calling Amfac Parks and Resorts or Mistix Reservations. See our Parks and Forests chapter for more information about Amfac, the concessionaire that runs most of the lodging and many of the activities in Yellowstone Park.

Four campgrounds, which total nearly 1,400 sites, have reserveable sites costing $14.50 per night in 1997. Non-reservation campgrounds cost from $8 to $10 per night in 1997. Fees can be paid to Amfac Resorts by either credit card or check.

You'll find at least minimal amenities such as tables, fire grills, drinking water and flush or pit toilets at all of the campgrounds. You'll also find amphitheaters or campfire circles where Park naturalists give presentations each evening. The reservation campgrounds generally have more amenities such as firewood for sale, showers and laundries. They are also close to general stores, post offices, restaurants and gas stations.

You can learn more about any of the Yellowstone National Park campgrounds by calling Amfac Resorts at (307) 344-7311.

In the Park

Madison Campground
$$ • West Entrance Rd., Yellowstone National Park

Only 14 miles east of West Yellowstone, the Madison Campground makes a good staging area for exploring Geyser country in Yellowstone Park. Away from the hustle and bustle of areas like Canyon or Grant Village, Madison provides a bit of that peaceful, woodsy feeling despite the fact that it has 280 campsites, all of which are filled almost nightly from Memorial Day to Labor Day. Below the campground you'll find a beautiful view and fishing in the Madison River. Each evening at the amphitheater, a naturalist presents programs on such topics as the bison, the mountains and rivers of the Park, geology and hiking.

The Information Station, adjacent to the amphitheater, is a log and stone structure built in 1929 and 1930 as a ranger station. It later became one of the first roadside museums in Yellowstone Park and now serves as a small information center that also sells educational books. Within easy biking or hiking distance is the turnoff for the one-way, 2-mile Firehole Canyon Drive where you'll see several cascades and waterfalls.

The average stay at Madison is three nights, just long enough to explore Geyser Country at a leisurely pace. To the south are several geyser basins with self-guiding trails that wind through them as well as other trails that lead away from them into the hills. To the north is Norris Geyser Basin, with more trails. In between are several points of interest including the Artists' Paint Pots and Gibbon Falls. To the west lies West Yellowstone and miles of landscape burned by the 1988 Yellowstone fire.

Madison Campground offers firewood for

sale. It also has flush toilets and an RV dump station. Madison is a reservation campground operated by Amfac Parks and Resorts. It is open from early May to late October.

Norris Campground
$$ • Mammoth-Norris Rd., Yellowstone National Park

Open mid-May to late October, the Norris Campground winds among the conifers bordering an open meadow that often sports elk. Just below the campground, at the edge of the meadow, is the Museum of the National Park Ranger. Take a stroll to this museum with your morning coffee. The large stone fireplace won't warm your bones, but a chat with the museum keeper is liable to warm the cockles of your heart and fire your imagination. Chances are you'll walk away from this old ranger station with a glimpse into the past, since it is staffed by a rotating crew of volunteers (some of whom are retired Park rangers) who are full of historical anecdotes.

We recommend taking a short (or long) hike on one of two trails leading away from the Norris campground. To the north, you'll find open meadows and Whiterock Spring. To the east, you'll follow Solfatara Creek through a burned area to a large meadow that is popular with elk during the summer months. From there, it's an uphill climb to Ice Lake. Norris Campground is also a good staging spot for forays into the Geyser, Mammoth and Canyon areas. Twenty-one miles to the north lie the Mammoth Hot Springs and Yellowstone National Park Headquarters. The Norris Geyser Basin is within walking or biking distance, and Norris is easy driving distance to the geyser basins south of Madison. The Grand Canyon of the Yellowstone is about 14 miles to the east. We suggest taking at least a day to see each of these areas. Evenings, you'll find talks by Park naturalists at the Norris Campfire Circle near the "C" Loop.

Norris has 116 campsites offered on a first-come, first-served basis. It is 12 miles to the closest full services, at Canyon Village.

Indian Creek Campground
$ • Norris-Mammoth Rd., Yellowstone National Park

Hidden among the conifers at the edge of a large meadow, Indian Creek Campground is a 75-space campground adjacent to the creek for which it is named. In a large meadow next to the campground you're apt to see wildlife like elk and bison. Just 8 miles south of Mammoth, Indian Creek is a good staging spot for both Mammoth and Geyser Country. It is also one of the more popular campgrounds in the Park and one of the few with a view. To the north, within easy walking distance, you'll find Sheepeater Cliff, once home of the Sheepeater band of the Shoshone Indians, Yellowstone Park's only resident Native Americans. Indian Creek is open from early June until mid-September. Firewood is for sale at this campground.

Mammoth Campground
$$ • Mammoth Hot Springs, Yellowstone National Park

Squeezed into a hairpin curve on the Mammoth-Gardiner Road, the 85 well-used campsites at the Mammoth Campground are doled out on a first-come, first-served basis. With binoculars you might be able to see antelope, elk or bison grazing in the distance. An amphitheater tucked into a draw at the head of the campground offers nightly educational programs. Plenty of other tours begin just up the hill at the Albright Visitor Center in Mammoth. We recommend leaving your vehicle behind while you explore the many attractions of Mammoth Hot Springs. You can start by touring the Albright Visitor Center, which contains an educational bookstore, a historical display with early era photographs and an interesting 25-minute film on Yellowstone Park. From there,

INSIDERS' TIP

Camping in or traveling through the backcountry? Carry a plastic bag or coffee can to receive used toilet paper. That way your family won't leave behind the little white clumps some folks call "mountain blossoms."

you'll want to walk the Mammoth Terraces (see our Attractions chapter).

Mammoth is the only year-round campground in Yellowstone National Park.

Slough Creek Campground

$ • Northeast Entrance Rd., Yellowstone National Park

The smallest and the most beautiful of the Yellowstone Park campgrounds, this one has 29 campsites that lie next to Slough Creek, renowned for its good trout fishing (see our Fishing and Hunting chapter). Eight miles northeast of the Tower-Roosevelt Junction and 1 mile north of the main road, this quiet area is only about a half-mile from the head of the Slough Creek Trail, which leads to the Park's northern boundary. After a short climb through a Douglas fir forest, the trail follows Slough Creek into a beautiful meadow. Besides finding great fishing here, you are apt to run across moose in the spring, coyote, trumpeter swans and birds of prey in the summer and elk and bison in the fall. Slough Creek is a good place to hole up and get away from the crowds for a while.

Slough Creek campground, open from late May until early November, lies at the northern edge of Lamar Valley, where wildlife is abundant and tourist traffic is relatively sparse.

Pebble Creek Campground

$ • Northeast Entrance Rd., Yellowstone National Park

Open mid-June to late July, Pebble Creek is one of the smallest campgrounds in Yellowstone Park. Situated next to — you guessed it — Pebble Creek, this 36-site campground has plenty of shade but not so many trees that you can't see out. Like the Slough Creek campground, Pebble Creek fills up fast during the summer. About 10 miles southwest of the Northeast Entrance at Silver Gate, Pebble Creek offers a quiet camp for those who want to hike or drive the Park. The Pebble Creek Trail leaves the campground and heads up a series of switchbacks to a small meadow. From there it heads up into the mountains and connects with the Bliss Pass Trail, which heads to the west, or it continues on to the Warm Creek Picnic Area a few miles west of the Northeast Entrance.

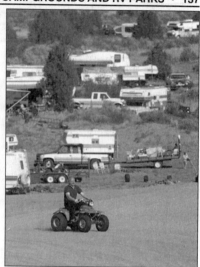

Photo: Steve Fischbach

Labor Day weekend in St. Anthony, Idaho, is a popular time to enjoy the dunes.

Tower Fall Campground

$ • Tower-Roosevelt-Canyon Rd., Yellowstone National Park

Hidden in the trees on a knoll 3 miles south of the Tower-Roosevelt Junction, Tower Fall is a popular campground with only 32 spaces. Right across the road from the campground is a Hamilton Store, and next to that is the trailhead to Tower Fall, a beautiful 100-foot waterfall that tumbles down between towerlike rocks. You'll find all kinds of hiking trails in this area. One of them, a 3.5-mile trail, leads from the campground to the Roosevelt Lodge where you can enjoy several different kinds of activities such as a stagecoach ride, horseback riding and a chuckwagon dinner (see our Attractions chapter). Another begins at the campground entrance and leads 3 miles up Tower Creek. Several more trails begin in the Tower-Roosevelt Junction area. One of them, the Yellowstone Picnic Area Trail, follows the Grand Canyon of the Yellowstone River for about 2 miles. For more information on these trails, we recommend contacting Yellowstone Park's backcountry office, 344-2160. This campground is open only in the summer.

Canyon Village Campground
$$ • Canyon Village, Yellowstone National Park

This is a full-service reservation campground with 271 spaces. Open from early June to early September, Canyon Campground is hidden in the trees away from the rest of the village. While you won't be able to see the bustling hamlet from your campsite, you may be able to hear it, and you definitely can walk to Canyon Village where you'll find a few stores well-stocked with gifts, groceries and outdoor gear. In case you're tired of your own cooking, the Hamilton Store in Canyon has a big lunch counter, and the Canyon Lodge has a cafeteria, a fast-food counter and a full dining room. Canyon also has a visitors center where you can get information and ideas for mapping out your stay in the Park. The most centrally located of all the campgrounds, Canyon makes a good staging area for anyone wanting one-stop camping (and shopping) in Yellowstone Park. From here you can choose a different direction in which to go each day.

You'll find a laundry at the campground office. Also available are firewood for sale, an RV dump station and hot showers.

Bridge Bay Campground
$$ • West Thumb-Fishing Bridge Rd., Yellowstone National Park

The largest of Yellowstone Park's 11 campgrounds, Bridge Bay is a huge sprawling reservations campground open from late May until late September. Don't be surprised if you wake up to an unexpected visitor here. Bison like to roam through the area. The main feature at this campground is Yellowstone Lake (see our Attractions chapter) and the marina adjacent to the campground. At the marina you'll find a boat launch, scenic cruises and guided fishing trips on the lake. Also, a biking and hiking trail leads to a natural bridge. This campground

is only 3 miles — an easy bike ride — south of Lake Village. Bridge Bay has 429 campsites.

Fishing Bridge RV Park
$$$$ • East Entrance Rd., Yellowstone National Park

This is the only campground in the Park where tents and pop-up campers are not welcome. This reservations campground, open from mid-May to early October, accommodates only RVs — 341 of them. That's because it's in bear country. The RV park is just a mile from the Fishing Bridge junction and a short walk to a Hamilton Store as well as a visitor center and a gas station. The Fishing Bridge RV Park is centrally located to use as a base camp for sightseeing in the lower portion of the Park. It is also close to the Pelican Valley Trailhead which leads into beautiful hiking (and bear) country and connects to several of the more remote trails in Yellowstone Park. You'll find showers and a laundry at this RV park.

Grant Village Campground
$$ • Grant Village, Yellowstone National Park

Campsites in this 425-unit reservation campground are strung out along the shore of Yellowstone Lake. While the sites are mostly in the trees, there are plenty of places where you can peek through the forest across the lake. You'll find showers, a laundry, a Hamilton Store, a gas station and a post office at Grant Village. This campground is also within easy biking distance of the geyser basin at West Thumb. Grant Village is a good staging spot for daytrips into both Geyser and Lake countries.

Lewis Lake Campground
$ • South Entrance Rd., Yellowstone National Park

Located on the west side of South Entrance Road, the Lewis Lake campground has 85

INSIDERS' TIP

August is yellow jacket season. Yellow jackets are aggressive bees attracted to bright colors, sweet smells and meat. Keep food-preparation areas clean and pay attention to the colors and lotions and cosmetics you wear if you want to avoid their company.

campsites overlooking Lewis Lake, renowned for its trout fishing. Open from mid-June to early November on a first come, first-served basis, Lewis Lake is the first campground you'll encounter if you enter Yellowstone Park from the south. It is a popular spot, so stake your claim to a site early. A boat launch adjacent to the campground provides access to Lewis Lake.

Entrance Communities

West Yellowstone, Montana

Baker's Hole Campground
$$ • U.S. 191, West Yellowstone, Mont. • (406) 646-7369

Because this full-service campground is frequented by black bears (and an occasional grizzly), no tents are allowed at Baker's Hole. (For more information about camping with bears, see our section on "Bear Safety" earlier in this chapter.) Otherwise this campground would be filled early each summer day with overflow campers from Yellowstone Park. Just 3 miles north of West Yellowstone, Baker's Hole has 72 sites strung out along the Madison River. Shaded with lodge pole pines, Baker's Hole features fishing in the nearby Madison River. A trail to streamside fishing platforms (to protect the vegetation) leads from the campground just north of unit No. 1. All facilities, including the fishing platforms, are wheelchair-accessible. Units 61 and 62 are situated closest to the river. Besides bears, you might see mule deer and osprey while camping here. The Forest Service has 19 reservation sites (see this chapter's introduction for more information about reserving campsites in U.S. Forest Service campgrounds) at Baker's Hole. Baker's Hole is open from Memorial Day to mid-September.

Rainbow Point Campground
$$ • Forest Rd. 6954, West Yellowstone, Mont. • (406) 646-7369

Tales of a 1983 incident in which a grizzly bear dragged a camper from his tent before killing (and eating) him may be why this campground remains underused to this day. Since then, only "hard-sided camping" has been allowed here — no tents and no pop-ups. Rainbow Point Campground is near Hebgen Lake about 10 miles northwest of West Yellowstone.

A quiet, wooded campground that features occasional visits by moose, deer, osprey and grizzly bears, Rainbow Point offers swimming, water-skiing, fishing and boating on Hebgen Lake. A beach and a boat ramp are adjacent to the campground. Open from Memorial Day to mid-September, the campground provides water, fire rings, grills, picnic tables, trash cans, vault toilets and paved loops. You won't find any RV hookups, though, and Rainbow Point has a 32-foot RV limit. Site 13 in loop C has a wheelchair-accessible toilet.

Cherry Creek Campground
No charge • Hebgen Lake Rd., West Yellowstone, Mont. • (406) 646-7369

Sip a cup of java and watch the rising sun splash daylight across the smooth waters of dawn. If you must, hurry a bit to beat the crowds in Yellowstone Park. We recommend taking a break, though. Lounge in the shade and read a good book or break out your float tube and fish on Hebgen Lake. Whatever you do, bring your own drinking water, because you won't find any well water here. Eight miles west of West Yellowstone and 6 miles north on the Hebgen Lake Road, Cherry Creek Campground is a free Forest Service campground with dispersed camping for about eight parties. It has a few fire rings, picnic tables and vault toilets. There are no RV hookups or wheelchair access.

Spring Creek Campground
No charge • Hebgen Lake Rd., West Yellowstone, Mont. • (406) 646-7369

When you get on a dirt road in Yellowstone country, you can be pretty sure you'll be leaving the crowds behind. Try this one: Drive 8 miles west of West Yellowstone on U.S. Highway 20, then 8 miles north on Hebgen Lake Road (it's a gravel road) to Spring Creek Campground on the west side of Hebgen Lake (see our Watersports and Fishing and Hunting chapters). You'll find wild grass and casual camping spots where you can bask in the sun or beat the heat in the shade on the shores of the lake. There are a few fire rings and picnic tables and vault toilets. There is neither drinking water nor hookups.

Lonesomehurst Campground

**$$ • Hebgen Lake Rd., West
Yellowstone, Mont. • (406) 646-7369**

If it's lake fishing you're after, Lonesomehurst offers a great camping and angling combo with a boat launch adjacent to the campground. On the banks of Hebgen Lake, Lonesomehurst is 8 miles west of West Yellowstone on U.S. Highway 20 and 4 miles north on the Hebgen Lake Road. The closest to West Yellowstone of several Forest Service campgrounds on the west side of Hebgen Lake, Lonesomehurst has 26 sites. Five can be reserved through National Forest Recreation Reservations (see "Reservations" earlier in the chapter), and one is wheelchair-accessible. You'll find shade, water, fire-ring grills, picnic tables, trash cans and vault toilets. And you'll find a pay telephone. Lonesomehurst is open from Memorial Day to mid-September.

Beaver Creek Campground

**$$ • U.S. Hwy. 287, Quake Lake, Mont.
• (406) 646-7369**

This quiet Forest Service campground overlooks the Madison River and Quake Lake (see our Attractions chapter). Moose, deer, elk, osprey, black bear and bald eagles frequent Beaver Creek campground, which is tucked into a wooded aspen and pine forest next to Beaver Creek. Open from June 10 until Labor Day, this campground has 64 sites with picnic tables and fire rings. Eighteen of the sites can be reserved through the National Forest Recreation Reservations (see "Reservations" earlier in the chapter). Site No. 13 in Loop C is wheelchair-accessible with a toilet. The rest are available on a first-come, first-served basis. You'll find drinking water here as well as vault toilets and paved loops, but no hookups. The campground is near popular hiking trails and is a mile from the Quake Lake boat ramp. The campground has a 32-foot RV limit.

Lionshead Resort

**$$$$ • U.S. Hwy. 20, 7 mi. west of West
Yellowstone, Mont. • (406) 646-9584,
summer (406) 646-7662**

In the summer, this hopping, happening year-round RV park 8 miles west of Yellowstone National Park turns into a mini-town. Set up to serve Yellowstone visitors, this little burg has 153 RV spaces, 18 tent sites and enough other amenities so that you can get out of your car and forget about errands at the end of the day.

Alice's Restaurant and Lounge, right in the middle of it all, serves breakfast, lunch and dinner. A Super 8 Motel at the edge of the RV Park has 44 guest rooms for those in your party who might prefer a motel room to camping. The Lionshead has a volleyball net, a playground, horseshoe pits and a pavilion for large groups. The Lionshead also has a gift store, a gas station, a grocery store and a guest laundry.

Wagon Wheel Campground and Cabins

**$$$, no credit cards • 408 Gibbon Ave.,
West Yellowstone, Mont. • (406) 646-7872**

Spic and span and neat as a pin! What this RV park and campground lacks in space, it makes up for in charm and attention to detail. RV spaces, tucked between mature conifers, are clustered near the (sparkling clean) restrooms, laundry and a game room. Tent sites, designated by numbered wagon wheels in the nooks and crannies of their own special yard, are equally snug. Older, well-maintained log cabins range from a heavenly honeymoon cabin to a three-bedroom, two-story cabin with a fireplace and Western decor. The owners also rent a heated sheep wagon by the night.

The Wagon Wheel is open only during the summer months.

Yellowstone Grizzly RV Park

**$$$$ • 210 S. Electric St., West
Yellowstone, Mont. • (406) 646-4466**

Mapped out, laid out, lined up — this new (in 1996) state-of-the-art RV park makes up for its lack of mature trees (the owners have planted 80 young conifers and deciduous trees) with carpetlike grass and an impressive array of amenities. The Grizzly RV Park, rimmed by a jackleg fence at the south edge of town, offers cable TV hookups, a convenience store, a game room, a groceries and gifts shop, squeaky-clean showers, a laundry, a dump station and even telephone hookups at some sites. Tenters will find soft sleeping on the lush lawn, and large groups, like Scout troops or families here for reunions, can cluster on one large island of grass. Asphalt roads lead to the 152 RV sites. Grizzly RV has 30 pull-through spaces and 16 individual tent sites.

Gardiner, Montana

Canyon Campground
No charge • U.S. Hwy. 89, Gardiner, Mont. • (406) 848-7375

East of U.S. Highway 89 about 18 miles north of Gardiner, cute little Canyon Campground has 12 units hidden behind big boulders and juniper trees at the base of a hill in Yankee Jim Canyon. Across the highway is the Yellowstone River. Despite the steep banks and poor access, quite a few people fish here. Yankee Jim Canyon is named after Jim George, who operated the first toll road into Yellowstone Park. On the other side of the Yellowstone River you can see traces of the old toll road as well as the old railroad bed and the Yellowstone Trail, the first automobile route into the Park. Other than a toilet, there are no services at this year-round campground. The vehicle length limit is 48 feet.

Timber Creek Campground
No charge • Jardine Rd., Gardiner, Mont. • (406) 848-7375

An open meadow splashed with wildflowers, a little creek, a lodgepole and Douglas fir forest and isolation — what more could you want? Open from June 15 through October 31, Timber Creek campground is about 9 miles northeast of Gardiner and 4 miles north of Jardine. You won't find water here so bring your own. The RV limit at Timber Creek is 48 feet.

Bear Creek Campground
No charge • Jardine Rd., Gardiner, Mont. • (406) 848-7375

Step out of your camper and fall into Bear Creek from one of five or six informal spaces next to the creek in this little campground northeast of Gardiner on the Jardine Road. We're exaggerating, of course, but several camping spaces are close to the creek. Hidden in a forest of spruce, Douglas fir and lodgepole, Bear Creek campground is 6 miles northeast

of Jardine and offers only scenic wonders and fair brook trout fishing in Bear Creek. You'll find enough room here for about 10 parties to squeeze in, but the RV limit is shorter than most at 34 feet.

Rocky Mountain RV Camp
$$$ • 14 Jardine Rd., Gardiner, Mont. • (406) 848-7251

If you're hot, tired and dusty, the neon "CAMP" sign of the Rocky Mountain RV Camp will look mighty welcome. Perched on a bluff overlooking Gardiner and Yellowstone Park, this campground offers 50 RV sites and 21 tent spaces with grass. This is a good spot for an overnight rest or for a base camp while you explore the Park. If it's a shower you're after, get up early to beat the crowd. You'll find the ladies' restroom packed with women showering themselves and their children, drying their hair and applying makeup at the sinks. Rocky Mountain has a coin-operated laundry (it's open to the public) and a store that carries an assortment of food and camping supplies. This RV Park has a dump station, and you can unload your garbage (just toss it into the back of the 1948 Dodge dump truck parked by the office). There is an afterhours registration box by the office door so latecomers can slip into the campground in the wee hours of the night. Rocky Mountain RV Camp is open May 1 to November 1.

Eagle Creek Campground
$ • Jardine Rd., Gardiner, Mont. • (406) 848-7375

If a day in the Park or on the road has you yearning for the soothing sound of a creek and the sweet smell of wild grass, head straight for the "CAMP" sign of the Rocky Mountain RV Camp, but don't turn in. Instead, bear to the left past the RV Camp entrance and drive north about 3 miles (the road leads to Jardine, a tiny mining town about 5 miles north of Gardiner) until you see a Forest Service sign on the left that reads, "Eagle Creek Campground." Turn left, slow down and cruise through this campground from top to bottom before choosing your home for the night. At the top, you'll find tent spaces tucked into the trees. At the bottom you'll find open spaces with mowed grass. To the east are a corral and plenty of room to pull through with a fifth-wheeler. No designated campsites, no signs, no campground host. And don't be surprised if an elk or two join you for breakfast. Bring your own water, pack out your garbage and don't count on finding firewood here. There is a toilet.

Silver Gate/Cooke City, Montana

Colter Campground
$ • U.S. Hwy. 212, Cooke City, Mont.
• (406) 848-7375

This is one of the few campgrounds you'll find that has a scenic view in this neck of the woods. Burned in the 1988 Yellowstone Fire (see the Close-up in our History chapter), the Colter Campground is thick with wildflowers and new young trees growing up through the rubble left by the fire. Open from mid-July until mid-September, the 23 sites in this campground fill quickly each summer day with overflow campers from Yellowstone Park 3 miles to the west. While you'll find few trees to screen your view of other campers at Colter, you will find there's plenty of space between each campsite. The campground has several toilets and drinking water. The RV length limit is 48 feet.

Soda Butte Campground
$ • U.S. Hwy. 212, Cooke City, Mont.
• (406) 848-7375

Big bear-paw signs warn visitors they're in grizzly country at Soda Butte, a popular staging campground for visitors to the Park. It is also the first campground to fill with overflow campers from Yellowstone Park's northeast entrance. Hidden among the conifers, dawn breaks slowly and night comes quickly. The cold nights (don't be surprised if it snows on July 4 or August 1) and the forest canopy make Soda Butte a good place to catch up on sleep. But, oh, it's hard to get up to the (usually) cold mornings here. You'll find water and trash pickup here. The RV limit is 48 feet, and there are 21 sites.

Grand Teton National Park

Grand Teton Park contains five campgrounds operated by the Park Service and two concessionaire-operated trailer parks. Gros Ventre, Jenny Lake, Signal Mountain, Colter Bay and Lizard Creek do not accept reservations. In summer, most fill by midafternoon. The most popular campgrounds, Jenny Lake and Signal Mountain, generally fill before 10 AM. Reservations are allowed at Colter Bay and Flagg Ranch trailer villages. These two campgrounds are also the only camping facilities in or, in Flagg Ranch's case, near, Grand Teton Park that offer full hookups.

Just as in Yellowstone Park, all Park campgrounds supply basic amenities: water, trash disposal, picnic tables, grills and flush or pit toilets. All have outdoor amphitheaters to house the regular naturalist-ranger evening presentations. All but Gros Ventre and Lizard Creek are close to concessionaire services like stores and cafes. Tenters may find they prefer Jenny Lake, where no RVs are allowed (no RVs means no noisy generators), or Lizard Creek, where you'll find walk-in sites, which offer more privacy and seclusion than is typical in busy campgrounds.

All campgrounds ask that you take seriously the bear-care restrictions explained previously. It's easy to make the mistake of feeling that wilderness is nowhere near. After all, you're surrounded by satellite dishes on big RVs, running children and tents of every size, shape and color. But wilderness is just past your nose, and the animals do amble through — despite the human zoo. We've seen it happen.

Jenny Lake Campground
$$ • Jenny Lake Loop at Jenny Lake

Popular and small, this tent-only campground often fills by 8 AM. The 49 sites are scattered among mixed aspens and pine. Small hills, jumbled boulders and dense brush provide privacy. A few sites, designated for hikers and bikers who don't have secure vehicles for food storage, are equipped with bear boxes. The Jenny Lake area is frequently visited by bears. Campground amenities include vault toilets, water and bear-proof dumpsters. A campground host is on-site. As with other Park Service campgrounds here, sites are not reserveable. Jenny Lake Campground is open by mid- to late May and closes in late September.

Lizard Creek Campground

$$ • U.S. Hwy. 89 at the top of Jackson Lake

Lizard Creek, with its 60 sites on Jackson Lake's north shore, is our favorite Park campground. The lodgepole forest shelters both conventional campsites and several walk-in sites. Walk-in sites require that you park out on the road and then take a short trail (30 feet to 30 yards) to your secluded, private site. Campground amenities are basic: water, picnic tables, dumpsters and vault toilets. Nearest services are about 10 miles south at Colter Bay or 8 miles north at Flagg Ranch. Lizard Creek opens in mid-June and closes in early September.

Signal Mountain Campground

$$ • Teton Park Rd. on south shore of Jackson Lake • (307) 739-3300

Views of Jackson Lake make some of Signal Mountain's 86 sites particularly pleasant. Others, tucked into the more densely forested south end of the campground, are pleasantly secluded in feel. Or, if you like sunny and open, camp in the sites on the thinly treed hill stretching away from the lake. In short, Signal Mountain has a site to match almost every camper's tastes.

RVers may find most sites a bit small. Campground amenities are basic. You'll have access to drinking water, dumpsters and vault toilets; a picnic table and grill are at your site. You also have access to the services of adjacent Signal Mountain Lodge: a restaurant and bar, gift shop, gas station and convenience store. There is a trailer dumping station here. This campground opens in late May and closes in early October.

Colter Bay Campground

$$ • U.S. Hwy. 89 on east shore of Jackson Lake

Colter Bay is the busiest service area in the Park. Part of the cause of all this traffic is the 310-site Park Service campground (second-largest in the Park) combined with the 112-site, concessionaire-operated Colter Bay Trailer Village. The campground offers standard Park amenities such as drinking water, picnic tables, dumpsters, grills and vault toilets. Some sites are for hikers/bikers only.

Some loops are tent-only, with no generator operation allowed.

Nearby Colter Village offers a gas station, showers, laundry facilities, trailer dumping and propane. There's a marina here, two restaurants, gift shops, a visitor center and a Grand Teton Lodge Company activity center to hook you up with horseback riding, lake cruises, raft trips and more. Much of the campground is so heavily treed that, even though 12,600-foot Mount Moran looms nearly at your shoulder, you only catch fragmented glimpses of it. Colter Bay Campground opens in late May and closes in late September.

Colter Bay RV Park

$$$$ • U.S. Hwy. 89 on east shore of Jackson Lake • (307) 543-2811, (800) 628-9988

This concessionaire-operated RV park is the only campground actually inside Grand Teton Park offering full hookups. Your other alternative, Flagg Ranch campground, is sandwiched between Yellowstone and Grand Teton parks. Expect to make your reservations up to a year in advance. All 112 sites have full hookups; no tents or open fires are allowed. Flush toilets are available in the campground, but you'll take your showers in the public facility for an additional $2. The best thing about this campground is its layout: Sites are clustered six to a loop so that you only have a few neighbors and a few cars driving by your site.

Everything's within walking distance at Colter Bay, including the gas station, showers, laundry facilities and a trailer dump. The park has a marina, two restaurants, gift shops, a visitors center and a Grand Teton Lodge Company activity center to entice you into horseback riding, lake cruises, raft trips and more. Security personnel drive through several times a night. Other likely visitors include deer, moose and bison. Bears are seen here as well, but less often than in other Park campgrounds. The RV park opens in late May and generally closes around the end of September.

Gros Ventre Campground

$$ • Gros Ventre River Rd. near Kelly

Sprawling through the cottonwoods in the riverbottom near the Gros Ventre River, this 360-site campground offers shady, spacious sites for RVers and tenters. It is also the National Park Service campground that opens earliest in the season (beginning of May), closes last (mid-October) and generally doesn't fill until evening, if then. Campsites have picnic tables and fire grates; some have gravel tent pads. Water, bear-proof dumpsters and flush toilets are available. Rangers say bears wander through the campground regularly, as many as three in one week last summer. Proper disposal and storage of food is important. A ranger staffs the tiny visitors center at the campground entrance.

Flagg Ranch Resort
$$$$ • U.S. Hwy. 89, John D. Rockefeller Jr. Memorial Pky.
• (307) 543-2861, (800) 443-2311

Although tent camping is allowed here, most folks are in RVs. Sites are open and sunny; each has a picnic table and fire grate. Clumps of lodgepole pine provide shade. All 77 sites have full hookups. The campground also has two shower facilities and a 24-hour laundry. Three minutes' walk from your site is Flagg Ranch lodge, with its restaurant, bar, convenience store, gas station and gift shop. At the end of the long parking lot is a small Park Service information center. The ranger here can point you to great area hikes. Flagg Ranch Resort offers a range of activities, including horseback riding and rafting. The campground opens in early June and closes at the end of September. The resort itself is open from June to mid-October and from late December to mid-March (see our Guest Ranches, Resorts and Lodges chapter).

Jackson Hole

Atherton Creek Campground
$ • Gros Ventre River Rd. at Lower Slide Lake • (307) 739-5400

This 13-site campground, choked with wild rose and sage and dotted with aspen and cottonwood, is often quiet when the nearby national parks are crammed with folks. The campground has drinking water and dumpsters. Some sites have paved pads for trailers and RVs and several offer views of pretty Lower Slide Lake. Campground roads are paved, as

is the boat ramp. The campground is open from early June until late October. Some sites are reserveable.

Red Hills and Crystal Creek Campgrounds
$ • Gros Ventre River Rd. at Crystal Creek • (307) 739-5400

Four and 5 miles, respectively, beyond Atherton Creek Campground lie these tiny campgrounds. Together they have 11 sites. What your white-knuckled perseverance on that jouncing, rocky dirt road bought you was peace and quiet: You may have the campground to yourself. You certainly won't see a lot of traffic going by. Both campgrounds offer drinking water, pit toilets and dumpsters. Trailers and RVs are not recommended, and no sites are reserveable. The campgrounds are open from early June until the end of October, which makes them and the Atherton Creek facility all popular with hunters. That late in the hunting season, the other Jackson Ranger District campgrounds are closed.

Pacific Creek Campground
No charge • Pacific Creek Rd. at wilderness boundary • (307) 739-5400

Head out of Grand Teton National Park on a nondescript little road called Pacific Creek that winds toward the Teton Wilderness and you'll end up at this primitive little campground on the edge of wild country. Pacific Creek Campground is often used by horsepackers heading into the wilderness. It has only six sites, drinking water and dumpsters. Sites are not reserveable, but we'd be surprised if you have a problem finding a tent spot here. Bear boxes are provided, and it's recommended you use them: You're definitely in the bears' backyard. Pacific Creek Campground is open from mid-June until late September.

Grand Teton Park KOA
$$$$ • U.S. Hwy. 26, Moran, Wyo.
• (307) 733-1980

Only six miles from Grand Teton Park, sprawling through the willow bottoms around the Buffalo Fork River, this year-round KOA offers a convenient alternative to national park camping. Remember that campsites in Grand Teton Park can't be reserved — but these can.

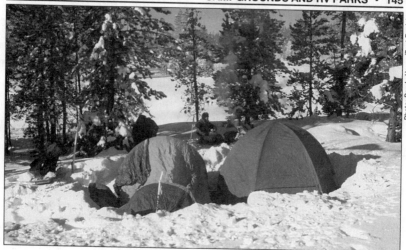

Photo: Randy Hayes/Post Register

Winter camping can be fun — just know your limits.

Most sites offer views of the Tetons. This KOA has a game room, an outdoor hot tub, a laundry, clean showers and a playground. Sites are generally open and sunny. Many are pull-throughs. All have picnic tables and grills. The attached store sells gas, firewood, fishing tackle, ice and groceries; it also rents videos. Winter visitors can rent snowmobiles, purchased new every year, with which to explore Buffalo Fork Valley, Togwotee Pass and even Yellowstone Park. In summer, guests can arrange whitewater and scenic Snake River floats or rent bicycles.

Wagon Wheel RV Park
$$$$ • 435 Cache, Jackson, Wyo.
• (307) 733-2357, (800) 323-9279

Part of the Wagon Wheel Village complex with its coin-operated laundry, restaurant, saloon and liquor store, gift shop and motel, the Wagon Wheel RV Park nevertheless offers an almost secluded feeling for an in-town facility. Flat Creek, wide and slow, meanders across the back of the grassy open campground (see our Kidstuff chapter for the goods on Flat Creek fishing). Busy Cache Street, which borders the complex, is out of view of most sites. The campground is small, with only 28 RV sites, and half of those are usually used by long-term residents and Wagon Wheel employees. The upshot for you is that you'll feel more like you've joined a small rural village than like you're camping in a campground smack in the middle of town. A bathhouse and campground manager are on-site. Jackson Hole's visitors center is directly across Cache Street.

Virginian RV Resort
$$$$ • 750 W. Broadway, Jackson, Wyo.
• (800) 321-6982 summer,
(800) 262-4999 winter

This modern RV park offers 103 full-hookup sites with cable TV. Sixty-eight are pull-throughs. A bit of thoughtful landscaping has placed a small aspen, red plum or evergreen at nearly every site. Sites also have picnic tables and grills. A Laundromat and bathhouse facility can be found at the center of the Park; nearby Virginian Lodge allows campers to use its swimming pool and hot tub. This Good Sam- and AAA-approved park closes down sometime in October and reopens in early May. It does not allow tent camping.

Hoback Campground
$$ • U.S. Hwy. 189 near Hoback Junction, Wyo. • (307) 739-5400

The nicest of these 14 sites are near the Hoback River where the water's rush can muffle road sounds. The campground road is paved as are parking pads; this makes Hoback

Dutch-oven Cooking

So, you and your family are camping in Yellowstone Country and you want to rough it without sacrificing scrumptious, easy-to-make food such as brownies or pot roast, homemade bread or biscuits. That doesn't mean you have to buy a camper, a travel trailer or a fancy whatchamacallit with an oven. Instead, we recommend you pack a Dutch oven or two (one for the entree and one for dessert). The only hard thing about Dutch oven cooking is wondering if you can do it. Once you try this old-fashioned but *easy* form of cooking, we're betting you'll make a special place for Dutch oven cooking on your patio back home.

Anything you can bake in an oven (or cook in a crock pot) you can cook in a Dutch oven with just a little bit — a very little bit — of practice. To get you on your way, we've given you a couple of recipes for easy, delicious one-pot dishes. Feel free to bring along your own favorite recipes. (If you're like us, you'll carry them in your head.)

But first, let's go over the ways to control the heat on your Dutch oven so it cooks perfectly every time. Because you may not always be in a place where you can build a campfire, we'll tell you how to cook with charcoal briquets. Feel free, though, to use a wood fire wherever possible.

To bake in a 12-inch Dutch oven you will need:

At least one Dutch oven
A small shovel
A pair of channel-lock pliers to lift off the lid and to pick up the pot by its wire handle
A pair of gloves (some people like to use them)
Charcoal briquets
A briquet starter

All you need to do is fire up those briquets — about 30 of them — then sit back and relax. Some folks like to cook slowly and carefully, and that's probably a good idea for a beginner. We like to go for the gusto. If you'd rather cook slowly, cut back the number of briquets to about 20.

For the best results, you should find a way to heat the Dutch oven lid over the briquets while they're on their way to becoming red hot. If your environment prohibits this, don't worry. Once the briquets are hot, just pour them on top of your Dutch oven, spread them over the lid and let the lid heat up. When the lid is hot, take about one-third of the coals from the top of your oven and evenly distribute them on the ground within the circumference of your Dutch oven. Place the Dutch oven over the coals and evenly distribute the remaining coals on the lid. Depending on what you're cooking and how close it is to the lid, you'll need to check your dish from time to time, especially after the first 15 minutes. If you sense it is getting too hot, lift your Dutch oven up off the coals and adjust them accordingly. Do the same with the coals on the lid (you're less apt to burn dishes from the top because heat rises).

Timing your cooking is fairly easy — just follow your nose. When you can smell it, it's done or close to it. Adjust the number of briquets up or down according to the size of your Dutch oven. Also, if you're using more than one Dutch oven, stack them one on top of the other, using fewer coals for the lids of the bottom ovens.

Birthday Casserole

This meal is hard to beat for a no-mess, no-fuss, plate-licking-good dinner. You'll need:

1 small cutting board
A paring knife

— continued on next page

4 large potatoes
5 large carrots
1 large onion
1½ pounds hamburger
1 large can tomatoes
Salt and pepper
1 12-inch greased Dutch oven
Slice and stack vegetables and meat in the order listed. Salt and pepper to taste. Bake about 1½ hours in medium-hot oven.

Peach Cobbler

Okay, so this is too easy to be good, you say. If you're traveling light and don't want to cart along all the fixings for a real cobbler crust, this peach cobbler will do in a pinch, especially if you have a batch of hungry kids. You will need:
2 boxes of yellow or white cake mix
2 large cans of peaches
Pour peaches and cake mixes into a greased Dutch oven and stir if you like. Bake at medium heat for about 1 hour.

Dutch-oven cooking is a great way to enjoy hearty, one-pot meals while camping.

Kitchen Sink Breakfast Casserole
Also known as: Gladys's Breakfast Casserole

For those mornings when everyone feels like eating a real meal instead of munching on granola or bagels and cream cheese, this great-tasting casserole fills the bill. It's deliciously filling, and prepared the night before. If you're like us, use this recipe as a good start and make your own creation using the leftovers that have been cluttering your cooler.
At least eight slices of bread (preferably French), cubed
½-pound grated cheese (your choice)
3 cups milk
6 eggs, beaten
¾-teaspoon dry mustard, a small squirt of regular mustard or a half cup of salsa
1 teaspoon salt
½-pound sausage or other cooked meat.
The night before: Mix eggs and milk in bowl. Brown sausage, then put the meat into egg mixture. Add grated cheese and the rest of the ingredients to the egg mixture. Put the bread on the bottom of the Dutch oven, cover with the egg mixture, place the lid on the Dutch oven, put it into the car away from bears and let set overnight. Bake at medium heat about 45 minutes. Serves 4.

---

unusual among area Forest Service campgrounds. Mosquitoes can be a problem in July, but winged biting things taper off as summer progresses. Among the amenities are bundled firewood for sale from the campground host, drinking water, dumpsters, picnic tables and grills. Some sites are reserveable; the campground opens in early June and closes in mid-September. Picnicking is pleasant here, but the host will charge non-campers $5.

Lone Eagle Resort
$$$$ • U.S. Hwy. 89 near Hoback Junction, Wyo. • (307) 733-1090, (800) 321-3800
Drive under the totem pole arch and down a

dirt road lined with buck and rail fence. Just after you cross the Hoback River on a narrow bridge, you'll enter civilization in the middle of wilderness: an RV and cabin resort. The grounds are immaculate and lit by lantern at night. Amenities include basketball and volleyball courts, an outdoor swimming pool, hot tubs, snack shop and convenience store, gift shop and casting pond (they're pretty serious about catch-and-release here — keep your fish and you pay $15). You could picnic in the tiled shower rooms, they're so clean. Lone Eagle offers three-day and overnight visits. Each includes whitewater fun on the Snake River and most meals prepared by staff. The resort closes down in early October and reopens the first of May. Also see our Resorts, Guest Ranches and Lodges chapter.

Granite Creek Campground
$$ • Granite Creek Rd. off U.S. Hwy. 191 • (307) 739-5400

A short drive from Granite Creek Hot Springs, this Forest Service campground in the Jackson Ranger District offers generously large sites in an open, sunny meadow and others tucked into groves of spruce and fir. Busy Granite Creek bustles by the edge of the campground, nearly at the base of the dramatic pinnacle folks call The Open Door (it takes a bit of imagination to see the door). Vault and flush toilets, drinking water and garbage disposal are available. Some pull-through sites are available for RVers. Best of all, that 10 miles of jouncing road you drove down after you turned off U.S. Highway 191 keeps many out. Even on summer weekends, this campground often doesn't fill. However, sites are reserveable, and it's not a bad idea to reserve yours to be sure.

Lazy J Corral RV Park
$$$ • 10755 S. U.S. Hwy. 89, Hoback Junction, Wyo. • (307) 733-1554

One of the least-expensive full-hookup RV parks in the area, Rod and Candy Huskey's place is also small, with only 12 to 14 smaller sites available for passers-through. Amenities, which Rod will describe if you call, are showers, laundry and several pull-throughs. He'll also tell you that his park, located right at Hoback Junction on the major thoroughfare, is convenient to all area services. The perk he may forget to mention is himself: Rod Huskey is from an old local family of artisans and business people. Rod is a jeweler; he also designs antler chandeliers. We think the best reason to stay at this sunny little RV park is so you can see his work and pester him into telling you about it.

Snake River Park KOA
$$$$ • 9705 S. U.S. Hwy. 89, Hoback Junction, Wyo. • (307) 733-7078, (800) 562-1878

The cabins face the Snake River. A grassy picnic area overlooks the pretty river, too, at the top of a wide trail leading from the bench on which most of the campground is built to the shore. Willow, aspen and fir dot the campground, creating pleasant shade. RV sites are up on the bench, but the tent sites get the best spots: along shady, rollicking Horse Creek and on the sandy bank of the Snake. More tent sites are on the bench, closer to restroom facilities. Also available are three canvas teepees pitched over wooden platforms. Families with kids love to stay in these. Campground amenities include showers, a small convenience store with a breakfast bar, a lounge with a pool table and a TV, a laundry room and a playground. The campground even has its own whitewater rafting company, which can load you up and take you through 8 miles of splashy fun through Alpine Canyon.

Astoria Hot Springs
$$$$ • U.S. Hwy. 89, Hoback Junction, Wyo. • (307) 733-2659

Full-hookup, pull-through RV camping is on

INSIDERS' TIP

Our streams and rivers are lovely and clear, but don't be tempted to drink from them without treating or boiling the water. No surface water is safe unless you're looking at the place it bubbles from the ground. Giardia, a particularly nasty microorganism that likes to set up housekeeping in your intestines and causes explosive diarrhea, is not uncommon.

a long grassy bench partly screened by cottonwoods from the highway beyond the Snake River. This campground is the only man-made thing on this side of the river. Tent sites are below the bench on a sandy area just above the river. The best sites are at the water's edge. All told there are more than 100. Up on the bench, you'll enjoy the playground and picnic area, the basketball court and, of course, the hot springs pool (more on this in the Attractions chapter). Showers, a laundry facility, a wading pool, horseshoes and sand volleyball are also available. The campground has a tiny snack bar. Sites are reserveable; the pool and campground close in September and reopen in May.

Cabin Creek Campground
$$ • U.S. Hwy. 89 between Hoback Junction and Alpine, Wyo.
• (307) 739-5400

It costs $5 to stop here and picnic. Facilities include pit toilets, barbecue grills and picnic tables at each site. No water is available. U.S. Highway 89 runs through a steep-sided, narrow river canyon here, so this campground and the next three are all close to the highway, but heavy forest screens the road from sight. Cabin Creek Campground is on a high bench overlooking the river. Sites are large, shady and private. The best ones sit right at the edge of the bench, with lovely views of the Snake River. Some of the 10 sites in this Jackson Ranger District campground are pull-throughs, and all sites at this campground are reserveable. The campground opens in late May and closes in mid-September.

Elbow Campground
$$ • U.S. Hwy. 89 between Hoback Junction and Alpine, Wyo.
• (307) 739-5400

The picnic area is lovely — a low sandy bar beside the Snake. It costs $5 to park here and eat your sandwich. Some sites are shaded by massive cottonwood trees; from your picnic table you can watch the river sweep past, clear and quiet, over rounded river rock. The campground is popular with boaters who drive in from Salt Lake City or Idaho Falls to float the upper Snake's whitewater stretch at Alpine Canyon. It's rare to find an open site here on weekends. The campground consists of nine sites, some of which are pull-throughs. Each has a picnic table and grill. The campground has an on-site host, pit toilets, dumpsters and drinking water. Some sites are shaded by massive fir trees. All are close to U.S. Highway 89, but tucked below it so you won't be awakened by headlights shining in your camper windows at night. Elbow opens in mid-June and closes in mid-September.

East Table Creek Campground
$$ • U.S. Hwy. 89 between Hoback Junction and Alpine, Wyo.
• (307) 739-5400

Of the four campgrounds in this area, East Table is our favorite. It's also the favorite of local rafters, so if you find an empty spot here on a summer weekend, be very, very glad. Each of the campground's 18 sites have picnic tables and grills. Sites are spacious, with some privacy. Drinking water, dumpsters and vault toilets are available. The campground stretches away from the road on a wide bench with a short access road, so the sites are farther from the highway than others in this canyon. East Table Creek winds across the bench. A small amphitheater hosts evening programs during summer weekends. Programs in 1997 often involved river management issues, since Jackson Ranger District is working with boaters right now to develop new guidelines and regulations for the heavily used upper Snake. Sites in East Table Creek Campground are reserveable; the campground opens in early June and closes in mid-September.

Station Creek Campground
$$ • U.S. Hwy. 89 between Hoback Junction and Alpine, Wyo.
• (307) 739-5400

In this narrow, steep river canyon it's hard to get very far from U.S. Highway 89 — there's nowhere to go. But Station Creek Campground is almost far enough. You can still hear the traffic vaguely, but you can't see it. The bench on which the 12 sites are scattered is wide and heavily forested. Sites are generous and well-shaded; some have tent pads. Other amenities include picnic tables, vault toilets, dumpsters and grills. A campground host is on-site. Station Creek opens in mid-June and closes in mid-September. Sites are reservable.

Teton Village KOA

$$$$ • 2780 N. Moose-Wilson Rd., Wilson, Wyo. • (307) 733-5354

Here you'll discover all the advantages of a KOA campground — clean facilities, full trailer hookups and pull-throughs, pleasant grounds, showers — with some nice surprises. This campground couldn't be in a more convenient spot. The Village Road (a.k.a. Moose-Wilson Road) shoots straight up through the ski mecca of Teton Village and into Grand Teton Park in 20 minutes, bypassing Jackson. (No RVs are allowed into the Park on this narrow road, though.)

Sample Jackson's summer bustle as you like; avoid it when you wish. Several restaurants serve great meals within a few miles in either direction (see our Restaurants chapter). Jackson is 6 miles away. Another pleasant surprise involves shade, plenty of it. Willows and shrubs splash cool shadows onto the lawn in almost every one of the 160-odd sites. And the long, thin shape of the campground means that most campers are so far from the busy road they can forget it's there.

Farthest toward the back are the Kamping Kabins, KOA's standard, economical bring-your-own-blankets cabins. Cabins sleep four to six. Teton Village KOA provides laundry facilities and a game room for its guests, who would be wise in summer to make a reservation, especially if looking for an RV hookup. The campground is open May through mid-September.

Surrounding Areas

Eastern Idaho

Idaho Falls, Idaho, Area

Idaho Falls KOA Kampground

$$$$ • 1440 Lindsay Blvd., Idaho Falls, Idaho • (208) 523-3362

This pleasant RV park was well-designed to screen Idaho Falls from view with walls of trees. You won't know you're in town; you probably will have a shaded site. About one-third of the more than 180 sites have full hookups; all have picnic tables and grills.

Special features of this KOA include its seasonally open swimming pool and miniature golf course, a year-round outdoor hot tub, showers, a playground, a game room and a store. In summer you can also enjoy nightly outdoor movies and barbecues. The campground is open year-round, a rarity around here.

Juniper Campground

$$ • 226 Meadowcreek Rd. at Ririe Reservoir, Ririe, Idaho • (208) 538-7443

This pretty little campground was a well-kept secret until recently, but its popularity is rising. Use has risen more than 400 percent in the last few years. Nevertheless, you can still expect to drive in and find an available site. Even at its busiest, Juniper still manages to seem quiet and peaceful. Sites are scattered among low, brushy juniper trees, some right at the edge of a cliff overlooking Ririe Reservoir.

Increased use has probably been spurred by recent improvements to the 21-year-old campground. Grass and junipers are watered so they're green and inviting. All but four of the 49 sites were recently upgraded to full hookups. There are showers, flush toilets and a new pavilion. Horseshoe pits, volleyball courts and a playground are planned. Also look for the 50 new boat moorings available near the boat ramp. Plans for the future include a small cafe and convenience store. Juniper is managed by Bonneville County (it was built and once was operated by the Bureau of Reclamation).

Months of operation are April through September, depending on weather. Golden Eagle Pass holders receive a discount here.

Jefferson County Lake Recreation Area

$ • U.S. Hwy. 20 near Rigby, Idaho • (208) 745-7756

Rumor has it that highway builders originally created Jefferson County Lake — by accident. Gravel mined to build roads eventually created a hole so deep it started to fill from below. You'll be pleased by the result. The recreation area includes a 1.25-mile path around the lake, shaded picnic and camping areas, picnic tables (scattered about but not in campsites), drinking water, showers and flush toilets. The charm of the campground is not in its amenities, though, but in that clear cool water and those tangled trees. When you call the number listed above, you're reaching not the campground but Jefferson County Clerk and Recorder's Office. They can take your reservation after January 1 for the current year. The campground opens in April and closes early in October, depending on weather.

Rexburg, Idaho, Area

Rainbow Lake & RV Park
$$, no credit cards • 2245 S. 2000 W., Rexburg, Idaho • (208) 356-3681

What makes Rainbow Lake a pleasant stop is not its convenience, although the man-made lake with 60-site campground on its treeless shore sits immediately adjacent to U.S. Highway 20, 1.5 miles from Rexburg. It's the fishing. The main lake is stocked and its fishing potential assured by the requirement that you catch and release and fly fish only. In fact, the odds of hooking into 20-inch plus rainbows are so high here that local anglers pony up $200 for season passes at Rainbow Lake.

You can rent paddleboats and canoes to get farther out on the lake. A smaller pond is catch-and-keep for 35¢ per inch. No Idaho fishing license is required to fish either of these bodies of water. Rods are available for rent. If you're not on a fishing trip but would like a hassle-free chance to try your hand at one of the region's best-loved pastimes, you've come to the right place. Everything you need, from gear to a barbecue pit on which to cook your catch, is here. The campground is equipped with recently renovated restrooms and shower facilities. Sites are open and sunny with no privacy. The owners plan to add laundry facilities.

Ashton, Idaho

Aspen Acres Campground
$$$, no credit cards • 4179 E. 1100 N., Ashton, Idaho • (208) 652-3524

Imagine 18 holes of golf on an aspen-dotted course rolling across low hills. Grouse chuckle from the shelter of the trees; at one point you think you see a bear pad silently out of view. Imagine finishing your game, hopping in your golf cart and driving to your campsite nestled into a large aspen grove tangled with wildflowers. Heaven? No, Aspen Acres. Most campers are here to golf, and most have RVs, although Aspen Acres is happy to accommodate tent campers, too. The campground offers showers, laundry facilities and firewood to its guests. The 40 sites are semi-private, tucked into the trees and underbrush.

Many visitors stay for quite a while, so Aspen Acres offers weekly and monthly as well as daily rates. Mosquitoes can be a problem, particularly down in the campground, so bring your repellant. Campers and golfers are welcome from early May through late October. A small pro shop and snack bar is on premises. Golf carts are available for rent (see our Other Recreation chapter for more on the golf course).

Jessen's RV Park
$$$, no credit cards • 1146 S. 3400 E., Ashton, Idaho • (208) 652-3356

Neica and Jack Jessen have created the kind of RV park that ends up serving more seasonal residents than passers-through. Convenient at U.S. Highway 20 near Ashton, the Jessens have 13 sites with shade and full hookups as well as a scattering of others with water and electricity. Many of these abut the irrigation canal that winds through the property. Even in the intense, high-altitude sunshine of Ashton, the massive willow trees keep things cool and shaded. Fruit trees and flower beds are scattered across the 10-acre property. A white gazebo, a big patio and a fire circle encourage campers to leave their RVs and tents and visit together. Amenities include shower and laundry facilities and a pop machine. Tent campers set up on the lawn festival-style without specifically designated sites. Firewood is provided.

Other accommodations options on the property include two bed and breakfast guest rooms in the old farmhouse and several small cottages at one end of the RV park. (Please see our Bed and Breakfast Inns and our Hotels, Motels and Cabins chapters.) The campground is open from May to November, depending on weather. Reservations are recommended.

Warm River Campground

$$ • Fish Creek Rd. off Mesa Scenic Byway • (208) 558-7301

This pretty little campground is the most parklike of the national forest campgrounds in the area. Sites are tucked among the willows on a parklike, grassy bench along the Warm River. There are nine tent sites and 10 RV sites, plus a few day-use picnic sites. Not all are available for reservation, so although this campground is very popular with local anglers and tourists-in-the-know, stop by if it's not too late on a weekend afternoon. There still may be sites available. Warm River Campground is equipped with vault toilets and potable water. A campground host lives on premises and can sell you bundled firewood. The shallow, crystal-clear river running by the campground is stocked every two weeks through the summer with rainbow trout.

Cave Falls Campground

$ • Cave Falls Rd. at Bechler, Idaho • (208) 652-7442

This campground has 23 sites — none can be reserved — tucked along the banks of the Fall River, which runs fast and deep in its steep banks. During the wildflower season (June and July, usually) both the long road in and the campground itself are spangled with color. No RV hookups are available. You can almost throw a rock from your campsite into Yellowstone Park. Although you can drive about 2 miles past the campground into Yellowstone in order to view Cave Falls, a giant, river-wide step in the Fall River, access to the Park beyond the falls is nonmotorized. This makes the Bechler entrance to Yellowstone the quietest, most secluded of them all. Until a couple of years ago, the National Park Service didn't even charge admission to those who entered Yellowstone here. All Cave Falls Campground's sites have picnic tables and fire pits, access to water, vault toilets and bear-proof storage boxes. The campground is in grizzly habitat, so pay attention to how you handle food and pleasant-smelling objects.

Riverside Campground

$ • Off U.S. Hwy. 20 near Ashton, Idaho • (208) 558-7301

This Forest Service campground, located on the blue-ribbon fishing waters of the Henry's Fork, is extremely popular with the fly-fishing set. Most of the desirable riverside sites are reserveable; the rest are first-come, first-served. Sites not near the river are tucked into lodgepole forest. The campground has 55 overnight sites arranged in three loops and a day-use parking area for anglers at a small fee. Campsites have picnic tables and fire pits. The campground is also equipped with vault toilets and potable water. A campground host lives on the premises. Bundled firewood is available for sale. This campground is in the Island Park Ranger District

Island Park, Idaho

Snowy River Campground

$$ • 3502 N. U.S. 20, Last Chance in Island Park, Idaho • (208) 558-7112, (888) 797-3434

This conveniently located campground was brand new in 1997. The shower, bathroom and laundry facilities are bright and clean. Some of the 57 sites are pull-throughs. The on-site convenience and gift shop is another bonus, as is the fact that owners Tom and Marleen Bowers are happy to let you send e-mail from the office computer. Even better, the Bowers work with a local mechanic to provide on-site RV repair while you're off fishing the famed Henry's Fork, right across the road. This is not a campground for folks who need seclusion: Sites are close, and there is little vegetation to provide privacy. However, the big community fire pit, the volleyball court and horseshoe pits tend to draw people

INSIDERS' TIP

If weather permits, make sure you sleep outside your tent or RV at least one night: Our high-altitude, low-humidity air makes fine star watching, particularly in August when meteors streak across the sky every few minutes. (You'll probably wake up damp in the morning from dewfall.)

out of their campsites and RVs anyway. The Bowers are in the process of building five tight, winterized cabins, but as of 1997, Snowy River was not a year-round campground.

Ponds Lodge

$$ • 3757 N. U.S. Hwy. 20, Ponds Lodge in Island Park, Idaho • (208) 558-7221

Most of the private RV parks in the area are large and busy, but Ponds Lodge offers an alternative. Just an easy walk from the lodge's grocery store, gift shop, cafe and bar, the 50 sites are scattered among stands of pine and clusters of wildflowers. They are refreshingly unimproved — no concrete pads, no pavement — and spread out more than most. Guests who come here to fish will appreciate being a stone's throw from the Buffalo River and five minutes from both Island Park Reservoir and the famous fly-fishing waters of the Henry's Fork. All sites have full hookups and, since the lodge has no bathroom or shower facilities, must be occupied by self-contained RVs. Weekly, monthly and seasonal rates are also available. The RV park closes in winter, but cabins are available year-round (see our Hotels, Motels and Cabins chapter). The lodge itself was built in 1935 by Charles and Myna Ponds; it's a massive log structure with vaulted ceilings. The solemn faces of its builders peer down from one wall.

Mack's Inn Resort RV Park

$$$ •U.S. Hwy. 20 at Mack's Inn in Island Park, Idaho • (208) 558-7272

This 69-unit RV park is attached to busy Mack's Inn Resort with its store, boat rental, playground, dinner theater, Laundromat and a recently remodeled shower facility. Recreational features include sand volleyball, horseshoes and an outdoor basketball court. None of this stuff is up at the RV park, however, which gives you the best of both worlds: access to the bustle without having to sleep next to it. All sites have full hookups.

Mack's Inn is popular because of its great location: right on the bank of the Henry's Fork of the Snake, just 10 minutes' drive from lovely (and very fishable) Henry's Lake. It also sits at the junction of Big Springs Road, which shoots away from civilization toward the valley's most interesting scenic attraction, Big Springs, where a whole river pours up out of the ground.

Sawtelle Mountain Resort

$$$ • U.S. Hwy. 20 and Sawtelle Rd., Mack's Inn at Island Park, Idaho • (208) 558-9366, (800) 574-0404

Twenty-five miles from West Yellowstone at the top of Island Park, Sawtelle Mountain Resort is the newest facility in the valley. It has 60 RV sites, all with full hookups, and 20 tent sites. A newer shower facility and laundry sit on the bench near the RV sites. Most of the sites are tucked far enough from U.S. Highway 20 that traffic sounds are distant. Stands of young lodgepole provide pleasant breaks in the grounds. Ten RV sites remain open in winter. The rest close down in October and reopen in May. Other services are available year-round. Sawtelle operates a gift shop, motel (see our Hotels, Motels and Cabins chapter) and small grocery. They also offer horseback riding, chuckwagon dinners and small watercraft rentals.

Grand Mountain Studio RV Park

$$$ • 50 N. Big Springs Rd., Mack's Inn at Island Park, Idaho • (208) 558-7863 in summer, (208) 354-2329 in winter

Carl Nelson's RV park is our favorite kind: small with a residential feel. In fact, most of his sites are used by folks who set up housekeeping for the summer. He makes sure to keep a few available for short timers, though. Park amenities include 20-foot-long cement decks next to RV spaces. Blue spruce, mountain ash, aspen and brush wall in each site. There's a coin-operated laundry across the street. No showers or toilet facilities are available, so you must be self-contained to stay here. RV sites have full hookups. The last benefit of Carl's park is location: Unlike almost every other commercial RV park in Island Park, this one is away from the main road while still being extremely accessible. Grand Mountain is open May through October. Be sure you make a reservation. And don't forget to check out Carl's jewelry shop on the premises. He works in gold and elk ivory, among other materials.

Flatrock Campground

$ • U.S. Hwy. 20, Mack's Inn in Island Park, Idaho • (208) 558-7301

This Forest Service campground is conveniently located just off U.S. Highway 20, five minutes from Mack's Inn with its restaurants, boat ramp, convenience store and gas station. Many campsites have views of the placid, trout-filled Henry's Fork. More private sites are farther from the river on a wooded hillside. Running water and flush toilets are available. Each campsite has a picnic table and a fire pit. Sixteen sites are reserveable; however, none of these have river views. A campground host lives on-site. Convenience tends to make this a busy, busy campground. Like all Island Park Ranger District campgrounds, this one opens in late May and closes in mid-September.

West End Dispersed Campground
No charge • Forest Rd. 167 at Island Park Reservoir • (208) 558-7301

"Dispersed" means that there are no real sites here. You pitch your tent or park your trailer under the tree of your choice. West End is an open area by a bend of Island Park Reservoir. The Forest Service charges nothing, but it provides vault toilets and a boat dock for your convenience. You must bring in your water and pack out your trash. Just because this campground is primitive doesn't mean it's not popular. Boaters love the freedom and seclusion enough to drive in 9 miles over a slow, winding dirt road to get here. So while you won't see any passing traffic, you will have plenty of company in the summer boating and fishing months. Many of the campers here are staying not for a day or two but for as long as the Island Park Ranger District allows, which is 16 days. This campground, like all Island Park Ranger District campgrounds, opens in late May and closes in mid-September.

Coffee Pot Campground
$ • U.S. Hwy. 20 near Mack's Inn in Island Park, Idaho • (208) 558-7301

Perhaps because it's 1.5 miles off U.S. Highway 20 on a dirt road, this small Forest Service campground tends to be quieter than others in the area. The setting is idyllic; most sites are within hopping distance of the Henry's Fork that slips quietly by, clear and dimpled. Picnic tables, fire pits, drinking water, vault toilets and bear-proof dumpsters are provided. There are only 15 sites here, and none of them is reserveable. It's not a great place for a large camper vehicle or RV since there's not much

turnaround room. Anglers and tent campers will love it, though. Trails leave from here to travel both up and down river. Hike down to look at Upper Coffee Pot Rapid, one of the few places up here where the Henry's Fork gets to make noise. This campground, like all Island Park Ranger District campgrounds, opens in late May and closes in mid-September.

McCrea's Bridge Campground
$ • Yale/Kilgore Rd. off U.S. Hwy. 20 near Island Park, Idaho • (208) 558-7301

The 25-site campground is situated on a thinly wooded hillside slipping down to Island Park Reservoir. U.S. Highway 20 with its traffic noise is nearly 3 miles away. Each site has a picnic table and fire pit. Vault toilets and running water are provided, as is a campground host. As with nearly all Forest Service campgrounds in the area, bear-proof dumpsters are available. Just across the water, visible from your campsite, is a small cafe. The nearest gas station and convenience store is 2 miles away. Reservations can be made for sites in this campground, and it, like all Island Park Ranger District campgrounds, opens in late May and closes in mid-September.

Big Springs Campground
$ • Big Springs Rd. off U.S. Hwy. 20 near Island Park, Idaho • (208) 558-7301

Adjacent to two of the area's most interesting attractions, Big Springs and the Johnny Sack Cabin, is this small, wooded campground. It has 17 sites, each with tables and fire pits. You'll have access to running water and bear-proof dumpsters, vault toilets and group picnic areas. The nearest gas station is nearly 5 miles distant, at Mack's Inn. West Yellowstone is 25 miles away. There is pleasant hiking and great wildlife viewing in the immediate area. A mile away is the Big Springs boat ramp, which marks the beginning of a lovely float along the nation's first wilderness water trail. And, of course, you must feed the fish at Big Springs. The only thing you can't do, tempting as it might be, is catch them. Fishing is prohibited here. This campground, like all Island Park Ranger District campgrounds, opens in late May and closes in mid-September.

Henry's Lake State Park
$$$ • Off U.S. Hwy. 20, north of Island Park, Idaho • (208) 558-7532

Parklike and open, this busy campground with a boat ramp has recently gone to an all-reservation system for its sites. Sites are planted with young trees; each has a gravel pad, a fire circle and a picnic table. The nicest sites are spacious and nearly at the water's edge. Showers are available to campers and, for a fee, to day-users. Attendants are available during business hours to answer your questions and keep an eye on things. The campground is open from early June to late September.

Swan Valley, Idaho

South Fork Lodge
$$$ • 40 Conant Valley Loop, Swan Valley, Idaho • (208) 483-2112, (800) 483-2110

This angler's campground is bounded by U.S. Highway 26 on one side and the famous trout fishing waters of the South Fork Snake on the other. These folks have 24 full hookups for RVs plus 15 with water and electricity only; 16 sites are pull-throughs. Tent camping is also allowed; the tent sites are on open pasture within sight of the river. There's plenty of grass, but no trees. Showers are available. Also on the premises is a locals' favorite restaurant/bar, a small motel, a fly-fishing shop and a fishing guide service (see our Restaurants chapter and our Resorts, Guest Ranches and Lodges chapter). Just down the road is a Bureau of Land Management public boat ramp. The campground is open mid-May through late September, but the office is open year-round to answer questions and take reservations for campsites and fishing trips.

Palisades Creek Campground
$ • Palisades Creek Rd., Irwin, Idaho • (208) 523-1412

Swan Valley's most scenic little campground isn't easy to find, but it's worth the hunt. Eight

Photo: Dave Sipe

These works are prime examples of woodsculpting in Jackson Hole.

generously large sites cling to the bank of Palisades Creek, 2 miles from U.S. Highway 26 on a well-maintained gravel road. The drive to the campground is pretty, but remember to watch out for horseback riders. The area is popular for trail riding. Pit toilets, running water and bundled wood for a nominal fee are the only amenities, but if you like to feel as if you're in the backcountry even though you've just stepped from your camper, this is your place. Walk from your campsite to the trailhead for one of the nicest hikes in the area: up Palisades Creek to upper and lower Palisades Lakes (see our Hiking chapter). The first several miles of the hike are on wide, level trail, perfect for trail runners and horseback riders. This campground opens in late June and closes in early September.

Palisades RV Park
$$ • 3804 Swan Valley Hwy., Palisades, Idaho • (208) 483-4485

This is a smaller, backyard-style RV park,

INSIDERS' TIP

We've said it before, but this is important: A fed bear is a dead bear. Please treat bears and other wild creatures with respect by *not* allowing them to learn that they like human food. Your safety and theirs depend on it.

the kind that tends to attract long-term visitors (about one-fourth of the 16 sites are occupied by folks staying for a big chunk of the season). All sites have full hookup and pull-throughs. There's a small laundry room, bathroom and shower. Two older, fully furnished pine-paneled cabins are also available. At Palisades, you're close to the recreational possibilities of the reservoir and to the world-class trout fishing of the South Fork Snake.

Huskey's Resort
$$ • 3781 Swan Valley Hwy., Palisades, Idaho • (208) 483-3581

All 25 RV sites at Huskey's have full hookups. The 15 grassy sites are a smidge larger and more pleasant. If you're here to fish the South Fork or to boat on Palisades Reservoir, the location is ideal and the price excellent. Huskey's also includes a gas station, a convenience store and a fishing supply shop. These folks can even rent you a boat to fish from and arrange your shuttle with a local shuttle company. The RV park closes in mid-October and reopens in May. While you're here, make sure you wander over to dad's jewelry shop. Pete Huskey's jewelry and antler art is like nothing you've ever seen: gold and silver inset with bear claws, elk antler, walrus tusk and bone (for more on Pete Huskey, see our Shopping chapter). The RV park is closed from mid-October to early May.

Teton Valley

Pine Creek Campground
$ • Idaho Hwy. 31 at Pine Creek Pass, Idaho • (208) 354-2312

This is the cheapest Forest Service campground in the area, mostly because it has no safe drinking water. Four dollars buys your site just below the summit of Pine Creek Pass. Some of the 11 sites are carved into dense underbrush and are very private. Most are shaded; a few are almost buried under heavy forest cover. A couple are accessed by small footbridges crossing Little Pine Creek, a tiny tributary to the Teton River. Some sites are closer to the road than we'd like. All have picnic tables and grills. Pit toilets are on-site; there is no campground host. The campground opens in early June and closes in late September.

Mike Harris Campground
$ • Idaho Hwy. 33 at Teton Pass, Idaho • (208) 354-2312

This national forest campground in the Teton Basin Ranger District is barely a mile off heavily traveled Idaho Highway 33, but the dirt road to the campground crosses Trail Creek, then winds around a hill and into a lodgepole pine forest. You'd never know there was a road anywhere near. Your fee buys you a spacious site in lodgepole forest dotted with wild geranium. Water and pit toilets are available; reserveable sites are not. Despite its attractiveness, convenient location barely 20 miles from Jackson and small size — only 11 sites are available — the campground is often quiet and empty, especially during the week. The campground has a trailhead to the Mike Harris trail, which is steep, rocky and, of course, lovely. The facility opens in early June and closes in late September.

Trail Creek Campground
$ • Idaho Hwy. 33 at Teton Pass, Idaho • (208) 354-2312

As Idaho Highway 33 begins the serious climb up and over Teton Pass, this little campground hides, almost out of sight, on Trail Creek below the highway. Don't miss it. Once you top the pass and drop over into Jackson Hole, you'll pay twice as much for Forest Service campgrounds. Trail Creek's 11 sites are not reserveable. Each has a picnic table and a grill; most enjoy shade. Pit toilets and drinking water are on-site. There is no campground host. The campground opens in early June and closes in late September.

Teton Valley Campground
$$$ • 128 Idaho Hwy. 31, Victor, Idaho • (208) 787-2647

Green, grassy and equipped with 32 pull-through RV sites, this 74-site campground is better suited to RVs than tents. Long-term visitors will appreciate the six sites with phone hookups. Teton Valley Campground is equipped with a heated outdoor pool (summer only), showers and a recreation room. Best of all, it's open year-round as sort of an experiment on the part of new owners Ruth and Gary Ellis. Nearly all area campgrounds shut down in September or October.

Teton Canyon Campground
$ • Forest Rd. 009, off Ski Hill Rd. near Alta, Wyo. • (208) 354-2312

Some of the best hiking in the area leaves from this campground, 4 miles out of Alta on a dirt road. The Alaska Basin and Table Mountain trails both wind toward heaven from here (see our Hiking and Backpacking chapter). The campground has several sites in deep forest. Shade keeps the undergrowth down for an oddly parklike feel. Other sites scatter about a sunny meadow ringed with aspen and dotted with wildflowers. Campers will appreciate raised gravel pads, picnic tables and fire circles, water and access to pit toilets. Some sites are equipped with the most intricate-looking grill systems we've ever seen on which you can hang pots or swing either of two grates over or away from the fire. Because of the hiking, Teton Canyon also offers trailhead parking and horse corrals. A campground host lives here, but not for much of the year: The campground is only open from early August to late September.

Southwestern Montana

Bozeman to West Yellowstone via the Gallatin Canyon (U.S. Highway 191)

Sunrise Campground
$$ • 31842 E. Frontage Rd., Bozeman, Mont. • (406) 587-4797, (888) 704-7966, pin 8162

If you're one of those people who has to check out the bathrooms before you check into an RV Park, then take your peek and park your car at the Sunrise Campground. Maryjo and Marty Stanek, owners since 1996, pride themselves on their glistening bathrooms. The Sunrise, on the eastern edge of Bozeman, is easily accessible from Interstate 90. Just take Exit 309, then turn left off the ramp onto Frontage Road. The Sunrise Campground is the second business on the right. About half this campground is shaded by mature trees planted 25 years ago when the RV park was first built. It has 52 RV spaces (all but three are full hookup) and a wide expanse of lawn where tent campers can pick their own spots to pitch their tents. Besides sparkling bathrooms, you'll

find laundry facilities, a TV room and a small playground. During the summer, it's a good idea to call ahead for reservations.

Bozeman Hot Springs KOA
$$$$ • 81123 Gallatin Rd., U.S. Hwy. 191, Bozeman, Mont. • (406) 587-3030

Location, location, location. Park your RV, hit the hay and sleep into the cool dawn. Then slip out of bed, grab your towel and your swimsuit and pick up the well-worn trail that leads from the KOA, through a hedge, to the Bozeman Hot Springs. Ahhh. Now, you have a choice. Do you want to swim in the giant blue inside pool? Or do you want to soak outside under Montana's big, blue sky? Besides their neighbors with the hot springs, this KOA has plenty of amenities including a playground, a laundry, showers, a convenience store, a game room and a miniature golf course. Located about 8 miles southwest of Bozeman, the Bozeman Hot Springs KOA has 130 RV spaces and 14 camp cabins.

Swan Creek Campground
$ • Swan Creek Rd., Gallatin Gateway, Mont. • (406) 587-6920

This nifty little 11-unit Forest Service campground is tucked into the trees and brush beside Swan Creek. You'll find water, outhouses, trash pickup and firewood here. You'll also have access to Forest Service Trail #186 at the top of the campground. It leads to the ridge above, where you can view the Gallatin Canyon. If you want to keep on hiking, this trail also leads into the Paradise Valley. Down the road, you'll find fishing in the Gallatin River. There is a 45-foot RV limit here.

Red Cliff Campground
$ • U.S. Hwy. 191, Gallatin Gateway, Mont. • (406) 587-6920

Forty-eight miles south of Bozeman on U.S. Highway 191, this Forest Service campground at the base of a red (of course) cliff has 68 campsites. Across the Gallatin River from the highway, it offers shade and seclusion. You'll find toilets, water, trash pickup and firewood. This campground offers fishing on the Gallatin River as well as hiking. It is easily accessible to Big Sky Ski and Summer Resort to the north and to Yellowstone National Park to the south.

Spire Rock Campground

No charge • Squaw Creek Rd., Gallatin Gateway, Mont. • (406) 587-6920

There's no water, no garbage and no fee at this little campground which offers hiking and fishing. To get to Spire Rock, drive 26 miles south of Bozeman on U.S. Highway 191, then turn east on the Squaw Creek Road. Spire Rock is about 2 miles up the creek, which runs happily beside the campsites. If you take the road up the creek a ways, you'll find a trail that leads to Rat Lake and good fishing. You'll probably find better fishing, though, down the road in the Gallatin River. This campground has 10 campsites and an outhouse and can accommodate a 50-foot-long vehicle.

Virginia City to West Yellowstone via the Madison Canyon (U.S. Highway 287)

Virginia City Campground and RV Park

$$$ • U.S. Hwy. 287, Virginia City, Mont. • (406) 843-5493

The only private campground in town, the Virginia City Campground and RV Park has 18 RV sites and 26 tent sites. It sits on the east edge of town, against the base of a hill where several campers and tents can squeeze into the shade near Daylight Creek. Besides hot showers, you'll find clean restrooms, a miniature golf course and horseshoe pits. There is an active cricket choir at the Virginia City Campground. And, in case you don't like cricket music, the campground is just around the corner from Virginia City, a restored and preserved historic mining town that offers entertainment (see our Attractions chapter).

Ruby Creek Campground

$ • U.S. Hwy. 287, Cameron, Mont. • (406) 683-2337

Just 3 miles off U.S. Highway 287 on a paved road pocked with potholes, the Ruby Creek Campground is smack-dab in the middle of a boulder field. The rocks offer no screen from the sight of other campers, but neither do they interrupt the view of the nearby Madison River and the Madison Mountains to the east or the Gravelly Range to the west. If you have a vanload of restless children, we suggest you pull out their bikes or skateboards (we hope you brought some along) and turn them loose on the paved road that weaves through the boulders. While anglers cast their lines into the waters of the Madison River (world-renowned for trout fishing), the family chef can cook up burgers and watch the setting sun play on the Madison Range. Later, climb into bed and let the river lull you to sleep. This under-used Bureau of Land Management campground has 28 spaces.

West Fork Cabin Camp

$$ • U.S. Hwy. 287, Cameron, Mont. • (406) 682-4802

This hopping place on the banks of the Madison River has 24 full-hookup RV sites and an array of other amenities including raft rentals, guided fly fishing and a fly shop. For more information about the West Fork Cabin Camp, please refer to our Hotels, Motels and Cabins chapter.

Madison River Cabins and RV

$$$ • 1403 U.S. Hwy. 287 N., Cameron, Mont. • (406) 682-4890

This small RV park has a great view and lots of amenities. For more information, please refer to our Hotels, Motels and Cabins chapter.

Livingston to Gardiner via the Yellowstone Valley (U.S. Highway 89)

Paradise Valley KOA Campground

$$$ • U.S. Hwy. 89, 8 miles south of Livingston, Mont. • (406) 222-0992

"Don't get the gumps. It's only a few more bumps to KOA," reads a sign posted along the way to the Paradise Valley KOA. This campground has it all: huge cottonwood, Douglas fir and quaking aspen trees and lush green brush to separate campsites, camp cabins, an indoor swimming pool, cheerful restrooms, a laundry, a gift shop and the standard KOA kiddie bikes. In the mornings, you'll find free coffee and a simple, inexpensive breakfast (a limited dinner menu is available, too). Sundays, you can attend a worship service at the campground chapel. The Paradise Valley KOA is on the banks of the Yellowstone River, about 1.5 miles east of U.S. Highway 89. It has 47 RV sites, 23 tent sites and 23 cabins.

Red Lodge to Cooke City or Cody, via U.S. Highway 212 or Wyo. Highway 296

Perry's RV Park and Campgrounds
$$ • U.S. Hwy. 212, Red Lodge, Mont. • (406) 446-2722

If you like cozy, comfortable and a just little bit wild with all of the amenities, you'll feel like you've come home or at least found your own little corner of the world when you stay at Perry's RV Park and Campground. Situated 2 miles south of Red Lodge on the banks of Rock Creek, this RV Park has plenty of cottonwoods and aspens for shade. Below the brow of a hill, it is also shielded from the highway. The only sounds you'll hear at Perry's are the creek, the chattering aspen leaves and the muffled voices of campers. You'll also find showers, electrical and water hookups, laundry facilities, a convenience store and a dump station at Perry's. There are picnic areas and barbecue grills for guests. Perry's has 20 RV units and space for 10 tent camps.

Sheridan Campground
$ • East Side Rd. #389, Red Lodge, Mont. • (406) 446-2103

Just 5 miles from Red Lodge, this little Forest Service campground is best-suited for tents and campers. Situated beside Rock Creek about a mile off U.S. Highway 212 on a dirt road, you'll encounter grass, a few trees and the comforting sights and sounds of the creek. Despite the fact that this campground is close to some small subdivisions, you'll still feel like you're in the wilds. Sheridan campground has a hand pump for drinking water and eight camping spaces. The campground has five reservation sites. For more information about the campground call the Red Lodge District office at the above number.

Parkside Campground
$ • Rock Creek Rd. #421, Red Lodge, Mont. • (406) 446-2103

Next to Rock Creek on the west side of U.S. Highway 212 about 12 miles south of Red Lodge, Parkside Campground is the largest of three Forest Service campgrounds in the Red Lodge District of the Custer National Forest. You'll find conifers, grass, wildflowers and cool mornings. (The elevation here is 7,200 feet.) The access roads are paved, and sites have back-in spurs. The RV limit is 40 feet. Of the 26 sites at Parkside, 15 can be reserved through the U.S. National Forest Reservation Center.

Island Lake Recreation Area
$$ • U.S. Hwy. 212 • (307) 754-7207

Camp on top of the world (elevation 9,600 feet) at Island Lake Recreation Area in the Clarks Fork District of the Shoshone National Forest. Sites in this beautiful and well-used campground are scattered between big round boulders, behind conifers, below and above the winding road and back in the trees. Adjacent to the campground you'll find a boat launch leading into the icy waters of — you guessed it — Island Lake, a popular float-tubing lake full of pan-size brook trout. (You'll need a Wyoming fishing license here.) Trail #620 is a popular trailhead leading across alpine meadows to scads of lakes in the Absaroka-Beartooth Wilderness.

Island Lake has 20 campsites. Generally, this campground and others on the Beartooth Highway are open from June 1 until September 1, depending on snow conditions. Expect snow and ice in September, though. The Beartooth Highway is closed during the winter.

Beartooth Lake Campground
$ • U.S. Hwy. 212 • (307) 754-7207

Situated on the shores of Beartooth Lake, the 21 units in this sparsely timbered campground are 9,000 feet up in the sky. That means cool mornings (and evenings). Beartooth Lake provides good brook trout fishing (you'll need a Wyoming license) and a spectacular reflection of Beartooth Butte, which looms above the lake. Two trails take off from this spot: Trail #621 leaves from the campground, while Trail #619 heads about a half-mile up Beartooth Lake at the inlet. Both trails lead to myriad other lakes and spectacular views (see our Hiking and Backpacking chapter). This campground is open only during the summer months. There are no firm opening and closing dates because they depend on the weather conditions, which can change in hours.

Crazy Creek Campground
$$ • U.S. Hwy. 212 • (307) 754-7207

Pull into the Crazy Creek Campground 6 miles south of the U.S. Highway 212 junction, and you're apt to think you've traded the wilds of Wyoming (the campground is just inside the Wyoming border) for a picture-perfect park. Tucked into the lush grass, lupine and lodgepole are 19 camping spaces with a 32-foot limit. A trail, which begins in the campground, leads to some tumbling falls on Crazy Creek.

Chief Joseph Group Campground
$ • U.S. Hwy. 212 • (406) 848-7375

Reserve this six-unit campground for your next family reunion or any other group outing. Four miles east of Cooke City, the Chief Joseph Campground is a favorite for groups, but if you happen along and don't see a cluster of tents here, help yourself. If you plan to stay for a while, check with the Gardiner Ranger District (the number is listed above) to see if it has been reserved.

Hunter Peak Campground
$ • Wyo. Hwy. 296 (Chief Joseph Pass Hwy.) • (307) 754-7207

Away from the highway and hidden in heavy timber, this small Forest Service campground makes a good stopover if you're traveling between Cooke City and Cody. Right next to the Clarks Fork River, this nine-unit campground promises good fishing. It also offers the possibility of at least seeing grizzly signs since they regularly cruise the river for food. You'll find full Forest Service amenities here, including water.

Northwestern Wyoming

Cody to East Entrance Yellowstone Park via U.S. 14-16-20

Gateway Motel and Campground
$$ • 203 Yellowstone Ave., Cody, Wyo. • (307) 587-2561

The lush lawn, mature trees and plentiful shade at the Gateway Motel and Campground will soothe your nerves and cool your cranky kids. About a mile west of downtown Cody, the Gateway is within easy walking distance of the Cody Nite Rodeo grounds and Old Trail Town (see our Attractions chapter). It's also right across the highway from Cassie's Supper Club, which features fine food and fantastic dancing (see our Restaurants chapter).

Next to the campground, owner Lura Showman's father offers horseback riding (see our Other Recreation chapter to learn more about the Gateway Ranch). Tucked behind the office and a row of motel rooms, the campground is quiet and countrified. A comfortable yard behind the office accommodates 87 tenters and is popular with large groups. It's so homey, you'll feel like the owner will show up at your camp any minute wearing an apron and carrying a jar full of your favorite cookies.

The Gateway has 29 electric hookups and 13 full-hookup sites. You'll find a laundry, clean showers and restrooms, a pay phone, UHF television reception and free coffee in the morning. The motel rooms and cabins, cute and clean, are older but adequate. Most have kitchenettes but no refrigeration. The motel and cabin units begin at $30. The Gateway is open from May 1 until October 1.

Ponderosa Campground
$$$ • 1815 B St., Cody, Wyo. • (307) 587-9203

What the Ponderosa Campground lacks in vegetation it makes up for with location. Just three blocks west of the Buffalo Bill Historical Center (see our Attractions chapter) and within easy walking distance of downtown, the Ponderosa Campground is a popular RV park and camping complex that's generally jam-packed. Besides easy access to restaurants, shopping and museums, the Ponderosa has an array of amenities including a large gift store, a video arcade, a laundry and a playground. In addition to 133 spaces with full hookups, the Ponderosa has 72-foot pull-throughs, several cabins, six tepees and special places for tenters. The Ponderosa is open from May 1 to mid-October.

Camp Cody Campgrounds
$$$ • 415 Yellowstone Ave., Cody, Wyo. • (307) 587-9730

Just look for the state flags — all 50 of them — flying in front of this campground on the north side of U.S. Highway 14-16-20 west of Cody. The new owners of Camp Cody Campgrounds (they took ownership in June of 1997) were busy planting grass and trees and building cabins to make their RV park more inviting. Until those trees grow big enough to make shade, you can refresh yourself in Camp Cody's heated pool. This RV Park has 60 RV spaces, 15 cabins, 15 tent spaces, free cable TV, a laundry and clean restrooms.

KOA Kampground of Cody

$$$ • 5561 Greybull Hwy., Cody, Wyo.
• (307) 587-2369

East of Cody on U.S. Highway 14-16-20, this was the first franchised KOA campground in the nation. Built in 1969, it is a couple miles east of town. The Cody KOA makes up for its distance from town by providing on-site amenities such as a swimming pool, a hot tub, a playground, showers and a laundry. Each morning during the summer, the staff serves a pancake breakfast under an awning. Monday through Saturday evenings they serve a chuckwagon dinner enlivened with entertainment by the Diamond C Chuckwagon crew. The campground also offers a free shuttle to the Cody Nite Rodeo and is a pickup point for Powder River tours (see our Getting Around chapter). You'll find plenty of grass, a few mature trees and a measure of peace and quiet here.

Eagle Creek Campground

$ • U.S. Hwy. 14-16-20, Cody, Wyo.
• (307) 527-6921

Paved with spurs and shaded by conifers, this Forest Service campground has a pressurized water system with spigots throughout. You'll find 20 units next to the North Fork of the Shoshone River. Remember — the signs here won't let you forget — this is bear country, and the Wapiti Ranger District has begun stepping up its efforts to avert human-bear conflict. You'll find good fishing in the North Fork. A trailhead and horse corrals are just a half-mile away. The trailer limit is 22 feet.

Newton Creek Campground

$ • U.S. Hwy. 14-16-20, Cody, Wyo.
• (307) 527-6921

You'll find several campsites right next to the North Fork of the Shoshone River here and bear signs to remind you to lock your food up. The Forest Service has made it easy by installing new, user-friendly bear boxes in which to lock up your food at night. The boxes are about waist-high, and the lids, hinged with chains, fold down to make a working surface adequate for a Coleman stove. This campground closes for a while each spring when the bears come out of hibernation and wander the riverbanks looking for food. Newton Creek has 31 campsites.

Three Mile Campground

$ • U.S. Hwy. 14-16-20, Cody, Wyo.
• (307) 527-6921

Three miles east of the East Entrance to Yellowstone Park, this Forest Service campground is a popular staging spot for visitors to the Park. Of the 33 campsites, four are isolated from the others on the banks of the North Fork of the Shoshone River and are reserved for day-use only. The area is a favorite corridor for grizzly bears during the night, especially in the spring and fall. The Forest Service has plans to install new bear-proof food boxes here by 1998.

It's not unrealistic to expect to visit the most well-known spots in the region — from Yellowstone to the Tetons to the St. Anthony Dunes to the Henry's Fork — in a week's stay from any home base within Greater Yellowstone.

Vacation Rentals

Ahhh, home away from home.

Take off your shoes, wander out onto the deck, fix a midnight snack or cha-cha through the living room in your bathrobe: In a vacation rental you can be as relaxed and comfortable as in your own home. The view out the windows is a bit different, though. Whether it's the rolling farmlands around Rexburg, Idaho, a broad ranching valley ringed by mountains or the marriage of glitz and down-home Western charm that is Jackson Hole, wherever you choose to hang your hat in Yellowstone country, you'll find yourself among pleasant, colorful people and within easy driving distance of magnificence.

It's not unrealistic to expect to visit the most well-known spots in the region — from Yellowstone to the Tetons to the St. Anthony Dunes to the Henry's Fork — in a week's stay from any home base within Greater Yellowstone. So don't limit your geographic choices too quickly as you read through these rental options. Also note that more cabins are described in the Hotels, Motels and Cabins chapter, particularly those that rent both by the night as well as for longer stays. Almost the only things you won't find are vacation rentals within the Parks themselves. Yellowstone Park is all public property, and although Grand Teton National Park has many private "inholdings," none that we know of are available for short-term rental. If you want to stay in the Parks, you'll camp, stay at guest ranches or resorts, or in hotels, motels or cabins. 'Nuff said.

The Yellowstone region encompasses everything from potato fields to 13,000-foot granite peaks to mysterious steaming holes filled with what looks like bubbling gray paint; its vacation rental possibilities are varied too. In general, you're choosing between condos, cabins and houses. All require minimum stays, but sometimes these can be waived or are for short periods like three or four nights. Minimum stays tend to vary with seasons, with longer stays required at busiest times. Monthly stays are sometimes required for houses. Rexburg's wonderful seniors program requests (but does not require) that participants plan to stay the entire summer.

Jackson Hole and Big Sky offer lots of condos, usually located in resort complexes, so additional services are available, such as spas, golf courses, tennis courts and swimming pools. Public transportation often is associated with condos too. These upscale areas are home to many large, luxurious houses, but the right to call them yours for a week or a month doesn't come cheap. They also might not be as close to ski hills and businesses since their locations were often chosen for aesthetic reasons more than for convenience.

In Teton Valley, Island Park and the broad valleys of southwestern Montana, log is the building material of choice, and most of what you'll find are best called cabins. Many are rustic. Often they lack amenities you may consider basic, like phones and televisions. However, much of the construction in our region has taken place in recent years, so just because a cabin is rustic doesn't mean it isn't fairly new. And an older cabin is often charming enough to offset any minor hassles such as driving out to make a phone call or do laundry.

The Northern Rockies are steep, and much of the land around here is national forest, wil-

---

INSIDERS' TIP

There is a 4 percent lodging tax throughout Montana. However, within the West Yellowstone city limits, expect to pay an additional 3 percent tax on accommodations.

derness or national park. This means that the secluded cabin in the pines you may have in mind is practically nonexistent. Most cabins, condos and houses exist in clusters on the valley floors. These accommodations look toward the magnificent mountains, but they're not in them. And if a property manager tells you a cabin or house is secluded, that doesn't necessarily mean you can't see other cabins and houses nearby. Our mountains are heavily wooded, but the valleys are broad swaths of sage, willow and wildflowers. Unless you're positioned along the cottonwood trees that line most of our rivers, you can usually see for miles in all directions.

The moral of the story: Ask a lot of questions and think in terms of luxury and amenities when you choose a location in which to search for your vacation home. If rustic is your middle name, don't look in Jackson or Big Sky, but rather try the outlying areas of Wyoming, Montana and Idaho. Note also that most rentals' pricing varies with the season. You can save a bundle by coming in the fall when the trees flame and the mosquitoes are gone. Or try late spring, when early wildflowers are just beginning to bloom. Summer is high season for most of Yellowstone country, but near ski resorts (Jackson Hole, Teton Valley, Big Sky and Red Lodge) and snowmobiling meccas (Island Park, Togwotee Pass, West Yellowstone, Cooke City and Pahaska Teepee), winter can be pricey too. Availability is slim around the entrance communities to Yellowstone Park because the towns are squeezed between the Park and national forest. With private land so hard to come by, most folks are living on theirs.

The subsequent listings are mostly property management companies and realties. The list is not all-inclusive, but it does cover most of the larger companies with the greatest selections of rentals. Some areas, particularly

Island Park, Swan Valley and Teton Valley in Idaho, are not yet well-represented by property management firms; there, homeowners may try to find their own renters. Phone books and chambers of commerce can sometimes help you hook up with these folks, as can classified ads in local papers and Internet classified ads. (Chambers of commerce are listed in our Resources chapter; local and regional newspapers are discussed in our Media chapter.)

When you call, be sure to ask about cigarettes, pets and children if you're planning on bringing one or more. Many properties do not allow smoking; most frown on pets. Unless noted, these companies will accept your credit card or check.

If you're planning a winter visit, also inquire about ski storage and firewood. Most properties provide firewood if they have fireplaces. Outdoor ski storage lockers will make your life easier.

Yellowstone National Park

Entrance Communities

West Yellowstone, Montana

The Cabin
West Yellowstone, Mont.
• (406) 646-7784

One block from downtown West Yellowstone and 250 feet from the Yellowstone Park boundary, this 70-year-old log cabin is a favorite among winter snowmobilers and summer sightseers. The Cabin, recently modernized, comes complete with a dishwasher, microwave and coffee maker. Furnished with a combination of antiques and comfortable

---

INSIDERS' TIP

Planning a family reunion? Larger cabins and houses, especially in outlying areas, can be ideal gathering places for the entire clan.

Western decor, it holds a maximum of eight people. In the summer, guests can enjoy a backyard barbecue. In winter, they can rent snowmobiles right down the block. A bargain at $135 per night, this cabin usually is booked months ahead of time. Owner Pat Henrie has a three-night minimum.

Sportsman's High Vacation Rentals
750 Deer St., West Yellowstone, Mont.
• (406) 646-7865

Wow! What a combo. He builds them. She decorates them. And are they beautiful. Together, Gary and Diana Baxter have created five rental homes that will accommodate from six to 12 people each. They also manage a neighbor's house adjacent to their property. All are 8 miles from the hustle and bustle of West Yellowstone in a country setting surrounded by aspen groves and wildflowers, and bordered by national forest. These homes, each designed and furnished with a different theme, rent from $145 to $305 per night, depending on the duration of your stay, the house and the time of year. There is a three-night minimum.

Yellowstone Village Rental Condominiums
West Yellowstone, Mont.
• (406) 646-7335, (800) 276-7335

Nine miles from the west entrance to Yellowstone National Park, these quiet, clean one- and two-bedroom units are near Hebgen Lake. They are open year round, and guests have access to an outdoor pool and two tennis courts. Yellowstone Village is about 4 miles west of Mont. Highway 191. If you prefer, in the winter you can snowmobile straight to town and into the Park. Because vacation rentals are scarce in the West Yellowstone area, these condos fill up fast. Rent ranges from $99.50 to $159 per night. While you can stay for just one night, the manager encourages longer stays.

Gardiner, Montana

Slip and Slide Ranch and Outfitters
U.S. Hwy. 89, 11 miles north of Gardiner, Mont. • (406) 848-7648

You'll need a four-wheel drive to get to this seven-year-old log cabin furnished with antiques and pine furniture. Two miles above the Slip and Slide ranch house, this cabin is surrounded by national forest and has a great view. The cabin, which has an upstairs loft with six beds, has electricity but is heated with a pellet stove. You'll find the kitchen stocked with dishes and food staples. The cabin goes for $150 a night for groups of six, and there is a three-night minimum. The owners are not equipped to handle credit cards but will take personal checks. Slip and Slide also offers bed and breakfast rooms as well as horseback riding, private fishing ponds and guided hunting trips.

Mountain Retreat
No credit cards • U.S. Hwy. 89, 10 miles north of Gardiner, Mont. • (406) 848-7272, (800) 727-0798

Mountain Retreat offers two homes 10 miles north of Gardiner and .75-miles east of Mont. Highway 89 on Cedar Creek. Built in the 1950s, this home accommodates six people and rents for $150 per night. The house is ready to live in but has no dishwasher or washer and dryer. A smaller 700-square-foot cabin built in the 1890s offers a taste of the Old West with a root cellar, smokehouse and a two-hole outhouse out back. It rents for $110 a night. The owners accept personal checks.

Jackson Hole

Alpine Vacation Rentals
Teton Village, Wyo.
• (307) 734-1161, (800) 876-3968

This property management company recently merged with the 15-year-old Jackson Hole Racquet Club Resort, adding even more vacation rental options for you. Choose from more than 175 properties ranging from condos to five-bedroom homes; rates range too, between $90 and $1,400 per day. Most rentals are in the pleasantly upscale West Bank, which means they're away from the traffic snarls of Jackson and a convenient drive to Teton Village and the back route into Grand Teton National Park. All rentals are fully furnished. You bring only yourself and a desire to enjoy "the Hole."

Black Diamond Vacation Rentals
Jackson, Wyo.
• (307) 733-6170, (800) 325-8605

These folks have condos, townhouses and family homes available in several premium locations. Teton Shadows is 10 minutes north of Jackson and adjacent to Jackson Hole Golf and Tennis Club, which you may enjoy for a fee. Black Diamond also has properties at the base of the lifts in Teton Village and at The Aspens, a resort area adjacent to Arnold Palmer-designed Teton Pines Golf Course. You may use The Aspens' athletic club with sauna, hot tub and swimming pool for a fee. These folks handle condos in the town of Jackson and houses scattered through the valley. Prices range from $75 to $280 for condos and vary even more widely for houses — from $3,000 to $8,000 per month. Minimum stays vary from property to property — anywhere from two days for some condos to 30 for houses. Black Diamond condos and houses have fully equipped kitchens, washer/dryer, fireplaces, color TV with cable hookup, telephone, linens and towels. Some properties also have hot tubs and garages.

First Cabin Rentals (Prime Properties of Jackson Hole L.L.C.)
1230 Ida Ln., Wilson, Wyo.
• (307) 739-9145, (800) 989-9145

Like the personal touch? First Cabin represents private homeowners who have decorated their houses to their unique personal tastes. A few of the properties are condos, but what First Cabin specializes in are homes, scattered through the valley but mostly in the desirable West Bank outside Jackson. A few of these houses are secluded enough that you can look through each window and not see another home. All are fully furnished. Most properties rent on a per-month basis — for $1,100 to $12,000 — but a few are available nightly. Approximately 40 properties are rep-

resented, but First Cabin promises that if they don't have what you're looking for, they'll look for someone who does.

Jackson Hole Central Reservations
Jackson, Wyo.
• (307) 733-4005, (800) 443-6931

Jackson Hole Mountain Resort, the area's world-famous ski hill, celebrated its 30th birthday last year — and so did Jackson Hole Central Reservations. The Hole's largest and oldest reservation service is hooked in almost everywhere; they book for 33 hotels, bed and breakfast inns, and property management companies. These folks charge a small fee for making your life easy, but especially if you're calling during the busy ski or summer seasons, you'll enjoy the convenience of one phone call instead of many. Jackson Hole Central Reservations specializes in complete and money-saving vacation packages, which include airfare, car rentals and lift tickets for Teton Village, Snow King and nearby Grand Targhee. (See our Winter Sports chapter.) Most accommodations are subject to minimum-stay requirements, which vary by season and property.

Mountain Property Management
175 S. King St., Jackson, Wyo.
• (307) 733-1684, (800) 992-9948

Mountain Property Management handles 14 houses and 28 condos. Some condos are at Teton Shadows, 7 miles north of town near Jackson Hole Golf and Tennis Club; this course is open to the public. Other condos are at The Aspens, also known as Jackson Hole Racquet Club Resort. Costs range from $90 per night to $300, generally with a five night minimum. The houses have two to four bedrooms and rent for a monthly charge of $4,000 to $10,000. Houses and condos are fully furnished, right down to the silverware and linens. All have cable TV and VCRs,

---

INSIDERS' TIP

If you're heading from Idaho Falls to your vacation rental in Island Park, take the Mesa Falls Scenic Byway outside Ashton, but leave plenty of time. The road is narrow and a bit bumpy, and you're going to want to stop and look at Upper and Lower Mesa Falls. This road is closed in winter.

washer/dryers and fireplaces with firewood provided. Some have hot tubs or hot tub access.

Reservations Network Inc.
Park City, Utah
• **(800) 255-6451**

Twelve-year-old Resnet, as it's called, is one-stop shopping for ski vacations in the intermountain West. With one phone call, book vacation rentals for your big ski tour through Jackson, Lake Tahoe and several Utah ski areas (see our Winter Sports chapter). In Jackson, Resnet can hook you up with hotel rooms, condos and any of about 50 private homes scattered through the valley. Most condos have hot tub access, many have fireplaces, and nearly all include laundry facilities. They range from $100 to $900 per night, generally with three-night minimums (peak travel weekends will have greater minimum stays). Homes rent from $500 to $1,500 per night, with varying minimum stays. All homes and condos are fully furnished and offer fully equipped kitchens. Resnet is not only convenient, but also can save you money; they charge no booking fee. Even better, on short notice, especially in the off-season, they've been known to offer discounts of up to 50 percent to folks with flexible travel plans. Call within 30 days of your arrival to try for these good deals. Resnet is also hooked into bulk airfare rates and discount car rentals.

Teton Village
Property Management
3285 W. McCollister, Teton Village, Wyo.
• **(307) 733-4610, (800) 443-6840**

The condo specialists in town, Teton Village Property Management handles more than 110 condos, nearly all in Teton Village. This puts you at the base of the ski hill, outside Jackson. All services are available either here or nearby — expect a bit more quiet and solitude than you'd likely to find in Jackson proper. Condos range in size from studios to four-bedrooms with lofts. All are privately owned. These rentals are all fully furnished; most have access to pools, hot tubs and, in summer, tennis courts. All provide winter transportation to the ski hill. These folks also make reservations for 11 private homes and two

A Canada goose airs out after being swept over the falls in Idaho Falls.

small hotels; these are also outside Jackson, and most are in Teton Village. The smallest condos start at around $120 per night in peak season; the highest-priced houses go for about $1,000 nightly. Prices during spring and fall can be up to a third lower. Minimum stays are seven nights in winter, three in summer. During spring and fall, you may be able to rent some properties for two nights.

Surrounding Areas

Eastern Idaho

Rexburg, Idaho, Area

Sunbird Program/Rexburg
Chamber of Commerce
420 W. Fourth S., Rexburg, Idaho
• **(208) 356-5700**

Back in 1978, some bright Rexburgian noticed that hundreds of off-campus student apartments sat empty when Ricks College students went home for the summer. Now in its 19th year, the Sunbird Program offers affordable summer accommodations to retired Southerners who want to escape to cool northern air. Approximately 2,000 senior citizens participate every year. The Rexburg Chamber of Commerce charges between $850 and $1,550 for the summer. The minimum stay is one month, but most folks come for the whole three-month availability. Many sunbirds have been migrating here every year since the program started. Accommodations are apartments and range from two to four bedrooms. Some have pleasant extras like hot tubs, swimming pools, computer rooms and pool tables on the premises; some have TVs and telephones. None provides linens or dishes. None has air conditioning.

Island Park, Idaho

The Henry's Fork Realtors of Island Park, Idaho
3404 Idaho Hwy. 20, Last Chance in Island Park, Idaho • (208) 558-7354

Norman and Doug Ellis handle 13 cabins scattered all over Island Park. These are people's vacation homes, but you're invited to make use of them when their owners can't, summer or winter. They rent nightly for $125 to $250 and weekly from $700 to $1,100. All are fully furnished; you bring only yourself and something to eat. Small cabins accommodate four people; the largest will hold 20. Some are on exclusive Bills Island, a limited-access tract of land surrounded by the waters of Island Park Reservoir. Some are on lovely, trout-filled Henry's Lake; others view the Henry's Fork. Opened just two years ago, Henry's Fork Realtors carries the first large-scale vacation-rental listing in Island Park. They also assist with discount car rentals out of Idaho Falls for guests who fly into that airport (see Getting Around).

Rainbow Realty
3376 Idaho Hwy. 20, Last Chance in Island Park, Idaho • (208) 558-7116

Tawnya Phillips rents eight fully furnished cabins for between $700 and $1,200 per week. One is on Island Park Resort Golf Course; three perch north of Henry's Lake with lake views; and one waterfront cabin looks out on Island Park Reservoir. These folks also handle a fishermen's waterfront cabin on the Henry's Fork near Last Chance plus two rustic cabins set back in the woods. Several are available year round. The folks at Rainbow are happy to serve as an emergency answering service for the cabins unequipped with phones.

Teton Valley

Grand Valley Lodging
Driggs, Idaho • (208) 354-8890, (800) 746-5518

This valley, although not yet a tourist destination of Jackson's scale, is just as pretty and perhaps a bit more, well . . . real. The cowboy hats are worn by cowboys, and the cracked leather cowboy boots weren't purchased that way. This broad, flat valley is lined on one side by the Big Holes and on the other by the Tetons. Liz Pitcher has 13 cabins, condos and homes to entice you into the valley. Most are newer log homes on the valley floor; some are more secluded. Each is privately owned and fully furnished. Most have color TVs, VCRs, microwaves and coffee pots, laundry facilities and woodstoves or fireplaces. Rates range from $135 to $375 per night, with weekly and monthly rates available. Most have minimum stays of at least three nights. Several have Teton views, hot tubs or creek access. One large five-bedroom, four-bath house sits on 10 acres with a deck that wraps around the entire house; this massive home sleeps 12 in kingly comfort.

INSIDERS' TIP

If you're coming in June or July, bring your mosquito repellant and citronella candles. Your vacation rental probably has a deck that you'll enjoy more if you can subdue the 'skeeters.

Southwestern Montana

Mountain Home – Montana Vacation Rentals
Bozeman, Mont.
• (406) 586-4589

Owner Suzy Hall is more of a concierge than a property manager. She has combed southwestern Montana for the very best rentals. Her criteria: well-maintained homes with character and a great view in the middle of a big chunk of private property. Once you make a reservation, she will send you an arrival packet telling where to stock up on supplies and how to find fun things to do. Her 15 homes range from a $400-a-week, 500-square-foot honeymoon cabin, to a seven-bedroom Big Sky home with an indoor swimming pool that rents for $4,000 a week. On the average, her homes will cost you from $1,500 to $2,000 per week. Each is stocked with necessities such as laundry detergent, dish and hand soap, toilet paper and paper towels.

Bridger Pines Property Management
15792 Bridger Canyon Rd., Bozeman, Mont. • (406) 587-3096

Bridger Pines manages four homes and one condo near Bridger Bowl ski area. Depending upon the size, rental prices range from $500 to $2,500 per week. Some of the homes are equipped with amenities such as hot tubs, steam showers and fax machines. These rentals are popular with fishermen in the summer months and skiers during the winter. Bridger Pines does not accept credit cards.

Intermountain Property Management
611 W. Main, Bozeman, Mont.
• (406) 586-1503, (800) 685-7196

Intermountain Property handles cabins, condos, cottages and country homes throughout Yellowstone country. While most are within a 25-mile radius south of Bozeman, a few are very close to Yellowstone Park. Among those closer to the Park are a split-level six-guest condo overlooking a golf course and with access to a swimming pool 6 miles from the Big Sky ski area. Intermountain also offers a new home overlooking Hebgen Lake, 15 miles from the Park, as well as the Eagle's Nest, a three-bedroom log home perched on a rock bluff 9 miles from Yellowstone Park's north entrance at Gardiner. All rentals have a one-week–minimum policy. Rates range from $400 to $2,000 per week.

The Innskeeper
119 S. Main, Livingston, Mont.
• (406) 222-5456, (800) 590-5456

The Innskeeper is a central reservation service that handles private accommodations of all kinds, including vacation rentals, mostly in the Yellowstone Valley. Homes range from the secluded rustic log cabins to the Lazy Heart Lodge, a remodeled farmhouse in the Paradise Valley. The Innskeeper also handles The Centennial, a beautifully appointed railroad car (now offered as lodging) that traveled to New York in 1963 for Montana's territorial centennial celebration. Now sitting on 16 acres next to the Yellowstone River, it once stood in Gardiner where it housed the chamber of commerce. These homes rent for an average of $125 per night, with discounts for longer stays.

Big Sky Chalet Rentals
Big Sky, Mont.
• (406) 995-2665, (800) 845-4428

Sally Welte manages about 45 condos and homes in the Meadows and Mountain villages at Big Sky. While she mostly caters to large groups, she does have rentals for singles. Her rentals run the gamut from studio apartments to six-bedroom homes. Demand for her rentals is increasing each year, so if you're hoping to rent one for next winter, you'd better call by midsummer. Homes are rented during the Christmas holidays, sometimes a year in advance. You'll find summer is an easier time to find a rental. In addition to proximity to Yellowstone Park, Big Sky offers an array of recreation including hiking, biking, golf, rafting, horseback riding, cross-country and downhill skiing, and snowmobiling.

4M Ranch Log Guest Cabin
E. River Rd., Emigrant, Mont.
• (406) 333-4784

What could be better? This spacious two-bedroom, one-bath log cabin is off the beaten path at the base of Emigrant Peak in the Paradise Valley. East of Mont. Highway 89 on E. River Road, this cabin is about a half-hour from Yellowstone Park and minutes away from Chico Hot Springs (see Resorts, Guest Ranches and Lodges chapter). Inside, you'll find games and books. Outside, you'll find a picnic table and barbecue to enjoy after a day of fishing, hiking or sightseeing in the Park. Rented by the day or week, this cabin goes for $115 and $725, respectively. 4M Ranch also offers bed and breakfast rooms. (For more information, refer to our Bed and Breakfast Inns chapter.)

Willows Inn
224 S. Platt, Red Lodge, Mont.
• **(406) 446-3913**

While the Willows Inn is a bed and breakfast in Red Lodge, proprietress Carolyn Boggio has two storybook cottages that she rents for a minimum of two nights and generally by the week. See our Bed and Breakfast Inns chapter for further information.

The Cedar Guest House
3450 Barley Cir., Billings, Mont.
• **(406) 656-5747, (888) 626-5747**

You've been there. You're in a cute little cabin just made for playing house, but when you open the cupboard doors they resemble Mother Hubbard's. Owner Sharon Cobetto has been there too. That's why you'll find spices and herbs, sugar, salt, pepper, flour, coffee and tea to get you started. She also sees that you have one package of pancake mix, and either pancake syrup or sparkling cider. The cider, by the way, is for you to enjoy while dipping in the hot tub on the multilevel deck.

This sunny cedar home in Red Lodge has vaulted ceilings and lots of windows to enjoy the beautiful views everywhere you turn. The dining room table seats eight, and Sharon caters to families, providing a high chair and a playpen. The Cedar Guest House is close to a golf course and a ski hill, and is 65 miles from Yellowstone National Park via the Beartooth Highway, one of the most beautiful drives in the world. While Sharon mostly rents her house by the week, she will let it go nightly for $125.

Northwestern Wyoming

Cody Guest Houses
1401 Rumsey Ave., Cody, Wyo.
• **(307) 587-6000, (800) 587-6560**

These eight guest houses aren't just places to stay — they're an experience. Take the Victorian House, with its graceful grounds and beautifully appointed interior. Romance is written in every detail. From the hardwood floors to the formal dining room, it is decorated with antiques, art and historical artifacts. The four-bedroom Western Lodge, where guests can indulge in barbecues and billiards, is different only in its theme — the best of Old West charm. The Country Cottage and two others, the Annie Oakley and the Buffalo Bill, are smaller but not shy on charm. Or choose from two air-conditioned suites equipped with laundry and kitchen facilities, a carport and a beautiful yard with a gazebo. One block from Main Street in a historic residential neighborhood, all eight rentals are within walking distance of the Buffalo Bill Historical Center, world-class shopping and fine dining. Single-night double-occupancies range from $95 to $405 per night. The Victorian Inn, the queen of the collection, can be rented either as a house or by the room (there are three of them). Situated mostly on the same street, these homes, rented collectively, offer a moderately priced — and priceless — opportunity for family reunions and conferences.

Kinkade Guest Cabin
87 Green Creek Rd., Wapiti, Wyo.
• **(307) 587-5905**

Guests at this off-the-beaten-path rental like to linger . . . and often offer to buy the place from co-owner Becky Kinkade, who grew up

---

INSIDERS' TIP

Some property management firms can help you figure out not only where you'll stay while you're here, but also what you might want to do.

here. The log cabin, which features open beams and skylights, sits next to Green Creek and is surrounded by a terraced lawn with rock walls. Becky, who lives in a basement apartment below the house, is so flexible that she'll find someplace else to stay if you want the cabin all to yourself. When she doesn't have the house rented, she takes in bed and breakfast guests. Two bedrooms, each with a bath, are separated by a sun room with a player piano. Both rooms open into a dining/living area. A native of Park County (her father was sheriff), Kinkade can clue you in to local lore and Insider information. The house rents for $170 per night.

THE WINE SPECTATOR'S
"Award of Excellence"
1994, 1995, 1996, 1997

THE AWARD
OF EXCELLENCE
FROM
DISTINGUISHED
RESTAURANTS OF
NORTH AMERICA

SNAKE RIVER GRILL

on the Town Square in Jackson,
WY

307-733-0557

web page: snakerivergrill.com

Restaurants

Picture Yellowstone National Park as the sun and Yellowstone country communities as tiny planets whipping in orbits around it. Without our sun, most communities in this region would loll in economic emptiness. Only a few larger towns, like Idaho Falls and Bozeman, don't seem to be shaped primarily by Yellowstone and its tourist dollars.

Local dining options directly reflect how heavily the town you're in relies upon Yellowstone sunlight and in what direction the town has grown under that light. In some towns, tourist services have bloomed into extravagance. Each in its small-town way surprisingly cosmopolitan, these towns are Jackson, Cody, Bozeman, Big Sky and Livingston. Treat yourself to Thai, Chinese or classical Italian food: It's all here. In these communities, fine dining often means meat, and not the kind you can buy from your butcher. Buffalo, elk, venison, duck, pheasant, ostrich and emu are standards, garnished with wild mushrooms, berries, nuts and leeks.

Another staple you're almost sure to find on the menu is trout. Even in the classiest restaurants, it may be pan-fried. You'll pay dearly for the trendy food in these towns, but you'll also get what you pay for: Topnotch chefs seem to lurk around every corner.

Elsewhere in Yellowstone country, menus tend to look a bit alike. Meat and potatoes are king, and good means plentiful but cheap. Idaho potatoes are famous, so the menu may proudly point out that the spuds served up fried, mashed, baked or diced into hearty salad or soup are local. The meat? Nearly every restaurant serves burgers and steaks, and prime rib or barbecue is every cook's specialty. Chicken and seafood options add variety.

A lot of folks call it home cookin' because even inexpensive restaurants in this region pride themselves on not buying preprepared food or relying too heavily on the microwave. It's a Western self-sufficiency perhaps born of a time when home cookin' was the only cookin' to be had. These folks bake their own breads and pies, make their own sauces, jams and breaded items. Some cut their own french fries. This may mean that service is friendlier than it is fast. It also means that when your plate comes out, you'll be happy to have waited.

We've tried to pick for you an entertaining range of dining options: It wasn't easy, and we've had to leave out plenty of good ones. Most of our picks have been around for years. In this volatile, tourist-driven market, restaurants can appear and disappear in a year. The restaurants that last almost invariably enjoy strong local support, which gets them through the slow times. We've also left off the extensive collection of chain restaurants that crowd shopping areas, particularly in Idaho Falls, Bozeman and Cody. We figure you know what they're serving.

Price Code

The price code below will help you plan your dining experience. Each category is based on an average-price dinner for two, without starts, dessert, alcoholic beverages, taxes or tip. At some restaurants, this includes salad and/or soup with your entree. At others, entrees stand alone. If an establishment doesn't serve dinner, we looked at their most expensive meal, usually lunch.

$	$10 - $19
$$	$20 - $27
$$$	$28 - $35
$$$$	$36 and more

Most establishments accept credit cards. If they don't, we let you know. Most of those that don't will accept personal checks no matter where you live, though. We also note for you the establishments that accept or recommend reservations.

Remember that in summer the fine dining restaurants with the highest reputations may have their most popular dining hours booked up days in advance. Make plans early if you want to enjoy justly famous meals at places like Jenny Lake Lodge in Grand Teton Park or the Snake River Grill, The Range or Stiegler's in Jackson Hole, or Franca's in Cody. We've also let you know what alcoholic beverages you can order with your meal. Nearly all of Yellowstone country's restaurants welcome children, and many offer children's menus to accommodate smaller stomachs and pickier palates. It never hurts to check when you make your reservation, however.

One last tip that might help you pack for your trip: Fine dining around here does not mean fancy dress. If it entertains you to put on a jacket and tie or a nice dress and heels, by all means do so. But you'd be hard-pressed in Yellowstone country to find a restaurant that would flinch at jeans, hiking boots and a T-shirt.

Happy eating!

Yellowstone National Park

Lake Hotel

$$$ • Lake Village, Yellowstone Park • (307) 344-7901

Supper will be served at 6 o'clock sharp mesdames et messieurs. Supper for two, just your sweetheart and you. It's not required, but we recommend that you dress for the occasion. The dining room, the lake, the hotel will make a dinner here special enough. But why not do it up big? Lounge in the sun room, sip a little gin, tap your toe to the piano music then float into the Lake Hotel dining room. We recommend the Blackened Prime Rib, an item that remains on the menu year after year.

The menu changes each season. Last year, you might have tried the quail with spinach, walnut and goat cheese stuffing, or breast of duck or scallops with sun-dried tomatoes. Open from May until the first week in October, the Lake Hotel is for the romantic and — let's face it — the hungry. Lake has a full bar and a long wine list.

Mammoth Hotel Dining Room

$$ • Mammoth Hot Springs, Yellowstone National Park • (307) 344-7901

It's big, grand, spacious and historic. There's something for everybody at the Mammoth Hot Springs Dining Room, from the all-American hamburger and orange roughy to tenderloins of turkey. You'll find the mix of diners here as varied — but probably not so colorful — as tourists during the stagecoach days who began and ended their stays in Yellowstone Park here. This is a popular supper spot in the Park. Complement your meal with wine and mixed drinks, if you like.

The Mammoth Hotel and Dining Room are open from the first week in May until mid-October. They reopen for the winter season about December 20 and remain open until the first week in March.

Old Faithful Inn

$$$ • Old Faithful, Yellowstone National Park • (307) 344-7901

At the turn of the century, when the Old Faithful Inn was built, ladies were required to dress — we mean *dress* in long silk dresses with sweeping hoops — for dinner. Anyone who was late for supper had to eat outside in a tent. After supper, diners removed themselves to the lobby where they danced until the wee hours. The band played from the Crow's Nest high above.

Times have changed at the Old Faithful,

INSIDERS' TIP

Fine dining in Yellowstone country doesn't mean you have to dress up. Dress is casual almost everywhere.

but the dining room still says "Western" and still rings of the frontier. The menu includes entrees like honey lemon chicken, fettuccine with mushrooms, artichoke hearts and olives, and Rocky Mountain trout. Take your time dining here; the pioneers did. Old Faithful has a full bar and a healthy wine list.

Strictly a summer hotel, the Old Faithful Inn is open from about May 1 until mid-October.

Roosevelt Lodge
$$ • Roosevelt-Tower Falls Junction, Yellowstone National Park • (307) 344-7901

Hang your hat and pull up your chair at Yellowstone Park's most comfortable Western dining room where the fare is simple and the atmosphere like a dude ranch. This turn-of-the century log dining room is reminiscent of the days when Teddy Roosevelt and his Rough Riders might have stood on the stoop smoking cigars and sipping whiskey before heading in for supper. The menu has changed somewhat since the early days. In addition to prime rib and rib-eye steaks, you'll find Cajun catfish, linguine with artichoke hearts, mushrooms and garlic, Cobb salad and the All-American burger. You'll find wine on the menu as well.

The Roosevelt is open only during the summer, mid-June until the first week in September.

Entrance Communities

West Yellowstone, Montana

Bullwinkle's Saloon and Eatery
$ • 19 Madison Ave., West Yellowstone, Mont. • (406) 646-7974

Besides homestyle food, you'll find good humor and easy camaraderie at Bullwinkle's Saloon and Eatery, which also happens to be West Yellowstone's resident sports bar. Jackie and Dennis LaFever have surrounded themselves and their customers with mementoes from their hometown in Sheboygan, Wisconsin: The walls in Bullwinkle's are lined with Green Bay Packers memorabilia.

Noted for their baby-back pork ribs, their Sicilian style tenderloins, and their Snowmobiler (a 20-ounce T-bone steak), Bullwinkle's serves an array of burgers, a few pasta dishes, frog legs and at least one wild-game entree, depending on the season. What Jackie really specializes in, though, is soup and appetizers. Expect to find soups like Grandma used to make: chicken dumpling soup, split pea, navy bean and ham. And her appetizers are legendary. They include Tater Skins smothered with cheese and topped with bacon bits, homemade Hay Stack Onion Rings, Winkle's Hot Wings and Nacho Supreme, piled high with fresh-cooked beans, beef, cheese, tomatoes, onions and olives — enough to make a meal for two.

The Coachman
$$$ • 209 Madison Ave., West Yellowstone, Mont. • (406) 646-7381

If it's meat and potatoes you're after, you'll find it at The Coachman in the Stage Coach Inn. But it's the seafood, especially the fresh salmon, that folks often favor here. Chef Jack Cole, who has been serving up consistently good meals at the Coachman since 1989, changes the menu according to the season and the situation. In summer, you might find a selection of steaks, homestyle pot roast or pesto chicken primavera. From late November through early December you'll find a menu designed for hard-working U.S. cross-country teams in training. On holidays — the Coachman is open seven days a week year round — Cole turns out traditional fare with a flair. Don't let the fresh flowers (when they're available) or the linen service scare you. It's strictly come as you are, breakfast, lunch and dinner. The dinner menu includes a long wine list. And you can order drinks from the hotel bar.

Doris's Cantina
$ • West Yellowstone Airport, West Yellowstone, Mont. • (406) 646-9533

Open seven days a week, June 1 through September 30, Doris's Cantina features fresh Tex-Mex cuisine in a small corner of the West Yellowstone Airport. The 3-mile drive from town doesn't deter locals bent on biting into Doris Barton's Pancho Villa chile relleno dinner, the hottest — read most popular — item on her dinner menu. Tuesday is traditionally 50¢ Taco Day. Doris, who hires extra waitresses to help her with the Tuesday crowd that shows up for the bargain lunch, says she sometimes sells more than 500 tacos in a couple of short hours.

In addition to standard breakfasts, Doris serves huevos rancheros and chorizo con huevos. Lunches include tacos, burritos, hot sandwiches and burgers served at the counter or at a table overlooking the airport runway. Doris closes her Cantina from 2 to 5 PM each summer afternoon.

Eino's Bar
$ • 8955 Gallatin Rd., West Yellowstone, Mont. • (406) 646-9344

The price is right, and the juicy burgers and big steaks are cooked to your exact order. That's because you are your own chef at Eino's, where customers get to grill their own steaks or burgers. Nine miles north of West Yellowstone on U.S. Highway 191, Eino's is more than a bar and burger stop. It's the inconspicuous place (the sign is so small you could easily miss it, so watch for it at the junction of U.S. Highways 191 and 287) where anyone can stop in and make themselves at home. Cook up your steak — they offer only T-bones and top sirloin — in the grill room. Sip a beer, then devour that steak while you gaze across the open landscape through Eino's giant picture windows. Or head downstairs with a pitcher of beer and try your hand at pool.

Eino's is closed for three weeks between Thanksgiving and Christmas. During the summer, it opens about noon. When snowmobilers are on the loose, though, the place opens in the morning. Eino's has a full bar and a friendly staff.

The Gusher
$ • Madison and Dunraven, West Yellowstone, Mont. • (406) 646-9050

Relaxed and comfortable, The Gusher is the sort of place where you can sink into a padded chair and stare after a long day in the Park or on the road. Read a newspaper or peruse a guidebook. Or sip a Guinness served Dublin style at 46 degrees. (The Gusher has a good selection of beer.) In addition to pizzas (they deliver) The Gusher has the biggest burgers in town as well as some seafood, sandwiches and a dinner steak. You'll find lunch and dinner here year round.

Nancy P's Baking Co.
$ • 29 Canyon Ave., West Yellowstone, Mont. • (406) 646-9737

Nancy Pfeiffer, owner of Nancy P's, doesn't do donuts. She does do huckleberry buckle, strawberry rhubarb bars, morning-glory carrot muffins and big bad brownies. And she serves a great cup of coffee — Torrefazione Italia (coffee lovers may recognize the brand) — in her cheery little bakery. Her showcase is loaded with so many goodies (three kinds of sweet rolls too) that you may forget to look up and around.

Depending on the day, you'll find an assortment of European specialty breads, and you'll always find focaccia bread. If you get there early, look for a basket full of lunch-sized pizzas — they're just right for two — atop her showcase. These are perfect for a picnic. So are her ham and cheese croissants, her Mediterranean rollups and humongous to-go sandwiches made on focaccia bread. Nancy P's is open from May through September.

Oregon Short Line
$$$ • 315 Yellowstone Ave., West Yellowstone, Mont. • (406) 646-7365

Tucked into a nifty nook adjacent to the 1903 Oregon Short Line Railroad Car (see our Attractions chapter for more information about this railroad car, the anchor around which the West Yellowstone Conference Hotel was built), this restaurant combines consistently good food with comfort and convenience, especially if you're staying at the Conference Hotel. Feel free to start your dinner hour at the Iron Horse Saloon next door (you can take your drink to the dining room). Be forewarned, though: You'll be sharing the room with a few wild animals — like a mounted pheasant, a bobcat, an antelope and a black bear.

You'll find a varied menu with entrees ranging from chicken pesto linguine to prime rib to broiled lamb chops. We recommend you try the Steak Durango, a grain-fed beefalo top sirloin steak. Top it off with a glass of wine.

Pete's Rocky Mountain Pizza Company
$$ • 104 Canyon Ave., West Yellowstone, Mont. • (406) 646-7820

Just try walking by Pete's Rocky Mountain Pizza on a summer's evening with the smell of an Incredible Edible pizza wafting out the door. This popular pizzeria makes up to 180 Italian pies a day at the peak of their season. Pete's also serves steaks, an assortment of chicken dishes and pastas with homemade sauces (their lasagna is delicious) as well as lunches during the summer. If you can't stand confinement on a summer's evening, try one of their tables on the sidewalk patio. Or, if you like, kick back in your motel room and order out. Pete's delivers.

Running Bear Pancake House
$ • 538 Madison Ave., West Yellowstone, Mont. • (406) 646-7703

Ask Insiders who serves the best breakfast in town and chances are they'll say, "The Running Bear Pancake House." Running Bear is such a popular breakfast spot that some summer mornings you'll find a line of people waiting their turn for their morning meal. Lunch favorites include real turkey sandwiches and half-pound, extra-lean, hand-shaped hamburgers. Owners Dixie and Mike Klostrich also serve breakfast for lunch.

This restaurant, which seats 75, closes from October 31 through December 25, and from March 31 through May 1.

Three Bear Restaurant
$$$ • 205 Yellowstone Ave., West Yellowstone, Mont. • (406) 646-7811

Come as you are and come when you can, says manager Tom Schaap. If you aren't the bashful sort, you'll want to wander about looking at the historic photos that line the Three Bear Restaurant's walls. You may have to peer over other peoples' tables, though.

This is a popular place. The food here is consistently good. And the decor, a combination of rustic with giant log pillars and soothing green carpet and wallpaper, is comfortable. It's just right for dining on the Three Bears' hand-cut steaks or slow-roasted prime rib. (We dare you to tackle the 16-ounce Cattleman's Cut. If you aren't into dares, we suggest the 8-ounce Petite Cut.) Besides a good assortment of steaks, the Three Bear menu includes chicken and seafood, pork and pasta.

The Three Bear closes from October 18 to December 15 and from March 1 to May 1. They serve breakfast, lunch and dinner. There is a lounge adjacent to the dining room. Feel free to bring your drink to the table.

Gardiner, Montana

Bear Country Restaurant
$$ • 232 Park, Gardiner, Mont.
• (406) 848-7188

After a day in Yellowstone Park drive straight to the Bear Country Restaurant. Have a piece of apple pie or chicken pot pie, lasagna or stir-fry shrimp. Everything here is homemade. Sometimes hopping until 11 o'clock on a summer's night, this place is casual. You may just feel like you're at Aunt Sue's potlucking with your long-lost relatives. The Bear Country serves breakfast, lunch and dinner.

Corral Drive Inn
$, no credit cards • U.S. Hwy. 89,
Gardiner, Mont. • (406) 848-7627

If you're a burger lover, chances are you've heard about this place. If you haven't, don't pass through Gardiner without stopping at the Corral Drive Inn. The burgers here, served up for 37 years by Helen Gould (the Corral is the oldest single-owner business in Gardiner) are legendary half-pound, handmade whoppers. Besides an assortment of regular hamburgers, Helen does a fine buffalo burger and an array of hot burger-type sandwiches.

You'll find a patio outside and three tables inside. More than a juicy hamburger, Helen dishes up a serving of old-fashioned straight-forward local color. Dining here is an experience. (Ask her about her "Hateful Hamburger" sign.)

Montana Blue's Chuckwagon Dinner Theater
$$$ • U.S. Hwy 89, Gardiner, Mont.
• (406) 848-9898, (800) 424-4445

Cooked country style and served family style at a dozen huge picnic tables, the food at Montana Blue's is just like Grandma used to make. In fact, chances are Grandma did make the homemade biscuits and the pots full of rich baked beans that complement the mounds of barbecued beef and chicken. Cooked by the Meyer family — read mostly Grandma Meyer — and served on tin plates, the meal includes apple sauce, spice cake, coffee and lemonade. It also includes an af-

ter-dinner musical performance by the Meyer brothers and their father, Bob. Children younger than 12 can buy the whole shebang for $6.50.

Montana Blue's is casual — a barn-like building with a gravel floor, cowboy memorabilia on the walls, and no windows (it makes for better lighting during the Meyers' performances). Dinner is served at 6:30 sharp Memorial Day through Labor Day, and reservations are recommended.

Silver Gate and Cooke City, Montana

Joan and Bill's Family Restaurant
$$ • U.S. Hwy 212, Cooke City, Mont.
• (406) 838-2280

Known by locals as "the pie place," Joan and Bill's Family Restaurant offers an impressive array of delicious homemade pies and other baked goods. Comfortable, with a casual rustic atmosphere a la Cooke City, Joan and Bill's is the kind of place where you might find yourself doubling up at a table with a stranger (the management would never ask you to do it, and you won't be strangers for long) to make room for a larger crowd. At your service, you'll find the second, third and fourth generations of Cooke City restaurateurs (Grandma's dad began the restaurant on Cooke Pass just after World War II). The menu offers pretty typical Western fare, and chicken-fried steak is their best seller.

The Prospector
$$$ • U.S. Hwy. 212, Cooke City, Mont.
• (406) 838-2251, (800) 527-6462

The Prospector is the only restaurant in Silver Gate/Cooke City that consistently stays open all year. While The Prospector is renowned for its great chili (they go through 15 gallons every other day no matter what the season), you'll find plenty of other entrees on the menu. For breakfast we recommend the Sunrise Breakfast Special: two eggs, two pancakes, two pieces of bacon for $2.99. If you're a bit hungrier, try their steak and eggs. Prime rib and Chicken Mediterranean (chicken breast cooked in white wine, shallots and garlic with

Photo: Robert Bower/Post Register

The dining room of the Old Faithful Lodge is probably what your hometown steakhouse modeled itself after.

marinara sauce) are the favorites. You'll also find an assortment of pasta dishes, three kinds of steaks, Mexican food and shrimp scampi. This busy place is open from early morning until pretty late at night.

Grand Teton National Park

Jenny Lake Lodge
$$$$ • Teton Park Rd. at Jenny Lake • (307) 733-4647, (800) 628-9988

It may be the only restaurant for hundreds of miles that has a dress requirement — men are asked to wear jackets to dinner — but with the food so well-coiffed, you won't mind. Garnishes and sauces include ginger chutney, wild mushrooms, cognac-laced jus, baby leeks and warm caviar vinaigrette. Entrees can be exotic: buffalo,

ostrich, antelope, venison and rabbit. But there are several upscale restaurants in the area serving creatively prepared wild game, so those menu items don't fully explain this spot's popularity. We suspect that so many people eat here because they love the rustic old log dining room, with its bright throw rugs on wood floors, white curtains and matching white linen tablecloths, fresh flowers and cowhide upholstered seats.

Jenny Lake Lodge serves breakfast and dinner from the end of May to early October. Dinner reservations are required. There are two seatings per night, both of which book solid. The Sunday evening buffets have achieved legendary status around here.

Dornan's Chuckwagon
$$ • 10 Moose St., Teton Park Rd. at Moose Junction • (307) 733-2415

Dornan's has been serving outdoor chuckwagon meals here in summer since

1948. Eat on the lawn when the weather's nice (believe us, the view couldn't be better), or pile into one of two big teepees if it's raining. You can get pancake and egg breakfasts and sandwich lunches. But it's the barbecued short ribs, roast beef and dutch oven fixin's, all you can eat, that pack the picnic tables.

The Chuckwagon closes in winter, but even after all the other Park concessions close, you can always find a meal at Dornan's. Across the parking lot, Dornan's Pizza and Pasta Company serve calzones, gourmet pizzas and pasta dishes for lunch and dinner year round. The well-stocked grocery store offers a third option with its deli and bakery goods.

Mural Room at Jackson Lake Lodge
$$$$ • U.S. 89 at Jackson Lake Junction • (307) 543-2811, (800) 628-9988

Mountains on one side and mountain men on the other, this is fine dining at its most Teton-esque. The Mural Room in massive Jackson Lake Lodge looks across distant Jackson Lake to Mount Moran and the Teton range. Other walls display murals of early fur traders, trappers and hunters. (The well-known creator of these murals, Carl Roters, became so enamored of his Western subjects' home that he moved to Jackson in 1968.)

The Mural Room serves breakfast, lunch and dinner. Dinner options include a scattering of Teton specialties like grilled buffalo strip loin or skillet seared Idaho trout as well as more traditional items. Reservations are recommended for dinner.

Other dining opportunities in Jackson Lake Lodge are the Blue Heron, a bar with the same stunning mountain views as the Mural Room and an extended bar menu, and The Pioneer Grill, a cafe in which you trade in the views (The Pioneer looks out the back of the lodge into lodgepole forest) for more affordable prices. Jackson Lake Lodge is open in summer only.

Signal Mountain Lodge
$$$ • Teton Park Rd. on south shore of Jackson Lake • (307) 733-5470

You spent the morning touring Jackson Lake and now you're hungry. It's time to participate in a Teton tradition: nachos and Margaritas (huckleberry, if you're adventurous) on the deck at Signal Mountain Lodge. The nachos come stacked so high you're sure to get your fill. The breeze off the lake provides perfect seasoning. You can also order soups, salads, sandwiches and burgers.

It addition to its cafe, Signal Mountain Lodge also offers fine dining in the evening at Aspens Restaurant. Reservations are recommended if you want to sample one of the daily trout and salmon specials prepared differently each night. A tempting array of pasta dishes is also available, along with options ranging from Italian to Chinese. Enjoy your meal with a drink from the fully equipped bar or a gourmet coffee beverage. Both Aspens Restaurant and the lodge's cafe offer children's menus.

Also at Signal Mountain are a clothing store, gift shop, service station, convenience store and marina. The marina offers scenic floats, boat rentals, guest buoys and guided fishing trips. Signal Mountain Lodge opens in mid-May and closes in mid-October.

Jackson Hole

Jackson, Wyoming

Bubba's Barbecue
$ • 515 W. Broadway, Jackson, Wyo. • (307) 733-2288

Big servings of affordable food have made Bubba's a popular place in Jackson. Ribs are the house specialty: baby back or spare. You can't make reservations, but the timing usually works out about right if you sign onto the waiting list, wander across the street to the grocery store for a six pack of beer (no alco-

---

INSIDERS' TIP

A culinary delight peculiar to this area is "fry sauce," a pale pink blend of mayo and ketchup for dipping french fries into.

hol is served at Bubba's) and wander back. In the off-season, you'll find the dining room busiest at breakfast. Even President Clinton enjoyed a generously sized Bubba's country breakfast on a recent visit. Bubba's serves breakfast, lunch and dinner seven days a week.

The Bunnery
$ • 130 N. Cache, Jackson, Wyo.
• (307) 733-5474

Locals know The Bunnery as a great breakfast shop and the home of OSM — Oatmeal Sunflower Millet bread. Other local favorites include chocolate cheesecake and flaky, nut encrusted sticky buns. Lunch (and in summer, dinner) includes gourmet burgers, hot and cold sandwiches, salads, soups and omelettes. With your meal enjoy fresh-squeezed juice, gourmet coffee beverages, soft drinks, beer or wine. From June through September, expect to wait in line during the breakfast and lunch rushes.

Make sure you grab a loaf of OSM on your way out. You can even get OSM pancake mix or the Bunnery cookbook, which includes the OSM recipe for your bread machine.

Cafe a Mano
$ • 45 S. Glenwood, Jackson, Wyo.
• (307) 739-2500

Imagine fast food that tastes gourmet and you've got Cafe a Mano. From the salsa bar, which always features five fresh-made salsas, to the fresh lime juice that goes into the margaritas, to the meat marinades and sauces made fresh daily, these folks go the extra. The menu is Mexican-ish to match the rounded doorways and faux adobe walls. The international burritos, which range from Thai chicken to barbecued tofu, deserve special comment.

Cafe a Mano serves lunch and dinner with no reservations necessary (although with only 14 tables, you may have to wait or take out during the lunch rush). In spring and fall the restaurant closes on Sundays. Oh, and in case you were wondering, the carved polka-dotted snakes on the walls are for sale.

Calico
$$ • Teton Village Rd., near Teton Village, Wyo. • (307) 733-2460

The menu at this family favorite ranges from macaroni and cheese to pizza to rotisserie-prepared whole chickens or prime rib, so a variety of palates and pocketbooks can be satisfied. Dining is casual. And the long deck is a perfect spot to sip wine and watch your kids play on the large lawn well off the road. Calico even provides the toy box. Before it was transported here, the tiny attached bar was a schoolhouse and later a church in nearby Kelly. Calico serves dinner seven nights a week. No reservations are necessary.

Camp Creek Inn
$$ • U.S. Hwy. 189, near Hoback Junction, Wyo. • (307) 733-3099

Some of the best things in life are incongruous . . . like wilderness U.S. 189 winding out to Pinedale with little but trees on the sides of the road and the relaxed fine dining offered by Camp Creek Inn, just 4 miles out of Hoback Junction on that highway. Flowered linen tablecloths under glass contrast with woven rawhide and peeled pine chairs.

You'll peruse a menu that features locally renowned prime rib (you order by the inch), while in the exposed rafters overhead, a stuffed cougar crouches in such a lifelike pose that you expect his dangling tail to twitch. Camp Creek Inn offers a children's menu with kid-sized portions. The inn serves breakfast, lunch and dinner in summer, lunch and dinner only in winter.

Gouloff's
$$$ • 3600 N. Teton Village Rd., near Teton Village, Wyo. • (307) 733-1886

We were charmed by the little restaurant's backyard. It's fragrant with raised beds of sage, chives, oregano, rosemary, cilantro, red romaine lettuce, three kinds of mint, thyme, tarragon and dill, all destined for your plate. Owner Vicky Gouloff even cultivates edible flowers for garnishes.

Vicky calls her food "Teton Cuisine," and the dining experience here, "a casual, affordable sort of fine dining." This means wild game, creatively prepared with lots of berries and nuts in an atmosphere as casual as dinner at your neighbor's house. Locals recommend the corn ginger soup and the pistachio nut chicken. Gouloff's serves dinner only, Tuesday through Saturday. The two dining rooms are small, so reservations are wise. The restaurant generally closes for several weeks in the spring and again in the fall.

The Granary at Spring Creek

$$$$ • **1800 Spirit Dance Rd., Jackson, Wyo.** • **(307) 733-8833**

Some swear the best fine dining in the valley isn't in the valley. It's at Spring Creek Resort on East Gros Ventre Butte, almost 1,000 feet above Jackson Hole. The Granary is open for breakfast, lunch and dinner, serving what it calls American cuisine. Reservations are advised.

You'll have trouble paying attention to the food, creative and complex though it is, because the huge windows seem to hang you off the cliff edge. Hawks soar below you and granite peaks saw off the horizon. But if you order an elk dish (the elk is from New Zealand not the Elk Refuge) or trout (this is local) from the ever-changing menu, you'll probably find you can tear your eyes off the windows after a couple of bites. A good bet for lunch is the Portobello mushroom sandwich with watercress and caramelized onion or the elk flank fajitas.

Horse Creek Station

$$ • **9800 S. U.S. Hwy. 89 near Hoback Junction, Wyo.** • **(307) 733-0810**

Eleven miles south of Jackson and perfectly located for fishermen and whitewater rafters is Horse Creek Station. Barbecue tops the menu: Locals love the baby back ribs, barbecued shrimp and barbecued pork chops. The on-premises sports bar offers a full range of beers, wines and mixed drinks and an abbreviated finger-food menu. In warm weather, enjoy lunch or dinner on the deck outside.

During football season, make this your Monday night stop. Every Monday night a drawing determines which lucky patron gets to enjoy the game from the plush recliner, drinking and eating gratis (even the chair is given away — at halftime during the Super Bowl).

Jedediah's Original House of Sourdough

$ • **135 E. Broadway, Jackson, Wyo.** • **(307) 733-5671**

Named for Jedediah Smith, early 1800s wanderer in these parts, this breakfast hot spot serves sourdough made from a culture born in that wilder century. Seventeen years ago when Mike Gieran and his partners opened this restaurant, they asked locals to bring in family sourdough cultures. Some of the sourdough starters were more than 100 years old. Mixed together and cultured in 60 gallon crocks in the basement, the bubbly result becomes biscuits and pancakes and other goodies every morning. Some summer days, the little log cabin restaurant goes through 30 pungent gallons of the stuff.

Jedediah's serves breakfast, lunch and, in summer, dinner. Reservations can be made for dinner. While you're in, check out the sign-up sheet for Jedediah's catalogue: You can order house jams and sourdough culture for your friends.

JJ's SilverDollar Grill at The Wort Hotel

$$$ • **Corner of Glenwood and Broadway, Jackson, Wyo.** • **(307) 733-2190, (800) 322-2727**

The Wort is a Jackson landmark. Inside the old hotel, decorated with photographs from Jackson's wilder days, JJ's SilverDollar Grill serves upscale Western meals in a family restaurant atmosphere. Folks come here for the meat. Whether it's lamb, pork, duck, buffalo or elk you've got a taste for tonight, you'll find it. SilverDollar Grill boasts that it serves the best prime rib in town, a tall claim in beef-happy Jackson. There are also seafood and vegetarian options. The restaurant serves breakfast, lunch and dinner; dinner reservations are recommended.

The Lame Duck

$$ • **680 E. Broadway, Jackson, Wyo.** • **(307) 733-4311**

So here you are in cowboy country, land of beef, beef and more beef, and what will you

---

INSIDERS' TIP

On a tight budget but want to sample some fine area cuisine? Many high-end restaurants serve a very affordable lunch.

enjoy for dinner? May we suggest sushi? Sylvia and Joe Dipriscio have been serving up their authentic Oriental dishes (mostly Chinese — Joe studied Oriental cuisine in Hong Kong) to Jackson Insiders for 16 years.

If you're planning a get-together at your condo or motel, consider ordering one of The Lame Duck's famous 30-piece sushi platters. Or call and reserve one of four private rooms. Each is separated from the main dining area by rice-paper screens. Two feature Western-style seating; two are traditional, their low tables equipped with floor pits into which you extend your legs for comfort. Each private room seats from four to 12.

The Lame Duck has a full bar, including, of course, sake. The drink menu is almost as fun as the food menu, featuring such concoctions as Disaster and Chinese Firedrill (sorry, you'll have to see for yourself what's in 'em). The restaurant serves dinner only. Reservations are accepted for the private tea rooms.

Nani's Genuine Pasta House
$$$ • 240 N. Glenwood, Jackson, Wyo.
• (307) 733-3888

Sicilian Carol Mortillaro Parker, padrona of this little restaurant, serves only authentic Italian cuisine. Olive oil, balsamic vinegar and other key ingredients are imported from Italy. Fresh herbs come from the restaurant's garden. The regular menu is classic Italian, but every month dishes from a different region of Italy are featured. Wine selections complement the region's style.

Reservations are recommended since there are only 15 tables inside, plus deck seating in summer. Dinner is served seven nights, except in spring and fall when the restaurant cuts back its hours.

Nora's Fish Creek Inn
$$ • 5600 W. Wyo. Hwy. 22, Wilson, Wyo.
• (307) 733-8288

If you're looking for the place locals love to love, you've found it. Nora's serves a breakfast so popular you'll probably stand in line for it on weekends (sorry, no breakfast reservations). But when you lay your fork into those huevos rancheros or blueberry pancakes, you won't mind the wait. Nora's serves breakfast, lunch and dinner seven days a week; the bar

draws crowds in the evenings. Classic country music plays through the speakers day and night.

Fifteen years ago, owner Nora Tygum took over what was once a dance studio and before that Wilson's general store and post office. The peeled logs of the 1930s building have been left exposed. Fresh flowers decorate the tables every day, 12 months a year. Pretty Fish Creek flows almost right past the door.

Although breakfast is the popular meal at Nora's, many locals say it's not the best. That honor goes to dinner. The black Angus beef gets rave reviews, but that won't surprise you out here in cattle country. The surprise is fresh — that's right, fresh — salmon, trout and halibut. Folks who live near the sea and ought to know say Nora's charbroiled salmon or pine nut crusted halibut taste about as good as fish can. Dinner reservations are accepted.

Pearl Street Bagels
$ • 145 W Pearl Ave., Jackson, Wyo.
• (307) 739-1218
$ • 1230 Ida Ln., Wilson, Wyo.
• (307) 739-1261

The original shop opened in Jackson in 1990 and quickly became a locals' coffee-sipping hangout. Recently owner Maggie Gibson decided to bring Pearl Street's products to little Wilson at the base of Teton Pass. Both locations feature old-fashioned boiled and baked bagels — none of that steam oven shortcutting. Fancy cream cheeses top the fresh, fragrant bagels, making a fine breakfast or lunch. You can even get bagels and lox. These folks also serve a variety of premium coffees and teas, including Chai ice tea. Stop by in the morning for a bag of discounted day-olds while they last.

The Range
$$$$ • 225 N. Cache, Jackson, Wyo.
• (307) 733-5481

Chef Arthur says that the designer who gave The Range its unique look was striving for "metropolitan prairie." You'll have to judge for yourself, but what's certain is that with that open-style kitchen, cherry wainscoting and unobtrusive street entrance, folks don't confuse The Range with any other Jackson restaurant.

The wine list will surprise you in its variety and quality. Selections range from American to French to Italian to Australian. The menu shows Chef Arthur's tendency to "take the usual and make it unusual." Nightly specials include an appetizer, salad, meat, fish and fresh trout. Those nightly trout specials mean The Range has offered more than 200 trout preparations since it opened in 1988.

The Range takes its food and wine seriously, but you'll be serenaded by music ranging from Jerry Garcia to Patsy Cline, and the kitchen staff wear brown baseball caps. These folks are open for dinner seven nights a week, except for one month closures in the spring and fall. A full bar is on premises.

Shades Cafe
$$, no credit cards • 75 S. King, Jackson, Wyo. • (307) 733-2015

They used to call it the Vuarnet Cafe, but Vuarnet, the snazzy sunglasses manufacturer with first claim to that name, apparently didn't much like that idea. Nine-year-old Shades is a coffeehouse and restaurant with more seating space on its shaded deck than inside its dining room. Breakfasts are bakery treats, Belgian waffles, eggs Benedict and more, washed down with a gourmet coffee. Lunches are foccaccia sandwiches, burritos, soups and salads. Dinner is a bit more surprising: It's Thai. Served Wednesday through Sunday in summer and shorter hours other seasons, the Thai menu is as authentic as these folks can make it.

This locals' favorite tends to fill fast for dinners, so reservations are strongly recommended. Shades serves no alcohol, but you may bring your own beer and wine. Expect a small corkage fee for wine.

Snake River Brewing Co.
$$ • 265 S. Millward, Jackson, Wyo. • (307) 739-2337

There are no logs here. No cowboy art and no elk mounts. Instead you'll see patterned concrete floors, cable bannisters and high ceilings crisscrossed by a profusion of shiny white steel beams. The bar is a huge black S curve. Blocks of light stream through tall, square-paneled windows. This popular microbrew pub looks more like a factory than a bar.

In typical Jackson style, the food is also a new take on an old thing: The menu features pizza baked in a wood-fired oven, but these pizzas are, well, different. For instance, there's the mozzarella and fontina pizza topped with duck sausage and fresh sage. Or the smoked chicken and sun-dried tomato pizza. You can also get pastas, salads and soups, plus a few eclectic surprises. Make sure you have the bartender pour you a pint of one of the pub's award-winning brews to go with your meal (we recommend the Zonker Stout).

Snake River Brewing Co. serves lunch and dinner seven days a week. The kitchen stays open late for the party crowd (see our Nightlife chapter for more).

Snake River Grill
$$$$ • 84 E. Broadway, Jackson, Wyo. • (307) 733-0557

Rumor has it that Harrison Ford owns this upscale restaurant. Actually he just eats here. The President and Mrs. Clinton have too. Winters, it's full of chummy, red-faced skiers. This is Jackson-style elegance, with log walls, wrought iron accents and a moss rock fireplace. The food is simple but artfully combined and presented; mashed potatoes, asparagus and mustard sauce might complement your seared salmon, or spicy cole slaw your rainbow trout with pecan-butter. Snake River Grill has a full bar and award-winning wine list. They serve dinner only, seven nights a week. In summer, it's a good idea to make your reservations well in advance. The restaurant closes during November and April.

Stagecoach Bar and Patty Cake West
$, no credit cards • 5755 W. Wyo. Hwy. 22, Wilson, Wyo. • (307) 733-7225

Strange things happen — and sometimes they end up strangely right. One such event occurred in November 1996, when upscale deli Patty Cake Patisserie (now renamed Patty Cake West) moved into Wilson's popular locals' hangout, a country-western bar (see our Nightlife chapter). Now you can play pool, listen to country music and sip a local microbrew while enjoying fine pastries, homemade bread or soup and tasty pasta salads. Long lines cue up at lunch for such favorites as the grilled chicken sandwiches or the made-to-order burgers. Don't forget to grab dessert, too: big chocolate chip cookies or pastries made fresh that morning. If you're not moseying over to the bar for a cocktail, add an espresso to wash it all down.

Steak Pub
$$ • 4125 S. U.S. Hwy. 89, near Jackson, Wyo. • (307) 734-8070

If it seems that the Steak Pub turns its back on U.S. Highway 89, obstinately facing its windows and cottonwood-shaded deck out toward the distant Snake River, it's actually the highway's fault. When the little roadhouse that is now Steak Pub's dining room was built back in 1938, the road was in front of the building. Lucky you: You'll enjoy the views and breezes on the deck, screened from U.S. 89 by additions to the old log building in the 60s, 80s, and in 1997.

We heard that Steak Pub's bar, which has its own sandwich and finger food menu, is the best place in town for hot wings. The dining room features beef but doesn't forget about chicken, shrimp, salmon and pasta. After dinner, enjoy a decadent homemade eclair — flaky and drizzled with chocolate, they're the size of a small loaf of bread. Reservations are recommended for dinner.

Stiegler's Restaurant and Bar
$$$$ • Teton Village Rd. at Jackson Hole Racquet Club • (307) 733-1071

Some will tell you this is the best fine dining in town. Austrian Peter Stiegler serves continental delicacies in a plushly carpeted, lace-curtained dining room. The tiny adjoining bar is warmed by a river rock fireplace; the bar itself is topped with beaten copper.

Peter is both head chef and maitre d' in this classy little restaurant with its own house china service and fresh flowers on every table. Some menu items are, as Peter says, "as Austrian as it gets." Like the Bauern Schmaus, a two-person platter of roast pork tenderloin, smoked pork, bratwurst, dumplings, sauerkraut and red cabbage. Or the Schlipfkrapfen, a ravioli dish from Peter's home province. Portions are exquisitely presented rather than large. Reservations are requested; Stiegler's serves dinner nightly except Mondays; it closes for a few weeks in spring and fall.

Vista Grande
$$ • 2550 Teton Village Rd., near Teton Village, Wyo. • (307) 733-6964

Twenty years ago, newlyweds Becky and Tom Schnell decided to build a restaurant. It became a family endeavor: Tom was his own contractor, the couple's mothers sewed the waitresses' dresses and their fathers made the tabletops.

They still spend much of their time at the restaurant they started their marriage with. Go there often and you'll find yourself greeted by name. The restaurant has grown several times, now seating 160 inside. A recent addition is the deck that wraps around the west and north sides of the building overlooking a spacious grassy area big enough for kickball or frisbee (which is what you're likely to find your kids doing while you sip that Margarita). The menu is extensive, but Becky says customers are particularly partial to the fajitas (made with skirt steak, the traditional cut) and the chimichangas. A full bar is on premises; Vista Grande serves dinner seven nights per week.

Surrounding Areas

Eastern Idaho

Idaho Falls, Idaho

The largest town in Greater Yellowstone, Idaho Falls has more than 120 eating establishments. A striking number are major chains or fast food joints, though, so the odds of finding a culinary surprise aren't as high as you

---

INSIDERS' TIP

Livingston is the home of Wilcoxson's Ice Cream, a homemade-tasting brand sold since 1912. Watch for Wilcoxson's ice cream when you're in Livingston, West Yellowstone and Yellowstone Park.

might think. The trend in recent years has been for new chains to locate on 17th Street near the mall, so if you want familiar food you can either grab a local phone book or just hop in your car and head toward Grand Teton Mall. (Broadway and the Northgate Mile also host their share of franchises.) Idaho Falls' originals are scattered about town. The following is a too-short list of longtime local institutions and other interesting alternatives to the national franchise scene.

Hawg Smoke Cafe

$$$, no credit cards • 475 Northgate Mile, Idaho Falls, Idaho • (208) 523-4804

Walk into this tiny, seven-table restaurant in your jeans and tee-shirt. Grab a beer from the cooler in the corner. Order off a menu chalked onto boards on one wall. Sit down, chat with your companions and prepare for a fine dining experience. This little restaurant specializes in the kind of high quality food and creative dishes most often associated with jacket and tie joints. For instance, there's the popular Steak Watsonville, a petite filet served with large succulent Mexican shrimp. On the side are artichoke hearts and leaves, drizzled with a gorgonzola cheese sauce. Or there's the house mole/curry, which spices up tenderloin or chicken breast.

One word of warning: There are no quick meals here. Plan to spend an evening, enjoying good friends and original, exquisite food. Hawg Smoke is open Tuesday through Saturday for dinner only. Beer and wine are available, but the cafe serves no mixed drinks. Reservations are recommended.

La Yaquesita

$ • 110 Science Center Dr., Idaho Falls, Idaho • (208) 523-1779

Ask a local where to go for good, authentic Mexican food, and they'll almost certainly say, "La Yaq." The Mendez family, from Sonora, Mexico, opened this old-fashioned Mexican restaurant 10 years ago. It serves dynamite chile relleno, chile verde, carne asada and chimichangas. Other items on the extensive menu are just as authentic and just as reasonably priced. Enjoy your meal with a cold Dos Equis, Tecate, Negro Modelo, Pacifico or Carta Blanca, or a wine cooler or margarita.

La Yaq serves lunch and dinner Monday through Saturday. A private banquet room upstairs can accommodate up to 50 people.

North Hi-Way Cafe

$ • 460 Northgate Mile, Idaho Falls, Idaho • (208) 522-6212

North Hi-Way Cafe is located across the street from Idaho Falls' stockyards. Open since 1947, it may be the oldest restaurant in town. Stockmen eat here when they're in town for Wednesday cattle auctions or on alternate Mondays when sheep auctions take place. You won't pay a lot of money for your rare beef sandwich (like a french dip only cooked up rarer), your prime rib sandwich (think slab, not slice, of meat inside the bun) or your Triple Crown burger with pastrami and Swiss, but you will get a lot of food. Two people could make a meal of some of those sandwiches. The cafe serves breakfast, lunch and dinner.

Sandpiper Restaurant

$$ • 750 Lindsay Blvd., Idaho Falls, Idaho • (208) 524-3344

Prime rib has been the house specialty for 25 years — these folks slow-roast and serve a minimum of 276 pounds of certified Black Angus every week. You can also choose from fresh halibut, chicken and pork dishes as well as a selection of pasta meals. Sandpiper serves only Idaho potatoes and has the most extensive wine list in town. Dine near the solarium windows, or in nice weather, enjoy your meal on one of two decks overlooking the Snake River and the greenbelt.

This restaurant has a full bar and serves lunch and dinner daily except Sunday, when no lunch is served. Banquet facilities are available for up to 100 people. The Sandpiper is locally owned and operated by longtime residents Ron and Rose Anne Obendorf. Reservations are accepted.

Smitty's Pancake and Steak House

$ • 645 Broadway, Idaho Falls, Idaho • (208) 523-6450

Smitty's is an Idaho Falls institution serving breakfast, lunch and dinner daily. Breakfast is probably the most popular meal here, although the relatively inexpensive rib eye, filet mignon and other dinners draw folks too.

Since soup, salad and dessert are included in your dinner price, Smitty's is a downhome good value. If you come for a weekend breakfast, you'll probably wait in line for your chance at the specialty pancakes like potato, baby Dutch and German. Smitty's has had only two owners in its 28-year history. In Idaho Falls' volatile restaurant market, that ought to earn these folks a prize.

The Snake Bite
$ • 425 River Pkwy., Idaho Falls, Idaho
• (208) 525-2522

Think of it as a yuppie burger joint. The Snake Bite was voted Idaho Falls' best lunch spot in 1997. It serves about 20 microbrews, premium wines from the West and Northwest, pasta dishes, gourmet burgers (made with ground sirloin) and steak. The fresh king salmon sandwich with creamy dill sauce is worth a visit all by itself. The Snake Bite serves lunch and dinner Tuesday through Saturday and lunch only on Monday. The restaurant is small and personable, with a Southwestern feel that matches the jazzed up, spiced up food.

Rexburg, Idaho, and Vicinity

The Relay Station
$$ • U.S. Hwy. 20, 2 mi. N. of St. Anthony, Idaho • (208) 624-4640

Owners Lynn Klein and Wanda Harshbarger named their restaurant in the rolling farm country between St. Anthony and Ashton after the old travelers' way stations on railroad lines. But they're more of a locals' joint than a travelers' stopover. Maybe it's the cozy log building, with its pine paneling and lodgepole pine rafters. Maybe it's the sunny deck where you can enjoy your meal on nice days. But more likely it's the food — homecooking, right down the line. Lots of folks like the generous steaks, but Lynn is most proud of her shrimp. It's the biggest she can find, peeled, cleaned and breaded right here.

The Relay Station serves breakfast, lunch and dinner every day but Tuesday. Beer and wine are available. It's a good idea to call in your reservation if you're planning on coming during the busy weekend evenings. These folks are open year round.

Ashton, Idaho

Big Jud's Country Diner
$ • 265 S. U.S. Hwy. 20, Ashton, Idaho
• (208) 652-7806

When Jud Niederer set out to open a restaurant, he aimed straight for the big time. Around here big thinking is appreciated; four years later Idaho supports four Big Jud's. The Ashton restaurant was his second. The original is near Rexburg.

What was Jud's big idea? Well, basically — bigness. There's the Big Jud, a one-pound burger housed in a specially made bun eight inches across. Finish yours and you'll get your picture on the wall with all those who've managed the same feat. Pound down a double and your photo will grace a much smaller board (how many people do you know who can eat two pounds of beef in one sitting?). Another big favorite at Jud's is the Hungry Heifer, a literal mountain of ice cream — 15 scoops — crowned with as many as five different toppings. Jud's serves lunch and dinner Monday through Saturday.

Glade's Plaza Restaurant
$$ • 1370 U.S. Hwy. 20, Ashton, Idaho
• (208) 652-7869

From the steady flow of doggy boxes walking out the door, you can tell that portions aren't small at Glade's Plaza. Folks don't walk away hungry. Although new in 1997, this clean, well-lighted family restaurant lost no time becoming a locals' favorite. What do the locals order here? Well, when the boneless rib special is on, usually Fridays, the kitchen can't make enough of the juicy morsels. Pork chops are a favorite too. Glade's Plaza serves three meals a day, seven days a week. Reservations are accepted but not generally necessary.

Island Park, Idaho

Elk Creek Ranch
$$$, no credit cards • 3906 Loop Rd., Island Park, Idaho • (208) 558-7404

A magical dining experience awaits at 400-acre Elk Creek Ranch. You'll eat in the 100-year-old lodge at one of an eclectic cluster of round oak tables, while outside a shallow manmade lake attracts trumpeter swans, osprey, sandhill cranes and great blue heron. See our Resorts, Guest Ranches and Lodges chapter for more about accommodations at Elk Creek Ranch. You'll feel like you're tucked into the backcountry (because you are), even though you're only a pleasant drive from Island Park on a good dirt road.

However, camp food this is not. Manager VeAnn Merrill calls it homecooking. Enjoy grilled halibut, stuffed prawns and the house specialty, beef, prepared a variety of ways. Breads, spreads and desserts are made from scratch. Reservations are required.

Henry's Fork Landing
$ • 4238 U.S. Hwy. 20, Mack's Inn at Island Park, Idaho • (208) 558-7672

Imagine pancakes so fluffy and light that a short stack is tall. Or a chicken-fried steak breaded in the kitchen behind you, not pulled out of the freezer and tossed in the fryer. Now imagine eating your plate of homecooked food while staring out the window onto the Henry's Fork of the Snake River, barely 5 miles from where it bubbles, clear and cold, out of the ground.

Henry's Fork Landing accepts reservations. These folks are open year round, except for about six weeks in the spring and fall when things are slow. While you're there, be sure to check out the local histories written by the late Dean Green, who owned Henry's Fork Landing and was informal historian to the area.

Henry's Fork Lodge
$$$$ • Off U.S. Hwy. 20 near Island Park, Idaho • (208) 558-7953

The dining room is hung with authentic woven Indian blankets; each heavy oak table is graced with fresh flowers. Outside, a wildflower-covered slope steepens into the Henry's Fork canyon. Dine on the patio if you'd like to watch trout dimple the river's surface as they feed.

Henry's Fork Lodge is a quietly luxurious fishing lodge just south of Last Chance. And from 6 to 9 PM, seven nights a week, it opens its dining room doors to the general public. The menu changes nightly, but we bet your

mouth will water with one example: Imagine sautéed salmon medallions topped with a Dijon mustard sauce, green peppercorns, bay shrimp and scallions. The chefs prepare all desserts and breads from scratch.

Reservations are required for this fine dining experience, but fancy dress is not. The restaurant, like the lodge, is open mid-May to mid-October.

Island Park Lodge
$$ • N. Big Springs Loop Rd., off U.S. Hwy. 20 at Island Park, Idaho • (208) 558-7281

Ask for a nice place to eat in Island Park and you're liable to get steered here, especially if you like pasta with homemade Alfredo sauce or tender, juicy ribs. Lighter meals like soups, salads and sandwiches are also available. The lodge serves lunch and dinner in a low-ceilinged log building dating to the 1940s. Enjoy your meal with beer, wine or a cocktail from the adjoining saloon. Island Park Lodge is open summer and winter, with a six-week hiatus in spring and fall.

Swan Valley

Bette's Coffee Shop
$ • S. U.S. Hwy. 89 at Alpine, Wyo. • (307) 654-7536

Bette says, "I wouldn't want to see anybody go away hungry." Not only are her portions generous, but almost everything, from the breads to the soups to the cinnamon rolls, is made right here. Bette's serves breakfast, lunch and dinner seven days a week. The standard cafe menu is jazzed up a bit: You can order not just hot cakes but strawberry hot cakes, banana-nut hot cakes and cinnamon and spice hot cakes. Or choose from 12 different kinds of burgers. Bette's little coffee shop on the northwest shore of Palisades Reservoir has been serving up meals for locals and travelers for 14 years.

Brenthoven's Restaurant
$$$ • U.S. Hwy. 26 at U.S. 89, Alpine, Wyo. • (307) 654-7545, (800) 343-6755

He once played Carnegie Hall. Now he performs seven days a week, breakfast and dinner, in the kitchen of Brenthoven's. Pianist

Photo: Randy Hayes/Post Register

Idaho's famous russet potatoes sit out on the ground exposed to the sun for a very short time before being loaded into a truck and placed in a climate-controlled cellar.

and chef Brent Johnstone's little restaurant has six tables, each adorned with fresh flowers. Entrees include Chicken Brenthoven, featuring the chef's special plum sauce, and Cod Parmesan, Norwegian cod fillet stuffed with crab and baked with a parmesan topping. It's hard to say which is more pleasant, the food or the intimate little dining room.

The little bar next door is also tiny and intimate; it offers a full range of alcoholic beverages. Brenthoven's closes in mid-October and reopens in June. If you start wondering whether he plays as well as he cooks, you can pick up one of his CDs in the adjoining gift shop.

Last Cast
$ • 40 Conant Valley Loop, Swan Valley, Idaho • (208) 483-2229

Moose and elk mounts watch you from the walls while you watch the Snake River

slide past the cottonwoods below your window. If it's a Friday or Saturday night, you're also probably enjoying the locally famous prime rib. Folks from as far away as Idaho Falls make a regular pilgrimage to Swan Valley for this South Fork Lodge feast. But perhaps the friendly staff and comfortable, casual lodge setting have got you craving a more downhome dinner. No problem. The lodge will be happy to serve you up a generous chicken-fried steak or, on some nights, a plate of liver and onions. Reservations are accepted but not required. Weekends during fishing season can be busy.

Sandy-Mite Fly Shop and Cafe
$$ • 3333 Swan Valley Hwy., Irwin, Idaho • (208) 483-2609

Since 1986 the Sandy-Mite has been serving up fresh breads and bakery goods, fluffy omelettes (served all day), burgers and sandwiches. Rumor has it that the breakfast trout, prepared with two cheeses, deserves special attention. Dinner offerings include steak and various chicken dishes. These folks will even box up a river lunch for you. If you're an angler, take a quick look at the fly selection after you order your meal: All of Sandy Mite's flies are tied locally.

Teton Valley

Knight's British Rail
$$ • 75 W. Depot St., Driggs, Idaho
• (208) 354-8365

This fine little restaurant is also a local landmark. In 1916 a family named Christensen built the place; they raised 11 children here. In fact, the present dining room was once a parlor and two bedrooms. Geneo Knight, current owner and reason why Knight's British Rail has such fine food, will tell you that two children died in the house and that the restaurant is haunted. Things move around by themselves sometimes, he says, and voices speak when you'd swear you're alone.

But don't come here looking for the ghosts. We eat here often after skiing at Grand Targhee, and although we always see a plate full of tasty food and a frothy microbrew, we've never seen ghosts. The menu is surprisingly varied, with an emphasis on Asian food. Desserts are sinful and go down best with a serving of the British Rail's fresh roasted, fresh ground coffee, brought to your table in a mini-french press with a carafe of milk on the side.

Eat in the bar, its walls encircled by Geneo's extensive beer can collection, or in the dining room. Reservations are recommended. Doors are open Tuesday through Saturday for dinner. The pub stays open until folks go home.

Knotty Pine Bar and Restaurant
$$$ • 27 E. Main, Victor, Idaho
• (208) 787-2866

One of the interesting tidbits about the Knotty Pine is that none of its many owners over the years (Knotty Pine received the second liquor license in Teton Valley) has been a valley native. Knotty Pine serves lunch and dinner seven days a week and breakfast Tuesday through Sunday. The dinner menu is heavily slanted toward beef, but baby back ribs prepared with homemade barbecue sauce are the house specialty. A bar menu is also available.

Lost Horizon Dinner Club
$$$$, no credit cards • Mile 6, Ski Hill Rd., Alta, Wyo. • (307) 353-8226

It's not dinner, it's a dining adventure. Locally famous Lost Horizon is a tiny, intimate restaurant serving a single seating of 12 people every Friday, Saturday and Sunday nights. The meal is 10 languorous courses of Japanese and Chinese delicacies. You'll spend about four hours here, eating your hot and sour soup, tempura, tori katsu, chicken and cashews and other courses and relaxing around the circular hooded fireplace between courses.

Owners Chuck and Shigeko Irwin know Oriental food. Shigeko is Japanese; Chuck spent a decade in Asia as a career serviceman. They named their restaurant after the book by James Hilton about a mythical Shangri-la, an Eden-like place where people never aged. Lost Horizon is open year round

---

INSIDERS' TIP

Occasionally, a menu will offer Rocky Mountain oysters as an appetizer or entree. These are bull calf testicles, normally removed each spring when the bulls are branded and castrated. When they come from young animals, Rocky Mountain oysters are very tender and tasty. Be sure to ask your waitress, though, about the source of the "oysters" listed on the menu. These days we've seen people cooking up slices of full-grown bull testicles and calling them Rocky Mountain oysters. What they most resemble are leather boot tongues.

except in May and October. As you no doubt guessed, reservations are required.

Mike's Eats

$, no credit cards • 10 N. Main, Driggs, Idaho • (208) 354-2797

You'll pass the jukebox on your way in. The linoleum is blocked in black, green, blue and red. Red upholstery highlights chromed bar stools and booths. A bar runs the length of the long, skinny dining room beneath an ornate silver ceiling. In short, Mike's is a flamboyant 1950s-style diner, smack in the middle of cowboy country.

Folks come here for the buffalo: buffalo chili, buffalo hot dogs, buffalo polish sausages, meat loaf and burgers. Probably they're not thinking of the health benefits of that choice, but they could be; buffalo meat is significantly lower in cholesterol, fat and calories than either beef or chicken. So you might as well order a shake or a root beer float to go with that burger, eh? Mike's Eats serves breakfast, lunch and dinner seven days a week in summer. Winters it closes.

Victor Emporium

$ • 45 N. Main, Victor, Idaho • (208) 787-2221

You could come here for fishing hooks, guide books, camping gear, plastic worms, hats, ice or beer. Or you could be after homemade shredded beef burritos, green chile chicken burritos or the wildly popular fish tacos (be flexible — daily specials vary and can sell out quickly). But if you're like Ronald Reagan, Supreme Court Justice Sandra Day O'Connor and about 12,000 locals and tourists each summer, you're here for a huckleberry shake. Made from real ice cream and handpicked local huckleberries, served up in a tall glass with the creamy leftovers waiting their turn in a chrome mixing cup, Victor Emporium's huckleberry shakes are famous in these parts. As they should be.

Bob and Marilyn Meyer serve lunch only. They're open from 8 AM to 7 PM most days, though, and between meals you can catch a cup of coffee, a cherry phosphate or a fresh lime freeze. Or a huckleberry milk shake. (You can also take home a souvenir tee-shirt, commemorating your shake experience.)

Southwest Montana

Bozeman, Montana

The Crystal Beer Garden

$ • 123 E. Main St., Bozeman, Mont. • (406) 587-2888

During fair weather, you can rise above it all at the Crystal Beer Garden, a rooftop cafe that serves beer and burgers. Enter from the outside via a wooden staircase that leads from the rear parking lot. Or treat yourself to a peek into Montana — not the dressed-up tourist version — by strolling through the Crystal Bar door on Bozeman's Main Street. The burgers are juicy. The beer is cold.

John Bozeman's Bistro

$$$ • 242 E. Main St., Bozeman, Mont. • (406) 587-4100

Since its owners opened John Bozeman's Bistro 15 years ago in the land of cowboys, this place has been on the cutting edge of fine food in the West. For example, when Chef Perry Wenzel creates a dish, he not only thinks about doing a delicious ballet on your taste buds, but he also envisions delivery, style, form. Just listen to him talk about a new dish and chances are you'll hear him wax eloquent about things like verticality and elevation.

On a given night, Wenzel might serve French, Italian and Cajun cuisine. The Bistro is known for its fresh — very fresh — seafood. While he changes the menu often (on a given night you might find seven or eight seafood entrees on the menu) there are a few house specialties, like the macadamia nut-crusted fresh catch served with mango sauce, black beans, fried bananas and a tiny pile of greens. The wine list here is phenomenal. So is the food.

MacKenzie River Pizza Co.

$ • 232 E. Main St., Bozeman, Mont. • (406) 587-0055

Livingston residents drive 26 miles to Bozeman just to get a taste of a MacKenzie River Pizza. This mom-and-pop-comfortable gourmet pizzeria has 23 different kinds of pizza, ranging from the Vegetarian to the Pesto Fajita to the Meat Lovers. The Rancher (a combo) and the pepperoni-packed Good Old Boy are still the all-time favorites with customers. On a Friday night you might find the place packed and a friendly crew cranking out as many as 500 Italian pies. You'll also find music and an assortment of sandwiches. MacKenzie River is open for lunch and dinner.

Gallatin Gateway, Montana

Gallatin Gateway Inn
$$$$ • U.S. Hwy. 191, Gallatin Gateway, Mont.• (406) 763-4672

You know the scene. The chef tastes the sauce, pinches all five finger tips together, kisses them just so, closes his eyes and listens to the delicate symphony playing on his taste buds. Chef Erik Carr at the Gallatin Gateway Inn uses only the very best ingredients then combines them in ways that defy the normal imagination. Carr's award-winning food might include entrees like Grilled Boston Cod with Pernod-creamed Red Lentils, or Chinese-Steamed King Salmon or Five Peppercorn Seared Certified Angus Tenderloin.

The dining room, set with linen and fresh flowers, is ringed with tall windows reminiscent of the early railroad days when tourists stopped over on their way to Yellowstone Park. Carr changes his menu often and offers an extensive wine list to complement it. The Gallatin has a full service bar.

Big Sky, Montana

Buck's T-4 Lodge
$$$$ • U.S. Hwy. 191, 1 mile south of Big Sky, Mont. • (406) 995-4111

If it's a taste of wild game you have a hankering for, Buck's T-4 has it. The menu here includes ranch-raised bison, New Zealand red deer, South Texas antelope and a wild game meat loaf that combines all of the above. Buck's also serves wild game stew in a burgundy sauce and wild game pate, a combination of buffalo, wild boar, venison and caribou layered with fresh herbs and pistachio nuts. Here's your chance to sample it all. (In case you're traveling with someone who can't stomach wild game, Buck's has plenty of other standards like steak, chicken, seafood and pasta.) You'll find a full bar and a decent wine list at this laid-back place.

The Corral Cafe and Steakhouse
$$$ • U.S. Hwy. 191, Big Sky, Mont. • (406) 995-4249

It's Western. It's comfortable. And it's reasonably priced. The Corral turns out juicy steaks and burgers in a casual atmosphere, making it the hot spot for Gallatin Canyon residents and visitors alike. We recommend you try the 25-ounce porterhouse . . . if you dare. You'll find a full Western bar at The Corral and a pleasant mixture of locals and visitors. You'll also find a friendly, welcoming staff and a taste of the Old West.

Rainbow Ranch Lodge
$$$$ • U.S. Hwy. 191, Big Sky, Mont. • (406) 995-4132

Resurrected, refurbished and revived, the Rainbow Ranch Lodge offers fine dining on the Gallatin River. Since the Lodge opened in 1995, Chefs Kim and Paul Cameron (they're a couple) have changed the menu twice a year to keep themselves "on their creative toes." There is at least one exception to the menu changes: Sesame-Crusted Salmon covered with creamy avocado-lime butter. Despite efforts to remove the dish, it remains on the menu by popular demand. Last winter's menu included Dim Sum Plate of Pan-Fried Dumplings, Tournedos of Beef with a Gorgonzola Sage Sauce, and Fresh Lemon Rotelle Pasta with Dungeness Crab.

A spacious lounge with deep chairs, sofas and a fireplace is a good place to begin or end your meal. If the weather's fair, you can dine on the deck. The wine list here is extensive. The Rainbow Ranch Lodge closes from November 1 to November 15, and from April 15 to May 15.

Livingston, Montana

Mark's In & Out
$, no credit cards • Park and Eighth Sts., Livingston, Mont. • (406) 222-7744

Carhops on Rollerblades? Who can resist? Mark's In & Out has been serving burgers and fries, malts and shakes, since 1954. Home of the Super Cheese — two patties with two slices of cheese and your choice of toppings for $1.99 — this cute little drive-in is a must for nostalgia nuts and families alike. Mark's is open from March 1 to November 1 depending on the weather. Check it out.

The Sport

**$$ • 144 S. Main St., Livingston, Mont.
• (406) 222-3533**

Little jeans, big jeans — we mean *big* jeans, like jeans with a 76-inch waist and a 45-inch inseam — old newspapers and cowboy memorabilia line the walls of this historic restaurant. Heck, the decor and a chance to hobnob with history are half the reason folks like Robert Redford and Peter Fonda pack into the old Sport.

Owned since 1983 by Livingston resident Suzanne Schneider, The Sport began as the "Beer Hall" in the late 1800s. Within the now-tame walls of this eating and drinking establishment, fortunes have been won and lost in poker games, and whole paychecks have been spent on a round for "the Boys" (women weren't allowed in The Sport until the 1940s).

The food at The Sport is reasonably priced with a menu that features the famous Sport Burger (some folks say it's the best in Livingston), Sport Bar-B-Q Baby Back Pork Ribs, several Mexican dishes, seafood and hot sandwiches. The Sport, open for lunch and dinner, serves Montana-grown steaks and veal.

The Stockman Bar

$$, no credit cards • 118 N. Main, Livingston, Mont. • (406) 222-8455

Wear your spurs, chaps and cowboy hat if you like. The Stockman is Montana as it used to be with a steakhouse stuck in the back of a cowboy bar. You'll find an assortment of juicy steaks and giant stacks of homemade fries at prices that even a family can afford. Burgers, one of The Stockman's top sellers, are big and super juicy. You'll find prime rib on weekends. The Stockman serves supper seven days a week, and lunch every day except Sunday. Carry your drink from the bar to the table or order it on the spot.

Uncle Looie's Ristorante

**$$$ • 119 W. Park, Livingston, Mont.
• (406) 222-7177**

"If you find yourself a quart low on olive oil, Uncle Looie's Ristorante offers some of the best Italian dishes this side of New York's Little Italy," wrote David Lyons in the May 1997 issue of *Northwest Airlines Magazine*. While the image may not appeal to weight watchers, if you're going to indulge, this is the place to do it. At Uncle Looie's, you'll feel like you're walking into a cozy New York restaurant minus that Eastern formality. Menu favorites include chicken scarpiello (a half-chicken sautéed in oil with Italian sausage, pepperoncini, capers, kalamata olives, onions and white wine) and veal del giorno (tender veal prepared in a different way each day). Uncle Looie's also features pastas of the day. Lunches include sandwiches, pasta and pizza. The wine list is extensive.

Lunch is served Monday through Friday, dinners seven days a week. Reservations are suggested.

Winchester Cafe and Grill

**$$$ • 201 W. Park, Livingston, Mont.
• (406) 222-2708**

The only things missing from a dining experience at the Winchester are the old cowpokes and Wall Street financiers who once lounged in the Murray Hotel lobby before taking supper at the Winchester. Refurbished and revived, the Winchester still echoes the understated elegance of its heyday as *the* hotel across the street from the Northern Pacific train depot.

Spacious and airy with high ceilings, this popular place combines the new and the old with dinner entrees ranging from a porterhouse steak (cooked the way you like it) to a shrimp cashew stir-fry and vegetarian dishes. The Winchester has an extensive wine list and a full-service bar. Open year round, The Winchester serves three squares a day.

Emigrant, Montana

The Livery Stable

**$$$ • U.S. Hwy. 89, Emigrant, Mont.
• (406) 333-4688**

Montanans love their steak. Half-rare or medium well-done, it doesn't matter. (If you order it well-done, though, the chef warns customers he's not responsible if you don't like it.) The Livery Stable, housed in what was once the Old Saloon, Pool Hall and Hotel, serves up steaks, prime rib and an array of chicken and seafood in fine Western tradition. Charbroiled steaks are their calling card. The Livery Stable, adjacent to the Old Saloon, serves drinks and wine. This is a popular place, so play it safe and make a reservation.

Old Saloon

$ • U.S. Hwy. 89, Emigrant, Mont.
• (406) 333-4482

Speeding between Livingston and Yellowstone Park, it would be easy to drive right by the Old Saloon at Emigrant. Don't. The Old Saloon serves up a taste of the West. You'll find a good old Western breakfast and lunch at old-fashioned prices. No matter that you'll be eating in a bar, where cowboys and other local residents may be sipping coffee (or whiskey) for breakfast. This is Montana, where movie stars and welders, cowboys and counts drop their titles at the drop of a hat.

The menu at the Saloon is simple: burgers, toasted sandwiches and saloon dogs for lunch.

Pray, Montana

Chico Inn

$$$ • Pray, Mont. • (406) 333-4933

Bon Apetit, *Gourmet*, *The New York Times*. They've all written about the food at the Chico Inn, the dining room at Chico Hot Springs. But words won't tell the story. "Fresh" means the rainbow assortment of lettuce in your salad came straight from the Chico garden. It also means fresh seafood is flown in daily, and the poultry dishes are made with free-range chickens raised by Montana Hutterites. Depending on the season, you might find sauces made with wild mushrooms, huckleberries, cherries, raspberries or other natural bounty from the area.

Their entrees — Beef Wellington and Rosemary Crusted Rack of Lamb are among the favorites — are nationally renowned. And their desserts are legendary, especially their Orange Flambe. A hollowed Valencia orange, lined with chocolate, is filled with Grand Marnier ice cream, topped with meringue then flamed at the table with Baccardi 151 rum.

Chef Jo Cobb has a crew of 25 to help him during the summer months. Expect an elegant wine list and drinks from the in-house bar. (For more information about Chico, refer to our Resorts, Guest Ranches and Lodges chapter.)

MacAllister, Montana

Bear Claw Bar and Grill

$$$ • U.S. Hwy. 287, MacAllister, Mont.
• (406) 682-4619

Built in 1923, the original part of this added-onto rustic relic from the past is now the main part of the bar. In back you'll find the dining room, a funky sort of addition used as living quarters by one of the past owners.

Owner Bob Miller serves up a mouth-watering array of steaks, crab, shrimp (two ways), chicken and swordfish or salmon. Comfortable and Western country verging on chic, the Bear Claw doesn't attract many cowboys during the summer. But as soon as the tourists leave, the ranchers and other locals take over and turn the place into a sort of community center. The Bear Claw Bar and Grill is open 364 days a year (the bar, but not the kitchen, is open Christmas Day). It serves lunch and dinner.

Ennis, Montana

Scotty's Long Branch Supper Club

$$$ • 125 E. Main, Ennis, Mont.
• (406) 682-5300

Some folks just don't like having to stroll through a bar to find a meal. If you want to eat at Scotty's Long Branch Supper Club, though, you'll have to bite the bullet and take that hike. The folks who frequent the Long Branch Saloon are friendly locals, and Scot Davidson's food, consistently good, is well worth the walk.

Scot doesn't do burgers and fries. He does do fresh seafood, an assortment of veal dishes, chicken, pork chops and steaks. His menu is small, but it changes often and includes weekly specials. Scot's French onion soup is legendary, and his desserts are all homemade. Hours

---

INSIDERS' TIP

Occasionally, you'll see a dish that uses "beefalo," low-fat, low-cholesterol meat that results from crossbreeding bison and cattle. Beefalo, developed 40 years ago by Montana rancher Jim Burnett, is 37 percent beef and 63 percent buffalo.

vary according to the season. We recommend calling ahead to check Scot's schedule.

Cameron, Montana

Grizzly Bar and Grill
$$$ • 1409 U.S. Hwy. 287, Cameron, Mont. • (406) 682-7118

You know the food is good when a restaurant that's in the middle of nowhere regularly has a crowd of cars parked outside. The Grizzly Bar and Grill, owned for 20 years by Eric Smith, is near the West Fork of the Madison, about 20 miles south of Ennis.

The menu is simple. The food is great. And the steaks, cooked over an Aspen-fired grill, are out of this world. Ask Chef Nikolai Fleeson about the Filet Mignon Du jour or have the house favorite, Filet Mignon Churasco. In addition to the regular steak menu, you'll find pasta, shrimp and chicken entrees as well as juicy burgers. Fleeson features two specials each night. The Grizzly Bar and Grill is open from April through November.

Red Lodge, Montana

Bogart's
$ • 11 S. Broadway Ave., Red Lodge, Mont. • (406) 446-1784

Bogart's has great pizza and magnificent Margaritas. In fact, when the doors open at 11:30 AM, Bogart's staff is prepared with a 15-gallon batch of Margarita mix. Years ago, owners Tom Leatherberry and Judy and Jodie Christensen enlisted friends to help them taste-test experimental recipes of the mix. It will soon be sold commercially along with Bogart's canned salsa, Ruggie's Rocky Mountain Salsa, and their fajita marinade.

Bogart's is a big brick building filled with old photos of Humphrey Bogart, mounted game animals and an abundance of antiques. Bogart's sells atmosphere (it's comfortable and Western) and good food. We recommend any

of the pizzas, the sour cream enchiladas and the Margaritas.

Greenlee's at the Pollard
$$$$ • 2 N. Broadway Ave., Red Lodge, Mont. • (406) 446-0001

Walking into Greenlee's at the Pollard in Red Lodge feels a little like entering the dining room of an exclusive Eastern or Midwestern club minus the high-priced tab. You'll find crisp linen tablecloths, fresh flowers, abundant oak woodwork, plush drapes, excellent service and delicious food.

Chef Scot Greenlee, who has been with the Pollard since it opened in 1994, keeps the menu interesting and himself interested by changing it often — like twice-a-week often. Among Greenlee's most popular dishes are Sage-Smoked Chicken, Risotto with Wild Mushrooms and Huckleberry Duck Breasts. Other signature foods include Greenlee's French bread and his Creme Caramel, a baked custard with caramel sauce. The wine list is tip-top.

The Round Barn
$$ • U.S. 212, Red Lodge, Mont. • (406) 446-1197

You'd never know this homey, old round brick building was once a dairy barn. Owner Dan Farrar has fixed it up as a restaurant and dinner theater. Dinner is served buffet style with four entrees (a range of meats and fish), homemade mashed potatoes, a fresh vegetable like steamed snow peas and dessert. A 15-foot salad bar features fresh salads, homemade soups and bread just out of the oven. For information about the theater upstairs in the hayloft (you don't have to eat dinner to get into the theater, but we recommend it), see our Nightlife chapter.

Bear Creek, Montana

Bear Creek Saloon
$ • 108 Main St., Bear Creek, Mont. • (406) 446-3481

You get to eat Mexican food and watch

pig races in the middle of nowhere. Open Friday, Saturday and Sunday from Memorial Day to Labor Day and from Christmas until Easter, the Bear Creek Saloon offers decent Mexican food at family rates in a Western bar. Owners Lynn and Pits DeArmond follow their meals with free family entertainment: pig races. For more information about the Bear Creek Saloon, see our Nightlife chapter.

Northwestern Wyoming

Cody, Wyoming

Cassie's Supper Club
$$$ • 214 Yellowstone Ave., Cody, Wyo. • (307) 527-5500

Owned in the 1920s by Cassie Waters, the renowned madame of a Cody sportin' house, Cassie's Supper Club has been recently resurrected by owners Steve and Melody Singer. Steve, who plays nightly in the house band, grew up down the street from Cassie's. As a boy, he frequented the place, playing piano tunes for the bar regulars. Since buying the place (Singer sang on the road for 20 years before buying Cassie's), Singer has become an enthusiastic collector of Cassie memorabilia. Look for her fur lap robe displayed in the entry way and the parrots above the bar.

Known these days for its steaks, prime rib and seafood, the house specialty at Cassie's is the 14-ounce prime rib. Singer serves only Choice USDA grade beef, along with homemade soups and breads. Lunches include a variety of sandwiches as well as a small rib-eye steak and prime rib. Cassie's is open seven days a week year round.

For more about Cassie's, read our Nightlife chapter.

Franca's
$$$$, no credit cards • 1421 Rumsey Ave., Cody, Wyo. • (307) 587-5354

Plan to spend the whole (romantic) evening at Franca's, a small Italian restaurant (it seats 24 people) on the main floor of a 1920s French colonial Cody house. Leave your watch at home. Bring your heart and a healthy appetite. Franca Franchetti — yes, she's Italian, accent and all — cooks all day then shucks

her apron and dons her big-hearted hostess persona. Pasta specials and homemade focaccine (an Italian specialty bread) are among her signature foods, and the house special is Tortelloni Verdi al Mascarpone (spinach pasta stuffed with an Italian cream cheese). Franca also serves daily specials like sausage and spinach ravioli, followed by salad and bread, or baked pork loin with rhubarb sauce (in the summer) with stuffed peppers.

Since Italians believe wine is married to the food, Franca provides endless marital combinations with a voluminous wine list including more than 100 selections. Three dining rooms (one is a converted sun porch and another has a fireplace) are joined by arched openings. Each table is set with linen, its own antique china pattern, real silverware and antique crystal. On the walls, you'll find art by Franca's husband, Joseph.

Franca's is open Wednesday through Sunday May 15 through January 15.

La Comida
$$ • 1385 Sheridan Ave., Cody, Wyo. • (307) 587-9556

The honey locust trees and patio outside this reasonably priced restaurant say "Mexican," and so does the menu, which features award-winning food. (Articles from *Bon Apetit* and *Gourmet* magazines are posted as proof on the wall.) Spinach enchiladas, fajitas and pechuga de ray (chicken over rice) are among the house favorites. In addition to their fine Mexican fare, the desserts at La Comida are legendary.

La Comida is open seven days a week year round. During the summer, dine outside under the stars on the patio. Inside, choose between the East and the West rooms — they're like night and day.

Our Place
$$ • 148 W. Yellowstone Ave., Cody, Wyo. • (307) 527-4420

Folks pack into Our Place for more than the 25-cent coffee. Waitresses here serve up hearty, low-priced meals with Western coffee shop flair — a few "honeys" and "how ya doin's" mixed with casual bustling service. Our Place serves three squares a day. We recommend the Rustler, Wrangler, Cowhand or the Huevos Rancheros for breakfast. (You can order breakfast from dawn till dark.) At lunch and dinner you'll find typical Western coffee shop fare at prices you can afford. (Try the prime rib on Friday and Saturday nights for $8.95.) Our Place is open year round seven days a week.

The Proud Cut Saloon
$$ • 1227 Sheridan Ave., Cody, Wyo.
• (307) 527-6905

The carved wooden sandwich sign outside this Western chic bar and restaurant advertises "Kickass Cowboy Cuisine." Whatever you call it, you'll find a long list of juicy steaks and shrimp at the Proud Cut, where the walls are lined with old photos and cowboy memorabilia.

Comfortable and crowded on weekend nights, the Proud Cut produces several choices that are popular among customers, such as the tenderloin and the 14-ounce prime rib. They also offer a 22-ounce porterhouse steak and Rocky Mountain oysters (breaded bull calf testicles). By the way, if you think Proud Cut refers to the steaks this saloon serves, ask an Insider. They'll tell you "Proud Cut" is the term used for stallions that have been castrated a bit late in life and so can't ever quite quit acting like studs.

This restaurant is for adults only.

Stefan's
$$$ • 1367 Sheridan Ave., Cody, Wyo.
• (307) 587-8511

He (Stefan Bennett) is the chef, and she (Nina Bennett) is the hostess at Stefan's, a softly lit restaurant that serves contemporary American food. That means that when Stefan cooks up Untraditional Traditional Meatloaf or Chicken Pot Pie, he adds a kiss of mysteriously mixed herbs and sauces that leaves the palate wishing for just one more taste. Everything, we repeat, everything, is made from scratch, much like the restaurant itself.

Stefan and Nina worked and slept in the building for three weeks while they transformed it from Queen Bee Fashions to an upscale restaurant with a Southwestern look. The walls (three layers of paint that make them look like they're covered with terra cotta-colored suede), ficus trees strung with white Christmas lights, a dark green ceiling and carpet, and the fountain at the front create a scene soothing to the soul.

We recommend you start with the seafood Delmar or the stuffed filet mignon. Stefan's serves lunch, dinner and Sunday brunch.

You may notice that in summer we start late, and in winter we tend to come out more often, except, of course, in summer tourist towns like Jackson, which hop all evening and nearly every night of the week, June through September.

Nightlife

Night falls in Yellowstone country, and a new realm unfolds. Diamond-edged stars wink into place and, even in July, a chill touches your face. Four-legged residents who spent the day tucked out of sight wander out into evening, into their time. What had begun to seem familiar — towering Douglas fir, misty steam rising from a hot spring, the jagged outline of the Tetons — becomes mysterious again. This is no time for sleeping, folks.

You're likely to find yourself a ways from the nearest bar, but closer at hand is another style of nightlife altogether, one many locals would choose even if a more conventional nightlife scene were available. It often starts with a campfire. Campfires seem to turn people in, toward each other and the flickering flames. Sometimes they take you into yourself: Maybe you'll remember old campfire songs you thought you'd forgotten. Or how to construct a s'more. Or the scary ghost stories you learned when you were a little kid. Or maybe you'll campfire-cook the trout you caught today — clean it, leaving the head on (no need to scale or skin trout), spit it on a stout willow stick, sprinkle with butter, salt and pepper, tie the body shut and roast it, belly up, above the coals until the eyes turn white. Eat with your fingers.

Perhaps you'd like to skip the fire and instead turn your attention outward. In this clear air, a full moon sheds enough pale light for strolling flat trails (note this is not a recommended activity in bear country) or for cross-country skiing with a bota bag of wine on your hip. Some even snowmobile, tree and hill shadows skating away before their headlights.

On August evenings, meteors put on a dramatic show. If you keep your eyes tipped up it's hard not to see at least one streaking meteor every minute or two. And any time of year you can watch satellites spin across the night sky, learn constellations or locate the North Star (sky charts are available at many outdoor shops and most bookstores). You can even turn your good binoculars onto the face of the moon to see its cratered, rough skin.

An eerie fall treat that lasts into November is the nightly concert of rutting elk. Bull elk bugle in long whispery whistles, hollow grunts and screaming sobs. You'll listen in awe as first one, then another and another of these massive animals lifts that thin, unworldly call into the darkness. It's hard not to think you're experiencing the voice of Wilderness itself. Bugling elk can be heard through much of Yellowstone country around sundown and again around sunrise. A few particularly good places to experience this are the Jenny Lake area and the Oxbow in Grand Teton Park, Harriman State Park near Island Park, and near Mammoth Hot Springs, Hayden Valley and Madison Junction in Yellowstone Park.

One of Yellowstone country's summer bonuses is nearly endless daylight. Full, pitch darkness falls after 10:30 on a June night, so summer sunsets are a late-evening attraction. Of course, the flip side is that in winter sunset precedes dinner. Summer and winter, sunset watching is a popular evening activity. If you happen to find yourself in one of our towns at sunset, try wandering a greenbelt. Jackson, Idaho Falls, Teton Valley and Bozeman all have pleasant, parklike walkways on which folks can stroll and exercise. Idaho Falls' greenbelt affords a particularly nice sunset show, since it runs on both sides of the Snake River through town. Two of the town's most popular photo opportunities, the Falls themselves and the monolithic Mormon temple, are along your route and look particularly fine around sunset, especially from the west side of the river.

One magical sunset spot in the Madison Valley is Sphinx Mountain. A quirk in the Gravelly Range to the west provides a notch through which the setting sun spotlights the Sphinx while her sisters stand in shadow. You can see the Sphinx from almost anywhere in the Madison Valley near Ennis.

Mountains in general look stunning in evening light, though. Part of the cause is a phenomenon called alpenglow. On clear evenings the mountains seem to pull a soft pastel light from the air and into their snow-covered slopes. It can make for the most beautiful photographs you'll take on your trip. (Early morning light is even sweeter, but it's hard to crawl out of bed at 5 o'clock on a summer morning to take photos.)

Nightspots

Crystal-bright stars, snapping campfires and alpenglow aside, sometimes nothing hits the spot like jostling, laughing crowds and music that makes your toes tap. You can find night crowds in Yellowstone country, although perhaps not the variety and numbers you may be accustomed to. You may notice that in summer we start late, and in winter we tend to come out more often, except, of course, in summer tourist towns like Jackson, which hop all evening and nearly every night of the week, June through September. College towns like Bozeman have a lively nightlife scene, too. In winter, the après-ski bars fill to their jammed maximum nearly every afternoon, but most of them clear out before dinner as tired skiers head for the hot tub and bed.

In smaller or quieter communities, more focused on going about their business than on tourists, the nightlife scene can be a bit . . . sparse. For instance, in West Yellowstone, where families are the main summer visitors, you'll find little nightlife except on special occasions like the Fourth of July. Most people leave the Park late with only enough time for dinner, a bit of shopping and then bed. West Yellowstone in winter is a bit livelier as snowmobilers replace families as the primary visitors. Only a little, though: Like skiers, snowmobilers mostly want to eat and then hit the hay after a day's ride.

But even if you can't find a band to listen to or a show to watch — a likely scenario outside the tourist hotspots — belly up to the bar at the local pub. You'll probably find yourself next to somebody who'll be happy to tell you a story or three about Yellowstone country. We've included here a selection of the more popular bars, particularly those that frequently host live music. We've also listed a few choice alternatives to the bar scene. You can, for instance, ski the night slopes at Snow King or attend a dinner show.

Another place to find evening diversions is our Annual Events chapter. Many Yellowstone communities are better at putting on periodic great parties (usually in summer) than maintaining a dynamic week-to-week, season-to-season night scene. Maybe it's because a relatively small segment of Yellowstone country residents frequent bars and nightclubs. Remember that nearly all eastern Idaho communities as well as many in western Wyoming and southern Montana are home to large Mormon populations that, for the most part, have little truck with the party scene. And many of the rest of us would rather grab hold of our weekends and take them out into the mountains.

If you do go out, you'll want to keep your eyes peeled for local talent such as Kip Attaway. He's a Wyoming native known for his outrageously funny songs and his top-notch country-western musicianship. You're equally likely to find him performing at a bar or simply camped out in the Hawg Smoke Café in Idaho Falls, playing for his friends and a lucky group of patrons. Kip's humorous stuff is usually topical — O.J. and such.

Unless noted, the establishments described below charge no admission and are open all year. Don't assume, though: Bars and playhouses in Yellowstone country live with a seasonal ebb and flow that can mean unexpected changes to door policies and even last-second fall or spring vacations for the entire staff. Credit card policies vary. Some folks will let you pay your tab with plastic, but not your door charge. If you plan to leave your cash in the motel room, call your intended party spot first.

Drinking laws vary in Yellowstone country's three states. Wyoming defines intoxicated driving as a blood-alcohol level greater than .10. In Idaho the law's a bit tougher; you're considered intoxicated over .08. But all three states take drunk driving seriously. In Wyoming, in fact, if you refuse a breath test, you automatically lose your driver's license for 180 days, whether you're a resident or a visitor. In Idaho, state police policy says there is no tolerance for intoxicated drivers and the absolute minimum penalty is a 90-day suspended license.

Bars in Wyoming and Montana are generally open until 2 AM. Idaho bars are required by state law to close at 1 AM, but individual counties may choose to allow their bars to stay open until 2 AM. No Idaho counties within Greater Yellowstone have done so, however.

Wyoming and Idaho both allow people younger than 21 to enter bars that are also restaurants, but in Montana kids can walk into any bar. They can't drink, but they can be there. Generally in Idaho and Wyoming, if a place has a bar area separate from the food-service area, kids won't be allowed in the bar.

Idaho, both Yellowstone and Grand Teton parks and many Wyoming counties have open-container laws that make it illegal for you to drive with an open bottle containing an alcoholic beverage. Teton County Wyoming allows no open containers on the streets, either, so if Jackson's town square looks like a perfect place for a bottle of wine, it isn't. Alcohol can be carried on the streets during some events; check with the local police or ask event hosts if you're uncertain. Wyoming also has an odd law called an "intoxicated pedestrian law." It allows enforcement officers to remove an intoxicated person from a public way, like a parking lot, a sidewalk or the side of a road.

Yellowstone National Park

Entrance Communities

West Yellowstone, Montana

Bullwinkle's Saloon
19 Madison Ave., West Yellowstone, Mont. • (406) 646-7974

Monday nights and Sundays Bullwinkle's is packed with folks watching ball games,

hockey, you name it, on the six TVs. Is it the food or the TVs that attracts sports fans to this bar? We think it's both. Decorated with Green Bay Packer uniforms, pennants and other memorabilia (the owners moved from Sheboygan, Wisconsin), Bullwinkle's offers a menu of appetizers that would please folks even without a ball game to watch. Among the treats that owner Jackie LaFever cooks up are smoked trout, shrimp cocktail, bratwurst with sauerkraut, a homemade haystak of onion rings and her enticingly good Nachos Supreme — so homemade she even makes the nacho chips. LaFever, who serves lunch and dinner, also has her soup pot filled with concoctions similar to those that Grandmother used to make on her wood cookstove. During the summer, Bullwinkle's is open from 11 AM until 11 PM. In winter, it closes closer to 9 PM. For more information about Bullwinkle's, see our Restaurants chapter.

Eino's Bar
8955 Gallatin Rd., West Yellowstone, Mont. • (406) 646-9344

Comfortable and casual are the bywords at this lonely outpost 8 miles north of West Yellowstone on U.S. Highway 191. During the winter, this full-service bar is packed with snowmobilers who have driven their sleds right up to the door. From West Yellowstone, it's an easy jaunt by car or snowmobile (we recommend the latter for a special night out). Customers cook their own steaks and burgers on a communal grill. Open and spacious, Eino's overlooks meadows leading to Hebgen Lake. Downstairs you'll find a pool table.

Happy Hour Bar
15400 Hebgen Lake Rd., West Yellowstone, Mont. • (406) 646-7281

If you see a bumper sticker that reads, "I was honked at the Happy Hour Bar," you'll know the folks in the car have been to this spot on the shores of Hebgen Lake. You won't find any happy hour discounts here, but owners Bud and Karen Klungervik were born to run a bar that exudes happy-hour hilarity. Housed in an old A-frame originally built as a home, the Happy Hour has huge windows that frame the lake below and the mountains beyond. During winter, snowmobilers and ice fishermen dot the ice-and-snow-covered lake. A deck shaped like the bow of a boat juts toward the lake. From this vantage point, the owners and customers honk an airhorn at passersby. They also launch water balloons with a giant slingshot that propels the bombs up to 200 yards.

A marina with four docks that belongs to the bar invites boaters to stop in at the Happy Hour for a meal or a quick drink. The Happy Hour, which seats about 50, serves lunch and dinner, including juicy half-pound hamburgers and an assortment of steaks. For more information about the Happy Hour, see our Restaurants chapter.

Iron Horse Saloon
315 Yellowstone Ave., West Yellowstone, Mont. • (406) 646-7365

Located in the West Yellowstone Conference Hotel, the Iron Horse offers an open-mike night on Tuesdays and a dance band on winter and summer weekends. The saloon itself doesn't have much of a dance floor, but a sliding door opens onto a ballroom big enough to accommodate hundreds. When things are slow in town, you generally won't find a band here, so it's best to check ahead to see what's happening.

Playmill Theater
29 Madison Ave., West Yellowstone, Mont. • (406) 646-7757

People regularly drive from as far away as Pocatello, Idaho, and Belgrade, Montana, just to watch a performance at the Playmill Theater. The 272-seat theater celebrates its 35th anniversary in 1998 with three shows: *Oklahoma*, *Love Rides the Rails* (a melodrama back by popular demand) and *Joseph and the Amazing Technicolor Dreamcoat*. Owner John Bidwell, who teaches theater and related subjects at Ricks College in Rexburg, first acted at the little

theater as a student in 1973. He bought the playhouse in 1989 and now hires about 20 players (mostly college students) each summer. Bidwell also has a regular steady staff that includes a director, a choreographer and costume maker. Students are provided with lodging and given a $2,500 stipend for the season.

From Memorial Day through Labor Day, the Playmill runs two shows each night at 6 and 8:30 PM Monday through Saturday. Tickets cost $10 for adults, $8 for children and $9 for seniors. Groups of 25 or more get a $1 discount on individual ticket prices.

Stage Coach Inn
209 Madison Ave., West Yellowstone, Mont. • (406) 646-7381

You'll have to wait for winter to dance here. On winter and summer weekends, the bar upstairs often has a piano player or some other light musical entertainment. During snowmobile season, though, you can find rompin', stompin' dance music downstairs in the Oak Barrel Bar. This place packs 'em in so fast that people often head downstairs hours ahead of time just to reserve a table. If you're into live poker, the Stage Coach is the only place in town that deals real cards.

Gardiner, Montana

Blue Goose Saloon
206 W. Park, Gardiner, Mont. • (406) 848-7434

Named the Blue Goose back in the 1940s, this local hangout has been serving beer and drinks since the 1920s. Now a favorite hangout for Park employees and locals alike, the Blue Goose has brought together its share of Park employees who later married.

The Blue Goose has two pool tables (you can play pool for free on Sundays), a large-

---

INSIDERS' TIP

If you're planning on a campfire in one of the National Park campgrounds or a well-used National Forest campground, expect to either gather your firewood (downed wood only, please) outside the campground or purchase it. Many campgrounds sell bundles of split, dry wood. So do area stores.

screen TV, 12 brands of beer on tap and an impressive array of mounted game animals.

Montana Blues Chuckwagon Dinner Theater
U.S. Hwy. 89, Gardiner, Mont.
• **(406) 848-9898, (800) 424-4445**

This is pure family entertainment. After a chuckwagon dinner of barbecued beef or chicken, homemade biscuits, baked beans, spice cake and lemonade, the Meyer brothers and their father, Bob, will treat you to a Western musical show.

Montana Blues is casual — a barn-like building with a gravel floor, cowboy memorabilia on the walls and no windows (it makes for better lighting during the Meyers' performances). Dinner is served at 6:30 sharp Memorial Day through Labor Day, and reservations are recommended. Adults eat for $14, and children younger than 12 can get the whole shebang for $6.50.

Silver Gate and Cooke City, Montana

Range Rider's Lodge
U.S. Hwy. 212, Silver Gate, Mont.
• **(406) 838-2359**

During the summer, this comfortable old log lodge comes to life when the sun goes down. On weekends June through August you can count on live music that'll set your toes to twitching. A rock fireplace, a pine bar and locals with a down-home hospitality will make you feel right at home here. If you're the sort who prefers to sit and watch others dance, there's plenty of space around the dance floor with tables for folks just like you. If you're a dancer with a hankering to step into the rhythm of the West, Range Rider's Lodge is a must.

Miner's Saloon
U.S. Hwy. 212, Cooke City, Mont.
• **(406) 838-2214**

If you're looking for local color, you'll find it at the Miner's Saloon. You'll also find a mini-museum hanging mostly from the walls and ceiling. The Miner's Saloon imports an occasional band. Otherwise, it's the juke box, conversation or the game room in back, which features pool tables, air hockey and those gambling machines.

The Ore House Saloon
U.S. Hwy. 212, Cooke City, Mont.
• **(406) 838-2251, (800) 527-6462**

Located in the Soda Butte Lodge, the Ore House Saloon is a sprawling bar overlooking the Clarks Fork River and a regular thoroughfare for bears. The Ore House is another one of those popular *Monday Night Football* hangouts. It has three TVs, one of them a big-screen. There are gambling machines here, but no pool table.

Grand Teton National Park

Dornan's Bar
Teton Park Rd. at Moose Junction
• **(307) 733-2415, Ext. 200**

Hootenanny (n): A gathering of folk singers, typically with participation by the audience.

Don't take the American Heritage Dictionary folks at their word: Come see a hootenanny for yourself Monday nights year round. Hear old-time folk, cowboy songs and bluegrass performed by local talent and others who wander in with a song and an instrument. You'll pay a $2 door charge.

In summer the hootenanny gets crowded fast. People begin arriving in late afternoon for the 7 PM show. When the house is full, folks spill out onto the deck and enjoy the music through speakers. Dornan's Bar hosts other concerts from time to time, so give them a call if you'll be staying in or near Grand Teton National Park and want to enjoy a little live music. Concert tickets cost around $10.

Signal Mountain Lodge
Teton Park Rd. on south shore of Jackson Lake • **(307) 733-5470**

Some nights when the crowd gets rowdy, it's hard to remember that you're buried in lodgepole forest at the base of some of the wildest looking mountains you've ever seen, and that you'll soon be headed through dark mountain chill to your tent or cabin. No better reason exists to order another Margarita and perhaps a mountainous plate of nachos. Signal Mountain Lodge is open from mid-May to mid-October. Two restaurants are on-site.

Jackson Hole

Jackson, Wyoming

Bar-J Chuckwagon Suppers & Original Western Show
Teton Village Rd., Wilson, Wyo.
• **(307) 733-3370**

Fortlike, the Bar-J buildings box a spacious patio and lawn. Paths lead across it to a memorabilia hall, a gift shop, and of course the giant dining room that seats up to 750 every night in summer. You'll enjoy barbecued beef, baked potatoes, beans, home made biscuits and more. The rest of the evening is given to the traditional western music, tall tales and cowboy poetry of the Bar-J Wranglers. The charge for adults in 1997 was $13, meal and all. The Bar-J puts on its supper shows from Memorial Day to the end of September. The ranch is located in a grove of cottonwoods about a 10-minute drive from Jackson.

Cadillac Grill
55 N. Cache, Jackson, Wyo.
• **(307) 733-3279**

Besides serving an interesting selection of what the menu calls "new American cuisine," Cadillac Grill puts on a fine late-night happy hour. Abstract paintings hang on the walls, black napkins rest on white tablecloths and oldies play through the speakers. Stop in for two-for-the-price-of-one drinks from 5 to 6 PM or 11 to midnight.

Since Cadillac Grill is right on town square, an easy walk from other local nightspots including the SilverDollar, the Million Dollar Cowboy Bar and the Rancher, lots of folks wander in for happy hour from other parties. If you're coming early for dinner, it's best to make a reservation.

The Clubhouse at Teton Pines Resort
3450 N. Clubhouse Dr., Jackson, Wyo.
• **(307) 733-1005, (800) 238-2223**

In summer, it's 22,000 elegantly appointed square feet of golf clubhouse, with a fine dining restaurant, pro shop, bar and lounge. In winter, though, the cathedral-ceilinged second floor, with its 35-foot-long leather couch and massive fireplace, becomes a busy après-ski sushi bar. Stop by on your way back to Jackson from the ski hill at Teton Village or after your cross-country ski tour of the golf course's 14-K groomed track.

Million Dollar Cowboy Bar
25 N. Cache, Jackson, Wyo.
• **(307) 733-2207**

This famous Jackson institution must be seen to be believed — from the glossy log-slab tables to the knobby pine pillars, railing and ceiling trim, and from the saddle bar stools (yes, they really are saddles) to the huge grizzly mount supposedly dispatched in a battle to the death with a weaponless man. For a moderate cover charge (usually $3 to $5) you can play pool or dance to live Western music Monday through Saturday nights, sipping on the beer or cocktail of your choice.

Stop by the gift shop out front for a T-shirt, mug, sheriff's badge or pair of Million Dollar Cowboy Bar panties. You can pick up a good steak dinner in the restaurant downstairs. The bar closes for a week or two in the spring and again in the fall.

Rancher Spirits and Billiards
20 E. Broadway, Jackson, Wyo.
• **(307) 733-3886**

The huge, mirrored hall is lined with rows of pool tables; the second floor deck looks over the hullabaloo in the town square. Rock music plays over the speaker system. Most of the folks at the Rancher are here to play pool, because that's what you do at the Rancher. In the fall of 1997 a grill was added downstairs that delivers to the second-floor bar, so now patrons can drink, play pool and enjoy nachos, burgers, wings and poppers.

Shady Lady Saloon
400 E. Snow King Ave., Jackson, Wyo.
• **(307) 733-5300**

Part of the Snow King resort complex, this four-level saloon hosts bands every Wednesday night and most summer weekend nights. You'll seldom pay a cover for the energetic rock, blues, ska and reggae music that thump the crowd of young people and hotel guests. Shady Lady serves a short bar menu; one item it practically dares you

Visitors to Greater Yellowstone should keep an eye peeled for one of the two dozen brewpubs and microbreweries in the region.

to try is the local version of the infamous Rocky Mountain oyster. The saloon is open seven nights a week.

SilverDollar Bar at The Wort Hotel
Corner of Glenwood and Broadway, Jackson, Wyo. • (307) 733-2190, (800) 322-2727

The long bar was designed in 1950 by a German cabinetmaker who embedded 2,032 uncirculated silver dollars into its surface. Why? In rough and tumble Wyoming, gambling, though illegal, was tolerated. The Wort Hotel had an active casino operation from the time it opened until a raid in the late 1950s, and apparently the shiny silver dollars celebrated that fact. The designs burned into the wooden bar tables commemorate another piece of western color: They are brands from working ranches across Montana, Idaho and Wyoming.

SilverDollar Bar serves a busy lunch. Tuesday through Saturday you can enjoy live music here with no cover charge. There's no room to dance, but the music is generally quite good, ranging from bluegrass and folk to country.

Snake River Brewing Co.
265 S. Millward, Jackson, Wyo.
• (307) 739-2337

This pub's award-winning beers are brewed in big shiny tanks behind the S-shaped bar. Enjoy Snake River Pale, Zonker Stout and other varieties while listening to live jazz on Tuesday nights or a local bluegrass band on Thursdays. Occasionally you'll catch a band on weekends, but only in summer and winter; during spring and fall the brewery hosts no bands. There's no cover charge.

Winter nights, you can sit by the fireplace and watch the night skiing at Snow King through tall windows. Snake River Brewing Co. is also a restaurant, serving lunch and dinner seven days a week. The kitchen stays open late for the party crowd (see our Restaurants chapter).

Stagecoach Bar
5755 W. Hwy. 22, Wilson, Wyo.
• (307) 733-4407

It's a classic local hangout: pool tables, dart board, a juke box on one wall. The building dates to the 1940s; it has a settled-in look that makes a beer go down just fine. The music is country and western, and the full bar features six tap handles, two of which are generally microbrews.

The food is a bit surprising. In November 1996, Patty Cake Patisserie, an upscale deli, changed its name to Patty Cake West and moved into the building. Now the folks tossing darts are also munching fresh pastries or pasta salads.

You won't see many tourists here except on Sunday nights when the Stagecoach Band performs. These boys are a piece of Jackson Hole history. Local legend has it that the band's founder, Bill Briggs, was the first guy to ski the Grand Teton. His country band has performed for fans at the Stagecoach on Sunday nights since 1969.

Mangy Moose Saloon
3825 W. McCollister Dr., Teton Village
• (307) 733-4913

It's got an entire antique shop stapled to the ceiling. Through the chaos above your head, a moose with dangling legs pulls a dangling sleigh. The house beer is — you guessed it — Moose Brew. Blues Traveler and Widespread Panic have played here. So has Leo Kottke. Arlo Guthrie spins through a couple times a year. Timothy Leary wowed the crowds. Did we say crowds? Oh, yeah. You can ski from the lifts at Teton Village to the door, so the Mangy Moose is, from 3 to 7 PM in winter, wall-to-wall skiers. In fact, *Snow Country's* reader poll has named the Mangy Moose the best ski bar in the country three years running.

You'll pay a cover for some of these acts, but they're generally worth it. The music plays most nights in winter and most weekends in summer. Mangy Moose is open seven nights a week. It closes in April.

Jackson Hole Playhouse
145 W. Deloney, Jackson, Wyo.
• (307) 733-6994

This playhouse exudes historical charm. It's the oldest theater in Wyoming, the oldest frame building in Jackson, a former livery stable, a former Western Union office, and a former bowling alley. In the 1950s it was made over into the Pink Garter Theatre. In 1969 a newer theater was built across the street. The old theater's name jumped the road, but the theater stayed.

What you'll see at the former Pink Garter is Western musical theater, mostly old Broadway musicals like *Seven Brides for Seven Brothers*, *Oklahoma*, *Shenandoah* and *Paint Your Wagon*. Performances are staged by a 12- to 25-member cast Monday through Saturday evenings, Memorial Day to Labor Day. Although the Playhouse has not historically done winter shows, they're considering it, so give them a call if you're in the area in December or January. Tickets are around $12.50.

Grand Teton Mainstage Theatre
50 W. Broadway, Jackson, Wyo.
• (307) 733-3670

If you happen to be passing the Pink Garter Plaza any night but Sunday and hear singing and laughing and a gathering crowd, you're probably witnessing the pre-show antics of Grand Teton Mainstage Theatre. In a few minutes the actors and their new fans will tromp up to the 340-seat theater that comprises the shopping center's third floor, hold a sing-along and then get down to the serious business of comedy. Shows are often musicals and always lighthearted. Members of the 16- to 20-member company hail from all over the country.

The theater is open for the summer season only. Tickets are $14 for adults. Same-day tickets are usually not a problem, although some weekend shows do sell out.

Snow King Resort
400 E. Snow King Ave., Jackson, Wyo.
• (307) 733-5200, (800) 522-5464

Snow King looms at the edge of Jackson, so the best part of night skiing its 110 acres of

INSIDERS' TIP

Many bars in Yellowstone country pride themselves on carrying a selection of regional microbrewed beer. If you're a beer lover but you haven't experimented with micros yet, ask for a few "tasters" so you can get an idea what you like. A tremendous range of flavors is possible.

lit slope is the sight of town lights glowing below you. Night skiing is available from 4 to 8 PM, Tuesday through Saturday, weather permitting. Tickets are $14 for adults. The mountain generally opens Thanksgiving weekend and closes March 29.

Surrounding Areas

Eastern Idaho

Idaho Falls, Idaho, Area

Alive After 5
498 A St., Idaho Falls, Idaho
• (208) 535-0399

Listen to music outside early Wednesday evenings June through September. Each week the town blocks off A Street from Capital to Park. Local musical groups perform, and a different local restaurant each week is invited to sell its specialty to the après work crowd. Beers, including Idaho Brewing Company's award-winning brews, are on tap. Street merchants get into the act with specials and sidewalk tables of merchandise. Between 300 and 500 attend. Attendance is free, but food and beer are not.

DB's Steakhouse
216 First St., Idaho Falls, Idaho
• (208) 529-4070

Wes Smith, this bar's owner, has a sister named Debbie. So for some reason, this establishment's first incarnation, 19 years ago, was as Debbie's Brother. Now it's DB's. Some of the better dance bands this town gets to hear play this bar on Friday and Saturday nights. The music is usually classic rock 'n' roll or blues. DB's can seat nearly 300 people; when a good band comes in, it often does. Smith and his wife book as many blues acts as they can and and have brought in such notables as Commander Cody and the Lost Planet Airmen. If Rebecca Scott is playing, don't pass it up. She's a Boise songstress and a regular here whom we think is headed for a recording contract soon.

You can generally expect to pay no cover, but special shows sometimes cost as much as $5 at the door.

A popular Friday stop for locals is DB's Power Hour from 5 PM to 7 PM You pay $6 for all the beer you can drink. All three bartenders spend those two hours pouring as fast as they can. DB's attracts a mixed crowd of partiers, mostly younger folks.

Dust Lounge
700 Lindsay Blvd., Idaho Falls, Idaho
• (208) 523-1865

Locals say this upscale country bar in the Stardust Motor Lodge is probably the friendliest place in town to kick up your cowboy boots and two-step the night away. Rodeo pictures line the walls and cowhide lines the barstools, but this isn't where folks go to get wild. Dust Lounge hosts country and western bands every Friday and Saturday night. There is no cover. In the past they've offered free line and two-step dance lessons from 6 to 8 PM to get you ready for the action. If you'd like to learn, it's worth a phone call.

Ford's Bar
444 A St., Idaho Falls, Idaho
• (208) 523-4840

Come here because play at the five pool tables is free, just like in the old days. Or come for the live country music, or for that unassuming, smoky atmosphere that every neighborhood bar used to have — or to check out the scrolled and intricate antique back bar. It was brought here by wagon in the late 1800s and installed as the building was constructed. Ford's has been around for nearly a century and has been under the same ownership for 33 years. Tourists don't come here much, but if you want a peek into the past, make this one of your evening stops. There is never a cover charge for the Friday- and Saturday-night bands.

Heise Hot Springs
5116 E. Heise Rd., Ririe, Idaho
• (208) 538-7312

Mineral-laden hot water bubbles out of the ground at 123 degrees at the Snake River's edge. The water fills a large mineral hot pool maintained at a pleasant soaking temperature of 105 degrees. Through heat exchangers, it also warms a freshwater pool that's kept at about 94 degrees. Both pools are outdoors and open until 10 PM, making for a pleasant evening diversion — especially in winter when you can watch the snowflakes melt on your steam-warmed arms. The cost is $5 for adults. The pools are open year round except for three weeks in November when they close for maintenance. Both are chlorinated.

There's lots more going on at Heise than hot water. See our Attractions chapter to learn about the golf course, summer pool and other features.

Peppertree Restaurant and Lounge
888 N. Holmes Ave., Idaho Falls, Idaho • (208) 523-5993

Thursday is the best night to come to the Peppertree: That's comedy night, when two comedians take the stage for the evening. Tickets are $5. There is no charge for admission other nights.

Weeknights tend to involve audience participation: karaoke, amateur sumo wrestling or amateur boxing (Peppertree provides appropriate sumo garb and oversize boxing gloves to brave volunteers). On weekends the lounge hosts a deejay. The Peppertree offers a full bar.

Island Park, Idaho

Jacobs' Island Park Ranch
Off Kilgore Rd., Island Park, Idaho • (208) 662-5567, (800) 230-9530

Get ready for an evening of Western entertainment. You begin around 5:30 with a ride in an authentic antique English-style carriage behind a Clydesdale or Belgian horse. Your driver delivers you to The Barn for an evening of Dutch-oven treats and barbecued meats. All this is followed by a Western variety show with comedy acts, singing and dancing.

While at The Barn, you'll be interested to know that the massive structure was actually built as a barn. But when it was finished, the Jacobs realized it was far too pretty to simply house carriages and horses, so they decorated with the Indian rugs you see before you, added the stage and — ta-dah! They had a perfect Western showplace.

Jacobs' Island Park Ranch hosts these reservation-only evenings every Friday and Saturday night in summer. The cost is $20 per person. The ranch also offers pleasant cabin accommodations and horseback riding (see our Resorts and Guest Ranches chapter).

Mack's Inn Dinner Theater
4111 Big Springs Rd., Mack's Inn at Island Park, Idaho • (208) 558-7871

All-you-can-eat roast beef and pork, Dutch-oven treats, homemade breads and jams — that would draw most of us from our campsites and fishing holes. Now add live drama (in 1997 the shows were Noel Coward's comedy *Blithe Spirit* and Philip King's *See How They Run*) in a casual dining atmosphere that welcomes your dusty jeans and hiking boots.

Needless to say, summer weekends are busy at the Playmill and reservations are recommended. Shows and dinner run Monday through Saturday all summer.

Swan Valley

Covered Wagon Saloon
No credit cards • Swan Valley Hwy. at Irwin, Idaho • (208) 483-2027

Bob Jackson retired, got bored and opened this saloon 10 years ago. Judged by the fact that the bar hasn't closed a day since, he's not bored now. He can seat about 100, and on the summer Saturdays and holidays when he brings a country-and-western or soft-rock band to town (no cover), those 100 seats are often taken.

Other nights, Covered Wagon Saloon is quieter. Locals and visiting fishermen drink at the bar and play pool or shuffleboard. You can get a bite to eat in the adjacent cafe.

The Saddlesore Saloon at The Fox's Corner'd Inn
2998 U.S. Hwy. 26, Swan Valley, Idaho • (208) 483-2501

If you're looking for somewhere to dance to old rock or new country, the Saddlesore is worth a try. It hires bands for holiday and other weekends, mostly in summer. If you're driving in from a distance, you can camp free on the 2-acre property after the party. And since this establishment is also a restaurant, kids are welcome. The well-ventilated room is kept relatively smoke-free. The look is new-rustic, with pine paneling, a log staircase and a fire in the dining room fireplace. The Saddlesore Saloon is open seven days a week for lunch, dinner and late-night fun.

Teton Valley

Knotty Pine Bar and Restaurant
27 E. Main, Victor, Idaho
• **(208) 787-2866**

In the 1920s it was a service station. Then it was a six-stool bar. Now it's got three TVs, a fireplace, a pool table, a dining room (see our Restaurants chapter) and a sunny deck outside. On most Friday nights the old log walls of the somewhat renovated, much-expanded Knotty Pine vibrate with the sounds of rock 'n' roll, country and western or pop music from local dance bands. There is no cover charge.

Pierre's Playhouse
27 N. Main, Victor, Idaho
• **(208) 787-2249 summers only**

What goes perfectly with the laughs and delightful overacting of an old-fashioned melodrama? How about an all-you-can-eat Dutch-oven dinner of chicken, potatoes, salad and homemade scones? Enjoy the show alone ($8) or take our suggestion and have dinner as well ($14) Wednesday through Saturday, mid-June through August. Two shows play on alternate days, each with a cast of six to eight players.

This is a family operation, so owner Peggy Egbert's son plays the villain, as did her husband before him. A daughter also acts in Playhouse productions. Two other daughters work behind the scenes. Pierre's Playhouse will celebrate 35 years of fun and good food in the summer of 1998.

Spud Drive-in Theater
231 S. Idaho Hwy. 33, Driggs, Idaho
• **(208) 354-2727, (800) 799-SPUD**

The giant potato on the old flatbed truck is a local landmark, and an outdoor movie at the Spud Drive-in is a local tradition. The summer of 1997 marked the venerable old drive-in's 44th year. Unlike many drive-ins, the theater only shows one movie per night. Most of the audience are families, and with summer darkness falling around 10 PM, a one-movie evening doesn't end until midnight.

The regular admission price in 1997 was $5 per adult, but the theater runs specials: Mondays are Family Nights, and you pay $5 per car; Thursdays are Cheap Date nights, and two get in on one $5 ticket. The season runs from mid-April to early October.

Trap Bar and Grille
Grand Targhee at Ski Hill Rd., Alta, Wyo.
• **(307) 353-2300, (800) TARGHEE**

Ski to the stairs and climb out of the cold into Trap Bar, which serves snacks, lunch and dinner. You can also enjoy 10 different tap beers and live music almost every night except during football games. (Football is broadcast on six TVs in Trap Bar.) There is never a cover, even for acts as fine as Peter Rowan, Sam Lee's All Star Band and U.S. Blues. Music is eclectic here at Trap Bar. It ranges from blues to bluegrass and Motown R&B to reggae, plus the uncategorizable, such as String Cheese Incident. But what it mostly is, is danceable.

Bands start playing around 4:15 PM during ski season. They break from 6:30 to 8 PM and then play until around 10 PM, when all good skiers go to their beds to dream the next day's turns. Trap Bar closes in spring and fall.

Southwestern Montana

Bearcreek Saloon and Bearcreek Downs
108 Main, Bearcreek, Mont.
• **(406) 446-3481**

The bell rings, the trumpet sounds, the gate opens, and the pigs race around a track to the finish line where a trough of food awaits. This could be the cheapest — and most memorable — entertainment you'll find anyplace in Yellowstone country: An inexpensive Mexican dinner followed by pig races. Economic desperation led owners Lynn and Pits DeArmond to come up with this outlandish idea for attracting crowds to their out-of-the-way saloon 7 miles east of Red Lodge. It worked. Friday through Sunday the pigs at Bearcreek Downs do their thing for crowds of up to 300 people.

In addition, the DeArmonds hold a pig-racing Calcutta (they had to get a special "pig racing bill" passed by the Montana legislature). Since the races began in 1989, proceeds from the calcutta have generated $32,000 for local scholarships. Weaner pigs race outside during the summer, while baby pigs do their thing in a glass-enclosed track during the winter.

The Bearcreek Saloon and Downs are open from Memorial Day through Labor Day, and from Christmas through Easter.

Cat's Paw
721 N. Seventh Ave., Bozeman, Mont.
• (406) 586-3542

The Cat's Paw is the cat's meow when it comes to good times and big crowds. It's a mostly blue-collar bar that attracts a healthy mix of clientele including college students, lawyers in suits, cowboys, teachers and even a 95-year-old regular who plays poker and dances when he can. At the Cat's Paw you'll find live music Thursday through Saturday and well-known bands that play during the week several times a month. (The Freddy Jones Band, Inner Circle and Norton Buffalo played here in 1997.)

The Cat's Paw seats nearly 400, including 60 patrons at the bar, which runs the length of the room. Happy hour runs from 8 AM until 8 PM daily. Thursday is free-beer night from 9:30 PM until 12:30 AM (there's a $6 cover charge), while Wednesday is $1-a-pint night. The Cat's Paw has 20 brands of beer on tap.

Firehouse 5 Playhouse
U.S. Hwy. 89 S., Livingston, Mont.
• (406) 222-1420, (800) SLAPSTICK

The Firehouse 5 Playhouse presents cabaret-style musicals and vaudeville shows year round. Using casts comprised almost entirely of community members, Playhouse owner Bill Conch changes the marquee once a month. In 1997, Firehouse Five's performances included the *Wizard of Oz*, *Fiddler on the Roof*, *The Denver Comedy Club*, *World War II Revue* and *Forever Plaid*.

Summer performances are Thursday through Saturday, while winter presentations are Friday and Saturday nights. You'll find Sunday matinees summer and winter.

Chet's
Mountain Village, Big Sky, Mont.
• (406) 995-5000

From 4:30 to 6 PM each day, more than 150 people — about a third of which are kids — pack into Chet's to see what the Crazy Austrians are going to do next. This duo, which is practically an institution in Big Sky, has the audience singing along, doing the polka and playing nearly 100 funky musical instruments including kazoos. Once the Crazy Austrians get your children up on stage to do silly things, they'll send them back out to drag you up there. Anyone hauled in front of the audience might end up in a funny little outfit or buffalo skull masks or weird hats. Before you know it, they'll have everybody in Chet's doing the Chicken Dance.

After 6 PM things calm down. From 9:45 PM until 1 AM, you'll find an acoustical guitar player making background music.

Half Moon Saloon
U.S. Hwy. 212, Big Sky, Mont.
• (406) 995-4533

This is the biggest bar in Big Sky (it seats 238), and it sells the most reasonably priced drinks. It also has a pleasant mix of locals and tourists. Huge bay windows overlook the Gallatin River on one side and the Madison Mountain Range on the other. The Half Moon imports a band most Saturday nights, and during the busier summer months it adds to that by a night or two each week. When they aren't using the dance floor, the owners cover part of it with a Ping-Pong table and a foosball table. The Half Moon also has three pool tables, shuffleboard, dart games and a few poker and keno machines.

The Half Moon serves lunch and dinner from 11 AM to 9 PM in the winter and from 11 AM until 10 PM in summer. Locals say this place serves the best burgers in the area.

INSIDERS' TIP

Both Jackson papers publish weekend editions that will give you an Insiders' scoop on the nightlife action in that partying town.

Milkie's Pizza and Pub
Westfork Meadows, Big Sky, Mont.
• **(406) 995-2900**

Milkie's is the local after-work bar. Since many employees work in restaurants and don't get off 'til after the dinner dishes are done, things don't really get going here until 9 or 10 PM. During dinner, though, you'll find families dining on Milkie's pizza, which, by the way, can be delivered. The walls are a regular museum, displaying photos and sports memorabilia such as old golf clubs, fishing gear, ice skates and fishing creels. Enhancing Milkie's casual atmosphere are a pool table, dart board, poker machines and a jukebox with an amazing selection of oldies.

Scissorbill's Bar and Grill
Mountain Village, Big Sky, Mont.
• **(406) 995-4933**

We think Scissorbill's has the best happy hour in Big Sky. From 4 to 6 PM seven days a week, you can ski right up to the bar and slurp $2 pints of beer or $2.50 Margaritas. Another late-night happy hour begins at 10 and ends at midnight. Too small for a dance band (it holds 80 customers), Scissor Bill's does feature live music from 4 to 6:30 each Saturday afternoon. Wednesday nights, stop in for open-mike night. For the slow times, you'll find dartboards and a few poker machines. Scissor Bill's is open November through April.

Chico Saloon
Old Chico Rd., Pray, Mont.
• **(406) 333-4933**

Located about 25 miles south of Livingston, the Chico Saloon at the Chico Hot Springs Lodge hires a different kind of band every Friday and Saturday night. Depending on the band, folks drive for miles to mingle with a mixed crowd of locals and visitors that might range from stove-up old cowboys to duded-up movie stars. Just off the dance floor is the Chico Hot Springs pool where you can either start or finish the night. The Saloon offers a special menu for patrons, and for those evenings when there's nothing much else going on, you'll find a couple of TVs, a pool table, darts and gambling machines.

The Lagoon
431 S. Third St., Livingston, Mont.
• **(406) 222-7937**

It's hard telling what might be going on at this spontaneously happening dinner gallery. One night you might find a jazz band, the next night there'll be a Mexican polka band from Butte, and the following night The Lagoon might be hosting a cast party (in 1997, the cast of Robert Redford's movie *The Horse Whisperer*, filmed in Livingston, held its opening party here).

Situated on the edge of Sacajawea Park in a big brick waterworks building from the 1880s, The Lagoon combines cozy and airy with fireplaces, couches and lots of tall windows. Tables situated on a stage overlook the lagoon, which often sports geese and swans. At one end you'll find an atrium. At another you'll find giant doors big enough to accommodate a dumptruck. Out the front, you'll find wildflowers, a patio, a Ping-Pong table and barbecue and horseshoe pits.

The dinner menu is simple with four entrees. Call two hours ahead to let them know you're coming, then make yourself at home. There's no liquor license here, so it's BYOB. Occasionally the owners simply serve wine gratis. The Lagoon is generally open all year.

Molly Brown
703 W. Babcock, Bozeman, Mont.
• **(406) 586-9903**

If pool is your passion, you'll find your match at the Molly Brown. Its 11 pool tables and sports theme attract a younger crowd enamored with skiing, snowboarding and skateboarding. A crazy collection of sports memorabilia and gear such as cross-country skis, bikes and a motorcycle hang on the wall. A gondola car dangles from the ceiling. Happy hour runs from noon until 8 PM Saturday, and Sundays are the Molly Brown's official Pint Nights.

Murray Lounge and Grill
201 W. Park Ave., Livingston, Mont.
• **(406) 222-1350**

Anything attached to the Murray Hotel, Livingston's oldest and most Western hotel, manages to mix the slightly upscale with the definitely down-to-earth. Belly up to the oval bar, play pool or dance to the band of the week. The Murray features music to match its clientele — eclectic, eccentric, egalitarian. Even the walls reflect the sometimes crazy combos. One sports brands from the movie, *Keep the Change*. The others display art by Livingston artists Parks Reese and Michael Simon.

Depending on the night — and the mood — you'll find rock and roll, country and western, blues or reggae music most weekends. (During the winter, bands play on Thursday and Friday. The Murray adds Saturday nights to the summer schedule.)

The Round Barn Restaurant and Dinner Theater
U.S. Hwy 212 N., Red Lodge, Mont.
• (406) 446-1197

The atmosphere here is worth the meal alone. And the food would be worth the drive (it's only a couple of miles from town) without the round red-brick barn built as a dairy by the Kent family in 1941. Owner Dan Farrar has converted this beautiful barn into a restaurant on the ground floor and a theater in the loft. June through September Farrar books professional actors, singers, musicians and comedians to perform in his "theater in the round."

Dinner, served buffet style, includes four kinds of meat, potatoes (often real mashed potatoes), a very fresh salad, vegetables, bread, soup and a dessert. The curtain rises at 9 PM. The rates are reasonable. The Round Barn is usually closed during January and February.

Stacey's
300 Mill St., Gallatin Gateway, Mont.
• (406) 763-4425

If it's cowboy kitsch you crave, don't go to Stacey's. This comfortable cowboy bar is the real McCoy. It hosts a country and western band every Friday and Saturday night, and it boasts a huge collection of rodeo photos given

to owner Stacey Crosby by his cowboy friends. Don't expect anything fancy at Stacey's (the sign will say the "Old Faithful.") Do expect a homey horseshoe-shaped bar with a fireplace and a pool table on one side and a dance floor on the other.

Northwestern Wyoming

Cody, Wyoming

Cassie's Supper Club
214 Yellowstone Ave., Cody, Wyo.
• (307) 527-5500

If it's dancing you're up to, this is the place to go in Cody. Owned by musician Steve Singer, a Cody native who played music on the road for 20 years before returning home, Cassie's is a classic country and western dancing bar. You'll find live music here six nights a week — Singer plays them all. Weeknights, you won't have to share the dance floor with quite so many others. Expect a jam on summer evenings. (Singer opens up the back bar and another whole room to make room for the crowds.)

Cody Nite Rodeo
421 W. Yellowstone Ave., Cody, Wyo.
• (307) 587-2992

Among visitors, the Cody Nite Rodeo has to be town's the No. 1 nighttime entertainment for young and old alike. Nearly 90,000 people attend this fast-moving rodeo every night from Memorial Day until Labor Day. For more information about the Cody Nite Rodeo, see our Spectator Sports chapter.

Gib's Sports Pub
1901 Mountain View Rd., Cody, Wyo.
• (307) 527-5253

Mondays and Sundays during football season, this place is packed with folks drinking beer and watching the ball games on the seven screens in the bar. Attached to the verging-

---

INSIDERS' TIP

The IMAX Theater and the Grizzly Discovery Center in West Yellowstone qualify for evening family entertainment. For more information refer to our Attractions chapter.

on-upscale Black Sheep restaurant, Gib's offers comfortable chairs and eight kinds of beer, including Guinness and Moose Drool, on tap. The bar, which is carpeted in plush almost-burgundy, has no dance floor, but the Black Sheep does, though dances here are sporadic. Drinks are reasonably priced — even better at the 50¢-off happy hour from 5 to 7 each evening.

Silver Dollar Bar and Grill and Angie's
1313 Sheridan Ave., Cody, Wyo.
• (307) 587-3554

You'll recognize this place by the big burger painted on the front window. The Silver Dollar, which hires a band nearly every Friday and Saturday year round, is a favorite local hangout that attracts revelers of all kinds and ages, as well as businessmen for lunch. (Some locals say this place serves the best burgers in town. The menu features seven varieties.) In front is the regular old Silver Dollar, while Angie's, a new addition with another bar,

is where the band plays and the customers dance. When summer comes, you'll find a tent over a patio bordering the sidewalk.

Weeknights from 5 to 7 PM, the Silver Dollar has a 50¢-off happy hour. The Silver Dollar has five pool tables and three TVs to wile away your time.

Skate Away
3534 Bighorn Ave., Cody, Wyo.
• (307) 587-6556

Skate away the day and evening at the 12,000-square-foot Skate Away roller rink. Or just turn the kids loose while you sit back and watch. Skating here costs from $3.25 to $3.50 depending on the time of day. For most sessions, the admission price includes roller-skate rental. (In-line skates will cost you $1.50 extra to rent.) Winter hours here are Fridays from 7 to 10 PM, Saturdays from noon to 4:15 PM and Sundays from 2 to 4 PM. Summer hours are restricted to Friday and Saturday nights from 7 to 10 PM, as well as a Saturday afternoon session.

Albertsons®
FOOD & DRUG

Idaho:
- 1901 South 2500 East — **Ammon**
- 1295 Parkway Boulevard — **Blackfoot**
- 1705 Broadway — **Idaho Falls**
- 590 East 17th Street — **Idaho Falls**
- 735 East Anderson — **Idaho Falls**
- 330 East Benton — **Pocatello**
- 940 Yellowstone Avenue — **Pocatello**
- 490 North 2nd East — **Rexburg**

Wyoming:
- 1825 17th Street — **Cody**
- 520 West Broadway — **Jackson Hole**

Montana:
- 1531 Main — **Billings**
- 1633 Grand Boulevard — **Billings**
- 6999 Jackrabbit Lane — **Belgrade**
- 200 South 23rd — **Bozeman**
- 1301 Harrison — **Butte**
- 1210 10th Avenue South — **Great Falls**
- North 3151 Montana — **Helena**
- 600 Fee Street — **Helena**
- 1906 Brooks Street — **Missoula**

Shopping

In the early days, visitors hacked away at geyser cones and petrified trees, bagged up the pieces and took them home to keep as souvenirs from Wonderland, an early nickname for Yellowstone Park. Today, visitors still like to bring home something from the towns surrounding the wild lands they've visited. Throughout Greater Yellowstone, and especially in towns such as Jackson and Cody, you'll find myriad shops displaying man-made creations wrought from and inspired by the area's natural resources.

Maybe you'll find a particularly pleasing painting of a familiar landscape or simply a pair of cowboy boots and a hat to match. Maybe it will be a chandelier made of antlers or a set of mugs made of local clay. Whatever it is you're looking for, chances are you'll stumble upon it if you spend some time in our shops. And, if you're not in the mood for buying, it's fun just to look and marvel at the inventive ways artisans have used local materials to create functional works of art.

In this chapter we've included plenty of the frivolous. And we've also listed a good representation of absolutely essential sources such as sporting goods and fly shops to outfit your recreational pursuits. And, of course, we've listed sources for the Greater Yellowstone fashion look. Or looks rather, because there are several. Let's take a look at them.

A funny thing happened on the way to the sporting goods store: The functional high tech fabrics and clothing designs of outdoor athletes and backcountry adventurers became Greater Yellowstone high fashion. For instance, there's fleece, designed to be light and retain warmth even when it's wet. It can be a lifesaver in the backcountry, but it's purchased more for town wear, in sweaters, jackets and tunics. Gore-tex, a fabric that repels rain but lets sweat evaporate, is equally important in the backcountry, and

equally common at the video rental store. Your Gore-tex coat (or "shell," if you're hip to gear wienie lingo) is even more fashionable if it's oversized and doesn't match the fleece jacket underneath.

In summer, add canvas, cotton or nylon shorts — baggy ones, please. Grab a mesh and nylon high-tech imitation of the old-fashioned ball cap. Sport sandals like Tevas or Alps, or leather sandals like Birkenstocks complete the ensemble. In winter, substitute jeans or nylon pants. These latter should zip up the outside as though you were just about to pull them off over plastic climbing boots, despite the fact that you're standing in the grocery store parking lot. Add Sorel snow packs, the ones with the cute fur strip around the top. Sorels are even cooler if you don't lace and tie them neatly.

Note that brand names, which in faux-sport couture are plainly visible outside your clothes, are important. You'll pay for the right manufacturer's tag, but hey, you can't be cool without it. Look for Patagonia, Gramicci, Kavu, Sorel, Teva, Marmot, North Face or any brand name you find stamped, embroidered or tagged onto the outside of a very expensive clothing item in a store which carries both climbing gear and skis.

One last tip: Remember not to match colors. It's the beginner's most common mistake and will immediately mark you as only a wannabe faux-sport fashion plate, instead of a genuine faux-sport fashion plate.

Now, perhaps you don't care to adopt the look made cool by frost-bitten Everest climbers and unbathed river guides. Another option is cowboy couture, available at trendy stores in Jackson. With this look, you most certainly match, from your silver-tipped, sharkskin boots and your hand-tooled belt to your satin appliqued, silk embroidered, pearl-snap Western shirt (which you will have paid a cool $150 for). Then you'll shrug into your matching, luxuriously fringed calf or deerskin jacket (kept short in women's styles to show off that belt). And don't forget the cowboy hat, which will be fur felt (consider nothing but beaver, please) with a hand-tooled hatband that makes liberal use of horsehair or antique trade beads. Women, your arms should drip with turquoise-encrusted silver bracelets. Men, you can go with bracelets, too, but don't miss out on a bolo tie, perhaps on a rattlesnake theme, also in silver and turquoise, but with a bear claw or pair of elk ivories thrown in.

Cowboy couture is pricey but fun, as fun to shop for as to wear. But keep in mind as you hunt for your costume that that's just what it is. Cowboys don't wear this stuff. They'd faint at the thought. You're buying a costume for strutting the streets of Jackson, and perhaps to wow your friends with back home, but you're not buying the clothing that will make you one of the boys (or girls). And you'll probably find that the look does not become part of your fashion riff. Like that lime-green plastic mini-skirt you bought when retro-'60s reared its ugly head a couple years ago, this stuff will be fun a few times — then it'll be relegated to the back of the closet.

If you're going for the authentic cowboy look, then head straight for the Wrangler jeans. Any color will do, but buy boot cut. Stay away from taper-legged jeans. They'll look like lumpy stuffed sausages pulled down over your boot tops. And after a session of sitting in the stands, they'll slide up your boot, pucker big-time at the knee, and stay there when you stand.

Justin and Tony Lama have the name when it comes to boots, but every cool cowhand goes for the casual comfort of Ariat's lace-up ropers and dress boots. Built like tennis shoes — flexible and easy to break in — Ariats mark you as a man or woman in the know. Justins or Tony Lamas will do in a pinch. See that you don't apply that pinch to your toes with pointed tips, though. Old-timers who grew up with pointy-toed boots and high, underslung heels can get away with wearing them still.

When it comes to belts and buckles, it's best to keep a low profile. Any color, with or without silver will pass as long it matches your hat and boots. You can't go wrong with a smallish Montana Silversmith buckle. Stay away from the giant plate-sized trophy-type buckles. Unless you've won the buckle, that silver plate across your belly button will mark you as a shining wannabe.

For the casual look, pretty much any shirt will do. If you want to top off the whole cowboy look, though, buy a long-sleeved, button-up shirt by Wrangler, Adobe Rose, Rocky Mountain Blaze or Mo' Betta. Don't bother with the bright, wild Brush Popper shirt. It's fading into the sunset.

Top that look off with a black, grey or cream hat by Stetson or Resistol. Buy a Montana Silversmith watch (they're hot) and all the jewelry you can. (Big earrings are in.) For those cool evenings, throw a double-breasted, military style jacket over your shoulder.

www.insiders.com

See this and many other **Insiders' Guide®** destinations online — in their entirety.

Visit us today!

INSIDERS' TIP

Crazy Creek Products, a company that makes padded camp chairs for backpackers, is headquartered in Red Lodge, Montana. Owner Robert Hart, an outdoor enthusiast and former Outward Bound instructor, spent a year perfecting a prototype. He planned to go on the road selling them from his van, but the chairs were instantly so popular among his friends that he did nothing but sew for three months (he could sew 34 a day). Now the bulk of Hart's chairs are made in China, and they're sold by more than 2,000 stores. Employees still do custom orders at the Red Lodge office on U.S. Highway 212, but Hart says you'll get a better deal on the chairs from local retailers than through the Red Lodge office.

Because we think you'll likely want to learn more about Greater Yellowstone, we've listed bookstores where you will find enlightening information (see our Resources chapter for suggested reading). We've also included a healthy menu of places where you can trade in your tenny-runners for a pair of shiny new cowboy boots. You'll find a few furniture stores under functional art, simply because they feature nifty Western-style creations like gnarly pine four-poster beds or intricate antler coat racks. And we've told you about a few extraordinary antique stores.

Our list of stores is not all-inclusive by any means. For your convenience, we have listed stores first according to category, then by geographic area. If, in your meanderings through Yellowstone country, you come across a shop that you think absolutely needs a write-up, we encourage you to let us know about it.

Sporting Goods

Yellowstone National Park

In the Park

Hamilton Stores
Various locations throughout the Park

Hamilton Stores, operated by the Park's oldest existing concessionaire, are located throughout the Park. (For more information, refer to the Close-up on Hamilton Stores in this chapter.) In some locations such as Tower Fall and Lake, you'll find a comparatively limited menu of food, supplies and gifts. At other stores, such as the one in Canyon, though, you'll find everything you could imagine you might need for camping, cooking, traveling, and more. Several locations also have lunch counters, especially the older ones, such as those at Fishing Bridge and Old Faithful.

At Mammoth and Canyon, Hamilton operates separate "nature" shops. In addition, the stores at Fishing Bridge, Old Faithful and the Canyon Nature Shop all have on-site one-hour

photo processing. You'll notice that most Hamilton Stores employees are senior citizens. Hamilton Store at the Fishing Bridge is a beautiful old place with a huge stone fireplace. At one time, a couple big sofas in front of the hearth used to be favorite conversation spots for locals. Merchandise has replaced the couches.

Hamilton Stores Inc. has offered its Yellowstone On-Line Catalog since June of 1997. In addition to such items as Yellowstone souvenirs and apparel, gifts, recreation products, jewelry and Native American handicrafts, you'll find information about road conditions, weather, fishing updates, campgrounds, hotels and employment. Hamilton Stores Inc. also has a web site: http://www.hamiltonstores.com.

Entrance Communities

Arrick's Fishing Flies
125 Madison Ave., West Yellowstone, Mont. • (406) 646-7290, (800) 646-7290

If you've never tied a fly before, you'll want to after walking into this small shop jam-packed with fly-tying paraphernalia. If owner Arrick Swanson isn't out guiding an angler on a nearby river, chances are he'll be tying flies behind the counter. If it's fishing information and esoteric fly-tying goodies you're after, this is the place to stop. This is also the place to stop for local fishing information.

Bud Lilly's Trout Shop
39 Madison Ave., West Yellowstone, Mont. • (406) 646-7801

It's trout and fly everything in this world-famous trout fishing shop. Even Trico, the shop dog — you'd be surprised how many businesses in Yellowstone country have canine companions — is named after a fly. Trico, a coal-black cocker spaniel, has a tip of white, just like her namesake. Besides a huge rod, reel and fly assortment, you'll find clothing, accessories and everything you'd want for a Yellowstone fishing expedition. Plan to spend some extra time looking at the photos of successful anglers. Lilly's features a ton of snapshots of local and visiting folks with the big ones that didn't get away.

Eagle's Store
3 Canyon St., West Yellowstone, Mont.
• **(406) 646-9300**

The selection of Western wear, outdoor clothing, fishing gear, cameras and gifts here is not the largest you'll see. But you will find a taste of the olden days that begins with the tiled counter of the soda fountain — and an old-fashioned chocolate soda. Parts of this store date back to 1910, but most of it was built from 1927 to 1930 to serve tourists. (The shop once had cabins attached to it.) The Eagle Store was one of the three original projects granted special-use permits by the Forest Service in 1908 when the Oregon Short Line of the Union Pacific Railroad reached the west entrance of Yellowstone Park.

Parks' Fly Shop
U.S. Hwy. 89, Gardiner, Mont.
• **(406) 848-7314**

Like the town of Gardiner, this fly shop is simple compared to some. Still, you can find what you need here and plenty of Insider information on area fishing. This shop has been around for decades, and the owners offer a wealth of information.

Jackson Hole

Gear Revival
854 W. Broadway, Jackson, Wyo.
• **(307) 739-8699**

If you're looking for a deal, stop on by Gear Revival's consignment section. Consignment items generally include kayaks, skis, snowboards, ski boots, outerwear, tents and sleeping bags. The retail section, which is stocked with outerwear, backpacking accessories and mountaineering equipment, aims to have the lowest prices in town. The sales

staff include experienced telemark skiers, as well as mountaineering and ice climbers. In winter, Gear Revival shortens its hours and closes Sundays.

High Country Flies
185 Center St., Jackson, Wyo.
• **(307) 733-7210**

Shop owner James Jones grew up fishing in Pennsylvania; he worked as a guide for High Country Flies before he bought the place in 1984. Jim's is the only fly shop in town that carries Patagonia brand clothing, as well as the shop in which the guy behind the counter is most likely to be the owner.

The shelves are stocked with all the supplies an angler needs, from rods to flies to clothing to books on fishing to odd gifts for the angler who has everything. Jim's shop is open seven days a week in summer but closes Sundays in November. See our Fishing and Hunting chapter to learn about High Country Flies' guiding services.

Jack Dennis Sports
50 E. Broadway, Jackson, Wyo.
• **(307) 733-3270**

This is the granddaddy of Jackson fishing shops. Fishing celebrity Jack Dennis Jr. opened his fly shop and guide service here in 1967. Seven years later he expanded into a full-blown sporting-goods store. Now the business even includes a gallery hung with wildlife and landscape art. But most important, Jack Dennis Sports carries the area's largest selection of fishing and fly equipment, including fly-tying supplies you may be accustomed to finding only in catalogs. Look for equipment and accessories by Sage, Scott, Winston and Loomis.

This shop is also home to one of the better known fishing guide services in town (see our Fishing and Hunting chapter).

Moosely Seconds
Dornan's at Moose, Wyo.
• (307) 733-7176
150 E. Broadway, Jackson, Wyo.
• (307) 733-7176

Both Moosely locations are owned by Skinny Skis; think of them as the sporting goods alternative for the wallet-conscious. Moosely carries less-expensive brands as well as discounted seconds and closeouts from makers such as Gramicci, Mountain Hardware, Marmot and Lowe Alpine. About 50 percent of the inventory is priced at full retail.

The Moose location focuses on climbing equipment, although it also has a good selection of sportswear and high-performance outerwear. The shop rents plastic boots, climbing shoes, crampons and ice axes. The Jackson location focuses more on soft goods: clothing, accessories and outerwear. The Moose store closes from early October through Memorial Day weekend.

Rendezvous River Sports/Jackson Hole Kayak School
1035 W. Broadway, Jackson, Wyo.
• (307) 733-2471

Rendezvous is Jackson's first all-paddle shop. Owner Aaron Pruzan says he stocks the best selection of paddle sports equipment in the area. A prospective kayaker can get completely outfitted here, from a helmet, paddle and pile sweater to wetsocks, kayak and nose plugs. Rendezvous carries boats by Dagger, New Wave, Perception, Prijon, Pyranha and Wave Sport.

Rendezvous is open every day but Sunday from March 15 to October 15. To learn about the associated Jackson Hole Kayak School, see our Watersports chapter.

Skinny Skis
65 W. Deloney, Jackson, Wyo.
• (307) 733-6093

Patagonia, Marmot, Mountain Hardware, Rossignol, Arcteryx, Dana, Lowe Alpine — if you're into outdoor gear, you're in the right place. The 23-year-old Skinny Skis is Jackson's snowshoe, nordic and skate ski headquarters in winter and a camping, climbing and jogging store in summer. The sportswear selection is worth stopping in for even if the most strenuous activity you're planning is a walk in the Park.

The staff tends to be practitioners of the sports for which they sell and rent equipment.

Teton Aquatic Supply/Snake River Kayak and Canoe School
155 W. Gill, Jackson Wyo.
• (307) 733-3127

Think of this shop as two stores in one: It houses diving gear, air and a five-star PADI training facility with certified instructors who can teach you to breathe underwater; it also stocks paddle-sports gear and offers kayak and canoe instruction for those who'd rather play on the surface. You can buy whitewater kayaks, sea kayaks and whitewater and lake canoes. Gear to outfit these crafts and their operators fills the store's shelves.

In summer, the shop is open seven days a week. In fall, winter and spring, hours are Monday through Wednesday, Friday and by appointment on Thursday. To learn about the Snake River Kayak and Canoe School or the PADI dive facility, check out our Watersports chapter.

Teton Mountaineering
170 N. Cache, Jackson, Wyo.
• (307) 733-3595, (800) 850-3595

Although Teton Mountaineering carries gear, from hiking books to camp chairs, for the casual outdoors person and the weekend camper, the specialty here is mountaineering and backcountry travel. The store carries the town's best selection of climbing gear and outdoor books and videos, stocks all the topographic maps of Greater Yellowstone and plenty of touring, camping, hiking and climbing guides to the area.

The staff tends to be knowledgeable and ready to help plan your routes and campsites. Teton Mountaineering rents gear, too. In winter, it's ski gear; in summer, almost everything for your backpacking or mountaineering trip is available. Fees are reasonable: $3 per day for self-inflating sleeping pads and $5 per day for backpacks.

Westbank Anglers
3670 N. Moose-Wilson Rd., Teton Village. Wyo. • (307) 733-6483

This fly shop carries outdoor clothing, reels and waders for your fishing adventure. About the only fishing supplies this shop doesn't sell, in fact, are fly-tying materials, but if you're a fly-tier, you can order anything you might want from their catalogs.

In summer the shop is open seven days from around 7:30 AM. In winter it closes Sundays. To learn more about Westbank's guiding services, see our Fishing and Hunting chapter.

Surrounding Areas

Eastern Idaho

Idaho Falls, Idaho

Canyon Whitewater Supply
450 N. Yellowstone Hwy., Idaho Falls, Idaho • (208) 522-3932

Dave's little shop in the old gas station has been a touchstone for area floaters for as long as we can remember. Dave sells rafts, kayaks and accessories. His inventory is small, but if he doesn't have it, he's happy to order it in.

Dave also custom builds catarafts, stable whitewater craft that have become popular for their maneuverability and willingness to stay upright . The shop is a one-man operation, so hours can vary, especially in winter. Call before you stop by. You can also call Dave for river-flow information.

Idaho Mountain Trading
Corner of Shoup and B, Idaho Falls, Idaho • (208) 523-6679

In summer you can purchase backpacking, climbing and mountain-biking gear and accessories. In winter the emphasis is on skiing, ski-touring and snowboarding. The rental and repair shop has ski mechanics on duty in winter

and bike and in-line skate mechanics in summer. Idaho Mountain Trading rents toys ranging from telemark skis to backpacks and in-line skates to mountain bikes.

The store, which has been here since 1978, is closed Sundays.

Teton Valley, Idaho

Mountaineering Outfitters
62 N. Main, Driggs, Idaho • (208) 354-2222, (800) 359-2410

At 26 years old, this is the grandpa of area sporting-goods stores. Part army surplus, part discount shop and part retail store carrying brands such as Columbia and Patagonia, Mountaineering Outfitters crams its shelves to the ceiling with high-performance outdoor clothing and outerwear. You can also pick up backpacking food, some camping equipment and Driggs' best souvenir: a T-shirt that proclaims the little town the "Cultural Hub of the Universe."

Mountaineering Outfitters is open Monday through Saturday year round.

Peaked Sports
70 E. Little Ave., Driggs, Idaho • (208) 354-2354, (800) 705-2354

The valley's alpine ski and snowboard shop in winter is its Schwinn bike headquarters in summer. Scott Prindle, who runs the shop, skied pro for seven years and currently coaches the local ski team. He likes to share his expertise with competitive skiers. If you're not a competitive skier, you may feel like one by the time you walk out the door with your newly tuned mind and skis .

The shop rents ski equipment in winter and mountain bikes in summer. Bike rental includes a helmet, an extra tube, a seat pack, a pump,

---

INSIDERS' TIP

Want to buy a Western hat while you're here? Check out these hat facts: Cowboy hats are made from straw, wool felt or fur felt. Straw is cheapest, wool felt a bit more and fur felt the most expensive. Fur-felt hats are made from beaver or from some combination of beaver and, say, rabbit. Beaver felt is prized because it's said to be more waterproof and better able to hold its shape than wool felt or other fur mixes. Straw hats can be had for $20; a high-end custom beaver felt hat can cost you $200 or more.

a patch kit, bottle cages and advice about where to go.

Peaked is closed on Sundays in summer, but the shop is open seven days a week during the busy winter season.

R.U. Outside
455 S. Main, Driggs, Idaho
• (208) 354-3455, (800) 279-7123

The newest sporting goods store in Driggs was born between the pages of a catalog. The store, which grew out of a catalogue company that began in 1994, carries outerwear and gear for snowmobilers and other outdoor enthusiasts. Particularly successful has been the line of orthopedic devices that address snowmobilers' aches and pains: back supports, knee supports and thumb supports (thumbing that throttle lever gets uncomfortable after a while).

If you're a "what's new?" type of gear lover, stop in: The store is a test ground for items the company may want to include in its catalogue. R.U. Outside is open every day but Sunday. During the winter ski season, it may open seven days a week.

Yöstmark Mountain Equipment
12 E. Little Ave., Driggs, Idaho
• (208) 354-2828

Think of it as one-stop shopping for your backcountry adventure. Clair Yöst owns this shop, which in winter specializes in telemark, cross-country and snowboard equipment for the backcountry. In summer Yöstmark becomes an Orvis fly shop and a hiking/backpacking store.

Look for Clair's own wide-shoveled and blunt-nosed telemark ski designs, named the Classic Noodle and the Mountain Noodle. Both are popular around here. Clothing/gear brands available here include Gramicci, Mountain Hardware, Lowe Alpine, Quest, Solstice and Burton.

Yöstmark also rents snowshoes, snowboards and touring, telemark and skate skis in winter. In summer it rents inflatable kayaks, an inflatable drift boat, fishing rods and reels, life jackets, wetsuits and other water gear, and camping and backpacking equipment such as sleeping bags and stoves.

Southwestern Montana

Northern Lights Trading Co.
1716 W. Babcock St., Bozeman
• (406) 586-2225
Meadow Center, Big Sky
• (406) 995-2220

Now Montana's largest outdoor store specializing in paddle sports, backpacking, climbing and Nordic ski equipment, Northern Lights is one of those great American success stories. Owner Mike Garcia began selling rafting equipment out of his garage in the early 1980s because nobody else in town was selling it. Before he knew it, Garcia had moved into a small store and had expanded his inventory to include other sports.

Northern Lights sells and rents rafting, backpacking and ski equipment. You'll also find a good selection of casual outdoor wear and name brands that include Marmot, Mountain Hardwear, Royal Robbins and Exofficio. Northern Lights carries the only complete line of Patagonia clothing in Bozeman. The staff here are friendly, knowledgeable and very helpful.

Dan Bailey's Fly Shop
209 W. Park, Livingston, Mont.
• (406) 222-1673, (800) 356-4052

Nostalgia may be enough to pull you through the door of Dan Bailey's Fly Shop in Livingston. Looking much the same as it did when legendary fly-fisherman Dan Bailey owned the place, this fly shop in the heart of fly-fishing country carries a full line of fishing gear: flies, ties, rods, reels, shorts and shirts. The Wall of Fame, as legendary as Dan Bailey himself, consists of three walls with wooden plaques bearing the penned outlines of four-pound-plus trout caught in Yellowstone country since the 1940s.

The shop has a mail-order catalog jam-packed with absolutely everything for the fly-fishing fanatic. To get a catalog, write Dan Bailey's Fly Shop, P.O. Box 1019, Livingston, MT 59047, or call.

The Powder Horn
35 E. Main St., Bozeman, Mont.
• (406) 587-7373

Even if you don't want to buy one thing, The Powder Horn on Bozeman's Main Street is a store worth gawking at. One side looks like an old Yellowstone lodge, with pine and stone floors and a 30-foot-high rock fireplace set into a log wall. It's the new side. Except for the giant log archway that joins the two rooms, the original half looks pretty much as it did when Ivan Dieruf's dad opened the store more than a half-century ago. Today, two carved, fish-bearing grizzlies hold up the arch, the gateway between the new and the old.

Dieruf, a Bozeman boy who ended up as a designer in New York City, paid big bucks to have masons create special effects with their rock work. (You'll have to see it for yourself.) Besides soft lighting and a dreamy atmosphere, you'll find plenty of other surprises at The Powder Horn. By the way, Dieruf's father believed that "only rich men could afford to buy junk." For that reason, you'll only find top-of-the-line fishing, hunting, and backpacking gear at The Powder Horn.

Sylvan Peak
9 S. Broadway, Red Lodge, Mont.
• (406) 446-1770, (800) 425-0076

Besides manufacturing Polartec clothing in-house, Sylvan Peak also sells a wide range of generally outdoor clothing on the main floor. Downstairs you'll find the mountain shop, which during the summer months is a full backpacking store. Come winter, the mountain shop turns into a ski shop where you can buy or rent almost any kind of snow gear you might want.

Owner Mary Ellen Mangus started Sylvan Peak in 1980 after years of making and designing custom outdoor and sports clothing for family and friends. She decided to either quit sewing altogether or to move someplace she liked and start a business. That's how she and Sylvan Peak ended up in Red Lodge.

Northwestern Wyoming

Cody, Wyoming

Foote's Mountaineering
1280 Sheridan Ave., Cody, Wyo.
• (307) 527-9937

Foote's Mountaineering is the new kid on the block when it comes to a specialty outdoor store. Don Foote, who opened his store in 1997, moved in January from a 550-square-foot location into a new 2,100-square-foot building down the street. For a buck a climb, you can scale the 35-foot climbing wall outside Foote's. The wall is equipped with ropes and harnesses, and an employee is on hand to help. In addition to rock and ice climbing gear, Foote's carries all the equipment you'll need for heading into the backcountry, including tents, sleeping bags and backpacks.

Rocky Mountain Sports
1820 17th St., Cody, Wyo.
• (307) 527-6071

If it has to do with hunting, fishing or camping, and it's not too trendy, chances are Rocky Mountain Sports carries the item. This 9,000-square-foot store is loaded with clothes and toys to tantalize sportsmen, including nearly 500 firearms, 1,000 pairs of gloves, gun safes, spotting scopes, binoculars, ammunition and reloading equipment. Rocky Mountain Sports also carries a large selection of outdoor clothing that includes an array of wool garments by Woolrich and Johnson, as well as boots by LaCrosse and Field and Stream. You'll also find a virtual museum of more than 35 mounted wildlife heads.

Tim Wade's North Fork Anglers
1438 Sheridan Ave., Cody, Wyo.
• (307) 527-7274

This serious fly-fisher shop carries everything from hooks to books, including polarized sunglasses so you can spot those trout under the water. In fact, the people at North Fork Anglers are so bent on pleasing that they'll arrange to have your prescription glasses polarized. Besides carrying the largest fly-tying selection in the Bighorn Basin, North Fork Anglers sells more than 1,000 kinds of locally tied flies. North Fork Anglers is a pro shop selling an impressive list of name brands including Sage, Winston, Diamondback, Bucks Bags, Simms (for waders) and Glacier (for gloves). The store's biggest asset, though, is the enthusiastic and courteous staff who spend every free moment fishing.

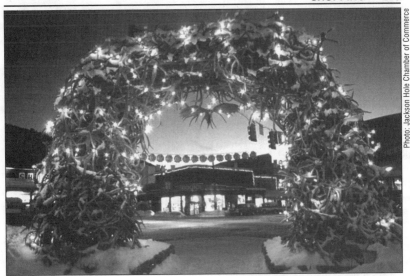

Arches made of elk antlers stand at the entrance of the square in Jackson Hole.

Sunlight Sports
1251 Sheridan Ave., Cody, Wyo.
• (307) 587-9517

This hometown sporting goods store, which features a huge handmade cabinet from a Fort Laramie hardware store, has been serving Cody residents for 27 years. Inside you'll find outdoor gear for backpacking, climbing, skiing, snowboarding, snowshoeing, and rock and ice climbing.

During the winter, Sunlight has a ski shop complete with rentals (Cody residents ski at Red Lodge). Sunlight is well-stocked with pepper spray. This repellant, packaged in bear-sized cans, is carried for self-defense in case of a bear attack. Sunlight sells about four cans per day during the summer. (For more information about pepper spray, see the Close-up on bear safety in the Fishing and Hunting chapter.)

Western Wear

Yellowstone National Park

Entrance Communities

Kellem's Montana Saddlery
U.S. Hwy. 89, Gardiner, Mont.
• (406) 848-7776

Oh, Mama. Take your honey into this shop and buy him some cowboy duds. While you're at it, ask him to buy you a pair of those smooth, red fringed leather gloves. This saddlery, owned for more than a dozen years by Les and Carol Kellem, has a relatively small selec-

INSIDERS' TIP

High-tech outdoor clothing maker Patagonia usually allows one or two vendors to sell their products in a town. Jackson has several, a nod to the importance of outdoor sports in the area and the huge market for high-performance outdoor clothing. Patagonia products are available at Skinny Skis, Teton Mountaineering and High Country Flies, all listed in this chapter.

Photo: Jackson Hole Chamber of Commerce

tion of Western wear. What you find, though, will be unique. In addition to clothes, belts, buckles and bridles you'll find a rack full of horseshoes.

Les makes saddles in the back room. Kellem's saddles are so popular that he doesn't have to advertise. They cost anywhere from $1,700 to $10,000 depending on the detail. His customers live as far away as Europe. Carol makes beautiful chaps (pronounced "shaps").

Jackson Hole

Baggit Men's and Ladies Western Boutique
35 W. Broadway, Jackson, Wyo.
• (307) 733-1234

What's with that name? Well, 20 years ago, Baggit was a bag store. If you wanted a bag, in canvas or leather, you came here. Baggit also carried a small selection of pretty women's clothing that other stores in the area didn't have. This corner of the store became so popular that it eventually took over. Now Baggit is the place to shop for a feminine, Victorian Western look as well as for non-Western men's and women's dressier clothes. You can buy a Western wedding dress here or a versatile Linda Lundstrom coat, wool with a detachable shell and detachable fur ruffs at collar and hood.

Locals shop here because the store carries a selection of midpriced clothing among its more upscale offerings. Many out-of-towners like the more low-key Western look of Baggit's clothing — much of Jackson's Western wear offerings are splendidly, unabashedly ornate.

Beaver Creek Hat and Leather Company
36 E. Broadway, Jackson, Wyo.
• (307) 733-1999, (800) 533-4522

Western felt hats in almost every imagin-

able shape line the walls. Floor space is filled with leather vests, wool, leather and canvas jackets, belts and belt buckles and, of course, hatbands. John Bickner Sr. makes his hats by hand on period equipment dating to 1904. He also makes the hatbands. In fact, the reason John makes and sells hats is because he was a hatband maker who kept getting asked to sell the hats he bought to display his hatbands on.

Hat prices range from $50 to $350, depending on the style and felt quality you choose. A favorite style among customers is the Old Timer hat, which John shapes and treats to make it look like it's been on a few cattle drives.

While you're shopping for your custom-shaped hat, make sure you wander toward the back of the store where two Bickner sons have set up shop. John Jr. runs Elkhorn Industries, which sells antler chandeliers, cutlery, cribbage boards and lamps. Elkhorn also carries mountain-man hats in silver fox, coyote, bobcat and beaver. Rick's enterprise is called Moo's Gourmet Ice Cream; the all-natural, all-organic ice cream is made by hand right here. The store also sells chocolate. Rick's ice cream is available in local restaurants and grocery stores.

Corral West Ranchwear
840 W. Broadway, Jackson, Wyo.
• (307) 733-0247
1527 W. Main, Bozeman, Mont.
• (406) 586-8671
1106 W. Park, Livingston, Mont.
• (406) 222-7473
1202 Sheridan Ave., Cody, Wyo.
• (307) 587-2122
1625 Stampede Ave., Cody, Wyo.
• (307) 587-4493

Working cowboys and Jackson locals shop here because the prices are moderate and the clothing ranges from Wranglers to fancy leather vests and Western dresses. Shop the large selection of Western jeans, shirts, boots, belts, jack-

INSIDERS' TIP

Were you about to hit the trail and found you forgot to pack the stove, or the tent, or your sleeping bag? Many area sporting-goods stores rent these items and more (see our "Sporting Goods" section in this chapter).

ets, vests and cowboy hats. Pick up a straw hat for as little as $10. Wool felt hats start around $30, fur felt around $80. There's even a kids' corner where you can outfit your little buckaroo.

While you're here, step back to the video corner and ask to see the hat video, which proves that anything can be fascinating, even the making of cowboy hats. These folks stay open until midnight Wednesdays and Saturdays during the summer so the post-rodeo crowd can shop.

Dixie's Custom Creations
72 W. Glenwood, Jackson, Wyo.
• **(307) 734-5111**

If you like fun, flamboyant Western wear but you don't like running into another woman in the same outfit you put on this morning, stop by. The artists who produce deerskin vests, moccasins, skirts and jackets for Dixie's don't sell anywhere else in Jackson Hole. The hand-cut, hand-laced jackets, some trimmed with horsehair, others with feathers, run from $750 to $2,200. Custom moccasins range between $600 and $1,800.

Jackson Hole Clothiers
45 E. Deloney, Jackson, Wyo.
• **(307) 733-7211**

Check out Western glamour wear from DD Ranchwear, Hairston Roberson, Clarissa Cassandra, Stubbs, Manuel and others. You'll find women's, men's and children's clothing, as well as jewelry, bedding and gloves, at this high-end boutique.

Some of the more popular gift items sold by Jackson Hole Clothiers are handmade beaded, painted leather belts by Charles G. Hunt. Hunt uses mostly antique seed beads in his creations; paints are produced by hand crushing mineral deposits found in Wyoming. His belts generally run from $114 to $1,140.

Jackson Hole Hat Company
255 N. Glenwood, Jackson, Wyo.
• **(307) 733-7687**

Marilyn and Paul Hartman are that rare breed: self-taught craftspeople. They build, service and restore fur felt hats (cheaper felt hats are made from wool). They can also sell you the braided-horsehair hatbands and Western shirts and vests to go with your new hat. The price for a custom hat is surprisingly reasonable, starting around $99.

Surrounding Areas

Eastern Idaho

Idaho Falls, Idaho

Bish's Western Wear
3855 N. 5th E., Idaho Falls, Idaho
• **(208) 522-5030**

Bish's sells Justin, Tony Lama, Nocona and other brands, and everything from jeans to boots to buckles. They're the only folks in town who carry Whites, which may be the best laceup work boot you can buy. Handmade and custom fit, a pair of Whites will run you around $325.

An Idaho Falls institution since 1966, Bish's helps sponsor the town's two largest rodeos, the Centennial and the War Bonnet. The store is closed Sundays.

Hunters' Creek Saddlery
629 W. Sunnyside, Idaho Falls, Idaho
• **(208) 529-4349, (800) 560-4349**

This little shop is the only English riding apparel and tack store between Jackson and Salt Lake City. They also sell Western saddles and tack, but little in the way of Western apparel. You can check out the used equipment, which owner Kathryn Curl takes on consignment.

Also expect to find veterinary supplies, including the Professional's Choice line of sports-medicine boots for both horses and humans, Ariat Western and English riding boots, Breyer model horses and other horse-related gift items. Riding videos and horse books are also available. Hunters' Creek is open every day but Sunday.

Southwestern Montana

Corral West Ranchwear
1527 Main, Bozeman, Mont.
• **(406) 586-8671**
1106 W. Park, Livingston, Mont.
• **(406) 222-7473**

If there's a Corral West that can meet your every Western clothing need, the Bozeman store is most likely the one. One of the big-

Hamilton Stores:
Park Concessionaire Extraordinaire

Many a concessionaire has come and gone in Yellowstone Park since its inception in the late 1800s. Only Hamilton Stores, though, has survived ever-changing political whims and the difficult economic times brought on by World Wars I and II and the Great Depression.

Founded in 1915 when Charles Ashworth Hamilton bought the Klamer Store at Old Faithful, Hamilton Stores Inc. is the oldest concessionaire in Yellowstone Park and one of the the largest privately owned concession in the country. At every major Yellowstone

Park attraction — and sometimes in between — you'll see these stores staffed by cheerful workers (almost all retirees) wearing blue-and-white checked shirts. Hamilton, a young man from St. Paul, Minnesota, who came to Yellowstone Park as a seasonal employee for another concessionaire, the Yellowstone Park Association, bought his first store in 1915 — months before the automobile was allowed in the Park. That same year, Park visitation jumped from 20,000 to 50,000.

Legend has it that when Hamilton heard the Klamer store was for sale, he traveled day and night from Minnesota without stopping until he reached Old Faithful. He paid $5,000 down on the $20,000 asking price, then rode like heck to Mammoth where his former employer and good friend Harry Child lived. Hamilton was hoping that Child, the chief hotel concessionaire in the Park, would loan him $5,000 to cover the rubber check he had just written — he only had $300 in his account. He was right. Once he got the money from Child, Hamilton rode nonstop to Livingston, Montana, so he could beat his bad check to the bank. The rest is history.

Until 1959, Hamilton's offices, headquarters, warehouse and living quarters were on the second floor of the Old Faithful store. The wall of his office was papered with canceled checks totalling more than $1.8 million. The first to be glued on the wall was

— continued on next page

This Hamilton Store in the Old Faithful area is a popular stop for visitors.

Photo: Robert Bower

his own check to Mrs. Klamer, framed by horse-race tickets — symbols of the gamble that had paid off. A gambler, a prankster and a tireless worker who refused to heat either employee dormitories or company delivery trucks, Hamilton spared none of the amenities for entertaining VIPs in his office. Though small, it was furnished with a comfortable armchair, an array of bearskin rugs and a full bar.

After cars were admitted to the Park, Hamilton got permits to build stores at West Thumb, Lake and the Fishing Bridge. As the number of Park visitors grew, so did Hamilton Stores. In 1927, Hamilton Stores began featuring soda fountains — an instant hit among tourists. After World War II, when tourism doubled then tripled, Hamilton's business followed suit. He built gas stations at each one. Always he kept in mind the needs and the pocketbooks of the average American, stocking his stores with necessities and souvenirs. For years, until the Park outlawed their sale, bearskin rugs (imported from Russia) were among Hamilton's top-selling souvenirs.

Hamilton's best workers (and his four children) were rewarded for their efforts and their ingenuity by climbing the Hamilton Stores ladder of command. Until recent retirements, many of the top executives at Hamilton Stores were those who began as soda jerks and winterkeepers. (Winterkeepers lived in the Park and patrolled buildings through the winter, removing snow from their roofs so they didn't collapse under the weight.) Today, Charles Hamilton's daughter, Ellie Povah, and her husband, Trevor Stewart-Povah, still personally pass out bonuses to store employees who lead in sales. They took over the Old Faithful Swimming Pool in 1948, living in a small room of the facility. The two took Hamilton Stores through some tough times. And in 1959, they built new headquarters outside the Park in West Yellowstone, Montana. Halfway through construction, the 1959 earthquake demolished it. So they rebuilt it. This disaster was only one in a long series that befell the Hamilton Stores business endeavors for a while. When the owners tried to expand their Hamilton Stores to a year-round business with concessions in Death Valley, California, an arsonist burned their building there. Later, another fire razed their newly purchased Smith and Chandler Store in West Yellowstone. The Smith and Chandler store and other businesses outside the Park are held and managed by a separate company called Ventures West.

Today, Hamilton Stores operates 14 outlets within the Park and employs about 875 workers each summer. As in the old days, the company must winterize each building, emptying the pipes, removing perishable and valuable stock from the shelves and battening the shutters. Winterkeepers must still tend the buildings (and others) in the Park, being sure to remove snow from the roofs before it gets too heavy. Many of today's Hamilton executives, who began their careers with the company as clerks or winterkeepers, remember those old days fondly.

---

gest and oldest Corral West stores in the country, it serves a wide variety of customers from ranchers in the outlying areas to Montana State University students. The Livingston location, a smaller version of Bozeman's, has fewer choices when it comes to fashion, but it has a collection of wildlife mounts worth seeing. This incredibly successful chain is headquartered in Cheyenne, Wyoming, and has stores all over the country. For more information about Corral West, read the entry under Jackson, Wyoming.

Northwestern Wyoming

Cody, Wyoming

Cody Rodeo Company
1291 Sheridan Ave., Cody, Wyo.
• **(307) 587-5913**

We've listed the Cody Rodeo Company under shopping, but this store is so unique it ought to be included in the Attractions chapter. For starters, you'll want to have your photo taken on Buford, the bucking Brahma bull. (He's stuffed.) Make that your family photo, because Buford is big and strong enough for the whole family to ride at the same time. Second, you'll want to wander around and take in all the cowboy humor — like the VW bug clown car (it came from the wrecking yard) with mannequins sprawled around inside and legs sticking out from underneath. Then there's the cowboy taking a bath in the livestock watering trough. Windmill power circulates the water in the "tub." (There's more, but we'll let you discover it for yourselves.)

The Cody Rodeo Company sells cowboy clothes, furniture, housewares, and accessories. The most popular place in this store, though, is Stetson country, where the cowboy hats live.

Owners Susan and Ev Diehl also have a shop at the Cody Nite Rodeo. (Refer to our Spectator Sports chapter for more information.)

Corral West Ranchwear
1202 Sheridan Ave., Cody, Wyo.
• (307) 587-2122
1625 Stampede Ave., Cody, Wyo.
• (307) 587-4493

Corral West, a chain of stores nearly synonymous with Western wear, finds its roots in Cody where a Red Lodge, Montana, businessman opened the Cody Corral in 1953. That's why you'll find two Corral West Ranchwear stores in Cody. What the smaller downtown store doesn't have, the bigger store on the hill does. Clothes and accessories here are reasonably priced, and the stores are thoroughly stocked with everything the well-dressed cowboy or cowgirl might need.

The bigger store on Stampede Avenue has a great collection of mounted animals including a Kodiak and an Alaskan grizzly bear, wolverines, caribou, moose and even a walrus. Corral West is a family-owned business headquartered in Cheyenne, Wyoming. In 1997, Corral West had 55 stores in 13 Western states. Be sure to check other geographic locations in this chapter for Corral West Ranchwear stores.

Bookstores
Yellowstone National Park

Inside the Park

Yellowstone Association
36 Mammoth, Yellowstone National Park
• (307) 344-2293

The Yellowstone Association sells a hefty selection of Park-related books through all Park visitor centers. You'll find books on birds, animals, hiking, fishing, geology, geysers and lots of other topics. Proceeds from book sales go toward the Yellowstone Association, a nonprofit group that helps Yellowstone National Park with funding, research and interpretive projects.

Entrance Communities

The Book Peddler
106 Canyon St., West Yellowstone, Mont.
• (406) 646-9358

Walk into this homey, hopping place and you'll get the message: read. Besides having a great selection of books, the owners and staff here are very friendly, helpful and laid back. Your nose will tell you there's a coffee bar somewhere in the house. Stroll straight to the back and you'll find the source of the aroma. Order a cup of java, pull your new

INSIDERS' TIP

You can purchase great souvenirs at some Jackson restaurants. For instance, Jedediah's House of Sourdough sells recipe books, its own homemade jams and dry sourdough starter. The Bunnery sells a book of recipes, OSM (oatmeal, sunflower and millet) mixes for breads and pancakes and other souvenir items.

book out of its bag, plop down at one of the tables and read on.

Grand Teton National Park

The Grand Teton Natural History Association
Grand Teton National Park, Moose, Wyo.
• **(307) 739-3403**

This nonprofit organization supports the National Park Service's educational, interpretive and research efforts. Funding comes from book sales at visitors centers in Grand Teton Park and ranger stations in Targhee National Forest, including the multi-agency Eastern Idaho Visitor Information Center in Idaho Falls, Idaho.

The Association stocks approximately 900 book titles, maps, posters and other interpretive literature to help you make the most of your visit. Browse the shelves at Moose, Colter Bay, Flagg Ranch or Jenny Lake or call to order materials or request a catalogue of selected titles.

Jackson Hole

Teton Bookshop
25 S. Glenwood St., Jackson, Wyo.
• **(307) 733-9220**

You could shop here for the books, of course, particularly the selection of Western and local titles. Or you could check out the posters and maps. You could be a collector here to peruse the tall bookshelf of old and rare books. But Jackson locals stop in to talk to owner Gene Downer as much as they do to shop.

Teton Bookshop was established in 1972. Hours vary depending on time of year, so if it's not summer, call before you stop by.

Valley Bookstore
125 N. Cache, Jackson, Wyo.
• **(307) 733-4533, (800) 647-4111**

Jackson holds about 6,000 people; its biggest bookstore boasts 40,000 titles. Valley Bookstore is known for its extensive collection of regional titles, especially in Western history. Also noteworthy is the "staff picks" shelf, where the avid readers who work here place recent discoveries, and "shelf talkers," cards containing book synopses and recommendations from staff members. Shelf talkers let you browse through the store feeling a little like a well-read clerk is hovering at your shoulder whispering suggestions.

Surrounding Areas

Eastern Idaho

Idaho Falls, Idaho

Barnes & Noble Booksellers
2385 E. 17th St., Idaho Falls, Idaho
• **(208) 522-1010**

These folks are the nation's largest bookseller, with 454 stores (not counting their smaller B. Dalton shops). The Idaho Falls location carries around 100,000 titles and, like other Barnes and Nobles, encourages its patrons to indulge in a library-esque browsing spree with the comfy chairs and tables scattered around the store. It also has a coffee shop that serves Starbucks coffee and treats from a local bakery. By the way, you are equally welcome to take books you haven't yet bought into the coffee shop or wander the stacks, latte in hand.

This is a store that prides itself on carrying not only front-list titles, but also those by more obscure authors, as well as lesser-known works by popular authors. Barnes and Noble also sponsors regular events with a literary tilt, such as their weekly Story Times, book signings and occasional concerts. Pick up the monthly calendar while you're here if you want to learn more (or check out our Kidstuff chapter to find out about Story Time).

B. Dalton Bookseller
2300 E. 17th St., Grand Teton Mall, Idaho Falls, Idaho • (208) 528-6401

These folks devote one whole bay — six shelves — to their regional book collection. B. Dalton also prides itself on its complete stock of best sellers and on the ordering system that helps the store keep major titles, even very popular ones, always in stock. The small staff of about six employees has good product knowledge because each works a lot of hours; they're here enough to see what sells and what ships in.

Deseret Book Company
2300 E. 17th St., Grand Teton Mall, Idaho Falls, Idaho • (208) 523-5061

Owned by the Church of Jesus Christ of Latter-day Saints, this bookstore is part of a 35-store chain scattered throughout the Midwest and West. The chain's original shop opened in Salt Lake City in 1866. Although Deseret is a full-line bookstore, carrying national best sellers and a range of both fiction and nonfiction, it is very family-oriented, and its titles reflect that. Make sure you check out the extensive children's section.

Other services offered by Deseret Book include mounting and framing of standard-size art. These folks can also emboss with gold lettering the books you purchase.

Teton Valley, Idaho

Dark Horse Books
55 N. Main, Driggs, Idaho • (208) 354-8882

Peter Andrews' 3-year-old bookstore is small — only 3,500 volumes in stock. Still, it offers a surprisingly eclectic selection of books and magazines, a comfortable sitting area where you can examine your potential buys and a small coffee bar so you can sip while you browse. Pick up CDs and tapes by local musicians here, too.

Andrews says he's happy to order books his customers want to look at. The shop is open Monday through Saturday, year round. Hours can be short in fall.

Southwestern Montana

Country Bookshelf
28 W. Main, Bozeman, Mont. • (406) 587-0166, (800) 621-7977

When this bookstore opened its doors in 1957, it was a tiny shop around the corner from its current location. Today, the Country Bookshelf has 75,000 titles housed in a 7,000-square-

foot, two-story building. Owner Mary Jane DiSanti stocks a wide variety of books including a large Montana and Western history section, a travel section and a large children's section. She also has frequent book signings and readings. Be sure to look for the special shelf of autographed books by Montana authors.

Hastings Books, Music and Video
1601 W. Main, Bozeman, Mont. • (406) 587-8024

This big bookstore has 90,000 book titles, 31,000 CD titles, 1,900 magazine titles and 3,000 video titles (for rent and for sale). In addition, the store stocks 1,850 different software titles for home and office. You can browse through numerous subject areas, including a New Age boutique and an extensive children's section.

Museum of the Rockies Museum Store
600 W. Kagy, Bozeman, Mont. • (406) 994-2252

Stacked among the children's games, the Native American crafts, T-shirts and general gifts at the Museum of the Rockies Museum Store is a healthy supply of books — about 5,000 titles worth. This store has an array of books on geology, history, natural science and travel. (For more information about the Museum of the Rockies, see our Attractions chapter.)

Phillips Bookstore Inc.
111 E. Main St., Bozeman, Mont. • (406) 587-3195

This Main Street bookstore celebrated its 100th anniversary in 1997. Established in 1897 and still in its original building, Phillips was once the biggest bookstore between St. Paul, Minnesota, and Seattle, Washington. Today, the store stocks 4,000 volumes, including a nice selection on Montana and the West in general. You'll also find art supplies, gifts, greeting cards, maps and computer software.

Poor Richard's News
33 W. Main, Bozeman, Mont. • (406) 587-9041

In business on Bozeman's Main Street since 1957, Poor Richard's has a selection of more than 700 magazine titles, two dozen tobacco blends and a fine selection of imported cigarettes. More than that, though, Poor Richard's has a cigar selection that's tough to beat. You'll find more than 200 brands of cigars. The shop also carries a selection of pipes ranging from a $3 corncob pipe to a $375 English-made Dunhill. Poor Richard's closes Christmas and New Year's.

Vargo's Books
One E. Main, Bozeman, Mont.
• (406) 587-5383

You'll want to drop into this place just to banter with the lively owner, book nut Francis Vargo. Besides carrying 30,000 titles, Vargo has a collection of first-edition, out-of-print, old and rare books for sale. He'll also hunt up hard-to-find books for you.

Vargo's also has a nice selection of jazz CDs. Chances are when you enter his domain, Vargo will be playing one of the lighter selections of his jazz collection.

Sax and Fryer
109 W. Callender, Bozeman, Mont.
• (406) 222-1421

Established in 1883, one year after the Northern Pacific Railroad laid its tracks and rolled into town, Sax and Fryer became an all-purpose store that sold books, musical instruments, stationery, sleds and bikes. It also had a soda fountain. Today, Sax and Fryer, owned by John Fryer, has a complete esoteric collection of books about Montana and Western history. If you can't find it at the library, chances are Fryer has it.

Northwestern Wyoming

Cody, Wyoming

Cody Newsstand
1121 13th, Cody, Wyo. • (307) 587-2843

The Cody Newstand offers 20,000 book titles, 4,000 magazine titles and a fine collection of cigars. In Cody since 1988, this bookstore carries a wide range of books for all ages.

Museum Selections, Buffalo Bill Historical Center
720 Sheridan Ave., Cody, Wyo.
• (307) 587-3243, (800) 533-3838

Located in the Buffalo Bill Historical Center, this store has a small selection of books aimed at art and Western history. You'll also find an array of gifts, posters and reproductions. The store has a coffee bar. Authors frequently make appearances here.

Functional Art

Yellowstone National Park

Entrance Communities

Homeroom
121 Madison Ave., West Yellowstone, Mont. • (406) 646-4338

A woman shouted to her husband as he headed into Arrick's Fly Shop in West Yellowstone, "I'll be in that store with the bathtub full of white balls." That would be Homeroom, a unique store filled with mostly art and functional furniture. Take the hand-painted antique trunk converted to a coffee table, or a lamp made of antlers. Besides a fascinating collection of hand-painted shelves, cupboards, chests and mirrors, you're apt to see a selection of William Herrick's "waterflow wood carvings." Herrick creates glass-topped tables that feature his beautiful wood carvings of stream life beneath the surface.

Off the Wall Creations
226 W. Park St., Gardiner, Mont.
• (406) 848-7775

For more than 20 years, folks in Yellowstone country have been returning to Off the Wall Creations for yet another piece of unique custom-made jewelry. Michael Furtney and Chris McIntosh handcraft everything in the store — from the customized elk-ivory rings to the silver bracelets set with Montana sapphires to finely spun silver earrings. You'll also find unusual versions of antler art and furniture.

Off the Wall is open from May through October. During the winter months, McIntosh and Furtney open the store by appointment. They also take orders by phone.

Silver Heels Jewelry
115 Yellowstone Ave., West Yellowstone, Mont. • (406) 646-7796, (805) 256-4010

If you have a set of elk ivories you want made into earrings for your sweetheart, the folks at Silver Heels can do it. They have a knack for working jewelry magic. Owners Ron and Beverly Huth make and repair jewelry on the spot. By the end of the summer, they're so swamped with orders they have to shut down and make jewelry (which they'll later ship to you).

The bulletin board at this custom-jewelry store is cluttered with thank-you notes from pleased customers around the world. A wall-to-wall case displays the owners' jewelry as well as the fine collection of gems they use in crafting bracelets, necklaces, earrings — you name it.

Jackson Hole

Jackson, Wyoming

Barlow's
164 E. Deloney, Jackson, Wyo.
• (307) 733-1649

We can almost guarantee you won't find anything you've seen before on the shelves at Barlow's. Innovative jewelry, pottery, art glass, candleholders, fountains and dinnerware make up most of the inventory. The shop also has educational and interactive toys, including some 1940s reproduction wind-up toys. The shop, which opened in 1993, closes on Sundays.

Beads Unlimited
87 W. Deloney, Jackson, Wyo.
• (307) 733-0761

Folk art, mostly by Wyoming artists, adorns the walls along with samples of the main business here: custom-made bead jewelry. Beads — porcelain, stone, amber, wood, bone, copper and sterling silver — fill the display cases.

You can buy the beads, but what Beads Unlimited is really about is creating from the masses of beads in inventory the exact necklace, bracelet or earrings you envision. For a custom necklace, you can spend from $20 to $2,000. You choose the price by choosing the

materials, and these folks create your masterpiece.

Ingrid Weber's shop is open seven days a week in summer, Monday through Saturday in winter and shorter hours in spring and fall.

Crazy Horse Authentic Indian Jewelry
133 N. Cache, Jackson, Wyo.
• (307) 733-4028

This small shop sparkles with polished sterling silver — jewelry, hair clips, bolos and belt buckles — from Southwestern Native American artists. Also available here is one of our favorite inexpensive gift choices, sterling-silver button covers to dress up your shirts. You can also find local beadwork in Crazy Horse's display cases.

Dan Shelley Jewelers
Gaslight Alley, Jackson, Wyo.
• (307) 733-2259

There's plenty to ooh and ahh over even if you're not buying: one-of-a-kind gemstones cut by award-winning gem cutters, museum-quality fossil specimens including massive stone panels practically swarming with the tiny fossilized fishes called kneightia, and original jewelry designs in 14- or 18-karat gold. Dan Harrison and Shelley Elser, both jewelers, own the store.

Elkhorn Designs
165 N. Center, Jackson, Wyo.
• (307) 733-4655

This is a great place to pick up well-crafted antler art of various kinds. You can get antler candleholders, chandeliers, tables and chairs. The largest chandelier Elkhorn makes weighs about 180 pounds and costs $10,000. The store also carries a selection of Western furniture, silver jewelry set with turquoise, lapis, hematite and other semi-precious stones. Walls are hung with moose, bison and elk mounts, as well as deer, bear and bison hides.

High Country Accents
265 W. Pearl, Jackson, Wyo.
• (307) 734-1301, (800) 736-1301

From the sublime to the silly, from the reasonable to the wildly expensive, this store has it all. High Country Accents is a Western-style home-furnishings shop in which lovely Bird's-eye maple chairs, elegantly simple of design, sit beside vases made from old cowboy boots. You can buy an $8,500 twisted-juniper leather club chair on which a stuffed cougar perches alertly, or perhaps a wolf-hide wall hanging. The selection also includes $10 accessories such as leather light-switch covers, drawer pulls, lamp finials and cabinet handles to add that little Western touch to a home that isn't quite ready for a stuffed cougar. High Country Accents closes Sundays.

Jackson Moore LTD.
130 E. Broadway, Jackson, Wyo.
• (307) 734-2425, (800) 667-4616

Who knows what you'll find to admire when you stop in, but we were floored by a bed. It was outfitted with a supple buckskin bedspread with a matching buckskin bedskirt and pillowcases, all rough-edged and hand laced. Three floors of such surprises await you in this upscale Western-furniture store. Nothing here is cheap, but we can almost guarantee you'll never again have this much fun looking at furniture.

Paint, Glaze and Fire Ceramics Painting Studio
No credit cards • 225 N. Cache, Jackson, Wyo. • (307) 733-6723

You're gonna love this. Paint, Glaze and Fire is a paint-your-own pottery studio that stocks a wide selection of unpainted pottery and all the supplies you need to indulge your artistic flair. Or, if you have artistic ideas but feel a bit short on flair, you can hire the staff to execute your original designs for you. Either way, displayed finished pieces and books of stencils and designs help you find inspiration.

Ceramic-ware prices range from $2 to $30; studio time runs about $6 per hour. It takes about seven days for your painted, fired pieces to be ready for pickup. If that's more time than you have, don't worry: they ship. Children are welcome. Paint, Glaze and Fire is closed Sundays in spring and fall.

Sweaters etc. International
95 W. Deloney St., Jackson, Wyo.
• (307) 733-6444

Jackson's crisp summer evenings and icy winters make this little store a perfect shopping stop. Sweaters etc. carries men's and women's fine wool and cotton sweaters from around the world. Shop for cozy wool warmth from Canada, Norway, Nepal, China, Bolivia, Peru and Scotland. Cotton sweaters are mostly American-made. Prices range from around $50 for a light cotton sweater to $200 for a bulky machine-knit Norwegian wool. Accessories include wool hats, vests, throws and scarves.

This shop closes Sundays in winter except during the Christmas season.

Warbonnet Indian Art and Jewelry
60 E. Broadway, Jackson, Wyo.
• (307) 733-6158, (800) 950-0154

This shop carries an impressive range of Native American folk art, jewelry, pottery and weaving. Artists come mostly from the Navajo, Zuni, Hopi and Santa Domingo tribes of the Southwest. Prices range from pocket change to serious investment. One nice feature of this shop is that it sizes jewelry to fit, at no charge, while you wait.

Surrounding Areas

Eastern Idaho

Idaho Falls, Idaho

Wild Country Creations
609 E. First St., Idaho Falls, Idaho
• (208) 529-0207

This is our favorite place to shop for Western-themed gifts. Wild Country Creations stocks Native American jewelry, including beadwork and sterling silver. Some polished, shaped mineral art is available; so are antler art, custom knives, dream catchers and more.

Teton Valley, Idaho

The Quilt House
No credit cards • 200 N. Main, Victor, Idaho • (208) 787-2220

The little robin's-egg-blue building houses the work of 12 area quilters, as well as 82-year-old native Bertha Gillette's biography, "Homesteading with the Elk." Both are worth the stop. Bertha has been selling quilts and quilting supplies since 1945. These days, you can buy a machine-sewn quilt from her for $450 to $600. Hand-sewn quilts cost more: $600 to $1,600.

Bertha closes up sometimes in winter when the snowplows push big hills of snow in front of her shop's door. Other seasons, she's generally open six days a week. The Quilt House is always closed on Sundays.

Southwestern Montana

Quest Gallery and Gifts
122 E. Main, Bozeman, Mont.
• (406) 586-0611

This combination art gallery and gift shop is worth checking into if you're looking for something unique to take home. Owner Gayle Green carries work by local artisans that includes leatherwork, limited-edition blankets, jewelry, wood carvings, artistic woodworking and pottery. The gallery, tucked into a nook on Bozeman's Main Street, is a refreshing change from other more cluttered shops in the area.

Northwestern Wyoming

Cody, Wyoming

Timbercreek Interiors Furniture and Design
1371 Sheridan Ave., Cody, Wyo.
• (307) 587-4246

Maybe it's the cushy denim sofas or the antler chandeliers. Or is it the selection of Mexican candles and Western-style dining tables? Aha, it must be the fountain and the fireplace. Whatever it is, walking into Timbercreek is like coming home. Arranged like a house with all its rooms, Timbercreek carries a wide selection of generally Western, casually sophisticated furniture and household accessories.

Even if you aren't in the market for new furniture, a tour through Timbercreek is like stepping into a stronghold of gracious Western hospitality.

Antiques

Jackson Hole

Beyond Necessity
335 S. Millward, Jackson, Wyo.
• (307) 733-7492

Look here for a broad range of contemporary American folk art, antique furniture and collectibles. These folks also offer restoration services. We were told that local antique dealers frequently get their restoration work done here.

Fighting Bear Antiques
35 E. Simpson, Jackson, Wyo.
• (307) 733-2669

If your brand of sweet tooth considers antique Western furniture tasty, this is your candy store. Terry and Sandy Winchell have been in business in Jackson since 1981; they handle no reproductions. Their specialty is the work of a whimsical Western furniture maker — sort of the Andy Warhol of Western design — named Thomas Molesworth. Trained at the Chicago Art Institute, Molesworth worked mostly in leather and fir. Dwight D. Eisenhower and John D. Rockefeller owned Molesworth pieces. These days his work brings anywhere from $800 for a simple brass-tacked leather armchair to $15,000 for a club chair of burled fir and leather with matching Native American woven upholstery patterns.

Shop here Monday through Saturday and Sundays by appointment. Fighting Bear usually closes for a bit in early spring and late fall.

Grandma's House
180 N. Center, Jackson, Wyo.
• (307) 734-5414

Cathy Edmiston's treasure-cluttered shop is a co-op of eight dealers and dozens of consigners. Merchandise is crammed into six small rooms and ranges from old saddles and tools to vintage clothing, books and old art supplies. Expect to find a bit of everything here.

Grandma's House is open seven days a week in summer, and Tuesday through Saturday in fall, winter and spring.

Western Collectibles
U.S. 89 near Hoback Junction, Wyo.
- **(307) 733-4285,**
  in winter (760) 326-2350

If you're looking for the area's down-home antiques and collectibles shop, head south out of Jackson about 10 minutes. You can buy, sell or trade here, for Western antiques such as saddles, boots and specialty bridles, old badges, belt buckles and Western children's toys.

Bill and Joan Lineberry's shop is open May to September.

Surrounding Areas

Eastern Idaho

Idaho Falls, Idaho

Antique Gallery
341 W. Broadway, Idaho Falls, Idaho
- **(208) 523-3906**

The area's largest antique mall sprawls over nearly 8,000 square feet of floor space, but still feels cluttered with treasure. More than 20 dealers display antiques and collectibles ranging from vintage clothing and antique tools to costume jewelry and furniture.

Country Store Boutique
4523 Ririe Hwy., Idaho Falls, Idaho
- **(208) 522-8450**

This old building north of Idaho Falls houses a wide selection of antique and refurbished furniture. Restoration services are available on site. One whole room is devoted to oak dining sets; another contains mostly dressers, bookshelves and chests. The front room is crowded with smaller antiques, oddities and collectibles.

Rexburg, Idaho

Main Street Antique Mall
52 E. Main, Rexburg, Idaho
- **(208) 356-5002**

A wide range of merchandise and good display makes this two-story antique shop a pleasant stop. Among the items here are furniture, pottery and military collectibles. You can also sell or consign your treasures to Randy and Rosan VanWagenen, the managers. Most merchandise is displayed in well-lit cases; everything is price-tagged.

The shop is open Tuesday through Saturday.

Teton Valley

Sioux Antiques
8 N. Main, Victor, Idaho • (208) 787-2644

Western and Yellowstone memorabilia dominate this antique shop. You can find rusted railroad nails, vintage hats and gloves, old rawhide-laced snowshoes and old basket-woven fishing creels. The only non-antiques the store carries are Frankoma pottery and a stoneware line that features earth-tone silhouettes of bison, moose and bear.

In summer Sioux Antiques is open Tuesday through Saturday. In winter, it's open Thursday through Saturday or by appointment.

Southwestern Montana

The Cowboy Connection
108 Second St., Livingston, Mont.
- **(406) 222-0272**

Long before they knew each other, Vangie and Jerry Lee fell in love with Montana. Then they fell in love with each other. They married and collected cowboy memorabilia. Now, they've turned their passion for the West into a booming business. The couple moved to Livingston from northern California to open The Cowboy Connection in 1994.

Among the cowboy collectibles and antiques in their shop in 1997 you would have found Jesse James' Smith and Wesson, sold in 1903 by his mother (she got $60 for it). The original bill of sale comes with the purchase of the gun. Or you might have seen an 1840s California mission saddle or a heavy silver parade saddle. The Lees also carry such items as an old wheel of fortune, bits, spurs, chaps and black-powder antique firearms.

My Home's In Montana
26 E. Main, Belgrade, Mont.
• (406) 388-9751

"My Home's in Montana, I wear a bandanna,

My spurs are of silver, My pony is gray.

When riding the ranges, My luck never changes.

Foot in the stirrup, I gallop away."

Three Montana girls grew up singing that song in grade school. Now they own a 10,000-square-foot antique store called, "My Home's in Montana." Inside, you'll find things you'd never expect, like an old smokehouse cabin and an outhouse, for starters. This antique store is so huge and so full of surprising antiques that we recommend bringing a picnic lunch so you can stay all day. (Owners Sandy, Mary Lou and Debi keep the coffeepot going.)

Miscellaneous

Yellowstone National Park

Entrance Communities

Cooke City Store
U.S. Hwy. 212, Cooke City, Mont.
• (406) 838-2234

You'll find a little bit of everything at the Cooke City Store. And you might need a little bit of everything by the time you reach this relatively out-of-the-way town. Among other things at this store are a small selection of better-than-average cheese, a few fresh fruits and vegetables, other kinds of food, tarps, camping supplies, fishing licenses, books and just about everything else you might need in an emergency. The building is on the National Register of Historic Places. The owner is friendly and full of information about where to go and what to do.

Jackson Hole

Crystal Falcon Rock Shop
50 W. Broadway, Jackson, Wyo.
• (307) 733-9158

Two cases of collectors' specimens brighten one wall — minerals such as rich, blue crystalline cavansite, root beer-colored wulfenite and a rare crystal form of the blushing pink mineral rhodochrosite. The rest of the store is full of polished, carved or cut pieces of such materials as geode, petrified wood and rainbow obsidian. You can even find a little jewelry. Look for the shop's selection of regional fossils. Under the display cases are cabinets holding more surprises.

Manager Scott Allison has been collecting minerals for more than 15 years, but he runs his shop so we noncollectors will feel at home (and find things to buy). Crystal Falcon is closed on Mondays and Tuesdays in winter.

The Hole Works
80 W. Broadway, Jackson, Wyo.
• (307) 733-7000

If you're shopping for something you've never seen before, you may find it at The Hole Works on the second floor of the Broadway Shops building. Anne Beaver's shop bucks Jackson's Western trend to bring you African art and artifacts, from trade beads in glass and amber to boldly painted, slit-eyed masks, spears and shields. The amber selection is particularly varied; some pieces look like solidified honey, others like opaque wood. Amber trade beads run from $24 to $700 a strand.

Jolly Jumbuck Leathers
Gaslight Alley, Jackson, Wyo.
• (307) 733-6562

Jumbuck is an Australian term for a young sheep. At Jolly Jumbuck, most of the high-end, custom-made outerwear you see has something to do with sheep. The shop carries

---

INSIDERS' TIP

See those "Open Range" signs on the side of the highway? Open range means that cattle are not fenced away from the road. If you hit one, you are responsible for the cost of the cow.

Photo: Cody Rodeo Company

No, he's not alive, but it darn sure looks that way.

handcrafted wool coats, lamb suede and sheepskin items. Other materials include deerskin and hand-knitted beaver. Looking for a gift that's a bit . . . odd? How about a designer dog collar studded with silver-plated conchos?

These folks are closed most of April.

The Main Ingredient
140 E. Broadway, Jackson, Wyo.
• **(307) 734-1210**

If you can't find The Main Ingredient, try Jackson Hole Mercantile, which may be the name of this fun kitchen and condiment store by the summer of 1998. Manager Stiofain Goff is planning a new concept as well as a new name. The store currently carries a range of hard-to-find treats including canned chanterelles and vichyssoise, Peking-duck sauce and burgundy snails. More conventional are the regional treats such as deersteak seasoning, jams, chocolate sauce, various huckleberry products and the increasingly popular arabica coffee beans sold by the Cowboy Coffee Company.

Goff plans to stock the new and improved store with an array of Americana, including antique phones (that work) and reproduction Tiffany lamps. But don't worry about the redo:

The great regional and international treats aren't going anywhere.

Wyoming Buffalo Company
135 N. Cache, Jackson, Wyo.
• **(307) 733-0636, (800) 453-0636**

What's lower in fat than chicken and higher in protein than beef? It's buffalo, and it's available in a variety of forms right here. Try a smoked buffalo roast or buffalo summer sausage, salami or jerky. Buffalo meat isn't cheap, though, mostly because compared to cattle, buffalo are difficult to raise. They'll walk right through an electrified fence that would put a horse on its knees, and they have a tendency to get a bit surly around humans.

Wyoming Buffalo Company also serves up regional treats such as canned smoked rainbow trout, Cowgirl Salsa and Smoked Jalapeño Cornbread mix. If you'd rather wait 'til you get home to purchase these treats, no problem: You can order by phone.

Wyoming Wear
20 W. Broadway, Jackson, Wyo.
• **(307) 733-2889**

Frannie Huff came here in 1969 after finishing high school. She started a company called Wyoming Woolens in 1981. Now the store, which sells a variety of fleece accessories and jackets, pants, high-tech outerwear and other items, has grown to four. Wyoming Wear products, made in Afton, Wyoming, are also available through the mail and in dozens of stores throughout the country.

The Jackson flagship store carries Woolrich and other clothing brands, in addition to its own Wyoming Wear products.

Yippee I-O Candy Company
84 E. Broadway, Jackson, Wyo.
• (307) 739-3020

Barrels, baskets and jars full of candy fill this store — every color and flavor you can imagine — plus a few that will surprise. These folks have more than 500 different kinds of sweet morsels, including hand-dipped chocolates, sugar-free candies, saltwater taffy and various kinds of huckleberry treats. The cream and butter fudge is made fresh in the store. So are the brownies.

Surrounding Areas

Eastern Idaho

Idaho Falls, Idaho

Blue Unicorn
233 First St., Idaho Falls, Idaho
• (208) 525-8604

Come here to find incense and aromatherapy products, massage oils and books on massage techniques, as well as Native American artifacts. The shop's small and offbeat book collection includes several titles dealing with astrology, color therapy and the healing arts. Blue Unicorn is closed Sundays.

Growers' Market of Idaho Falls
501 W. Broadway, Idaho Falls, Idaho
• (208) 522-7336

Now in its 10th year, this farmers' market opens in May with about 15 vendors and swells to more than 30 vendors by August. The market runs through October. You'll find bedding plants, berries, exotic mushrooms, emu meat and craft items. The market is also a good source of fresh herbs, cut flowers, honey, seafood and more kinds of potatoes than you might have known existed.

Various food vendors supply the walking-around munchies. For a small fee and the time it takes to preregister, you can even set up a booth of your own for the weekend or the season. Hours are Saturday mornings and Wednesday afternoons. The location is the Key Bank parking lot adjacent to the Snake River.

Made in Idaho Inc.
2300 E. 17th St., Grand Teton Mall, Idaho Falls, Idaho • (208) 529-5118

If you haven't found the right souvenirs for your friends back home yet, you might want to drop by the Made In Idaho store. One of three such stores in the state (there's also one in Twin Falls and another in the state capital of Boise), most of the merchandise is made in Idaho or is somehow related to Idaho. Best sellers are Idaho Spud candy bars, made by the Owyhee Candy Company in Boise, and the huckleberry candies, syrups and other specialty foods. Anything on the potato theme is available here, including such products as potato hand lotion, potato bath salts, baked-potato sprinkles and potato refrigerator magnets.

Swan Valley

Huskey's Gallery and Trading Post
3787 U.S. Hwy. 26, Palisades, Idaho
• (208) 483-2582

Pete and Dorothy Huskey say they've lived in Swan Valley for more than 40 years, and this cram-packed little shop makes that easy to believe. Pete is a jeweler who works in some unusual materials: sinew, coyote and elk bones, semiprecious stone beads, elk ivory and bear, wolf and coyote claws. The shop features his work as well as that of other artists. One case displays raw materials for jewelers. You can occasionally find fossilized walrus teeth, carved walrus tusk or fossilized wolf teeth. Another room houses collectibles and antiques.

Pete does custom work, which he's happy to ship to your home. His prices are extremely reasonable: Some simpler jewelry items run less than $10. The store is open from May to October.

Teton Valley, Idaho

Teton Jade and Gem at Driggs Plumbing and Heating Supply
140 N. Main, Driggs, Idaho
- **(208) 354-2562, (208) 787-2483**

Teton Jade and Gem is a real old-fashioned rock shop. Much of the material was gathered on family vacations by shop owners/collectors David, Janeane, Jack and Neta Driggs. These folks know the area and its rockhounding possibilities, but they carry material from all over the country. The selections of Wyoming jade and Idaho opal are particularly nice. Local Bitch Creek jade, a pale to nearly blackish-green mineral, is available both polished and rough. You can also find glass-clear quartz crystals, collected near Dillon Montana. The shop carries some jewelry and can provide basic jewelry repair services.

Teton Jade and Gem is open weekdays in winter; in summer the shop is also open Saturday mornings.

Southwestern Montana

Montana Candy Emporium
7 S. Broadway, Red Lodge, Mont.
- **(406) 446-1119**

Willie Wonka, eat your heart out. While the Montana Candy Emporium makes 22 kinds of fudge as you watch, this store's real claim to fame is the volume of confections packed inside its turn-of-the-century walls. The Montana Candy Emporium has 2,300 kinds of sweets, including more than four tons of hard candy contained in bushel baskets. In this case, seeing is believing. Even if you aren't a candy lover, we recommend you stroll the aisles of this store on Red Lodge's main street just to experience the mind-boggling and mouth-watering sight of so many goodies. While you're here, you might want to try the killer fudge or huckleberry bark.

White Buffalo Lodges
522 E. Park Ave., Livingston, Mont.
- **(406) 222-7390**

Plains Indians once lived in them. Now Don Ellis makes them for people around the world. They are tipis, and Ellis makes four types: the Sioux, the Cheyenne, the Crow and the Blackfoot. The Sioux, though, is the most popular. Tipi sizes and prices range from $330 for a 9-foot children's tipi without poles to $2,073 for a 24-foot tipi with poles.

Inside White Buffalo Lodges, about five blocks east of town, you'll also find a gift shop featuring an assortment of Native American work including jewelry, drums, dresses, rugs and small bags.

Northwestern Wyoming

Cody, Wyoming

Wyoming Buffalo Company
1276 Sheridan Ave., Cody, Wyo.
- **(307) 587-8708**

So, you've been wanting a taste of buffalo ever since you hit Yellowstone country. If you step inside the Wyoming Buffalo Company, someone will treat you to a tiny taste of bison jerky for starters. Once you're inside, you won't believe all of the different buffalo-meat concoctions and pre-packaged cute cowboy foods. Step right in.

Opened in 1997, this store is owned by the same Wyoming Buffalo Company featured earlier in the "Jackson" section.

Indian powwows,
mountain-man
rendezvous, frontier
days, rodeos and
shootouts are examples
of events that have
grown out of our
fascination with
"the way it was."

Annual Events

Throughout Greater Yellowstone you'll find events that are a celebration of our Western myths. Indian powwows, mountain-man rendezvous, frontier days, rodeos, and shootouts are examples of events that have grown out of Westerners' fascination with "the way it was." For visitors, these events can be both fascinating and educational. For locals, they are also social events. Some have grown so big that locals head for the hills until they're over.

You'll find celebrations of the arts throughout the region. In some cases, we've listed purely community celebrations such as the New Year's Eve Ball at the Gallatin Gateway Inn near Bozeman, Montana. Affairs like this are reminiscent of the frontier days when families would drive miles in a team-pulled wagon to dance with their neighbors. Sometimes they met at the local grange or one-room schoolhouse, as a few of the very small communities in the Greater Yellowstone still do. Other times, a family with a "big" house (small by today's standards), would push back the furniture, roll back the rugs, tune the fiddles and throw open their doors.

Carnivals and snowmobile expos take place in winter in such places as Red Lodge and West Yellowstone, Montana, and Jackson, Wyoming. And you'll find a few other surprising events like skijoring and dogsled racing.

We invite you to join us in our festivities, whether it's a New Year's Eve ball, a gun show or a music festival. Stepping into the circle of celebration is a good way to get an Insider's look at life in Greater Yellowstone.

We organized this chapter like a calendar, with events laid out month-by-month; look for our familiar geographic arrangement within each month's section. Also, as you will note in our entries, the dates of these annual events are not always the same each year. Generally, they all fall on weekends, and often they fall on the same weekend year after year. But, as each community adds more and more events to their attractions list, the dates of even well-established events occasionally are moved. We urge you to call the information numbers we provide or contact the local chamber of commerce to get more particulars on events that interest you. You'll find the addresses and phone numbers of area chambers in the Resources chapter.

January

Jackson Hole

International Rocky Mountain Stage Stop Sled Dog Race
Various locations in the Jackson Hole area • (307) 734-1163
This 10-day race draws world-famous mushers and topnotch sled teams. The race begins and ends in Jackson Hole. The first stage is best watched from Jackson's town square. The final push, another good show, brings contestants barreling into Teton Village. A closing dinner banquet happens at Snow King Resort in the town of Jackson.

Southwestern Montana

New Year's Eve Ball
Gallatin Gateway Inn, Bozeman, Mont. • (406) 763-4672
Each New Year's Eve, several hundred people from the area push back the furniture and dance into the New Year at the Gallatin Gateway Inn (see our Hotels, Motels and Cabins chapter). Dress ranges from casual to formal. A swing band usually provides the music. The Gallatin Gateway Inn offers a package for those who want to spend the night, dance and eat breakfast on New Year's Day. Admission to

the ball in 1997-98 was $15, while a dinner and dance ticket cost $50 per person.

February

Jackson Hole

Jackson Hole Shrine Club Cutter Races
Off U.S. Hwy. 26, 5 miles south of Jackson, Wyo. • (307) 733-3316

This weekend of action-packed chariot races brings crowds out into the weather to cheer, boo and bet. Always President's weekend, the 27-year-old event will cost you around $5 per day. Food and drink are available at the arena. (See our Spectator Sports chapter for more.)

www.insiders.com
See this and many other **Insiders' Guide®** destinations online — in their entirety.
Visit us today!

Cowboy Ski Challenge
Jackson Hole Mountain Resort, Teton Village, Wyo. • (307) 733-2292

The Old West and the new meet in mid-February for a Western music concert, novelty ski races, a rodeo, a Dutch-oven cookoff, cowboy poetry and a barn dance. Ski activities on the mountain are the focus on day one. Day two, centered around the outdoor snow arena, is devoted to snow-rodeo events such as skijoring, in which two-person teams race, one on horseback pulling the other on skis. You can watch events at no charge; a chance to compete costs $30 per person. Generally, locals enter and visitors watch. Some events, like the Dutch-oven cookout, will cost you.

Eastern Idaho

Ashton, Idaho, Area

Ashton American Dog Derby
Main St., Ashton, Idaho • (208) 652-3377

Sled dogs waiting to pull bark excitedly and nonstop. So during the third week of February every year, Ashton fills with the energetic yipping of up to 34 six- and 10-dog teams. During the two-day derby, six-dog teams will clock around

80 miles, and 10-dog teams more than 120. The scenes at start and finish lines are most exciting. Other canine competitions round out the weekend's entertainment. (See our Spectator Sports chapter for more.)

Swan Valley

Yamafest
40 Conant Valley Loop, Swan Valley, Idaho • South Fork Lodge
(208) 483-2229, Swan Valley Chamber of Commerce (208) 483-2060

The snowmobile course runs through forest, hill and open field for 38 to 45 miles. Start and finish lines are at South Fork Lodge, where post-race drawings, prizes and dinner prizes and dinner await the more than 300 snow-machine drivers who roar in, ready to warm up and party. The one-day Yamafest normally takes place in the first week or two of February. Since snow conditions have to be good, the date's often not set until late January. Last year's first prize was around $700; entry fees are generally $15.

Northwestern Wyoming

Buffalo Bill Birthday Ball
Cody Auditorium, Cody, Wyo. • (307) 587-2777

In Cody, it's Buffalo Bill everything — even in winter long after the tourists have gone home. If you happen to be in town on the Saturday before Buffalo Bill's February 26 birthday, dress up for his Birthday Ball. It's the locals' celebration of the frontiersman's birth. By day, residents cover the front of the Cody Auditorium with a Western façade of old barn wood. A sign on the front reads "Wolfville Hall." By night, 500 folks don their turn-of-the-century attire, dance until the wee hours and howl 'til the hens come home. In 1998, they ended the ball with a buffalo roast. The mounted head of the buffalo and the hide were auctioned off to the highest bidders. Admission in 1997 was $13 per person.

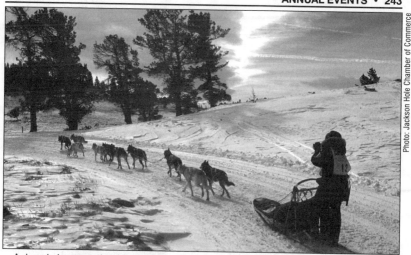

Photo: Jackson Hole Chamber of Commerce

A dog sled racer makes his way along the trail during the annual 10-day, 350-plus-mile Rocky Mountain Stage Stop Dog Race held near Jackson, Wyoming.

March

Yellowstone National Park Entrance Communities

West Yellowstone, Mont.

World Snowmobile Expo
Various locations in West Yellowstone, Mont. • (406) 646-7701

Fifteen thousand people showed up in 1997 for the World Snowmobile Expo, a kaleidoscopic event held in conjunction with the World Championship Snowmobile Races in West Yellowstone. (See our Spectator Sports chapter for more information.) In addition to the four major snow-machine manufacturers that display next-year's models, about 70 vendors set up booths and tempt the crowds with their wares. If it's related to snowmobiling, you'll find it at this show: helmets, hats, coats, boots, goggles, mufflers, tracks, skis — you-name-it. Even if you only go to watch the people, this end-of-the-season hurrah is worth watching. A weekend in mid-March is set aside for the expo, which charges an admission fee ranging from $8 to $15.

Jackson Hole

World Championship Snowmobile Hillclimb
Snow King Ave., Jackson, Wyo.
• (307) 734-9653

Snowmobilers from all over the country compete in what is perhaps the nation's best-known hillclimb competition, a four-day event at the end of March. You can buy a lift ride up the mountain to your viewing spot, but if you're willing to hike up you don't have to pay. When you have seen enough roaring, racing snowmobiles, check out the circus-like camp of vendors at the bottom of the mountain. (See our Spectator Sports chapter for more.)

Southwestern Montana

National Finals Skijoring
Red Lodge Rodeo Grounds, Red Lodge, Mont. • (406) 446-1718

They used to do it out in the snow-covered hayfields. Now, horse, cowboy and skier hook up the second weekend every March to compete in a crazy competition that pulls skiers around a 250-yard-long course marked by 16 to 24 gates and several jumps. In 1997, 128 teams from six states showed up for the competition held at the Red Lodge Rodeo grounds. In order to place, competitors must be upright with at least one ski on the ground when crossing the finish line. Admission in 1997 was $3.

Red Lodge Winter Carnival
Various locations in Red Lodge, Mont.
• (406) 446-1718

While this carnival sometimes features snow sculpting (depending on the snowfall), the highlight of the entire weekend festival is the Cardboard Classic Race down Red Lodge Mountain. Costumed racers ride the hill in their glued-together cardboard "vehicles," waving to fans and family. Another favorite is the Firehose Race featuring teams of firemen from as far away as Minnesota. Dressed in firemen's garb, the skiers race in teams down the hill holding a 50-foot section of firehose. Other fun events include a Friday-night parade, a costume contest and obstacle races and treasure hunts for children. The festival, well-attended by regional residents, ends with a torchlight parade down Red Lodge Mountain. Admission prices vary by event.

April

Jackson Hole

Pole Pedal Paddle
Various locations in Jackson Hole
• (307) 733-6433

Cabin fever can produce some strange ideas, like the one someone had 23 years ago that grew into this race. Hundreds of teams and individuals alpine ski, cross-country ski, bike and kayak or canoe from Teton Village to Astoria Hot Springs below Hoback Junction, a combined distance of more than 39 miles. All skill levels are welcome. Weird costumes are encouraged for the untimed fun class. Par-

ticipation will cost you between $25 and $35. Watching is free but kind of tough: This race moves fast. Pole Pedal Paddle is held the last weekend Jackson Hole Mountain Resort's ski lifts run — usually mid-April.

Northwestern Wyoming

Cowboy Songs and Range Ballads
Buffalo Bill Historical Center, Cody, Wyo. • (307) 587-4771

Each spring, cowboys duded up in Brush Popper shirts, leather vests and Wrangler jeans ride into Cody to yodel, croon and boom tunes learned at home on the range. One of the oldest in the country — 1998 will be its 16th season — this gathering of cowboy songsters and balladeers catches them fresh out of their winter cabins where most have had time to pen a few new poems and practice some old tunes. The old favorites can stand the re-telling and the re-singing. Dates vary from year to year, and admission prices range from free to $7.50 depending on the show.

May

Jackson Hole

Elk Antler Auction
Town Square, Jackson, Wyo.
• (307) 733-5353, 733-4467

Local Boy Scouts gather some 3 tons of shed antlers from the nearby National Elk Refuge every year. Antlers are auctioned off to the public the third Saturday in May in the world's largest public antler auction. Private sales (of shed antlers only) are conducted simultaneously on a neighboring street. Much of the product, sold in lots that range from two matched antlers to 40-pound bundles, ends up in Asian markets where ground antler is believed to have aphrodisiacal properties. In this country, elk antler decorates homes, becomes furniture and chandeliers, or is carved into belt buckles and bolo ties. The average price has hovered around $10 per pound. Jackson Hole Historical Society cooks up meals at Town Square so you can nibble as you watch or bid.

Old West Days
Various locations in Jackson, Wyo.
•(307) 733-3316

Jackson celebrates the Old West with parades, a rodeo, street dancers, an amateur Western swing contest, stagecoach rides, Native American dancers, shooting matches, plays, movies, concerts and more. Up in Teton Village outside Jackson, a Mountain Man Rendezvous keeps the mood of the weekend with muzzleloader shoots and tomahawk throws. This Memorial Day weekend celebration, Wyoming's second-largest festival, draws crowds from all over the region. Contact the Jackson Hole Chamber of Commerce at the number above for more information.

Eastern Idaho
Rexburg, Idaho, Area

Free Fisherman's Breakfast
Keefer Park, St. Anthony, Idaho
• (208) 624-3540

More than 40 years ago, a group of St. Anthony business people decided to provide coffee and donuts to anglers traveling to favorite waters for Memorial Day weekend's Saturday season opening. That nice idea gradually escalated into the full-scale event it is today. Every Friday before Memorial Day weekend, 1,200 pounds of pancake mix and 500 pounds of sausages feed more than 5,000 folks — for free. The meal is courtesy of the community and in honor of the opening of fishing season. Speakers include local politicians, representatives from the Forest Service and Idaho Fish and Game. Local musicians perform.

June
Jackson Hole

Town Square Shootout
Town Square, Jackson, Wyo.
• (307) 733-3316

Look down the barrel of six-gun justice. From Memorial Day to Labor Day, every night but Sunday, watch the longest-running shootout in the country (it's 40 years old). The Jackson Hole Shootout Gang supplies five to 12 "gunslingers" at a typical show.

J.H. Rodeo
Fairgrounds on Snow King Ave.,
Jackson, Wyo. • (307) 733-2805

Bull riding, bareback and saddlebronc riding, team roping and other cowboy competitions rollick across the arena every Wednesday and Saturday, Memorial Day to Labor Day. Reserved seats are under cover in case of bad weather. In 1997 those cost $10. You'll pay $8 at the door for festival seating under the sky. (See our Spectator Sports chapter for more.)

Eastern Idaho
Idaho Falls, Idaho, Area

Mountain Brewers Beer Festival
McDermott Field, Idaho Falls, Idaho
• (208) 523-1010

Started in 1994, this event draws around 70 breweries and a couple hundred beers for your sampling pleasure. Food vendors sell brats, chicken sandwiches and burgers. Root-beer stands take care of non-beer lovers. Festival organizers also provide an inexpensive designated-driver rate for those who aren't planning to sample brewers' wares. The rest of us pay around $15 for entry and sampling rights, with all profits going to charity. While you sip, you can listen to live music, check your fast ball with Idaho Falls Braves' radar gun, participate in a silent auction and more. In 1997, 3,000 attended the one-day event, held the first Saturday in June.

Idaho Falls Centennial Rodeo
Sandy Downs, 6855 S. 15 E., Idaho Falls, Idaho • (208) 522-5030

One of the region's first rodeos every year is the Centennial Rodeo, which draws big crowds and plenty of cowboys and cowgirls. Tickets are around $7; the rodeo is usually scheduled for early June. (For more, see our Spectator Sports chapter.)

Free Fishing Day
All of Idaho • (208) 525-7290

One Saturday, usually in June, Idaho Fish and Game invites you to pick up a rod and drop a line into some of the world's best fishing waters without picking up a license first. This goes for non-Idaho residents and locals alike.

Downtown Idaho Falls Street Festival
Various locations in downtown Idaho Falls, Idaho • (208) 535-0399

Around 75 retail and food vendors unpack their goodies into carts and booths for this one-day event. Five streets are blocked off from vehicle traffic in the core downtown area for the 10,000 to 15,000 wandering festival-goers to wander on. Two stages host music and other entertainment. The festival normally takes place the third Saturday in June.

Northwestern Wyoming

Plains Indian Powwow
Robbie Powwow Garden, Buffalo Bill Historical Center, Cody, Wyo.
• (307) 587-4771

Beads, feathers, buckskin and leather fly to the rhythm of the Northern Plains Indian powwow drums each mid-June in Cody. Sponsored by the Buffalo Bill Historical Center (see our Attractions chapter), the Plains Indian Powwow — "powwow" means medicine man — has been held for the past 16 summers. Adults and children alike will be mesmerized by the movement and color as dancers compete for prize money. Admission in 1997 was $3.

July

Jackson Hole

Grand Teton Music Festival
Walk Festival Hall, Teton Village, Wyo.
• (307) 733-1128

The 1998 season marked the 37th year for this composite orchestra made up of 175 talented musicians. Performances are highlighted by special appearances of world-class guest conductors, soloists and artists. Concerts begin June 30 and end in late August. Some events are free, but most run between $15 and $30 per seat. (For more, see our Arts chapter.)

Fourth of July Celebration
Snow King Resort, Snow King Ave., Jackson, Wyo. • (307) 733-3316

Jackson hosts a parade, a rodeo and a barbecue for the nation's birthday, but the best part is the culminating event: Snow King Mountain's spectacular dusk fireworks show.

Music in the Hole
1855 High School Rd., Jackson, Wyo.
• (307) 733-1128

This Fourth of July event starts in midafternoon with food concessions and regional musicians playing outside at Jackson Hole High School's Alpine Field. It culminates in a free performance of the renowned Grand Teton Music Festival orchestra, featuring the "1812 Overture." Appropriate crashings are provided by the howitzers of the Wyoming Military Department's 300th Field Artillery Battalion. Six thousand people attended in 1997; organizers expect closer to 10,000 this year. The concert is scheduled early so you don't miss the fireworks show on Snow King Mountain.

Mountain Artists' Rendezvous Art Show
275 N. Willow Dr., Jackson, Wyo.
• (307) 733-8792

This nationally-recognized, juried arts and crafts fair is held on the lawn at Redeemer Lutheran Church. Too fun to happen just once a year, it runs two weekends each summer: once in mid-July and again in mid-August. There is space for 134 artists, but hundreds apply every year. Most, if accepted, will exhibit in both shows. You'll enjoy browsing through the displays, shopping, munching goodies and taking in the schedule of live entertainment. The 1998 show marks its 33rd year.

Teton Village Summer Festival Event: Antique Show and Sale
Teton Village, Wyo. • (307) 733-2292

This three-day event is said to be Wyoming's biggest antique show and sale.

At West Yellowstone, thousands of professional and amateur racers gather every spring for the Snowmobile Exposition.

More than 40 vendors bring out their best treasures for display in tents and under the sun, making this mid-July weekend a great time to be in Teton Village.

Teton Village Summer Festival Event: Indian Art Show and Dance
Teton Village, Wyo. • (307) 733-2292

About 500 people per day wander through the exhibits of Native American arts and crafts on this late-July weekend. Enjoy Native American dancing, singing and foods. Many of the approximately 35 exhibitors are nationally recognized artists.

Teton County Fair
Snow King Ave., Jackson, Wyo.
• (307)733-5289

In 1997, evening events such as bull riding, a rodeo, pig wrestling and the demolition derby cost $8. Most events are free, however. Listen to live music and watch clowns and other acts. Wander the food booths or peruse exhibits that include winners from dozens of contests ranging from cut flowers to cut hay. You can also enjoy canine-obedience competitions and horseback events. The event runs for a week at the end of July.

Eastern Idaho

Idaho Falls, Idaho, Area

Fourth of July Fireworks
Greenbelt, Idaho Falls, Idaho
• (208) 523-1010

Thousands crowd the greenbelt on both sides of the Snake River for an impressive fireworks display that begins right after dark (around 10 PM) every Fourth of July. Come early if you want a comfortable patch of grass. Viewing is good from both sides of the river between Broadway and Science Center Drive at Freeman Park. If you want to do as the locals do, bring blankets, chairs, ice chests and a radio you can tune into KLCE, the station that broadcasts the accompanying music.

Eagle Rock Art Guild Sidewalk Art Show
Greenbelt at Memorial Dr., Idaho Falls, Idaho • (208) 522-4409

Up to 100 exhibitors from states as distant as Oklahoma and California display their best at this juried show: painting, jewelry, pottery, woodworking, photography and more. This event is more than 40 years old, but it got a big boost in 1990 when it moved from a local park to a more visible and pleasant location — the greenbelt that runs through town alongside the Snake River. Organizers estimate some 8,000 people wander through the event, held every year the fourth weekend in July.

Rexburg, Idaho, Area

Idaho International Folk Dance Festival
Various locations in Rexburg, Idaho
• (208) 356-5700

During this nine-day festival the first week of August, little Rexburg throws open its doors to more than 300 dancers and musicians from around the world, as well as to the thousands who come to enjoy the dancers' art. In previous years, teams have come from Malaysia, New Zealand, Denmark, Sweden, Israel, China, Russia and other nations. Free events include a parade and a street dance, Youth Culture Day at Ricks College and a community picnic and band concert. You'll pay between $5 and $12.50 for seats at the evening indoor performances and matinees. Western traditions are honored with a rodeo one night during the festival.

Teton Valley

Teton Valley Balloon Festival
Various locations in Teton Valley, Idaho
• (208) 354-2500

Crayola-bright hot-air balloons hover above the green valley floor; mountains frame every photo you attempt. This is the weekend to be in Teton Valley, with a 30- to 40-contestant hot-air balloon race, an arts festival and other fun events. The festival always falls on Fourth of July weekend.

Rockin' the Tetons Festival
Ski Hill Rd., Alta, Wyo. • (307) 353-2300, (800) 827-4433

Grand Targhee Resort's music festivals bring crowds from around the region, and this one is no exception. Enjoy rock, blues and reggae music, a street breakfast and chairlift rides. Regional microbreweries' beers are available for sampling in the sun. Previous years have featured Poco, the Marshal Tucker Band and Jefferson Starship. Tickets for this three-day event, held the second weekend in July, are around $20 per day. For an additional $10 per person, your group can set up camp for the weekend within walking distance of the party. Generally 4,000 to 5,000 attend.

Southwestern Montana

Livingston Roundup Rodeo
Park County Fairgrounds, Livingston, Mont. • (406) 222-3199, (406) 686-4232

The Livingston Roundup Rodeo is one of three "Gateway Rodeos" (Livingston, Red Lodge and Cody) held over the Fourth of July. Admission in 1997 was $12 for reserved seats, $8 for general admission and $4 for children ages 6 to 12. For more information see our Spectator Sports chapter.

Home of Champions Rodeo
Red Lodge Rodeo Grounds, Red Lodge, Mont. • (406) 446-1718

This rodeo is one of three followed each Fourth of July by some of the top rodeo hands on the circuit. Admission in 1997 ranged from $8 to $16. For more information about it, refer to our Spectator Sports chapter.

Big Sky Arts Festival
Meadow Village Pavilion, Big Sky, Mont. • (406) 995-2742

From July through August, the Big Sky Association for the Arts sponsors a series of weekend performances on the lawn at the Meadow Village Pavilion. In 1997, events included a picnic and dance, a performance by the Missoula Symphony and a bluegrass festival. For specific dates and times for this season's events, we suggest you call the above number. Admission prices vary.

Mountain Man Rendezvous
Locations vary in Red Lodge, Mont. • (406) 446-1718

Pitching their tents and tepees the first weekend in July, mountain-man enthusiasts set up camp and display their wares, which include wrought-iron goods, jewelry, trade beads, beadwork, black-powder rifles and pistols, knives, clothing and a kaleidoscope of other goods. Stroll through their camp and ask questions. Buy if you must. Afternoons and evenings you'll find a variety of events for adults and children, as well as black-powder shootouts and lectures on the era. Admission in 1997 was $3 for adults, $1 for kids ages 6 to 12 and free for kids younger than 6. Persons dressed in fur-trade-era costumes are admitted free. Contact the Red Lodge Chamber of Commerce (the number is above) to find out the 1998 location for the rendezvous.

Taste of Bozeman
Main St., Bozeman, Mont.
• **(406) 586-5421**

Belly up to a block-long table that stretches up and down Main Street. City officials block off the road for the occasion, allowing diners to enjoy their suppers purchased from and served by a number of Main Street restaurants. Diners who want a taste of Bozeman must purchase tickets ahead of time from the restaurant of their choice. While the crowd at the table dines, residents milling on the outskirts can indulge in a "Bite of Bozeman" by paying for samplings offered at sidewalk stands. Ticket prices vary depending on the restaurant you choose. The taste fest is always held the Wednesday before the Sweet Pea Festival (see our August listings).

Northwestern Wyoming

Stampede Rodeo
Stampede Park Rodeo Grounds west of Cody, Wyo. • **(307) 587-5155**

This is the richest Fourth of July rodeo in the country in terms of prize money. Admission in 1997 was $14 July 1 to 3 and $15 on July 4. For more information, see our Spectator Sports chapter.

Yellowstone Jazz Festival
Locations vary in Cody, Wyo.
• **(307) 587-3898**

This two-day event in mid-July treats music lovers in Cody and Powell, Wyoming, to a park performance, an evening concert at Cody High School's Wynona Thompson Auditorium and a performance at a local bar. The 1997 roster of players included Maxine Carr and the T-Bones, the Yellowstone Big Band and

an array of singers, pianists and other instrumental musicians. Admission prices vary depending on the performance.

Frontier Festival
Buffalo Bill Historical Center, Cody, Wyo. • **(307) 587-4771**

This two-day event in mid-July is a celebration of frontier life and culture. It features outdoor activities and demonstrations of the skills people needed to survive way back when. Watch for the pack-horse race in which contestants pack one horse, then hop onto another horse and lead the packed animal on a merry gallop around the track. The first rider who crosses the finish line with the pack still intact wins. The festival also features a campfire-cooking contest in which cooks are each given a uniform set of ingredients with which to concoct a culinary delight. Judges taste them all. Kids will find plenty to do: gold panning, rope making, cattle roping and a petting zoo. Admission in 1997 was $2 for adults and $1 for children.

Winchester Gun Show
Sweitzer Gym, Cody, Wyo.
• **(307) 587-2777**

Since 1976 collectors have been converging on Cody in mid-July to sell, buy, try or simply drool over the guns on display at the Winchester Gun Show. Whether you're a collector or not, the numbers and varieties of old guns — 90 percent of them are Winchesters — will astound you. The 1997 admission was $4 (free for kids 12 and younger).

August

Yellowstone National Park Entrance Communities

Gardiner, Montana

Buffalo Days
Downtown Gardiner, Mont.
• **(406) 848-7971**

A combination end-of-the-season celebration and fund-raiser for the Gardiner Ambulance

Service, Buffalo Days is one of those typical small town weather-dependent affairs where officials rope off Main Street for dancing and dining. Wear your old jeans, though. And prepare to dine on burgers — they used to be made of buffalo meat, but organizers decided the burgers weren't juicy enough — cole slaw, potato salad and an array of other delights. The music starts at noon, and the celebration continues into the wee hours. Children will hoot and holler at events just for them, and everyone will enjoy the dunking booth where, if your aim is good, you can dunk local celebrities. Buffalo Days is held the Saturday of Labor Day weekend. The admission price varies.

Jackson Hole

Grand Teton Music Festival
Walk Festival Hall, Teton Village, Wyo.
• (307) 733-1128
For more on this 175-member orchestra and its summer performances, see the July listing.

Mountain Artists' Rendezvous Art Show
275 N. Willow Dr., Jackson, Wyo.
• (307) 733-8792
This nationally recognized arts and crafts show is held one weekend in mid-July and again in mid-August. Please see the show's listing under July events.

Storytelling in the Huyler Tradition: Them's What's Gone
5450 W. Wyo. Hwy. 22, Wilson, Wyo.
• (307) 733-2214
A 30-year tradition for Hole residents Jack and Margaret Huyler, this annual potluck and storytelling event draws 35 to 100 storytellers

and story lovers, mostly locals. The stories represent four decades of Jackson Hole lore beginning in the 1920s. Snake River Institute, host for the last several years, provides drinks; Jack and Margaret emcee. Everyone brings blankets and potluck dishes. This event is usually held the afternoon and evening of the third Sunday in August.

Eastern Idaho

Idaho Falls, Idaho, Area

War Bonnet Roundup
Sandy Downs, 6855 S. 15 E., Idaho Falls, Idaho • (208) 523-1010
The state's oldest rodeo is held the first weekend in August. In 1997, adults paid $7 for advance seats and $8 at the door. On Thursday kids 11 and younger get in free. Sponsored by American Legion Bonneville Post 56, the rodeo raises money for Legion projects and charities (for more, see our Spectator Sports chapter).

Island Park, Idaho

National Cutting Horse Show
Jacobs' Island Park Ranch off Kilgore Rd., Island Park, Idaho • (208) 662-5567, (800) 230-9530
Cutting horses are cow ponies, bred and trained to be fast and smart. Come to the National Cutting Horse Show at Jacobs' intimate outdoor arena and see just how fast and how smart horses can be. The event, free to spectators, takes place the second weekend in August. (See our Spectator Sports chapter for information on rodeos and other Western events hosted by the Jacobs family on their 2,000-acre Island Park ranch.)

INSIDERS' TIP

You'll find Fourth of July fireworks displays in almost every town throughout Greater Yellowstone. Usually, the bigger the town, the larger the display. We recommend watching the Silver Gate/ Cooke City display. It's small by comparison to those in larger towns, but these folks get a lot of bang for their bucks when the booms from the fireworks echo off the narrow canyon walls. Following the display, you can dance the night away at the Range Rider Saloon. (See our Nightlife chapter.)

Island Park Wild Horse Stampede
Idaho Hwy. 67, north side of Henry's
Lake at Island Park, Idaho
• (208) 754-4271

The first weekend of August at Crystal Brothers Ranch Arena overlooking Henry's Lake, all hell busts loose. This three-day rodeo attracts around 7,000 spectators. The cost has been $7 per adult (for more, see our Spectator Sports chapter).

Teton Valley

Grand Targhee Bluegrass Music Festival
Ski Hill Rd., Alta, Wyo.
• (307) 353-2300, (800) 827-4433

Imagine three days of live bluegrass under the crisp blue skies of the Tetons. You'll also find crafts and food booths. This event, which marks its 11th year in 1998, attracts first-class musical talent and festive crowds. Previous years' performers include String Cheese Incident, the David Grisman Quintet, Vassar Clements and Peter Rowan. The festival falls on the second weekend in August. Tickets are about $20.

Southwestern Montana

Sweet Pea Festival of the Arts
Locations vary in Bozeman, Mont.
• (406) 586-4003

Art, music, dance and flowers mark this festival of the arts held at locations throughout town. Listen to bluegrass music or learn to country dance in Lindley Park. Decorate Main Street sidewalks at Chalk on the Walk, race in the Sweet Pea Run, compete on your bike, watch Shakespeare in the Parks or listen to a big-name band. This three-day festival the first full weekend in August regularly attracts 18,000 people. Join the fun and get lost in the crowd. The 1997 cost of a Sweet Pea Button, allowing access to all events, ranged from $5 to $7.

Festival of Nations
Locations vary in Red Lodge, Mont.
• (406) 446-1718

Begun in 1949 as a community celebration of the town's rich cultural diversity, the

The Pole, Pedal, Paddle race is an annual rite of spring in the Jackson Hole area.

Photo: Steve Fischbach/Post Register

Festival of Nations has become Red Lodge's biggest tourist event. The weeklong celebration, held the first week of August each year, will take you back to the days when Red Lodge was a mining town with tight-knit neighborhoods of German, Scandinavian, Finnish, Italian, Slavic, Scottish, Irish, English and Welsh families. During the event, festival-goers celebrate the food, clothing, arts, crafts and dancing of each nationality. It's all yours for the sampling. Admission is free.

Northwestern Wyoming

Buffalo Bill Celebrity Shootout
Cody Shooting Complex, Cody, Wyo.
• (307) 587-2777

In a town that houses the largest collection of American firearms in the world, it seems natural to have a celebrity shootout. Naturally, in Cody, that shootout would be named after Buffalo Bill. This growing event at the end of August attracts celebrities who compete with amateurs and professionals in a series of shooting events. There's no better place to watch the big boys shoot. Admission is free.

September

Jackson Hole

Jackson Hole Fall Arts Festival
Various locations in Jackson Hole, Wyo.
• **(307) 733-3316**

Every year from mid-September to mid-October, Jackson, Wyoming, hauls out its best arguments for naming the town Wyoming's arts center. Most major galleries — Jackson has more than 30 — feature special exhibits. Arts for the Parks, an international competition in which artists celebrate the United States' national parks and monuments, juries thousands of entries and selects the top 100 for local display. You can also enjoy concerts, poster signings, fiber-arts exhibits, workshops and more.

Jackson Hole Shrine Club Cutter Races
Off U.S. Hwy. 26, 5 miles south of Jackson, Wyo. • **(307) 733-3316**

Local Shriners, who have been hosting a February weekend of chariot races for 27 years, added a September event. Its popularity encouraged them to try again in 1998. You'll pay around $5 per day. Food and drink are available (see our Spectator Sports chapter for more).

Eastern Idaho

Idaho Falls, Idaho, Area

Eastern Idaho State Fair
97 Park St., Blackfoot, Idaho
• **(208) 785-2480**

Beginning every Labor Day Saturday and running through the following Saturday, exhibitors and contestants from 16 eastern Idaho counties park their pickups in Blackfoot. This fair, which began in 1925, attracts some 250 commercial exhibitors, 65 food concessionaires and around 30 rides. More than 200,000 visitors wander through exhibits and sample events such as a rodeo, a demolition derby, a tractor pull, horseracing and concerts with acts that have included REO Speedwagon and Alabama. Agriculture is important in eastern Idaho, and the fair doesn't forget this: You can view more than 2,000 animals of different types, most here for competitive judging. Food booths feature fresh corn on the cob, elephant ear deep-fried breads and Dutch-oven chow as well as the usual country fair fare. Adults pay $3 to enter.

Northwestern Wyoming

Western Design Conference
Cody Auditorium, Cody, Wyo.
• **(307) 587-2777, (888) 685-0574**

Furniture, fashion and accessories with a Western flair are the heart of this high-energy conference held in Cody at the end of September each year. The conference begins with a fashion show followed by a dance at the Irma Hotel, Buffalo Bill's historical lodging. In 1997, more than 50 craftsmen displayed their work gallery-style at the Cody Auditorium. Admission to exhibits was $3 in 1997; the fashion show and dance tickets were each $10.

November

Jackson Hole

Jackson Town Square Lighting Ceremony
Town Square, Jackson, Wyo.
• **(307) 733-3316**

Santa Claus shows up to help light up the square; elves provide homemade cook-

---

INSIDERS' TIP

Bridger Bowl and Big Sky ski areas hold Easter Sunrise services. For more information, call the local chambers of commerce, which are listed in our Resources chapter.

The cowboy ski race is held at Jackson Hole Mountain Resort every spring.

ies, hot cider and coffee. The Jackson Hole Community Band and Chorale fill the air with the music of the holiday. Garlands bedeck the boardwalks and lights twinkle in the trees and antler arches of Jackson's town square. This event is always scheduled right after Thanksgiving to get folks focused on the next holiday in line.

Eastern Idaho

Idaho Falls, Idaho, Area

Festival of Trees
640 E. Elva, Idaho Falls, Idaho
• (208) 524-1550

Get in the Christmas spirit early and help raise money for disabled Idahoans. Festival of Trees, held each year at the Idaho Falls' Elks Lodge, starts in mid-November and runs four days. Purchase a decorated tree (or

donate one), visit 30 to 40 holiday booths and take part in an Elves' Workshop stuffed with stuff for the kids. Enjoy live entertainment ranging from elementary-school choirs to cloggers and other dance groups. You'll pay about $10 at the door for your family. Meals are available for purchase: soup, bagels, bread, baked potatoes and more.

Swan Valley

Brenthoven's Restaurant
U.S. Hwy. 26 at U.S. Hwy. 89, Alpine, Wyo. • (307) 654-7545, (800) 343-6755

From mid-November through mid-December, owners of The Nordic Inn and Brenthoven's Restaurant host a truly unique experience. Groups of eight are invited to an eight-course meal served on Lennox china and Waterford crystal, with wine at each course. Dinner is followed by a private piano concert. The setting is the gracious, becolumned Southern Colonial-style home of Anne and Michael Clinger and partner Brent Johnstone. The surroundings are the tiny town of Alpine at the top of Palisades Reservoir on the Idaho/Wyoming border. Brent, a chef as well as a concert pianist who has performed at Carnegie Hall, prepares the meal and provides the music. Michael serves. In 1997, about 180 people experienced a holiday evening with the Clingers and Johnstone. All made their reservations months in advance at a cost of about $75 per person.

December

Yellowstone National Park Entrance Communities

West Yellowstone, Montana

Christmas Dinner and Dance
Locations vary in West Yellowstone, Wyo. • (307) 646-7701
Locals kick off the winter season with a dinner and dance held either at the old Union

Pacific Dining hall — a massive log and stone building used to feed passengers coming to and from the Park — or the Yellowstone Conference Hotel Holiday Inn. For a peek into the world of those who serve tourists and keep the town going, and for a chance to dance away the night, step inside and trip the light fantastic with West's best. It's held the first or second weekend in December. Admission in 1997 was less than $20.

Jackson Hole

Community Visual Arts Association Christmas Bazaar
Snow King Center, Snow King Ave., Jackson, Wyo. • (307) 733-8792
On the first Saturday of December, usually the day the ski lifts at Jackson Hole Mountain Resort open, locals have a tough decision to make. Should they head for the mountain or the 121-artisan craft show at Snow King? Historically a locals'-only event, recent years have seen more visitors from nearby communities as the word gets out that this is a primo Christmas-shopping opportunity. No admission is charged, but you have the opportunity to donate a buck or so to the Arts Association.

Photo: Andy Bronson/Post Register

At the Mountain Man Rendezvous near Chester, Idaho, latter-day mountain men demonstrate primitive woods skills, including musketry, leather crafts, cooking and teepee camping.

Torchlight Parades
At Jackson Hole, Snow King and Grand Targhee Ski Resorts
• Jackson Hole (307) 733-2292,
• Snow King (307) 733-5200,
• Grand Targhee, (208) 353-8148

A torchlit parade of skiers snakes down the dark mountain, surrounded by their own spreading glow. This visual treat is available at Grand Targhee and Jackson Hole on December 25. All three resorts sponsor a parade on New Year's Eve. Starting times depend on the weather.

Eastern Idaho

Island Park, Idaho

Island Park Snowcross
Henry's Lake Flats, U.S. Hwy. 20 at mile marker 396, Mack's Inn at Island Park
• (208) 558-7818

Imagine a moto-cross race on snow and ice, with low-slung snowmobiles executing those jumps and whipping turns. That's snowcross. Sanctioned by the Rocky Mountain Cross Country Racing Circuit and hosted by Sawtelle Sales, Service & Rentals, this race is now in its fourth year and growing fast. The first weekend of December can find as many as 200 racers in Island Park competing in categories that range from junior novice to pro. Spectators pay around $5 per day for a standing-area view of the action on the track.

Swan Valley

Brenthoven's Restaurant
U.S. Hwy. 26 at U.S. Hwy. 89, Alpine, Wyo. • (307) 654-7545, (800) 343-6755

Owners of The Nordic Inn and Brenthoven's Restaurant host a holiday meal and concert for small groups from mid-November to mid-December. See our description under November listings.

Southwestern Montana

Bozeman Christmas Stroll
Main St., Bozeman, Mont.
• (406) 586-5421

On the first Saturday in December, from 4 to 7 PM, Bozeman's Main Street turns into a Christmas wonderland with sparkling lights, carolers, sleigh rides, food booths, arts and crafts and a gingerbread house decorating contest for children. Admission is free.

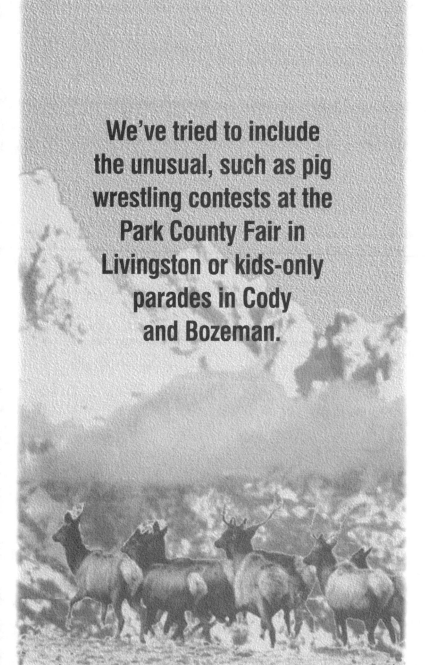

We've tried to include the unusual, such as pig wrestling contests at the Park County Fair in Livingston or kids-only parades in Cody and Bozeman.

Kidstuff

Skip rocks across a slow stretch of river. Or see how far you can throw them. Build yourself a fire and roast a hot dog. Better yet, roast marshmallows or make s'mores. Tell tall tales or play "Telephone" and laugh at how your secret has changed. Climb a tree. Walk a log. Hop from rock to rock. Play tic-tac-toe with a stick in the dirt. Carve yourself a walking stick. There are plenty of things for kids — and families — to do in Yellowstone country.

Besides all the fun you may discover on your own along the way, this book is chock-full of organized activities for kids and the young-at-heart to seek out — like horseback riding, dog sledding or riding in an old stagecoach. (See our various recreation chapters and our Attractions chapter to learn more about these things.)

Just to top it off, this chapter is a kaleidoscopic alphabet of just-for-kids stuff. We've tried to include the unusual, such as pig wrestling contests at the Park County Fair in Livingston or kids-only parades in Cody and Bozeman. As you will quickly see, this chapter is not arranged geographically, but we have listed the phone numbers and addresses for each entry to help you on your way.

Parents, you'll be happy to know that many kidstuff events listed in this chapter are either free or very inexpensive. And some are unusual enough that you may just want to veer off your planned course to be where the kid action is.

A

is for adventures in art, like drawing chalk pictures on Bozeman's downtown sidewalks during the Sweet Pea Festival each August. Or check out the **Emerson Cultural Center** and **Beall Park Art Center**, (406) 587-9797, 111 S. Grand in Bozeman, Montana, where you'll find a rainbow of art activities for kids after school and on Saturdays. In 1997, they offered classes in such activities as clay sculpture, dance, singing, painting and weaving. In Jackson, stop by **Paint, Glaze and Fire Ceramics Painting Studio**, 225 N. Cache, (307) 733-6723, for the chance to paint your own ceramic masterpiece. You can create mugs, vases, platters and plates. Bring your imaginations — the staff will provide everything else you'll need.

B

is for the **Buffalo Bill Fast Draw Championship** at the Buffalo Bill Festival on a weekend in August each year in Cody, Wyoming. Besides the Fast Draw Championship, which is held both days, you'll find a special festival just for you. At this same festival in 1997, kids participated in a bike rodeo, practiced roping and fly fishing, rode on a fire engine, had their faces painted and went for carriage rides for starters. To learn more about the Buffalo Bill Festival, call the Cody Chamber of Commerce at (307) 587-2777.

C

is for cowboy hats. Grab Mom or Dad by the hand and don't let go until they've bought you a cowboy hat. You'll find a good selection at prices Mom might be willing to pay if you go straight to a **Corral West Ranchwear**. You'll find these stores in Cody, Wyoming, at two locations: 1202 Sheridan Avenue, (307) 587-2122; and 1625 Stampede Avenue, (307) 587-4493. In Bozeman, Montana, Corral West is at 1527 W. Main, (406) 586-8671, and in Livingston, Montana, Corral West is at 1106 W. Park Avenue. In Jackson, Wyoming, you'll find one of these jam-packed cowboy stores at 840 W. Broadway, (307) 733-0247. In Idaho Falls, go to Corral West at Grand Teton Mall, (208) 535-0326. Or try **Teton Kids**, 1820 S. Park Route, Jackson, (307) 739-2176. They can outfit even the tiniest buckaroos. Or just keep your eyes open. There are ranch supply stores and even old-style dry goods mercantiles that sell hats in every town in Greater Yellowstone.

D

is for diving into a commercial hot-springs pool. This country is full of them. No matter where you go, look for the cool pool, too. Nothing's better than going back and forth between the two extremes. Bozeman KOA is great for this — the lip between the pools is curved and smooth so you can sort of slither (see below).

Try **Bozeman Hot Springs**, 81123 Gallatin Road, Bozeman, (406) 586-6492. Located right next to the Bozeman Hot Springs KOA, this hot spring features a small pool outside under the big sky or a big blue pool inside. In the Paradise Valley near Livingston, Montana, you can dip into the **Chico Hot Springs**, (406) 333-4933, at Pray, Montana. If Mom and Dad aren't in the mood for swimming, they'll love sitting poolside sipping lemonade while they watch you dive. Near Jackson, Wyoming, try **Granite Creek Hot Springs**, way out in the woods with shaded picnic spots along nearby Granite Creek. It's 10 miles into the woods on Granite Creek Road off U.S. Highway 191, (307) 739-5400. More convenient is **Astoria Hot Springs**, also near Jackson. Located on U.S. Highway 89 outside Hoback Junction, (307) 733-2659, Astoria has camping, a snack bar and lots of grass to run and play in when you get tired of the water. It also has a nice patio overlooking the pools for parents whose idea of a good time is a long, slow soak in the sun. Near Idaho Falls, Idaho, check out **Heise Hot Springs** at 5116 E. Heise Road, Ririe, Idaho, (208) 538-7312. At the foot of bluffs that box the Snake River Canyon, Heise has a soaking pool and two play pools, along with camping and picnicking. Best of all is the big waterslide.

E

is for elk bugles. Buy one at a sporting goods store almost anyplace in Yellowstone

country and drive your parents crazy while you learn to produce the whistling call of a real elk bugling. Cow calls are cheaper and easier to use than the bull elk bugles, by the way. Don't bugle in the Parks, though, because it's illegal.

F

is for fishing in easy-to-catch-a-fish ponds. If you throw your line into the **Bozeman Pond** on the west end of town next to the Main Mall, 2825 W. Main Street, chances are good that you'll hook onto a rainbow, brook or brown trout. String your fish on a stick, Tom Sawyer-style, pick a piece of grass to hold in your mouth like a giant toothpick, then take your fish home and ask Ma to cook them up for dinner. (If you aren't a fish eater, ask her, "pretty please," if she'll cook you up a hot dog — then watch her eat the fish you caught.) Teton Valley, Idaho, and Jackson, Wyoming, both have kids-only fishing spots. In Jackson it's Flat Creek, which meanders sedately across town and is reserved just for kids within city limits. In Teton Valley, it's the **Trail Creek Pond** at the base of Teton Pass, fenced safely away from Idaho Highway 33, surrounded by blooming yellow mules' ears and bright green picnic tables. Wherever you are, call a local fishing shop. The folks there will know where to send you.

G

is for golf — miniature golf, that is. In Cody, Wyoming, you'll find the lush **Cody Mini Golf Course**, (307) 587-3685, right across from the Chamber of Commerce on Sheridan Avenue. Owned by the city, this golf course is open from Memorial Day until Labor Day. In summertime in Jackson, Wyoming, you can play miniature golf at the base of **Snow King Mountain**. Call (307) 733-5200. In Idaho Falls, Idaho, the indoor **Land of Enchantment** is open year round at the Plaza Lanes Building, 1811 N. Yellowstone Highway, (208) 523-3985.

If you like miniature golf and your folks are looking for a place to camp in Idaho Falls, tell them to check out the **Idaho Falls KOA Kampground** at 1440 Lindsay Boulevard, (208) 523-3362. This place has its own private course for patrons. One really fun course in Idaho Falls is at **Tautphaus Park Funland**, 395 Sunken Diamond Drive, (208) 525-9814. Shoo your little brother toward the merry-go-round and try your hand at 18 challenging holes. Putt into a fiberglass rabbit, through four revolving barrels or up a ramp to jump a sticky obstacle. Some longer holes have multiple obstacles. No two are alike.

Photo: Steve Fischbach/Post Register

A young buckaroo hangs on for dear life.

H

is for horseback riding. Put on that new cowboy hat, boots and belt, look that wrangler square in the eye and tell him, "Pardner, I've got a hankerin' to ride one of your hosses." You'll find horses waiting for you at **Bill Cody Ranch**, 2604 Yellowstone Highway, Cody, (307) 587-6271. The wranglers here will take you for a ride right into the mountains where the elk roam. After the ride, you and your parents can eat a delicious dinner in the log lodge or outside chuckwagon style, depending on what day you go. In West Yellowstone, Montana, try out the horses at the **Parade Rest Guest Ranch**, 7979 Grayling Road, (406) 646-7217, about 9 miles north of town. (See our Other Recreation chapter for more on these ranches.)

Other good bets are at **Flagg Ranch** near Yellowstone's south entrance, (307) 543-2861; at Snow King Resort in Jackson, Wyoming, (307) 733-5781; at **Jackson Lake Lodge** within Grand Teton National Park, (307) 543-2811; and with **Jackson Hole Trail Rides** in Teton Village, (307) 733-6992. In Island Park, Idaho, there's great riding within **Harriman State Park**, (208) 558-7077. A short drive from Idaho Falls can find you near Ririe at **Granite Creek Ranch**, a real working cattle ranch that also rents horses for short rides. Call (208) 538-7140.

I

is for "I scream, you scream, we all scream for ice cream!" If you've got that ice-cream screaming urge, look in any **Hamilton Store** in Yellowstone Park for **Wilcoxson's Ice Cream**, made in Livingston, Montana, at 314 S. Main, (406) 222-2370. This old-fashioned creamy ice cream comes in 50 flavors and has been made in Livingston since 1912. Try the Peanut Butter Chip, Huckleberry, Cookies and Cream or Pecan Praline. You'll also find Wilcoxson's outside the Park, in West Yellowstone and other Montana towns.

In Swan Valley, Idaho, the I-scream stop is at the **Swan Valley Commissary**, locally famous for its hand-dipped, square ice creams. Look for the Commissary at the intersection of U.S. Highway 26 and Idaho Highway 31, (208) 483-2151. Teton Valley may be the Huckleberry Shake capital of the world, so make sure you stop at the **Victor Emporium** for an old-fashioned treat made with hand-picked local huckleberries and lots of smooth, rich ice cream. Victor Emporium is at 45 N. Main in Victor, Idaho, (208) 787-2221.

J

is for jumping into the **Firehole River Swimming Hole** in Yellowstone National Park. Pack a picnic and steer your parents toward Firehole Canyon Drive (you'll see it on the Yellowstone National Park map they give you at the entrance gate). The road is just south of

Madison Junction on the west side of the Madison-Old Faithful Road. Keep on going until you come to the Firehole River Swimming Hole. You can't miss it unless you have your eyes closed. Wear your lifejacket and float in the water from one end of the hole to the next. Or stick to the swimming hole off the tiny beach.

If the weather's not right for outdoor swimming, do your jumping at the **Teton County/ Jackson Parks and Recreation Center**. Summer and winter, you can play on the two-story water slide, hide behind the waterfall, swirl in the whirlpool or giggle on the geyser. Find this watery playground at 155 W. Gill Street in Jackson, Wyoming; call (307) 739-9025.

K

is for kids-only parades. Dress your dog like a clown, put him in your little red wagon, don your most outrageous gypsy outfit and head for Main Street with all the other kooky kids in town. Cody, Wyoming, has a kids-only parade every July 2 during its **Stampede Rodeo**. Bozeman, Montana, has a kids-only parade the first Saturday of December when the town holds their Christmas stroll. We suggest you check with the Cody Chamber of Commerce, (307) 587-2777, 836 Sheridan Avenue, and the Bozeman Chamber of Commerce, (406) 586-5421, (800) 228-4224, 1205 E. Main Street, to learn the exact times and starting points for these parades.

L

is for learning more about the ins and outs of Greater Yellowstone. In Cody, Wyoming, you can catch hands-on, kids-only workshops at the **Buffalo Bill Historical Center**, 720 Sheridan Avenue, (307) 587-4771. If your family is planning to be in Cody for a while, check into multi-day workshops offered July through August. In 1997, kids learned to paint with Western artists and wrote songs with cowboy songsters. They also learned to powwow

dance with Native Americans, and they tooled leather with a saddlemaker.

Both **Teton Science School** and **Snake River Institute** offer classes for kids, too, mostly in summer (Teton Science School also has great winter programs for area schools and school groups). Teton Science School, located within Grand Teton Park, is all about nature: Lucky students spend as much as six weeks learning hands-on about ecology and the natural world while they live in cabins within the Park. Nonresidential programs are also available for kids and adults. Call (307) 733-4765.

Snake River Institute, located at the foot of Teton Pass in Wilson, Wyoming, is an experiential arts and humanities center. It offers nonresidential classes for adults, families and kids. Enjoy guided hikes, wildflower-seed gathering, learning about nature photography, fishing, animal tracking and how to cook with the sun. Call (307) 733-2214 for a catalog, or stop by the Snake River Institute at 5450 W. Wyo. Highway 22, Wilson, Wyoming. See our Education chapter for more about these two programs.

Last but not least, Yellowstone and Grand Teton Parks are home to ranger-naturalist programs that can teach you about elk, bears and bison, geysers and forest fires and how the mountains were formed. In Yellowstone Park, check the *Yellowstone Today* newspaper that the ranger will give you at the entrance gate; Grand Teton's newspaper, available at all visitors centers and Park entrances, is called *Teewinot*. Inside you'll find descriptions of available programs. You can also check the bulletin board at your campground for a schedule of evening campfire talks. Often the evening programs are geared for children and adults.

M

is for museums. Hold on a minute. Before you say "Yuck," "Yawn" and "Do we have to?", we know of a couple museums that are pretty darn fun for kids. At the **Museum of the**

INSIDERS' TIP

In Yellowstone Park, fishing permits are required for children older than 11.

Rockies, 600 W. Kagy Boulevard, Bozeman, Montana, (406) 994-2251, you'll see T-Rex, one giant dinosaur skeleton (he takes up a whole big room) pieced together from bones found near Jordan, Montana. In the rest of the museum, you'll find lots of buttons to push and handles to pull. Upstairs may be the best part, though. The Martin Discovery room, equipped with puzzles, puppets and other activities, is made especially for kids.

Or get your parents to bring you to the **National Museum of Wildlife Art** north of Jackson, Wyoming. The children's gallery wants to let you interact with art; for instance, you get to redesign famous wildlife art masterpieces just the way you like them — all the paintings' parts have been cut apart and made into magnets. You're the artist! The museum is at 2820 Rungius Road off U.S. Highway 26, (307) 733-5771.

The **Bonneville Museum, 200 N. Eastern Avenue,** Idaho Falls, (208) 522-1400, is cheap and worth the visit just for the Main Street Eagle Rock display downstairs, where a series of storefronts chock-full of cool old stuff recreate the town of yesteryear. Plus the museum features hands-on displays, most recently, a chance to run the kind of remote control grippers used to move nuclear waste from behind thick glass walls. Admission is $1 for adults. The museum is open Monday through Friday, and Saturday afternoon. See our Attractions chapter for more about the Bonneville Museum.

N

is for navigating the **Children's Fire Trail** near Mammoth Hot Springs in Yellowstone National Park. This trail is only a half-mile (that's about six city blocks). It winds through forest that was burned in 1988. Signs along the way tell you about the fire and invite you to get down on your hands and knees to look for the new life that is sprouting up through the burn. If you get tired of looking at the signs, you can always race your parents or your brothers and sisters back to the car.

O

is for ordering dinner at Jackson, Wyoming's, **Calico** or **Vista Grande**, at

Choices in Idaho Falls, Idaho, or at **Dornan's Chuckwagon** in Grand Teton Park. All four are extremely kid-friendly. Calico, Vista Grande and Dornan's offer outdoor seating (in season) and run-and-play space. Calico and Vista Grande face each other across a huge lawn safely away from the road. Kids are welcome to use the contents of the toy box on Calico's deck. Find Calico, which serves Italian food, on Teton Village Road near Teton Village, (307) 733-2460. Vista Grande, a Mexican restaurant, is next door, (307) 733-6964. Dornan's Chuckwagon, open in summertime only, serves up its selection of barbecued sandwiches and treats at 10 Moose Street off the Teton Park Road at Moose Junction, (307) 733-2415. Choices has no grassy lawn to play on, but it does serve the most varied, family-favorites menu you're likely to find: burgers, pizza, prime rib and steak. Find them at 1869 N. Yellowstone Highway in Idaho Falls, or call (208) 523-2131.

P

is for pig races at the **Bear Creek Saloon**, 108 W. Main Street, (406) 446-3481, in Bearcreek near Red Lodge, Montana. People drive from all over to this tiny town so they can eat a Mexican dinner (these dinners are so inexpensive that Mom and Dad will jump at the chance to take you) then watch the pig races outside. The pigs run from their cages to the other end of the track where a trough of food is waiting.

P is for also for pig wrestling contests at the **Park County Fair** in Livingston, Montana. On Friday of fair weekend (it's either the last weekend in July or the first weekend in August, depending on when the fair board can schedule a carnival) 40 teams of four wrestle muddy pigs into a 55-gallon drum. The teams jump into the very muddy pen with a 150-pound pig, then have 30 seconds to get it into the barrel and stand the barrel upright. It's a hoot to watch.

Q

is for quiet time with books from stores that feature a strong selection of kids' favorite reading material. Some of our favorites are

Valley Bookstore in Jackson, Wyoming, 125 N. Cache, (307) 733-4533; **Deseret Book Company** in Idaho Falls, Idaho, at the Grand Teton Mall, 2300 E. 17th Street, (208) 523-5061; or Idaho Falls' **Barnes and Noble Booksellers**, 2385 E. 17th Street, (208) 522-1010.

In addition to selling great books, Barnes and Noble hosts a year-round Saturday morning Story Time for kids. A staff member shares a favorite children's book every Saturday morning at 11 o'clock. A scattering of other literary activities for kids is available as well. Call Barnes and Noble for a calendar or stop by.

Visitor centers in both Yellowstone and Grand Teton parks sell an enticing array of kids' books that can teach you about wildlife and Park wonders.

R

is for rodeo — for kids. Nearly all area rodeos offer a kids event. Sometimes it's mutton busting, where participants try to ride a sheep. Sometimes it's calf riding. Sheep bolt and calves buck, so it's hard to say which is more fun to watch or harder to do. You usually have to sign up in advance if you want to rodeo, but in Cody, Wyoming, at the **Cody Nite Rodeo**, 421 W. Yellowstone Avenue, (307) 587-2992, announcers invite kids out of the stands to join in the rodeo fun. In the calf scramble, a calf with dollar bills stuck to it (sometimes it's someone's pet milk cow) is turned loose in the arena. A herd of kids chases the calf around the arena trying to grab the bills off the calf.

At Jackson Hole's twice-weekly **J.H. Rodeo**, the two calves have ribbons tied to their tails. Fifty to 100 kids ages 4 to 11 try to capture the ribbons to win. J.H. Rodeo is held at the Fairgrounds on Snow King Avenue in Jackson, Wyoming, (307) 733-2805, from Memorial Day to Labor Day. Check our Spectator Sports chapter for other rodeo times and locations.

S

is for skating on ice. In Bozeman, Montana, you'll find three free ice-skating rinks. At **Southside Park** on West College Avenue at South Seventh Avenue, you can play hockey or just skate. **Beall Park** at Villard and Black streets offers broomball on certain days of the week

and recreational skating the rest of the time. Or play hockey at **Bogert Park** at 325 South Church.

In Jackson, Wyoming, you can pay a few bucks to skate at the indoor **Snow King Center Ice Rink** at 100 E. Snow King Avenue, (307) 733-5200. Dad and Mom can relax with a hot chocolate or a snack while you skim across the ice. The rink is open from August to mid-April. Call first, though, because the rink hosts a range of events and isn't always available for public use.

You can also ice skate at the **Tautphaus** (say it TOFF-us) Park hockey rink in Idaho Falls, Idaho, (208) 529-0941. Hours can vary, but usually there's public skate time every day, winter only.

T

is for tubing at Snow King's new tubing park in Jackson, Wyoming. For just a few bucks an hour, kids get to ride up a modified rope tow on a special, canvas-covered innertube, then barrel back down the snowy slope on the same tube. Small children can leave the tow halfway up for a shorter, easier ride. You can even tube at night Monday through Thursday. **Snow King Resort** is at 400 E. Snow King Avenue, (307) 733-5200.

U

is for utterly confusing your parents on **Uncle Tom's Trail**. Make them (or your siblings) count the steps leading down into the Grand Canyon on Uncle Tom's Trail in Yellowstone National Park. Can you count past 300? (To find the Grand Canyon of the Yellowstone River, look at that map you'll get at the Park's entrance.) Turn east off the Canyon-Lake road onto South Rim Drive. Stop at Uncle Tom's parking lot, pile out of the car and look for the signs telling where to go. We must warn you, this is a very strenuous walk, so if anybody in your family has a health problem, you'd better skip this one.

V

is for **Virginia City**. This is one great old mining town with plenty for kids to do. Ride the train from Virginia City to Nevada City. Play the nickelodeons in the Bale of Hay Saloon. Go to a melodrama (you get to hoot, boo and hiss with the rest of the crowd) at the Virginia City Players. Fish in the kids-only fishing pond at Nevada City. Go to Boot Hill and check out the headstones of the Plummer Gang.

W

is for whitewater rafting and flatwater canoeing. Local river companies will take you down Jackson's fun whitewater stretch, called **Alpine Canyon** (see our Watersports chapter for names and numbers). You spend about two hours on the water. This activity is appropriate for most physically active families, although at higher water levels, some companies institute minimum age limits you'll want to pay attention to.

Or ply your paddle in a canoe on Grand Teton Park's String, Leigh, Jenny and Jackson Lakes, or on the Oxbow section of the Snake River, also in Grand Teton Park. Canoeing is a great way to see the scenery and the wildlife. Boat rentals are available from several shops (see our Watersports chapter for names and numbers).

X

is for x-ing off the pictures of each animal on page 8 of your Yellowstone Park Junior Ranger Activity Paper for kids 8 to 12 years old. (They have one for younger kids, too.) At the end of your Park visit, you can turn your activity paper in. If you've done everything required, you can become a Junior Ranger and get a patch to prove it. In order to qualify, you must attend at least one ranger-naturalist program, view a visitor center or roadside exhibit and tell about it, take a walk on a Park trail, read and understand the Junior Ranger pledge and understand six basic Park rules. You must also do a certain number of pages of your activity paper. For $2 you can buy one of these activity papers at any one of the visitor centers in Yellowstone Park.

Y

is for yummy candy. The **Montana Candy Emporium**, 7 S. Broadway Avenue, Red Lodge, Montana, (406) 446-1119, has 2,300 kinds of candy. While you're drooling over the other candy, you can watch the owners make Killer Fudge or Gooseberry Bark right in the store.

In Jackson, Wyoming, don't miss the **Yippee I-O Candy Company** at 84 E. Broadway, (307) 739-3020. This shop is lined with barrels, baskets and jars full of candy — every color and flavor you can imagine plus a few that will surprise — including hand-dipped chocolates, sugar-free candies, saltwater taffy and various kinds of huckleberry treats. The cream and butter fudge is made fresh in the store.

In Idaho Falls, stop by **Candyland** near Grand Teton Mall at 2289 E. 17th Street, (208) 528-0499, or at 651 N. Skyline Drive, (208) 528-0778. These folks carry truffles, hard candies, chocolate roses, Jelly Bellies and yummy imported treats from around the world. They even deliver!

Z

is for **Tautphaus Park Zoo**, 2725 Carnival Way, (208) 529-1470, and **Tautphaus Park Funland**, 395 Sunken Diamond Drive, (208) 525-9814, in Idaho Falls, Idaho. The zoo houses more than 250 critters, including endangered snow leopards, Siberian tigers and ring-tailed and red-ruffed lemurs. In the Children's Zoo, you can feed goats and sheep and pet the donkey. Funland is more than 50 years old. Its first ride, still operating today, was a merry-go-round with 30 leaping horses and two chariots. Now it has four more rides and an 18-hole miniature golf course (see "G" for golf, above). You pay by the ride; it's free to walk about the amusement park or wander to the concession stand for a sandwich or a snack. Both zoo and Funland are open seven days a week in spring and summer, and many weekends through the fall. Both close for the winter.

In Montana alone, there are more than 200 nonprofit arts organizations, more than 200 art galleries and more than 130 museums.

The Arts

In 1982, Joel Jahnke, artistic director of Bozeman's Montana Shakespeare in the Parks, was setting up for a production of Moliere's *Imaginary Invalid* atop Poker Jim Butte in eastern Montana. Next to the stage were the Poker Jim Fire Lookout, a small campground and a one-holer outhouse. The closest town was Birney, Montana, population 23. Jahnke looked at his cohorts, shook his head and said, "This is crazy. Nobody's going to come here." About an hour before show time, from every direction far below the butte, tiny plumes of dust shot up behind pickup trucks full of ranchers speeding to Poker Jim Butte. By show time, there were nearly 200 people perched on lawn chairs and sprawled on picnic blankets, awaiting a taste of culture under Montana's big sky.

While Birney is a stretch outside Greater Yellowstone (it's just south of the Northern Cheyenne Indian Reservation in eastern Montana), the thirst for culture is not. In Montana alone, there are more than 200 non-profit arts organizations, more than 200 art galleries and more than 130 museums. In Southwestern Montana, and in Greater Yellowstone, Bozeman is the center for the arts. Nurtured by the students and staff of Montana State University, the arts community has grown (mostly in the last 25 years) to include several dance and acting groups, a couple of orchestras, the Emerson Cultural Center (see its write-up in this chapter) and a rich menu of arts workshops and presentations each year.

In the outlying areas of Greater Yellowstone, you'll find a few towns with tiny, volunteer-driven arts councils and organizations working hard to bring artists, musicians, actors, dancers and entertainers to their communities. In some communities, you'll find people making their own music through chamber orchestras, old-time fiddler groups, community plays, dance groups, choirs, cowboy poetry gatherings, artist workshops and music camps. At county fairs you'll see a sampling of artistic endeavors in booths where locals have entered their work for judging. In many cases, the art grows out of the local lifestyle and the pursuit of personal passions. Flower arranging, photography, watercolors and oil paintings, quilting and even canning and baking entries display skills honed to artistic achievement.

Bozeman's not the only cultural hot spot. At the southern end of Greater Yellowstone is Jackson, Wyoming, a town that prides itself on its art galleries (there are more than 30). Clustered around Town Square, these galleries represent both undiscovered and nationally known artists working in every medium imaginable. To the north in Montana, art galleries have sprung up in Livingston, Bozeman and Red Lodge; to the east, the number of galleries in Cody is also growing. In large part, gallery owners in Jackson (and elsewhere in Greater Yellowstone) are promoting and selling the same thing: a piece of the West in general, and Greater Yellowstone in particular.

In many places, including eastern Idaho, the arts scene isn't as readily visible as in Jackson or Bozeman. If you dig, though, you'll find a budding (and sometimes struggling) cultural renaissance all over Greater Yellowstone. Inside the Parks, there are few organized artistic programs. However, endless opportunities to study the artistry of nature exist everywhere in Yellowstone country.

In this chapter, we'll tell you, by region, where to find dance, music and other artists who practice and perform in the Greater Yellowstone. We'll also tell you about some of the art galleries along the way. Our list of galleries is by no means all-inclusive. Because so many galleries rise and fall within a relatively few years of opening, we have first chosen to list those that have been in business the longest. We have also included galleries that Insiders appreciate for their unique artwork. We suggest that as you tour Greater Yellowstone, you keep your eyes peeled for art that suits you. It is often hanging quietly in restaurants, office buildings, banks, gift shops and furniture stores. Finally, we have featured a few of the arts organizations in the region that have been (and still are) instrumental in making the arts happen.

www.insiders.com
See this and many other Insiders' Guide® destinations online — in their entirety.
Visit us today!

Jackson Hole

Jackson, Wyoming, Area

Art Organizations

The Art Association
260 W. Pearl, Jackson, Wyo.
• (307) 733-6379

The Art Association showcases experimental juried non-Western art, attracting talented artists from around the country. One popular annual show exhibits the top entries from the Arts For the Parks contest. This international competition draws thousands of entries, all scenes from the nation's national parks and national monuments. The top 100 tour the country with a stopover here. The top five become postage stamps. At least four shows a year are oriented toward the local art community. The Art Association also sponsors art outreach into local schools and open studio sessions in which you can draw, paint or sculpt from a nude or clothed model for a small fee ($6 in 1997). An associated art school offers short courses in photography, darkroom technique, watercolor and oil painting and more. Classes for kids are available, as is a computer for public access to the Internet.

Performing Arts

Grand Teton Music Festival
Walk Festival Hall, Teton Village, Wyo.
• (307) 733-1128

Now in its 37th season, the Grand Teton Music Festival is a composite orchestra made up of talented musicians from all over. The 175-member company spends most of July and August playing traditional and contemporary music in the shadow of the Tetons. Appearances by world-class guest conductors, soloists and artists ice an already sweet cake. Last year Minnesota Orchestra's Eiji Oue (a former protege of Leonard Bernstein) debuted as music director. Full orchestra, spotlight and chamber music concerts alternate days, Tuesday through Saturday. In addition to concerts, you may attend pre-concert talks with composers, post-concert talks with the music director, open orchestra rehearsals, Fourth of July celebration and two young people's concerts. Ticket prices range from around $15 for chamber music concerts to almost $30 for full-orchestra concerts.

Museums

National Museum of Wildlife Art
2820 Rungius Rd. off U.S. Hwy. 26 near Jackson, Wyo. • (307) 733-5771

This museum building, whose startling, award-winning design will remind you of a crumbling pueblo or an ancient castle, opened in the fall of 1997. It has been completely funded by donations from more than 600 individuals, foundations and corporations. The museum is located next to the National Elk Refuge, as though to place the art as close to its inspiration as possible. Twelve exhibit rooms house special shows and a permanent collection that includes the work of greats like John Clymer, C.M. Russell, Carl Rungius and George Catlin. The auditorium is home to an enticing array of films, symposiums and lectures, some of them free. Last year they included a Wildlife Film Festival, a weeklong Photography at the Summit workshop, a lecture and slide show on saddlemaking and another on the history of Navajo textiles (ask for a calendar at the desk).

The museum is open seven days a week, summer and winter. In spring and fall, Sunday hours are shortened. Adult entry fees are $5. The on-premises Rising Sage Cafe serves light meals during museum hours.

Galleries

Jackson prides itself on its art galleries, most focusing on high-quality Western and wildlife art. There are more than 30 galleries in the Hole, with new ones opening every year. Most of our picks were recommended by gallery owners and artists; nearly all are an easy walk from each other and town square, so park your car and spend an afternoon enjoying the impressive Jackson art scene.

Center Street Gallery
110 Center St., Jackson, Wyo.
- **(307) 733-1115**

Its sculptures are of wildlife, all right, but they're slant-lined, elongated, shaped from poly-resin, stone and steel as well as the traditional bronze. Eleven years ago when Beth Overcast opened Center Street, no local gallery focused on abstract expressionism, bold colors or startling shapes. She decided to do something about that. Much of the work Overcast displays is one-of-a-kind. She selects pieces that seem to her stimulating, alive and active. Two of her more popular artists are Taos-based painter Malcolm Furlow, who renders traditional Western subjects in startling colors and simple lines, and Colorado-based Mary Jane Schmidt, who paints large, bold colored abstracts and florals. Center Street closes on Sundays during the spring and fall.

Gerald Anthony Shippen Sculpture Studio
185 N. Center St., Jackson, Wyo.
- **(307) 733-6171**

Shippen's little gallery isn't easy to find unless you know it's on the second floor of the Home Ranch building, accessed through a sort of back door. You're not stopping here to take in an extensive collection of painting and sculpture. What you'll see is Shippen's work and that of a few friends and select acquaintances — and probably Shippen. He creates much of his bronze sculpture in the little studio attached to this little gallery. His subjects are both human and animal, slightly stylized and intricately detailed.

This Wyoming native, whose work is held in private collections and museums around the world, has been sculpting Western figures for 20 years. When he's not working in one of his two studios, he often goes out into nearby mountains and works on location. Shippen conducts summer art workshops for those with a hankering to become artists. The gallery is open Monday through Saturday in summer, and Tuesday through Saturday with abbreviated hours in winter, fall and spring.

Images of Nature
170 N. Cache, Jackson, Wyo.
- **(307) 733-9752**

Thomas Mangelsen's wildlife photography is internationally famous and locally beloved. Of his 12 galleries in six states and Hong Kong, the Jackson location was first. Mangelsen sells limited edition prints of his striking wildlife images. If your budget is tight, you can shop the gallery for his cards, books and posters. Upstairs you may view videos that teach you more about Mangelsen and his photography. The large Jackson gallery is open seven days a week, year round (for more, see our Close-up on Mangelsen in this chapter).

The Legacy Gallery
150 Center St., Jackson, Wyo.
- **(307) 733-2353**

Like many Jackson galleries, The Legacy specializes in traditional, representational Western art. Wildlife, landscape, Native American and cowboy subjects abound, as does sporting art featuring anglers and hunters. You'll find Teton scenes here as well. Showcased on a table with legs made from the arcing horns of Texas Longhorns, several award-winning jewelers are represented in silver and gold, turquoise and other semiprecious gems. Jewelry ranges in price from $80 to $10,500. The Legacy prides itself on catering not only to the experienced art collector, but also to the novice: Staff members help you educate yourself about specific artists and the collecting world. The Legacy closes on winter Sundays.

Light Reflections
35 E. Deloney, Jackson, Wyo.
- **(307) 733-4016, (800) 346-5223**

One of two photo galleries we recommend in Jackson, Light Reflections showcases the work of landscape photographer Frederic Joy. Not only has Joy done some breathtaking work with the local breathtaking scenery, but his photos of farm country and Utah sandstone also turn the contours of land, sky and rock into abstract compositions of shape and color. Joy hand prints all of his work, so what you see on the wall is exactly what the artist envisioned in his mind. Another good reason to stop by Light Reflections is the affordable options available here if you're looking to buy but don't want to max your credit card. Small matted prints of Joy's work, full-sized posters of his and other fine Western photography, even greeting cards, can satisfy your desire to own lovely art without paying gallery prices. Light Reflections generally closes on winter Sundays.

Martin-Harris Gallery
60 E. Broadway, Jackson, Wyo.
• (307) 733-0350, (800) 366-7814

Gallery owner Marty Kruzich says, "It took hundreds of years to bring the West this far." We say it's about time. This 7,000-square-foot gallery hosts modern Western art at its most striking and whimsical. There's nothing here without surprise capability, but the most fun pieces aren't the paintings or even the sculptures, though some of them are bigger than you. It's the furniture. Fourteen furniture artisans showcase work here — leather, wood and forged steel pieces ranging from fanciful to stolid. Every piece is unique. All of these artisans will also work with you, creating your offbeat dream couch, chair or armoire. Among the more than 40 artists represented by this gallery are John Nieto, Nelson Boren, Bill Schenk and Anne Coe.

Mountain Trails Gallery
172 Center St., Jackson, Wyo.
• (307) 734-8150

The newest gallery we've listed here belongs to bronze sculptor Vic Payne. His work and that of other bronze artists is well represented here. So are works by the very collectible Russian artist Oleg Stavrowsky, whose oil paintings Payne displays by special arrange-

ment. Although themes and subjects tend toward traditional Western, some treatments are more impressionistic than representational. Mountain Trails also showcases the work of emerging young artists (often available at precast prices). Sometimes you'll find them working on their pieces in the gallery. When we were there, 20-year-old Chris Schiller was putting the finishing touches on the clay version of a rioting elk sculpture. The self-taught young artist's work, several pieces of which are on display at Mountain Trails, shows Schiller's fast slide from traditional representational sculpture to a more impressionistic, individualistic feel. Mountain Trails closes Sundays in winter.

Trailside Americana Fine Art Galleries
105 N. Center, Jackson, Wyo.
• (307) 733-3186

This is one of the oldest galleries in Jackson and one of the largest Western galleries in the country. Trailside specializes in representational treatments of Western scenes, wildlife, mountain landscapes and Native Americans. Work from more than 60 artists, many of them members of the Cowboy Artists of America, cycles through here. Some of these artists are very collectible: Clyde Aspevig, a landscape painter of increasing renown, and G. Harvey, whose busy but somehow cozy 19th-century city scenes are a pleasant contrast to cowboys, elk and mountains, are both represented here. You can also view many smaller table sculptures. The showcased artists work in monumental scale as well.

Two Grey Hills Indian Arts & Jewelry
Corner of Broadway and King, Jackson, Wyo. • (307) 733-2677

Two Grey Hills names both an area in New Mexico and the fine Navajo weavings produced there. It's a perfect moniker for this high-end gallery, now in its 21st year, which specializes in one-of-a-kind Native American art. Pottery,

---

INSIDERS' TIP

According to the 1990 census, one out of every 83 Montana residents is a working artist.

The Whitney Gallery of Western Art shows the work
of artists who captured the West's mythical beauty.

weavings and jewelry, much of it museum quality, cram the little shop. You'll find jewelry you can easily afford and pieces you'll want to keep in your safety deposit box; you'll find weavings ranging between $100 and $16,000. Two Grey Hills closes some Sundays in winter.

Wilcox Gallery
1975 N. U.S. Hwy. 89, Jackson, Wyo.
• (307) 733-6450

If you're wondering why we'd send you clear out of town, nearly to the Wildlife Art Museum, you won't after you've wandered through the work featured here. First, it's not all Western. If you've been to other galleries in town, you're probably ready for paintings from two popular Chinese artists, or wooden bowls so finely carved they're translucent, or unique wooden boxes whose only decoration is the scalloped live edge, sometimes with bark still attached, wavering across the front of the lid. But the biggest reason to come out here is Jim Wilcox, local landscape painter, whose work is showcased here and whose son manages the gallery. Wilcox's work has received seven awards from the Arts for the Parks competition, where artists from around the world celebrate this nation's national parks and monuments. One piece is

part of the permanent collection at the Cowboy Hall of Fame in Oklahoma. If you're looking for an inexpensive souvenir rather than fine art, check out the Jim Wilcox T-shirts and posters.

Wilcox first came here in 1959 for the series of summer jobs that put him through college. He fell in love with Jackson then, and when the time came to open his own gallery in 1969, he opened it here. Wilcox Gallery is open Monday through Saturday year round, with shorter hours in winter.

Eastern Idaho

Idaho Falls, Idaho

Arts Centers and Organizations

Eagle Rock Art Guild
P.O. Box 2542, Idaho Falls, ID 83403
• (208) 522-4409

The guild's primary events are their three annual arts shows. The juried summer Eagle Rock Art Guild Sidewalk Art Show is the biggest (see our Annual Events chapter for more); the fall show is also juried for non-guild members; and the spring show is dedicated to work by members only. The guild has about 100 members. Most, but not all, are artists. In addition to their art shows, the Guild sponsors scholarships and art contests for kids.

Idaho Falls Arts Council
498 A St., Idaho Falls, Idaho
• (208) 522-0471

If you want to learn about the local arts scene, this is a smart first stop. The Arts Council can hook you into the more than 15 local performing and visual arts groups, among which are the American Guild of Organists, the Eastern Idaho Photographic Society, the Snake River Woodcarvers, the Weavers and Spinners of Idaho Falls and the Idaho Falls Opera Theatre. Idaho Falls Arts Council has two other important roles in town. First, they maintain a 2,700-square-foot art gallery, the only public showcase of its kind in town, with parquet floors, stained-glass windows and high ceilings. The gallery is located in the Miles and Virginia Willard Arts Center. Second, the council spearheads the effort to refurbish the old theater, formerly called the Colonial Arts Center, a 1,000-seat house dating to the 1920s and expected to open in December of 1998. Once the home of vaudeville and silent film performances, the Willard Arts Center will provide Idaho Falls with a more intimate venue for plays and other performances than the Civic Auditorium can. To date, more than $4 million has been raised to refurbish and reopen the new arts center and its gallery.

Performing Arts

Actors' Repertory Theater of Idaho Inc.
P.O. Box 50423, Idaho Falls ID 83405
• (208) 524-1489

This active volunteer theater group has performed 25 full-length shows over its 11-year history. They schedule four shows a year, usually classics by playwrights like Neil Simon, Oscar Wilde or Ira Levin. You can catch a performance at the Stardust (around $18 for dinner and the show or $10 just for dessert and the show) at 680 Lindsay Boulevard, Idaho Falls Idaho. Opening night at the Stardust is popular because it often coincides with a wine tasting. One weekend of every show usually happens at University Place Auditorium, located at 1776 Science Center Drive, Idaho Falls, Idaho. Tickets there are around $6. ARTI occasionally does charity performances and one-acts for holiday parties. In summer you can sometimes catch a free performance at the band shelter in Freeman Park. If you're moving to town, remember that these folks can always use help; they'd love to tap your acting, set building, writing or management skills. Call ARTI for show schedules and locations.

Idaho Falls Opera Theatre
P.O. Box 50204, Idaho Falls, ID 83405
• (208) 522-0471

Greater Yellowstone residents are willing to drive for their dose of culture: Idaho Falls community opera theater draws over one-fourth of its audiences for the twice annual shows from out of town. Audience members are from Montana, Wyoming and Utah, as well as from down the street. The company's spring productions tend to be light operettas or musicals; fall shows are heavier opera selections. One of the things this group prides itself on is a reservoir of singers talented enough that lead roles are generally performed by local amateurs, not guest professionals. Most Idaho Falls Opera Theatre shows involve about 30 performers and 120 orchestra members, set builders, costumers, etc. The 20-year-old organization also hosts one Broadway show per year, usually in January or February. Reserved seats for operas run around $15; general admission is around $8. Seat prices for the Broadway shows vary according to the acting company involved. Shows are generally held at the Civic Auditorium, located at 501 S. Holmes Avenue, Idaho Falls, Idaho.

The Idaho Falls Symphony
498 A St., Idaho Falls, Idaho
• (208) 529-1080

This volunteer symphony began in 1949. In 1991 a chorale was added, expanding the symphony's range. The Idaho Falls Symphony plays a five-concert season, including one Pops concert. Guest artists are often world-class; they've included names like violinists Daniel Heifetz and Nadja Salerno-

Thomas Mangelsen, Nature Photographer

Thomas Mangelsen learned to love wildlife as a boy, hunting and fishing along the Platte River in his native Nebraska. That love led to undergraduate and graduate work in biology and zoology and later to jobs shooting educational wildlife films. He first saw Jackson Hole in 1978. Its rugged beauty and plentiful wildlife stuck in his mind.

Even while he worked in films, Mangelsen pursued his first love, still photography. By 1981 he had a sizable collection of prints under his belt; he decided it was time to open a gallery in Jackson Hole. Most photographers who manage to make a living at all do it by selling their work to magazines, books and calendar companies. "I had this idea that maybe you could sell limited-edition photographs," Mangelsen told a reporter for the *Jackson Hole Guide*. At first it wasn't easy. Mangelsen house-sat in winters and spent his summers living alternately in a shack in Black Canyon, a barn in Ditch Creek and a garage room in Wilson, Wyoming. None of these havens had running water, and a couple had no electricity. For nearly a decade Mangelsen supported his work more than it supported him.

But the man produced beautiful images. Maybe, as one writer put it, it was his commitment to "capture creatures on film while they are immersed in the arduous business of survival." His images record polar bears, backs to a wind that whips snow into icy tongues around their feet; an Alaskan brown bear at the top of a waterfall, jaws extended to snap shut on a huge leaping salmon; a bald eagle, soaring against an ominous sky. "I'm not interested in the cutesy wildlife image," Mangelsen says.

The days of unheated housing with no running water are past. Now Mangelsen has 12 galleries, including one in Hong Kong. Probably his most famous work has been with polar bears, but the prolific photographer has also created spectacular images of bald eagles, grizzly bears, trumpeter swans, cheetahs, Teton landscapes and more. In fact, with a half-million slides in his photo library, there's probably not much Mangelsen hasn't photographed — except captive animals. According to Mangelsen, many wildlife photos and most shots of wary predators like wolves and cougars are taken at game farms. Mangelsen says that 99 percent of the mountain lion photos you see in magazines were not shot in the wild. Despite the fact that a morning at a game farm could produce a year's worth of marketable images, Mangelsen shoots all of his photos in natural, wild settings.

For more on Mangelsen's Jackson, Wyoming, gallery, called Images of Nature, see the listing in this chapter.

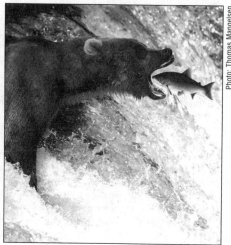

Photo: Thomas Mangelsen

Nature photographer Thomas Mangelsen captures compelling images of everyday events in the natural world.

Sonnenberg and pianists Misha Dicter and Alexander Toradze. Adult tickets range from $10 to $18. Season tickets range from $45 to $70 . Concerts are held at the Civic Auditorium, 501 S. Holmes Avenue, Idaho Falls, Idaho, except for the Pops concert, which is held at the Shilo Inn, 780 Lindsay Boulevard, Idaho Falls, Idaho.

Snake River Chamber Orchestra
620 Moonlite, Idaho Falls, Idaho
• **(208) 542-0577**

This pleasant recent addition to the Idaho Falls performing arts scene is the brainchild of conductor David Rutherford, who moved here from Afton, Wyoming, and noticed that Idaho Falls lacked a chamber orchestra. Chamber orchestras range in size from two to 20 musicians; Rutherford's group consists of about 25 volunteers who, he promises, will have paid positions within two years. The more delicate, intimate performances of a chamber group have been well received here. Since the orchestra's first performance in the fall of 1997, corporate sponsors have offered support; concerts are well attended.

The orchestra has a five-show season from September to May, with a special January show that combines silent films and vaudeville with the chamber orchestra as musical accompaniment, a combination Rutherford says is authentic early 20th-century film presentation. Tickets for adults are $7 in advance and $8 at the door. Concerts are currently staged at University Place, 1776 Science Center Drive, Idaho Falls, Idaho. However, the orchestra hopes to move to the soon-to-be-completed Willard Arts Center in the fall of 1998.

Southwestern Montana

Bozeman, Montana

Arts Centers and Organizations

Emerson Cultural Center
111 S. Grand Ave., Bozeman, Mont.
• **(406) 587-9797**

This cultural mecca housed in an old Bozeman school building is home to not only 40 studios, but also about 10 galleries. On any given day, the halls ring with the sound of music from musicians in their upstairs studios teaching piano, string and horn instrument workshops. A hub of art, music, dance and design studios rented by local artists, Emerson Cultural Center is a living, changing gallery of the artists' work. A dozen or so shops and galleries, including the Indian Uprising Gallery, Botannica Fine Art, A Thread Runs Through It and the Tibetan Trader, offer the wares of local artists. In addition, the Emerson Cultural Center has an auditorium that hosts regular theatrical events.

Montana Arts
321 E. Main St., Bozeman, Mont.
• **(406) 585-9551**

Founded in 1948 as the Montana Institute of the Arts, this nonprofit organization acts as an umbrella bookkeeper, grant administrator and conference organizer for several arts organizations. In the 1960s, Montana Arts was instrumental in bringing arts groups together, and was set up to accept money from the National Endowment for the Arts for the state of Montana. The organization served in this role for 8 years until the Montana Arts Council came into being.

Each year Montana Arts organizes an artist showcase for the Montana Performing Arts Consortium. Montana Arts also acts as a nonprofit umbrella for emerging arts organizations, it sponsors special projects including artist exchange programs with Russia. An offshoot of this exchange program is an exhibit from the Brodsky Museum in St. Petersburg, Russia that is to be displayed in the fall of 1998 at the Yellowstone Museum of Art in Billings, Montana. Montana Arts also sponsors the Mary Brennan Clapp Memorial Poetry Contest for Montana poets.

The Montana Arts Council
316 N. Park Ave., Helena, Mont.
• **(406) 444-6430**

This state agency is charged with promoting and expanding the role of arts and culture in Montana. The Arts Council administers grants and other programs that benefit all arts endeavors in Montana.

Photo: Winslow Studio

The Vigilante Theatre Company showcases popular performances, such as this production of *Sherlock Is That You?*

Performing Arts

Big Sky Dance Center
2304 N. Seventh Ave., Bozeman, Mont.
• **(406) 586-1880**

Operated by Jeff and Cathy Giese, the Big Sky Dance Center offers ballet, dance, modern and tap classes to dancers of all ages. The Gieses also operate the Montana Dance Alliance, a nonprofit organization designed to raise funds to help defray costs so that area students can enjoy top-quality dance workshops with nationally known instructors.

Bozeman Symphony Orchestra and Symphonic Choir
104 E. Main, Bozeman, Mont.
• **(406) 585-9774**

Concerts presented by the Bozeman Symphony Orchestra have become so popular in the past few years that it's best to buy tickets well ahead of time. Celebrating its 30th anniversary this year, the Bozeman Symphony is a nonprofit orchestra that began in the Montana State University School of Music, then crept into the community. Each year, the 80-member symphony presents five concerts. In addition, the symphony offers a family concert that costs only $10 per household, a gala fund-raising event and a free concert for fourth graders. An 80-member choir also performs — sometimes with the symphony, and sometimes alone.

The Bozeman Symphony performs in the Willson auditorium, 404 W. Main. Except for an annual gala performance, which is more costly, tickets generally cost from $10 to $22 and can be purchased by stopping by or calling the office. Tickets for the family performance cost $3 for adults and $2 for children. Student tickets are discounted.

Montana Ballet Company
221 E. Main, Bozeman, Mont.
• (406) 587-7192

There are two arms to this group. The first is the Montana Dance Company, a nonprofit endeavor that produces and presents three to five performances each year. The Montana Dance Company also offers workshops each year taught by some of the nation's finest dancers. And it organizes an educational outreach program for rural students. Two or three of their annual performances use local and Montana dancers, while one or two are presented by outside dance companies.

The second arm of Montana Ballet, the Montana Dance School, was founded 20 years ago and now has 200 students from 3 to 50 years old each year.

Montana Shakespeare in the Parks
MSU Sub Rm. 354, Bozeman, Mont.
• (406) 994-5885

For 25 years Montana Shakespeare in the Parks has performed in the parks and prairies of Montana. A part of Montana State University's College of Arts and Architecture, this troupe of a dozen or so professional actors plays in communities across the state from Polson to Miles City, from Libby to Livingston. Their performances are free to the public.

In addition to about 50 tour dates scheduled for 1998 in small Montana towns, Shakespeare in the Parks will present *A Midsummer Night's Dream* in June at Montana State University's Grove east of the Duck Pond on 11th Street. The company will also present *A Winter's Tale* at the Grove and will perform at Lindley Park during the Sweet Pea Festival (see our Annual Events chapter). Other 1998 performances include *A Midsummer Night's Dream* at MSU's Strand Union Theater and *A Winter's Tale* at the Strand during Shakespeare in the Parks, which ends the '98 season. For information about their tour schedule, call 994-3901. The Strand Union is on Grant Street, west of South 11th Avenue.

Vigilante Theater Company
111 S. Grand Ave., Bozeman, Mont.
• (406) 586-3897

For 17 years, four actors calling themselves the Vigilante Theater have toured Montana and the Northwest with original productions indigenous to the Northwest. While only two of the four founding actors are still with the company, their style is the same. They bring it all — lights, sets, costumes, props — presenting unique productions like *Who Shot the Sheriff*, the story of a 100-year-old shooting, and *Wuf!*, the satirical story of wolf reintroduction in Yellowstone Park. Since this company tours a lot, and often does private performances, it's best to call Joanne Eaton at the above number to find out how you can catch their act.

Galleries

Frame Work Designs
119 E. Main, Bozeman, Mont.
• (406) 586-3626, (800) 533-9396

Owned for nearly 15 years by founder Skip Tubbs, Frame Work Designs on Bozeman's Main Street, features Western wildlife and landscapes by mostly Montana and Bozeman artists. In addition to original oil and watercolor paintings, Tubbs carries sculptures with a Western theme and limited edition prints by Bev Doolittle and other Western artists. Frame Work Designs is a dealer for three print publishing companies: Greenwich Workshop, Mill Pond Press and Hadley House. These days, it's the original oil landscapes that are hot at this gallery, open year-round from 10 AM until 5:30 PM, Monday through Friday, and from 10 AM until 4 PM on Saturdays.

Artifacts
308 E. Main, Bozeman, Mont.
• (406) 586-3755, (888) 586-3755

One of the first craft galleries in the area, Artifacts still features finely crafted art 20

INSIDERS' TIP

In Livingston, Montana, you can sip wine and walk between several downtown galleries during three summer gallery walks scheduled each June, July and August. For more information call the Livingston Chamber of Commerce at 222-0850.

years after Patricia Bloom opened its doors in Bozeman. Sandwiched between John Bozeman's Bistro and O'Brien's, a restaurant serving fine continental cuisine, Artifacts takes advantage of the dinner crowd through an arrangement made between Bloom and a former owner of O'Brien's. Diners can mosey over, with wine in hand, from O'Brien's into Artifacts and browse through the gallery items while waiting for their dinner. Current owners Jim and Linda Brown are the second to own Artifacts since Bloom sold it in the mid-1980s. At Artifacts, open seven days a week, from 10 AM until 9 PM, you might find one-of-a-kind jewelry, ceramics or wood work.

Emerson Cultural Center
11 S. Grand Ave., Bozeman, Mont.
• (406) 587-9797

There are about a dozen galleries and shops in the Emerson Cultural Center that feature a range of art media by local artists. For more information, see the previous entry under Arts Centers and Organizations.

Grey Fox
23 W. Main St., Bozeman, Mont.
• (406) 587-9778

If it's local landscapes or nostalgic Western scenes and buildings you're looking for, chances are you'll find it at the Grey Fox way out West on Bozeman's Main Street. When owner Pam Coleman bought this gallery four years ago, it was called La Petite, a gallery that sold only miniatures. The Grey Fox is open year-round from 9:30 AM until 5:30 PM.

Old Main Gallery and Framing
246 E. Main St., Bozeman, Mont.
• (406) 587-8860, (888) 587-8860

The oldest gallery in Bozeman — it's been there since 1964 — the Old Main is both a gallery and a booming framing shop with five full-time certified picture framers, more than any other gallery in Montana. In addition to the framing, the Old Main handles mostly two-dimensional Western, wildlife, Native American and fishing art as well as antique paper art, with a wide range of prices in both prints and originals. Among the artists handled by Old Main are Native American artist Kevin Red Star, Daryl

Poulin and Gary Carter. You'll also find prints by wildlife artist Nancy Glazier and originals as well as prints by fish artist Michael Stidham. The Old Main is open seven days a week from 9 AM to 7 PM Monday through Friday, and from 9 AM until 5 PM on Saturday and Sunday.

Livingston, Montana

Performing Arts

Blue Slipper Theater
113 E. Callender St., Livingston, Mont.
• (406) 222-7720

Since 1964, this nonprofit volunteer community theater has been presenting three plays per year (mysteries, dramas and comedies) to the residents of Livingston. Supported by patrons and housed in a turn-of-the-century sandstone building in downtown Livingston, the Blue Slipper Theater seats 85. Reservations can be made by calling the above number. Tickets cost $7.

Yellowstone Ballet Company
109 S. B St., Livingston, Mont.
• (406) 222-0430

This nonprofit ballet company, owned by Rick Pittendop and Kathleen Rakela, both former professional dancers, instructs about 50 local Livingston dancers September through May. Yellowstone Ballet Company puts on one major production each year, making their own backdrops and scenery.

Galleries

Burl Jones RocheJaune Galerie
5237 U.S. Hwy. 89 S. #1, Livingston, Mont. • (406) 222-8719

You'll recognize the Burl Jones RocheJaune Galerie by the bronze eagle in front of the building. Jones, a Livingston dentist who retired in 1991 to devote full time to sculpting, is just one of the artists featured in the RocheJaune (which, by the way, is French for "yellow stone"). In addition to Jones' sculptures, you will find oil paintings and limited edition prints with a — you guessed it — Western and wildlife theme. The RocheJaune is open seven days a week from 9 AM to 5 PM Monday through Saturday, and from

10 AM to 3 PM on Sundays. To get to this gallery from Interstate 90, take Exit 333, turn south on U.S. Highway 89. The bronze eagle flies about a half-mile south on the West side of the highway.

Danforth Gallery
106 N. Main St., Livingston, Mont.
• **(406) 222-6510**

Operated by the Park County Friends of the Arts, the Danforth is Livingston's oldest gallery and its only nonprofit art gallery. From June through December, the Danforth features about 60 mostly Montana artists. All proceeds from their sales go back into the arts program, which includes a two-month film festival each winter and the Main Street Theater, a series of winter variety shows. During their summer season, the Danforth is open from 10 AM until 6 PM seven days a week.

Visions West Gallery
108 S. Main, Livingston, Mont.
• **(406) 222-0337**

Open since 1991, Visions West features Western wildlife and sporting art, including original paintings, photography, sculpture, ceramics or pottery and gifts. During the summer of 1997, owner Evelyn Walinchus had several shows including the work of Montana ranch photographer Barbara Van Cleve and a set of 50 original watercolors of fish painted by her husband, artist/guide/author Rod Walinchus. During the winter, Visions West is open from 10 AM until 5 PM, Monday through Saturday. Summer hours are flexible, but generally extended to seven days a week.

The Wade Gallery
116 N. Main St., Livingston, Mont.
• **(406) 222-0404**

Established in 1986 and open year round, the Wade Gallery features fine art by regional artists and has Montana's most complete selection of photographs and photogravures from *The North American Indian* by Edward Sheriff Curtis. Owner Kelly Wade, who has built a reputation for offering top-quality work by local artisans, also features a selection of pottery, weavings and jewelry. Wade provides a complete framing service and is open seven days a week during the summer months. The rest of the year, she recommends calling to find out seasonal hours,

since store hours during slow times can be subject to the weather and other mercurial factors.

Red Lodge, Montana

Performing Arts

Red Lodge Chamber Orchestra
P.O. Box 456, Red Lodge, MT 59068
• **(406) 446-3419**

This group, which performs monthly winter concerts in groups ranging from small ensembles to a 14-member orchestra (depending on the composer), mushroomed after one individual decided he wanted to get together with others to make music. The orchestra plays in various locations including Red Lodge's Roman Theater, the Carbon County Arts Guild and a local resort. They also perform with a local chorus. The orchestra plays in various locations including Red Lodge's Roman Theater, 120 S. Broadway Avenue.

Carbon County Arts Guild
11 W. Eighth St., Red Lodge, Mont.
• **(406) 446-1370**

This nonprofit arts organization and gallery is housed in the old railroad depot where it operates an art gallery featuring the work of members. The guild also exhibits monthly shows by well-known area artists. The Carbon County Arts Guild also sponsors workshops for both adults and children.

Northwestern Wyoming

Cody, Wyoming

Galleries

Big Horn Galleries
1167 and 1414 Sheridan Ave., Cody, Wyo. • **(307) 527-7587**

At one time Bob and Nancy Brown's Big Horn Gallery was the only art gallery in Cody. Now one of a dozen or so, the Big Horn has split into two galleries on Sheridan Avenue, Cody's main street. The Big Horn Galleries feature fine art and limited edition prints with

Western and wildlife themes. These shops are the only places in the country where collectors can buy James Bama's work. Bama, a nationally known Western artist from Cody, used to display his work exclusively at a gallery in New York City. The Browns have owned and managed several galleries in the Greater Yellowstone area. The Big Horn is open year round from 9:30 AM to 5:30 PM.

Jordan Gallery
1349 Sheridan Ave., Cody, Wyo.
- **(307) 587-6689**

Known as "the guy with the good eye," Jerry Jordan features four types of art in his gallery: turn-of-the-century Indian artifacts, rare Western books and historic ephemera, Dan Begg sculptures and historic Navajo rugs. Begg is a multi-award-winning Canadian sculptor whose work is reasonably priced. Jordan Gallery, open since 1992, is one of only two galleries in the United States that carries Begg's work. For serious collectors, Jordan will dig until he comes up with that hard-to-find piece you've been hunting for. The gallery is open 9 AM to 9 PM June though September, and 9 AM to 5 PM the rest of the year. Jordan closes on Sundays.

Simpson Gallagher
1115 13th St., Cody, Wyo.
- **(307) 587-4022**

Owner Sue Simpson Gallagher returned several years ago to her hometown of Cody, then opened a gallery. She features the work of her "gang of friends," who happen to be nationally known artists from across the country. Featured work includes the oil paintings of plein-air artist Clyde Aspevig and watercolors by cowboy artist William Matthews. She also carries sculptures by Walter Matia. The gallery specialty, though, is a collection of etchings with traditional sporting, wildlife, cowboy and landscape themes. The Simpson Gallagher stays open all year. The gallery is open 10 AM to 6 PM Tuesday through Saturday during the winter. The hours are the same for the summer, with the addition of being open Monday.

Whitney Gallery of Western Art
Buffalo Bill Historical Center, 720 Sheridan Ave., Cody, Wyo.
- **(307) 587-4771**

This gallery has one of the most extensive collections of Western art anyplace. A separate wing houses a collection featuring Frederic Remington. His replicated New Rochelle, New York, studio brings the artist and his work to life. Charles M. Russell, turn-of-the-century "cowboy artist," also rates his own wing in the Whitney. Other names you may recognize include early 19th-century painter George Catlin; William Tylee Ranney, a self-taught artist determined to capture the Native American culture in oil; and Thomas Moran, a 19th-century artist who traveled with the 1871 Hayden Expedition and whose sketches helped convince Congress to establish Yellowstone Park. You'll also see James Earl Fraser's "The End of the Trail," the famous bronze sculpture that depicts a stooped-over, spear-carrying Indian sitting on his sagging, wind-blown horse. Recently, the Whitney has begun aggressively collecting contemporary Western art as well.

A two-day admission ticket to the Buffalo Bill Historical Center costs $8 for adults, $6.50 for senior citizens, $4 for students 13 and older, $2 for children ages 6 through 12 and free for kids 5 and younger.

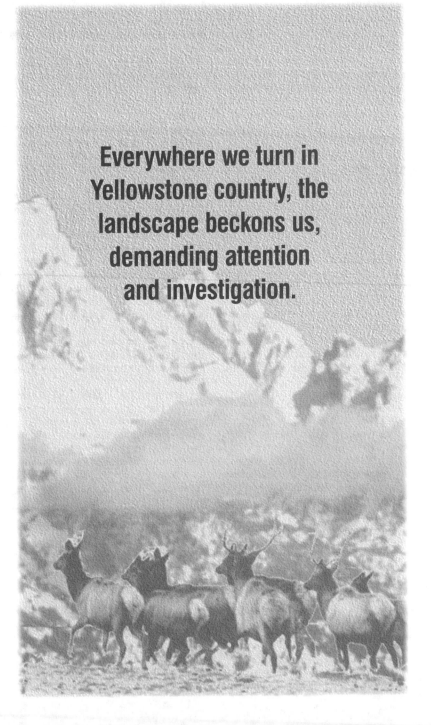

Everywhere we turn in Yellowstone country, the landscape beckons us, demanding attention and investigation.

Attractions

"A thousand Yellowstone wonders are calling, 'Look up and down and round about you!'"

— John Muire, *Our National Parks*, 1909

Who can resist stopping to watch the clear waters of mountain streams cascading down a boulder-strewn gorge? Or the sun setting on snow-frosted peaks? Or a bull elk, his antlers in velvet, basking in the morning sun? For that matter, who but the most hurried wouldn't be attracted to a grassy spot by a river winding through a meadow? Everywhere we turn in Yellowstone country, the landscape beckons us, demanding attention and investigation.

Oddly, it's the determination to see the "Attractions" that drives so many people so fast past those smaller, unannounced attractions. As you drive through Greater Yellowstone, we urge you to answer the call to explore the unexpected. We're betting that you'll gain the same sense of wonder that made early tourists dub this wild place "wonderland."

In this chapter we have lifted the veil only slightly on some of the natural mysteries of Greater Yellowstone, like geysers and mountain ranges. We've also listed some of the region's human-created attractions like museums, commercial hot springs and winter sleigh rides. As you will see, for your convenience we have chosen mostly roadside attractions. They're our favorites, but they're not all that's out there waiting for you. Explore. Enjoy.

Yellowstone National Park

General information about Park admission fees, services and more can be found in the Parks and Forests chapter. Highlighted attractions are listed below.

In the Park

Geothermal Features

Geothermal features are what first attracted expeditions to this wild country. And, with the exception of a stray bear, it's the brewing, bubbling bowls and cones that still attract most visitors today. That's why we've devoted a little extra attention to geothermal features in this chapter. We've provided the highlights, and leave you to decide which basins you want to visit. Before you tour the basins, we recommend you read our Natural World chapter for a brief explanation of what's happening below the surface.

We haven't told you how to get to these places because they're well-marked on the map you'll get as you enter the Park and on road signs. Generally, though, they're along the western edge of the Park.

Mammoth Hot Springs

Mammoth Hot Springs is a mysteriously beautiful steaming, growing, living sculpture made of travertine (calcium carbonate). These springs, emanating from a hillside above Park headquarters, discharge about 500 gallons of hot water per minute. The water deposits about 2 tons of travertine limestone per day, which means that these incredibly beautiful terraced formations grow. Unfortunately, they don't always grow where Park managers want them. East of the Mammoth Road, for example, you'll see the very white Opal Terrace near a house. This terrace, which grows at a rate of a foot per year, took over a tennis court in 1947 and now threatens a historic home built in 1908 and designed by famous Park architect Robert Reamer.

Minerva Terrace, the centerpiece of the Lower Terraces, includes a rainbow of bright colors and ornate travertine formations. Several other terraces and springs cover the hillside and provide a landscape that records the changing flow of the springs' waters. Boardwalks wind around the terraces, and a one-way road loops around the Upper Terraces.

Norris Geyser Basin

The Norris Geyser Basin is the only basin with acidic water, which means it doesn't have the varied and beautiful coloration created by algae that other geyser basins have. The water here is much hotter (a drill hole in this basin came upon 459-degree water only 1,087 feet below the surface), and the geyser activity, more violent. For some reason, during late summer, all of the Norris springs and geysers become simultaneously muddy.

The Porcelain Basin in the northern half is full of very active, constantly changing geysers. More than 40 geysers dot this basin; some are inactive, others suddenly rear their heads. The 1-mile trail through this area is well-signed and explains the various thermal features.

The Back Basin on the southern end of Norris contains more than 60 geysers interspersed among the trees. One of the most interesting is Steamboat Geyser, which didn't become active until 1878. Then it exploded with such force it blew huge rocks into the air killing nearby trees and plants with its burning mud. Steamboat behaved itself until 1911, when it rocked the area again in a series of violent eruptions. For the next 50 years, the geyser was again docile. From 1961 until 1969, Steamboat erupted 90 times, often very vigorously. Steamboat has been relatively inactive since 1985, but since 1969, some eruptions — no one can ever predict when this monster will go off — have been so violent that the geyser has shot as high as 380 feet into the air, more than three times as high as Old Faithful. The roar during its eruption is so loud people nearby cannot even shout at each other and make themselves heard. Legend has it that one winter eruption could be heard 14 miles away at Madison Junction.

Echinus Geyser is a favorite for several reasons. It is large and beautiful, and it erupts often and fairly regularly — every 20 to 80 minutes. Also, you can get very close to it.

The Veteran Geyser is a teaser that often keeps people watching it expectantly because it always looks like it's about to erupt. If you watch long enough, you won't be disappointed. This geyser erupts at irregular intervals from 20 minutes to three hours.

Lower Geyser Basin

The Lower Geyser Basin is the largest in Yellowstone Park and contains a dozen geyser groups including the Fountain Paint Pots, so called because they contain creamy mud that resembles thick latex paint.

This Basin has a number of interesting geysers. Among them is the Great Fountain Geyser, first geyser to greet the Cook-Folsom-Peterson Party (see our History chapter to learn more about these explorers). Great Fountain erupted just as they came upon it. Journals from the expedition indicate that to a man, they whooped and threw their hats in the air. Just down the road is White Dome, a geyser so old the cone is about 20 feet high while the spout has been nearly sealed off by mineral deposits.

Farther down the road is the Pink Dome Group containing Bead Geyser, the most regular erupter in the Park. In the Firehole Lake Group you'll see Firehole Lake, the largest and hottest of several pools with a total water output of about 3,500 gallons per minute. Below it is a larger hot pool, Hot Lake, which actually contains the runoff of Firehole Lake and has a much lower temperature than its upstream neighbor.

The Fountain Group is the largest in the Lower Basin, and the activity here increased dramatically after the 1959 earthquake. The activity at this spot indicates that these geysers are all interrelated underground because their eruptions are dependent on those of their neighbors.

The Thud Group is an interesting complex, mostly because of the history associated with them. This area was the site of the former Fountain Hotel, removed in 1927. Amazingly, the hotel's employees used these springs as dumps. In 1948, when Park officials tried to

www.insiders.com

See this and many other **Insiders' Guide®** destinations online — in their entirety.

Visit us today!

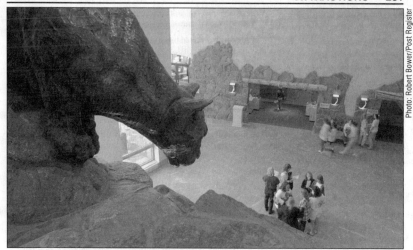

A larger-than-life bronze cougar peers down across the lobby
at the National Wildlife Art Museum near Jackson, Wyoming.

clean them, they removed up and removed an outrageous list of foreign objects including a 40-gallon drum, crocks, a pitchfork, wagon braces, a stew kettle, bath mats, an apron, a broom, a kerosene lamp, an oven rack and a whole lot more.

Midway Geyser Basin

There is one main attraction here: Grand Prismatic Spring, an expanse of amazingly beautiful water that comprises the largest hot spring in the Park and the third-largest in the world. In addition, you'll see Excelsior Geyser, once the most impressive geyser in Yellowstone Park. Excelsior discharges 4,000 gallons of hot water a minute. Now relatively inactive, from 1882 to 1888 it sprayed as high as 300 feet and had a 300-foot-wide base. Excelsior, which in those days erupted every 20 to 120 minutes, rumbled and roared so violently beneath the ground that those who camped nearby couldn't sleep. Scientists theorize that Excelsior blew its plumbing apart in the 1800s and can no longer build the pressure it needs to explode.

Upper Geyser Basin

With 150 geysers clustered in a square mile, the Upper Geyser Basin has the highest concentration of geysers anywhere in the world. It is also the home of Old Faithful and a number of other spectacular geysers. If you want to take in the entire Upper Basin, you'll have to spend two or three days to see all the majors erupt. As of 1991, more than 46,000 Old Faithful eruptions had been recorded with an average interval of 65 minutes. (Intervals varied between 33 and 120 minutes.) Eruption heights average about 120 feet with a duration of 1½ to 5 minutes.

A loop trail will take you around nearby Geyser Hill where nearly 50 big geysers are clustered. Among them you'll find Beehive Geyser, which has a beautifully shaped cone with a narrow vent that spews hot water up to 200 feet in the air like a fire-hose nozzle. Once fairly regular, Beehive now erupts infrequently. You'll be lucky to see this beaut spout.

Solitary Geyser was a quiet pool until 1925 when permission was given to use it as a swimming hole. Then it suddenly turned into a geyser erupting about 25 feet into the air.

The Giantess Geyser is a hummer. It came to life in 1997 after decades of relative dormancy and has been erupting every three to five days. Members of the Washburn Expedition of 1870 described the eruption of Giantess as one of the grandest experiences of their visit to Yellowstone country. Giantess bubbles and boils, sometimes for several days, before blasting up to 200 feet toward the sky. Its eruptions have a visible effect on neighboring geysers.

Castle Geyser is very old, as evidenced by its 12-foot-high cone that resembles a castle tower. Over the years, its eruptions have changed. Most recently, it likes to splash like a fountain for a few hours before erupting into a 20-minute display up to 80 feet high.

The Castle-Grand Group includes more than 40 geysers and is the best place to catch a multitude of major geyser eruptions. Some folks think Grand Geyser is the most impressive in the world. Grand erupts in a series of bursts. The first is about 100 feet high and lasts for about nine minutes. After completely shutting down, Grand erupts again, this time up to 200 feet, usually with succeeding spectacular bursts — sometimes only two, but in 1983 up to 11.

Lone Star Geyser Basin

Lone Star's regular eruptions (every three hours) last 30 minutes. But we think the nicest thing about Lone Star is you have to walk 2.5 miles away from the crowds to get there. The trail (an old road) begins on the highway near the Kepler Cascades of the Firehole River.

Throughout this basin you will find several springs and minor geysers. Probably the most interesting geyser besides Lone Star is the Buried Geyser, which erupts frequently and with violent force.

West Thumb Geyser Basin

In the West Thumb Geyser Basin (named for a thumb-shaped bay on the southwestern end of Yellowstone Lake) you'll find the famous and well-photographed Fishing Cone, an odd little gray structure filled with boiling water in the lake's shallows. Historians claim early explorers and visitors caught fish in the lake, then dipped them into the cone to cook in the boiling water. Visitors even donned aprons and cook's hats for photos at the Fishing Cone. Apparently, the Fishing Cone used to erupt fairly regularly to heights of up to 40 feet earlier in the century. Cooking fish in the cone isn't allowed these days.

Near the Fishing Cone you'll find a series of hot springs including Abyss Pool and Black Pool, both beautiful blue-green pools as alluring as any in the Park.

Other Park Attractions

Yellowstone Lake

Cradled atop the Yellowstone Plateau at 7,333 feet are the pure, frigid waters of Yellowstone Lake — 20 miles long and 14 miles wide. Amazingly, warm water rises out of fissures in the bottom of the lake, creating champagne-like bubbles. Despite these thermal features, the ice and snow that blanket the lake during the long winter months keep this lake so cold — the average temperature is 41 degrees — that swimming in it even in summer is discouraged.

Fishing is encouraged, however. Yellowstone Lake is home to the largest inland population of wild cutthroat trout in North America. Unfortunately, it also contains a growing population of lake trout, a non-native species that may threaten cutthroat populations in the lake.

For most people, the allure of Yellowstone Lake is its pristine beauty. On a clear day, the lake presents a huge expanse of glittering ripples with snow-capped peaks in the background. On other days the wind whips the lake's waters into churning, ocean-like waves. On the northern shores, you may see bison

INSIDERS' TIP

There's one attraction in the Greater Yellowstone that no one can predict: cattle drives. Once a common sight in the spring and fall on rural highways, cattle drives have become more rare. If you happen to see green splats on the highway, that's your clue that around the next bend there may be a sea of cattle. Slow down and enjoy a truly Western experience.

© John Church

© Dan Johnson

© Peters

GRIZZLY DISCOVERY CENTER
A BEAR AND WOLF PRESERVE

Located in Grizzly Park at the West entrance of Yellowstone National Park. Come experience this unparalleled *educational facility* devoted to the preservation of these threatened wildlife species. Here you'll discover firsthand the habits and surprisingly playful behaviors of grizzly bears and a gray wolf pack. The center also presents a broad range of interactive exhibits, films, presentations and a wildlife themed gift shop suitable for all ages.

Open all year, from 8:30 a.m. until 8:30 p.m., with wildlife viewing until dusk. For more information call or write: *Grizzly Discovery Center, P.O. Box 996, West Yellowstone, MT 59758. (406)646-7001 or (800) 257-2570. Visit our Web Page; www.grizzlydiscoveryctr.com.*

grazing around the Lake Hotel or soaring bald eagles searching the waters for trout.

Near West Thumb, a steaming pocket of thermal springs, mud pots and geysers on the western lake shore, you might see river otter playing in the water.

You have several options for viewing Yellowstone Lake. Some like to just sit inside the Lake Hotel sunroom and gaze out from the comfort of their wicker chairs. On pleasant summer days, some folks picnic on the lakeshore. If you happen to stop at the Fishing Bridge visitor center, you'll discover a nice little beach out the lakeside door and a handy bench where you can read, gaze at the scenery or have a bite to eat. At Bridge Bay Marina regularly scheduled scenic cruises depart throughout the day from June through September. From mid-June through mid-September at the marina, you also can rent outboard motorboats and canoes or take a guided fishing trip on the lake (see our Watersports chapter). Private outfitters also offer guided fishing, kayaking, canoeing, horsepacking and back-

packing trips on or around Yellowstone Lake. You'll also find a fine selection of campgrounds - especially along the eastern shore of the lake.

On the Molly Islands in the southeast arm of Yellowstone Lake is a white pelican rookery, one of only seven such breeding areas in North America. Motorized boats are prohibited near it, and landing on the Molly Islands with any kind of boat is prohibited. Feel free to use your binoculars, though.

Old Faithful Inn

While Old Faithful, the geyser, is the No. 1 attraction in Yellowstone Park, we urge you to spend time exploring the Inn. You can take one of the regularly scheduled tours of the place, during which your guide will give you a colorful and fascinating account of its construction and early use by tourists. Designed by Seattle architect Robert Reamer, Old Faithful Inn is sometimes referred to as the only building that looks like it grew up in the Park. It was built in 1904 using giant Douglas fir logs, with a massive four-sided stone chimney in the center of the lobby. Two railed balconies overlook the lobby. Old Faithful Inn survived the 1959 earthquake and the Fires of 1988 and is still open to overnight guests as well as diners during the summer months. (See our Hotels, Motels and Cabins chapter.)

Up in the rafters of the 92-foot ceiling webbed with a log framework is a crow's nest where musicians once played for the after-dinner dancers twirling in black ties and ball gowns below. Equipped with running water and electricity, the inn even had a spotlight on the roof, which was used to illuminate night-time eruptions, bears raiding the garbage and "rotten loggers" stealing a few kisses in the shadows.

The Inn is so close to Old Faithful Geyser that visitors can watch the eruptions from a second floor veranda.

Fishing Bridge

Old-timers say they didn't dare drive across this bridge in a convertible for fear of being snagged by the flying hook of some angler casting from its side. In the early days, especially in June when the cutthroat trout were spawning, each side of this bridge was edged with elbow-to-elbow fishermen. These days, fishing is prohibited from the bridge. If you stop by in June and look into the waters of the Yellowstone River that pass beneath it, you'll see why: It's a major spawning bed for native cutthroat trout.

Lamar Valley

This valley, which generally lies in the Lamar Creek drainage in the Northeast corner of the Park, is called the Serengeti of North America. It's also wolf country, especially in the winter when the range is teeming with elk and the wolves stand out against the white snow. The wolves, reintroduced into the Park in 1995, can often be seen from the road and are a growing attraction. Even without its wild-life, Lamar is a beautiful open valley with a couple of campgrounds, including those at Slough Creek and Pebble Creek (see our Campground and RV Parks chapter). Slough Creek, a world-famous trout stream, also runs into the valley.

Several miles from the northeast entrance, you'll find the Buffalo Ranch on the north side of the road. It was here that early buffalo keepers brought bison populations from the brink of extinction by breeding and feeding bison as if they were cattle.

Mount Washburn

If the promise of an astounding view isn't enough to make you climb this mountain, then maybe the pay telephone on top will tempt you. Call your mom or a friend from the top of Mount Washburn — plenty of other people do. The Park's best-known mountain rises 10,243 feet above the West edge of Yellowstone's Grand Canyon. Named after Gen. Henry Dana Washburn, a teacher, law-yer and auditor who led the 1870 expedition to Yellowstone country, the mountain is a popular hiking spot. Once you reach the sum-mit and see the view, you'll know why. Along this 3-mile hike (no matter which of the two trails you take) you'll see fields of wildflowers and possibly bighorn sheep. On top there's a fire lookout. You can get out of the wind in a shelter on the bottom floor of the tower.

Grand Canyon of the Yellowstone River

This canyon — 24 miles long and 4,000 feet wide in places — left many an early ex-plorer speechless with its yawning walls col-ored in hues of red, brown, white and orange. (Add pink and salmon to that at sunset.) The Yellowstone River rushes through the Grand Canyon 800 to 1,200 feet below. The elements of nature have exposed seven geologic lay-ers, including those formed by volcanic ash, sediments formed by an inland sea and gla-cial gouging — a treasure-trove of geologic history for the educated eye.

You can view the Grand Canyon from sev-eral vantage points. The most famous of these is Artist Point on the south rim. Bring a camera, watercolors or a pen and paper to Artist Point. Take a photo, paint a picture, pen a poem. We defy you to capture the breathtaking beauty of the Grand Canyon and the Lower Falls. Inspi-ration Point on the north rim probably offers the best display of colors, especially at sunset. Nearby, a hiking trail leads to Seven Mile Hole, where you'll find a couple of camping sites. It takes a day to hike in and another to hike out, which means you'll have to spend the night. If

The Cody Firearms Museum claims the largest collection of American firearms in the world.

you think you want to attempt this hike, you'll have to get a permit from the backcountry office (see our Hiking and Backpacking chapter). Lookout Point also offers a spectacular view into the Canyon from the north rim.

Lower Falls, the highest waterfall in the Park, plunges 308 feet into the Grand Canyon. It is a pounding, roaring monster during spring runoff in June. By August, it is still awesome, but tame compared to its June glory. You can view the Lower Falls from a variety of spots. If you want to see it up close, take the Brink-of-the-Falls Trail, which switchbacks down the hill from the southernmost parking lot on the North Rim Road to the lip of the falls. Uncle Tom's Trail (just follow the signs on the South Rim Road) leads down more than 300 metal steps to the foot of the Falls. (Warning: The walk back up is very strenuous. Folks with health problems should be cautious.)

The 109-foot Upper Falls tumble into a quiet

pool above the Lower Falls. You can reach these with a quarter-mile round-trip hike from the upper Falls Parking Lot.

The area is laced with all kinds of hiking trails and a number of well-used cross-country ski trails. Depending on the time of year, the trails may be closed because of ice and snow. Park officials warn visitors not to leave the paths, not to throw things into the Canyon and to remember that the Canyon is bear country.

Specimen Ridge

Near Tower Junction, Specimen Ridge is as mysterious a place as any in the Park. Here scientists have discovered as many as 27 separate petrified forests, one on top the other. Some of the trees are still standing and indicate that at one time the climate was much warmer. Among the identified species are redwood, pine, magnolia, dogwood, oak, maple, hickory and walnut. The best way to see Specimen Ridge is through a tour led by one of the Park's naturalist-guide Rangers. Check at any visitor center to find out when you can catch one of these tours.

Firehole Canyon Road

This 2-mile side trip south of Madison Junction takes you along a stretch of the old road. Among other sites, you'll see Firehole Falls and Firehole Cascade. You'll also come across the Firehole River Swimming Hole, a delightful stop any day, but especially on a hot day — and there aren't many of those in the Park.

Stagecoach Rides and Chuckwagon Dinners

Headquartered out of Roosevelt and run by Amfac Parks and Resorts, these stagecoach rides and chuckwagon dinners have been among the favorite attractions in the Park for decades. The colorful stagecoaches will give you a taste of what the earliest tourists endured on their bumpy, dusty rides through the Park. The chuckwagon dinners, which are regular feasts served from an outfitted chuckwagon pulled by a team of horses, make a really special night out. See our Other Recreation chapter for details.

Museum of the National Park Ranger

Located on the edge of a meadow below the Norris Campground, this old log ranger station was once an outpost for Fort Yellowstone soldiers guarding the Park, and later became a ranger station. See our History chapter. This museum is often staffed by a volunteer who knows the Park well and can tell you tales about the area.

Outside the Park

Entrance Communities

Oregon Short Line 1903 Executive Rail Car
West Yellowstone Conference Hotel, 315 Yellowstone Ave., West Yellowstone, Mont. • (406) 646-7365
This beautifully appointed executive suite on rails is the centerpiece of the West Yellowstone Conference Hotel. When it rolled out of the shop at a cost of $16,424, the Oregon Short Line was the pride and joy of Union Pacific Railroad officials. For the next 32 years, the car traveled back and forth across the country carrying Union Pacific bigwigs and other dignitaries. In 1935, after the car's last trip to West Yellowstone, the Oregon Shortline 1903 was retired along with Superintendent of Transportation Edward C. Manson. Set on a concrete foundation three blocks from where it now sits, the old railroad car changed hands many times before ending up in the care of Clyde Seely, one of the owners of today's Yellowstone Conference Hotel. Seely and his family lived in the old railroad car while they built their house. Later, employees and guests stayed there. To get to this museum on wheels, you must go inside the Hotel. Admission is free.

Quake Lake Visitors Center
U.S. Hwy. 287, 8 miles north of West Yellowstone, Mont. • (406) 646-7369
August 17, 1959: It was the night the earth shook and the mountain fell into the path of the Madison River. Hebgen Lake tilted north, houses and chunks of highway dropped into the river. Cars were washed away, and so were unsuspecting campers asleep in their beds. Twenty-eight men, women and children died that night, and many others were trapped between the slide that blocked the rising river and the missing sections of road behind them. Women saw their husbands and children blown away by a blast of air, then carried away by the raging river. Others clung for their lives to trees as a wave roared upstream from the collision of mountain and river. Rescuers worked through the day to save the stranded survivors. Today the scene at Quake Lake, formed when the mountain slid, is calm, but the scars remain. For a $2 charge, you can learn more about the 1959 earthquake by stopping at the Quake Lake Visitors Center. Besides a collection of old photos and interpretive maps and signs, the center shows a movie about the earthquake. Quake Lake Visitors Center is open from Memorial Day through the end of September.

Roosevelt Arch
North Entrance, Yellowstone National Park, Gardiner, Mont.

Busloads of visitors to Yellowstone Park pile out to have their pictures taken in front of this 50-foot-high basaltic stone arch. Designed by Park architect Robert Reamer, the arch has a 20-foot-wide and 30-foot-high opening, with 12-foot-high wing walls extending 50 feet on either side. Built in 1903, it was designed to make up for the unspectacular terrain greeting tourists as they entered the Park. The arch was dedicated that same year by President Teddy Roosevelt before a crowd of thousands. Inscribed on the arch are the words: "For the benefit and enjoyment of the people."

Grizzly Discovery Center
201 S. Canyon St., West Yellowstone, Mont. • (406) 646-7001, (800) 257-2570

Before Yellowstone Park officials began closing dumps and retraining bears to fend for themselves in the wild, bears were one of the main attractions in the Park. They would hang out by the roadside and beg food from passing motorists. Today, if you want to be sure of seeing a bear, you'll have to go to the Grizzly Discovery Center, a zoo-like facility that offers visitors a chance to watch bears (and wolves) in an outdoors setting 365 days a year.

Six bears take turns doing their thing for the public in a 1.8 acre pen. A pack of 10 wolves does the same thing in a separate 1-acre pen. The bears, mostly adults orphaned as cubs, would otherwise have died or been destroyed. The center stresses bear education through exhibits, six different videos shown daily in a 50-seat theater and live presentations.

Admission to the Grizzly Discovery Center is $7.50 for adults, $6.50 for seniors, $3 for children ages five to 15 and free for children younger than 5. The Center offers a family rate of $19.50 and a group rate of $6 per person for groups of at least 15 during the summer and 10 during the winter. The Discovery Center opens at 8:30 AM and closes at twilight, about 5:30 PM in mid-winter and 8:30 PM in mid-summer.

National Geographic Theater
101 S. Canyon St., West Yellowstone, Mont. • (406) 646-4100

Stepping into the National Geographic Theater can't match the real Yellowstone Park, but the 45-minute movie *Yellowstone* will take you into parts of the Park that few people ever see. It's also a total experience in movie technology. The IMAX theater has one of the largest movie screens in the world — it's 54 feet tall and 76 feet wide — with a six-channel sound system surrounding the 350-seat theater. (The film for the movie weighs between 350 and 400 pounds.) Shown hourly 365 days a year,

Yellowstone not only depicts the history but also captures the natural world in living color that some folks say is bigger than life. The movie was written and directed by Academy Award-winner Keith Merrill, who is known for other works about the American West.

In the past, this theater has shown Yellowstone every hour on the hour from 9 AM with the last show which begins at 9 PM in the summertime. When a new manager took over in the fall of 1997, she started showing other films like The Rolling Stones and Whales and Alaska. Look for a variety of movies in the summer of 1998. Yellowstone shows several times daily winter and summer. In winter, showtime begins at 11 AM and ends after the 7 PM show. On Thursday, Friday and Saturday nights, IMAX added an 8 PM show to their winter schedule. In 1997, admission was $6 for adults, $4 for children 5 to 18, and free for children 4 and under. It's best to call ahead for showtimes.

Grand Teton National Park

General information about Park admission fees, services and more can be found in the Parks and Forests chapter. Highlight attractions are listed below.

The Tetons

The Grand Tetons are some of the youngest mountains on the continent. The range owes its sharp-edged silhouette to that fact, as well as to the geologic fault that threw this mountain range so high from its valley floor 9 million years ago. Vigorous carving by a series of recent ice ages finished the sculpting. The Tetons include seven peaks more than 12,000 feet above sea level and four more over 11,000. The resulting skyline, even seen from a valley floor 7,000 feet above sea level, is awesome.

These days, most tourists are content to stare at or photograph the Tetons, or perhaps hike around their bases and ascend a little ways into the wild, rugged canyons that lie at their feet (see our Hiking chapter). But almost from explorers' first encounters with these harsh peaks and continuing today, many visitors respond to the mountains' awesome spectacle by wanting to climb to the top. The first unsuccessful attempt to summit the Grand Teton, the range's highest mountain, may date to 1843. If so, many more failed attempts followed.

The first successful ascent was in either 1872 or 1898, depending on whose stories you believe. Most accept the 1898 date and credit the first ascent to William Owen, Franklin Spalding and two other men. The reason these men get the credit is because three of them returned to the summit several days later, built a rock cairn and chiseled their names into the summit boulder while Owen took photographs from below. The 1872 attempt, made by 14 members of the Hayden Expedition, had no photographic evidence and no names carved in stone, only the stories of the two men who said they'd reached the summit.

If you look at the Grand, as locals like to call it, and find yourself dreaming of conquest, you're certainly not alone, but your dream is not one to be acted upon lightly. Climbing this mountain, or any peak in the Tetons, is a deadly serious endeavor. The Tetons claims at least one unfortunate or ill-prepared victim almost every year. Appropriate equipment and skill, as well as good physical condition, are musts for Teton climbers. Many believe that, without previous Teton experience, even knowledgeable, competent climbers should hire a professional guide. (To learn about the Tetons' two Park-approved climbing services, see our Other Recreation chapter.)

INSIDERS' TIP

Springtime is branding time in cattle country. Since brandings are generally a local affair, you'll be lucky to be invited to one. Still, keep your ears open in cafes or haunt local hardware stores or feed stores if you're bent on attending a branding. There's nothing like it.

Teepees give visitors a taste of what's to come at the Buffalo Bill Historical Center.

Below are information about what are perhaps the range's two most famous peaks.

The Grand Teton

The Grand Teton's dramatic, craggy head rises to 13,770 feet. Often draped in clouds, always at least partly covered in snow, the mountain is visible from the Idaho (western) side of the range at Teton Valley, from Grand Targhee Ski and Summer Resort and from Jackson Hole on the Wyoming (eastern) side.

The Grand Teton is home to year-round ice fields called glaciers. South of Jenny Lake is a road turnout that allows good viewing of the Teton Glacier. Glaciers are ice fields so thick and heavy that they behave in some ways more like liquids than solids, flowing in ultra-slow motion downhill. Ice in the middle of Teton Glacier moves downslope at a rate of nearly 40 feet per year, but melting at the bottom edge has kept the glacier in roughly the same position since the 1950s. It's believed, though, that all of the Teton range's glaciers were larger 100 years ago than they are today. Photos taken by William Owen in 1898 seem to show the Teton Glacier about 200 feet thicker and 500 feet longer than the present version. Teton Glacier is a smaller cousin of the vast glacier fields that carved out the signature shapes of the Tetons, as well as the valley floor you're driving on.

The Grand has a distinctive shape sometimes referred to as a horn. Another famous mountain with a similar shape is Switzerland's Matterhorn. Both were carved into their sheer, dramatic lines by multiple glaciers simultaneously chewing on their flanks. Height and the abrupt drama of the Grand's shape draw climbers from around the world: 1,500 to 2,000 summit the mountain each summer. A few more serious adventurers challenge the Grand at its most forbidding, in winter. Climbers have explored and named more than 90 routes and variations on routes to the summit.

The South and the Middle Tetons, both immediately south of the Grand, along with the Grand itself, make up the famous Trois Tetons (three breasts), the peaks from which early French trappers borrowed the whole mountain range's name.

Mount Moran

The Grand Teton towers above other peaks of the Teton range from most angles, but if you approach the Tetons from the north or northeast, 12,605-foot Mount Moran takes over the skyline. From the famous picture windows of Jackson Lake Lodge's hotel lobby, bar and dining room, it's Moran, not the Grand, that takes your breath away.

Mount Moran is named for landscape artist Thomas Moran, who accompanied the 1872 Hayden Expedition through Yellowstone and Grand Teton parks. Together with the photographs of expedition member William Jackson, Moran's paintings of the wonders of Greater Yellowstone helped sway President Grant to sign into existence the nation's first national park.

Moran is unique among the Tetons in having a massive, flat summit. It measures about 600 feet by 1,600 and covers more than 15 acres. The mountain also has five active glaciers, the most famous of which, Skillet Glacier, is readily visible from Jackson Hole. It's called that because some people (we don't know any) think it looks like a skillet with its handle pointing up. Another unique feature of this mountain is the readily visible dark band that runs through its east face. This intrusion of darker rock, called a dike, measures 125 feet across and runs nearly 7 miles west through the mountain.

First summited in 1919, Moran was once one of the most frequently climbed mountains in the Teton range, but that was when a road still ran to the north end of Leigh Lake, ending almost at the mountain's foot. The road was closed in 1953 to protect wilderness values; now the easiest way to approach Mount Moran is to paddle a canoe about 3 miles across Leigh Lake.

The Cathedral Group

If you're driving along Teton Park Road (the inner loop) near Jenny and Leigh lakes, look south and west at the biggest peaks you can see. You're looking at what is often called the Cathedral Group, which includes the Grand, Mount Owen and Teewinot, all higher than 12,000 feet. From this angle, the three stack together, framed by Nez Perce Peak and the Middle and South Tetons into a breathtaking and much photographed vista.

Wildlife Viewing

The best times to see the Park's larger wildlife (and many smaller species as well) are at dawn and dusk. Spring, winter and fall tend to be better than summer, partly because of the mass of human traffic and partly because food, water and adequate cover are

more easily obtained away from the valley floor in summer. Plus most animals are more visible against a background of snow.

Binoculars and a telephoto lens on your camera will come in handy, because if you're close enough to see and photograph wildlife well without magnification, you're probably too close for its comfort (and perhaps your own). Park officials say if you make an animal move, you're too close to that animal. That goes double in the winter, when the difference between life and death for a creature may be the energy it expends getting away from you.

According to helpful folks at the Jackson Hole Chamber of Commerce, the following are some of your best wildlife viewing bets.

Antelope Flats

Drive out Antelope Flats Road from the main Park road, turn south toward Kelly and loop back in on the Gros Ventre River Road. Elk and bison migrate through this area in spring and fall. In winter and early spring, moose may be seen feeding on grasses.

Sawmill Ponds

Just south of Moose on the Moose-Wilson Road, the Park's back door, are a series of small ponds. Moose feed year round on the willows and alders that grow at the water's edge. In spring and fall, this is a popular hangout for waterfowl until the ponds ice over. Elk may be seen on hillsides west of here during spring and fall, feeding on the grasses.

Buffalo Fork Meadows

The Buffalo Fork River, which flows into Grand Teton Park from the east, meanders through a broad valley choked in spots with willow. Moose, which love to eat willow, often graze along the river near Moran in fall, winter and spring.

Oxbow Bend

You have two options for enjoying this wildlife-rich area. One is to simply pull over into the large parking area about halfway between Jackson Lake Lodge and Moran Junction, where the Snake River slows and swings a wide turn. Or you can rent a canoe and paddle out into the still waters of the Oxbow, which will bring you much closer to the plentiful waterfowl and the river otters fishing for their next meal. Watch for the moose that may be munching willow on the side of the river, the elk that may be browsing on grasses during spring and fall in the nearby meadows or the bald eagles carving circles overhead. Expect to see great blue herons standing as if frozen into long grayish statues on the river's edge. In the fall, the Oxbow is a great place to hear bull elk bugling at dawn and dusk.

Willow Flats

East of Jackson Lake Dam is an area of beaver-engineered ponds and freshwater marsh. Beaver ponds are often home to a wide range of wildlife, and this area is no exception. Waterfowl congregate here in spring and fall. Moose munch on the tangled willows year round. And, of course, there are the beavers. The Park Service asks that in winter you observe the wildlife from roads and pullouts only: The Willow Flats area is closed to human access in winter to protect the wildlife.

Gros Ventre River near Lower Slide Lake

Drive up the Gros Ventre River Road to just outside Grand Teton Park during fall, winter and spring, watching the ridgetops and south-facing hillsides. You may see Rocky Mountain bighorn sheep grazing. Males carry a heavy, curled rack of horn. Females and young males have goat-like spikes on their heads. Any time of year, watch for mule deer and, among the cottonwoods and willow near the riverbank, moose. Black bears are regular visitors to the Gros Ventre Campground (see our Camping and RV Parks chapter).

Other Attractions

Jackson Lake and Jackson Lake Dam

Seventeen-mile-long Jackson Lake was not created by its dams; the dams merely enlarged its water storage capacity for the benefit of irrigators downstream in Idaho. The first Jackson Lake Dam was a log structure, built in 1906, that washed out in 1910. The earthen dam that replaced it was gradually heightened over the years to increase the reservoir's storage capacity. These days, the maximum depth of Jackson Lake is more than 400 feet.

Marinas at Colter Bay and Signal Mountain Lodge offer a variety of ways to enjoy this huge body of water. You can rent canoes, fishing boats and cruisers. You can sign up for scenic cruises of the lake at Colter Bay, including breakfast tours and steak-fry cruises. Both marinas provide guided fishing, and both, with tiny Leek's Marina, provide services and supplies to those who own their own boats. Colter Bay has a particularly well-equipped marina store (see our Watersports chapter).

Fishing is generally good on Jackson Lake. Another place to drop a line is below Jackson Lake Dam on the Snake River. You'll often find yourself in the company of osprey, also fishing the waters below the dam. A boat launch and picnic area are situated below Jackson Lake Dam. On the south shore overlooking the dam are interpretive signs worth checking out.

Jenny Lake

This glacier-carved lake at the foot of Mount Teewinot was named for the Shoshone wife of Beaver Dick Leigh, the guide for the Hayden Expedition of 1872. In 1876, Jenny and her six children died of smallpox contracted when the family took in a sick traveler. Nearby Leigh Lake is named for old Beaver Dick himself.

Recreation opportunities abound in this area. Teton Boating Company (see our Watersports chapter) has a dock on Jenny Lake. The company rents fishing boats and provides regular shuttles across the lake, as well as scenic cruises. Hikers and climbers both take advantage of the inexpensive ferry across the lake, cutting miles off their journey into the wild country behind Jenny Lake.

One popular short hike accessed from the ferry drop-off (see our Hiking and Backpacking chapter) is the Hidden Falls/Inspiration Point hike, which is less than 2 miles round-trip from the ferry landing. See our Hiking chapter for more.

Jenny Lake is also known for its excellent fishing. Lake trout weighing up to 40 pounds have been pulled from these pristine waters.

Leigh and String Lakes

Also gouged out by glaciers, these two linked lakes provide pleasant hiking, canoeing and picnicking, as well as lovely photo opportunities. Try your photos in the morning when the lakes are still and Mount Moran, Rockchuck Peak and the Grand Teton herself are reflected on their calm surfaces.

You can launch canoes, available for rent at several locations in the Park (see our Watersports chapter), in shallow String Lake. Your course then takes you for a half-hour paddle to the clearly marked portage that leads to the much larger Leigh Lake. Or hike from the String Lake Trailhead north of Jenny Lake Lodge; you can go completely around String Lake, or skirt the south shores of both String and Leigh lakes to tiny Bear Lake, and return as you came. (For more Teton hikes, see our Hiking and Backpacking chapter.)

Gros Ventre Slide and Lower Slide Lake

Mountains and rivers are always changing, but usually they do it so slowly we can't see it happening. In 1925, though, Sheep Mountain and the Gros Ventre River remodeled themselves, literally overnight, when the whole side of the mountain slipped down into the river's channel. The resulting dam rose 180 feet above the natural streambed, creating a lake about a half-mile wide and 4 miles long. The lake contained about 65 thousand acre feet of water (an acre foot would cover an acre of land with 1 foot of water). The lake came to be called Lower Slide Lake, since a similar but much smaller slide years before had created a tiny lake upstream of the new impoundment.

Two years after the Sheep Mountain slide, much of the new dam gave way. The resulting flood wiped out homesteads and little towns in its path, killing six people and leaving more than 100 homeless. Today you can still observe the fresh-looking 2,225-foot-long slide scar on Sheep Mountain south of the Gros Ventre River and drop your boat in Lower Slide Lake. Interpretive signs on the Gros Ventre River Road tell the story.

Signal Mountain

A couple miles south of the Jackson Lake Junction on the Teton Park Road, a narrow, paved side road takes off to the east and then rapidly begins climbing flat-topped Signal Mountain. The road is 5 miles long; no trailers are allowed.

The drive up affords great views of Jackson Lake; at the top are picnic sites and two viewing areas. One viewing area, at the very pinnacle of Signal Mountain, faces down into the Hole to show you the winding Snake far below and the distant Gros Ventre and Hoback mountain ranges. The other, lower viewing area is at the end of a short ridgeline hike. You wind up staring massive, blocky Mount Moran right in the face — or perhaps the belly button. Interpretive signage at both viewpoints is well-worth stopping to read.

Menor's Ferry
In Grand Teton National Park, near Moose, Wyo. • (307) 739-3300

In 1894, Bill Menor, who lived on the eastern shore of the Snake River near what is now Moose, built a ferry for crossing the swift channel, then a formidable obstacle to travel. His was the only dry crossing-place for 40 miles (there was a bridge at Moran to the north), so he was able to charge passengers up to a dollar for the ride. The ferry was made obsolete by a bridge built near Moose in 1926. Bill's old cabin was later refurbished and outfitted with antiques and exhibits as an interpretive attraction. The trail through Bill's old property is less than a half-mile-mile long; in summer, you can even take a free ride on a replica of his ferry.

Colter Bay Indian Arts Museum
In Grand Teton Park, Colter Bay, Wyo. • (307) 739-3300

Part of the National Park Service visitors center in Colter Bay Village, the Indian Arts Museum contains artistically displayed examples of art and artifacts by Native American tribes from around the country. Some of the well-preserved, carefully crafted items — moccasins, bags, boomerangs, hide paintings and more — date to the 19th century, when local Native American cultures were still largely intact.

The bottom floor houses one or more guest artists, Native American craftspeople who will show you their work and answer your questions. The museum is open in summer only. There is no admission charge.

The valley of Jackson Hole, encompassing much of Grand Teton National Park as well as the towns of Jackson, Wilson and Teton Village, is packed with both natural and manmade attractions. Those inside the Park are covered above. Most of the rest that we've selected are in or near the town of Jackson. For more on the valley called Jackson Hole, see our Area Overview chapter.

Jackson Hole

Town Square
Jackson, Wyo. • No phone

Before Jackson was hip, this little park was surrounded by locally owned souvenir shops and restaurants. Then booming tourism caused town square shops to become the most expensive commercial properties in a very expensive town. Now the square is home to factory outlets for major chains like Coldwater Creek, Ralph Lauren and Eddie Bauer, as well as upscale art galleries and restaurants. Town square dates to 1932. Its official name is George Washington Memorial Park, to commemorate the 200th anniversary of the death of America's first president — though most folks around here don't recall that.

In summer, the square is home to one of the town's longest-running attractions, the Town Square Shootout. For more than 40 years, the Jackson Hole Shootout Gang has put on its show. The action starts around 6:30 every night but Sunday, barring torrential rains. Shows last about 20 minutes. Typically, five to 12 gunslingers are sprawled in the streets when the dust clears. After they come back to life, performers shake hands and sign autographs. Big crowds are typical, so arrive early if you want to see the action up close. The closer you are to the intersection of Center and Broadway, the better.

The antler arches that bracket each of the park's four sidewalk entrances are attractions in and of themselves. They were built between 1953 and 1969 by the local Rotary Club; nobody could think what else to do with antlers, which in those days were plentiful — and worthless. Every winter, bull elk drop the antlers they have sharpened and battled each other with.

Thousands of antlers lie like dead branches across the National Elk Refuge just outside of town. Since the refuge's grasslands are tended to produce maximum browse for the wintering herds, the antlers must be removed. These days elk antlers are worth significant money, but back then nobody wanted them, so they were warehoused. For a while in the 1920s, antlers were handed to tourists as free souvenirs of their visit to Jackson Hole. The arches were another solution to a sticky problem.

The southwest arch consists of approximately 500 antlers. The number has to be approximate because the southwest arch, like the other three, gradually becomes smaller over the course of the summer as tourists steal a chunk here and a bit there. Every year the Rotary Club replaces the missing bulk with new antlers salvaged from the National Wildlife Refuge. Antlers not used for this purpose are sold at auction by the Rotary Club and the Boy Scouts (see our Annual Events chapter).

What also happens every year is that the Jackson Chamber of Commerce receives letters of protest from folks who believe the town killed hundreds of animals to create this tourist attraction.

National Museum of Wildlife Art
2820 Rungius Rd. off U.S. Hwy. 26 near Jackson, Wyo. • (307) 733-5771

Squatting 100 feet above the National Elk Refuge like a medieval castle overlooking its kingdom, the National Museum of Wildlife Art is worth stopping for even if you're not a wildlife art lover. We can guarantee you've never seen a structure like this before. The roughly fitted stone slabs of the exterior walls still host living lichen. Rooflines are rough and uneven, following the uncut shapes of the stones. Inside, the sandstone floor is imprinted here and there with animal tracks, as though deer had wandered through just minutes ahead of you. A massive 700-pound bronze cougar, sculpted by Colorado artist Ken Bunn, crouches above the wide entrance stairway. One wall of the lobby area is formed by a huge window facing toward the National Elk Refuge, where thousands of elk congregate in late fall and through the winter.

Fanning out from this lobby are 12 exhibit rooms, a gift shop, a 200-seat auditorium and The Rising Sage Cafe, which serves light meals during museum hours. The exhibit rooms house special shows and a permanent collection that includes the work of greats like John Clymer, C.M. Russell, Carl Rungius and George Catlin. The auditorium is home to an enticing array of films, symposiums and lectures, some of them free (ask for a calendar at the desk).

The museum is open seven days a week, summer and winter. In spring and fall, Sunday hours are shortened. You only pay the $5 entry fee if you're going into the exhibit rooms; wandering the foyer or visiting the cafe are free.

National Elk Refuge and Elk Refuge Sleigh Rides
U.S. Hwy. 89 north of Jackson, Wyo.
• (307) 733-0277, (307) 733-5386

Created in 1912 to resolve winter conflicts between ranchers and starving elk, the nearly 25,000-acre National Elk Refuge provides a winter home to elk herds that once had the entire valley floor for forage. Most of the best winter range in the area is now inhabited by humans, so for about 10 weeks in the heart of winter, the 7,000 to 12,000 elk that find a winter home here are fed pelleted alfalfa; for the rest of their stay, the huge herds eat the native grasses and shrubbery as they did all across Jackson Hole before homesteaders arrived in the late 1800's.

View the elk from October to April from turnouts along U.S. Highway 89 or in comfort and style from the lobby of the National Museum of Wildlife Art (see the previous write-up).

Better yet, try the popular sleigh rides, which depart from the National Museum of Wildlife Art every 15 minutes between 10 AM and 4 PM from mid-December through mid-April. Purchase your ticket from the museum desk and head for the waiting room to see slide shows and ask refuge staff your questions. The sleigh rides, provided by Bar T 5 Ranch, take about an hour and in 1997 cost $10 for adults. Your wagon is drawn by two horses; it will circle the herd, coming sometimes as close as 25 or 30 yards. Best times are late in the winter, when the elk are accustomed to humans and sleighs and allow closer approach, and early in the day, when the alfalfa pellets put out at 8 AM are still being consumed.

On your way back into town, make sure you stop at the visitors center just north of Jackson. It doubles as an interpretive site for the refuge and a travelers information and chamber of commerce center. Visitors center personnel tend to be very knowledgeable people.

Other times of year you won't see elk on the refuge, but trumpeter swans are known to frequent ponds at the southern tip of the refuge near the visitors center. This means the visitors center and the U.S. Hwy. 89 pullout just north are still good stops.

Jackson National Fish Hatchery
1500 Fish Hatchery Rd., Jackson, Wyo.
• (307) 733-2510

One of 75 federal hatcheries in the country, this facility stocks local waters with cutthroat and lake trout and ships some 2.5 million cutthroat eggs across the country. Cutthroat spawn from March to June, making a visit during those months particularly interesting. Trout at this facility are hand-spawned alive, not killed for their eggs and sperm. Other times, enjoy the interpretive displays, the outdoor and indoor runways full of fry, fingerlings and ready-for-release 8- to 10-inch-long fish. The facility is located 4 miles north of Jackson on U.S. Highway 26/89/191. It's open daily. Your visit is free.

Wyoming Balloon Company
335 N. Cache, Jackson, Wyo.
• (307) 739-0900

If you're in Teton Village and you look up to see a hot air balloon floating against blue sky, a silhouette of the Teton range stenciled on its canopy, you're looking at something you could be doing. Wyoming Balloon Company has a four-balloon fleet. The largest, 10 stories tall, will lift 12 people not including the pilot. The smallest takes two. You can be picked up anywhere in Jackson or Teton Village. You get to observe the cold-air inflation of the balloon and then the heating process

that lifts the inflated balloon off the ground. Your flight will begin as the morning sun slips down the face of the Teton Range toward the valley floor.

Rates in summer run $185 for a one-hour flight topped off by a continental breakfast and champagne on the ground afterward. In 1997-98, the company plans to offer shorter winter flights at discounted rates.

Summer and winter, the flight corridor is about 4,000 acres, which is an area about 2 miles wide and 4 to 5 miles long. This area reaches almost to the south border of Teton Park and allows the balloon to overfly the Snake River.

Rainbow Balloon Flights
P.O. Box 20066, Jackson, WY 83001
• (307) 733-0470, (800) 378-0470

Hot-air balloon flights in Teton Valley, just on the other side of the ragged wall of the Teton Range, give you the opportunity to find out where you stand on the old Idaho-versus-Wyoming controversy: Which side of the Tetons is prettier? Rainbow will drive you from Jackson Hole to Teton Valley and back, so you also get the scenic trip over Teton Pass before and after your flight. Get more information on this attraction in the Teton Valley listing in this chapter.

Teton Rock Gym
1116 Maple, Jackson, Wyo.
• (307) 733-0707

Maybe you've been wondering what rock climbing is all about, but you'd like to try it under controlled conditions. Or maybe you're an experienced climber itching to get your hands on some rock, but it's winter, so you'll just have to wait, right? Wrong. Teton Rock Gym is a pleasant newer facility with room for more than a dozen climbers at a time to navigate its artificial holds and vertical and overhung walls. Climbing walls surround an open, gravel-floored area. Climbing holds are arranged into new routes every week.

Ropes and some other equipment are provided or are available for rent. There's also a small weight room and a shower facility on premises. Novice climbers must take a quick lesson before they can climb. Lessons range from $22 to $33 and include the $10 entry charge. Teton Rock Gym is open afternoons and evenings.

Jackson Hole Museum
105 N. Glenwood, Jackson, Wyo.
• **(307) 733-2414**
Teton County Historical Center
105 Mercill, Jackson, Wyo.
• **(307) 733-9605**

Jackson Hole Museum, which opened in 1958, displays items of local historical interest dating from prehistoric times through the days of the fur traders and mountain men and into modern ranching times. Jackson Hole's history is even more colorful than its current incarnation, so expect to be entertained.

The museum is open in summer only. Its collection of historic photographs alone are worth the $3 price of admission.

The affiliated Teton County Historical Center is a Western researcher's dream. On display in this historic log cabin are artifacts and old photos. In the stacks are shelves of archival volumes, recorded oral histories from locals and thousands more photographs. Some of these photos depict a nineteenth century Jackson, a rough and tumble town with a reputation for harboring horse thieves, gamblers and no-goods. Staff are happy to assist serious researchers or the merely curious. The Historical Center is open weekdays year round. There is no admission charge.

Alpine Slide
Snow King Resort, Jackson, Wyo.
• **(307) 733-7680**

The Alpine Slide snakes 2,500 feet from the top of Rafferty Chairlift to the resort hotel below, dipping into and out of the trees and slipping past wildflower meadows. You'll ride the lift up and pilot your own brakeable toboggan down the cement channel. Choose your speed: Your trip down can be as sedate or as exhilarating as you like. Adults ride for $7. Kids 6 and younger must ride with an adult.

Red Velvet Swing Old Time Photos
36 E. Broadway, Jackson, Wyo.
• **(307) 733-6467**

David Dunn's place, tucked into the basement of Cache Street Square, will bring out the exhibitionist in you. He has more than 50 complete, hat-to-shoes costumes. You can pose in the clawfoot bathtub, behind the saloon doors, in the saddle or against the wagon wheel. The walls, lined with photos of other sudden exhibitionists, will help you decide who you want to be.

Photos can be developed and framed while you wait. Dunn says he creates around 100 old-time photos a day in summer and about five a day after the snow flies. While you're in, make sure you say "hi" to Lady, the 70-pound, sleepy-eyed Alaskan Malamute that is the shop's mascot.

Red Velvet Swing closes on Tuesdays and Wednesdays between Labor Day and Memorial Day.

Granite Creek Hot Springs
End of Granite Creek Rd., off U.S. Hwy. 189, near Hoback Junction, Wyo.
• **No phone**

Granite Creek Road ends at a parking area. From there, pack your towel, your favorite pool toys and an ice chest loaded with drinks and lunch down the hill. Cross crystal-clear Granite Creek on a footbridge and walk up the short trail to heaven in the wilderness: a pool full of

INSIDERS' TIP

Jackson town square's four antler arches may seem huge, and they are: More than 1,700 elk antlers were used in their construction. A single antler can weigh up to 20 pounds, so the four arches together weigh well in excess of 10 tons. But there's a bigger arch in Afton, Wyoming — the biggest in the world. It spans U.S. Highway 89, stands 18 feet high and consists of more than 3,000 antlers.

warm, clear water enclosed by a wooden deck and spectacular scenery.

About 50 feet in diameter and 8 feet deep at its deepest, Granite Creek Hot Springs is a great place for adults to relax and kids to play. Above you towers 10,808-foot-high Pinnacle Peak. Just outside the fence are picnic areas and a bathhouse with pit toilets. Down by the creek are more picnic sites. The pool was constructed in 1933 by the Civilian Conservation Corps and is operated by a Forest Service concessionaire. Summer temperatures dip down to around 93 degrees as snowmelt percolates into the ground somewhere above the hot springs pool to cool the naturally hot water. In winter, when up to 400 inches of snow accumulates on the ground, pool temperatures can be higher than 110 degrees, hot enough to make steam rise from your arms and legs and make rolling around in the snow feel good.

Pool attendants say that winter use often exceeds that of summer, as snowmobile, dog sled and sleigh tours all take the 10-mile trek in from Highway 189 to bask in the steamy heat. Ironically, the gravel-and-dirt Granite Creek Road, which slows cars down in the summer, makes for faster winter travel — the trail is not plowed, but rather groomed for snowmobilers. Despite its isolation, Granite Creek Hot Springs is not a quiet place; it sees an average of 120 visitors every day in summer.

The adult admission for a one-day pass in 1997 was $5.50.

Astoria Hot Springs
U.S. Hwy. 89, near Hoback Junction, Wyo. • (307) 733-2659

The Snake flows by, clear and cold, but the equally clear water of the concrete-lined swimming pool is warm, around 95 degrees. This is thanks to a natural hot spring that bubbles out of the ground here. It flows into and through two pools, creating warm, clean fun. The large pool is about 40 feet wide and 80 feet long. The smaller, triangular kiddy pool is about a foot deep. Astoria Hot Springs provides lifeguards, dressing rooms with hot showers, lockers and even swimming suit and towel rentals.

Don't come here looking for solitude. The

pool, adjacent picnic grounds and camping area are busy in summer. Both pool and campground close in September and reopen in May. In 1997, the adult charge was $5 to use the pools for the day. Camping is at additional charge (see our Camping and RV Parks chapter).

Surrounding Areas
Eastern Idaho
Idaho Falls, Idaho, Area

Stone Walls
751 S. Capital, Idaho Falls, Idaho • (208) 528-8610

This indoor climbing gym draws folks looking for a good workout, curious adventure seekers who want a safe way to learn about rock climbing, and serious climbers honing their muscles and skills. Rock gyms used to be where climbers went when weather wouldn't permit access to real rock, but these days indoor climbing is almost a sport in itself.

Stone Walls can rent you all necessary gear. They also provide ropes and basic instruction. Routes are up to 30 feet high; many are overhung and difficult, but there's something for every skill level here. Stone Walls is open Monday through Saturday evenings and Sunday afternoons. A one-day pass will cost you $7. If you need to rent a harness and climbing shoes, expect to pay an additional $4.

Heise Hot Springs
5116 E. Heise Rd., Ririe, Idaho • (208) 538-7312

Choose your water temperature: The soaking pool is kept at 105 degrees, the small swimming pool runs about 94 degrees and the 10 foot-deep summer pool with its 350-foot water slide stays around 75 degrees. Adults pay $5 to use all of these outdoor facilities. You can even make a day of it, picnicking on the banks of the Snake River and then playing a round of golf at Heise's little nine-hole course. You'll pay a greens fee at the golf course.

The two warm pools are open year-round until 10 PM except for three weeks in November. The golf course and summer pool close in fall and reopen in spring.

Idaho Falls Greenbelt and Falls
Snake River near Broadway Bridge, Idaho Falls, Idaho • No phone

The little town of Eagle Rock changed its name to Idaho Falls in 1891 on the advice of Eastern developers, who thought the new moniker more marketable. At that time, the Snake River flowed smooth and swift through the center of town — without a single splash. Decades later, a 1,500-foot-wide falls was built to generate municipal power and, coincidentally, create a namesake for the town.

In winter the falls are festooned with icicles; spring and fall find rows of Canada geese perched at the lip of the maelstrom. Early summer, when the river runs high, the cascade of Idaho Falls roar, foam and spit mist into the air.

Situated on either side of the river is the town's greenbelt. The 2¹/3-mile walk from the Broadway bridge to the U.S. Highway 20 bridge and back will take you along the river's grassy bank, past picnickers, in-line skaters, bicycle riders, joggers, and of course, the falls. You can also catch a stunning view of the local Mormon Temple, blocky and grand, topped with a golden statue of the angel Moroni. (If you're curious about the Mormon faith or just want to see the pretty grounds, guided tours are available through the visitors center. Only Mormons can walk into the temple itself. The visitors center is located at 1000 Memorial Drive, (208) 523-4504, right along your Greenbelt walk.)

Bonneville Museum
200 N. Eastern Ave., Idaho Falls, Idaho
• (208) 522-1400

This historical museum tries to depict Bonneville County from prehistoric times up to the Atomic Age. Permanent displays focus on pioneer living, agriculture and natural history. Because the nearby Idaho National Engineering and Environmental Laboratory was home to the first nuclear reactor, a detailed exhibit traces the development of nuclear energy. Researchers can make use of the reference room's wealth of historic documents, some quite rare and fascinating.

Museum admission is $1 for adults. The museum is open Monday through Friday, and Saturday afternoon.

Idaho Potato Expo
130 N.W. Main, Blackfoot, Idaho
• (208) 785-2517

If, for some reason, you wanted to encircle the world in french fries, how many would you need? These and other pressing potato issues are addressed at this fun stop just off I-15 in Blackfoot. Learn everything you ever wanted to know about Idaho potatoes; buy surprising products like potato lotion, potato soap, Darth 'Tater T-shirts and more. Then wander over to the kitchen to pick up your complimentary baked potato with butter and sour cream. Or buy potato fudge, potato cinnamon rolls and cookies.

The Expo is located, appropriately, south of Idaho Falls in Bingham County, the county that grows one-third of the nation's potatos. While you're there, don't miss the world's largest potato chip. Even better, commune with the Dan Quayle potato, personally signed by a former Vice President of the United States who is famous in Idaho for his inability to spell the name of that all-important tuber. This attraction is open May through September, seven days a week. Admission is $2 for adults.

Lava Hot Springs Inn and Spa
94 E. Portneuf, Lava Hot Springs, Idaho
• (208) 776-5830, (800) 527-5830

These hot springs on the Portneuf River near Soda Springs, Idaho — some 80 miles south of the area covered in this book, but we couldn't resist — carry 22 dissolved minerals, more than any other hot springs in the country. The water is said to have medicinal properties. Right now the facility maintains three pools that range in temperature from about 90 degrees to more than 106. A cold plunge pool is available for cooling down after a long soak.

Big changes are in the works here, though. By the summer of 1998, 12 new pools should open — nine private soaking tubs available for hourly rental and three whirlpool tubs, one specially outfitted for hot-water massage therapy. The new spa facility, offer-

Photo: Randy Hayes/Post Register

Throwing himself off a galloping horse onto a running steer, a wrangler tries to bring the animal down in one fluid motion during a steer wrestling competition.

ing body treatments, aromatherapy and hydrotherapy, should also be open.

Right now, expect to pay $5 for an all-day pass. Spa treatments and private pool rental prices haven't been set yet. Lava Hot Springs Inn and Spa are open year round, seven days a week. Lava Hot Springs is a tiny town with all amenities and services, including motels and camping.

Rexburg, Idaho, Area

St. Anthony Sand Dunes
North of St. Anthony, Idaho
• **(208) 524-7500**

St. Anthony Sand Dunes are a startling anomaly among the fertile fields and sage-covered hills of the St. Anthony area. These quartz sand dunes range from 10 to 600 feet high, rolling one after another along an area

35 miles long and 1 to 5 miles wide. No services are available at the dunes besides parking and restrooms. Off-road vehicles, dirt bikers, hikers and picnickers frequent this surreal sea of sand.

To find the dunes, follow the signs from U.S. Highway 20 near Rexburg for about 15 miles. The Bureau of Land Management asks that you stay on the open sands; damage to the vegetation that stabilizes some dunes could force the closure of this sandy playground. You are also asked to use a safety flag if you plan to drive your dune rail or ATV here; please leave your glass containers back at the car.

A portion of the area is closed from December through March every year to protect wildlife. Before you come, it's a good idea to call the number listed above and ask the BLM about other regulations you should be aware of.

Teton Damsite
Off Idaho Hwy. 33 between Rexburg and
Tetonia, Idaho • No phone
Teton Flood Museum
51 N. Center, Rexburg, Idaho
• (208) 356-9101

People in Rexburg, Sugar City and other
nearby communities divide their histories like
this: Before the Flood and After the Flood.
They're talking about the day — June 5, 1976
— the brand-new Teton Dam failed. When Bureau of Reclamation engineers noticed clear
springs of water spurting from canyon walls
below their recently filled dam, it was already
too late to divert disaster: 17 miles of the Teton
River had become a reservoir containing 85
million gallons of water. Then cracks formed in
the face of the dam itself. Desperate attempts
to plug them with earth were unsuccessful: First
the bulldozers were engulfed, and then the dam
disintegrated like soggy cardboard. The towns
of Wilford, Sugar City, Roberts and Rexburg
were inundated first but floodwaters eventually
reached as far south as American Falls over
120 miles away. In the aftermath, 11 were dead,
hundreds injured, 25,000 homeless and the repair bill sat at about $400 million.

You can visit the Teton Dam site and stare
at what remains of the earth and rock structure.
Then look down into the river channel from the
canyon edge (you can also hike down into the
canyon) and see the effects of the tremendous
flood. What was once a cottonwood-shaded
river with a swift, riffly channel is now a series of
stagnant pools and sharp drops. In some places
the new river channel is yards from where the
old one was. Experts say it'll be 10,000 years
before the river returns to anything like its former
state. Fishing, although still interesting, is not
what it used to be.

When you finish thinking about the forces
of nature unleashed upon man by himself,
drive back to Rexburg and stop by the Teton
Flood Museum. The first thing you'll see as
you walk in the door is a flood-line on the wall
to your right, showing how high the waters
rose that day. Downstairs, along with all the
cluttered mysteries of a small-town historical
museum, are interpretive materials and personal recollections from the flood. The museum is open Monday through Saturday in
summer, and Monday through Friday the rest
of the year. You'll pay a small donation.

Ashton, Idaho

Hess Heritage Museum
3409 E. 1200 N., Ashton, Idaho
• (208) 356-5674

This 15-year-old local history and lifestyle
museum is open by appointment and, when
the gate is open, for drop-ins. Find it a mile
south of Ashton on Fish Hatchery Road (a.k.a.
1200 N.). Pioneer descendants Dan and Mary
Hess are the curators of this remarkable,
homegrown collection. Mary's grandfather was
personal secretary to the 19th-century founder
of the Mormon church, Joseph Smith. Her
grandmother traveled from St. Louis to Salt
Lake City in 1852, pushing her possessions in
a hand cart. Dan's parents homesteaded what
are now the museum grounds in 1909, moving into an old dirt-floored, sod-roofed cabin
that had been built on this land in the 1890s.
This cabin is now part of the main farmhouse,
the coldest room in the house in summer.

Enjoy the museum's collections of old wagons, the reproduction one-room schoolhouse,
the period clothing, antique furniture, old farm

INSIDERS' TIP

In 1920, Jackson, Wyoming, made history by electing an all-
woman town council, perhaps the first in the country. Before the
air had cleared, the five councilors balanced the town's books
and had Jackson's streets graded with new culverts in the
woefully inadequate drainage ditches. They commissioned board
sidewalks, established a town dump and passed health laws that
banned garbage dumping in vacant lots or in the streets. They
also had a road built up to the town cemetery so pallbearers
would no longer have to struggle up a steep, brush-choked hill.

equipment, historical photos and more. But what you won't be able to tear yourself away from are Mary's stories. She's the real repository for the past she doesn't want forgotten. When Mary or Dan can't guide you around, they usually have volunteer curators on-site, also local, also full of stories.

You can make an appointment most days except Tuesday and Sunday from mid-April to mid-October. Entry costs $3 for adults. If you happen to be in the neighborhood on the Fourth of July, don't call — just stop on by the Hess Museum for the annual Pioneer Country Fair. You can learn about local history and pioneer skills like rope plaiting, listen to cowboy poets and hear stories from around 30 docents, some of whom are as old as the exhibits themselves.

Ashton Fish Hatchery
3330 E. 1200 N., Ashton, Idaho
• (208) 652-3579

Run by Idaho Fish and Game, this hatchery was constructed in 1920 to take advantage of a bubbling spring that flows out of the ground at a steady (and very fish-friendly) 50 degrees year round. Wandering through the facility's fish runs, which produce 50,000 pounds of grayling and trout per year, will take only a few minutes. You may find yourself down at the feeding pond for an hour or more, however. Buy special fish food from a pond-side dispenser for a dime; trout weighing up to 14 pounds swirl into view when the first pellet hits the water.

Fish stocked from this hatchery into the Buffalo River, Warm River and the Henry's Fork are generally much smaller than these display fish. Idaho Fish and Game charges no fee for entering the facility. A staff member who can answer your questions is generally about.

Upper and Lower Mesa Falls
Idaho Hwy. 47 (Mesa Falls Scenic Byway) • No phone

Upper and Lower Mesa Falls on the Henrys Fork of the Snake River are the two best reasons to drive Idaho Highway 47, the Mesa Falls Scenic Byway. This *long* shortcut between Ashton and Island Park is dirt for part of its length, skirting the sheer edge of the Snake River gorge through lodgepole forest. Camping and canyon-rim hiking are available along the byway. Be sure to stop and view Lower Mesa Falls, 65 feet high, and the upper falls, which is more than 100. As you view the lower falls from Grandview Campground, the almost-visible Upper Mesa Falls kicks mist into the air like distant smoke.

The upper falls has a paved loop trail and viewing area that takes you right to the smooth, glassy lip of the cascade and into the mist rising from the narrow canyon. The falls' big voice rises from the canyon like a physical force. You could almost imagine that the force that destroyed the bridge spanning the river here at the turn of the century was the river's roar (really it was a winter flood). Big Falls Inn, a historic old roadhouse built around 1915, is being renovated into a visitors center.

Island Park, Idaho

Big Springs
Big Springs Rd., Island Park, Idaho
• (208) 558-7301

It's a river's birthplace. One hundred and twenty million gallons of pure water a day — enough to meet the water needs of a million people — surge out of the ground here. Just below the glassy pool is a bridge. Toss breadcrumbs into the water from it, and you'll see that constant flow (at a year-round temperature of 52 degrees) and the clean gravel bottom make for perfect trout habitat. Big Springs' trout get BIG. Leave your fishing pole in the car, though: No fishing is allowed until below the outlet to Henry's Lake, several miles away.

Take the short walking trail around the pond to reach Johnny Sacks' cabin. Johnny was a German immigrant who built his cozy cabin and its furnishings by hand out of local trees. He also built a water wheel turned by spring water tumbling out of the hillside. The wheel provided electricity and brought water uphill to the cabin. Johnny's old place is now a visitors center and an attraction in its own right.

Your other Big Springs alternative is to rent a boat from Henry's Fork Landing or Mack's Inn and float the gentle Henry's Fork's 5-mile-long National Water Trail. For more on the Big

Springs National Water Trail, see the Close-up in the Watersports chapter.

Harriman State Park Railroad Ranch
U.S. Hwy. 20 near Island Park, Idaho
• **(208) 558-7368**

Harriman State Park contains 15,000 acres of prime habitat for moose, bear, deer, trumpeter swans and more. The Henry's Fork of the Snake, a world-class fly-fishing river, runs through the park. An additional 10,000 acres of neighboring national forest lands are managed as a wildlife refuge, so game is plentiful.

Railroad Ranch is the park's main tourist attraction. Railroad Ranch was born in 1902 as a working ranch whose main objective was not profit, but recreation for the ranch's owners, who were mostly railroad management from the Union Pacific. In 1977, the Harriman family deeded the ranch and its property to the state of Idaho. Most of the buildings still stand, and the ranch still hosts an active cattle operation.

You can take a self-guided tour of the ranch any time; just pick up one of the detailed brochures from the visitors center. They'll describe the 28 buildings and building sites and explain their purposes. Guided tours are also available. Park entrance fees are $3 per vehicle. Learn more about Harriman in our Parks and Forests chapter. Also check out the park's cross-country ski trails, some of the area's best, in our Winter Sports chapter. A riding stable rents horses in summer (check out our Other Recreation chapter.)

Teton Valley, Idaho

Teton Aviation Center
675 Airport Rd., Driggs, Idaho
• **(208) 354-3100**

On blue-sky days, summer or winter, you can get the bird's-eye view of the Tetons from a glider plane. Teton Aviation flies its two planes daily from around 8 AM to around 4:30 PM, weather permitting. Gliders have no engines of their own — they are pulled into the air by a tow plane. Once the tow plane detaches from your glider at 11,700 feet, you are surrounded only by the sound of the wind.

Just above you are the peaks of the Tetons, most of them at or just over 12,000 feet. In summer, the glider pilot seeks out and uses thermal air masses to lift the kite-like plane high above Teton Valley. In winter, there are no thermals; instead pilots catch what they call "wave lift" off the ridgelines; winter rides are shorter because wave soaring won't carry you as high as summer thermals.

The longest summer flights last about an hour and cost $135 per person. Flights are limited to a 25-mile radius of the airport. Scenic airplane rides are also available for from 15 minutes up to an hour.

Rainbow Balloon Flights
P.O. Box 20066, Jackson, WY 83001
• **(307) 733-0470, (800) 378-0470**

Rainbow launches its balloons from Driggs' fairgrounds seven fair-weather days a week. Balloons are nine stories tall and 90 feet in diameter, striped in rainbow shades. Flights are peaceful and silent; the balloon has no choice but to move with the speed and direction of the winds. The one-hour rides can take you as high as 3,000 feet, or, in cooperative wind conditions, as low as necessary to check out a fox, deer or moose.

Balloons hold seven adults plus the pilot, but generally the pilot takes a maximum of six passengers. The pilot may be able to bring you down nearly at your starting point, or the company's chase vehicle may have to come pick you up as many as 20 miles away. Flights begin at sunrise, when air is most stable.

Rainbow will pick you up in Jackson or meet you in Teton Valley. By balloonist tradition, flights always end with a champagne toast. The season runs June to September; rates are $175 per person.

Moon Mountain Ranch Dog Sled Tours
Grand Targhee Ski and Summer Resort at Ski Hill Rd., Alta, Wyo.
• **(800) 827-4433**

Make reservations early, preferably at least a week in advance, for your half-day or moon-light dog sled tour in Targhee National Forest. You sit on the sled, cocooned in blankets, while the eight- or 10-dog team runs ahead through the snow. You can also try guiding the sled from the musher's spot on the back runners. Tours stop at the Trapper's Teepee where snacks and hot drinks are served. Larger groups (four or more) can arrange to have a full barbecue cookout at the Teepee. The dogs rest while you eat, then carry you back to your starting point.

Moonlight tours are magical, but require a clear night sky within a few days of the full moon. This means you need to be willing to reschedule or even get cancelled.

Rides are available, weather permitting, from December through April. Each sled can carry 350 pounds. Daytime rides cost $190 for two people, assuming they can share a sled. Moonlight tours cost a bit more.

Martin's Sleighride Dinners
Grand Targhee Ski and Summer Resort at Ski Hill Rd., Alta, Wyo.
• **(800) 827-4433**

Here's an attraction and dinner rolled into one. The big horse-drawn, flat-bed sleigh, loaded with hay bales and warm blankets carries you and 19 other guests to a toasty-warm, canvas-and-wood tent called a yurt. The ride takes about 15 minutes. Dinner is cooked for you on one of the yurt's two stoves (the other is for warming hands). You'll eat steak, chicken or a vegetarian entree with fixings and dessert. Hot tea, cider, coffee and water are provided. You're invited to bring your own alcoholic beverages.

There are two seatings per night, Tuesday through Saturday. Special arrangements can be made for large groups on Sundays and Mondays. Dinner runs $30 for adults.

Southwestern Montana

Museum of the Rockies
600 W. Nagy, Bozeman, Mont.
• **(406) 994-2251**

Established in 1965, the Museum of the Rockies is a multifaceted hub of learning enriched by its connections with Montana State University. At the heart of the Museum these days is a T. Rex dinosaur skeleton unearthed in 1990 near Jordan, Montana. Jack Horner, the curator of paleontology at the museum, was the scientific adviser for the movie *The*

Lost World, the sequel to *Jurassic Park*. He is also author of *Dinosaur Lives: An Evolutionary Saga*. Horner and his staff have collected more than 15,000 fossil specimens from the badlands of Montana.

In other wings you'll find interactive exhibits on geology as well as the Taylor Planetarium and the Tinsley Homestead, a living-history farm. The focal point of the farm is the two-story log farmhouse built in 1921 by Oliver and Annie May Beiring. Now edged by newer subdivisions, a 12.5-acre piece of the family farm was purchased by the museum in 1995. The Living History Farm, open daily from 9 AM to 4 PM, Memorial Day through Labor Day, employs costumed interpreters who carry on 19th-century living at the farm. You might find them cooking on a woodburning stove, forging iron in the blacksmith shop, gathering eggs or plowing with a team of horses.

The Museum of the Rockies is open year round and offers a multitude of classes, workshops and educational tours. In 1997, admission to the Museum of the Rockies was $6 for adults, $4 for children ages 5 to 18. Children 4 and younger are admitted free. Memorial through Labor Day, the museum is open from 8 AM to 8 PM seven days a week. The rest of the year, the Museum of the Rockies operates 9 AM to 5 PM Monday through Saturday, and 12:30 to 5 PM Sunday. The Taylor Planetarium regularly shows films with such titles as *The Dinosaur Chronicles*, *Rocky Mountain Skies* and *Laser's Southern Cooking*. It also features children's programs on Saturday mornings. The cost is $2.50 per person.

American Computer Museum
234 E. Babcock, Bozeman, Mont.
• **(406) 587-7545**

Prepare to be amazed. In this 6,000-square-foot museum, you can ponder the dinosaurs of the computer world in a program that takes you back 4,000 years. You'll see calculating devices from ancient Babylonian and Egyptian times, as well as a 1950 electronic calculator that weighs in at a ton and has more than 18,000 vacuum tubes. And you'll see everything in between.

This museum, open all year, could enlighten even the most computer-apathetic in your family. There's no doubt it will interest cyber-tech nuts. June 1 through August 31, the museum is open seven days a week from 10 AM until 4 PM. September through May, it's open Tuesday, Wednesday, Friday and Saturday from noon until 4 PM. In 1997, admission to the museum cost $3 for adults, and $2 for children ages 6 to 12. Children younger than 6 are admitted free of charge. Ask about group rates.

Park County Museum
118 W. Chinook St., Livingston, Mont.
• (406) 222-4184

Park County collected relics for 10 years before opening its museum in an old school building. Open Memorial through Labor Day, the Park County museum features two replicated archeological digs, a Native Cultures room with an extensive arrowhead collection, a Yellowstone National Park collection, fire engines, an 1889 caboose and a blacksmith shop.

This museum is not very wheelchair accessible.Open from June 1 until Labor Day, the Park County Museum operates from noon until 5 PM, and from 7 until 9 PM. During the off season, curator Mark Baker will open the museum by special appointment. Admission is $3 for adults, $2 for juniors ages 12 to 17 and $1 for children younger than 2.

Livingston Depot Center
200 W. Park, Livingston, Mont.
• (406) 222-2300

Livingston was founded in 1882 as a base for Northern Pacific Railroad workers who ran the railways and maintained the shops in the region. Later, the town became the jumping-off point for Yellowstone travelers. To accommodate them, the railroad built a three-building brick complex for its depot. Today it has been restored and is the home of the Livingston Depot Center, a combination museum, meeting hall and convention and cultural center. On permanent display is "Rails Across the Rockies," an extensive exhibit on railroading. The Depot is also a destination for the Montana Rockies Railroad, which originates in Sandpoint, Idaho, stays the night in Livingston and buses guests to Yellowstone Park for the day.

Lewis and Clark Caverns State Park
Mont. Hwy. 2 between Cardwell and Three Forks, Mont. • (406) 287-3541

Guided trips through more than 2 miles of a limestone labyrinth will lead you down 600 steps from one cavernous "room" to the next. Along the way, you'll see stalactites and stalagmites created by the slow drip of mineral-

Photo: Robert Bower

Granite Creek Hot Springs near Hoback Junction, Wyoming, is a popular spot to soak your weary bones.

bearing water. You'll also see and learn about bats that make their home in the caverns, which were once totally dark but now are lit during tours. Once under the care of the National Park Service and Yellowstone Park, the Lewis and Clark Caverns were so forgotten that a local man named Dan Morrison built 2,000 steps into the caverns then charged for tours. Each summer he would break the Park Service lock and replace it with his own. Authorities at Yellowstone Park were too busy and too far from the caverns to do anything about it. In 1937, the Caverns became Montana's first state park.

This trip is worth a drive way out of the way. To get to the caverns from West Yellowstone you must drive about 100 miles north on U.S. Highway 287. In 1997, a tour of the caverns cost $7 for adults, and $3 for children ages 6 to 11. There are also group rates for parties of 15 or more that make reservations at least two weeks ahead. The caverns are open from Memorial Day through Labor Day. On-site you'll find a 44-space campground with several camp cabins.

Virginia City, Montana
U.S. Hwy. 287, Virginia City, Mont. • (406) 444-9682

Once a booming mining town with tens of thousands of residents, Virginia City was the Montana territorial capital in 1865. By 1870, though, the gold had played out and most of the people had left. In 1890, the town could boast only 125 full-time residents, and the buildings that lined Main Street were frozen in time. In the 1940s, Charles and Sue Bovey began buying the old buildings one by one, while importing other gold-rush structures to Nevada City, a mile down the road. The couple also collected mining and pioneer artifacts from around the state.

Each summer for many years, the Boveys — and later, their son, Ford — opened Virginia City to the public. In addition to the displays in each old building, the "town" was home to the Wells Fargo Cafe, the Bale of Hay Saloon with old nickelodeons, the Virginia City Playhouse, a museum and the Fairweather Inn, all connected by boardwalks. Above the town is boot hill, where the notorious Plummer Gang lies buried after being chased down and hanged by local vigilantes. The Plummer Gang, led by Virginia City's own sheriff, had been caught robbing and murdering miners.

In 1997, the state of Montana bought the Bovey's portion of Virginia City. The attraction is being managed through the Montana Historical Society. Beginning in 1998, it will be run by a concessionaire. Badly needed repairs to the buildings have already begun. Plan to spend one long day meandering through this old mining town.

There are plans to re-open a narrow-gauge train in 1998 that runs from Virginia City to Nevada City, where you'll find another hotel, a cafe and several other attractions. While local residents remain for the winter, the tourist parts of the two towns are only open from Memorial Day through Labor Day.

Carbon County Museum
Broadway Ave. and Eighth St., Red Lodge, Mont. • (406) 446-3912

This hometown museum had plans to move by the 1998 season from its former home in a very old log cabin into the Labor Temple Building, the abandoned home of the local miners' union. Started in the 1950s by rodeo personality Alice Greenough, the museum was taken over by Carbon County in 1980. Exhibits in the museum include the Greenough collection, old bootlegging stills, a rodeo collection, the town's first telephone switchboard, a general store, an old printing press and a grand piano used in the Pollard Hotel. The museum board also has plans for a simulated coal mine in the museum's basement.

The Carbon County Museum is open daily from 10 AM until 6 PM, Memorial Day until Labor Day. Admission is free.

Beartooth Highway
U.S. Hwy. 212 between Red Lodge and Cooke City, Mont.

Throughout this book you'll see references to the Beartooth Highway, which has made many a tourist quiver with its narrow, winding road. Charles Kuralt called this the most beautiful drive in America. Built in the 1930s, this road seems to crawl to the top of the world, where rocky crags jut out of lush alpine meadows in summer. At once rugged and fragile, this wild terrain is ruled by the stormy whims of winter. In summer, snow clings to north facing slopes. Diehard skiers and snowboarders pack their snow-sliding toys to headwalls, and bomb down vertical snowfields on the Fourth of July. Trails etched into the grassy meadows lead everywhere into the wilderness.

The weather at this elevation is so unpredictable that in 1947, after the road had been opened for the summer, a sudden snowstorm caught motorists unawares. When a snow-plow slipped into the ditch and blocked the the road, motorists were caught in the snow for the night. By morning, the cars were buried in snow, and three men in a trapped pickup truck were found dead, frozen by the sudden summer storm.

At the summit, you'll find the Top of the World Store, open only in summer. The owners, former school teachers, return each June to dig their store out. In 1997, when they reached the store in mid-June, it was buried under a 23-foot snowdrift.

Northwestern Wyoming

Buffalo Bill Historical Center
720 Sheridan Ave., Cody, Wyo.
• **(307) 587-4771**

There is so much to do and see in this world-class museum that it could take you more than a day to work your way through it. Don't worry or hurry: Your BBHC ticket is good for two consecutive days. Along the way you will likely find films, gallery presentations or tours for you and your children. Stop and enjoy them — especially the hands-on demonstrations scattered throughout the center.

The original Buffalo Bill Museum, housed in a log building similar to Cody's ranch house, opened in 1927. Today, that little museum has become the 237,000-square-foot Buffalo Bill Historical Center, with four wings housing an art gallery and three museums. The Whitney Gallery of Western Art features an extensive collection by artists who have documented and interpreted the West since the 19th century. The Buffalo Bill Museum contains the frontiersman's memorabilia. The Plains Indian Museum captures the past and present of the natives to the land, and the Cody Firearms Museum, the complex's newest wing, has the largest collection of American firearms in the world.

Also included in the Center is the Harold McCracken Research Library, which contains nearly 15,000 books and manuscripts as well as 250,000 photographs.

A full-time staff of 70 and a part-time staff of 125 work to not only run the museum, but also plan cultural events and educational workshops for all ages. The BBHC also has a special educational program designed for local schools.

The Buffalo Bill Historical Center is open year-round, but the hours vary dramatically depending on the time of year. We suggest you call ahead to find out for yourself. Admission is $8 for adults, $6.50 for senior citizens, $4 for youth ages 13 to 21 and $2 for children ages 6 to 12. Children younger than 6 are admitted free.

Cody Nite Rodeo
421 W. Yellowstone, Cody, Wyo.
• **(307) 587-2992**

Started in the 1930s to entice travelers to spend a night (and some of their money) in Cody, the Cody Nite Rodeo is one big attraction that runs nightly from Memorial Day through Labor Day. For more information on the Cody Nite Rodeo, see our Spectator Sports chapter.

Heart Three Carriage Service
1701 Sheridan Ave., Cody, Wyo.
• **(307) 587-3595, (307) 899-1485**

Step back in time and leave the driving to Ken Larew and his crew as they carry you through Cody in a carriage. You'll find Heart 3 Carriage Service on Sheridan Avenue (Cody's main street) somewhere near the Irma Hotel or at the Holiday Inn up the street during the summer only. (If you don't spot him right away, listen for the clip clop of his horses' hooves on the pavement.) For $10 per person, Larew will take you on a one-hour historical tour of Cody June through mid-September.

If a historical tour isn't your bag, Larew will take you most anyplace you want to go. Each year 15 to 30 wedding parties ride to and from the church in his carriages. And around the holidays, locals book Larew to take them on a one-hour Christmas lights tour. Larew also carries Santa Claus to the Buffalo Bill Historical Center each Christmas. Larew runs carriages from 3 PM until the sidewalks are empty.

Old Trail Town
Yellowstone Hwy. west of Cody, Wyo.
• **(307) 587-5302**

This may be the most reasonably priced attraction and the most interesting in all of Greater Yellowstone. For sure, it's a labor of love.

Situated on either side of an old wagon road are 26 pre-1900 cabins, 100 horse-drawn vehicles and an extensive collection of frontier memorabilia. Behind the town you'll find the graves of frontiersmen such as Jeremiah "Liver-Eatin'" Johnston and Phillip Vetter, a trapper killed by a grizzly. The bones of these notables were exhumed and moved to the Old Trail Town graves.

Husband-and-wife team Bob and Terry Edgar began collecting cabins in 1967. Bob, an archaeologist, historian and Western artist, disassembled and reassembled old cabins in the townsite. Meanwhile, he and Terry lived in one of the cabins without electricity or running water. Admission to Old Trail Town was $3 in 1997.

Spirit Mountain Aviation
3227 Dugglby Dr., Cody, Wyo.
• **(307) 587-6732**

For a change of scenery, get above it all with Spirit Mountain Aviation, a charter flight service that offers scenic air tours over Yellowstone Park. From the air, you can see how Yellowstone Country fits together, how the Grand Canyon is tied to Yellowstone Lake by a ribbon of river and how Yellowstone Park is protected by massive mountain ranges. From above, the changing colors of the Park's hot springs come more into focus. Joe Siligato will also fly you anyplace else you want to see from a bird's-eye view. A flight over Yellowstone will cost you $100 each if there are two of you. Bring some friends along and save money. The cost is $67.50 per person for three people and $50 per person for four people.

Buffalo Bill Dam Visitor Center
4804 North Fork Hwy., Cody, Wyo.
• **(307) 527-6076**

The Buffalo Bill Dam blocked the North Fork of the Shoshone River, giving life to the dry lands of the Bighorn Basin. One of the first three major dams built by the newly formed Bureau of Reclamation, the Buffalo Bill Dam was the highest in the nation (328 feet) when it was built in 1910.

Six miles west of Cody, the little visitor center/rest area depicts the story of the dam's construction. Standing on the walkway above the dam, you also get a sense of how dramatically the dam changed the river. This visitor center is open from May through September. There is no admission charge.

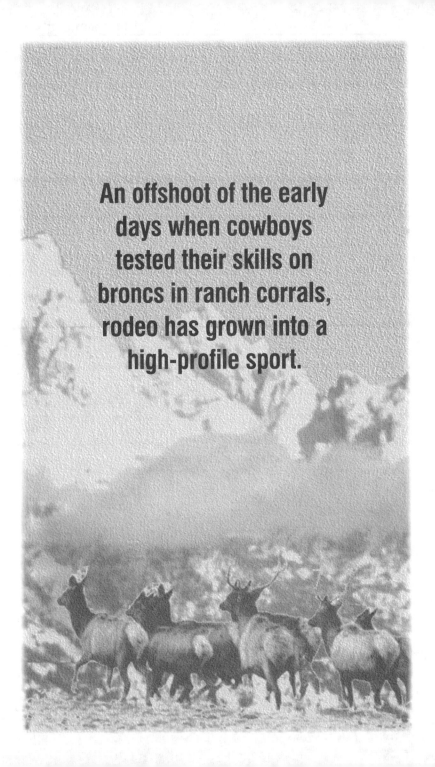

An offshoot of the early days when cowboys tested their skills on broncs in ranch corrals, rodeo has grown into a high-profile sport.

Spectator Sports

Rodeo and the endangered cowboy culture it glorifies have penetrated the psyches of folks from Jackson to Germany, from Japan to New Jersey. An offshoot of the early days when cowboys tested their skills on broncs in ranch corrals, rodeo has grown into a high-profile sport that glorifies the skills once depended upon and now seldom used in cattle ranching. These days, you'll find that top hands on the rodeo circuit are often city boys with a talent for riding or roping but no ranch experience.

The riding events are remnants of the days when cowboys replenished their remudas (string of saddle horses) with wild horses fresh off the range. Cowboys wasted no time breaking their horses. They just jumped on and rode — and hit the dirt plenty often before they had a bronc lined out. Those who could ride a high-pitching horse quickly built reputations repeated around the lonely campfires of the range. In today's rodeo riding events — bareback, saddle bronc and bull riding — competitors climb astride animals born to buck. They have to ride the critter for eight seconds. And they have to look good doing it. The better they look and the harder the animal bucks, the higher the score.

Even the best horseman wasn't worth a hoot if he couldn't throw a lariat. On the range and in the corral, cowboys depended on their lariats to rope, brand and doctor calves, yearlings, cows and even bulls. Today's calf-roping events, in which both calf and rider break at full speed out of their respective chutes, requires a fast, reliable horse and consistently good roping. (We've seen team ropers practicing in airports while waiting to catch a plane to their next rodeo.) The slower team-roping event is a timed event in which one rider ropes the head and the other ropes the hind feet of a steer. Each "takes a dally" (wraps the rope around the saddle horn), before stretching the animal out on the ground. On the range, a few cowboys still use these skills to doctor livestock. Steer wrestling or bull doggin', is a crazy timed event in which the rider leans off his galloping horse, grabs a running steer by the horns, slides off his horse, then wrestles the steer to the ground. In barrel racing — the major event for women — riders race around three barrels then back to the finish line, trying to beat the clock.

At some rodeos, you'll see calf scrambles and mutton busting during a break in the regular action. In a calf scramble, a 150-pound calf (or even somebody's milk cow) is turned loose in the arena with dollar bills glued to it. A herd of kids chases after the cirtter, trying to grab the money. Each rodeo committee varies the details on the same theme. In mutton busting, kids try to ride bucking sheep. Other half-time events may include wild cow milking or a wild horse race. Each can be plenty dangerous. The wild horse race, though, may be the worst. Six teams are each assigned to the wild horse, which they must saddle, then ride.

In some smaller towns of Greater Yellowstone, like Gardiner and Ennis, you'll find less polished amateur rodeos with an earthy hometown flavor. For locals, these rodeos are an annual celebration. Clubs, businesses, kids, firemen, bands and cheerleaders dress up and parade down Main Street. The rest of the town watches them. At the smaller rodeos, you're apt to see hometown boys and girls entering events. You'll also eat a bit more dust — we said they were down to earth — and be exposed to whatever the weather brings. Afterward, chances are good you'll get swept into post-rodeo celebrations on local barroom dance floors.

At professional rodeos — especially the bigger ones like those in Red Lodge, Livingston, and Cody, all held on the Fourth of July — you'll find better bucking stock and nationally ranked rodeo cowboys. Most of the hands who compete in these rodeos are working up to a dozen rodeos in a six-day period around the holiday. They'll fly into a rodeo (Red Lodge has an airstrip adjacent to the grounds) just in time to ride, then fly away again as soon as they've ridden.

Most rodeos are annual events, and many in Greater Yellowstone happen on the Fourth of July. For more regularly scheduled rodeo shows, you can go to Cody and Jackson. In Cody, the self-proclaimed Rodeo Capital of the World, you can see a show every night from Memorial Day through Labor Day. Each summer up to 100,000 spectators crowd into the Cody Nite Rodeo, a show that has dominated the Cody tourist scene for 60 years. In Jackson, you'll find a twice-weekly rodeo during the summer months.

Besides rodeo, you'll find a few other Yellowstone Country sports to watch, mostly in the winter. Jackson Hole hosts races of all kinds, including snowmobile, dogsled and cutter. In West Yellowstone, a snowmobile race attracts nearly 15,000 spectators. In Red Lodge you'll find the National Skijoring Finals. And baseball fans can take themselves out to the ballgame to watch the Idaho Falls Braves, a farm team for the San Diego Padres.

Mostly, though, as you will soon discover, folks in Greater Yellowstone are more into doing than spectating.

In this chapter, we continue our geographic organization, and then group our spectator sports categories within those regions. Needless to say, "Rodeo" is the only category in some places.

Yellowstone National Park Entrance Communities

Rodeo

Upper Yellowstone Roundup
Gardiner Rodeo Grounds, Gardiner,
Mont. • (406) 848-7971
This amateur rodeo, sanctioned by the

Northern Rodeo Association and held on Father's Day weekend, is one of those hometown rodeos that's a little more like Montana "used to be." You're apt to see more people draped on fences, kids wearing cowboy hats half their size and hamburger stands. In the arena, things are little more casual. Instead of featuring high-powered professionals who may have grown up in Brooklyn, you'll be watching mostly homegrown cowboys and diehard grandpas who rodeo close to home because they just have to — it's in their blood. Besides its small town ambiance, the Upper Yellowstone Roundup is known for its long lineup of bull riders — 30 to 60 of them per rodeo — and its long, interminably long slack time during which extra contestants compete after the rodeo. The stands are exposed to the elements. In Gardiner in June, that means you could be going sleeveless, or bundled up or both. Bring a blanket, a cooler and sunscreen. And bring your friends. Admission is around $10.

Winter Events

SnoWest SnoCross and ISOC Cross Country Snowmobile Races
Old Airport, West Yellowstone, Mont.
• (406) 646-7701
Each mid-March, 13,000 people pack into West Yellowstone to watch 250 professional, semipro and amateur racers buzz, whine and jump their way through the SnoWest SnoCross races. It's here that the huge jumps and high-flying sleds separate the pros from the Sunday drivers. The fans love it. This race is one of the top-10 snowmobile races in the snowbelt and the last big one of the season. The top racers in Canada and the United States show up for this one. The ISOC (International Series of Champions) sanctions another one-day, 100-mile cross-country race on the Friday of this event. The sponsor (*SnoWest Magazine* in Idaho Falls) starts preparing the track days ahead of time.

Eastern Idaho

Rodeo

Idaho Falls Centennial Rodeo
Sandy Downs, 6855 S. 15 E., Idaho Falls, Idaho • (208) 522-5030

In 1997 this Intermountain Professional Rodeo Association rodeo was voted best rodeo of the year by Association cowboys. It drew more than 500 competitors and 7,000 spectators. And although most spectators came to see the eight timed and roughstock events, from bronc riding to barrel racing, the calf riding probably got the most laughs: 5- to 11-year-old kids trying to ride skittish 150-pound calves. The calf-riding winner each night is awarded a trophy that probably stands higher than the kid's cowboy hat. Tickets for this rodeo, held in early June, are around $7.

War Bonnet Roundup
Sandy Downs, 6855 S. 15 E., Idaho Falls, Idaho • (208) 523-1010

One of only four professional rodeos in eastern Idaho, the PRCA-sanctioned War Bonnet is also the state's oldest: The bucking chutes first blew open on this rodeo in 1911. More than 250 contestants compete in seven events for prize money and the rodeo's trademark award: Winchester .30-.30s for each event's high score or best time. Around 7,500 spectators usually catch one or more of the three days' show. For kids, the best show is the mutton busting: Ten kids each night climb aboard a sheep, lace their fingers into the woolly back and, when the gate flies open, try to stay on. The rodeo's best mutton buster is

also awarded a BB gun. The event is held the first weekend in August (in 1998, that means it begins July 30). In 1997, adults paid $7 for advance seats and $8 at the door. Thursdays, kids younger than 12 get in free. The rodeo is sponsored by American Legion Bonneville Post 56, and proceeds fund Legion projects and charities.

Jacobs' Island Park Ranch Events
Off Kilgore Rd., Island Park, Idaho • (208) 662-5567, (800) 230-9530

Jacobs' intimate outdoor arena, 6 miles from U.S. Highway 20 on a 2,000-acre working ranch, hosts several Western events every summer. Some of these are bull wars, in which bull riders attempt to stay seated on huge animals 10 times their weight. Others include rodeos featuring a variety of other rough stock as well as timed events. Best of all is the National Cutting Horse Show in which highly trained cow ponies and their riders get to show their stuff. One of the best things about watching a bronc rider or calf roper at Jacobs' is the fact that the grandstands are small and close to the action: You won't need your binoculars here. Admission for rodeos and bull wars was around $7 in 1997. The National Cutting Horse Show, which takes place the second weekend in August, is free to spectators. Call for other dates and times.

Island Park Wild Horse Stampede
Idaho Hwy. 67, north side of Henry's Lake at Island Park, Idaho • (208) 754-4271

It all started 52 years ago, when actress Jane Russell, in Island Park to make a movie, told local rancher Vern Crystal she'd love to see a rodeo. He and other area ranchers

---

INSIDERS' TIP

Idaho's biggest rodeo and your best chance to see world-class talent ripping up the rodeo arena takes place every March in Pocatello, Idaho, about 50 miles south of Idaho Falls. More than $400,000 is up for grabs, making the Dodge National Circuit Finals Rodeo one of the most lucrative in the Pro Rodeo Cowboys Association, rodeo's most venerable sanctioning body. Area motels and grandstand seats fill fast for this five-day event, so make your plans early. Call Pocatello's Holt Arena at (208) 236-2831.

Cody Nite Rodeo

In 1938 a group of Cody, Wyoming, businessmen started the Cody Nite Rodeo hoping the event would entice Yellowstone Park visitors to spend the night — and some money — in their town. The idea stuck, and the town has put on a nightly rodeo from Memorial Day through Labor Day each summer since, earning Cody the title of Rodeo Capital of the World. Rodeo, often the only English word clearly spoken by foreign visitors, has become Cody's hallmark.

Close-up

Gathering folks up for an evening of rompin', stompin' rodeo fun has become a science with a sense of humor. Each summer, rodeo contractors Jim and Cathy Ivory hire a young cowboy to cruise main street for 10 hours a day, seven days a week, in a gold 1978 Cadillac. Draped across the hood of the slow-moving cruiser is a set of 5-foot-wide longhorns. Perched on top of the Cadillac is a loudspeaker blaring cowboy music interrupted by frequent announcements from the driver. Each evening the Ivorys send a bus to Cody motels and campgrounds to pick up fans.

Behind the chutes at the rodeo grounds west of town are the animals, the cowboys and the contractors — the Ivorys — that keep the show rolling night after night. By day, Jim cares for his stock as carefully as if they were his football team in training. Their care doesn't end with feeding. Jim says he is so attuned to his horses — 150 of them, each with a different disposition — he notices immediately if one of them is feeling out of sorts. Jim bucks them according to their age and personality. Some horses like to buck once a week, while others do better bucking every other week. Some horses perform better when they're packing a bit of extra weight, and others do better when they're slim and trim. It's Ivory's job to know which is which. Some are older horses that have been to the National Finals but are too old to

— continued on next page

Photo: Cathy Ivory

Bull-riding and other rodeo events at The Cody Nite Rodeo attract about 90,000 spectators each summer.

withstand the stress of traveling weekly in a semi-truck with a stock contractor who follows the regular rodeo circuit. Other horses are young ones just learning to buck.

That's right, there's an art to bucking. Like an athlete, horses develop their own techniques over time to best buck off those pesky riders. Just watch them in the arena after they've succeeded. They'll gallop or trot around the arena, head high, tail up, looking proud as can be. Often, a rancher will bring in a horse that nobody can ride and ask Jim to try him out in the rodeo. Ivory only has to watch the horse buck one time to learn whether or not it has potential.

Once horses have passed the born-to-buck test, Ivory looks for other qualities, such as straightforward "pretty" bucking that makes both horse and rider look good. (Some horses are dirty duckers, divers and whirlers. They look bad, they're hard to ride, and they can hurt the rider.) Next, he looks for a horse that will give a cowboy a soft landing. Some horses have a knack for throwing their riders high in the air. Ivory cares for his bulls the same way. And he looks for bulls that look good bucking and won't hurt the riders.

Ironically, Ivory's string of regular cowboys match his stock string: They're mainly either young and improving or older and staying close to home. Some of them are college kids bent on improving their riding and roping skills so they can follow the Professional Rodeo Cowboys Association rodeo circuit. While some of them work regular jobs by day, others simply rodeo each night and live on their winnings. A few PRCA riders rodeo in Cody during the week and at PRCA rodeos on the weekends. Like the older horses in Ivory's string, some of the riders are older family men who don't want to travel but can't get rodeo out of their blood.

Each day during the summer, Ivory and his crew work and draw stock for the night's rodeo. The announcer simultaneously encourages the budding young riders and educates newcomers in the audience. Two clowns — one a bullfighter and the other a clown — fight bulls and fill in the gaps. Clown Tony Martoglio is one of the best in the business, says Cathy Ivory. He works the Cody Nite Rodeo so that he can be home with his family. (Following the pro rodeo circuit means kissing your family good-bye for most of the year.)

A tight-knit brotherhood, the rodeo hands hang out at the grounds by day, hauling hay, talking horses and helping out with the stock. For many, the rodeo grounds are home — so much so that they hold their own weekly church services there. Behind the scenes, Jim and Cathy Ivory round up visitors, stock and cowboys for 90 straight days of the Cody Nite Rodeo.

---

obliged; it was so much fun they've been doing it ever since. Crystal Bros. Ranch hosts this three-day professional rodeo the first weekend of every August in an arena overlooking the clear waters of Henry's Lake. It begins with bull wars on Friday, fine excitement since bull riders are arguably the smallest contenders in rodeo and bulls are the largest critters. Eight regular timed and rough stock rodeo events make up the action on Saturday and Sunday. Other events include calf riding for kids (Crystal Bros. provides the bicycle helmets) and wild-cow milking and wild-horse racing for adults. Wild-horse racing is particularly wild, since as many three-person teams as enter (usually around six) are

in the arena at the same time catching, saddling and then riding the same number of unbroken horses. About 7,000 people attend the Stampede at a cost of around $7 per person.

Winter Races

Ashton American Dog Derby
Main St., Ashton, Idaho • (208) 652-3377

In good snow conditions, a six-dog team can cover a 40-mile course in less than six hours. Every year in the third week of February, up to 34 six- and 10-dog teams try to do just that. The race runs two days, during which six-dog teams clock around 80 miles, and 10-dog teams travel more than 120. Hundreds and sometimes thousands show up to watch the start and finish-line excitement on Main Street. Others come for the silliness of the Mutt Races one block off Main. One year two Chihuahuas participated in this short race, one of them pulling a tiny sled driven by a Barbie doll. Other events include weight pulls and junior dogsled races.

Island Park Snowcross

Henry's Lake Flats, U.S. Hwy. 20 at mile marker 396, Mack's Inn, Island Park, Idaho • (208) 558-7818

Imagine a motocross race on snow and ice instead of dirt, with low-slung snowmobiles executing those jumps and whipping turns with the same screaming intensity as a motorcycle. That's snowcross. Sanctioned by the Rocky Mountain Cross Country Racing Circuit and hosted by Sawtelle Sales, Service & Rentals, this race notched its fourth year in 1998, and it's growing fast. The December race draw more than 200 racers to Island Park, competing in categories that range from junior novice to pro. Spectators pay around $5 per day for a standing-area view of the action on the track.

National Finals Skijoring

Red Lodge Rodeo Grounds, Red Lodge, Mont. • (406) 446-1718

Cowboys on horseback with skiers in tow, gallop around a 250-yard-long course with 16 to 24 gates and several jumps. In 1997, 128 teams from six states entered the competition, which is held the second weekend in March. In order to place, competitors must be upright with at least one ski on the ground when they cross the finish line. This event, held at the Red Lodge Rodeo Grounds, is an offshoot of old-time ranch entertainment. Admission price in 1997 was $3.

Other Sports

Idaho Falls Braves Baseball

McDermott Field, 568 W. Elva, Idaho Falls, Idaho • (208) 522-8363

It's professional baseball with an old-fashioned, kick-back-and-enjoy-a-summer-evening flavor. Braves games don't often sell out, but nearly 60,000 fans attended 36 home games last year. A farm team for the San Diego Padres, the Braves have 400 season-seat holders, 150 corporate sponsors and 300 to 500 members of the Junior Braves Club. The season opens in mid-June and ends around Labor Day weekend. Better seats are $6; general admission is $4.50. A variety of contests and mascots enliven the evening including last year's addition: a chipping contest in which fans try to hit a golf ball into a regulation-size hole from 20 yards. Last year one woman came within 6 inches, but so far nobody has won the prize: a $10,000 car.

Sandy Downs Off-Track Betting

6855 S. 15 E., Idaho Falls, Idaho • (208) 529-0671

Especially in winter when not much is going on around here, folks meet under the grandstands at the local horse track for simulcast betting. Sandy Downs broadcasts five different horse tracks and one dog track on more TVs than you'll take the time to count. Bettors meet Wednesday through Sunday afternoon and evening year-round. No food is available, but you can get a soda or beer. On a weekend afternoon, you'll be sharing the action with perhaps 30 other race enthusiasts.

INSIDERS' TIP

Bucking horses and bulls wear a flank strap, a sheepskin-lined strip of leather that cinches snugly behind the rib cage. It's equipped with a quick release buckle to protect the animal in case of freak accident. Pro Rodeo Cowboy Association spokespeople and veterinarians say the flank strap doesn't cause pain or make the animals buck. They say roughstock animals buck because they want to. The flank strap apparently just provides something more to fight against.

Southwestern Montana

Rodeo

Livingston Roundup
Rodeo Park County Fairgrounds, Livingston, Mont. • (406) 222-3199

This fast-paced rodeo features Kesler Rodeo Stock. Insiders know that means top-of-the-line bucking horses and bulls. (Kesler ranks among the top three stock contractors used at the National Finals Rodeo.) They also know that good stock attracts top hands. Combine those two ingredients with a crew that knows how to keep the action rolling and an award-winning announcer and you have one of the best little pro rodeos in the West. The Roundup, held July 2 through July 4, is one of the three Gateway Rodeos held over the Fourth of July each year in Yellowstone Country. That means professional cowboys travel back and forth between Livingston, Red Lodge and Cody, riding at each place to increase the odds of winning prize money. (The purse at Livingston totaled $44,000 in 1997.) In addition to the traditional rodeo contests, the event features skydivers who land in the middle of the arena. Fireworks are also launched each night at the end of the rodeo events. Admission in 1997 was $12 for reserved seats, $8 for general admission and $4 for children ages 6 to 12.

Home of Champions Rodeo
Red Lodge Rodeo Grounds, Red Lodge, Mont. • (406) 446-1718

Red Lodge is the small town with the big rodeo. Marking its 70th season in 1998, the Home of Champions Rodeo has been so called because of the hometown boys and girls who have made good on the rodeo circuit. Most notable are the Greenoughs and the Lindermans. Sisters Alice and Marge Greenough, who grew up on a ranch outside Red Lodge, were champion bronc riders who went clear to Madison Square Garden in New York. Their brother, Turk, and Alice rode into fame from the 1920s clear into the 1950s. In the early days, the Crow Indians used to come from the reservation, set up their tepees and hold races on the track that then circled the rodeo grounds.

These days, you'll see a crew of champion riders emerging from a Lear jet that's just landed on the runway adjacent to the rodeo grounds. If you pay close attention, you'll note that they arrive just in time for the grand entry. And they'll stay just long enough to compete before flying off to another rodeo. Besides the usual menu of events, Red Lodge features a wild-horse race and a calf scramble for kids. In Red Lodge, the rodeo doesn't begin or end in the arena. The parade is legendary, and the saloons are packed after showtime.

Admission in 1997 ranged from $8 to $16. The rodeo is held July 2 to 4.

Ennis Rodeo
Ennis Rodeo Grounds, Ennis, Mont. • (406) 682-4388

You're in the heart of ranching country here. Don't expect the high-powered, polished bucking stock of bigger rodeos. Do expect the unexpected and a much more homey feeling than at the bigger pro rodeos. And remember that many of the riders you'll see at this amateur rodeo have come right off the ranch. Like the horses, they're a little less sophisticated. Besides the rodeo, there's lots to see behind the scenes and in the stands. Unlike some of the bigger rodeo grounds that make it difficult for you to connect with Locals, you can wander about among the pickup trucks and trailers catching glimpses of contestants caring for their horses, gear and families.

The Ennis Rodeo is always held on July 3 and 4. On July 3, the performance begins at 8 PM; on July 4, the show is at 2 PM. The weather at this rodeo is pretty consistent — it either rains or snows, or it's 120 degrees. Tickets cost $8 for reserved seating and $6 general admission.

Northwestern Wyoming

Rodeo

Cody Nite Rodeo
Stampede Park Rodeo Grounds, Cody, Wyo. • (307) 587-2992

Pack into the Cody Nite Rodeo just once

and you'll know why this town is called the Rodeo Capital of the World. Every summer's night for the past 60 years, fans have sat on the edges of their seats watching bucking stock twist, twirl, buck and duck the cowboys who dare to ride them. Geared for tourists, many of whom don't speak English, the announcer at this rodeo colors his comments with educational tidbits that only Insiders know. Contractors Jim and Cathy Ivory, who own the stock and run the show, produce more than a nightly tourist attraction. Behind the scenes, they're helping young rodeo hands hone their skills. And they're cultivating cayuses that are born to buck. (Some of them have been to or are headed for the National Finals Rodeo.) Besides bareback and saddle bronc riding, the nightly show includes calf roping, team roping, bull dogging, barrel racing for cowgirls and steer riding for the younger cowboys. Kids in the stands are also invited to join in a calf scramble and stick-horse races. The Ivorys make getting to the rodeo easy: A rodeo bus will pick you up at your campground or motel.

In 1997, grandstand seating for adults cost $10 ($4 for children). Seats in the Buzzard's Roost above the chutes cost $12 for adults and $6 for kids. Tickets for the 8:30 PM show can be purchased at the gate after 7 PM, at the ticket booth wagon in City Park, at many Cody businesses and at the chamber of commerce office (see the Resources chapter). The rodeos begin June 1 and end August 31.

Stampede Rodeo
Stampede Park Rodeo Grounds, Cody, Wyo. • (307) 587-5155

Let's face it. Cody folks just like to be the best. And when it comes to rodeo, you'd be hard-pressed to find one better than the Cody Stampede, held July 1 to July 4. Celebrating its 79th consecutive season in 1998, Cody's four-day Stampede is the richest Fourth of July rodeo in the world. A $240,000 purse in 1997 drew 450 professional cowboys. Among them were most of the top hands on the national circuit. Attracting the best cowboys doesn't stop with the purse. At the grounds, the Stampede Board provides a hospitality room for riders where they can lounge in comfort, eat homecooked meals and watch the rodeo on closed-circuit TV. The board also chauffeurs

cowboys flying in and out of Cody's Yellowstone Regional Airport. You'll find the best horseback-riding announcer, a top rodeo stock contractor and a state-of-the-art sound system. What you won't notice is how the chutes, gates and working corrals are set up to make the whole show run smoothly. This topnotch rodeo is a fast-moving show with world-class stock. Besides the usual events, Cody features a wild-horse race described in the introduction to this chapter. In addition to the rodeo itself, the Stampede features two parades (one just for kids) and music in the City Park. Admission in 1997 was $14 for the July 1 to July 3 shows and $15 for the July 4 show.

Jackson Hole

Rodeo

J.H. Rodeo
Fairgrounds on Snow King Ave., Jackson, Wyo. • (307) 733-2805

Most rodeos run once a year; this one goes twice a week, Memorial Day to Labor Day. Practice makes perfect: J.H. Rodeo runs snappy, with little hang time between events. The cowboys aren't pros, but some of them are headed that way. Right now they're competing for fun, for practice or for the couple hundred dollars in the winners' purses. All events except steer wrestling are represented. The rodeo owns its own stock: roughly 30 bulls, 70 horses, 30 roping steers and 25 calves. The audience-participation event is a calf scramble for kids ages 4 to 12. Two calves with ribbons tied to their tails are set loose among 50 to 100 kids from the audience. Winners snag the ribbons. Reserved seats were $10 last year. Tickets at the door cost $8 for festival seating.

Winter Events

Jackson Hole Shrine Club Cutter Races
Off U.S. Hwy. 26, 5 miles south of Jackson, Wyo. • (307) 733-3316

Cutters are sleighs pulled by horse teams, but you won't see any at this race.

Photo: Jackson Hole Chamber of Commerce

Every President's Day Weekend, the Jackson Hole Shrine Club
sponsors cutter races on snow at a track south of Jackson.

Instead you'll cheer two teams of two horses each as they thunder wheeled chariots across the finish line. At least 20 races are staged each day. Food and beverages are available. So is Calcutta betting, where tickets representing the two teams are auctioned to the highest bidder. The holder of the winning team's ticket also wins. Contestants come from all over the Intermountain West. Spectators come from across the country. The event is held every President's Weekend, usually the second weekend of February. In 1997, attendance cost $5 per day. Make sure you bundle up: You'll be sitting outside and even on a sunny day, Jackson in February is not warm. The popular event raises money for Shriners' programs and hospitals. For the second year in a row, the Shriners will host a second cutter racing event sometime in September 1998.

International Rocky Mountain Stage Stop Sled Dog Race
Various locations in and around Jackson Hole, Wyo. • (307) 734-1163

This 10-day race draws world-famous mushers and topnotch sled teams. The race begins and ends in Jackson Hole. The first stage is best watched from Jackson's town square. The final push, another good show, brings contestants barreling into Teton Village. The closing banquet is held at Snow King Resort in Jackson.

World Championship Snowmobile Hillclimb
Snow King Ave., Jackson, Wyo.
• (307) 734-9653

This snowmobile event draws enough spectators to fill every motel in Jackson to its roof. Starting from the base of Snow King Resort's steepest ski run, contestants from all over the country barrel up the hill at top speed through a challenging course. The "Kings/Queens of the Mountain" climb highest or get to the top fastest. Jackson Hole Snow Devils, a nonprofit snowmobile club, sponsors the event, which attracts more than 200 contestants every year. More than 10,000 spectators daily ride the lifts to a viewing spot or hike up from the bottom of the mountain. Some pay a couple of bucks to stand in the ballpark at the base of the mountain. The hillclimb runs from the last Thursday through the last Sunday in March. Sunday is arguably the wildest day, since that's when the finals are run, and only about 30 percent of each class qualifies to participate.

We've included only the
most wonderful of
wonders: the animals,
mountain terrain and
hydrothermic fireworks
that seem to stand out
in people's minds
before they arrive
and after they leave.

Our Natural World

It happens the first time you see the ponderous swagger of a grizzly, the jagged grandeur of the Grand Teton dressed in tattered clouds or the improbable loveliness of Yellowstone Park's Opalescent Pool: You're hooked. And you realize that those interesting restaurants, cozy bed and breakfast inns and picturesque ski resorts — in fact, all the great tourist attractions and diversions Yellowstone country offers — are just at the surface of things. Underneath is the really glamorous stuff. This region hosts natural wonders so unique that the stories of Yellowstone's first explorers were disbelieved, so rare and fine that the people who saw them with their own eyes wanted this place preserved forever. This chapter is about these Greater Yellowstone wonders — what makes them tick and how they came to be.

We've included only the most wonderful of wonders: the animals, mountain terrain and hydrothermal fireworks that seem to stand out in people's minds both before they arrive and after they leave. We'll tell you about the Yellowstone hot spot and Yellowstone National Park's hydrothermal magic. We'll tell you a bit about the rugged landscape of this region and how it formed. The plant communities upon which everything else depends get a glance, too.

We give much of our space, though, to the wildlife. This region contains the last nearly intact ecosystem in the country. The variety of creatures here is astounding, including once-common animals that now exist in few other places.

Grizzlies, bald eagles, gray wolves, bighorn sheep and bison live in this one place much as they once did across the West. Another reason wildlife is worth looking for here is that it can be found. These animals may exist in other wild areas, but they are likely to be nearly impossible to glimpse, either because they're extremely wary or because they're rare. Because Greater Yellowstone hosts so many visitors each year, much of its wildlife has learned to tolerate humans, especially in the region's two national parks. So although Yellowstone's wildlife *is* wild, some creatures are easier to view here than anyplace else you might encounter them except, perhaps, in a zoo.

Our Geothermal Features: The Yellowstone Hot Spot

Geologists believe the earth consists mostly of molten rock, so what looks like solid land to us actually are thin plates floating like vast life rafts on this fiery ball of a planet. Where they meet, one plate slips under another, and the diving edge melts back into the molten sea. Sometimes they slide, in fits and starts, past each other. From the human perspective, this giant-scale rearranging of the planet's surface happens in agonizing slow motion — inches or less a year — except for the sudden corrections that are earthquakes and the sudden release of melted plate material that probably trigger some volcanic eruptions.

Geologists further theorize that there are places in this molten ball that act as pipelines to the even hotter material of the earth's center. The ball and its heat-conducting pipelines don't move but the life rafts above do. This means residents of life rafts currently passing over one of these hot spots are going to experience some weird phenomena — as weird as, say, Yellowstone Park, where between 150 and 200 geysers spout steam and hot water into the air; where a scientific team can dig 265 feet into the earth and encounter temperatures in excess of 400 degrees; where 107 known groups of hot springs percolate; and where, all told, there are at least 10,000 individual thermal features. Like a pot on a hot stove, Yellowstone simmers and steams.

One mark of a good theory is the number of questions it can answer. The hot-spot theory addresses questions such as, "Why does the Park radiate enough heat to melt 19 tons of ice every second?" and "Why is there a path of old volcanic activity stretching across what is now the Snake River plain of southern Idaho and leading straight to Yellowstone Park — a path consisting of craters, dead volcanoes and old lava flows?" It also explains why volcanoes get younger as they get closer to Yellowstone and why, just west of the massive collapsed lava dome of the Yellowstone Plateau, exists an even larger collapsed dome, called the Island Park Caldera.

The hot-spot theory can't account for the wonder of Yellowstone by itself, though. A similar hot spot is supposed to exist under the Hawaiian Islands, and they don't have an Old Faithful or a Mammoth Hot Springs. The missing ingredient is water. Yellowstone's unique features are hydrothermic ("hydro" means water and "thermic" means hot). Groundwater is plentiful here, and volcanic rock is porous. The water percolates into the rock, getting increasingly warm and pressurized as it descends. Pressure keeps water liquid, even in its superheated state, even in an increasingly superheated state, in some cases probably hotter than 500 degrees. Some water may penetrate as deeply as 2 miles. How hot it gets and how it returns to the surface determines what sort of hydrothermal feature you see.

Hot Springs

In one sense, all hydrothermal features in the Park are hot springs because they all involve heated water, but the phrase is commonly used to talk about two kinds of features: the trickling springs that form terraced hillsides like those at Mammoth and pools of warm or even boiling water like Doublet Pool, Blue Star Spring and Crested Pool in the Upper Geyser Basin.

At Mammoth and places like it, the subterranean water runs through calcium carbonate (limestone), dissolving the mineral as it goes. When the solution reaches the surface and trickles downslope, the calcium carbonate is deposited into those pale, lumpy walls and terraces you see. The material of which the walls are made is called travertine and is similar in composition to marble.

Hot springs pools in Yellowstone are often lovely shades of blue, black or green. The blue color comes from the geyserite (also called sinter) that lines the walls of the pool. This coating consists mostly of silica dissolved out of the volcanic rock from which the water emerged. The full spectrum of light enters the water, but only the blue light waves bounce off the geyserite and are reflected back through the water. Dissolved silica in the water can change the color to baby-blue.

All but the hottest springs contain or are surrounded by living creatures: orange, green, red and yellow bacteria, green and yellow algae mats or blood-red hot-springs mites. These living elements, coupled with the chemicals dissolved in the pools and the minerals that line them, make possible all the colors of the rainbow. Orange bacteria coupled with water that would appear blue will create the appearance of a pool of black water. Yellow algae in what would otherwise be blue water creates a pool that appears bright green.

Geysers

Yellowstone's most famous feature is probably Old Faithful, a geyser that erupts about every 74 minutes. But only 3 percent of the Park's hydrothermal features are geysers. To be a geyser, a hot spring must occasionally or regularly eject steam and water. This requires some fairly odd plumbing: Geysers run on a combination of superheated water — water that would like to boil but doesn't have room — and steam explosions.

To create superheated water and to withstand the explosions, a geyser's plumbing needs to consist of an almost vertical chimney or series of chimneys leading down probably at least 200 feet. The walls must be fairly smooth and made of resistant rock. Walls will be further smoothed and strengthened by the gradual formation of geyserite from silicas suspended in the water. These chimneys must also be extremely narrow in order to create the tremendous pressure required to hold water in a liquid state above its boiling point. Geyserite helps here, too, since as it accumulates it gradually narrows the chimney walls. Eventually it will seal the geyser chimney altogether.

At the bottom of the whole plumbing system must be a constantly replenished reservoir of water because water is what the whole system runs on. Exposed to high temperatures and violently restricted at the bottom of this long, narrow chimney, water becomes superheated. The only place it can go is up, so it tries to rise. Pressure from water in the narrow chimneys above prevents this until the pressure from below becomes too great. Then up comes a bubble of superheated water.

What you see when you're standing at the geyser's mouth isn't much — maybe a surging current or a small fountain of water. But that exiting water means that, suddenly, there is more room available below. The pressure that corked the chimney decreases. The superheated water flashes into steam, which instantly increases in volume and has nowhere to go but up in a hurry. Water above the steam explosion is flung into the air on a rising column of steam. As soon as pressure is reduced to below the flashpoint, the geyser quiets and begins to build pressure for next time. This can take seconds or hours.

To imagine the explosive force that produces that lovely, seemingly magical geyser display, imagine this: A cup of boiling water

Wind-chill temperatures near 50 degrees below zero turned Old Faithful's boiling water column into freezing fog and ice.

instantly converted to steam would increase 1,700 times in volume. It would nearly fill two 55-gallon drums.

Mud Pots

A mud pot looks like liquid caulking material someone put on the stove in a big soup pot as a joke. Below the bubbling mess you see, a vent extends through the surface rock, leading to a reservoir of water far below your feet. Steam from this reservoir rises through clays created when acidic ground water dissolved surrounding rock. The watery clays, forced up to the surface by steam pressure from below, burble and spit contentedly as more steam rises through them.

Some, however, explode violently. At Mud Volcano, a giant mud pot existed for a short time that could be heard a mile away in Hayden Valley when its huge clay bubbles burst. In dryer periods when clay consistency becomes thicker, mud pots can hurl clay bombs up to 200 feet.

Also called mud volcanoes or paint pots, the walls of these formations are generally colored by minerals, not algae and bacteria as are many hot springs. Yellows come mostly from sulphur; oranges, reds, browns and blacks come from iron oxides and iron sulfides. These minerals also exist inside the mud pots themselves, accounting for the many colors painted by these bizarre formations.

Fumaroles

Like a geyser or mud pot, this hydrothermal feature runs on steam. But there's very little water in the plumbing system of a fumarole, and what little there is converts to steam as fast as it reaches boiling temperatures. What you see is a smoking hole in the ground. The roaring, hissing sounds, like the "smoke," are from steam exiting the vent.

A Yellowstone Time Bomb?

Geologists study slow-moving phenomena — events that occurred in such a distant past they are recorded only in stone. But the ponderous rhythm of geologic time doesn't seem to apply in Yellowstone. Here the hot spot keeps things hopping. Changes large and small happen almost in the blink of a geologist's eye. New mud pots and geysers form; old ones dry up or become something else, say a hot spring or fumarole.

Thousands of tiny earthquakes are recorded here every year, and between two and 167 annually are strong enough to feel. The last major earthquake in this area created a lake and modified hydrothermic features of the Park, some permanently. It occurred in 1959 and measured 7.5 on the Richter scale. The epicenter was just west of Yellowstone Park, and the temblor was felt across 500,000 square miles. Resulting rock slides in Madison Canyon, Montana, killed 28 people. The largest slide tumbled a mountainside into the Madison River and formed Quake Lake, which still exists today. The lake is narrow but long and backs up the Madison River canyon for about 4.5 miles. After the main shock, around 300 geysers in Yellowstone Park suddenly erupted. At least 160 of these had never been known to erupt. At least one blew so violently it threw 50- and 100-pound slabs of geyserite 50 feet from its vent.

Yellowstone's petrified forests are more distant reminders of the region's potential for dramatic geologic change. Yellowstone Park alone has about 25 square miles of petrified forest. Other patches exist beyond Park boundaries, particularly in the Gallatin National Forest. These eerie sites were created when volcanic eruptions and subsequent mud and ash buried whole forests. Silica, which was dissolved in ground water, percolated through the mummified trees, preserving them right down to their cell structure, including some of their leaves, needles and cones. Specimen Ridge in Yellowstone Park contains layer upon layer of petrified forests. Like a wave rolling up on a beach, volcanic material would inundate a forest. Then the resulting rich volcanic soil gave birth to new trees, which were themselves destroyed by the next wave. The youngest petrified trees here are about 50 million years old. Scientists cluster the volcanic events that created these successive stone forests together, calling it Yellowstone's first volcanic episode.

We seem to be in the middle of the second one. Scientists who study the Yellowstone hot spot say this episode's pattern includes cataclysmic eruptions on a scale that makes Mount St. Helens look like a good neighbor. These eruptions occurred along the hot spot's path at least three times, each at roughly 600,000-year intervals. It's been 600,000 years since the last one. It left a 28-mile-by-47-mile caldera, one of the largest in the world, now partially filled by Yellowstone Lake. It's thought that before the explosion, a huge lava-filled dome formed. Measurements show that, in Yellowstone, the earth's surface is doming again — the area between Old Faithful and Canyon rises about an inch a year.

Our Geology: The Yellowstone Plateau

Just as beautiful as the world-famous hydrothermal features, if not so astounding, are the mountain ranges, high plateaus and glacial valleys of Greater Yellowstone. The Yellowstone Plateau itself is at a high elevation, about 8,000 feet, but the terrain is rolling and, with the exception of the Grand Canyon of the Yellowstone, fairly unimpressive. The plateau was formed primarily in two volcanic episodes. One occurred about 38 to 50 million years ago and also formed much of what are now the Absarokas and the Gallatins. The other, which is ongoing and began about 2 million years ago, is what really gave the plateau its shape. It's believed that the Yellowstone Plateau formed when a gigantic magma bubble spewed its molten interior out onto the earth. The dome collapsed as its contents were depleted. Then it partially refilled, creating the fairly flat terrain of the Yellowstone Plateau.

Basin and Range

Our most impressive mountains are not volcanic in origin, however. At about the same time the plateau was being created — about 50 million years ago — much of what is now the Rockies formed as the earth folded into row after row of mountains separated by row after row of low, flat basin country. Geologists theorize that the cause was the North American plate colliding with the Pacific plate along a line near what is now the Idaho-Oregon border. The collision created the accordion-like folding you might find on a car's hood after a head-on collision — the crumpled topography of much of the western United States. Others have speculated that this part of the North American plate is currently floating atop a massive lump in the magma sea. The result is crustal extension — a stretching of the North American Plate — that created weak spots, or faults, which in turn allowed the folding action to take place.

Whatever its cause, geologists call this vast region "basin and range." The term describes the terrain of parts of Nevada, Utah, Oregon, New Mexico, Arizona, Idaho, California and Wyoming. The Tetons are its eastern edge.

As we said, most of the north-south mountain ranges and wide basins of this region formed about 50 million years ago, but not so the Tetons. They're only 9 million years old. That's why, even in the middle of rugged,

mountainous country, they stand out. They seem to shred the clouds and steal scalloped bites out of the moon. The Grand Teton is not the tallest mountain in Greater Yellowstone — that honor, by about 100 feet, goes to Wyoming's Gannett Peak — but its impossibly steep profile and its soaring leap nearly 7,000 feet from the flat valley floor make it arguably the most spectacular.

Like many mountain ranges in the Rockies, the Tetons formed along a fault, visible now as the sharp divide between the steep slopes of the Teton range and the flat floor of Jackson Hole. This weak spot allowed a massive granite block 40 miles long and 15 miles wide to rise and the valley floor to drop. It's believed the Teton uplift has been much greater than the current height of the Teton range, perhaps as much as 5 miles.

Glaciation

While stony fire is the defining force of the Yellowstone Plateau and Yellowstone Park, folding and lifting are the mechanisms that formed most of the region's mountain ranges. To finish the picture we still need one more sculptor: ice. Geologists find evidence of three ice ages in this region. The first began around 160,000 years ago. The last ended a mere 13,000 years ago. When ice advanced, most of the higher elevations in Greater Yellowstone were inundated. Geologists believe that about 15,000 years ago, at the height of the last ice advance, some 90 percent of what is now Yellowstone Park was buried in an ice blanket perhaps as much as 3,000 feet thick.

Slow-moving glaciers ground the valleys of Greater Yellowstone into big, rounded Us. Glaciers work like massive sandpaper sponges, scouring the earth across which they slowly creep and then incorporating the dislodged sediment into themselves. The more rock and dirt they accumulate, the better shapers of land glaciers become, just as coarse sandpaper removes paint faster than fine. As the Yellowstone glaciers retreated, sediment that had become part of the ice blankets was transported and then deposited in valleys by melt-streams. This further leveled the valley floors. Jackson Hole is a classic glacial valley, wide and flat-bottomed with steep, mountainous sides.

One valley not shaped into the classic glacial U is the famous Grand Canyon of the Yellowstone. Twenty miles long and 1,000 to 1,500 feet deep, the Grand Canyon of the Yellowstone was formed by the power of water, with a little assistance from heat. The rock of the canyon walls was weakened by heat from a series of volcanic events, making it more vulnerable to the cutting force of the Yellowstone River. The result is a narrow, sheer-sided canyon with almost no flat area on the valley floor. The canyon walls' golden color is a result of chemical changes from the same heat which made them so vulnerable to erosion.

As glaciers retreat, they leave behind some of their accumulated rocks and sediment in long, low ridges. Sometimes these ridges, called moraines, became dams, and long-profiled lakes formed behind them. All of the major lakes in Grand Teton Park, including Jenny and Leigh Lakes, are glacial moraine lakes.

High up on the mountainsides, glaciers carved their signature cirques: flat-bottomed, steep-sided bowls scooped out of bare rock. The Grand Teton, a steep, sharp-edged spire, is a mountain with multiple cirques scalloping its faces. The Wind River range and the Gros Ventre range are thought to have been buried under continuous ice sheets, much as Yellowstone Park was. Smaller cirque glaciers were common in the Absarokas, Palisades, Centennials, Madison, Gallatin, Salt River and Hoback ranges, among others. These ranges' ice-clear mountain lakes are typically pools that have collected in glacial cirques.

Yellowstone still has glaciers, although they are probably not remnants of the mighty ice fields that carved this country into its lovely, rugged shape. Geologists believe those glaciers melted and these formed later. The Wind River Mountains, in the seldom-visited southeast corner of Greater Yellowstone, get the glacier prize. Their extreme high altitude has allowed the formation of at least 24 named glaciers. This range has the largest glaciers in the lower 48 states.

The Tetons harbor several small glaciers, including one on the Grand itself. Glaciers grow and shrink with small fluctuations in climate. Photos taken of the Grand in the late 1800s show a much larger glacier below its north face than the one you see there today.

Our Plant Communities

We refer, as many do, to a Greater Yellowstone ecosystem, as though it were a homogeneous place. Don't let us mislead you into thinking of Greater Yellowstone as a seamless expanse. It's a crazy quilt of wet and dry zones, lowland valleys and above-the-treeline alpine crags. Species like elk, bison, bear and moose do move across the region with the seasons and the availability of food, and Greater Yellowstone's landscapes and animal and plant communities can be seen to interlock like puzzle pieces. But this region is nothing if not diverse. In a moment we want to introduce you to what we believe is the third most-popular main attraction of Greater Yellowstone: the wildlife. But first let's look at the world these animals live in — or, rather, the worlds.

Plant communities in Greater Yellowstone vary with altitude. Other factors are important, too, like soil type or a hillside's orientation to sun and prevailing winds. But in general, look for the driest areas at the lowest elevations.

In many of Greater Yellowstone's low valleys, sagebrush and bunch grasses dominate; they are green in spring but gray and straw-colored by midsummer. Although 30 inches of annual precipitation fall in some parts of Greater Yellowstone, these lower elevations may see only 10. About 160 species of grass grow here, mostly in lower elevation meadows and valleys. Grass is the preferred forage for most grazing animals, but they'll eat sage if they have to, for instance in winter when grasses are buried too far under the snowpack to reach.

Along these same low-elevation valleys run rivers. Where you find these rivers, you'll find deciduous trees, the broad-leaved species that shed their leaves in winter. The three most common are cottonwood, willow and aspen.

Find any of these three deciduous trees and you've also found water, either at or just below the surface.

Cottonwoods grow along river channels at lower elevations; in some areas they practically line the banks. This is a result of cottonwoods' inclination to drop their fluffy, floating seeds just in time for spring runoff. The seeds travel downstream, lodge on exposed gravel as the river recedes and begin to grow. In return for the free ride, cottonwoods stabilize river banks.

Aspen grows in pockets where groundwater accumulates rather than near sources of surface water. Aspen is important in this ecosystem because of an anomaly in its makeup: Its bark contains chlorophyll, nutritious for elk who love to browse on aspen shoots and nibble at aspen bark, especially in winter when little else is available.

Willows are among the most abundant small trees in Greater Yellowstone. At higher elevations, they take the place of cottonwoods, stabilizing riverbanks and lakes and providing cover for small animals. Willow, one of the moose's favorite food sources, is particularly common on the marshy, flat valley floors that glaciers tend to leave behind.

Scattered across Greater Yellowstone are the region's lakes and ponds, including huge bodies of water such as Montana's Quake Lake (some maps call it Earthquake Lake) and Wyoming's Yellowstone Lake, the largest high-mountain lake in the country. Also included are tiny ponds such as Kelly Hot Springs and the lakelike waters of the Snake River Oxbow in Grand Teton Park. Then there are the natural lakes that have been enlarged by dams to store more water, including Henry's, Jackson and Hebgen, as well as man-made reservoirs such as Palisades and Island Park. All together, about 10 percent of Yellowstone Park is water.

The fish-bearing waters of Greater Yellowstone make up one of the world's most productive fisheries. Rare white pelicans and trumpeter swans, as well as more common waterfowl, also rely on these bodies of water. So do land mammals that find shelter in water, such as otters, or that feed on its abundant plant life, such as bear and moose. Warm water from the region's hydrothermal features keeps many of these waters ice-free in winter. This benefits species like trumpeter swans that otherwise could not survive winter here.

At slightly higher altitudes away from the rivers, but where more precipitation falls or where deeper or more well-drained soil favors deep-rooted plants like trees, the spruce, fir and pine forests begin. Like many areas that have been shaped by glaciation, the soil here can be very thin in places and therefore not suitable for trees. But much of the soil of Greater Yellowstone is also volcanic in origin, which tends to make it nutrient-rich and fertile. Where a thick enough layer of well-drained soil and ample water exist, trees grow densely, despite long harsh winters that may prevent them from growing fast.

Much of Greater Yellowstone is not forested. As we said earlier, areas at low elevation with low moisture or areas with thin soil or poor drainage won't grow trees. Trees can't thrive at extremely high elevations, either. Above tree line, as it's called, growing conditions are too harsh and the growing season too short for anything but shrubs, grasses and wildflowers. The reason plants up here are often miniature versions of species that exist below is that they don't have time to grow large: They must flower and reproduce in too short a time to mess around getting big for no purpose. In fact, if a flowering plant "thinks" it doesn't have time to flower, go to seed and reproduce itself before the winter snows hit, it will skip a year's flowering and wait until the next. For this reason, most of the tiny plants above the timberline are perennials, plants that regrow from their root systems every spring, rather than annuals, which die every fall and rely on their seeds to produce next spring's plants.

But most of us spend little time at those windswept altitudes. We play in the mid-elevation forests, made up mostly of lodgepole pine. In Yellowstone Park, 80 percent of the forested areas is lodgepole. You also find Douglas fir at lower elevations; at higher elevations grow subalpine fir, whitebark pine and Engelmann spruce. But throughout the ecosystem, the predominant evergreen is tall, spindly, fast-growing lodgepole. Lodgepole forests cause a gamut of problems for land managers, not the least of which is that lodgepole

National Elk Refuge

Elk spend their summers in high country, but heavy winter snows force them to migrate to friendlier elevations or starve. Much of the traditional summer range of Greater Yellowstone's elk herds is protected as national forest or national park. Their winter range, however, is nearly gone, carved up into recreational acreages, grazed by cattle or gridded into towns. Even where fertile, lower-elevation grasslands still exist untouched, they're difficult for elk to access because towns stand across the old migration routes.

Elk feeding and the National Elk Refuge in Jackson Hole exist today as an uneasy compromise between the needs of humans and those of elk. Feeding began here during the harsh winter of 1908, but it was a local effort — too little and too late to prevent hundreds of animals from dying. The next winter was, if anything, worse. Starving elk marauded ranchers' haystacks and competed with their cattle, then died in the trampled snow anyway. Ranchers, barely eking a living in the tough conditions of a Jackson Hole winter, couldn't afford the losses to their cattle. Nor could they easily dispose of the rotting corpses in the spring.

The National Elk Refuge and the funding that subsidizes its feeding program have their roots in photos taken by a man named Stephen Leek. One of Leek's most-famous pictures shows the crumpled forms of dead elk and a desperate few, still alive, stretching toward life-giving hay too high overhead to reach. The heartbreaking photos prompted Congress in 1912 to allot 1,000 acres and feed money to Jackson Hole's winter elk herds.

Now the refuge contains nearly 25,000 acres of prime grassland and supports a winter herd of somewhere between 7,500 and 12,000. Funding for the roughly 30 tons of alfalfa pellets the herd requires after the natural vegetation has been grazed off comes from two sources. Wyoming Game and Fish provides about half with profits from the

— continued on next page

Photo: Jackson Hole Chamber of Commerce

The Elk Refuge north of Jackson Hole provides
a close view of elk during the winter months.

sale of hunting licenses. Local Boy Scouts provide the other half, their share generated by their annual antler auction in Jackson, Wyoming. The cost of feeding one animal for the winter is about $50. Limited hunting is allowed on the refuge to control the herds, since the animals' natural predators don't exist in significant enough numbers to limit herd sizes to what the available land (with supplemental feeding) can support.

The refuge is home to one of the area's more interesting winter attractions: a horse-drawn sleigh ride out into the huge herds of elk (see our Attractions chapter). In summer, the elk return to the high country, and the dirt Elk Refuge Road is used by joggers and mountain bikers. Ponds at the southern end of the refuge near U.S. Highway 89 host a variety of waterfowl, including the endangered and lovely trumpeter swan.

Many people don't know that more than 20 elk-feeding sites exist between the refuge and Pinedale, Wyoming. The better-known of these are the one between Jackson and Hoback Junction and another near Alpine, Wyoming, at Palisades Reservoir. Additional feeding locations are necessary because the broad valley floors south of Jackson are also traditional elk wintering grounds. The elk that winter at the refuge constitute only a portion of the Yellowstone herds, many of which seek refuge in low grasslands that have become almost totally the domain of humans.

Another thing visitors may not know is that winter feeding is controversial around here. Every human intervention, whether well-intended or not, impacts ecosystem balance. For instance, some amount of winter kill has always been part of the lives of Greater Yellowstone's ungulate herds. In early spring, grizzlies and other predators rely upon the ready supply of meat provided by winter-killed elk, bison and deer. Supply feed to the herds, and few will die. Then it's the grizzlies, wolves, wolverines and coyotes that suffer hardship.

For more about the National Elk Refuge, see its listing in the Attractions chapter.

---

forests are designed to burn. These trees are fairly short-lived, and when they die, they become fodder for the inevitable fire.

Before the coming of Euro-Americans, this was fine. In fact, just as gardeners today may burn off their garden plots to make the next crop more productive, Native Americans once burned wild lands to increase the productivity of plant communities. Similarly, fire is good for lodgepoles, which at maturity tend to fall victim to the mountain pine beetle, sicken and die. After a fire, burned wood replenishes nutrients in the soil. The lodgepole's special cones, which open in response to the intense heat of a fire, reseed the burned area. So fire begins the conversion of a mature, dying forest to a vital young one. Fire also spurs the production of new aspen shoots, which sprout from a communal root system that survives all but the hottest fires. Fire benefits other plant species as well, because a mature lodgepole forest is homogenous. The trees, all about the same age and height, grow close together,

canopies overlapping. Little underbrush can grow because little sunlight breaks through. Young trees of any species don't stand a chance. Fire makes room for a greater variety of plant species, particularly the grasses and brush that wildlife browse upon.

The massive fires that swept through Greater Yellowstone in 1988 were seen as tragic by many. Vast hillsides of charred trees look like destruction to us. A human lifetime is too short to make appreciation of the forest cycle easy, especially when close to half the nation's first national Park is involved. The logging industry wasn't happy either: Harvestable timber is not the endlessly available commodity it once seemed to be, so to watch forests go up in smoke hurt. Some 400,000 acres of trees in nearby national forests also burned. But throughout Greater Yellowstone, and most strikingly in Yellowstone Park, the lodgepole forests were and are mature — ready to burn and make room for more plant diversity and the greater animal diversity that inevitably follows.

Our Wild Inhabitants

From its lowest elevations to its highest, Greater Yellowstone is rich with wildlife. Its vast tracts of relatively wild lands contain a wide range of environments that support an even greater range of animal life. All together, Greater Yellowstone harbors seven species of ungulates (hoofed animals), two species of bears, three kinds of wild cats, three canids and about 70 smaller predator and prey species. The area is also home to 22 kinds of fish, more than 120 species of butterfly and more than 20 species of reptiles and amphibians. You will almost certainly see one or two of Greater Yellowstone's 90,000 mule deer along roadsides. Driving in the grassy sagelands, you're likely to spot the white-sided pronghorn antelope, the fastest North American mammal. An incredible number of bird species — more than 300 — call this area home at least part of the year. Among these are osprey, kingfisher, ouzel and magpie.

But the stars of the show, the animals so many come hoping to see and photograph, are the elk, moose, bison, bears, wolf, bald eagle, trumpeter swan and bighorn sheep. The fish that anglers are most interested in catching is the colorful native cutthroat trout. Some of these stars, like the bald eagle and grizzly, are making their final curtain call in this wild country. Others, like elk, exist all across the West.

The sections that follow provide an introduction to each animal, so you can feel acquainted if you are lucky enough to see these residents of Greater Yellowstone. We've also included information that should help you know where to look, since wild creatures, just like humans, live where they can find food and protection. Knowing a little about an animal's needs and habits helps you know where to find it.

Elk

Elk are not an endangered species, although around the turn of the century their survival was questionable. Nationwide, there are about 900,000 elk, 10 times as many as in 1900. In Yellowstone country, elk numbers seem to be at an all-time high. About 40 percent of Greater Yellowstone's 90,000 to 120,000 elk live inside Yellowstone Park at least part of the year. But the high, snowy Yellowstone Plateau would make for hungry winters, so the elk head for lower elevations in October. About 7,000 to 12,000 of these (depending on whom you ask) spend their winters at the National Elk Refuge near Jackson. Elk refuges and winter feeding grounds attempt to address the problem that for nearly six months a year, elk need to live in the same sheltered, low-elevation grasslands that make good sites for towns, ranches and farms.

Bull elk begin growing their impressive antlers early in spring (cow elk don't have antlers). The bull's antlers grow from two permanent bones called "pedicles" that attach to the elk's skull. The antlers take about four months to grow. They harden over the summer, fall and winter until, dry as old wood, they snap off close to the bull's head in late winter or in early spring. Then the next set begins to grow. Of the four subspecies of elk that still survive in the United States, the Rocky Mountain elk found in Yellowstone country have the largest racks. A pair of antlers from a big bull may weigh 40 pounds.

INSIDERS' TIP

If you look sharp, you may see an osprey, or fish hawk, winging away from a river with a trout slung aerodynamically head-first beneath him. And if you know that birds of prey have four toes, three forward and one back, you may be puzzled: how he can hold that slippery trout any way but sideways in his talons? The answer? The osprey's third forward toe is double jointed to bend back when he holds a trout. This enables him to clasp the fish with one talon, and use the other to grab the branch he chooses for his picnic area.

Wintering elk flee a helicopter carrying biologists who are conducting a winter survey.

Elk like green grass, so they're often seen on open grassy hillsides. In fall, when grasses dry up, elk will eat more small, leafy plants and even bushes and shrubs. In winter, elk paw through the snow and eat anything they can find: bushes, dried grasses, tree bark (especially aspen) and lichens hanging from pine trees.

Especially in tough winters, some elk will not survive. Without the feeding programs that began soon after the turn of the century, even more elk would starve to death in winter, since most of what was once their winter range has been developed for human use. This means that, despite the fact that elk populations in this area are probably much lower than before the coming of Euro-Americans, herd sizes are currently maintained at artificial highs based on what remaining wildlands can support. If we left them alone, there would be many, many fewer elk in Greater Yellowstone. (To learn more about elk and the National Elk Refuge, see our Close-up in this chapter.)

Grizzly Bear

Some estimates say that in 1800, 100,000 grizzlies lived in North America. Now experts think fewer than 1,000 live on two tiny fragments of their former range. Grizzlies are generally solitary animals that require huge, sprawling wilderness — something that no longer exists throughout nearly all of their former range. One area still large enough and wild enough to contain grizzlies is Yellowstone country; the other is a loosely defined area that contains northwestern Montana's Glacier National Park and several wildernesses jigsawed together much like those of Greater Yellowstone. The Greater Yellowstone grizzly population is variously estimated between 170 and 350.

The name "grizzly bear" comes from the animals' fur, which is dark brown tipped with gray, giving them a grizzled appearance. On all fours, a grizzly is likely to stand 4 feet at the shoulder. Males can weigh 900 pounds or more; females, 400. Belying their ponderous size, grizzlies can run up to 25 mph (that's *much* faster than you) and can climb certain kinds of trees. They can smell a carcass 3 miles away; their claws are more than 4 inches long.

Despite their fearsome appearance, grizzlies eat mostly plants — grass, dandelions, berries and roots — and small creatures from insects to spawning cutthroat. The only time of year they regularly eat large animals like elk or deer is in spring, when the carcasses of winter-killed animals are generally plentiful and weakened or infant animals even more so. Grizzlies aren't real hibernators, but they do sleep deeply through most of the winter. Real hibernators can't be awakened by disturbance, but bears can, as researchers who've visited them in their winter lairs know. In winter, sleeping bears lose much of the 8-inch-thick layer of fat accumulated in the fall. At times their pulses fall to eight beats per minute.

One reason the seemingly invincible grizzly is in such danger from man is that it reproduces slowly. Females don't mate until they are 6 to 8 years old. Mature females are only ready to mate for two or three weeks out of a year — and the bears' huge ranges make that small window of opportunity easy to miss. Plus, cubs stay with their mothers for up to four years, and only females without cubs will mate. Females produce only one or two cubs at a time. Wildlife managers fear that we're killing grizzlies as fast as they can reproduce, despite best efforts to the contrary.

Park Service and Forest Service rangers destroy dangerous "nuisance" bears every year; others are killed in encounters with hunters or backcountry travelers, or mistaken by hunters who thought they were shooting at black bears (hunting black bears is legal; hunting grizzlies is not). One study found that between 1975 and 1988, 86 grizzlies, 39 of them females, were killed by humans in Greater Yellowstone. That may be nearly half the current grizzly population. Despite the fact that Yellowstone grizzly numbers seem to be stable, some experts say that such a small population in such an isolated pocket of land is too vulnerable to further habitat reduction, mismanagement or act of nature. These people predict extinction for the Yellowstone grizzlies within 100 years.

Seeing a grizzly in the wild is a privilege and a risk. It's also a rare event: Grizzlies in Greater Yellowstone stick generally to meadows and alpine basins in roadless areas, as far from human intrusion as they can get. Even if you're in their territory, a grizzly can scent your presence at several hundred yards and will generally retreat without you ever knowing he was near. If you want to look at grizzlies, you'll need binoculars. If you stood close enough see a grizzly well with the unaided eye, you'd be standing too close, both for your safety and the bear's. Remember that bears forfeit their lives when they lose their fear of man or when they come to associate our cars, campsites and backpacks with food. (See our Close-up on bear safety in our Fishing and Hunting chapter). In the Parks, report grizzly sightings to the rangers.

Black Bear

They're more likely to be brown, cinnamon or blond, but some black bears actually are black. Black bears weigh from 125 to 500 pounds and usually stand less than 3 feet tall at the shoulder. They have curved claws that allow them to climb trees more easily than their larger cousins, grizzlies, whose claws are nearly straight. Black bears, like grizzlies, are competent swimmers; also like grizzlies, they can run at much higher speeds than you can, belying their fat and clownish appearance. Unlike grizzlies, who generally stick to higher, wilder country and are therefore seldom seen by human visitors, black bears are common and can be spotted in forested areas all over Greater Yellowstone. Some estimates place black bear numbers in Yellowstone Park alone at 600.

A black bear's diet consists mostly of vegetation, perhaps as much as 80 percent. Grasses are a mainstay. This means that black bears are partial to forested areas interspersed with the open meadows that grow their dinner. Bears also like bulbs, berries, the inner bark of some trees, as well as rodents, insects and carrion. Bears are most active at night, so dusk and dawn are likely sighting times. If you happen to see a black bear, do not approach it except with your binoculars. Black bears look pudgy and cute, but take them seriously: They're wild and potentially dangerous animals. They have been known to attack and kill humans. The National Park Service asks that you report bear sightings in the Parks, particularly those near areas with significant human traffic. Bears that have been taught by careless visitors that food can be found in campgrounds or cars or backpacks are moved if possible and destroyed if necessary.

For more on how to treat both yourself and the region's bears with care, please see our Close-up on bear safety in the Fishing and Hunting chapter.

Moose

The moose is the largest member of the deer family. Adult males can stand 6 feet at the shoulder and weigh up to a half-ton. Like elk and deer, bull moose grow velvet-encased antlers every spring. The velvet supplies blood to the growing bone; if you could touch an antler in summer it would feel warm from the blood coursing through the velvety sheath. The velvet dries and is scraped off in late summer. Fall is the rut, a time when female moose are receptive to mating and bulls become aggressive. This is the purpose of the massive antlers — sparring and fighting over females. The agitated males will lose up to 30 percent of their body weight during the rut, which ends in mid or late October. The heavy antlers, their usefulness outlived, harden until they snap off close to the animal's head, usually sometime in December or January.

Except in early spring when males lack antlers, the distinctive shapes of these bony appendages make for easy identification of local members of the deer family. If you see antlers at all, know you're looking at a male. If the antlers are cylindrical like tree branches and point mostly upward, you're watching a deer. If the main stem of the antler branches back on a line almost parallel with the animal's back, you're seeing a bull elk. If the antlers are great, flat plates edged with finger-like tines, the ungainly brown beast in your binoculars is a bull moose.

There are thought to be about 6,000 moose in Greater Yellowstone. Some hypothesize that the big ungulate did not historically live in significant numbers here, but was pushed into the area as man took over lower-elevation habitat.

Moose eat twigs, pine and fir needles, and tree bark in winter, but what they like is water vegetation and the tender willow shoots that grow alongside rivers and streams. They also like aspen and new, fresh grass. Long legs make moose good water foragers. A common sight in Greater Yellowstone is a big brown body, apparently headless, hip-deep in a pond or slow-moving stream. When the big head rises above the surface, it cascades water and trails soggy green water plants. Those long legs also make winter snows less an obstacle for moose than for many other Greater Yellowstone ungulates: Moose can move more easily and are less likely to die off in winter than elk or deer.

In summer, look for moose near water, especially in willow thickets, cottonwood bottoms or plant-clogged ponds. In winter, peruse the south-facing hillsides where the snowpack is not so deep or in thick trees, which also keep snowpack down.

Moose are not as sedate as they may appear, particularly if they feel cornered. Bull moose in rut have been known to attack hikers with little provocation. Moose aren't terribly afraid of humans. They'll avoid you if they can, but if they can't get away from you without going through you, they're coming through. Early one morning in Gros Ventre Campground in Grand Teton Park, we watched from behind a big tree as a young bull moose accidentally demolished a tent that had been pitched illegally out of bounds. The moose bolted through the campground, tentfly tangled in its antlers. Twice it stopped to confront humans. The animal seemed to be flipping a mental coin: heads, run some more; tails, trample the puny creature. Although it came up heads both times, we were glad for our tree.

Trumpeter Swan

In the 1930s, the trumpeter swan balanced precariously at extinction's razor edge: Fewer than 70 were known to exist in the United States. The largest waterfowl in North America, the trumpeter swan was known by the graceful curve of its neck, its snowy feathers, and (unfortunately) its tasty flesh. Now about 2,500 swans make their home in Greater Yellowstone and neighboring areas in Wyoming, Montana and Idaho, and another, larger flock lives along the Pacific coast. A moratorium on hunting and egg collecting helped, but more importantly, marshy winter habitat was preserved at places like Red Rocks National Wildlife Refuge in Montana and Idaho's Harriman State Park.

One negative aspect of recovery efforts involves winter feeding. As their numbers increase, trumpeter swans are overfilling the few areas we've set aside for them, but 50 years of winter feeding at Red Rocks has discouraged the flocks from seeking other winter havens farther south. The birds are currently using or overusing most of the available winter habitat in Greater Yellowstone. They need open water to survive, and this far north that means spring water, which stays warm enough not to freeze even in the harshest winters — so their continued recovery hinges on finding new winter habitat.

Trumpeter swans weigh around 30 pounds and have wingspans of up to 8 feet. They fly at speeds of 50 mph. Trumpeters' black bills help set them apart from the domestic mute swan commonly seen in zoos. Tundra swans, the only other swan species seen in this area, also have black bills and are most easily distinguished from trumpeters by guesswork. Only about 1 percent of swans seen around here are tundra swans, so if you guess that a black-billed swan is a trumpeter, you're probably right. (If you want to get serious about this and you have a pair of binoculars handy, look for the telltale yellow spot on the tundra swan's bill just in front of the eye.)

A few trumpeters spend the whole year here, particularly at Harriman State Park, but most migrate from Canada in October and head back north in mid-March. Swans, like Canada geese, mate for life and return to the same nesting area every year. Swans prefer shallow, stagnant or slow-moving water, where they feed on shallow water plants, seeds and roots. Those long necks mean that swans can stretch down to plants too deep underwater for squattier ducks to reach, so ducks sometimes like to follow swans, cleaning up plant debris stirred up by the larger birds.

Because new migration patterns are key to the birds' continued recovery, you're asked to report sightings of neck-collared swans. Please note the location and date of the sighting, color of neck collar, and color and location of any dye on the bird. If you can, note also the letter and numbers on the neck collar. Call U.S. Fish and Wildlife Service at (208) 237-6616 with your sighting.

Bison

Once there were millions, traveling in herds as unstoppable as hurricanes and as lifegiving as rain for humans and other predators. The deliberate and uncontrolled hunting of the massive bison herds in the 19th century was partly about hides but mostly the result of bounties promised by the government. Officials guessed, correctly, that eliminating bison would starve the Plains Indians onto reservations. American bounty hunters were extremely effective. So was a policy of handing out ammunition to wagon train members and others along herds' migratory routes. By 1900 bison were nearly extinct. What is now the last wild herd in the United States grew out of the few dozen animals that remained in Yellowstone Park at the turn of the century, coupled with an infusion of new blood from small captive populations elsewhere.

Today's Yellowstone herd is about 2,200 head. A smaller herd in Jackson Hole may number as many as 400, although estimates vary. Bison also seem to be recolonizing areas adjacent to Jackson Hole. The bison's successful recovery in Greater Yellowstone causes problems for wildlife managers, though, as the animals begin to move outside the Park, particularly in winter. Foraging bison damage fences and frighten ranchers concerned that their cattle will contract a disease called brucellosis from their wild cousins. Brucellosis, which causes cows to abort their fetuses, is costly. Hundreds of bison are shot every winter as they wander beyond Park boundaries, outraging some and barely satisfying others.

Unlike other Greater Yellowstone ungulates, both bull and cow bison have horns, although the males' horns are larger. Horns, unlike antlers, are not shed and regrown every year — a bison keeps its horns for life. The material that makes up horn is keratin, the same stuff your fingernails consist of. Rut begins early for bison, running from mid-July to mid-August. Bulls paw the ground, butt and shove each other. Occasionally altercations become serious, but generally they involve a lot of bullying and little real force. Hikers sometimes mistake the enraged bellowing of bison bulls during the rut for grizzly bear growls.

Bison weigh up to 2,000 pounds and can gallop at an eye-popping 40 mph. Most of the time, though, they seem as sedate as cattle. Like cattle, bison are grazers, eating mostly grass year round. In winter they bulldoze through the snowpack with their big, blocky heads to reach the dried grasses and sedges below. Look for bison in large meadow areas like Hayden Valley and the Madison Plateau in summer and in lower-elevation open areas in winter. Some move into areas with thermal features in winter, taking advantage of the fact that little snow accumulates on the heated ground. Every winter one or two break through a thin earth shell over boiling water and die.

Most of Greater Yellowstone's bison are found in and immediately around Yellowstone Park. They tend to herd, so if you see one, look for more. As we said, bison look sedate and a bit dumb, which may be why the most common serious human-vs.-animal encounters in Greater Yellowstone involve bison. Every year, visitors who approach too closely or too carelessly are gored.

Wolf

Wolves, once common throughout the continental United States, were systematically trapped and poisoned to the brink of extinction for their bushy, plush hides and later to make room for domestic livestock. Unlike most species, wolves were not protected after the creation of Yellowstone Park. If anything, extermination efforts were stepped up in the early part of the 20th century. The last known wolves in Yellowstone Park, two pups, were killed in 1924 near Soda Butte. The last known resident wolf in Wyoming was shot in 1943. In 1995, after nearly two decades of debate, 14 wolves were captured in Canada and reintroduced to Yellowstone Park. Fifteen more were released in central Idaho. The next year, 38 more Canadian wolves were released in this country, 17 in Yellowstone Park.

There are no plans to introduce more wolves to Yellowstone. As of May 1997 roughly 100 wolves roamed Yellowstone country. It's hoped that a healthy population of the pack-hunting carnivores will exert natural control over the numbers of elk and bison; right now special hunts are the only way for wildlife managers to control ungulate numbers. Wolves were once the area's major predators.

As expected, the new residents of Yellowstone have reproduced and dispersed from the Park, sometimes onto private land. Also as expected, the newcomers have killed domestic livestock — about 60 sheep and five calves, by one report. A fund exists to reimburse ranchers for livestock depredation. Several wolves have been killed in turn, some by other wolves, a couple by poachers, one by burns sustained in a hot spring or geyser, several by cars or trucks and several more by either ranchers or wildlife managers. Ranchers may legally kill wolves that attack livestock, and wildlife managers have agreed to kill wolves that prey upon livestock, whether on national forest or private land.

If you want to see a wolf, the best area so far has been in the northeast corner of Yellowstone Park, along the Park road in the Lamar Valley. You'll need binoculars or a spotting scope, though; wolves generally stay at least a mile from humans. What should you be looking for? Imagine a gray, whitish or black German shepherd with extra long legs, an extra bushy tail and oversized feet, weighing

If you have net access and are interested in Greater Yellowstone's wildlife and wonders, try the following sites: www.poky.srv.net/~jjmrm/maughan.html, www.idahonews.com, www.nps.gov/grte/ or www.wyoming.com/~yellowstonejournal/TOC.html

about 125 pounds. That's the gray wolf, newly returned to Yellowstone country.

Cutthroat Trout

Cutthroats get their name from reddish-orange slashes under the lower jaw. Yellowstone's only native trout has 13 subspecies, but only two exist here: Yellowstone cutthroat and West Slope cutthroat. The West Slope variety are found primarily in Montana, but even there their numbers are sharply limited, so it's the Yellowstone cutthroat you're likely to encounter. Some believe the Snake River Finespotted cutthroat is a third Yellowstone subspecies, but Finespotted cutthroats differ from Yellowstone cutts only in appearance (the spots along their backs and sides are smaller).

All other trout in these waters — hard-fighting rainbows, long-lived, massive browns and scrappy little brook trout — were imported, beginning in the 1880s. Lake trout, which grow to truly monstrous size, are also imports, unwanted since they threaten the survival of native cutts in Yellowstone Lake and other waters. Studies have shown that when Lake trout colonize or are introduced to cutthroat habitat, the cutts gradually disappear. Lake trout were found in Yellowstone Lake, a cutthroat stronghold, for the first time in 1994.

Most visitors who come to Greater Yellowstone to fish hope to catch these colorful native trout, but the interest in preserving native wild fisheries is recent and still not universal. Rainbows, browns and hatchery hybrids like cutt-bows are larger than cutts and are often perceived as a tougher and therefore more satisfying catch. Cutthroats have a reputation for being foolhardy and ready to bite anything, which makes them easy to hook, and for being less feisty on a fisherman's line than, say, rainbows.

Cutthroats eat plankton when young, then mostly insects, although larger ones may eat other fish. A 4-pound cutt would be a large fish. They were once the most widely distributed trout in the West, but wild native cutthroat fisheries are becoming few and far between. Cutthroats are not very resistant to competition from non-native fish or to habitat modification like that on the South Fork of the Snake since the construction of Palisades Dam. Believing that native wild fisheries suffer when hatchery stock is introduced, Montana stocks no cutthroat into its streams. Idaho stocks Henry's Lake with cutthroat and hybrid cutt-bows, but Idaho's most robust native fisheries, like the South Fork of the Snake, are left alone. Wyoming regularly stocks hatchery cutthroat into its lakes and streams, which makes that state your best bet for catching cutts, if not your best bet for catching wild, native cutts.

The best places to see trout, including cutthroat, if you're not an angler are the National Fish Hatcheries in Jackson Hole, Wyoming, and Ennis, Montana; smaller state-run hatcheries at Henry's Lake and Ashton, Idaho; and fish-feeding areas such as Big Springs and the Warm River, both near Island Park, Idaho. Watching has replaced fishing at Fishing Bridge in Yellowstone Park because the water is so clear and the fish so easy to see. In fact, thousands more visit Fishing Bridge to *watch* fish than ever did to wet a line there.

For information on Yellowstone country's fishing opportunities, turn to our Fishing and Hunting chapter.

Bald Eagle

His wings can measure up to 7 feet from wingtip to wingtip. He may weigh 14 pounds. He eats mostly fish, which he catches himself or steals from osprey. He also eats carrion and other easy pickings, such as the young of other birds or animals. We witnessed what was probably a young bald eagle attacking Canadian goslings on the Blackfoot River last spring. He was beaten back by the honking parents while the young scampered across the river in hasty retreat, proof that what appear to be easy pickings sometimes aren't.

Younger bald eagles are difficult to distinguish from brown-headed, brown-bodied golden eagles, but at about 5 years of age, bald eagles develop the signature white head that leaves no question. Young birds tend to leave this area until they reach maturity, at which time they return to stay. They'll use the same nests year after year; nests, called eyries, can be 5 feet across.

Recently the numbers of bald eagles have been on a reassuring upswing. Nearly 100

Photo: Robert Bower

A trumpeter swan on the Firehole River searches for food as it paddles steadily against the current.

nesting pairs have been identified in the region. If you keep your eyes peeled toward the cottonwood-lined South Fork of the Snake as you drive between Ririe and Palisades Reservoir, odds are you'll see at least one of these rare birds. Two other likely spots are the Oxbow in Grand Teton Park and Yellowstone Lake in Yellowstone Park.

Bighorn Sheep

Greater Yellowstone probably contains the greatest remaining concentrations of bighorn sheep, some 7,700 spread across three national forests: the Shoshone, Gallatin and Bridger-Teton. A few live in Grand Teton and Yellowstone parks. In other areas of the Rocky Mountain West, bighorns have been nearly eradicated.

What has made survival and recovery difficult for the Rocky Mountain bighorn sheep, our local subspecies, is the way these creatures are bound by habit and social rules. They follow the same trails and stop at the same salt licks, watering holes and grazing areas like clockwork. Older animals lead, and younger animals learn the trails from their elders. Innovation has no place in a bighorn sheep herd. This has always made them easy to hunt. More recently, when cattle and domestic sheep overran their traditional ranges, it left them completely unequipped for finding new habitat. So they stayed on overgrazed habitat and eventually starved. Bighorns are also dramatically susceptible to the diseases of domestic livestock, so where domestic sheep and bighorns have contact, bighorns rapidly begin to die.

Both male and female bighorns have horns, but the females wear only spikes. Males, as they grow older, carry an increasingly heavy, ridged rack. Some grow to more than 30 pounds, or about 10 percent of the animal's body weight, and curl into a complete circle on each side of the animal's head. A male bighorn's rack can weigh more than his skeleton. Rams are also equipped with a double-layered skull, thick facial skin and a powerful tendon that connects skull with spine. All this is necessary because every fall the big rams battle for ewes and social standing by hurling themselves into crashing head-to-head contact. Their bodies are adapted to take the terrible pounding, generally without significant injury. In fact, injury is not the goal of either participant. The ritual battles, which can go on for hours, involve only this head-to-head pounding.

Look for gray-bodied, white-rumped bighorn sheep on open, south-facing mountainsides, high plateaus and ridgelines. Bighorns eat mostly grasses, so you won't often see them in or near forested areas. Since they protect themselves from predators by retreating to rocky, steep terrain, bighorn grazing areas are nearly always near rocky slopes and cliffs. From a distance, which is how you're most likely to see them, bighorns are easily mistaken for deer. Look for the larger, more prominent white patch on the rump and the stockier, barrel-bodied shape.

Easy-to-miss Residents

Many of Greater Yellowstone's most interesting creatures don't get the attention they deserve, either from visitors or this travel guide. Some are small or quiet and therefore easy to overlook. Others are secretive or rare and unlikely to cross paths with humans. In the easy-to-overlook category are creatures such as shrews, bats, beaver, porcupine, weasel, squirrels (including a species of flying squirrel!), mink, marmot, river otter and badger.

Shrews are the tiniest predator mammals, eating their weight in spiders, slugs and carrion every day. Marmots waddle when they walk, so intent are they on fattening up for their 8-month hibernation. True hibernators like marmot will not awaken even if they're starving, so it's critical that they crawl into their dens with enough fat reserves to survive the winter. It's thought that marmots constitute up to 70 percent of golden eagles' diets.

Beavers are the largest rodents in the West, weighing up to 100 pounds. Once trapped nearly to extinction for their plush, water-repelling fur, beavers are recovering some of their former range. They benefit other species in Greater Yellowstone by creating ponds that control flooding and provide habitat for waterfowl, moose and others. High quality fur-felt hats are still made from beaver harvested, these days, from fur farms.

Secretive and probably very rare in Greater Yellowstone are species such as the fisher, wolverine and lynx. The fisher looks like an elongated, chocolate-colored cat with a bushy tail. It measures about 2 feet from stem to stern. The fisher seems to require old-growth forest to live. Since there's little of that left, this small predator has disappeared from most of its former range. A few fishers have been sighted in Greater Yellowstone.

Lynx live at the mercy of their partner species, the snowshoe hare. When snowshoe hare populations are healthy, generally so are lynx populations. When snowshoes become scarce, lynx starve until there are the right number of cats to prey upon the smaller hare population. This medium-sized cat weighs up to 40 pounds and is built to hunt on snow: Long legs and huge, paddled feet allow it to stay on the snow's crust in pursuit of the hare. A lynx may eat as many as 200 snowshoe hare a year, although it will also take grouse, as well as small mammals and birds. Lynx also seem to need old-growth forest to live, so they're rare as well. Only a few lynx have been sighted in Greater Yellowstone; they're less uncommon in Canada where more old-growth forest remains. If in your backcountry travels you see what looks like a long-legged, clown-footed bobcat, count yourself among a very lucky few.

Wolverines look a little like small bears. They weigh up to 60 pounds and walk on all fours with a rolling, swaggering gait. Wolverines don't seem to tolerate human contact well. Females have been known to abandon their carefully hidden, remote dens merely because a human passed within eyeshot. Wolverines

INSIDERS' TIP

If you have an emergency, the number to call is always 911. But if it's information or non-critical assistance you need, check our Parks and Forests chapter for ranger station and Yellowstone/ Grand Teton National Park dispatch numbers. Many other government entities, from the Bureau of Land Management to the U.S. Fish and Wildlife Service, are happy to assist visitors. Find some of those numbers in our Resource section.

are aggressive hunters with powerful jaws. This solitary hunter has been known to take down deer nearly twice its weight, but it also eats grouse, smaller mammals and carrion. There are about three reports per year of wolverine sightings in Yellowstone Park. Nobody knows how many wolverines the region supports — probably nobody ever will. They are believed to be quite rare.

Secretive but not so rare is the mountain lion, also known as the cougar and puma. This big cat, which once lived all over what is now the United States, can weigh more than 200 pounds and reach a length of 9 feet if you count its long, bushy tail. It's practically extinct in the East, but cougar populations seem sound in the Western United States. Mostly nocturnal and very secretive, the cougar has been difficult to study. Less is known about this fairly common predator than about the wolf we once nearly eliminated from the United States. It is known that the mountain lion is one of few species besides man that will regularly kill its own kind. Mature males will kill cubs, intruding males and even females they haven't mated with. Solo and highly effective hunters, cougar regularly kill deer and even adult elk much larger than themselves. These big cats were hunted into invisibility in Greater Yellowstone for the same reason wolves were: to protect livestock. But unlike wolves, cougars have recovered spontaneously — leading some to speculate that perhaps they were never gone.

Secretive and sly — but as common as pennies — are coyotes. The most abundant canine in Greater Yellowstone weighs 30 to 50 pounds and is found in nearly every part of the ecosystem. Coyotes have distinguished themselves by surviving. The intense trapping and poisoning programs that eliminated wolves from the lower 48 states only made the coyote smarter. Coyotes, working in packs, occasionally take large animals like deer or bighorn sheep, but more often they live on mice, rabbits and gophers. They're smart enough not to move when you walk or drive by. You've probably been watched by many more coyotes than you've seen. Outside Yellowstone and Grand Teton parks, in which coyotes and other predators are protected with the rest of the wildlife kaleidoscope, ranchers, trappers and the federal USDA agency Animal Damage Control (ADC) regularly kill coyotes. George Wuerthner writes in *Yellowstone: A Visitors Companion* that in 1989, ADC trapped, poisoned or shot 76,000 coyotes on public and private lands in the West. The goal is to protect ranchers' livestock, which the small hunters occasionally kill. One day last spring, we hiked along a Greater Yellowstone dirt road in search of sunshine and wildlife, dogs at our heels and binoculars swinging around our necks. When looking for wildlife, you watch for movement, so we were very close to the still shape in the road before we realized what it was. The flyblown coyote carcass was attached by one mangled leg to an ADC trap. A nearby trap, baited with meat, lay waiting for spring. It was, ironically, the closest we had been to one of these elusive, shy predators: We usually count ourselves lucky to glimpse a furry tail as one drops over a ditchbank or dives into shrubbery.

The more you learn about the creatures that inhabit Greater Yellowstone, the issues that threaten them and the wildlife managers' efforts to save or control them, the more you will appreciate the complexity of this place. You are also more likely to see what you know to look for. But remember, with the exception of the big ungulates like moose and elk, most of Greater Yellowstone's inhabitants are rarely seen from the region's roads. After all, as crowded and cosmopolitan as Yellowstone Park can seem on a busy summer day, only 3 percent of it is accessible by road. There's real wilderness out there, just beyond the sounds of car engines and camera shutters. A good wildlife guidebook, a pair of binoculars, stout hiking boots or skis and some time will take you into a world most only see on the Discovery Channel.

Walk carefully, though. We're visitors here, but these animals are in the only home they have.

Explore Yellowstone with

A FALCON GUIDE ®

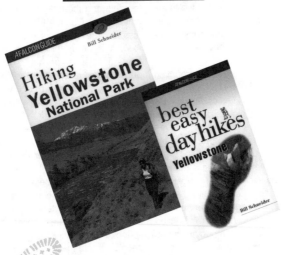

Best Easy Day Hikes Yellowstone
Hiking Yellowstone
Family Fun in Yellowstone
Fishing Yellowstone
Paddling Yellowstone & Grand Teton
National Parks
Scenic Driving Yellowstone

FalconGuides lead the way to adventure, and are available for most U.S. destinations and locations. Call the number below for a complete list of FalconGuide titles.

Parks and Forests

Only 19 percent of Greater Yellowstone's 18 million acres are privately owned. That small slice of the region's pie contains our towns and farms. The rest is public land. This huge chunk, by far the bulk of the pie, has been carved into chunks for managing by various public agencies.

Yellowstone and Grand Teton parks contain 14 percent of Greater Yellowstone; they're managed by the National Park Service, a branch of the United States Department of the Interior. In addition to preserving and protecting the wildlife and the Parks' natural features, the Park Service manages visitors, educating, policing and entertaining them.

National forests hold the lion's share of Greater Yellowstone lands, some 62 percent. The region's seven national forests are managed by the U.S. Forest Service, which is a branch of the U.S. Department of Agriculture. Each forest has its own administration. National forests are managed under a multiple use concept that allows logging, mining, livestock grazing, oil and gas drilling along with recreation.

The Wilderness Act of 1964 protects some of the nation's wildest national forest lands. Managed by the Forest Service, these lands are supposed to be kept as pristine as possible. Logging, road building and the use of motorized equipment is prohibited in designated wilderness. In a few cases, where legitimate mining claims exist, mining can occur. Livestock grazing is also allowed. So are hunting, fishing, hiking, rafting, camping, mountain climbing, cross country skiing, and snowshoeing. Greater Yellowstone is home to some of the nation's largest wilderness areas.

Two national wildlife refuges exist within Greater Yellowstone; they are managed by the U.S. Fish and Wildlife Service. The Red Rock Lakes Wildlife Refuge, funded through duck-stamp sales, is west of West Yellowstone

and was set aside primarily to protect trumpeter swans, although recreation, trapping, mining and grazing are also allowed. The other is the National Elk Refuge near Jackson, Wyoming, set aside to protect critical winter habitat for the region's huge elk herds.

State parks make up 2 percent of Greater Yellowstone's lands. They're managed in Montana by the Department of Fish, Wildlife and Parks; in Idaho by the State Department of Parks; in Wyoming by the Department of Parks and Resources. Generally state parks serve the recreational needs of visitors, providing such amenities as campgrounds, cabins and trails.

What follows is a close look at the two most famous slices of Greater Yellowstone pie, Grand Teton and Yellowstone National Parks. Look here for information about the Parks' visitor services. Then take a glance at our national forests, state parks and wildlife refuges. Contact numbers are included for each.

National Parks

Yellowstone National Park

Visited each year by nearly 3 million people, Yellowstone Park was established in 1872 as a "public park and pleasuring ground for the benefit and enjoyment of the people." Our country's first national park, Yellowstone covers about 2.2 million acres in northwestern Wyoming as well as little strips of Montana and Idaho. Initially it was the 10,000 steaming, bubbling, spraying geothermal features — hot springs, fumaroles, mud pots and geysers — that made Yellowstone stand out among other lands.

The region has other extraordinary features: rugged mountains, crystal clear lakes and streams (one-tenth of Yellowstone Park is under water) and a rich abundance of wildlife.

Yellowstone Park is home to the biggest elk herd in North America. It also has one of only two grizzly bear populations in the lower 48 states. In fact, Yellowstone Park is still home to nearly all of the animal species found by early explorers.

The heart of the Park is a volcanic plateau with an average elevation of about 8,000 feet. (Elevations range from 5,000 at the north entrance to 12,000 at Eagle Peak on the Park's east boundary.) This means winter comes early to the Park, and growing seasons are short. That's one reason you'll find only nine kinds of trees among the 1,700 plant species that grow in and around the Park.

In addition, you'll find about 300 species of birds, 18 fish species and nearly 100 different mammals. Among them are the black bear and the endangered grizzly whose populations are widely disputed. Estimates for the numbers of grizzlies in Greater Yellowstone range from 170 to 350. Black bear estimates are around 600. That means you'll be lucky to see a bear of any kind while you're visiting the Park.

In the next sections, we describe how to enter the Park and how to get around once you're in. We also provide information on visitor centers and other features. See our Attractions chapter for descriptions of some of the amazing sights you can see during your visit. And read the chapter, Our Natural World, for introductions to some of the flora and fauna you're likely to spot in this natural playground.

Entering the Park

When you enter the Park (see more about its entrances below), a ranger will give you a map and a Park publication full of useful information about where to go and what to do. Park entrance fees went up in 1997 to help offset budget cutbacks. (For more information about Park fees, see the gray box.)

For general information about Yellowstone National Park, call (307) 344-7381.

National Park Entrance Fees

New rates were instituted in 1997. They are:

$20 per private car
$15 per individual snowmobile or motorcycle
$10 per single entry (bike, foot or ski)

All these passes provide entrance to both Yellowstone and Grand Teton national parks for seven days. You can purchase an annual pass, also good for both Parks, for $40. Golden Eagle Passports cost $50 and offer additional benefits to the seniors who purchase them, including discounted camping fees.

All except the northeast entrance are open from about May 1 through October 30 round-the-clock. The northeast entrance is generally open from June 1 until September 30, depending on snowfall on the Beartooth Highway northeast of Cooke City. (This pass closes during the winter.) In mid-December, when the Park reopens for winter recreation, snowmobilers and snowcoaches line up at the West Entrance and about 150 miles of snow-covered roads are used for snowmobile traffic.

Once inside the Park you'll find 350 miles of roads winding mostly around the center of the Park past major attractions and through villages. The roads, which often follow those built in the 1800s, are well-marked and generally called by the names of the attractions they lead to and from, such as the Mammoth-Norris

INSIDERS' TIP

A sixth road in the southwest corner penetrates Yellowstone Park to Bechler Ranger Station and to Cave Falls, a scenic attraction. Popular trails lead off from both places, heading up the Fall River and deep into the Park. Horsepackers particularly like to use this entrance although difficult creek crossings limit the season to mostly July through September. The Cave Falls campground is not in the Park but rather in the national forest outside the Park, so it's cheaper to stay there.

Road, the Mammoth-Tower Junction Road or the Madison-Old Faithful Road. In Park lingo the central roads are called the Grand Loop, Lower Loop and Upper Loop. Tours offered by a number of companies feature these three routes.

West Entrance
West Yellowstone, Mont.

West Yellowstone, the Park's number one entrance (1.1 million visitors in 1996) is easily accessed by three routes: U.S. Highway 20, which leaves north-south Interstate 15 at Idaho Falls; U.S. Highway 191, which leaves east-west Interstate 90 at Bozeman, Montana; and U.S. Highway 287, which leaves I-90 near Three Forks. During peak season in summer or winter, by car or by snowmobile, you can expect to wait in line first thing in the morning at this entrance. The town of West Yellowstone, packed with motels, campgrounds, restaurants and attractions of its own, makes a good place to stay while touring the Park.

South Entrance
Via Grand Teton National Park

This entrance, the second-most used with 813,000 visitors in 1996, is accessed by the north-south highway through Grand Teton Park.

North Entrance
Gardiner, Mont.

Once the main entrance, Gardiner is a relaxed town with mostly dirt streets and a distinct Western flavor. In 1996, 578,000 visitors traveled through this gate. It's also the only entrance kept open year round, but the road is only plowed to Cooke City 57 miles to the east. About a quarter-mile west of the actual gate is the very grand Roosevelt Arch. From the north, U.S. Highway 89 leaves I-90 at Livingston, Montana.

East Entrance
U.S. Hwy. 20

Just east of this entrance, which admitted 315,000 visitors in 1996, you'll find Pahaska Tepee, an all-in-one motel, restaurant, gas station and convenience store. During the summer, they offer horseback rides and other recreation. During winter,

this entrance is closed to auto traffic, but not to skiers and snowmobilers. Fifty-three miles to the east is Cody, Wyoming, a hopping little town with lots to do. To get to Cody you'll drive U.S. Highway 20 through the North Fork Canyon. The scenery is outstanding, and so is the fishing in the North Fork of the Shoshone River.

Northeast Entrance
Near Cooke City

To the east is Cooke City, a little old mining-turned-tourist town that has nine months of winter. Farther east is the Beartooth Highway (U.S. Highway 212), which climbs over a 11,000-foot summit. During the summer the entrance offers spectacular views and access to awesome hiking and fishing. It's closed during the winter, though. Unless you want to snowmobile about 10 miles to plowed road, the only winter exit from Cooke City is through Yellowstone Park to Gardiner. In 1996, 189,000 people traveled through this entrance.

Visitors Centers

Yellowstone Park's eight visitors centers are touchstones of information for wandering visitors, and many of them act as repositories of Park legend and lore. Most have nearby amenities such as shopping, refueling and dining options. See the pertinent accommodations chapters for details on lodging and camping within the Park. Other chapters will fill you in on stores and restaurants doing business in the Park.

Each center has an extensive bookstore run by the Yellowstone Association, a nonprofit organization that has supported educational, historical and scientific projects in Yellowstone Park since 1933. The Yellowstone Association has contributed more than $5 million to the Park.

Albright Visitor Center
Mammoth Hot Springs

Albright may be the hoppin'est visitors center in the Park. Besides friendly rangers who will answer your every question, you'll find an informative historic display, movies shown every half-hour about Yellowstone's history and fairly regular ranger-naturalist programs that originate on the center's front steps.

Mammoth is home to the Yellowstone Park headquarters, which is housed mostly in old Fort Yellowstone buildings. Besides the administrative buildings, Mammoth has a hotel, cabins, campground, a bar and two restaurants operated by Amfac, Yellowstone Park's main concessionaire. Hamilton Stores, the oldest established concessionaire in the Park, operates two stores here. You'll also find a gas station, a post office and ice machines.

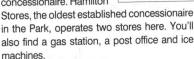

www.insiders.com

See this and many other **Insiders' Guide®** destinations online — in their entirety.

Visit us today!

Canyon Visitor Center
Canyon Village near West Entrance

This place can be a zoo sometimes, simply because it is the first visitors center you'll encounter if you're entering the Park via the West Entrance at West Yellowstone, Montana. Canyon Village is also a full-service stop that attracts campers, diners, shoppers and those needing gasoline. Neatly crammed into a horseshoe-shaped complex are two Hamilton Stores (one is a new "nature" store), a post office and a gas station. In addition, you'll find a restaurant, a cafeteria, fast-food places, a hotel, cabins and a campground. Laundry facilities and showers are attached to the campground office.

Old Faithful Visitor Center
Old Faithful Geyser

This old visitors center is spacious, airy and staffed by friendly individuals who know what they're talking about. Inside the center you'll find a board that lists the next projected eruption time for Old Faithful as well as other neighboring geysers. Old Faithful is a bustling place with two hotels, a lodge, more than 100 cabins, two gas stations, a post office and shower facilities. Other features include several restaurants, a couple of gift shops and two Hamilton Stores.

Grant Village Visitor Center
Grant Village

This center has a wonderful display about the Yellowstone Fires of 1988. There is also a backcountry office where you must register and buy a permit for overnight camping in this part of the Park. Grant Village facilities include one Hamilton General Store, a post office, showers, a laundry facility and an ice machine. You'll also find a motel-style lodge and a large campground by the lake.

Bridge Bay Ranger Station
Bridge Bay

The center is right next to the marina on Yellowstone Lake, and its staff answers hundreds of questions each day about fishing and boating here. At the marina, you'll find boat slips, boats for rent, scenic cruises and guided fishing trips. A campground is just a stone's throw away. You can get ice at the marina and groceries at the Hamilton Store.

Lake Ranger Station
Near the Lake Hotel in Lake Village

Log beams and a huge stone fireplace will catch your eye in this quaint old ranger station. Rangers here will answer your fishing questions (and any others you might have) from dawn until dark. Besides this ranger station, you'll find the Park's only hospital, a post office, the Lake Hotel and cabins and a small Hamilton Store.

Fishing Bridge Visitor Center
North Shore of Yellowstone Lake

Designed by Seattle architect Robert Reamer, this visitors center is one of our favorites. Besides having a wonderful collection of stuffed birds from Yellowstone Park, the center offers a spectacular view from its lakeside steps. Because it's in the middle of grizzly

---

INSIDERS' TIP

Idaho Department of Fish and Game has estimated the cutthroat trout population of the South Fork of the Snake at 3,500 fish per mile and the whitefish population at 30,000 per mile.

country, the Fishing Bridge is not the village it used to be. Still, you will find a Hamilton Store, an RV Park, a gas station and a lunch counter. The center also has showers and a laundry.

Norris Geyser Basin Museum
Norris Geyser Basin

Don't confuse the stone building on the hill above the Norris Geyser Basin with a visitors center. The building you're looking for is the small log structure across the way. Inside, you'll find an informative museum on geothermal features in the Park. We recommend stopping here before venturing into the Basin.

Grand Teton National Park

Geothermal springs, geysers and mud pots were the original impetus for preserving Yellowstone Park in 1872. For Teton Park, it was the 7,000-foot sweep of the Teton range as it flings itself upward, with no false starts, no foothills, from the valley floor. Those dramatic mountains and the string of glacial lakes that lie like mirrors at their feet awed 19th-century viewers, such as painter and explorer Thomas Moran, and continue to awe today's visitors.

Old Faithful and the mounted Ranger Patrol are still both alive and well.

A north/south fault that split some 9 million years ago, its Western side rising and its eastern side dropping, was the beginning of the Tetons (see the Attractions and Our Natural World chapters). Glaciers, water and wind have done the rest. From shortly after the creation of Yellowstone Park, calls went out to protect the magnificent Tetons as well. The first, most obvious impetus was the mountains' grandeur; the second was the growing awareness on the part of Yellowstone's admirers and managers that a significant aspect of the region's natural beauty lay in the abundant wildlife, and that Yellowstone wildlife would need more room to survive. In 1929, the rocky heart of the Teton range became a separate national park. This preserved the peaks themselves, but didn't address the issue of wildlife preservation. It also didn't control what was quickly becoming rampant tourist development on the shores of Jackson and Jenny Lakes.

With the encouragement of some local ranchers who saw their lifestyles and livelihoods better protected by a larger Grand Teton National Park, John D. Rockefeller Jr. began quietly acquiring land in the shadows of the Tetons; he bought rich winter rangeland, scenic lakefront property and important riparian areas along the braided channel of the Snake River. Against fierce local resistance — most Jackson residents saw only a ghost town in their future if the national park were allowed to grow — President Franklin D. Roosevelt added lands to the Park by decree. Much of the rest of Jackson Hole was added to the Park in 1950, when Rockefeller's purchases were given to the nation. In 1972, the last big chunk required to connect Grand Teton and Yellowstone parks was added; this chimney of land is named John D. Rockefeller Jr. Memorial Parkway.

All told, Grand Teton Park contains 485 square miles. Its borders contain one of the youngest mountain ranges in North America, eight large lakes and numerous smaller ones, several active glaciers, extensive fir, spruce and lodgepole pine forest and game-rich valley grasslands. One of the West's most important rivers, the nearly 1,000 mile-long Snake, meanders through the Park.

Getting Around

Teton Park's piece-by-piece birth makes it a different kind of place from Yellowstone. For instance, unlike Yellowstone Park, Grand Teton Park's roads were not designed to detour through a tourist area but rather to facilitate through-traffic, so there are fewer traffic jams than in Yellowstone. However, it is also true that a car tour of Grand Teton Park leaves many of the best sights unseen. The main Park road, U.S. Highway 191/89/287, enters Teton Park from the north. It skirts the east edge of Jackson Lake before U.S. Highway 287 joins U.S. Highway 26 and veers out the Buffalo Fork Valley through the Moran Park entrance. U.S. Highway 191/26 continues south and a little west across the broad valley floor to and through the south boundary of the Park and the town of Jackson, Wyoming.

At one point the 25 mile-long Teton Park Road — called "the inner road" by locals — loops away from U.S. 191/26/89 to bring you closer to Jackson, Leigh and Jenny lakes. Other side drives well-worth the taking include the Gros Ventre River Road, and the lower Jenny Lake loop. Signal Mountain Road dead-ends on top of Signal Mountain and leaves you staring up at Mount Moran or down at the flat valley floor and its scalloped braid, the Snake River. The Moose-Wilson Road, narrow and winding and inappropriate for trailers or recreational vehicles, is a lovely alternate route out of the Park.

In winter most Park roads are closed, but the "outer loop," U.S. Highway 191/89, and its offshoot, U.S. Highway 26/287, are plowed all winter. Unplowed roads are open to skiers and snowmobilers in winter, but Grand Teton Park receives nowhere near the winter traffic that Yellowstone does. Winter is actually quiet in the shadows of the Tetons. The quiet is in stark contrast to the pollution and noise created by tremendous numbers of snowmobilers drawn by Yellowstone Park's winter trails.

Summer or winter, it is possible to drive through Grand Teton Park, almost from end to end, without paying the entrance fee at either of the Parks stations. Take U.S. Highway 191/26/89 from Jackson past the National Elk Refuge. Now you're in the Park, but you haven't paid yet. The southern entrance station is on the inner loop road, also known as Teton Park Road, and you're on the outer loop. Continue north and east until you reach Moran Junction. Turn left here, and you'll hit Grand Teton Park's second entrance, where you'll have to pay to continue north. Or turn right on U.S. Highway 26/287 toward Dubois, and you'll exit the Park without passing an entrance station.

Entrance stations provide useful information, but even better are the Park's four visitors centers/ranger stations, including the one at Flagg Ranch, which is technically not part of Yellowstone or Grand Teton park but is equipped to provide resources and information about both. See our descriptions of these centers in the sections that follow.

In addition to ranger services, concessionaire-run tourist services are available in various locations. The biggest clusters are at Colter Bay, Signal Mountain Lodge, Jackson Lake Lodge, Jenny Lake and in Moose. Colter Bay, Jenny Lake and Moose have Park Service visitors centers in addition to their commercial services. More limited services are available at Kelly and Leek's Marina. Limited services are available just outside the Park's Moran Junction. Teton Village and Jackson offer complete services, including accommodations, gas, medical care, groceries, entertainment and dining.

Besides the two concessionaire-run RV parks, Grand Teton Park has five Park Service campgrounds. Other lodging options within the Park range from canvas-walled cabins to log cabins to hotels. See our accommodations chapters for more on where to stay.

Activities and Visitors Centers

Unlike Yellowstone, which is one solid blanket of public land, Grand Teton Park is checkered with private inholdings as well as lands that have been sold to the government but leased back to the former owners. More than 100 privately owned tracts exist within the Park boundaries, some as large as 400 acres. This means, for instance, that cattle and horse grazing is allowed in limited areas within the national park. Jackson Hole's municipal airport is even inside Grand

Teton Park — making it the only airport in the country completely surrounded by a national park.

All this grows out of the piecemeal manner in which Grand Teton Park was created. The main benefit to you is the range of activities available in the Park. Several dude ranches (see our Resorts and Guest Ranches chapter) operate here, and a variety of concessionaires offer activities such as scenic raft trips, ferry rides and horseback riding. Yellowstone has one primary on-site concessionaire and two smaller ones, but Teton Park has nine. Luckily, you can sort all this out on the inside front page of the *Teewinot*, Grand Teton Park's newspaper, available at entrance stations and visitors centers. Or you can call Park Dispatch at (307) 739-3300.

Here is a quick summary of what's available at the major tourist centers and Park visitors centers.

Flagg Ranch Visitors Center and Flagg Ranch Resort
John D. Rockefeller Jr. Memorial Pky.
• resort (307) 543-2861, (800) 443-2311

The visitors center is a tiny log building at one end of the Flagg Ranch Resort parking lot. Staffed by a National Park Service employee, the center provides brochures, maps and information. You can select from a limited supply of books for sale here as well.

Flagg Ranch Resort is operated by a single concessionaire that offers camping, cabins and motel accommodations as well as a variety of summer and winter diversions. You are between the two national parks, literally a few minutes' drive. You can catch a snowcoach or snowmobile into Yellowstone Park from here, go horseback riding and rafting in summer, or fish, hike and camp. The resort has laundry, grocery and dining facilities as well.

Completely surrounded by the John D. Rockefeller Jr. Memorial Parkway, Flagg Ranch is the only source of tourist services between Yellowstone's south gate and Grand Teton Park's north one.

Colter Bay Visitors Center
Colter Bay Village on Jackson Lake

This is our favorite visitors center, with a good selection of books and posters for sale, a backcountry ranger to provide information about and permits for backpacking expeditions and, best of all, an impressive collection of Native American arts and artifacts. On the bottom floor of the museum area is often a guest artist, a Native American craftsman who can show you the skills that produce his art and sell you a piece. The village itself is run by Grand Teton Lodge Company and offers two restaurants, a laundry, a gas station, public showers and a grocery store. There's even a marina here where you can sign up for cruises or rent a canoe. Call Grand Teton Lodge Company at (307) 543-2811.

Jackson Lake Lodge
On Jackson Lake • (307) 543-2811

Jackson Lake Lodge has no Park visitors center, but the headquarters for the Park's largest concessionaire, Grand Teton Lodge Company (phone number listed above), is a busy place. Many services are available here, including an ATM, the Park's single medical clinic, a service station, a swimming pool and two restaurants. You can catch bus tours, horseback rides and Snake River float trips from here. You can also pick up a *New York Times* or shop for men's and women's clothing.

Signal Mountain Lodge
On Jackson Lake • (307) 543-2831

Many services are available at Signal Mountain on the shore of Jackson Lake. The complex lacks a Park visitors center but little else. You can eat at either of two restaurants, hang out on the deck and sip Margaritas, shop for gifts or fill your gas tank (emergency gas is available year round here, although technically the lodge is closed in winter). Signal Mountain also has a convenience store and marina. You can rent a craft or a buoy or hop on a guided fishing boat. You can also sign

INSIDERS' TIP
Ten million board feet sounds like a lot of timber, but it only builds 100 houses.

up for a scenic float trip on the Snake River nearby.

Jenny Lake Visitors Center
South Jenny Lake Area

This center is smaller than Colter Bay and Moose visitors centers but carries the expected selection of books and posters, as well as a bird's-eye topo map of the region. The interpretive material in this visitors center addresses the formation of the Teton Range. The Park's climbing rangers also have an office, just across from the main visitors center, where you can obtain information about backcountry conditions. Until a couple years ago, you were required to register here to climb in the Tetons.

The South Jenny Lake area offers limited services, including a general store stocked with camping supplies, groceries and T-shirts, a marina run by Teton Boating Company, (307) 733-2703, and Exxum Guides, a climbing service and school, (307) 733-2297. Exxum is one of two climbing companies licensed to guide and teach within Grand Teton Park. For more information on Exxum and Jackson Hole Mountain Guides, see our Other Recreation chapter. Teton Boating Company is the only concessionaire plying the clear waters of Jenny Lake; these folks can ferry you across to the unroaded side of the lake, where the Tetons rise like a wall nearly from the water's edge.

Moose Visitors Center
Near Dornan's at Moose

Moose Visitors Center is big and busy. It features interpretive information about the Park's wildlife. The book and poster section is satisfyingly large. Backcountry rangers are available to supply you with permits for backcountry travel or to help you plan your trip. This is the only visitors center in Grand Teton Park open in winter.

Dornan's is two minutes from the visitors center. It offers most services including an extremely well-stocked grocery store, an ATM, sporting and mountaineering goods and gift shops, boat and bike rentals, two restaurants and a package liquor store with a fine selection of wines. The service station is open year round, as are most services.

National Forests

This country is home to 156 national forests containing 191 million acres in 44 states. Terrain ranges from high-altitude lodgepole forest, like what you find in much of this region, to ice-gilded crags, sage covered hills and scrub juniper. What all national forests have in common is that they're public land. They belong to you — to all of us.

The whole national forest system started here in Greater Yellowstone more than 100 years ago, which perhaps accounts for the fact that this region encompasses seven national forests that fit around Yellowstone and Teton parks like puzzle pieces.

What follows is a thumbnail sketch of Greater Yellowstone's seven national forests. These national forests encompass vast reaches of land and nearly unlimited recreational opportunities. The best way to approach them is first by phone, so we provide numbers for each forest's ranger districts and its overseeing forest headquarters. Think of forest rangers as the folks who have the instruction manual for one of your most prized possessions: your national forest lands.

Shoshone National Forest

America's first national forest grew out of lands set aside by Congress in 1891. Shoshone National Forest is a huge swath of land along Yellowstone Park's eastern border, extending south to well below Grand Teton Park and north to the Montana border. Its 2.4 million acres contains more than 1,000 miles of rivers and wide sweeps of sagebrush and grassland — more than any other Greater Yellowstone national forest. Forty-five percent of the Shoshone is protected within five federal wilderness areas, making this the most wilderness-full national forest in Greater Yellowstone.

INSIDERS' TIP

Most of the trees cut in Greater Yellowstone are lodgepole pine.

For general information, write the Forest Headquarters, 225 W. Yellowstone Avenue, Cody WY 82414, or call (307) 527-6241.

Shoshone National Forest contains four ranger districts:

• Clarks Fork Ranger District, 1002 Road 11, Powell, WY 82435, (307) 754-7207

• Greybull Ranger District, 2044 State Street, Meeteetse, WY 82433, (307) 868-2379

• Wapiti Ranger District, 203 A Yellowstone, Cody, WY 82414, (307) 527-6921

• Wind River Ranger District, 209 Ramshorn, Dubois, WY 82513, (307) 455-2466

Bridger-Teton National Forest

Named after its most dramatic mountain range, the Grand Tetons, and its most flamboyant 19th-century mountain man, Jim Bridger, this national forest is Greater Yellowstone's biggest. Bridger-Teton contains 3.4 million acres stretching from Yellowstone Park's southern boundary down Grand Teton Park's eastern edge, encircling the valley of Jackson Hole. One of its two long southern "arms" embraces the wild, glacier-sculpted Wind River range. The other stretches nearly to Utah to encompass the Salt River and Wyoming ranges. The forest is completely contained within Wyoming.

For general information, contact the headquarters for Bridger-Teton National Forest at 340 N. Cache, Jackson, WY 83001, (307) 733-2752.

The forest contains six ranger districts, with offices scattered from middle-of-nowhere Moran just outside Grand Teton Park to middle-of-nowhere Kemmerer near the Utah/Wyoming border:

• Jackson Ranger District, Box 1689, Jackson, WY 83001, (307) 733-4755

• Kemmerer Ranger District, Box 31, Kemmerer, WY 83101, (307) 877-4415

• Big Piney Ranger District, Box 218, Big Piney, WY 83113, (307) 276-3375

• Greys River Ranger District, Box 338, Afton, WY 83110, (307) 886-3166

• Buffalo Ranger District, Box 278, Moran, WY 83013, (307) 543-2386

• Pinedale Ranger District, Box 220, Pinedale, WY 82941, (307) 367-4326

Targhee National Forest

Greater Yellowstone is not a region easily contained by clean lines. Some would say, for instance, that nearly one-fourth of the Targhee National Forest's 1.8 million acres is not part of Yellowstone country. Others, including us, would happily fold the whole forest into Greater Yellowstone. Either way, the Targhee marks the western edges of the region from Idaho's Centennial Range down to the Caribou National Forest. The Targhee owns the western view of the majestic Tetons, as Bridger-Teton National Forest owns the eastern one. East, southeast and south of the Targhee is the end of wilderness, where a mighty swath of fertile farmland gives Idaho its famous potato reputation.

The Targhee is home to two wilderness areas. The Jedediah Smith Wilderness runs along the western slopes of the Tetons. Little-known and seldom-traveled Winegar Hole Wilderness — 10,750 acres tucked against the unroaded southwest corner of Yellowstone — is prime grizzly habitat.

For general information about Targhee National Forest, contact Forest Headquarters at Box 208, St. Anthony, ID 83445, (208) 624-3151.

The forest has four district offices within Greater Yellowstone:

• Ashton Ranger District, Box 858, Ashton, ID 83420, (208) 652-7442

• Palisades Ranger District, 3659 E. Ririe Highway, Idaho Falls, ID 83401, (208) 523-1412

• Teton Basin Ranger District, Box 127, Driggs, ID 83422, (208) 354-2431

• Island Park Ranger District, Box 220, Island Park, ID 83429, (208) 558-7301

Beaverhead-Deer Lodge National Forest

In 1996, the nearly 100-square-mile Deer Lodge National Forest was folded into the Beaverhead forest, which is nearly twice its size. The result sprawls across much of western Montana. Arguably, only a fraction of this complex of forestlands is contained within

Greater Yellowstone. What lies within our region takes the Snowcrest range for its western boundary, Red Rock Lakes National Wildlife Refuge on the Montana/Idaho border as its base and the Madison range for its eastern boundary. Also included are the lovely Tobacco Root mountains near Ennis, Montana.

One of Beaverhead-Deer Lodge's most compelling features is stark contrast: With a low elevation of around 4,000 feet and a high of more than 11,000, wildlife and vegetation vary dramatically. Low areas are covered in sage and bunch grasses. Moderate elevations are heavily forested in lodgepole pine with a bit of Englemann spruce and Douglas fir. High elevations are glacier-carved studies in rock and ice.

For general information about the forest, contact Forest Headquarters at 610 N. Montana Street, Dillon, MT 59725, (406) 683-3900. The only Greater Yellowstone ranger district within this forest is the Madison Ranger District, 5 Forest Service Road, Ennis, MT 59729, (406) 682-4253.

Gallatin National Forest

Gallatin is the most popular national forest in Montana. It wears the Madison and Gallatin ranges on its western side, the remote and rugged Absarokas and Beartooths to the east and the Bridger range to the north. An isolated chunk of this forest encompasses Montana's Crazy Mountains. The forest sits like a hat atop Yellowstone Park. It absorbs 2.5 million visitor days annually, more than Wyoming's massive Bridger-Teton National Forest. Two large wilderness areas protect 41 percent of the forest from development and resource extraction.

For general information, contact Gallatin National Forest Headquarters, Federal Building, Box 130, Bozeman, MT 59771, (406) 587-6701.

Gallatin Forest also maintains five ranger districts:
- Big Timber Ranger District, Box A, Big Timber, MT 59011, (406) 932-5155
- Livingston Ranger District, Route 62, Box 3197, Livingston, MT 59047, (406) 222-1892
- Gardiner Ranger District, Box 5, Gardiner, MT 59030, (406) 848-7375
- Bozeman Ranger District, 601 Nikles Avenue, Box C, Bozeman, MT 59715, (406) 587-6920
- Hebgen Lake Ranger District, Box 520, West Yellowstone, MT 59758, (406) 646-7369

Custer National Forest

Custer National Forest abuts Gallatin National Forest east of the Yellowstone Valley. The forest touches Yellowstone Park's northeastern corner to the south and splits the craggy, glacier-capped Beartooths with Gallatin. It's mountainous, jagged country.

INSIDERS' TIP

The mountain pine beetle is a natural part of a lodgepole forest's life cycle. Mature trees are susceptible to the beetle, which lays its eggs under their bark. Larvae eventually kill infested trees by feeding on their inner bark. You can see signs of mountain pine beetle infestation where there are stands of mature lodgepoles with reddish-brown foliage. Trees killed by pine beetles generally stand for about five years, then fall and create fuel for the fires that are also part of the lodgepole forest's life cycle: After a fire new lodgepole seedlings sprout and begin to regenerate the forest. If a fire does not occur, the next turn in the natural cycle is likely to be a spruce/fir forest. Much of the logging in the Targhee, Gallatin and Shoshone national forests, the area's most heavily logged, has been done in the name of controlling pine beetle infestations by removing infested trees and the mature stands that would eventually become infested. Like fire, logging and reseeding can result in new stands of lodgepole.

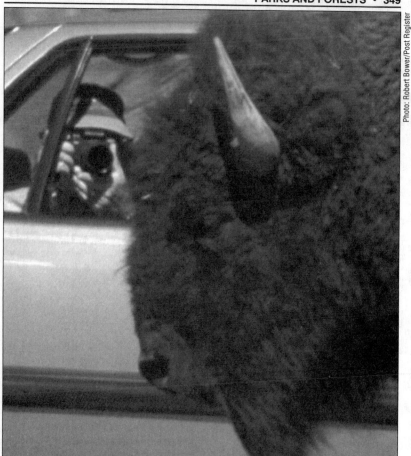

Photo: Robert Bower/Post Register

A Yellowstone park visitor gets a real close up of a herd of bison surrounding his car as they cross the highway near Flood Geyser.

Twenty-five peaks in Custer National Forest, most of them in the Beartooths, reach above 12,000 feet. Dozens of active glaciers survive in the thin, cold air — tattered grandchildren of the massive blanket of ice that covered this region more than 10,000 years ago. On its eastern side, Custer drops abruptly into prairie at about 4,000 feet above sea level.

Custer Forest Headquarters is located at 2602 First Avenue N., Box 2556, Billings, MT 59103, (406) 657-6361. Beartooth Ranger District can be reached at Route 2, Box 3420, Red Lodge, MT 59068, (406) 446-2103.

Caribou National Forest

Caribou National Forest lacks the sky-piercing crags of other Greater Yellowstone national forests — its highest point is Mead Peak at only 9,957 feet. Caribou is a long, narrow forest extending from northern Utah along the west slope of the Salt River valley and up 22-mile-long Palisades Reservoir. Away from its western edge roll the fertile volcanic farmlands of Idaho's Snake River Plain. East of the forest are stacked the Salt and Wyoming ranges, both contained within massive Bridger-Teton National Forest. Most of the forest's 1.2 million acres lies outside what experts call Greater Yellowstone. The area within Greater Yellowstone is administered by Targhee National Forest managers.

For general information, contact Caribou Forest Headquarters at 250 S. Fourth, Pocatello, ID 83201, (208) 236-7500.

Caribou has four ranger districts, none of which overlaps Greater Yellowstone. For information about Greater Yellowstone's chunk of the Caribou, contact the Palisades Ranger District of the Targhee National Forest at 3659 E. Ririe Highway, Idaho Falls, ID 83401, (208) 523-1412.

National Wildlife Refuges

National Elk Refuge

When human development began to threaten critical elk and bison winter range, and building in and around the town of Jackson, Wyoming, blocked winter migration routes, the trapped animals ravaged ranchers' hay in the northern half of Jackson Hole and then starved in pitiful heaps on the snow. The result, in 1912, was Wyoming's National Elk Refuge, which runs along the east side of U.S. Highway 89/26 north of Jackson for about 6 miles.

The refuge is home to somewhere between 7,500 and 12,000 elk in winter, depending on whom you ask. The elk are fed when necessary to ward off starvation. When necessary, they are also hunted selectively to thin their numbers.

You won't see much out there if you come by in summer, but from about October until the snow melts, the flat valley floor is home to more elk than you ever thought you'd see in one place. At the south end of the elk refuge is a visitors center.

Red Rock Lakes National Wildlife Refuge

If you're a bird watcher, the Red Rock Lakes National Wildlife Refuge near Monida, 276-3536, is a good place to hang out. A total of 232 species have been identified here, including the trumpeter swan for which the refuge was created.

The U.S. Fish and Wildlife Service established this 45,000-acre refuge in 1935 to protect and preserve trumpeter swans. About 9,000 acres of the area are comprised of lakes and ponds that are home not only to swans, but also to numerous other species.

The only way to get to this refuge is by a not-very-well-marked dirt road that leads from U.S. Highway 20 west of West Yellowstone, Montana, to Interstate 15 near Monida. The drive is beautiful and will lead you to two campgrounds.

State Parks

Henry's Lake State Park
Off U.S. Hwy. 20 north of Island Park, Idaho • (208) 558-7532

This busy campground and boat ramp are easily accessed from U.S. Highway 20 just north of the main business areas of Island Park. On a typical summer day, 100 vehicles may pass through the gates on their way to the boat ramp. Attendants are available during business hours to answer your questions and keep an eye on things (see our Camping chapter for more).

Henry's Lake is renowned both for its prime fishing — the most common catch is the cuttbow, a volunteer hybrid of cutthroat and rainbow that grows to tackle-busting size — and for its sudden storms. Weather sweeps down from the surrounding mountain ranges, the Henrys Lake Mountains, the Centennials and the Gravelly Range. Smart boaters keep an eye on the skies.

INSIDERS' TIP

National Forest managers distribute a wide range of free brochures that can tell you everything from how to survive a bear attack to how to stay on the right side of local fishing regulations. Stop by any ranger station or national park visitors center.

Harriman State Park
Off U.S. Hwy. 20 south of Island Park, Idaho • (208) 558-7368

Harriman State Park consists of 16,000 acres of land also protected as a wildlife refuge. No camping is available within the park, but plentiful camping opportunities exist in the vicinity. During summer visitors tour the Railroad Ranch buildings, 27 of which still stand. You can also fish, hike, bike and horseback ride from the riding stables. In winter, cross-country skiers take over.

The park hosts plentiful wildlife, including endangered trumpeter swans. One-third of the Rocky Mountain population of these huge birds spend their winters here. You can also see bald eagles, osprey, moose, deer, coyote and more. In fall, locals head here to listen to the unearthly whistling call of bull elk.

Facilities include a visitors center, equipped to provide interesting handouts about the area's wildlife and other features, and an outdoor interpretive center that also focuses on area wildlife. The riding stables are open in summer only. The visitors center is open as a warming hut on weekends in winter.

Buffalo Bill State Park
Yellowstone Hwy. west of Cody, Wyo. • (307) 587-9227

This state park, established in 1957, is tucked into the North Fork Canyon. Features include the Buffalo Bill Reservoir (8,500 surface acres) and 3,500 land acres surrounding it. The shores of the reservoir and the state park facilities changed in 1993 after the dam was raised by 25 feet.

You'll find several campgrounds, boat ramps and plenty of water for fishing and boating.

Removed from
development and
relatively undisturbed
by man, the rivers and
the wildlands of Greater
Yellowstone are home to
nearly all of the species
existing here more than
125 years ago.

Fishing and Hunting

In its February 1998 issue, *Sports Afield* named Island Park Idaho's premier outdoor sports town. This recognition follows Idaho Falls' designation as a hidden gem by *Outside* and *Outdoor Life* magazines in 1995. Outdoor sports are so much a part of our lives that some business owners, on a warm cloudy day when the insects are hatching and the fish are biting, will hang a "Gone Fishing" sign on their doors and head for the river. In the not-too-distant past, a few schools even closed on the opening day of hunting season. Administrators knew there wouldn't be enough kids (or teachers) in school to bother with classes.

Nowhere else in the lower 48 states will you find an area of wildlands as massive as in the 18 million-acre expanse of Greater Yellowstone. Rivers and streams, fed by spring waters and snow melt, run pure and fast — carrying 21 fish species, among them the trout that have made this region so famous. (The filming of Robert Redford's movie, *A River Runs Through It*, in Greater Yellowstone, definitely helped.)

Living in the shadow of a time when Greater Yellowstone's human inhabitants depended for their survival on the bounty of the mountains, folks in this region are still very much tied to the idea — if not to the actuality — of the mountains being a living pantry. Many who catch a mess of fish eat what they can then freeze or can the rest for winter use. Locals trade elk sausage recipes. And children take homemade deer jerky to school in their lunches. Smoked fish makes a fine hors d'oeuvre, and cut-up elk sirloin is excellent in Chinese stir-fry. One mark of friendship here is the sharing of elk tenderloins, called backstrap. If a resident of Greater Yellowstone offers you some, consider yourself blessed. Then eat it.

Though the fish populations in Yellowstone Park and the region were restored partially through catch-and-release fishing, for many in this region it's a difficult concept to swallow. Fish were made for catching — and eating.

In this chapter we'll give you just a taste of fishing and hunting opportunities. If you find yourself wishing for more, there's a rich menu of literature on fishing and hunting in our region. You'll find a few of them listed in our Resources chapter.

For more information on fishing and hunting in Greater Yellowstone, we refer you to the Montana Department of Fish, Wildlife and Parks, P.O. Box 200701, Helena, MT 59620, (406) 444-2535, (406) 994-4042; the Wyoming Department of Game and Fish, Attention: Information Section, 5400 Bishop Boulevard, Cheyenne, Wyoming, (307) 777-4600; and the Idaho Department of Fish and Game, P.O. Box 25, Boise, ID 83707, (208) 334-3700.

Fishing

Some fly fishers call it nirvana. Others call it the Golden Triangle of Trout. Whatever you want to call the web of trout-filled rivers, streams, creeks and lakes in Greater Yellowstone, it's a fact that from any town in Yellowstone country you can fish a different stream every day all summer if that's your pleasure.

The fast-moving rivers of the Rocky Mountains were made for fly fishing and waders. And the succession of insect hatches in Yellowstone country were made for studying, copying and following with a fervor. If you're a fly fisherman, you know bugs and fish go together like honey and bears. Among local fly fishers, a few have so fine-tuned the art and science of the sport that their names — such as Dan Bailey and Bud Lilly — have become legendary.

Chances are, though, you'll want to use your spinning rod in bodies of flatwater such as Yellowstone, Lewis and Jenny lakes and the Buffalo Bill Reservoir. You may also want to fish from a boat in these lakes, although anglers have plenty of success from the shores, especially early in the summer. An increasing number of folks fish from float tubes, but they don't venture very far from shore, and they generally learn the wind patterns first. The wind can sweep out of nowhere and stir the alpine lakes of the Rockies into ugly monsters.

Judging by the number of fly fishing outfitters and guides, there are plenty of anglers seeking nirvana. Newspapers carry regular columns written by local fishing experts. Radio stations broadcast daily fishing reports, including information about such things as the latest stonefly and caddis fly hatches and muddied high water to avoid. Hotel chalkboards carry shortened versions of like information. And small motels frequented by anglers post photos of their regular guests showing off their prize fish.

At the heart of this fishing paradise is Yellowstone Lake, home of the world's largest wild cutthroat fishery. Running down the draws and through the canyons are blue-ribbon rivers such as the Yellowstone, Gallatin and Madison, as well as the Gibbon, Gardner and Bechler. Other notable rivers include the Lamar, the Fall and the Firehole. And just as remarkable are the Henry's Fork, Buffalo Fork and South Fork of the Snake. With more than 100 lakes and 1,000 miles of streams within Yellowstone Park's 2 million acres alone, the list of fishing possibilities is seemingly endless. Outside Yellowstone's boundaries, the list — and the rivers — grow longer.

Comparatively unaffected by pollution and serious habitat degradation, Yellowstone's fisheries are in better shape than almost anyplace in the country. A number of factors account for this. The first is a lack of irrigation diversions in Yellowstone Park, which means the rivers aren't either dewatered or warmed and the fish aren't diverted onto croplands. Also, underwater hot springs not only bring up nutrients from within the earth, they also warm river and lake waters through the winter, which in turn makes fish grow much faster. The warmer winter water raises the cold-blooded fish's body temperature and its metabolic rate. The warm water also feeds aquatic vegetation on which the fish feed. Finally, the heavy snows in the region act as a reservoir to rivers, not only keeping water levels up during the hot summer months, but also keeping the water temperatures down during late summer. (Trout can not survive in water that is too warm.)

Within Yellowstone Park, anglers will encounter seven varieties of game fish: cutthroat, rainbow, brown and lake trout as well as grayling and mountain whitefish. Cutthroat, the only native species, are so named for the red slash under their throats. The other species — plus a few that didn't survive transplanting — were introduced mostly by government agencies beginning in 1890. A few species, such as the chub, sucker and shiner, were planted accidentally by bait fishermen who dumped their unused minnows into Yellowstone's waters. Inside Yellowstone, bait and lead have been outlawed in all but a couple of places. Children can still fish with bait in Panther, Indian and Obsidian creeks as well as the Gardner River.

Several problems have resulted from stocking, which Park officials stopped doing in 1958. First, some species such as rainbows and cutthroat have crossbred, creating hybrids called cutt-bows. In other cases,

---

INSIDERS' TIP

Headed this way on a fishing trip? Be sure you check our Resorts and Guest Ranches chapter for information on fishing lodges in the area. Many of these lodges are willing to supply guides to non-lodge guests.

Photo: Randy Hayes/Post Register

The South Fork of the Snake River flows through the Byington Landing area.

the exotic species prey on the natives. In 1994, Park officials discovered that someone had introduced lake trout to Yellowstone Lake. While lake trout grow big and are fun to catch, they also destroy the native cutthroat. Each spring, fisheries biologists now have to seek out and destroy all the eggs they can find in lake trout spawning beds. They also require anglers to keep and record each lake trout they catch in Yellowstone Lake. For other species in the Park, fishing is either catch-and-release or restricted to minimal possession limits.

When the Hayden party explored Yellowstone in 1871, one man fishing from shore caught 42 fish in just a couple of hours. Cutthroat in Yellowstone Lake were so plentiful their eggs began to be collected in massive quantities. Hatched and reared in captivity, the cutthroat fry were released into waters across the country. In addition, the Park opened a hatchery near the Lake Hotel. The Yellowstone Park Hotel Company caught nearly four tons of fish each season to serve in hotel dining rooms. In 1919, commercial fishing was stopped altogether. In 1973 even sport fishing was severely restricted in Yellowstone Lake and the Yellowstone River.

The Yellowstone Park Hotel Company caught nearly four tons of fish each season to serve in hotel dining rooms. In 1919, it was stopped altogether. In 1987, catch-and-release restrictions were applied to both cutthroat and rainbow trout in most Park waters. Today, you're allowed to keep two cutthroat of less than 13 inches on Yellowstone Lake. Park officials say that could change if they see fish-eating critters such as pelicans, grizzlies and otters aren't getting enough.

To fish in Yellowstone Park, you must buy a permit if you're 16 years or older. A 10-day permit cost $10 in 1997 ($20 for the entire season). Children ages 12 to 15 must get a non-fee permit. Montana, Idaho and Wyoming each have different regulations related to fishing and the purchase of licenses. Generally, the regulations are voluminous and require some study. You'll find regulations and licenses at any sporting goods store that sells fishing equipment.

Reams of books have been written about fishing in Greater Yellowstone. A few of them are suggested in our Resources section at the end of this book. In the meantime, in case you've never fished here before, we've described just a very few of the most popular lakes and streams. We've also given you the names of a few fishing outfitters and guides who can get you started on regional waters.

Our list is by no means complete, and there are plenty of good ones that we haven't listed.

Lakes, Rivers and Streams

Yellowstone National Park and Surrounding Area

To fish in Yellowstone Park, you need to pick up a set of regulations and a permit. You can get a copy of the regulations at almost any fly shop or sporting goods store in towns surrounding the Park. Anglers 16 and older must buy a fishing permit. Ten bucks will buy you a 10-day permit. Twenty bucks will buy a season permit. Permits are available at ranger stations, visitor centers, and Hamilton Stores.

Except for Yellowstone Lake, the Park's fishing season begins on the Saturday of Memorial Day weekend and continues through the first Sunday of November. On Yellowstone Lake, the season opens June 15, while the lake's tributary streams open July 15. For complete information on Park fishing, we suggest you pick up a set of the regulations. For more information you can write the Chief Ranger's Office, P.O. Box 168, Yellowstone National Park, WY 82190, or call (307) 344-2107.

Yellowstone, Lewis and Shoshone Lakes

About 50,000 anglers (nearly half of all those who fish in the Park) cast their lines into the icy waters of the 136-square mile Yellowstone Lake each year. Those who fish from boats are slightly more successful (they catch about 1.4 fish per hour) than shore anglers (their average is .8 fish per hour). Those who fish from boats, though, should keep in mind that winds come out of nowhere and can turn Yellowstone Lake into a small sea with dangerous waves. Home to the famed Yellowstone cutthroat trout (and the illegally introduced lake trout), this lake is the gauge for fishery health in all of Greater Yellowstone. Despite more than a century of heavy fishing, and scandalously high egg collection rates by early fish hatcheries, Yellowstone Lake still has a pretty high cutthroat population for today.

Most anglers fish from shore between Sedge Bay and Grant Village. In June, when the ice is still melting, lake trout hug the slightly warmer waters along shore. Cutthroat hang out in shallower waters near sandbars and inlets.

Lewis Lake, which has a campground and a boat launch, has large lake trout and browns, with a few brookies and cutthroat. High winds and wavy water on this 2,000-plus-acre lake can make it dangerous to canoe, but fishing is fine from the shores. If you're canoeing, float tubing or kayaking, hug the shoreline even if you're headed up the Lewis River Channel to Shoshone Lake.

Shoshone, the second-largest lake in Yellowstone Park (it's surface covers more than 8,000 acres), is also home to lake, brown and brook trout. You'll find the fish bite here all summer. There are some wonderful backcountry campsites around the lake. In both lakes, you can keep two lake trout and two browns. In the Lewis River below Lewis Falls, however, it's catch-and-release only for brown trout. Browns spawn in this area.

Firehole River

Beginning at Madison Lake south of Old Faithful on the north side of the Continental Divide, this 35-mile river wanders like a curious spectator through the Upper and Midway geyser basins before tumbling through the canyon leading to the Madison Junction. Ken

INSIDERS' TIP

Anglers, remember: You're in bear country, so don't set up camp near spawning streams. Gut your catch away from camping areas and, after puncturing the air bladder, throw entrails into the water. Wash hands thoroughly after handling fish. Pack out or burn completely other fish remains. Don't leave them lying around camp, and don't bury them.

Retallic, author of *Greater Yellowstone Flyfisher's Stream Guide*, says the fish in the Firehole River are smart and require "tiny flies for scholarly fish."

It's fly fishing only on the Firehole. You can't keep rainbow, but you're allowed two browns smaller than 13 inches as well as five brookies. There is no fishing at all from Old Faithful to Biscuit Basin. Where the road leaves the river near Fountain Paint Pots, you'll find a side road leading to Goose Lake to the west. Trails lead from Goose Lake to the Firehole. In spring, though, this area could be reserved for grizzlies.

Gibbon River

This capricious 38-mile river begins as a small ribbon leading from Grebe Lake, the small lake in Yellowstone Park and home to some large rainbow as well as the feisty grayling. The Gibbon splashes down Virginia Cascade, wanders through the Norris Geyser Basin, winds through Elk Park and Gibbon Meadows, shoots through a narrow canyon, then plunges over Gibbon Falls. (The pool below this waterfall sometimes holds big rainbows and browns.) The Madison-Norris Road parallels much of this river. A 5-mile stretch that winds through Gibbon Meadows will take you away from the road where you'll find good-size rainbows and brook trout. The water here can be deceptively deep. Bigger browns and rainbows live below the falls, while smaller brookies and rainbows hang out closer to the source in the vicinity of Virginia Meadows.

Only fly fishing is allowed below Gibbon Falls — catch-and-release for rainbows and a two-fish limit for browns (they must be 13 inches and smaller), five for brook trout. Above the falls, though, you can keep two rainbow. At Grebe Lake (it's a 3.5 mile hike from the trailhead on the Canyon-Norris Road), you can't keep grayling, but you can keep two rainbow.

Slough Creek and Lamar River

Give a fly-fishing fanatic only one stream to dip a line into in Yellowstone Park and chances are it'll be Slough Creek. Trails from the Slough Creek Campground lead to a series of three meadows through which Slough Creek slowly slithers before tumbling down to

the next lazy crawl. Hidden in the pools, glides, riffles and side channels of this world-famous stream are plenty of large cutthroat (up to 24 inches).

The Lamar River, into which the Slough flows, falls from the east out of the Absaroka Mountains. Fifty-five miles long, it dumps into the Yellowstone River near Tower Junction after rushing through the canyon. Upriver in the Lamar Valley, where transplanted wolves were released in 1995, the river not only offers great fishing in its winding channels, but also a wonderful view and a chance to see wildlife.

Both streams are home to good-size rainbows and have easy access to meadow fishing. The fishing season is from Memorial Day weekend through October 31. Cutthroat are catch-and-release, but anglers can keep two rainbow and five brook trout.

Grand Teton National Park

To fish in Grand Teton Park, you'll need to be familiar with Park fishing regulations, which you can pick up at the Moose Village Store, Signal Mountain Lodge, Colter Bay Marina and Flagg Ranch Village and many locations outside the Park. Unlike Yellowstone, Grand Teton Park does not require its own fishing permit. In general, fishing rules are the rules of Wyoming, with a few special restrictions.

Snake River in Grand Teton Park and Lower Jackson Hole

The Upper Snake flows into, then out of Jackson Lake, braiding its way south through the long valley of Jackson Hole, and eventually flowing into Palisades Reservoir at Alpine, Wyoming. Loaded with big cutthroats, this river is fishable by boat, with waders or from shore. Most commonly fished areas include stretches just above and just below Jackson Lake Dam, the Oxbow area and the stretch between Wilson Bridge and West Table (the latter commonly fished by boat). Access is good, with U.S. Highway 89 roughly paralleling the river for much of the journey. The area offers 12 boat ramps on the 130-mile-long section between Jackson Lake in Grand Teton Park and Palisades Reservoir far to the south of the Park.

Fish this river from April 1 to October 31. Only baitless fishing is allowed in Grand Teton

Park, and the entire section is subject to a three-fish limit. Other regulations may apply.

Jackson, Jenny and Leigh Lakes

Jackson Lake's 31 square miles yield mostly lake trout, some of which can grow to 30 pounds and more. You can also catch cutthroat stocked by the federal fish hatchery south of Grand Teton National Park. Smaller Jenny and Leigh lakes also contain lake and cutthroat trout, as well as a scattering of brook and brown trout. All three can be fished from shore at several trail access points: Jenny Lake has a trail that contours around its shore, and Leigh Lake's trail runs nearly half its perimeter. U.S. Highway 89 and the Teton Park Road run along the east shores of Jackson and Jenny lakes. Leigh Lake is not accessible by road. Boaters reach this lake by paddling up shallow String Lake and portaging across a hilly tongue of land.

Shore fishing is best in spring and fall; fish tend to head for deep waters in summer. Ice fishing is popular on all three lakes. Jackson Lake has three marinas. Jenny Lake has several potential launch points for smaller craft (motor craft over 7.5 horsepower are prohibited).

The limit on all three lakes is six fish per day; Jenny and Leigh lakes are open all year; Jackson Lake closes for the month of October. Other regulations may apply.

Jackson Hole

Wyoming fishing regulations apply throughout Jackson Hole. Pick up regulations and other fishing information, whose local office is at the Wyoming Department of Game and Fish, 360 N. Cache, Jackson, Wyoming, (307) 733-2321.

Gros Ventre River

The Gros Ventre is floated by whitewater enthusiasts and fished from shore by small stream lovers. Its 80-mile length flows into and then out the bottom of a natural dam at Lower Slide Lake. Then it roars and riffles its way east toward its confluence with the Snake 5 miles north of Wilson.

The Gros Ventre offers good rainbow trout fishing, especially just below Lower Slide Lake, but cutthroat are the dominant trout. Road access is reasonable, but some hiking is often involved in order to reach the water. For part of its journey, the Gros Ventre has carved itself a respectable canyon that makes river access a strenuous matter, but both the Gros Ventre River Road and U.S. Highway 89 cross the river at convenient access points. A dirt forest road parallels the upper reaches of the Gros Ventre.

Slide Lake itself is also fishable. A free boat ramp is available at Atherton Creek Campground, and a dirt forest road provides access to the north shoreline. The bag limit on the Gros Ventre River is six fish per day; the season runs from May 21 to October 31.

Hoback River

This bouldered mountain river is almost always fished from shore or by wading. U.S. Highway 191 runs alongside and provides ready access, although much of the lower Hoback is sandwiched by private land. The upper section runs beside a forest road nearly to its headwaters. Lesser-known than the Snake, this is a river for fishermen who like solitude more than they do fish (the fishing is not as good here as on more famous area waters). The river runs rocky and shallow through sagebrush flats and faster through its narrow canyon section until it reaches its confluence with the Snake River at the bottom of Jackson Hole. Its total length is 43 miles.

Catch cutthroat and a few brook trout here. This river can be fished year round. Anglers tend to focus on the lower section above the river's confluence with the Snake.

Eastern Idaho

Idaho contains more than 2,000 lakes and 16,000 miles of streams; by a generous count, it's home to 39 species of game fish, including trout, mountain whitefish, chinook, kokanee salmon, bass, white sturgeon, steelhead trout, yellow perch, crappie and catfish. In the small chunk of Idaho that belongs to Greater Yellowstone, though, you'll find mostly trout, whitefish and kokanee. One notable exception is Ririe Reservoir near Idaho Falls, which is warm enough to host smallmouth bass and perch.

Rainbow trout provide some of the most exciting catches. Cutthroats, with their striking red-orange-slashed throats, are some of the most satisfying, in large part because they're natives. The cutthroat you catch may be a hatchery fish, but the species itself is local to the area, unlike rainbows, lake and brown trout. Popular cutthroat waters are Henry's Lake and the South Fork of the Snake River. Arguably the best rainbow fishery is the Henry's Fork of the Snake. Whitefish are not a prized catch but are easily catchable; they often outnumber trout in the streams in which they live. In this section, we describe a few eastern Idaho fishing hot spots. Remember as you read that almost every lake and stream in eastern Idaho contains trout and would reward your careful cast.

Before you wet a line, be sure you either hire a guide or talk to a local fishing shop, a local ranger or Idaho Fish and Game at 1515 Lincoln Road, Idaho Falls, Idaho, (208) 525-7290. The shop where you pick up your license should be able to provide you with information on regulations and limits that apply where you intend to fish. Some rivers allow only fly fishing. Most have bag limits; some don't allow anglers to keep any fish.

The rivers and lakes described below provide fantastic fishing in large part because fishermen and regulatory agencies protect them.

South Fork of the Snake River

This big, high-volume river is dry-fly heaven and home to native cutthroat and record-breaking (but imported) brown trout. Rainbows and rainbow-cutthroat hybrids are also caught. Idaho doesn't stock this river with hatchery fish, so all the fish you catch are wild, if not all native (most Western waters were stocked at one time, either by official agencies or private sports enthusiasts.) Much of the river is road-accessible for those on foot, but drift boating is a popular way to fish this river as well. The river has 11 public boat ramps in the 64 miles between Palisades Dam and the Henry's Fork confluence, so boating trips can be of various lengths. The Conant Valley section is particularly picturesque, with its dramatic basalt canyon walls.

Fish this river from Memorial Day to November 30, except the section from the Heise measuring cable to the Henry's Fork confluence, which is open for fishing all year. This river has a two-trout limit. Other regulations, such as wildlife closures, may apply.

Henry's Fork of the Snake River

The meandering, riffly Henry's Fork is world-famous for its monster rainbows and prime fly fishing; it also promises great wildlife watching. The river winds across the Island Park Caldera, is impounded in two reservoirs and roars through scenic, waterfall-stepped Cardiac Canyon. About 120 miles downstream of its headwaters, the Henry's Fork joins the South Fork of the Snake to form the Snake River. Boat access is abundant — there are 12 boat ramps — but wading and bank fishing are extremely popular here. Road access is good for the non-canyon sections of the river, since first Big Springs Road and then Idaho Highway 47 and U.S. Highway 20 run alongside the river for much of its length. Cardiac Canyon is not floatable.

This river can be fished from Memorial Day weekend through November 30, except at Harriman State Park, where fishing season doesn't open until June 15, and Harriman Bird Sanctuary, which is open June 15 to September 30. From Vernon Bridge down, the river is open for fishing all year.

The catch is mostly big rainbows, plus browns and a few brook trout, cutthroat and cutthroat/rainbow hybrids called cut-bows. Efforts to maintain the spectacular quality of the fishing here despite heavy use have created complex regulations. Limits and allowable fishing techniques vary from section to section. For instance, Box Canyon to Riverside Campground is catch-and-release only, and Harriman State Park is fly-fishing only. Check with the Ashton, St. Anthony or Island Park ranger stations for the most recent regulations before you drop a line in the water. (You will find their numbers in our Parks and Forests chapter.)

Henry's Lake

The Targhee, Centennial and Gravelly ranges arc round and bald eagles overfly the trophy-trout-filled waters of Henry's Lake. This natural lake, like Grand Teton Park's Jackson

Bear Safety

When Bozeman, Montana, contractor Mark Methany was attacked in 1992 by a grizzly, it changed his life and his career. Methany now makes and markets UDAP, a high-powered pepper spray designed to repel bears. Methany and a friend, who were bow hunting near Big Sky, were hiking the main trail back to their pickup truck after shooting an elk. They startled a sow grizzly feeding on a carcass with her three cubs. Within seconds she had charged the 35 yards between her and the two hunters and had Methany's head in her mouth. Meanwhile, Methany's partner managed to get to his 4-ounce can of pepper spray designed for law enforcement. A shot into the bear's mouth from 5 or 6 feet, sent her away — for a moment. It took a second shot (and the rest of the can) to send the sow packing after she returned and bit Methany's arm.

When Methany had recuperated, he tried to return to his contracting business but could think only of developing a pepper spray especially designed for bears. In addition to the spray itself, Methany has designed quick-draw holsters.

While pepper spray is no substitute for being alert, knowledgeable and careful, evidence is mounting that it is an effective bear repellent in case of attack. Newspapers in Greater Yellowstone carried story after story of pepper power during the hunting season of 1997. Near Bozeman, a hunting guide turned a sow and her cub away with pepper spray after it charged first his client and then him. Near Cody, Wyoming, a Forest Service crew sprayed a grizzly when it charged into their camp. After rolling around on the ground bawling, the bear got up and left. Near Jackson, a hunter surprised a grizzly in a berry patch. While the bear was biting his leg, the hunter shot it in the face with pepper spray that was attached to his belt. The bear fled.

By the way, most human-bear encounters occur during hunting season when hunters are sneaking around alone in the woods. It's also when most grizzlies are killed. In 1997, eight grizzlies in Greater Yellowstone were killed by hunters being charged after surprising the bears. Pepper spray has a 10- to 15-foot range and can be rendered ineffective by adverse weather conditions like rain and wind. It's also not much good if you don't know how to use it. (In other words, if you choose to carry it, practice using it in your yard.)

Now that we have your attention, relax. Yellowstone country is not crawling with grizzlies, and not all grizzlies are going to charge you. In fact, the vast majority of visitors never see one. (A radio-collared male grizzly, tracked and studied in Montana over a period of years, once spent two peaceful days just 100 yards from the Dairy Queen in Big Fork, Montana. Only the trackers knew he was there.)

There are some things that you can do to avoid close encounters. First of all, we recommend you read as much as possible about grizzlies if you plan to hike or camp in their territory. Bill Schneider, a Yellowstone Institute instructor and author of *Bear Aware*, says knowledge is your best weapon against bears. Another good book is *Learning to Talk Bear* by Roland Cheek, an outfitter for more than 20 years in grizzly country. (See our Education chapter for information on the Yellowstone Institute.)

Schneider and other bear experts recommend defensive behaviors. Be alert — look for bear sign such as tracks, droppings or diggings — and look ahead. Be noisy — talk, sing, or clap. And be social. A bigger group makes more noise and looks more formidable than a single person. Travel between 11 AM and 3:30 PM when wildlife is

— continued on next page

Photo: Robert Bower

A grizzly pauses to sniff the air and check out the situation as it forages.

likely to be bedded down. Stay on trails, since bears tend to avoid them during the day because they know that that's where humans travel. If you happen to smell or see a dead carcass, steer clear. It could be a grizzly's food cache, which it will aggressively defend. If you see a bear cub, know that its mama is somewhere nearby. Back off. Avoid smelly foods or scented deodorants, etc.

In camp, you can do other things to discourage bear visits. The most common cause of serious injuries or fatalities occur at night in camps where attractants are present. To avoid these situations, hang your food from poles or from a tree. Next, pitch your tent at least 100 yards from your cooking site and your food cache. Don't cook in your tent or keep food in it — and don't wear your cooking clothes to bed. Don't leave food unattended during the day. People who sleep outside their tents are more likely to be attacked by a bear than those who sleep inside. If a bear does come into camp, especially during the day, be concerned. That's a clear indication that it has no fear of humans. If it has come into camp and gotten a reward, you can be sure it will return the next night expecting more. Move your camp.

If you encounter a bear, Yellowstone Park officials recommend backing away slowly, talking quietly to the bear, refraining from sudden movements and avoiding eye contact with the bear. A bear can outrun you so don't run for a tree. Black bears, young grizzlies and some adults can also climb trees. If a bear charges you, a Yellowstone publication for campers recommends you freeze since charges often turn out to be bluffs. In the event of an actual attack, most authorities recommend dropping to the ground, putting your knees to your chest and your hands behind your neck and playing dead. Usually, a bear will bite and swat a couple of times before running off. Don't move until you are sure the bear is gone. If a bear comes into your camp at night, most experts say not to play dead in that situation.

Before you go into the backcountry, it's a good idea to check with the agency involved. In Yellowstone Park, call the backcountry office at (307) 344-2160. In Grand Teton Park, call (307) 739-3399. If you're planning to hike on public lands managed by the Forest Service, call the local ranger district that manages the area you'll be hiking. Forest maps indicate the ranger districts, and our Resources chapter lists the numbers of ranger districts in Greater Yellowstone.

Lake, has been enlarged by a dam at its outlet. It measures about 4 miles wide by 5 miles long. The lake is best fished with boats or float tubes, since it is mostly surrounded by private land, which limits lakeshore access somewhat. Eight boat ramps exist on the lake. Half charge a fee for launches and sometimes for parking; half are free.

Henry's Lake is as well-known for its sudden winds and high waves as it is for its fishing, so keep an eye tipped skyward.

Catch trophy cutthroat (about half are wild, half stocked from nearby hatcheries), cuttbows and brook trout. The limit is two fish, at which point you must stop fishing. You can fish Henry's Lake between Memorial Day weekend and October 31, daytimes only. The lake's tributaries are open only for the month of August except Hatchery Creek, which is closed to fishing.

Teton River

Access to the Teton River is not as convenient as with most eastern Idaho rivers; it exists mostly at bridge crossings, since no road runs alongside the Teton. Float fishing is popular, although boating is not recommended between Idaho Highway 33 and Spring Hollow. You can put in at seven boat ramps between the Teton's start, where Pine Creek and Trail Creek combine, and its confluence with the Henry's Fork 75 miles downstream. Most access points allow wading and bank fishing, but the Rainey site is probably best. The upper sections of the river run through scenic Teton Basin, with its flat valley floor, sandhill cranes and views of the Teton range. The lower section has carved a narrow canyon.

Fish for cutthroat, wild rainbow and cuttbows (cutthroat-rainbow hybrids), as well as a few hatchery rainbows. This river is open Memorial Day weekend to November 30, except for Teton Creek and its tributaries, which can't be fished until July 1. There's a two fish limit on cutthroat. Other regulations may apply.

Southwestern Montana

Perched on the banks of the Madison River, the small town of Ennis displays a sign that reads, "Home of 640 people and 11 million fish." In the wadeable waters of the Madison, Gallatin and Yellowstone rivers, you'll see Robert Redford look-alikes casting their lines into the rippling waters, fishing and dreaming themselves into the script of *A River Runs Through It*, filmed on the Yellowstone and the Gallatin. Drift boats full of fly-fishers sit in the water like stuckup ducks staking out their pieces of the river. Chances are good that even a beginning fly fisher will be rewarded with that hoped-for but always-surprising jerk on the line. Landing a wiggling, jumping rainbow or native cutthroat is the ultimate reward. But even if you don't get a nibble, fishing is a good excuse to stand in the river, to listen to its soothing hum, to forget about the world you left behind.

If you look at a map, you'll see that the Gallatin, the Yellowstone and the Madison rivers originate in the Park before flowing into Montana's valleys. Since most of their waters lie outside Yellowstone Park, we've listed them that way. Keep in mind, though, that there's excellent fishing in these rivers where they're within the Park. Outside the Park, you'll need a Montana fishing license, a set of regulations and someone to interpret them for you. Inside the Park you'll need a permit.

Hebgen Lake

You'll see plenty of people putt-putting around this manmade lake bait and lure fishing for rainbows and browns below the surface. Locals, though, don't bother because the catch rate for this kind of fishing is low. They also know that 20 miles down the road at Henry's Lake they can fish the same way and catch much bigger fish. Experienced fly fishers like this lake, especially in the Madison Arm where the Madison River comes in and where the weed growth is good. Conditions are just right for

---

INSIDERS' TIP

The Foundation for North American Wild Sheep says that no state, including Alaska, has more Rocky Mountain bighorn habitat than Idaho. Numbers of bighorns in the state are low, but the potential for herd growth is tremendous.

good hatches. From about May 10, when the lake ice has melted, fish are cruising in packs looking for big midges. Their speed and spookiness combine to make spring fishing a challenge for the experienced and impossible for beginners. It's best to use a boat this time of year since you need some speed to find and catch up with the roving packs. By the end of May, the midges have gotten smaller.

In mid-July, Tricos start coming off the water early in the morning, while Callibaetis hatch about 10:30 AM. This is a good time to take your boat or float tube to the Madison Arm. Fishing in this technical lake falls off about mid-September. A few people ice fish during the winter months, mostly near the mouth near the dam and close to the Happy Hour Bar on the north side of Hebgen Lake. There are three free public boat launches on Hebgen. Another five (one on the south side and four on the north) are privately owned and available to the public for free.

Madison River

The Firehole and the Gibbon rivers give birth to the Madison right at Madison Junction in the Park east of West Yellowstone, Montana. From there this world-renowned river winds its way like a seductive serpent through Park meadows before flowing into (and out of) Hebgen and Quake lakes. In the spring, big rainbows swim from Hebgen up the Madison to spawn. Browns do the same in autumn, stopped only by the waterfalls of the Gibbon and Firehole rivers. Within the Park, avoid wading in the sucking, silty muck in the marshy area above Seven Mile Bridge.

Below the lakes, the river flows through a canyon before streaming into the wide open spaces of the Madison Valley, where U.S. Highway 287 parallels it. Fishing and access along this stretch of the river is good, especially at hot spots such as the confluence of the West Fork and a 10-mile stretch from the Varney Bridge to Ennis. Rainbows, browns, brookies, grayling and whitefish all call these waters home. Until whirling disease reared its ugly head, anglers could count on catching several fish an hour in this stretch of the Madison, the hardest hit by the disease. Catch rates still average a bit more than one per hour, and fishing is improving.

About 10 miles below Ennis Lake, the water slows down. Four accesses, beginning with one near the Norris Hot Springs, will get you near this mostly wadeable stretch of river. It's also a popular piece of water for drift fishing. If you fish the Madison in the Park, restrictions call for fly fishing only. Rainbow fishing is catch-and-release. But you can keep two brown trout smaller than 13 inches. There are some real whoppers in these waters.

Gallatin River

This 115-mile-long river, which originates just inside the northwest corner of Yellowstone Park, has so many diversion dams, logjams and crossfences that boat fishing isn't allowed until the last 12 miles before it empties into the Missouri River. However, the Gallatin is small enough to be very wadeable, though you'll have to remember to stay in the stream bed or below the high-water line to avoid trespassing. In addition to the five river accesses along a 12-mile whitewater stretch downriver from Big Sky, you'll find about eight public accesses along the river. Once outside the Park, the Gallatin parallels U.S. Highway 191.

Just outside the Park is the confluence of Taylor Creek, which pretty much dictates fishing conditions by running either clear or muddy depending on the weather. Below Taylor Creek, the waters hold rainbows, browns and hatchery grayling. In the Park, you can add cutthroat and hybrids to that list. Fishing on the Gallatin in Montana is possible year round. In the Park, it's closed during the winter. In Montana you must release grayling; otherwise the limit is five trout, with only one longer than 18 inches allowed. In the Park, it's catch-and-release for cutthroat, with a two-fish limit on rainbows and browns.

Yellowstone River

When fishing season opens July 15 above the falls of the Yellowstone, the river's waters along a 9-mile stretch are dotted with almost as many fishermen as there are fish in the river. It's easy enough to understand why. Large native cutthroat 16 to 24 inches long lurk in these wadeable waters. The granddaddy of them all, the 678-mile Yellowstone is the longest free-flowing river in the lower 48 states. Once you get past the Grand Canyon where the Yellowstone crashes over two waterfalls before tearing through the bottom of the deep gorge, you'll find two more hot spots before this river leaves the Park. One is in the canyon near Tower Fall and the other is in Black Canyon where trails lead into the river. A 20-mile stretch from Emigrant to Pine Creek south of Livingston, is a locals' favorite for drift and wade fishing.

Northwestern Wyoming

The fishing here is as good as anyplace in Greater Yellowstone and you'll generally find the same species in Wyoming as you will in the Yellowstone Park. We've listed only one lake in this section, but there are several good fishing lakes in the Cody area. Ask about them at one of the fly shops listed in this chapter. And check with the Wyoming Game and Fish for regulations on waters within their state.

North Fork of the Shoshone River

Before the North Fork of the Shoshone leaves Yellowstone Park, it races out of the Absaroka Mountains like a locomotive running wild. U.S. Highway 20 parallels this cold, rushing river for 40 miles between Pahaska Tepee and Buffalo Bill Reservoir, making it easily accessible and the most fishable stretch of the river. Open year round, the North Fork spawns fair-size Yellowstone cutthroat and rainbows, with brook trout at the top end and browns down below. In the spring, grizzlies coming out of hibernation make their own appearances to fish along the river's banks.

Besides offering good fishing, the scenery in this canyon, with its red-rock spires and minarets shaping the landscape, makes this one of the more beautiful fishing spots. An incredible number of tributaries flow out of the surrounding mountains into the North Fork from Pahaska to Wapiti. Some of these streams, such as the Grinell, Clearwater, Sweetwater, Elk Fork and Eagle creeks, also offer good fishing.

Below the reservoir, created in 1910 with the completion of the Buffalo Bill Dam, the North Fork runs through a deep rocky canyon that's difficult to access. You can catch and keep three trout per day; only one can be more than 20 inches.

Buffalo Bill Reservoir

Used almost exclusively by locals, this lake on U.S. Highway 20 west of Cody requires a boat for success, except in early spring when you can do well from the shore. Those who come here use both flies and bait. The mix of fish in the Buffalo Bill Reservoir includes rainbows, browns, cutthroats, and lake trout, which can grow up to 30 pounds. Browns run as high as 10 to 12 pounds, while rainbows and cutthroat weigh in from 2 to 8 pounds. Ice fishing is not good on this lake because of chinook winds that come through often to make "rotten" ice. You'll find campgrounds and boat launches here.

Clarks Fork of the Yellowstone

This 140-mile river begins in the Beartooth Mountains above Cooke City, dips into Wyoming where it cuts its way through one of the most beautiful canyons in Yellowstone country, then curls back up into Montana. There it flows through an amazing number of diversions before reaching the Yellowstone River near Laurel, Montana. U.S. Highway 212, and then Wyo. Highway 296, follow the Clarks Fork from Colter Pass to nearly Crandall Creek. From the Montana-Wyoming state line to Crandall Creek, you'll find a 16-mile stretch of fishable, mostly wadeable water winding through a high-mountain forested valley. From there the river disappears into a deep canyon then emerges to run across the sagebrush desert of the Bighorn Basin.

Since the regulations on this river vary considerably depending on which stretch you're fishing, we recommend you check with Wyoming Department of Game and Fish, (307) 777-4600 or (307) 527-7125, to find out the specifics. The upper Clarks Fork has mostly rainbow with a few cutthroat and brook trout; the canyon offers rainbows. In the lower stretch you'll find brown trout, cutthroat, rainbows and a few grayling. Crandall Creek holds good-size cutthroat, while Sunlight Creek has some hefty brookies.

Fishing Outfitters

Hiring a fishing outfitter can solve several problems for the visiting fisherman. Local guides have the local expertise that makes record catches more likely. They know where the fish have been biting and what they've

Photo: Chip Rizotto/High Country Outfitters

Rainbow trout are the mainstay of southwestern Montana's fishing water, as they are in many of Greater Yellowstone's blue-ribbon streams.

been biting on. They know the regulations, so you won't accidentally end up on the wrong side of the law. Plus most guide services supply transportation to and from the fishing area, a boat , meals and drinks, and sometimes even equipment. If equipment isn't available to loan, it's generally available for sale at the outfitter's shop. One day of guided fishing in Greater Yellowstone will cost between $200 and $300 per person. Package deals that combine lodging or breaks for additional people are common.

Yellowstone National Park's Entrance Communities

West Yellowstone, Montana

Blue Ribbon Flies
315 Canyon Ave., West Yellowstone, Mont. • (406) 646-7642

You won't find independent guides working out of Blue Ribbon Flies — just eight or so regular guides with years of experience under their waders. Owner Craig Mathews and his staff try their darnedest to steer you into having a good time fishing. That doesn't necessarily mean fishing 10 hours a day and bagging every fish in the river. It does mean that they'll try to teach you about bugs and fish psychology so when you go fishing without a guide, you'll have a better idea of what you're doing. They'll also try to lead you into the finer art of fly fishing.

In addition to a staff of veteran guides, Blue Ribbon has a complete selection of top-of-the-line, hard-to-find fly-tying materials. Mathews and his partners at the store have written several books as well as a weekly (in the summer) column called "The Fish Wrapper." Blue Ribbon guides on the Madison and Gallatin rivers as well as all of the streams in Yellowstone. Blue Ribbon is open year round. Blue Ribbon's 1998 fees are the same for wade and float fishing daytrips: $265 for one person, $285 for two and $350 for three people.

Bud Lilly's Trout Shop
39 Madison Ave., West Yellowstone, Mont. • (406) 646-7801, (800) 854-9559

It's true. Bud Lilly's Trout Shop has been a household word among fly fishers for 45 years. Bud Lilly no longer owns this shop, but the staff strives to maintain his sterling reputation in the fishing and guiding world. Besides being able to load you up with every bit of gear and tackle you need, Bud Lilly's has six full-time guides who can lead you to smaller Park streams or larger rivers in and out of the Park. This is a busy place, so it's best to reserve a guide months ahead of time if you plan to be in the area during the peak season. Occasionally, though, you can walk in and catch a guide on pretty short notice even in the summer time. Float trips cost $285 per person, while a walk-and-wade guided daytrip is $240 for one person, $250 for two people and $260 for three people. This shop is open year round.

Jacklin's Fly Shop
105 Yellowstone Ave., West Yellowstone, Mont. • (406) 646-7336

Bob Jacklin, who happens to own the oldest established fly shop in West Yellowstone, has been guiding fishing folks out of West Yellowstone since 1967. While he specializes in the Henry's Fork and the Madison rivers, Jacklin knows and guides on all the rivers in Montana and the Park. Jacklin's, a full-service fly shop across from the Old Union Pacific Depot, uses six to 10 guides each summer day. It'll cost you and your partner $295 to go fishing with one of Jacklin's guides. Lunch is included. Sunday evenings Jacklin gives free fly-casting lessons at 7:30 PM on his pond behind the police station (across the street from his shop).

Grand Teton National Park

Grand Teton Lodge Company at Colter Bay Village
U.S. Hwy. 89, Grand Teton Park, Wyo. • (307) 543-2811

Fishing boats depart four times a day from the marina at Colter Bay. Fish Jackson Lake for lunker trout while the non-anglers in your party enjoy the scenery. Grand Teton Lodge Company will also rent you a 9.9 horsepower boat or an aluminum canoe if you don't need a guide. Make advance reservations.

Signal Mountain Lodge
Teton Park Rd., Grand Teton Park, Wyo. • (307) 543-2831

Signal Mountain Lodge, perched on the shore of Jackson Lake, offers daily guided fishing trips on 425-foot-deep Jackson Lake. You may also simply rent your own fishing boat from these folks. Canoes and oar boats are available at $8 per hour; Signal Mountain also rents fishing skiffs with outboard motors. Reservations are suggested.

Jackson Hole

One thing worth knowing about the guided fishing scene outside Grand Teton Park is that minimal regulation has resulted in a local reservoir of anglers with boats who guide part-time, particularly on unregulated sections of the Snake. Although many are extremely capable anglers and oarsmen, they may or may not be insured. Ask lots of questions before you hire a guide in Jackson Hole. Or choose one of the guide services listed below. Each has a good local reputation and is conveniently associated with a fly shop.

Westbank Anglers
3670 N. Moose-Wilson Rd., Teton Village, Wyo. • (307) 733-6483

This guide service maintains its own fly shop for your convenience. The shop carries outdoor clothing, poles, reels and waders to take with you on your fishing adventure. You can arrange fishing adventures for nearby Flat Creek, the South Fork of the Snake (in cooperation with an Idaho outfitter), the Firehole, Gibbons, Madison and Yellowstone rivers; Yellowstone and Lewis lakes in Yellowstone National Park; the Green and New Fork rivers in the Pinedale area; and several stretches of private water. Half-day, full-day and overnight trips are available.

High Country Flies
185 Center St., Jackson, Wyo. • (307) 733-7210

Float the Snake River near Jackson and the

INSIDERS' TIP

Panther, Obsidian and Indian creeks in Yellowstone Park are reserved especially for bait fishing by children.

Green River to the south. Fish the famous waters of Yellowstone Park, the Firehole and Madison rivers and Yellowstone and Lewis lakes. Shop owner James Jones worked as a guide for this fly shop and guide service before he bought the place in 1984. Jones can also arrange instructional trips that emphasize casting, entomology, knot tying, and playing and releasing fish. Trips are catch-and-release only. James runs a fly shop near town square in Jackson to complement his guide service.

Jack Dennis Fishing Trips
50 E. Broadway, Jackson, Wyo.
• (307) 733-3270

Fishing celebrity Jack Dennis Jr. opened his fly shop and guide service here in 1967. Now Jack Dennis Sports is home to one of the better-known fishing guide services in town. Guides can take you to the brushy little New Fork, the Green, the rivers and lakes of Yellowstone Park and the Snake River through Jackson Hole. Through an Idaho outfitter, you can also book trips on eastern Idaho's famous South Fork Snake, a fantastic native cutthroat fishery. Trips can be walk-in or float. This company also offers seminars and fly-casting instruction, besides organizing a well-known fishing event: a one-fly trout derby.

Eastern Idaho

For information about Idaho's fishing guides and outfitters, write the Idaho Outfitters and Guides Association, P.O. Box 95, Boise, ID 83701, or call (208) 342-1438 or (208) 342-1919. Idaho was one of the first Western states to require that outfitters and their guides must be licensed.

Island Park, Idaho

Henry's Fork Anglers
Last Chance in Island Park, Idaho
• (208) 558-7525, winter 624-3590

Mike Lawson was born in this area and has fished here his whole life. In the off-season, he writes for fly fishing magazines and presents lectures on the sport. But when the rainbows are biting on the Henry's Fork, he's home fishing. Mike and his guides also offer trips on the Madison, Firehole, Gibbon,

Yellowstone and Gallatin rivers in Yellowstone Park, Island Park Reservoir, Henry's and Hebgen lakes and a variety of small area streams. A full-service fly shop is on premises.

Hyde Outfitters Inc.
3408 N. Hwy. 20, Last Chance in Island Park, Idaho • (208) 558-7068

Hyde Outfitters uses local guides and locally built Hyde drift boats. These folks offer daytrips to the South Fork of the Snake, the Henry's Fork, Teton River, Henry's Lake, Palisades and Island Park reservoirs and even Yellowstone National Park, all for about the same price. Your base price includes the guide, lunch, a Hyde drift boat and transportation. Guides are often available on short notice, but don't count on it. Hyde's has a complete fly shop.

Swan Valley

South Fork Lodge
40 Conant Valley Loop, Swan Valley, Idaho • (208) 483-2112, (800) 483-2110

Welcome to fishing heaven. The South Fork of the Snake River winds past South Fork Lodge through cottonwood flats, literally jumping with trophy-size native cutthroats. South Fork Lodge has been in Swan Valley native Spence Warner's family for more than 45 years. Trips can involve float or wade fishing (or both), depending on your preference. Float trips vary between 8 and 15 miles in length. Spence recommends anglers make guide and accommodations reservations well in advance. The full-service fly shop probably carries everything you forgot.

Southwestern Montana

Bozeman, Montana

R.J. Cain & Company Outfitters
24 E. Main St., Bozeman, Mont.
• (406) 587-9111, (800) 886-9111

Besides employing several full time guides, R.J. Cain uses contract guides throughout southwestern Montana. Operating out of their shop in Bozeman, owners Rod, Pam and Garry King tailor their guide service to your needs whether you're a beginner or a seasoned fly fisher. R.J. Cain offers lessons, guided float fishing on area rivers outside the Park, walk-and-wade trips and backcountry fly fishing trips by horseback.

In 1997, a day of guided float or walk and wade fishing cost $265 for one or two people. A third person could come along for an extra $75.

Big Sky, Montana

Gallatin Riverguides
U.S. Hwy. 191, Big Sky, Mont.
• **(406) 995-2290**

In business since 1981, Gallatin Riverguides is the longest-operating fly shop in Big Sky. Owners Steve and Betsy French offer a variety of low-cost casting clinics at their 2-acre pond behind the shop. The pond is equipped with a casting platform and target rings, not to mention some hefty rainbows. They employ eight guides, almost all of whom have at least five years of experience on Southwest Montana waters. (Some of the guides have been with the Frenches for more than a dozen years.)

Gallatin Riverguides fish the Madison, Yellowstone and Gallatin rivers and the rivers and streams of Yellowstone Park. They also do overnight trips on the Beaverhead and Missouri rivers. A day of guided walk-and-wade fishing costs $275 for two people. Fishing from a drift boat costs more: $300 for two. Gallatin Riverguides also rents rods, reels and waders.

Livingston, Montana

Dan Bailey's
209 W. Park Ave., Livingston, Mont.
• **(406) 222-1673, (800) 356-4052**

Located in Livingston, Dan Bailey's is synonymous with fly fishing. This hopping fly fishers hot spot taps into a battalion of independent guides to complement three or four in-house guides. You'll find that Bailey's guides mostly fish the Yellowstone River, the Madison River above Ennis and spring creeks in the Paradise Valley. It's best to reserve a guide ahead of time, although at times you may get lucky as a walk-in. Dan Bailey's, featured in our Shopping chapter, is a full-service fly shop.

George Anderson's Yellowstone Angler
U.S. Hwy. 89 S., Livingston, Mont.
• **(406) 222-7130**

While Bud Lilly and Dan Bailey may have been the big fly fishing names of the past, George Anderson is giving them a run for their money these days. Operating out of a 4,500-square-foot shop stocked with a broad selection of trout and saltwater tackle and rods, Anderson uses about 15 guides. Each has an area of expertise: Some prefer spring creeks, while others like to fish Yellowstone Park or the bigger rivers. In addition to fishing the Yellowstone, Anderson takes anglers to the Bighorn, Missouri, Boulder and West Boulder rivers as well as to the river and streams of Yellowstone Park.

Anderson's 1998 fees for two are $300 for a day of float fishing and $285 for a walk-and-wade trip.

Pray, Montana

High Country Outfitters
158 Bridger Hollow Rd., Pray, Mont.
• **(406) 333-4763**

This guide comes with a private cabin and casting pond, a lodge (Chip and Francine Rizzoto's home) and fine dining. While Chip takes you on a fishing experience tailored to your desires and your ability, Francine will cook up incredibly delicious meals in her country kitchen, then serve them when you're ready. She'll also tailor the menu to your tastes, keeping a computerized record of your favorite foods.

High Country offers a five-night, four-day package for two people that costs $3,140. The cabin comes complete with a queen-size bed and a set of bunkbeds, fly-tying equipment, a complete fishing library and a music system. In June, they hold a women's fly fishing clinic and will take only four students. It costs $1,200.

High Country is at the base of the

Absaroka-Beartooth Wilderness and is a six-minute drive from the Chico Hot Springs Lodge. (See our Resorts, Guest Ranches and Lodges chapter to learn more about Chico.)

Northwestern Wyoming

Cody, Wyoming

North Fork Anglers
937 Sheridan Ave., Cody, Wyo.
• (307) 527-7274

Operating out of its store on Cody's main street, North Fork Anglers not only has a full-service fly shop with hand-tied flies customized for the area, but also offers a range of guided fishing trips in and out of Yellowstone Park. Tuned into fishing conditions, Tim Wade and his guides weigh your needs and capabilities with hatches and high water. Wade also offers two weeklong "Cowboys and Cutthroats" horsepacking trips each July, as well as a "Cast and Blast" (fishing and hunting) trip in the fall.

Permitted to fish in Yellowstone Park and the Shoshone National Forest, North Fork Anglers charges $275 per day (for two people) for drift fishing and $250 per day for walk-and-wade.

Hunting

When we talk hunting in Yellowstone country, we first think *wapiti* — the mighty elk. Sure, there are plenty of other big-game animals in our neck of the woods, and we'll talk about those later. But the elk, bugling from across the meadow, herding his harem of cows, is the most sought after big game in Greater Yellowstone. Besides being beautiful to behold, elk are elusive enough to require stalking and studying. And they live in country remote enough to make the hunt a challenge. Elk hunters not only have to exert themselves physically, but they also have to learn something about the wapiti to find him, then think like an elk to outsmart him.

Elk also make good eating. The meat is high

on flavor, low in cholesterol and untainted by food additives. Having a freezer full of wild game is so much a way of life for many in Yellowstone country that they can't rest until they've filled that freezer. In small rural towns where the economies have always been depressed, the wild game that haunts the nearby hills is insurance against lean times. Often dependent on seasonal work, people might not be able to pay their bills through the winter months, but their families won't go hungry when meat is so close at hand, especially if they've raised and put up a big garden during the summer.

While many still look to game to supplement their larder, others simply relish the hunt: long days of hiking steep terrain in cold weather; stalking and outsmarting wild animals able to move much faster than a human being; making a clean shot. And bugling in a bull elk carries its own thrill. Headed your way, bugling himself with blood in his eyes, he has mistaken your call for that of an intruding bull. His instincts aren't ruled by reason.

Shooting a trophy bull or buck has always been cause for celebration — for the household as well as the hunter. In stores, restaurants, homes, even medical clinics in Yellowstone country, you'll see mounted heads of elk, deer, moose, bear, bison, and a whole slew of other animals. On main streets in small towns, clusters of men gather around a pickup truck, admiring an especially big bull draped across the spare tire in the back. While an increasing number of locals and almost all out-of-state hunters now have their kill cut, wrapped and frozen by local butcher shops or packing plants, some still butcher their own, setting up an assembly line on the kitchen table at home. Old-timers used to use every scrap of meat. The neck and head, discarded these days as waste, was pressure-cooked before the meat was removed to be canned up as mincemeat. The ribs, also often discarded, were sawed into slabs and saved for barbecued ribs. The bones were saved for soup.

We pride ourselves on passing the hunting tradition on to the next generation. Young boys and girls are given guns at an early age — and taught how to use them responsibly. They can start hunting at age 12 after a course in hunter safety. Men and women drive pickup trucks with rifles mounted on racks across the back window. Guns in the window racks of pickup trucks

during hunting season are so prevalent that when a federal law passed a few years ago outlawed guns on school grounds, students and their parents were outraged. Teenagers, especially those who live miles out of town, hunt on their way to and from school during the fall.

For insights into why people in our region hunt, read *Blood Ties* by Ted Kerasote. Kerasote, a Jackson author, is one of the region's top environmental reporters writing for a number of national outdoor magazines. Kerasote makes a compelling study of the ancient human urge to hunt.

Because Greater Yellowstone has such an extensive concentration of wild lands, it's a hunter's mecca. In addition to elk, Montana, Idaho and Wyoming all have healthy mule-deer populations. Bighorn sheep, mountain goats, moose and mountain lions are scarcer, partially because they are limited by the existing habitat. That means hunting for these species is limited to comparatively few permits each year. The same is true of black bears. Antelope, which are prevalent across Wyoming in general, are relatively rare on the Yellowstone Plateau. (There's a herd of about 230 on the northern range near Gardiner.) Anywhere you find water in Greater Yellowstone, though, you'll likely find great duck and good goose hunting. Other game birds can be pretty plentiful depending on the year.

Thinning the Elk Herds

Hunting is forbidden in Yellowstone National Park, and Grand Teton Park has only a brief hunt. Yellowstone Park officials count on hunting outside the Park to keep the herd's numbers down. In Yellowstone, the Park's summer elk population ranges from 75,000 to 90,000 with about 18,000 of them calling the Park's northern range their summer home. Except for a few isolated pockets of elk that hang out year round near thermal areas, the rest of the elk in the Park begin to trickle off the Yellowstone Plateau as soon as the first snows fall. To the South they head into Grand Teton Park and onto the Snake River Plain. To the west they migrate over Targhee Pass and into the Targhee National Forest. To the east, many are blocked by the towering Absaroka Range, but some find their way to the eastern slopes of the Absarokas and into Sunlight Basin.

These anglers ply the waters of the south fork of the Snake
River below Fall Creek in Idaho's Swan Valley area.

When Yellowstone Park was first formed, President Teddy Roosevelt recognized that the Park's elk herds, though decimated at the time by poachers, would multiply so fast that they would overpopulate the Park if they weren't hunted. He was right. In 1951, Yellowstone Park officials tried to reduce the northern herd size from 11,800 animals to 5,000, the number they felt the range could support. The same range today is currently carrying about 18,000 elk. Live-trapping and removal of the animals to other areas failed to fix the problem. In the winter of 1955-56 Park officials removed more than 6,000 elk from the northern herd. Nearly 2,000 of them were shot. The program was wildly unpopular.

Yellowstone and Grand Teton Park officials now use hunters to try to control herd sizes. If numbers are an indication of success, it's not working. Outside Yellowstone's boundaries, battalions of hunters wait to pick off migrating elk. To the north, where the country is more open and elk more plentiful, the animals have learned from experience not to step over the boundary line. That means fewer of them are killed. It also means that more elk are staying longer on their summer range in the Park, which some believe will cause habitat degradation.

Management of the migrating herds, which come under the jurisdiction of three state and federal agencies, is complicated. Yellowstone Park manages for natural regulation by predators and winter kill. The Montana State Department of Fish, Wildlife and Parks, on the other hand, manages for high populations to meet hunters' demands. If they sell too many elk tags, though, the public attacks them. The Forest Service, in charge of managing the land, doesn't always take game into consideration. For example, much of their money lately is supposed to be used for burns. While a prescribed sagebrush burn may promote increased grass growth, it also wipes out the sagebrush, a winter food source for mule deer.

Grizzlies and Hunters

Before you head for the hills, a word about grizzlies: Hunters + ursus horribilis = trouble. In 1997, 13 grizzlies were reported killed in human-bear encounters outside the Park. Eighty percent of them were killed by hunters.

Think about it. Except during hunting season, humans in Greater Yellowstone — and in the Parks in particular — walk in groups on trails during the day and make a lot of noise. Grizzlies have figured out human behavior and so generally stay off trails during the day. Come hunting season, though, lone camouflaged hunters are sneaking around off-trail, sometimes in the predawn dark. While their intent is to sneak up on an elk, some end up surprising a grizzly — and scaring the heck out of themselves. To compound the problem, gut piles left by hunters and hanging elk carcasses in camp act as magnets to grizzlies.

The Interagency Grizzly Bear Committee offers the following advice for hunters:

• Travel in pairs.
• Use horses when possible.
• Make a wide circle around dead carcasses or gut piles. After you've made a kill, gut, pack and remove the carcass as soon as possible. Don't leave a gut pile near a trail.
• Hang the carcass if you have to leave it, but leave the carcass where you can see it from a distance or approach it from upwind. When returning to a carcass, be wary; if a grizzly has claimed it, let him have it.
• Keep a clean camp with food inaccessible to bears.

Guided Hunting

Hunting seasons vary by state, areas, species and weapon. And regulations, different in each state, are so complicated that it darn near takes an attorney to decipher them. Generally, the seasons begin with bow hunts in late August or early September. A general season that begins about October 1 is followed by late hunts for black powder rifles and/or bow hunters that runs through December. Scattered throughout the seasons are special hunts. In some places where elk are overpopulated, state fish and game managers will extend a season if hunters haven't harvested enough animals. If you want the scoop on regulations and hunting licenses, we recommend you call the state agencies responsible for managing fish and game. They're listed at the end of the general introduction to this chapter.

When it comes to hunting, non-residents

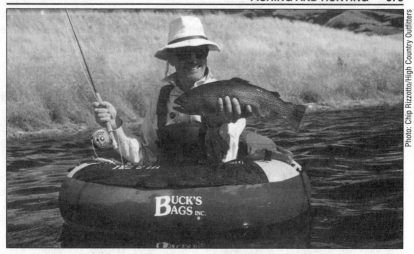

Photo: Chip Rizzotto/High Country Outfitters

A happy fisherman shows off a 4 pound rainbow he has just caught in a private high mountain lake near Emigrant, Montana.

pay for being outsiders. In Wyoming, it cost an out-of-stater $410 to hunt elk in 1997, and $195 for deer. The same permits cost Wyoming residents $35 and $22. Each applicant is assigned a number. Numbers are thrown into a pot from which permits are drawn.

In Idaho, non-residents paid $101.50 for a 1997 license, and extra for tags: An elk tag ran $326.50, while a deer tag was $226.50. Idaho Fish and Game plans to increase resident licenses this year. They sell out-of-state elk tags on a first-come, first-served basis. Sales for the 1998 season began on December 1, 1997. Fish and Game officials report that elk tags are usually sold out by April. In 1997, residents bought a license for $7.50, then paid an additional $16.50 for an elk tag, and $10.50 for a deer tag.

In Montana, 1997 non-resident fees cost $478 for a big game combo license. Applicants are assigned a number, which is thrown into a pot for drawing. Non-residents can bypass the drawing and secure a license by booking with an outfitter and paying $835 for a license.

If you're contemplating coming to Yellowstone country to hunt, we recommend you consider going with an outfitter. Most outfitters set up backcountry tent camps, often in the difficult-to-access wilderness. That means while many locals are combing national forest lands in their pickup trucks, you'll be tucked miles away from the nearest road. Outfitters not only know where to find the game, they have all the equipment (except the rifles and the clothing) you'll need for a hunt.

Montana, Idaho and Wyoming each have an Outfitters and Guides Association with lists of the licensed outfitters in their state (see the list below). If you do come hunting in Yellowstone country, we recommend you arrive looking forward to all aspects of the hunt — the hike, the scenery, the fresh mountain air — rather than the kill or a trophy. It's amazing how many hunters ruin their own hunts because they've come all the way across the country believing they can't go home without a trophy elk or deer.

By the way, if you call Fish and Game departments in any of Greater Yellowstone states, chances are good the first thing they'll tell you is, "Get in shape." The Rockies are steep. Their high elevations also mean your lungs will have a harder time finding oxygen in the air. And, if you target practice at home, you're less apt to miss your only shot at a big bull or a fat cow.

Guided hunts can be expensive. Weeklong guided elk hunts range from $1,500 to $3,800, while a guided bighorn sheep hunt can cost up to $8,000.

In the following sections, we tell you about a number of outfitters who guide in Greater Yellowstone. Cody alone has more than a dozen licensed hunting outfitters. We recommend you call the respective state's Outfitters and Guides Association for a complete listing. And we suggest that when you're trying to decide on an outfitter, you ask for (and check out) references. The associations are listed below.

• Idaho Outfitters and Guides Association, P.O. Box 95, Boise, ID 83701, (208) 342-1438 or (208) 342-1919.

• Montana Outfitters and Guides Association, P.O. Box 1248, Helena, MT 59624, (406) 449-3578.

• Wyoming Department of Commerce, Wyoming State Board of Outfitters and Professional Guides, 1750 Westland Road, Cheyenne, WY 82002; call (307) 777-5323 or (800) 264-0981.

Yellowstone National Park Entrance Communities

Cooke City, Montana

Beartooth Plateau Outfitters Inc.
U.S. Hwy. 212, Cooke City, Mont.
• (406) 838-2328 June through September
HCR 48, Box 1028, Roberts, MT
• (406) 445-2293 October through May, (800) 253-8545

Operating from a pack station in Cooke City, Beartooth Plateau Outfitters offers two early hunts: an early rifle bugling hunt from mid-September through the first week in October; an archery hunt from September 1 through mid-October; and a rifle hunt from October 1 through mid-October. The first hunt is in Montana, while the second two are just over the state line in Wyoming. Both are adjacent to the Park.

The best part about these hunts is you only have to ride horseback for two hours before reaching the base camp — a deluxe setup of wall tents housing sleeping, cooking and dining quarters. Outfitter Ronnie Wright offers later hunts

near Dillon, Montana. Wright also offers day and overnight pack trips out of Cooke City. For more information, see our Other Recreation chapter.

Jackson Hole

Jackson, Wyoming

Darwin Ranch
P.O. Box 511, Jackson, WY 83001
• (307) 733-5588

Loring Woodman hunts elk on horseback from his private ranch surrounded by the Bridger-Teton National Forest. Loring has been guiding horseback hunting trips since 1965.

Jackson Peak Outfitters
P.O. Box 1074, Jackson, WY 83001
• (307) 733-3805

Charlie Petersen Jr.'s operation features family-operated hunting camps and limited numbers of clients. Hunts are for elk, deer, moose, bighorn and bear. Charlie, his wife and two grown sons usually put on five or six hunts a season along Cache Creek east of Jackson.

Moran, Wyoming

Two Ocean Pass Outfitting
P.O. Box 182, Moran, WY 83013
• (307) 543-2309, (800) 726-2409

John Winter guides elk, deer, antelope, moose and bighorn sheep horseback hunts in the remote backcountry of the Teton and Washakie wildernesses.

Diamond D Ranch Outfitters
Buffalo Valley Rd., Moran, Wyo.
• (307) 543-2479

Rod Doty operates a comfortable little guest ranch in summer, but during hunting season he's on horseback in the Teton Wilderness, guiding clients to bighorn sheep, elk, moose and deer.

Turpin Meadows Ranch
P.O. Box 379, Moran, WY 83013
• (307) 543-2496, (800) 743-2496

At the top of Buffalo Valley, this summer guest ranch becomes a comfortable base or a jump-off for your hunting expedition in the Bridger-Teton wilderness. Dale Castagno and his three sons, Stan, Steve and Ryan, can show you elk, moose, bighorn sheep and deer. This family operation guides 30 to 50 hunters per season.

Eastern Idaho

Idaho's hunting seasons run around 65 days. Success rates are high and permits generally not difficult to get. Idaho's public lands support a wide range of game animals, from elk, mule deer and bighorn sheep to pronghorn antelope, bear, moose, cougar, mountain goat, whitetail deer, upland game birds and waterfowl. In the past 15 years, elk populations have increased and elk harvests have quadrupled. Deer harvests have doubled in the past decade. Many believe the population growth and the increased hunter success are tied to a string of mild winters through the late 1980s and early '90s.

Lyle Beard/Beard Outfitters
Leigh Canyon, Tetonia, Idaho
• **(208) 576-2694**
Hunt with a Teton Basin native for elk, deer, moose and bear on the west slopes of the Teton range and in the Jedediah Smith and remote Winegar Hole wildernesses. Lyle has been leading hunts in this region since 1963. His sons, Gary and Joe, also guide.

Anderson Outfitting
5646 Sorrell Dr., Pocatello, Idaho 83202
• **days (208) 237-6544, evenings (208) 237-2664**
Bob and Mary Anderson offer a range of outdoor activities, including trophy big-game rifle and bow hunts for moose, cougar, grouse, deer, bear and elk in the Caribou National Forest of southeastern Idaho. They specialize in one-on-one hunts.

Haderlie Outfitters
P.O. Box 175, Freedom, WY 83120
• **(800) 253-2368**
Vaughn Haderlie and his three sons lead archery, rifle and muzzle-loader hunts for elk, deer, moose, cougar and bear. They also offer summer trail rides and pack trips. The company has been in the family since 1968.

Southwestern Montana

Hunting seasons run from the first part of September through December depending on where you go and what your weapon of choice is. Based on observed rather than estimated animal counts, Montana is home to more than 100,000 wapiti and over 300,000 mule deer. In 1996, hunters bagged over 30,000 elk and more than 55,000 mule deer. In addition to deer and elk, Montana offers good populations of upland game birds, waterfowl, antelope, bears, moose and bighorn sheep, among others. For specific information about Montana's regulations, licensing and hunting opportunities, write or call Montana Department of Fish, Wildlife and Parks, listed at the end of the introduction to this chapter.

Bozeman, Montana

Medicine Lake Outfitters
Box 3663-TP, Bozeman, MT
• **(406) 388-4938**
Tom and Joan Heintz outfit in the Absaroka-Beartooth wilderness north of Yellowstone Park and the Madison Range to the west. While elk and mule deer are what most of their hunters are after, Heintz will also help you bag a moose, mountain goat or whitetail if you draw a permit for one. Heintz employs seasoned, professional guides whose average age is 40. And he operates with a string of 70 horses. During the summer months, Heintz leads pack trips into Yellowstone Park, the Absaroka-Beartooth Wilderness and the Madison Range.

Livingston, Montana

Cayuse Outfitters
Box 1218, Swingley Rt., Livingston, Mont. • **(406) 222-3168**
In the summer months you'll find Larry Lahren leading folks into the archaeological crannies of the Yellowstone Valley or taking them on horseback into the Absaroka-Beartooth Wilderness for fishing. Come fall, though, Lahren leads hunters to the elk and deer in the same region. These days he takes them on day hunts from his ranch where you'll find hearty ranch meals and a comfortable bed

waiting for you each night after the hunt. Lahren charges $250 per day or $2,500 to $3,500 for a five- to seven-day hunt, depending on the hunter-to-guide ratio and what you're hunting.

Bear Paw Outfitters
136 Deep Creek Rd., Livingston, Mont. • (406) 222-6642

This family-run outfitting business operates out of Tim and Cindy Bowers' homeplace 8 miles south of Livingston. While these days Tim specializes more in horseback rides in and out of the Park during the summer, he does a good hunt from his ranch. After a day in the Absaroka Mountains, he'll take you home, Cindy will feed you, and you'll sleep in a warm, comfortable bed. Tim doesn't guarantee his hunters an elk. He does promise a rich hunting experience — and he promises to send you home well-fed and tired. For more information about Bear Paw's per-hour, daylong and overnight horseback rides, see our Other Recreation chapter.

Gallatin Gateway, Montana

Broken Hart Ranch
73800 Gallatin Rd., Gallatin Gateway, Mont. • (406) 763-4279

Lee Hart has been leading hunters to big game in the Gallatin since 1969. While his specialty is elk, he'll also guide you to bighorn sheep, moose or any other big game for which you hold a permit. See our Other Recreation chapter for information on horseback riding here.

Northwestern Wyoming

At the turn of the century, antelope had almost taken their last dash across the prairie. Since then, though, Wyoming game managers have brought antelope populations back to nearly half a million. And that's after about a third of the population was wiped out by the severe winter of 1992-93. Elk numbers are also at record highs with an estimated state-wide population of 105,000. In 1996, hunters harvested about 21,000

Photo: Robert Bower/Post Register

Fly fishing in the Firehole River is very popular in Yellowstone National Park.

elk compared to about 15,000 in 1997. Game managers attribute the decreased harvest to late a late snowfall needed to drive them out of the higher elevations where they're easier to hunt. Wyoming is home to about 450,000 mule deer. In 1996, hunters harvested about 30,000 elk.

Wyoming Department of Game and Fish, which manages the state's wildlife, can be reached at 5400 Bishop Boulevard, Cheyenne, WY 82006, (307) 777-4600. Wyoming's elk hunting seasons begin in September and runs through most of December. Since they vary hugely depending on the area and the type of weapon you're using, we refer you to Wyoming Game and Fish. The address and number are listed at the end of this chapter's introduction.

Lost Creek Outfitters
31 Cedar Mountain Dr., Cody, Wyo.
• (307) 587-8584

You may never go back to tent hunting after a hunt with Lost Creek Outfitters operated by Greg "Griz" and Carla Turner. Midway between Yellowstone Park and Cody, the Turners offer a wilderness elk hunt combined with luxury accommodations at the Bill Cody Ranch. While you're riding the mountains on horseback, stalking that trophy bull, folks at the Bill Cody Ranch will be plumping the pillows in your cabin and cooking up a hearty ranch supper. Well-known locally for his own guiding abilities, Griz Turner prides himself on having the best guides in the area and limits his trips (both hunting, fishing and packing) to small groups.

He specializes in elk and mule deer hunts, but also guides spring bear hunts (both archery and rifle) in the spring, as well as antelope hunts in the fall. In the summer, he guides two- to 10-day pack trips as well as overnight fishing trips.

Yellowstone Park contains more than 1,000 miles of designated, marked trail. Grand Teton Park has a mere 200 miles, but off-trail hiking and mountaineering add nearly endless opportunity. And if you really want solitude, hike in the national forests.

Hiking and Backpacking

It's been said that only about 3 percent of Yellowstone Park is available to visitors who stay on Park roads. If you want to see the other 97 percent, you have to step out onto the maze of trails that lace Yellowstone's backcountry. The added bonus is that you leave most of the crowds behind. Yellowstone Park contains more than 1,000 miles of designated, marked trail. Grand Teton Park has a mere 200 miles, but off-trail hiking and mountaineering add nearly endless opportunity.

And if you really want solitude, leave the Parks altogether. The seven national forests that surround Yellowstone and Grand Teton parks each have at least a couple hundred miles of trail, and some much more. Heavily trailed Gallatin, Bridger-Teton and Shoshone forests together boast some 6,300 miles of designated hiking trail.

Both day-hiking and backpacking are popular in Greater Yellowstone. This chapter describes some of the better-known hikes in Yellowstone and Teton parks and outlying areas in Idaho, Montana and Wyoming. At least a couple in each area are appropriate for multi-day treks. The fact that these trails are particularly well-known can mean they are also particularly busy. Our picks aren't your best bets for solitude. Usually September clears the trails dramatically, and at any time of year, sunrise hikes allow you to enjoy even the most popular trails in near solitude.

Another way to find quiet is to seek what, for the most part, we've left out: hard-to-access or longer trails. Learn about them from hiking books or ranger stations and visitors centers. We like Jerry Painter's books. He's an avid hiker and author of *The Tetons: Great Trails for Family Hiking*, *Backcountry Hiking and Biking Trails in the Idaho Falls Area* and a hiking newsletter called *BackCountry Trail Guide*. Painter suggests many of the hikes described in this chapter. You can find his books at the *Post Register* in Idaho Falls, 333 Northgate Mile, (208) 522-1800. The newsletter can be obtained from Backcountry Trail Guide, 1439 Riviera Drive, Idaho Falls, ID, 83404.

Remember: The more remote your chosen trail, the better prepared you need to be with information, maps and equipment.

General Information

Backcountry Camping, National Forest Style

On national forest lands near paved roads, camping is typically restricted to designated campgrounds (see our Campgrounds and RV Parks chapter). Camping restrictions like these protect plant life, resources and scenic attractions from heavy use. Signs by the side of the road will alert you to roadside camping restrictions.

Once you're in the backcountry, you may camp almost anywhere you choose. This places some responsibility on you. Choose a campsite others have used, rather than damaging vegetation in a new site. Keep fires small and in existing fire circles, or better yet, don't build a fire at all unless somebody is chilled and needs warming. Some areas at some times of year don't allow fires, so bring and use a camping stove. Don't cut vegetation or trench your tent or modify the site in any avoidable way. As much as possible, leave no trace that you've been here: Pack out all garbage. Bury human waste 6 inches deep and at least 200 feet from any water source (toilet paper is not human waste and should be burned or packed out with the trash).

It's tempting to camp streamside, but your presence can cause bank erosion and prevent wild creatures from reaching water. Camp at least 100 feet from water (some high-use areas will require that your site be even farther from streamsides and lakes).

www.insiders.com

See this and many other **Insiders' Guide®** destinations online — in their entirety.

Visit us today!

If you're in Greater Yellowstone, you're probably in bear country, so food and any sweet-smelling toiletries (toothpaste, for instance) must be stored appropriately. It's said that a grizzly bear can smell tuna inside an unopened can. Take bear precautions seriously for your own safety and the bear's. If you're not familiar with the safety rules for travel in bear country, read our Close-up on bear safety in our Fishing and Hunting chapter. You can obtain additional information from ranger stations and national park visitors centers.

Greater Yellowstone's backcountry can get a bit busy, especially on popular trails like Teton Valley's Alaska Basin or Table Mountain. Remember that the groups you encounter probably shouldered their packs seeking solitude. Don't camp within sight or earshot of another group if you can help it. If you find yourself camping near others, be considerate and quiet. This goes double for pets: The wild creatures of Greater Yellowstone's national forests run free, but dogs are not wild creatures. Leash or otherwise control your dog, for the sake of the dog (mountain lions are said to *love* dogs), for the sake of horsepackers and other human travelers on narrow trails and for the sake of wildlife that it may amuse your dog to chase or disturb. The line between survival and death for many wild creatures is a thin one; having to rebuild a demolished den can take a creature across that line.

Check with the local ranger district or the national forest administrator's office before entering Greater Yellowstone backcountry (see our Parks and Forests chapter). Ask about the varying maximum-stay regulations, special restrictions on fires and the occasional trail closures. Special transportation restrictions apply in designated wilderness and some national forest lands. The trail you've chosen may enforce restrictions on mountain biking or motorized vehicles. Motorized vehicles are allowed in some areas, but their use is restricted to established trails in order to limit damage.

Rangers can also provide maps and share key information like how voracious the mosquitos and black flies have been, which stream crossings are difficult, how much snow remains at high elevations, which water sources have dried up, whether trails are too muddy to navigate without damage, etc. Find phone numbers and addresses for national forest ranger stations in our Parks and Forests chapter.

Backcountry Camping, National Park Style

Extremely heavy demand for backcountry sites in Grand Teton and Yellowstone national parks necessitates restrictions that don't apply elsewhere in Greater Yellowstone. For instance, no pets are allowed in national park backcountry. Neither are firearms (many visitors carry bear-repellent sprays, said to be safer and more effective than a gun). Other regulations apply, including maximum-stay limits for particular areas. Jackson Lake in Grand Teton Park, for instance, carries a three-day maximum. In Yellowstone Park, whole trails are closed at certain times to provide bears with solitude and to protect humans. Campsites near bear kills are routinely closed, since bears generally return to kills until the meat is gone.

A backcountry permit is required if you plan to stay out for more than a day. In Grand Teton Park, this permit is free and must be obtained in person at Moose, Colter Bay or Jenny Lake visitors centers. In Yellowstone Park, pick up your permit at a Park ranger station (and some entrance stations, if the ranger has time). Part

This waterlogged grizzly bear rests on a rock in West Yellowstone, Montana.

of the reason for the permit system is to give the rangers a chance to provide you with information about how to use the national park backcountry safely and responsibly.

Your campsite must also be reserved. In Grand Teton Park, 30 percent of backcountry campsites are reservable in advance at no charge; the rest are available on a first-come, first-served basis. Reservations may not be made by phone, so you need to write the Grand Teton National Park Permits Office, P.O. Drawer 170, Moose, WY 83012, or stop by the Moose Visitor Center. For more information about backcountry travel and camping in Grand Teton Park, call Park Dispatch at (307) 739-3300 or stop by any Park visitors center.

In Yellowstone Park, the drill is similar. Advance Yellowstone campsite reservations may be made in person or by mail for a charge of $15. Write to Backcountry Office, P.O. Box 168, Yellowstone National Park, WY 82190. You can speed the process by calling (307) 344-2160 or (307) 344-2163 to request advance forms by mail. Not all Yellowstone sites are reservable in advance. If you wait until you arrive and book your site less than 48 hours in advance, the $15 fee is waived.

In both Parks, rangers can help you select sites, but they appreciate it if you have several plans in mind when you show up. It helps us

as we navigate these requirements to remember that they exist to make our backcountry experience more pleasant. Users would overrun more popular sites and trails in no time without some sort of turnstile at the trailhead.

Do Your Homework

A friend of ours has a great definition for adventure: When, in the middle of an experience, you're wishing you were safely home regaling your friends with it, that's an adventure. To avoid backcountry adventures, do your homework before hitting the trail. Novice hikers/backpackers should make use of available books that help beginners select and pack gear, plan trips and have maximum fun with maximum safety. One we recommend, although it contains much more information than a casual hiker needs, is called *Mountaineering: The Freedom of the Hills* (see our Resources chapter). This is one of the most comprehensive resources available for backcountry travel. It's aimed mostly at climbers, but the first part is applicable to any would-be backcountry traveler. It discusses how to find safe creek crossings, how to select hiking boots, how to plan menus for a longer trip, what kind of camp stove to buy and more. If you only plan to day-hike, the introduction to a good hiking book should provide most of the information you need. Also make sure you stop in at the nearest ranger station or visitors center before you hike, particularly if you've selected a longer or more challenging trail or if you're going in overnight. Be sure to pick up a map of the area you're planning to hike

Your preparation and knowledge will, in large part, determine whether you enjoy an exhilarating experience rather than fall victim to adventure. At least as important a reason to study up before you hit the trail is the fact that Greater Yellowstone's backcountry is rare and fragile. Few such wild places still exist in this country. Only a knowledgeable traveler can walk lightly and with the care required to protect the wonders that await you here.

Yellowstone National Park

Yellowstone's hydrothermal attractions often involve short, well-marked hikes. They range in length from several hundred feet to a couple of miles. To find these, simply use the map handed to you at the entrance gate or watch the signs on the side of the road. However, most of the Park's 1,000-plus miles of trail are not so easily stumbled upon. What follows are some of the best shorter and longer hikes in the Park. Most of these hikes are more memorable for their scenery, wildlife opportunities and wilderness than for hydrothermal features. Perhaps their biggest attraction is their quiet: Although it's not as easy as you might think to find real solitude in Yellowstone Park, you can expect to leave 90 percent of Park visitors behind when you get more than 2 miles from a road or parking area.

Much of Yellowstone Park is grizzly country, particularly backcountry areas with few or no roads, such as the southeast and southwest corners of the Park. Learn appropriate precautions. Read about bear safety in our Camping and RV Parks chapter, or pick up

any of several bear safety brochures at visitors centers or ranger stations on neighboring national forest lands. Visitors planning to spend a night or more in the backcountry must register and reserve their site. Backcountry permits and site registration materials are available at all Park visitors centers.

Mount Washburn
Off Canyon-Tower Rd.

Mount Washburn is one of those must-do short hikes. You'll hike 3 miles and gain 1,500 feet of elevation as you ascend Mount Washburn. The payoffs are colorful wildflower meadows, a likelihood that you'll see bighorn sheep and views from the summit of Yellowstone Lake, the Tetons, the Yellowstone River, its Grand Canyon and more. You'll find a hikers' wind-shelter at the lookout tower atop the more than 10,000-foot-high mountain.

Two trails climb Mount Washburn, each about 6 miles round-trip, which gives you the option of hiking up one and down the other if you don't mind arranging a shuttle vehicle. One trail starts at Dunraven Pass and the other at the Chittenden Road parking area. Both trailheads are reached via the Canyon-Tower Road.

Fairy Falls and Fairy Falls Trail
Fountain Flat Dr., 1 mile south of
Firehole River Bridge

Of several quick approaches to Fairy Falls, we like this one best. It begins at the Imperial Meadows trailhead off Fountain Flat Drive and meanders through green meadow alongside Fairy Creek (watch for elk), arcs up to visit restive Imperial Geyser, then meets another trail and heads east to the base of Fairy Falls. Round-trip distance is 6 miles. Two hundred feet high, the thin, delicate cascade of Fairy Falls is one of the tallest waterfalls in the Park. You'll spend some time in lodgepole forest burned in the fires of 1988.

The long way into Fairy Falls is perhaps the most rewarding. It involves a shuttle, since you

---

INSIDERS' TIP

In Grand Teton National Park, most hiking trails start at about 6,800 feet and then go up. If you're not accustomed to high altitude, give yourself extra time.

begin at the Biscuit Basin trailhead and emerge 13.5 miles away just south of Midway Geyser Basin. Fairy Creek Trail runs beside the Little Firehole River, loops through a bison summering area called Little Firehole Meadows then drops off the edge of the Madison Plateau. Watch for trail markers, since we hear people occasionally get lost on this steep stretch. Below the plateau, you pass Imperial Geyser and come to a fork in the trail. The northern route follows Fairy Creek to Fountain Flat Drive. The other takes you to the base of Fairy Falls and then the Midway Geyser Basin trailhead.

Canyon Rim Trails
Grandview or Artist Point

You were planning to stop here anyway; why not take the time to see this canyon's golden walls and thundering waterfalls from a few more angles? This hike starts at either Grandview or Artist Point and links together the North Rim and South Rim trails for a one-way distance of just under 4 miles. If you start at Grandview, you'll begin on the North Rim Trail. At just more than a mile, you'll reach the Upper Falls parking area. Just beyond it, cross the Yellowstone River on a highway bridge. Turn left and head downstream along the South Rim Trail which takes you to Artist Point.

Several interesting side-hikes exist along your route. The scenic overlook at Red Rock Point, the spur trail to Crystal Falls, and Uncle Tom's Trail, which uses a steep stairway to reach an observation platform at the lip of the Lower Falls, are three of the best. Uncle Tom's Trail is worth doing by itself, although the steel platforms bolted to the canyon wall generally host a steady stream of hikers. Uncle Tom's Trail has its own parking area on the South Rim Trail about 1 mile before Artist Point. Park here and your one-way hike is only about .25 miles. You'll drop 500 feet below the canyon rim in that distance though, so this is not a casual stroll. Nor is it likely to be appreciated by those fearful of heights.

Hellroaring Creek
Tower Junction

This 10-mile out-and-back hike begins at Tower Junction. Start by heading northwest on the dirt road used for stagecoach rides. After about 1.5 miles the trail turns north (right)

and descends toward the Yellowstone River. A steel suspension bridge takes you across the narrow gorge cut by the Yellowstone. From there the trail crosses sagebrush flats, then runs alongside Hellroaring Creek before ending at Hellroaring Ranger Station.

Fishing for cutthroats is excellent along Hellroaring Creek. If you want to spend more time here, wander upstream of the ranger station about a half-mile. You'll find a footbridge that will allow you to safely cross the boisterous creek and continue exploring. Backcountry campsites are available to make this into a short overnight trip.

Shoshone Lake and Shoshone Geyser Basin
DeLacy Creek Trailhead off West Thumb Rd.

This 20-mile hike makes a perfect two-day backpacking trip, taking you past lovely Shoshone Lake and Shoshone Geyser Basin (which many call the Park's best backcountry thermal site). The 10-mile days are only moderately strenuous, even with full packs, because the trail is well-maintained and generally level. Find the DeLacy Creek Trailhead at a pullout 9 miles south of Old Faithful on the road to West Thumb. The trail follows DeLacy Creek, reaching Shoshone Lake in about 3 miles. Turn right at the fork in the trail and continue along the north side of Shoshone Lake, passing several backcountry campsites. At 11 miles the trail forks again. To your right is the route you'll follow to leave; a couple minutes' walk down the left fork is Shoshone Geyser Basin.

After you've checked out the geyser basin, head back to the fork and turn onto the main trail. You can either follow this trail clear to Old Faithful on the Howard Eaton Trail, or, when you reach another fork at about 17 miles, turn right. Your trail becomes an old road that runs beside the Firehole River, passing Lone Star Geyser before coming out at the Lone Star Geyser Trailhead, 2 miles east of Old Faithful. Either way you'll need to arrange a shuttle for your vehicle.

Thorofare Trail and Parts Beyond
East Entrance Rd., 9 miles from Fishing Bridge Junction

Thorofare Trailhead connects to a nearly endless array of remote, longer multi-day hikes, including a couple of loop hikes. The Thorofare Trail itself is one of the easiest ways to access the remote reaches of the Upper Yellowstone Valley. Amfac Parks and Resorts, (307) 344-7311, makes it easier yet with a boat shuttle on Yellowstone Lake that cuts some 9 miles off your trail distance at a cost of about $60 per hour.

Thorofare Trail begins by hugging the shore of Yellowstone Lake's southeast arm. At Terrace Point, the trail leaves the lake, offering panoramic views of the Upper Yellowstone Valley. Not far south of Terrace Point, you begin to have choices, many of which will have led you to shuttle a vehicle to the point at which you plan to exit the backcountry, possibly as far as Pahaska or Wyo. Highway 291 past Ishawooa Pass in Wyoming, or Pacific Creek Road in Grand Teton Park, or the Heart Lake Trailhead on the Park's South Entrance Road. Many of the forested areas from Terrace Point south are burned, but don't let that keep you off these long wilderness trails.

At about 19 miles, Thorofare Trail intersects Trail Creek Trail, which can take you to lovely Heart Lake and from there out to Heart Lake Trailhead on the South Entrance Road. You can also build a loop out of Trail Creek, Two Ocean Plateau and South Boundary trails and return the way you came on Thorofare Trail. Or continue beyond Trail Creek Trail to the next loop possibility, which swings around Bridger Lake before returning to Thorofare for the more than 30-mile journey back to your starting point.

If you stay on Thorofare Trail, you'll pass the backcountry Thorofare Ranger Station at about mile 32, cross the Park boundary a few minutes later and head toward the Continental Divide and Grand Teton National Park or continue along Thorofare Creek east and then north over Ishawooa Pass. On this route, the first road you intersect is Wyo. Highway 291, which runs from Cody to its dead end here in the Absarokas.

Many other options exist among the trails that intersect Thorofare. The important thing to know about these hikes is that they're remote — there are *no* roads in the southeast corner of Yellowstone Park — and they involve long distances. Be sure to ask lots of questions when you sign up for your backcountry campsites, and be sure you carry good topographic maps.

Grand Teton National Park

Hikes in Grand Teton National Park can be broken into two types: shorter loop trails on the valley floor, often encircling lakes, and strenuous longer loops that lasso steep-sided mountain canyons, traverse ridgelines or thread through mountain passes. The ease of the valley floor trails makes them popular — and crowded — on summer days. The best way to lose the crowds is to head into the mountains, but some care is required. Mountain trails in Grand Teton Park start at about 6,800 feet — then they go up. Though exhilarating, these trails should be approached with care and planning. Weather changes, routefinding problems, exhaustion or poor timing can turn a day's outing into an overnight fiasco.

Bears are more commonly seen in Grand Teton Park's backcountry, mountain and valley, than near its roads. Learn appropriate precautions. See our Close-up on bear safety in the Fishing and Hunting chapter, or pick up any of several bear safety brochures at visitors centers or ranger stations on neighboring national forest lands. Visitors planning to spend a night or more in the backcountry must register and reserve their site at a Park visitors center.

Swan Lake and Heron Pond
Off U.S. Hwy. 89 at Colter Bay Village

This 3-mile hike is a perfect dawn or dusk excursion. Wildlife viewing is almost a certainty at that time of day, and the fishing is good in Swan Lake, Heron Pond and Third Creek. You have a good chance of seeing moose, elk, beaver, sandhill crane, bald eagles, pelicans and other waterfowl. This easy hike is also popular with horseback riders, so don't expect to have the trail to yourself during the day in summer. You'll loop down the west shore of Swan Lake and back beside the east shore of Heron Pond. Elevation gain is nearly zero.

Many options exist for longer hikes, including a trek out to Hermitage Point (a backcountry campsite exists along this route on the shore of Jackson Lake) or looping east of Swan Lake. The Hermitage Point hike is about 10 miles long on level trails; it's suitable for novice hikers.

To find this hike, pull into the Colter Bay Village complex from U.S. Highway 89. Turn left at the visitors center. The trailhead is at the south end of the marina parking lot. In summer the visitors center provides free maps to the maze of trails in this area.

String Lake Trail
Jenny Lake Loop Road

Scattered at the base of the Tetons like discarded jewels, Jenny, Leigh and String lakes provide plentiful opportunities for hikes. The shortest hike loops around shallow String Lake for 3.4 miles. Longer hikes head out past Leigh Lake to Bearpaw Lake and Trapper Lake (about 9 miles one way), or completely around lovely Jenny Lake past Hidden Falls and Inspiration Point, two of Jenny Lake's more popular scenic stops (see hike description in this chapter). None of these hikes offer solitude except in spring and fall or extremely early in the mornings.

The String Lake hike is particularly nice for families. It's partially paved and has two footbridges, one across the lake's inlet and the other across its outlet. Elevation gain/loss is about 200 feet. On warm summer days, kids swim and innertube the placid shallow water and families picnic on the shores. A segment of String Lake's east shore is paralleled by a road that links the trail's two parking and picnic areas, so access is good.

Jenny Lake, Hidden Falls and Inspiration Point
Near Jenny Lake Visitors Center

You can do this trail a couple of ways: Either you hike the 6.6-mile loop completely around the pretty glacial lake or you use the ferry to shorten the journey. From the East

Shore boat dock to the watery veils of Hidden Falls is 2.5 miles. Inspiration Point, an overlook that allows you to view Jenny Lake, Jackson Hole and the Gros Ventre River range, is another half-mile beyond the falls. If you hike up to see the falls and look out over Jenny Lake, you'll gain and lose about 220 feet. Otherwise elevation gain is mimimal.

You can pick up maps at the Jenny Lake visitors center and at the trailhead. This hike is wildly popular, as is the ferry ride. You could almost imagine the park service installing passing lanes and traffic lights. But don't let that discourage you from taking this hike: The scenery is truly marvelous, and in late summer the huckleberries are sweet. Early morning and late evening are your best bets for a little solitude.

Find this trailhead near the East Shore boat dock below the Jenny Lake visitors center. You can also reach this hike from the String Lake loop trail (see previous above). There are no backcountry campsites on the perimeter of Jenny Lake.

Two Ocean Lake
Two Ocean Rd., off Pacific Creek Rd.

This trailhead off Pacific Creek Road leads to several loop trails, two of which trace the perimeters of Two Ocean and Emma Matilda lakes. Lake views, wildflower meadows, beaver dams, fishing and wildlife viewing are attractions, but the biggest reason to hike here is that few do. The dirt road that takes you to the trailhead means that, compared to other trails in Grand Teton Park, these are quiet.

The hike around Two Ocean Lake is flat and about 7 miles long. A short connecting trail takes you to the more popular Emma Matilda Lake trail, about 8 miles around. Horseback riders from the stables at nearby Jackson Lake Lodge make frequent use of parts of this trail, since it can also be reached from the lodge.

Find the trailhead by turning east off U.S. Highway 89 onto Pacific Creek Road. After

---

INSIDERS' TIP

Yellowstone National Park trails are marked with square orange metal markers which the National Park Service has nailed to trailside trees.

Emergency Gear: Think Ahead, Be Prepared

We think of it as plan-B gear. It goes in the backpack before tent, cookstove or clothing. It gets tucked behind the car seat and tossed into a daypack before a hike. Exactly what it consists of depends on many factors, but the principle is always the same: Plan-B gear answers the "what if" questions: What if the car broke down? What if you got sick? What if I fell and hurt my ankle? What if we got lost and had to spend the night?

Close-up

If you looked in our daypacks before a typical all-day summer hike in Yellowstone backcountry, the Plan B gear would probably consist of:

• a flashlight (preferably a headlamp with an elastic headband that allows us to work or walk with hands free)
• a knife, pliers and nylon cord for various repairs and projects
• matches and firestarter
• a watch, compass and good map of the area
• at least one extra piece of warm, non-cotton clothing, plus a wool hat
• water-repellent jacket
• extra water (or water purification tablets) and extra high-calorie food
• a first-aid kit

A word here on wearing a watch: We have friends who never hike with watches. They say they're escaping their schedule-bound lives. Sounds great, but people who know how long they've been hiking are more likely to know how far they've come. This makes it easier to use maps or to make plans if you become lost. And people in an emergency can make better decisions if they know exactly how much daylight remains.

All plan-B gear, first aid kit included, should vary from person to person and trip to trip. Two good rules for plan-B gear are: Don't pack it if you don't know how to use it; and don't pack it if something else you've already packed could make do. The farther into the backcountry you plan to go, the harsher the weather or the longer your stay, the more carefully and thoroughly you should pack your plan-B gear. For instance, we take winter backcountry travel seriously, so for a full day in winter backcountry, we'd almost certainly add to the above list:

• a head-to-toe extra non-cotton set of warm clothes, including extra gloves (extra doesn't include the clothes we plan to wear. If we start with one warm shirt but plan to wear two, we bring three)
• spare batteries for that flashlight
• chemical hand-warmer packets
• a bivy sack or "space blanket"
• duct tape for ski and other repairs
• tools for adjusting ski bindings
• even more extra food — without fuel the machine can't produce heat.

As first-aid kits go, ours is minimal because we've found that heavy first-aid kits tend to get left in the car where they can't do much good. Besides, when minor backcountry injuries occur, there are often items in our packs or jacket pockets from which solutions can be improvised, eliminating the need for specialty items in the first-aid kit. For

— continued on next page

instance, we never carry commercial splinting devices: a padded stick or ski will do. And we don't pack much medication unless we plan to be in the backcountry for several days or weeks. On a daytrip we figure we can walk out if we're bothered by a headache or stomachache. What our kit almost always contains are recently checked and replenished supplies of the following:

• standard-size, water-resistant band-aids (to protect a wound that has been cleaned and disinfected)

• knuckle and/or fingertip bandages (tabs on these bandage styles allow good coverage for wounds on fingers, toes and heels)

• sterile gauze pads, about 4 inches square (to scrub out and cover larger wounds or injured eyes)

• athletic tape (sticks better than medical tape and can be used to make makeshift butterfly bandages or wrap sprains and strains)

• povidone-iodine solution for disinfecting wounds

• individually wrapped antiseptic towelettes (to wash hands before treating a wound, to clean the area around a wound, etc.)

• moleskin for treating blisters and blisters-to-be. To slow down a developing blister, use moleskin when you start to feel a "hot spot." Duct tape from your plan-B kit is a good last step here: it holds moleskin on and decreases friction because it's slippery against your boot.

• 6-inch athletic wrap (for sprains, strains, attaching splints or use as a constricting band in case of snake bite)

• safety pins (for removing splinters, attaching the athletic wrap, securing a sling, fixing a broken pack strap, etc.)

• sharp scissors (not a razor blade — scissors are a safer tool in shaky hands)

• tweezers

It's a good idea to add a book on backcountry medicine. We recommend Buck Tilton and Frank Hubbell's *Medicine For the Backcountry* if you're going on a longer trip. Short booklets that would be more appropriate for a day-hiking first-aid kit are also available. Such books and booklets are even more useful if you read and re-read them periodically.

████████████████

about 1.3 miles turn left (north) on gravel Two Ocean Road. Two more miles takes you to a picnic area and trailhead. Two Ocean Road can be impassable after heavy rain or snow.

Surprise Lake and Amphitheater Lake
South Jenny Lake Junction on Teton Park Road

This is a classic Teton hike: The trail rises nearly 1,000 feet per mile and before about mid-July you're likely to find yourself walking through patches of snow. The prize at the end of your trek are two lovely mountain lakes — Surprise and Amphitheatre — tucked away from prying eyes on the valley floor. On the way up, enjoy views of Jenny, Taggart and Bradley lakes far below. Check out the creek

fed by Teton Glacier, its waters opaque and bluish from rock particles ground up by the glacier's inexorable weight.

Twice you'll pass left-forking trails. One takes you to Bradley Lake and beyond. The other is the Garnet Canyon climbers' trail, which heads up sheer-walled, waterfall-stepped Garnet Canyon and is considered "off-trail" hiking. Backcountry campsites exist between Surprise Lake and Amphitheatre Lake less than a half-mile beyond, so this trip can be made into an overnight. The round-trip distance is about 10 miles.

This hike is not recommended for young children. Find the trailhead by turning onto an unpaved road a mile south of the South Jenny Lake Junction. About 1.5 miles in, a restroom and parking area mark the trailhead.

Cascade Canyon and Lake Solitude
East Shore Boat Dock at Jenny Lake

The hike up glacier-carved Cascade Canyon is both lovely and loaded with hiking options. You can begin from Jenny Lake's East Shore boat dock or, for a small fee, shave 2 miles each way by hopping on the ferry. From Inspiration Point near the West Shore boat dock, a moderately strenuous 4.5 mile hike brings you to the forks of Cascade Canyon. You gain more than 1,000 feet in elevation and enjoy views of Teewinot and Mount Owen, and of cascading waterfalls. In late summer, allow a little time for berry picking. You can turn back at the forks, but if you're backpacking or looking for a more strenuous day's adventure, you have two choices.

Hiking up South Cascade Canyon beyond the forks can take you eventually to the Teton Crest Trail which traverses the southern half of the Teton range. This allows the possibility of a long backcountry trek. Or you can turn up the North Fork trail, which climbs another 1,200 feet in just under 3 miles one way and carries you to alpine Lake Solitude, surrounded by sheer rock. Don't let the name fool you: This hike is popular, and solitude is not likely at your destination. Camping is available near the lake.

The North Fork trail can be made into a loop hike. You can continue beyond Lake Solitude over Paintbrush Divide, past Holly Lake, down to String Lake on the valley floor and back along the shore of Jenny Lake to the West Shore boat dock. This loop hike is extremely strenuous — it climbs another 1,700 feet above Solitude and generally involves crossing large snowfields. Ice axes are often required. Talk to the rangers at Jenny Lake before heading up to Lake Solitude or the Paintbrush Divide loop.

Jackson Hole

Ski Lake Trail
Off Wyo. Hwy. 22 west of Wilson, Wyo.

Getting to see pretty alpine lakes usually involves strenuous hiking, but not at Ski Lake near Wilson, Wyoming. This hike is easy to moderate and only 4.6 miles round-trip. You get to hike through wildflower meadows, enjoy great views of Jackson Hole and the Gros Ventre range and, only 2 miles from your car, relax by the crystal clear waters of Ski Lake. The trailhead is often busy, since it's also a popular access point for the Teton Crest Trail, a long trail which traverses the southern half of the Teton range. To access the Teton Crest here, take the right fork to Phillips Pass when the trail divides about one mile in. To get to Ski Lake, take the left.

Find the trailhead by driving 4.5 miles west out of Wilson on Wyo. Highway 22. At the sign for Phillips Canyon, pull off into a parking lot on the south side of the road. Walk up the Jeep trail for about .3 mile. You'll see the trailhead sign on your left. For more information, call the Jackson Ranger District at 733-4755.

Gros Ventre Slide Nature Trail
Off Gros Ventre River Rd.

This easy interpretive hike makes a great addition to a day of picnicking, swimming and fishing at Lower Slide Lake outside Grand Teton National Park. Lower Slide Lake created itself in 1925 when the north side of Sheep Mountain sheared off and tumbled into the Gros Ventre River. Within a few minutes, 50 million cubic yards of debris had buried the river and created a natural dam. Frequent signs

INSIDERS' TIP

Be sure to tuck an all-purpose bandanna or two into your pack. These handy squares of fabric can be used for slings or bandages and as a sweat band. They can also be used to tie back your hair or to protect it from wind and dust. On a hot day, if you dip your bandanna in water, you can tie it loosely around your neck. The evaporating water on your neck will help cool you. We even know someone who has used a bandanna for makeshift sunglasses. He cut two slits big enough to see through while keeping out the bright light.

along the half-mile loop trail describe common plants, the slide itself and other points of interest.

Find the trailhead by turning east on Gros Ventre River Road from U.S. Highway 89. After 6 miles, watch the south side for the Slide display. The trail starts near the restrooms below the interpretive signs. For more information, call the Jackson Ranger District at (307) 733-4755.

Eastern Idaho

Island Park, Idaho

Coffee Pot Rapids Trail
Off U.S. Hwy. 20 at Upper Coffeepot Campground

This hike begins at Upper Coffeepot Campground and wanders alongside the dimpled, crystal clear waters of the Henry's Fork for about 2.5 miles. At Coffeepot Rapids, the river gets to show its teeth. You'll travel through lodgepole and subalpine fir. In late summer look for huckleberries along the sides of the trail. You may also find our favorite flower, the sego lily. It's a creamy cuplike bloom on a slim stem with grass-blade leaves.

This is an out-and-back trail suitable for families with young children. Find the trailhead near Mack's Inn by turning from U.S. Highway 20 onto the road marked for Upper Coffeepot Campground, a small and often quiet Forest Service facility. At the entrance to the campground is day-use parking for anglers and hikers. Call the Island Park Ranger District (208) 558-7301.

Old Railroad Bed Trail
Various access points

Along the Union Pacific's old tourist-train route to Yellowstone Park now runs one of the easiest hiking and biking trails in the area. The gentle grade required by trains makes for mellow walking, if not for fascinating terrain. Sometimes short sections are boggy and crossed by downed timber early in the season, but by late summer this trail is a backcountry sidewalk. The 55-mile-long route parallels the Warm River for 6 miles, leaves it and then re-

turns for several more. It crosses Toms Creek and the Buffalo and Henry's Fork rivers, slips over the Continental Divide and drops into West Yellowstone, Montana. It winds through lodgepole forest and open meadows, over trestle bridges and even through a tunnel long enough that you can't see the end from the beginning. It gains about 400 feet in the 10 or so miles between West Yellowstone and the divide, then loses about 1,500 feet as it gradually drops toward the trailhead at Warm River Campground.

Pick up a map at the Island Park or Ashton ranger districts to see how you can break this hike into short or long pieces by leaving a shuttle vehicle at any of several spots where the trail meets or parallels various forest roads. If you plan an out-and-back hike, try the section above Warm River Campground. Another short scenic section starts at the Black Canyon Loop Road and heads downhill to Big Springs.

You get to the Warm River trailhead from Warm River Campground just off of Idaho Highway 47, the Mesa Falls Scenic Byway. Reach the Black Canyon Loop Road from Big Springs Road which meets U.S. Highway 20 at Mack's Inn. For more information, call the Island Park Ranger District (208) 558-7301 or the Ashton Ranger District at (208) 652-7442.

Swan Valley

Palisades Creek Trail
Palisades Creek Rd. off Idaho Hwy. 26 near Irwin, Idaho

Ask folks in Swan Valley for a good hike and they're going to point you toward this one. Your destinations are Lower and Upper Palisades lakes, although if you hike beyond the upper lake the options become nearly endless. Travel also becomes more difficult — the creek crossings in particular can require care — and travelers much less common. Both lakes offer good trout fishing and pleasant campsites, although the popularity of this trail means that the lower lake's sites get snatched up fast, particularly on weekends. Bridges over creek crossings on the way to the lower lake make this hike particularly pleasant for families, bike riders and horseback riders. One-way distance to Lower Palisades Lake is 4 miles; the upper lake is 7 miles from trailhead, with an elevation gain of about 1,000 feet.

Find the trailhead by turning northeast onto tiny Palisades Creek Road from Idaho Highway 26 near Irwin. The road runs up the canyon for about 2.5 miles before ending at a small Forest Service campground (see our Campgrounds and RV Parks chapter). Palisades Creek Trail takes off from just beyond the campground. Park in the parking area just outside the campground on the far side of Palisades Creek. To learn more, call the Palisades Ranger District at (208) 523-1412.

Bear Creek Trail
Off Idaho Hwy. 26 near Palisades, Idaho

Bear Creek is a great trail system for folks who don't like to retrace their steps. You have at least four ways to make this journey a loop and even more options for building a multiday trip. The first few miles parallel pretty, fishable Bear Creek with level, well-maintained trail (you must wade the shallow creek in a couple places). After about 4 miles the trail divides to follow the creek's north and south forks; families with young children or hikers not looking for strenuous activity should pack up their fishing poles and head back. Travel becomes more difficult, with more stream crossings and steeper stretches. The side trails off the North and South Fork trails are steeper yet as they climb out of Bear Creek Canyon and can involve route-finding difficulties. This keeps most mountain bikers and horseback riders on the main trails.

Find the trailhead by turning off Idaho Highway 26 to cross Palisades Reservoir Dam near the tiny town of Palisades. About 6 miles after crossing the dam you'll see Bear Creek. Follow the road a quarter-mile north of the creek past the campground. Park among the willows at the trailhead parking lot. To learn more, call the Palisades Ranger District at (208) 523-1412.

Teton Valley

South Darby Canyon Wind Cave
Off Idaho Hwy. 33

This is a well-made but steep trail that climbs 1,800 feet in its 3.4-mile, one-way length. About 3 miles in, the trail forks. The unmaintained trail that continues along the creek joins eventually with the Fox Creek trail. The main trail continues past a monument erected in memory of five people killed here by lightning. Your destination is just beyond: a cave that runs for about .75 mile through the mountain. The mysterious wind that rushes from its mouth is the result of air pouring in from holes further up the canyon — as the air cools, it rolls downhill toward where you stand.

Negotiating the cave itself involves technical rock and ice climbing, but its entrance can be examined by hikers with flashlights. If the steep scramble up to the cave's mouth is still snow-covered, skip it and view the cave from more stable footing below, especially if you're hiking with kids.

Find the trailhead by turning east off Idaho Highway 33 onto a paved road marked with signs for Darby Girls Camp. After 1.5 miles the road, now gravel, forks. Take the right fork about 6 miles to a parking area. Your trail heads up the south fork of Darby Creek. For more information, call Teton Basin Ranger District at (208) 354-2431.

Table Mountain
Off Ski Hill Road near Teton Campground

One of the area's most popular and strenuous short hikes, the Table Mountain hike is 12.5 miles round-trip, with an elevation gain of more than 4,000 feet. To enjoy this hike, you need to be in good condition and allow plenty of time. The payoff is at the top of a nontechnical scramble onto the flat top of Table Mountain, elevation 11,106 feet, just below the razor-edged summits of the Teton range. With binoculars, you can watch from your rocky vantage as climbers challenge the Grand Teton — with nothing between you and them but thin mountain air. Most people do this as a day hike, but nice campsites exist along the north fork of Teton Creek.

Find the trailhead by turning right from Ski Hill Road, which leads to Grand Targhee Ski and Summer Resort, onto a dirt road marked with a sign for Teton Campground. Drive 5 miles to the trailhead parking area at one end of a Forest Service campground. For more information, call Teton Basin Ranger District at (208) 354-2431.

Alaska Basin
Off Ski Hill Rd. near Teton Campground

Alaska Basin is one of the loveliest backpacking and horsepacking trails in the Tetons. The last 4 miles up to an alpine basin studded with lakes are steep and strenuous. It is possible to add 2.5 miles to this 8-mile hike by heading past the Basin Lakes to Sunset Lake and beyond to Hurricane Pass. This adds significant elevation gain to the 2,400 feet you already climbed to reach the basin, but from the top of Hurricane Pass the views of the stark Teton range are breathtaking. Head back out the way you came or take the loop that winds down the Devils Stairs (a narrow, steep trail not recommended for children), returning to the main trail after about 4 miles. If you don't mind arranging a shuttle, a longer route crosses over Hurricane Pass, hooks up with the Cascade Canyon trail and back to civilization at Jenny Lake in Grand Teton National Park. At a little more than 20 miles, this makes a comfortable three-day trip or a strenuous two-day one.

Find the trailhead by turning right from Ski Hill Road, which leads to Grand Targhee Ski and Summer Resort, onto a dirt road marked with a sign for Teton Campground. Drive 5 miles to the trailhead parking area at one end of a Forest Service campground. For more information, call Teton Basin Ranger District at (208) 354-2431.

Author's note: We haven't included a detailed description of the Teton Crest Trail here. But, in case you're interested, it's a 28-mile trip from the Jenny Lake Ranger Station to the Granite Canyon Trail parking area. Depending on your stamina, it's a two- or three-night trip, one of the most popular multi-day trips in the Tetons. Some hikers save a stiff climb out of Granite Canyon by riding the Jackson Hole ski area tram to 10,400 feet.

Southwestern Montana

Before heading out onto southwestern Montana's trails, check in with your local Forest Service office. On the Beaverhead Forest, call the Madison Ranger District office west of Ennis at (406) 682-4253. For trails on the Gallatin Forest, check in with the recreation specialist at the Bozeman Ranger District Office, (406) 587-6920. Many of the trails numbered on Forest Service maps aren't necessarily numbered the same way or at all on the ground. Take along good maps and a compass to help find your way around this mountainous terrain.

Beaverhead National Forest, Madison Ranger District and Gravelly Range

Elk River Trail #79
Off U.S. Hwy. 287 on F.S. Rd. 209

This 10-mile roundtrip hike climbs gently through the timber paralleling Elk River, then heads up onto Lobo Mesa where the timber opens into grass lands. Elk, bear, moose, and mule deer frequent these meadows that are loaded with idyllic campsites. (Be sure to read sections on low-impact camping in this chapter and in the Campgrounds and RV Parks chapter if you plan to stay overnight.) If you're really fit and get an early start, you can hike this in a day. We recommend spending the night on top so you can watch the sun set and rise on the Rockies.

About 2 miles into the hike you'll meet Trail #29. Head south on #29 and prepare for steep switchbacks, the price of admission to the upper world of the Gravelly Range. The climb is worth it. Once you reach the top of the mesa,

---

INSIDERS' TIP

Since it's more difficult for horses (especially pack strings) to step off the trail, they have the right of way. Step off to let them pass, and don't make any sudden movements while they're angling by you. We've seen some hellacious wrecks caused by spooked mules and horses.

you can see forever, it seems. On a clear day, you can see the distant Tetons, as well as the Madison, Centennial and Snowcrest mountains. We recommend you take along a map to help you find your way and to help identify the surrounding mountains.

The trailhead is above Miller Flats up the West Fork of the Madison River about 45 miles northwest of Yellowstone Park.

Gallatin National Forest/ Bozeman Ranger District

Hyalite Lake Trail #427
Hyalite Reservoir, 15 miles south of Bozeman, Mont.

This 10-mile round-trip trail takes off from the head of Hyalite reservoir and climbs 1,800 feet to Hyalite Lake. Along the way, you'll pass 11 waterfalls. For the first 1.5 miles, the trail is wide and wheelchair-accessible. It's also very busy. Don't let that discourage you. Once you get past the first waterfall, the traffic thins out dramatically. In addition to seeing people, your chances are good of seeing lots of wildlife including a bear or two.

To get to the trailhead, take the right fork of the Hyalite Canyon Road at the head of the reservoir. You'll find some parts of this trail are pretty steep, but it is well worth reaching the top. If you feel inclined to keep on going once you reach the lake (we wouldn't), you'll have all kinds of options for continuing on. To do this, though, means you'll have to do some planning ahead of time and leave a vehicle at another trailhead. Included among the trail options are a few that head into the Yellowstone Valley to the east. For more detailed information we suggest you contact the Bozeman Ranger District at 3710 Fallon Avenue, Bozeman, Montana. The phone number is 587-6920. And take a map.

Lee Metcalf Wilderness (Spanish Peaks Unit), Gallatin National Forest

Spanish Lakes Trail #407 and #411
Spanish Creek Rd. off U.S. Hwy. 191

This 14-mile round-trip hike will take you into the beautiful Spanish Peaks. About 20 miles south of Bozeman on U.S. Highway 191, you'll come to the Spanish Creek Road headed west. Follow this road until you come to the trailhead. Trail #407 is the main thoroughfare for a whole system of trails leading into the wilderness. About 3 miles up, the trail forks. Stay to the left. About 1.5 miles farther, the trail forks again. This time stay to the right. Just a little ways farther, you'll come to another fork in the trail. Stay left. Now you're on your way, and it isn't all that much farther — about 2.5 miles.

From the Spanish Lakes there are several options for loops. They all take off from Trail #412, which heads north from Spanish Lakes. A couple of trails (#401 and # 410) will add only a few miles and new vistas to your trek.

The Absaroka-Beartooth Wilderness

The Absaroka-Beartooth Wilderness — Montana's third-largest with 943,377 miles — is legendary for its ruggedness, its alpine beauty and a multitude of mountain lakes filled with hungry trout. Twenty-seven peaks in this wilderness exceed 12,000 feet. Hundreds of miles of trail lead across huge alpine meadows, across breathtaking (literally) mountain passes and to more than a thousand lakes. One of the unique things about this wilderness is that in many places from Cooke City to Red Lodge, you can practically step out of

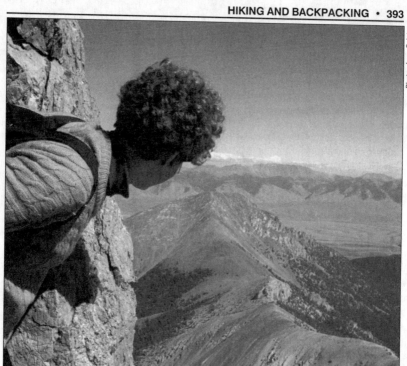

Photo: Jerry Painter

A hiker surveys the scene from atop Ten Peaks.

your car and be within the wilderness boundaries. (See our chapter on Parks and Forests to read about special restrictions in wilderness areas and to read more about the Absaroka-Beartooth Wilderness.) While it's a known fact that the deeper you go into wilderness, the fewer people you'll see, there are still plenty of beautiful, relatively people-free trails fairly close to the road. Following are a few either within or adjacent to the wildnerness. Remember (signs in the area won't let you forget), even though they're outside Yellowstone Park, the Beartooths are still very much in grizzly country.

Before heading off into the Beartooths, stop and pick up a map and carry a compass. We've given you the trail numbers as they're marked on the Gallatin National Forest Map, but on the ground, trails often aren't marked by number. To add to the confusion, different maps put out by the Gallatin Forest use different numbers for the same trail. We also recommend checking with the local ranger district for information on creek crossings, especially in early summer during runoff. If there's a problem bear in the area, they'll also tell you about that. To make contact with the ranger district, you'll have to think ahead. The office is more than 50 miles away in Gardiner.

Kersey Lake Trail

Trailhead 6 miles east of Cooke City, Mont., at Chief Joseph Campground on U.S. Hwy. 212

If you don't have much time, you can consider several options on this trail for in-and-out day hiking or camping combined with great fishing. Two miles in is Kersey Lake and another 2 miles down the trail is Rock Island Lake. Both offer good fishing and easy day hiking.

This well-signed trail (#567) begins at the parking lot across from the Colter Pass campground east of Cooke City on U.S. Highway

212. If you take the whole trail, it ends at the spectacular Crazy Creek Falls adjacent to the same-named campground on U.S. Highway 212 (about 7 miles east of where you'll start). About 3 miles into the hike, though, you'll intersect trails #3 and #565. Here's where you'll have to make your first decision. If you take #565, it will lead you 1.5 miles to Rock Island Lake. Chances are good you'll catch enough brook trout or cutthroat to cook up for dinner. Trail #3 — the main trail you'll be following for the rest of your hike — leads to the Crazy Lakes, so named because they are connected by the white waters of Crazy Creek. About 4 miles from the trailhead and a mile or so east on trail #624, you'll come to Fox Lake in the timber (elevation 8,055 feet and full of brook and rainbow trout).

Another 1.5 miles down the trail (about the halfway mark of your trek) you'll find Widewater Lake — 100 acres big and full of brookies. From there the trail meanders past Big Moose Lake on the Montana-Wyoming line. Ivy Lake (elevation 7,998 feet), is 4 miles from U.S. Highway 212 and pretty much the last fishable lake on your journey. You'll need a Wyoming fishing license here, though. (You can buy a one-day Wyoming license for $3.) Once you pass Little Moose Lake (it's hard to fish and plagued with mosquitoes, so keep on going), the rest of the trail winds through sagebrush grasslands with scattered timber and aspen patches.

Glacier Lake Trail #160
At the end of the Rock Creek Road southwest of Red Lodge, Mont.

This 2-mile hike is not for the faint of heart (literally). It begins at the end of the Rock Creek Road and makes a steep ascent to Glacier Lake, the queen of a string of alpine lakes ranging from 9,800 to 10,040 feet in elevation. If you're a low-lander, travel slowly to avoid altitude sickness (a major headache, nausea and lethargy caused by a lack of oxygen). Fields of alpine flowers, old wind-carved trees still standing after many years of fire and a spectacular view of the Beartooths make the climb well worth the effort.

Tucked into the base of a steep talus rock mountain, Glacier Lake is home to some lunker brook trout as well as rainbows and browns.

There are a few campsites near the outlet (there's an irrigation dam here) at the eastern end of the lake. If you cross the outlet, you'll find a clump of trees that act as a wind break. You'll also be pretty close to Emerald Lake, which is just a stone's throw from Glacier. If you follow the northern shore of Glacier, you'll come to the inlet creek. Follow the trail up the drainage to find Triangle, Mountain Sheep and Mountain Goat lakes. The weather at these lakes can change quickly for the worse, so take extra clothes. And take your fishing pole. By the way, Emerald Lake is in Wyoming, but Montana fishing licenses are honored here.

Grasshopper Glacier (Trail #569)
Off U.S. Hwy. 212 near Colter Campground east of Cooke City, Mont.

Jeep Road 3230 heads north from U.S. Highway 212 just before the Colter Campground east of Cooke City. At the end of the road (about 6 miles) you'll come to the trailhead of Trail #569. From here it's about a 3.5 mile climb to Grasshopper Glacier. This giant snowfield facing the Rosebud River is worth seeing.

Northwestern Wyoming

Chain Lakes Trail
Trailhead on Beartooth Hwy. (U.S. Hwy. 212) east of Island Lake

This 12-mile loop takes you on a pretty gradual up-and-down hike through beautiful open alpine plateaus dotted with lakes and timbered pockets. You can see many of the lakes from the road which, for more timid hikers, is encouraging. Don't be so encouraged, though, that you forget to take a day pack along filled with extra food, clothing and matches. A snow storm or fog can blow in any month of the year.

Once you're off the road, you'll forget about the world of cars above. The hillsides, covered with every wildflower imaginable — lupine, arrow leaf balsam root, asters, buttercups, monkey flowers — dip and climb between 9,650 and 9,200 feet. Across the highway from Long Lake (you can't miss it) you'll see an old Jeep trail (#120) heading down the hill. The old road leads to Duck Lake about

3 miles below Long Lake. From Duck, you can head south to Sawtooth Lake or east to Top Lake. We're taking you past Top Lake, so stick with us. The nice thing about this country is, except for a few draws that you drop into, you can really see where you're going. Follow the trail past Top Lake. Just after the creek crossing, there's a trail (#613 1A) that heads north to Stockade, Loosekamp, Solar and Hauser Lakes. The fish bite at these lakes — some are catch-and-release while others are catch-and-keep. Be sure to check the regulations first. This trail also takes you back to U.S. Highway 212. It reaches the highway about a mile east of the Jeep road where you parked your car. If you're short on time, you can start the hike in reverse and hike in and out of Hauser, Loosekamp and Solar lakes with plenty of time for fishing.

Beartooth Lake Trails
Beartooth Lake Campground, about 20 miles east of Cooke City, Mont., on U.S. Hwy. 212

While this hike is in Wyoming, it's only 20 miles east of Cooke City, Montana, just south of the Absaroka-Beartooth Wilderness. Again, the options in this neck of the woods are endless and the views stupendous. This 5 mile loop leads up Beartooth Creek and past several lakes including Grayling, Beauty and Crane lakes. Park at the Beartooth Lake Campground. (It's beautiful with good fishing and a wonderful view of Beartooth Butte.) Then hike up Trail #619 around the marshy east side of Beartooth Lake. At the north end, you'll have to cross Beartooth Creek (before July, this can be challenging if not treacherous). About 2 miles up the trail — it's a gradual ascent through meadows with rock outcroppings — you'll come to a junction with Trail #620, which heads east past Grayling and Beauty Lakes. Each of them boasts good fishing.

On the north end of Beauty Lake, you'll come to Trail #621. If you go left, you'll head northeast to Island Lake. (It's beautiful, with a campground and a whole new set of trails leading into the Beartooths.) If you turn right on #621, the trail will follow the eastern shore of Beauty Lake, heading south back to the Beartooth Lake campground. This hike can easily be done in a day. If you want to fish and explore, though, make it an overnighter and be sure to take your rod and your mosquito dope.

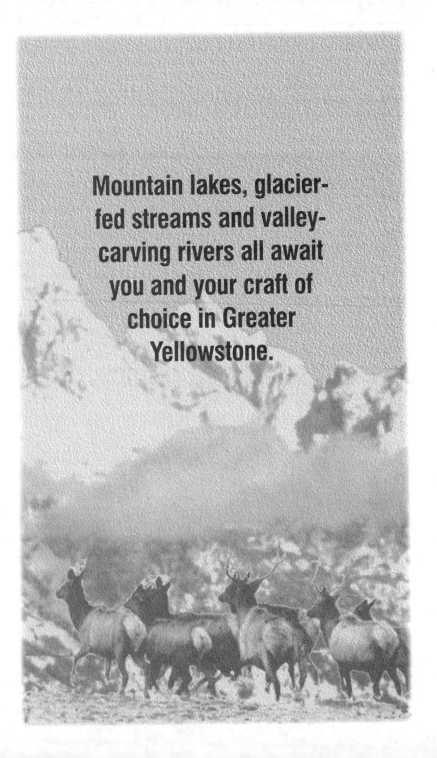

Mountain lakes, glacier-
fed streams and valley-
carving rivers all await
you and your craft of
choice in Greater
Yellowstone.

Watersports

Shimmering, shifting, splashing water — Greater Yellowstone has more than its share. Mountain lakes, glacier-fed streams and valley-carving rivers all await you and your craft of choice. We've selected a few of the region's more popular motor and paddle destinations for this chapter. First read about rivers and lakes well-suited for paddlers, then about outfitters who offer guided trips on these stretches of water. In the next section we list a few popular sites for motorized watersports and some companies that rent those craft.

Before you grab your paddle or pull out the choke, though, be sure you get current information about local conditions from area sporting goods stores, paddling schools and outfitters (see our listings later in the chapter). Park rangers, the Bureau of Reclamation and the Forest Service can also be helpful. Find Forest Service contact numbers in our Parks and Forests chapter and other useful numbers in our Resource section. These folks can provide detailed information about launching points and local services, as well as providing you a heads up for current conditions.

Remember that rivers and lakes change constantly. Old obstacles wash away and new ones are created as trees wash downstream or boulders slip from their earthen sockets and tumble into the river. Afternoon winds funnel through a notch in the mountains and peel 4-foot-high white-capped waves from the surface of what was a placid lake at breakfast time.

Even if you've seen a river or lake before, you should collect current local information before you launch. Use previous experience and the information below as general guidelines only. We've seen brand-new rapids created in the aftermath of one gully-roaring storm and tons of log obstacles added to a river section during one high-water spring.

Many of the campgrounds mentioned in this chapter are described in detail in our Camping and RV Parks chapter.

Whitewater and Flatwater Paddling

When describing rivers, we'll refer to the international rating scale (see the gray box), which provides a general idea of a river section's difficulty. Ratings can change with water flows. The difficulty of your run is also tied to the craft you choose and your proficiency with that craft, so the information provided by this scale is vague at best.

River Rating Scale

Class I: practiced beginner — Easy moving water with small or no waves.

Class II: beginner-intermediate — Regular waves, fast current, unobstructed rapids; may require some maneuvering.

Class III: advanced-intermediate — Large waves and obstacles, maneuvering required; clear route exists, but may not be obvious.

Class IV: expert — Large, chaotic waves, maneuvering difficult but required; route often not obvious; clear route may not exist; scouting recommended.

Class V: expert with previous class IV experience — No beginners on board; scouting strongly recommended; most people choose to portage.

Class VI: expert with previous class V experience — No beginners or intermediates on board; extremely dangerous; most people choose to portage.

Rivers and Lakes

Yellowstone National Park

Before you get out your rafts or your motorboats, be advised that, with the exception of the Lewis River channel between Lewis and Shoshone lakes, there's no boating on Yellowstone Park rivers, and limited motorized boating on the Park's lakes. Motorized boats are allowed on Yellowstone and Lewis lakes. Non-motorized vessels, including float tubes, are allowed on all lakes except Sylvan, Elenor and Twin lakes as well as Beach Springs Lagoon.

All vessels must be permitted with a sticker displayed. You can buy boat permits at several places in the Park. For motorized boat permits stop at the south entrance, the Lewis Lake Campground, Grant Visitor Center, Bridge Bay Marina and the Lake Ranger Station. For non-motorized boat permits, you'll have to go to the Bechler Ranger Station, the west entrance, the northeast entrance or the backcountry offices at Canyon and Mammoth visitors centers. In 1997, an annual motorized permit cost $20, while a seven-day permit cost $10. An annual non-motorized permit cost $10, and a seven-day permit cost $5. For information about boat or slip rentals, call the Bridge Bay Marina from the first week in June until the end of September, at (307) 242-3876. The rest of the year, call (307) 344-7901.

Yellowstone Lake

This lake, described in greater detail in our Attractions chapter, is 20 miles long and 14 miles wide. Even on a day in August, the waters of this lake are deathly cold (officials estimate you could die of hypothermia after 20 minutes in its 41-degree depths). They're also unpredictable. In the blink of an eye, gale force winds can descend on Yellowstone Lake and whip its waters into a frothy monster. Yellowstone Park officials discourage any kind of watersport that involves being in the water for any length of time (even with a wet suit). They also discourage crossing the lake in

smaller watercraft. Every once in a while a canoe capsizes and the lake swallows its unwary occupants. Canoeists and kayakers should hug the shoreline. However, if you want to kayak or canoe the "other side of the lake," you can hire an Amfac shuttle boat (for $60 per hour) to cart you, your friends and your gear across the lake or to its southern arms. An abundance of primitive campsites can provide you with base camps so you can explore the area by water.

Since motorized boating is allowed on Yellowstone Lake, you can expect to see and hear them buzzing around the lake. You'll find launch sites at Bridge Bay and Grant Village.

Lewis Lake

Twelve miles from the south entrance, Lewis is the only lake in the Park besides Yellowstone that allows motorboats. At the southeast end is a campground and boat launch. At the opposite end is the mouth of the Lewis Channel, which leads from Shoshone Lake. If you're into quiet water, paddling this lake in early morning or late evening will satisfy your longing for peaceful surroundings. From the lake, you can catch the pinks, peaches and grays of sunrise and sunset, as well as the faint smell of smoke rising from the campfires in nearby Lewis Lake campground. This is a popular brown trout and lake trout fishery with a smattering of brook trout and cutthroat. The lake is 3,000 acres big.

Shoshone Lake

Accessed only by trail or by a 4-mile channel from Lewis Lake, Shoshone Lake is still popular with canoeists, kayakers, and float tubers. From the launch site near the Lewis Lake campground, you'll have to paddle about 4 miles just to get to the mouth of the Lewis channel. The upstream climb from Lewis to Shoshone ends with a swift shallow stretch that requires getting out and pulling your craft the rest of the way. A few folks gain access by paddling up the Lewis Channel. If you want to relish your arduous journey to Yellowstone's second-largest lake, reserve ahead of time one of the 26 campsites on the lake's shores.

Grand Teton National Park

No real whitewater exists within the Park, but plenty of scenic paddling awaits. Canoes and kayaks are quiet craft and may allow you to see wildlife that might otherwise startle away before you could see it. The park's waterways also allow you to leave busy roads and experience a bit of Teton backcountry without a pack on your back.

Park permits are required to float lakes and rivers in Grand Teton Park. You can buy them at Moose or Colter Bay visitors centers. A one-week non-motorized permit costs about $5.

Snake River in Grand Teton Park

The Snake River slides out of Jackson Lake Dam, then meanders and braids its way for 25.5 miles of Class I-II before reaching Moose at the southern end of Grand Teton National Park. (Two floatable sections of the Snake are located above Jackson Lake as well, but they're less popular. One reason is that the lower run necessitates a slow paddle on Jackson Lake to the takeout at Lizard Creek.)

The upper Snake is a river well-suited to canoes, but it's also floated by kayakers, rafts and drift boats. The first section, about 4.5 miles, is appropriate for beginners: Parts are almost currentless and have few obstacles. Included in this section is a fine wildlife viewing area, the lakelike Oxbow. The takeout for

this upper run is called Pacific Creek. The next section runs from Pacific Creek to Deadman's Bar, about 11 miles. Chances of seeing wildlife are excellent here, since the river parts ways with U.S. Highway 26/89/189. Snags and braided channels are common. Neither this section nor the third, from Deadman's Bar to the Moose Visitors Center, are recommended for beginners. They look easy, but visitors get in trouble on them every year. The 10-mile lower stretch has more current and more braiding, snags and log jams than the upper two. Statistically, this part is the most dangerous. Before you float, be sure to ask the rangers about which channels to stay in and any new obstacles that may have snarled themselves into place.

If you plan to take out at Deadman's, Schwabacher or Moose, take a minute to familiarize yourself with conditions at the takeout before you put in. Deadman's, for instance, is unobtrusive and easily missed; the Moose takeout has surprisingly fast current some times of year. Before launching, read the bulletin board at your put-in for latest information about water conditions. No motorized craft are allowed on this river within the park.

Jackson Lake

Most paddlers will hug the shores of this 31-square-mile lake out of concern for frequent gusty winds that can kick up intimidating waves. Access to the lake is good, so you have many options for paddling trips. One popular trip begins at the Spalding Bay access and takes you to Moran Bay, on the secluded, unroaded side of the lake. Hikers like to paddle across the northern arm of the lake from Lizard Creek Campground to reach backcountry trails not easily reached from a road. Paddling this lake is unlikely to feel like a wilderness experience. Powerboats are thick on Jackson Lake on sunny weekend days in summer, and water-skiing, personal watercraft, sailboats and windsurfers are allowed nowhere else in Grand Teton Park.

Jenny Lake

This lake, only 2 square miles in size, would seem large if it weren't dwarfed by the watery sprawl of Jackson Lake. Jenny Lake allows motorized traffic, but motors must be less than 7.5 horsepower. No personal watercraft, sailboats and windsurfers are allowed. Besides Jenny and Jackson lakes, the only other park lake that allows motors is Phelps (not described here) near the southern park boundary.

The best access point is at the lake's East End boat dock at South Jenny Lake. Since Jenny Lake is completely ringed by trail, your canoe will take you nowhere that hikers aren't. However, your destination can be the West End boat dock if you'd rather paddle over to Hidden Falls than take the ferry or walk around. (Read about Hidden Falls in our Hiking and Backpacking chapter.) You may find, though, that the most pleasant boat trip to take on Jenny Lake is out to the middle, where you can relax and enjoy the sight of the Tetons reaching more than a vertical mile above the mirrored surface on which you float. Mountain lakes are often perfectly still in early morning, so that's when we'd recommend a trip, with camera, to the middle of Jenny Lake.

Leigh and String Lakes

Motorized craft are prohibited on these two lakes. In fact, Leigh Lake isn't even reachable by road. Visitors reach Leigh Lake on foot, or by dropping a canoe or kayak into shallow String Lake at either of two parking areas on the lake's southeast shore. Paddlers head up the lake until reaching a boulder-clogged inlet. A short portage on a well-maintained trail leads to the much larger Leigh Lake. One of the more popular canoe trips on Leigh Lake takes you from the put-in and past two fine backcountry campsites — if unoccupied, stop and enjoy the beach — to the base of Mount Moran, a trip of about 2.5 miles one way. Climbers who wish to scale Moran generally canoe, although a foot trail leads to the mountain's base as well. Unlike placid String Lake, Leigh is deep and large enough to kick up respectable waves. Many canoeists choose to stay close to shore, especially when the wind's up.

Jackson Hole

Snake River in Lower Jackson Hole and Below

As the Snake River leaves Grand Teton Park and meanders toward Wilson, Wyoming, then south down the wide valley floor, it grows gradually deeper and less braided. Eddies can be powerful, but for the most part, the river is forgiving with regular waves, plenty of flat but generally fast-moving stretches and infrequent obstacles. This part of the Snake River is rated Class II.

From Moose to South Park Bridge, the river is controlled by dikes on both sides to prevent erosion. Most of the houses are concentrated in the 14-mile section between Moose and Wilson. Beyond Wilson Bridge the river moves through relatively undeveloped land for 13 miles to the next take-out point, South Park Bridge. Between South Park Bridge and the local whitewater run, called Alpine Canyon (see the next section), are three possible take-outs: Astoria Hot Springs, East Table and West Table. The total distance between South Park and East Table is 18 miles. West Table is about a mile downstream of East Table.

Local whitewater paddling schools use the area between Wilson and South Park Bridge for beginner kayak instruction because there are plenty of manageable river features to play in and learn from. Jackson's Pole Peddle Paddle relay uses the South Park to Astoria section for its boating leg. Canoes, kayaks, dories and rafts all run the Snake in Jackson Hole. These stretches also see a lot of fishing traffic, so in season be prepared to share the river with the hook and line folks.

Snake River in Alpine Canyon

This 8-mile, Class III section is the local whitewater playground. Local outfitters float raftloads of guests down it; thousands of private floaters ply it. Jackson, Wyoming, residents stop by after work for a couple hours of hole riding and wave surfing. This is no secluded wilderness float — it's more like a whitewater highway.

The put-in is called West Table, and the take out is Sheep Gulch. Because of heavy waves in rapids like Lunch Counter and Big Kahuna, the most common craft here are kayaks, whitewater canoes and rafts. At higher spring flows, some rapids become Class IV; intermediate floaters should think twice before trying this section when the water is running more than about 13,000 cubic feet per second.

Hoback River

The 12-mile run between Granite Creek put-in and the Hoback Junction takeout is a little sister to Alpine Canyon (see the previous section). The river is narrower and shallower. With the exception of log jams on some outside corners and underneath bridges, rapids are straightforward Class II and small Class III, with some rock dodging. You can shorten or lengthen your trip, since lower put-in points exist, as well as a second, lower takeout at Astoria Hot Springs on the Snake. This section is most popular with kayakers and whitewater canoeists. At higher spring flows, the river becomes solid Class III, and the log-jam obstacles more significant.

Gros Ventre River

The narrow Gros Ventre drops steeply through sharp-edged boulders for 2 miles of technical, continuous Class III and IV. Then the gradient levels and the next 2 miles are fast-moving Class II. On the lower section, shallow boulder gardens necessitate more maneuvering than you might generally associate with Class II. Put-in for the upper section is just below the natural dam at Lower Slide Lake off the Gros Ventre River Road. Takeout is 2 miles downstream at a turnout at the National Park boundary. This is also the put-in for the lower section. The next takeout is at the town of Kelly.

This river is recommended for skilled paddlers only, particularly the upper section and most particularly at high water when the few eddies disappear and turn this run into one long stomping ride. Rafters don't find enough maneuvering room here — this is a kayakers' river.

Eastern Idaho

Ashton, Idaho, Area

Fall River

Depending on which map, sign or resident you believe, this river is called Falls River or Fall River. Either way, it's home to a fun class III or III/IV whitewater run and a longer, fast-moving scenic float upstream of the whitewater section. A recently completed private diversion project pulls enough water from the 6-mile lower run to make it unfloatable most of the year, so catch this one during spring runoff. The upper run, called the Cave Falls run, is rated Class III but is mostly without defined whitewater. Its river bed is wide and gravelly, so even its 44-foot-per-mile gradient doesn't kick up a lot of waves. It does require several portages during its 16-mile length, however; it also holds a lot of wood. Put-in for the Cave Falls run is at Cave Falls Campground just south of Yellowstone Park's only unroaded entrance. Take-out is at a C.C.C. bridge on 4525 E. near Ashton. This is also the put-in for the lower run. Takeout for the lower run is at the Kirkham Bridge spanning the river.

Rafts, dories, kayaks and whitewater canoes float the lower section. The upper run is best suited to kayaks because of the shallow sections, a few tight moves and the multiple portages. It's possible, especially on a weekday, that you'll have these runs to yourself.

Island Park, Idaho

Henry's Fork, Coffee Pot Run

Drift-boat anglers go to great lengths to get their oars into many sections of this blue-ribbon fishery, but if you want fun whitewater and convenient logistics, try Coffee Pot. This 6-mile run is the only Class III water on the Henry's Fork without difficult portages or put-ins. Most of this stretch is fast, shallow Class I and II water dropping between 13 and nearly 40 feet per mile over gravel bottom. Much of the gradient comes from the occasional big waterfalls. The Coffee Pot stretch, however, includes about 1.5 miles of fun pool-drop Class III. Watch for logs. Most of the run is flat, but the scenery, the fishing and Coffee Pot Rapids make up for that.

Put in at Mack's Inn, where you can also get supplies or a meal. Take-out is at McCrea Bridge, a stone's throw from Island Park Reservoir on the McCrea Road. Kayaks, canoes, drift boats and rafts all float this stretch, although not in anywhere near the numbers you'll see on, say, the Upper Snake.

Henry's Fork, Big Springs National Water Trail

It's the prettiest Class I we've ever floated. Splash-full of waterfowl, trout and landlocked Kokanee salmon, its water so clear you can imagine you're suspended on shimmering air, this 4-mile run is a scenic floater's dream. It's also heavily used in summer, to the point that concerns have been raised about damage to the local fishery. If crowds don't discourage you, turn to our Close-up on the Big Springs National Water Trail in this chapter. There's also a description of this float in the Attractions chapter.

Island Park Reservoir and Henry's Lake

These two large reservoirs — Henry's Lake is actually a natural lake substantially enlarged by a dam at its outlet — are not generally paddled by non-motorized craft, mostly because of their size. Fishermen in motorized craft tend to gravitate toward the superb fishing in Henry's Lake; powerboating, sailing and personal-watercraft enthusiasts generally head to Island Park Reservoir. If you do choose to canoe or kayak on Henry's Lake, be aware that its reputation for sudden winds and high waves is earned on a regular basis. Both reservoirs are also described in the motorized boating section later in this chapter.

Teton Valley, Idaho

Bitch Creek, Canyon Run

This 12-mile-long experts-only run seems a magical thing the first time you see it: a dramatic basalt canyon tucked beneath the rolling potato fields of Teton Valley. The whitewater is Class IV and has two Class V drops. Log jams and blind corners are frequent. The put-in is at the Idaho Highway 32 bridge over Bitch Creek. Take-out is on the Teton River. Bitch Creek drops a steep 70 feet per mile. Below the confluence with the Teton, the canyon walls fall away a bit and the whitewater action slows. Get the complicated directions to put-in and take-out while you're soliciting more information about this run (see the resource phone numbers in this chapter). If you don't like to share your whitewater with lots of wood, don't consider floating Bitch Creek. This is a kayakers' run.

Southwestern Montana

Hebgen Lake

About 15 miles long and surrounded primarily by Forest Service land north of West Yellowstone, Hebgen Lake is boated mostly by anglers, but you'll find folks playing with just about every kind of water toy on this 13-mile long lake. Exploring the shores of the lake by canoe or kayak, especially in the more protected Madison and Grayling arms, can lead you to wildlife that you might otherwise miss. In addition to waterfowl of all kinds, you're apt to see deer, elk moose, bears, and some of the smaller critters like coyotes, raccoons or weasels. The lake, a living pantry for land-loving wildlife, is also their drinking fountain. Animals like to tank up on water mornings and evenings. And lake waters are generally calmer at these times. Like other big lakes in the Greater Yellowstone, the wind can quickly turn Hebgen into a dangerous sea of whitecaps.

Hyalite Reservoir

About 15 miles south of Bozeman and about a mile long, Hyalite Reservoir is the center of recreation for Bozemanites. A no-wake regulation means motorboaters must putt-putt on this lake, so mostly anglers boat here. But there's also some canoeing, kayaking and float tubing. A couple campgrounds are scattered about the lake shore. You'll find a boat ramp at the Hood Creek Campground and an infor-

Rafters go through rapids on the Middle Fork of the Salmon River.

Photo: Rocky Barker

mal launch site near the Blackmore trailhead. Bring your own gas.

Drop into almost any specialized sporting goods store in Bozeman, Montana, and the clerks there will likely tell you that the main reason they live in this town is because it's location is central to an unlimited field of recreational opportunities. Watersports, especially river rafting, kayaking and canoeing rank high on their list of fun things to do. From Bozeman, they have easy access to the Madison, Gallatin and Yellowstone Rivers. For those who windsurf, Ennis, Dailey and Hebgen lakes are just a short drive away.

You'll find easy access to southwestern Montana's rivers and lakes. And a long list of outfitters who will treat you to thrills if you aren't into paddling your own vessel. If you're visiting and need to rent a boat and some gear, you'll also find plenty of places to meet your needs.

For stream flow on the Jefferson, Madison, Yellowstone and Gallatin rivers call the U.S. Geological Survey in Helena, Montana, at (406) 441-1319. For readings on the Boulder, Stillwater and Clarks Fork of the Yellowstone rivers call (406) 652-1916.

Gallatin River

Pouring out of Gallatin Lake in Yellowstone National Park, the Gallatin River winds about 100 miles and drops 3,000 feet in elevation before joining the Madison and Missouri rivers at the Missouri River Headwaters State Park east of Three Forks, Montana. Park regulations prohibit floating within the Park, which covers the first 26 miles of this river. Technically, you can begin floating the Gallatin as soon as it leaves the Park, but most people who want to paddle this 20-mile, Class I stretch, begin a few miles downstream at the Taylor Creek Access. (During low water, it's best to put in downstream at the Red Cliff Campground or the West Fork.)

Local river outfitters frequent a 13-mile stretch of Class III and IV that begins a few miles downstream from Big Sky at Deer Creek and ends at Squaw Creek. Over the next 23 miles, you'll face eight irrigation diversion dams, fences and logjams, all of which require a heads-up and some of which require portages. You'll encounter easier Class I and II water without obstacles on the last 19 miles of the Gallatin, beginning at the Central Park Access near the Interstate 90 bridge.

The river follows the road all the way (U.S. Highway 191 mostly), but wildlife is nevertheless abundant, and along the way you'll find several campgrounds and 18 public accesses, five of which are on the whitewater stretch in the canyon. Because of the number of diversions and downfalls on the Gallatin, fishing from a vessel is prohibited in all but the bottom 12 miles of the river. And the speed limit is 10 mph on the river.

Yellowstone River

The Yellowstone River spills off the Yellowstone Plateau into Montana's Paradise Valley before winding its way east across the prairies of Montana. Since boating Yellowstone Park rivers is prohibited, you won't be able to put in until Gardiner, Montana, where a 16-mile stretch of mostly Class III whitewater begins and runs through Yankee Jim Canyon. (There's a 5-mile piece of flatwater in the middle.) Easily handled by experienced rafters, kayakers and whitewater canoeists, this stretch from Queen of the Waters access to Carbella is frequented by river outfitters. Six accesses are available along this piece of the Yellowstone.

Once you hit Carbella, you may want to trade your paddle for a fly rod. The water slows down (good water for practiced beginners) and turns into blue-ribbon fishing for cutthroat, browns and rainbow. Suitable for kayaks, rafts, dories and canoes, this 48-mile section of peaceful river runs through the bottomlands of the Paradise Valley. Even though the river mostly follows U.S. Highway 89, you can expect to see a variety of wildlife and waterfowl since there are few homes along the river. Local paddlers warn about a treacherous bridge just before Livingston. Because the river hits it at an angle, paddlers can get sucked into the bridge supports. Navigating this stretch is for only accomplished paddlers.

Madison River

Interrupted by three reservoirs totalling 23 miles (Hebgen, Quake and Ennis lakes are featured in another section of this chapter), the Madison River winds through narrow canyons, across wide open meadows, along U.S. Highway 287 and through a remote section of the Lee Metcalf Wilderness before dumping into the Jefferson River and then the Missouri.

The wilderness section, just below Madison Dam, is called Bear Trap Canyon. This very popular 9-mile run of Class IV rapids can be accessed via the Ennis Lake Road, which runs east of the reservoir then into a narrow rocky canyon to the Madison Dam. Water discharges from the dam vary hugely from 900 to 10,000 cfs. If you're new to the river (and even if you aren't) check the flow gauge up from the power plant before putting in. Portaging around the rapids is possible, but check with local experts to find out which side is best for each one. Unless you are highly skilled with a good raft or kayak, we recommend you float with a guide service. (Some folks tackle these rapids in whitewater canoes.) Some of the outfitters listed below run the Bear Trap.

The Madison River serves up 3.4 miles of raging Class V and VI whitewater that even the highly skilled steer clear of, and that's from the Quake Slide Dam to the Highway 87 Bridge. The Quake Dam was formed when a mountain slid into and blocked the Madison River during the 1959 earthquake. (See our Attractions chapter for more information on Quake Lake.) Below this treacherous water are 7 miles of Class II water.

Once you leave the faster water, prepare for 41 miles of world-class fishing from Madison Campground to Ennis. Along this stretch you'll see all kinds of watercraft from dories to rafts full of fishermen casting for browns and rainbows. The biggest fish live in the river's waters from the Varney Bridge to Ennis Lake. To avoid the lake, though, it's best to take out at the Ennis Campground just below the Highway 287 Bridge. Just below the Bear Trap Canyon is the Mont. Highway 84 access, popular as a takeout because of its proximity to the Norris Hot Springs. Below this access, the river lines out into 31 miles of calm water OK for practiced beginners to paddle. You'll find 24 accesses to the Madison River and numerous campgrounds along the river's length.

Ennis Lake

Reached by the Ennis Lake Road which heads east from U.S. Highway 287 north of Ennis, this man-made lake is surrounded mostly by private ranch lands. That means you'll have to look at a map carefully and plan your route, especially if you want to put in at Valley Garden access just north of Ennis. Some folks canoe or kayak the braided channels of the Madison River as it winds from this access down into the lake. You'll find a small public campground with a boat launch on the northwest shore that would be your best bet for taking out. The Lake Shore Cabins and Campground on the north shore also has a launch. Since this lake is heavily silted, it's shallow and warm. Cruising the undeveloped shoreline in a quiet canoe or kayak can pay high dividends when it comes to wildlife viewing.

Northwestern Wyoming

North Fork of the Shoshone River

The North Fork comes tumbling out of the Absaroka Wilderness east of Yellowstone Park where it rushes through the upper stretch from Pahaska Tepee 42 miles to the Buffalo Bill Reservoir. While some very experienced river runners raft or kayak the upper stretches, it's characterized by frequent downfalls and logjams coupled with unexpected elevation drops. Early in the year, the rapids are rated anywhere from Class III to Class V depending on the stretch. The most popular rafting segment is from the Wapiti Valley near the Rimrock Ranch to a take-out 12 miles downriver just above the Buffalo Bill Reservoir. During highwater, this run can be rated as high as Class IV, but it quickly drops with the water. By summer's end, it's pretty tame. Access to the river below the dam is difficult because of the narrow rocky canyon.

Shoshone River

A few very experienced kayakers put in at the Hayden Arch Bridge about a mile below the Buffalo Bill Dam, then take out 4 miles downstream at the Old Bronze Boot below the rodeo grounds. Saner rafters and professional outfitters use a combination of smaller whitewater that runs from the Old Bronze Boot (DeMaris Hot Springs) to a takeout just above Corbett's Crossing before the Powell Bridge. Just past the bridge, the river is blocked by an irrigation diversion. Wyoming River Trips has an exclusive on the put-in at DeMaris (members of the public can put in there as long as they haven't rented the raft). It runs either half or all of the 11 miles of a Class III stretch (it tames to I and II late in the summer). From the Corbett's Diversion Dam, the Shoshone flows

another 50 miles to Bighorn Lake east of Lovell where you'll find frequent diversion dams.

Clarks Fork of the Yellowstone

This river begins in the Absaroka-Beartooth Wilderness above Cooke City, Montana, and flows 65 miles into Wyoming through the Clarks Fork Canyon before curving back up into Montana. As the river enters the canyon, you'll encounter a 5-mile stretch of floatable whitewater used by some local rafters and kayakers. But at the end is a very dangerous stretch of Class V, so it's best not to tackle this run without a knowledgeable guide, lots of experience, plenty of nerve and a life-insurance policy for your family. The very rocky, bumpy Clarks Fork Canyon Road will take you to the put-in.

Red Canyon River Trips picks up the Clarks Fork as it leaves the canyon and offers a scenic 12-mile float for those more interested in watching wildlife and learning about history. Once you reach the Montana border, the Clarks Fork is riddled with diversion dams that either cross a good portion of the river or block it entirely.

For stream flow on the Jefferson, Madison, Yellowstone and Gallatin rivers call the U.S. Geological Survey in Helena, Montana, at (406) 441-1319. For readings on the Boulder, Stillwater and Clarks Fork of the Yellowstone rivers call (406) 652-1916.

River Outfitters

Boating with an outfitter offers many advantages. The outfitter provides most of the gear — usually you show up with the clothes you'll wear, plus sunscreen, sunglasses and perhaps a camera. Outfitters also supply the food, transportation and local expertise. You can generally count on boats and other gear to be reliable and the guides trained and familiar with the water they pilot you down. Many companies pride themselves on their guides' knowledge of local history, flora and fauna.

Grand Teton National Park

Float trips in the park are on the Snake River. Expect most scenic tours to take two to four hours and cost in the neighborhood of

Big Springs National Water Trail

Imagine water so clear it slips over rocks like liquid light. Imagine an underwater forest of flowing green water plants, laced with lanes of clean gravel. Picture trout as long as your arm, so close you can watch their eyes swivel. Hear the sandhill crane's distant bellow, like seized-up machinery, then another that picks up the cry from just over there. You're on the Big Springs National Water Trail, a 5-mile long section of the Henry's Fork that begins a mile after the river spills from the ground and ends at Mack's Inn and Henry's Fork Landing below the point where the Henry's Fork swallows the slightly cloudy water of the Henry's Lake Outlet.

It's a river, but trail-like in that you can't get lost and the going is easy. The river runs shallow and gentle down an unbraided channel which requires no route-finding skills. You need only your binoculars, camera, warm clothes, fishing gear and snacks. Henry's Fork Landing and Mack's Inn provide the rest: boat, oars or paddles, life jackets and a ride to the put-in. Either establishment will sell you snacks, ice and beverages for the trip, and allow you to park in their lot. Crafts available for rent include canoes, rowboats, flat-bottom skiffs and rubber rafts (see more about these businesses at the end of this Close-up).

You're likely to see bald eagles, ospreys and kingfishers. Waterfowl of all descriptions paddle into startled flight as you sweep slowly around the river bends. You may see elk or moose. Come in the fall and, after you pass the Henry's Lake outlet, watch for the red-bodied, slope-faced kokanee salmon, a landlocked fish that, unlike his cousins the Chinook and sockeye, doesn't need to reach the ocean to complete his life cycle. Water flows vary little during the year, since the main source of the flow above Henry's Lake is Big Springs itself. That's why the water is so ethereally clear, too: Little or no stream sediment is present. It's also why the trout are so large. The steady year-round

— continued on next page

Photo: Jo Deurbrouck

A couple enjoys a quiet September trip on the clear
waters of the Big Springs National Water Trail.

water temperature is chilly enough to hold lots of dissolved oxygen and warm enough to support lots of food sources for trout. Less sediment means that the Henry's Fork provides the clean gravel beds that trout and salmon need to spawn in. Despite the enticing size of the fish, please don't wet a line until you pass Henry's Lake Outlet (you'll know because the water will become less clear and because you'll see a sign). In order to protect the fishery, fishing is not permitted above the outlet.

Expect to take about four hours if you stop much to fish or explore, or even if you simply float the current. If you row or paddle downstream and don't plan to stop, the trip will take about two hours. Depending on the craft you choose, expect to pay between $25 and $35 for two people, including shuttle costs. If you own a craft and equipment appropriate to a cold, shallow river with slow-to-moderate current, you can just head for the put-in off Big Springs Road (watch for the sign on your left about 5 miles off U.S. Highway 20). Both Mack's Inn and Henry's Fork Landing offer their unguided boat trips from as soon as the Big Springs Road is clear of snow, usually May, until October. Summer days on the Big Springs National Water Trail can be crowded, but even as early as September you can expect to have the whole glorious thing to yourself.

Check with Henry's Fork Landing, 4238 U.S. Highway 20; Mack's Inn at Island Park, Idaho, 558-7672; or Mack's Inn, U.S. Highway 20, Mack's Inn at Island Park, Idaho, 558-7272. Reservations are a good idea but often not necessary.

$35 for one adult. Extras such as Dutch-oven dinners or private boats, of course, cost more. Be sure you ask what section or sections the outfitter floats. Read our previous descriptions of the three sections of the Snake below Jackson Lake. All but one of the outfitters listed here float one or more of these. Flagg Ranch floats the smaller, rockier Snake River above Jackson Lake.

Triangle X-Osprey Float Trips
U.S. Hwy. 89 in Grand Teton Park, Wyo.
• (307) 733-5500, (307) 733-6455

The Turner brothers, who also run a guest ranch called Triangle X Ranch, offer sunrise, afternoon and evening scenic floats on the Snake in Grand Teton Park. Some trips travel the 10 miles between Deadman's Bar and Moose, but trips as short as 5 miles are possible, as are extra-long 20-mile floats. All trips are on Class I or II water. You can also arrange a dinner float.

Barker-Ewing Scenic Tours
Moose in Grand Teton Park, Wyo.
• (307) 733-1800

A real raft-guiding old-timer, this company has been providing scenic raft tours in the park since 1963. Trips run from Deadman's Bar to Moose, a 10-mile float on Class II wa-

ter. Some trips include a Dutch-oven cookout.

Flagg Ranch Float Trips
John D. Rockefeller Jr. Memorial Pky., Wyo. • (307) 543-2861

Flagg Ranch offers the only commercial trips on the upper Snake above Jackson Lake. The river is smaller and less traveled here. Both Class III whitewater and Class I and II scenic trips are available.

Signal Mountain Lodge
Teton Park Rd., Grand Teton Park, Wyo.
• (307) 543-2831

Signal Mountain Lodge, perched on the shore of Jackson Lake, offers scenic trips on the Snake below Jackson Lake Dam. You can also arrange for a guided fishing boat on 425-foot-deep Jackson Lake.

Grand Teton Lodge Company at Colter Bay Village and Jackson Lake Lodge
U.S. Hwy. 89, Grand Teton Park, Wyo.
• (307) 543-2811

Some Snake River float trips include picnic lunches or dinners at Deadman's Bar. Several morning and afternoon departures from both Colter Bay and Jackson Lake Lodge are scheduled daily for the 10-mile scenic float. Transportation to the put-in is provided. Colter Bay also runs regularly scheduled scenic and fishing cruises on Jackson Lake. Their most popular cruise includes breakfast or dinner on Elk Island.

Jackson Hole

Commercial outfitters in Jackson Hole generally float a Class III stretch of the Snake called Alpine Canyon and/or a scenic Class I and II run just above Alpine Canyon. Each run is about 8 miles long. Outfitters charge between $25 and $35 per person for a run down one of these sections. Breakfast and dinner floats will, of course, cost more. Most outfitters will help you rent cold-water gear, primarily wetsuits and booties, if you ask for them. If you get cold easily or it's June and the water's high, be sure to inquire about protective clothing. Also inquire about the type of craft available and how many it will hold. Paddle rafts allow you to participate under the direction of a guide, oar rafts let you sit back and be taken down the river, and inflatable kayaks put you in the driver's seat with nobody to blame for your good time but you. Rafts generally hold between eight and 15 people. Smaller rafts will make the wave action more fun. Larger craft are stable and less likely to flip or toss people into the water.

Barker-Ewing Jackson Hole River Trips
45 W. Broadway, Jackson, Wyo.
• **(307) 733-1000, (800) 448-4202**
Paddle boats and oar boats are both available on Barker-Ewing's trips down Alpine Canyon. Other trips offered by this company include scenic floats through the Snake River's South Park area and scenic and whitewater combos that run 16 miles of the Snake, encompassing the 8-mile Alpine Canyon and the scenic Class II section above it.

Breakfast and overnight trips can be arranged as well.

Dave Hansen Whitewater
455 N. Cache, Jackson, Wyo.
• **(307) 733-6295**
Alpine Canyon runs and scenic floats on the pretty stretch above the whitewater run are both popular. Sometimes the company runs a combined photo and whitewater trip on the entire 16 miles. At the end of the scenic run, guides pull the oar frames out of their crafts, turning their boats into whitewater paddle rafts. You can choose to ride in 12- to 14-person rafts or the smaller, more exciting eight-person craft.

Lone Eagle Whitewater
U.S. Hwy. 89/191, near Hoback Junction, Wyo. • **(307) 733-1090, (800) 321-3800**
Lone Eagle runs Alpine Canyon. Trips are paired with a hot breakfast, lunch or dinner cooked up at the company's outdoor kitchen and dining area on the Hoback River. The resort's hot tubs are waiting after your ride. Lone Eagle promises no more than eight to 10 guests per raft on the Alpine Canyon section. Scenic floats are also available.

Mad River Boat Trips
1255 S. U.S. Hwy. 89, Jackson, Wyo.
• **(307) 733-6203**
Special touches here include guaranteed self-bailing rafts (so you don't have to clear water out of your raft with a bucket), barbecue cookout trips that cap off your whitewater adventure with a hearty meal, and a stop at Mad River's River Runners Museum, a small collection of interpretive material designed to show you the roots of rafting in this region.

Charlie Sands River Trips
110 W. Broadway and 1450 S. U.S. Hwy. 89, Jackson, Wyo. • **(307) 733-4410, (800) 358-8184**
This company's been in business since 1967, plying Class III Alpine Canyon. Pri-

vate groups can arrange breakfast trips and cookout trips. Also by special arrangement, a group can take an overnight excursion with camping at Pine Bar in the Bridger-Teton National Forest. Sixteen-mile combined scenic and whitewater floats are available as well.

Jackson Hole Whitewater
650 W. Broadway, Jackson, Wyo.
• (307) 733-1007, (800) 648-2602

Enjoy breakfast or a steak/trout dinner in conjunction with your whitewater adventure in Alpine Canyon.

Lewis & Clark Expeditions
335 N. Cache, Jackson, Wyo.
• (307) 733-4022, (800) 824-5375

Lewis & Clark is a smaller company running Alpine Canyon and the 12-mile South Park scenic stretch of the Snake River. Guides are trained by a Forest Service naturalist. The company says it averages fewer people in its rafts than other companies: 11 in standard-size rafts and six in small rafts. Some trips are capped with a steak dinner at a riverside campsite.

Southwestern Montana

Yellowstone Raft Company
406 Scott St., Gardiner, Mont.
• (406) 848-7777, (800) 858-7781
Big Sky, Mont. • (406) 995-4613,
(800) 348-4376

In business since 1978, Yellowstone Raft Company offers half-day and full-day trips on the Yellowstone and Gallatin rivers and a full-day raft trip through the Bear Trap Canyon Wilderness on the Madison. They also offer kayak instruction for a couple of hours or a full day. Ask about their guided fishing trips.

Wild West Rafting
Yellowstone Outpost Mini Mall
(Headwaters Angler), U.S. Hwy. 89,
Gardiner, Mont. • (406) 848-7110,
(800) 565-7110

H.A. Moore, owner of Rendezvous Outfitters charges $33 for a run through the whitewater near Gardiner. He runs morning and afternoon trips as well as a few in the evenings.

Geyser Whitewater Expeditions
47200 Gallatin Rd., Gallatin Gateway,
Mont. • (406) 995-4989, (800) 914-9031

Located on U.S. Highway 191 just south of the Big Sky turnoff, Geyser Whitewater Expeditions runs half- and full-day floats on the upper and lower sections of the Gallatin River. In addition, Geyser offers half-day inflatable-kayak trips and a rafting and horseback-riding combo that includes some of each.

Adventures Big Sky
U.S. Hwy. 191 at the Big Sky Resort
entrance, Big Sky, Mont.
• (406) 995-2324

Whitewater or flatwater? Take your pick because Adventures Big Sky offers both on the Gallatin River. Ride in a paddle boat, an inflatable kayak or a raft with a frame and oars. Barbara and Patrick Dillon offer half- and full-day trips. In 1997, a half-day on the river cost $39 for adults (all gear is included), and $71 for a full day (lunch and gear are included in the price). A half day in an inflatable kayak cost $44. (You must be at least 15 years old to make the kayak trip.)

Montana Whitewater
Bozeman, Mont. • (406) 763-4465,
(800) 799-4465

Montana Whitewater offers a menu of options including half- and full-day whitewater and

---

INSIDERS' TIP

Altitude sickness is a serious condition, but feeling short of breath does not mean you are suffering from altitude sickness. Most cases of altitude sickness occur above 10,000 feet. Common symptoms are nausea, vomiting and severe headache. The treatment is simple and effective: Head for lower elevations right now.

scenic floats on the upper and lower Gallatin as well as dinner and breakfast floats. They also have a "Paddle and Saddle" package with a half-day of riding followed by a half-day float on the Gallatin. In addition they offer half- and full-day floats on the Yellowstone.

Beartooth Whitewater
P.O. Box 781, Red Lodge, MT 59068
• (406) 446-3142, (800) 799-3142

Beartooth offers half- and full-day trips on a stretch of water that includes three rivers: the Rosebud, Stillwater and Yellowstone. The company conducts four regularly scheduled half-day trips each summer's day. It also has a three-hour trip on the Stillwater with one-person rafts.

Montana River Expeditions (Canoe Montana)
26 Cedar Bluffs Rd., Livingston, Mont.
• (406) 222-5837, (800) 500 4538

Russell Young promises guests a "soft adventure" paddling canoes or touring kayaks (a special kind of kayak that's hard to roll) on quiet river waters in Greater Yellowstone. Instead of hooking you up to your adrenaline, Young aims to connect you to the river so it soothes your hurried soul. Young offers trips at dawn, sunset, by moonlight and overnight on a variety of rivers. He charges $60 for a half-day and about $175 per day for overnight trips depending on group size and destination.

Northwestern Wyoming

Wyoming River Trips
233 Yellowstone Hwy., Cody, Wyo.
• (307) 587-6661, (800) 586-6661

Wyoming River Trips offers five different raft and kayak trips in the Cody area. Four of them, including an inflatable-kayak trip, are on the Shoshone River. A fifth is on the North Fork of the Shoshone. Trip lengths range from 1½ hours to a half-day. Wyoming River Trips operates out of two locations: The Holiday Inn complex on Sheridan

Photo: Robert Bower/Post Register

This kayaker negotiates some rapids on the Snake River.

Avenue and on the Yellowstone Highway west of Cody. They pride themselves on their experienced guides.

Red Canyon River Trips
1374 Sheridan Ave., Cody, Wyo.
• (307) 587-6988, (800) 293-0148

Red Canyon River Trips offers four different trips, including two-hour rafting and "Duckie" trips on the Shoshone River. (A Duckie is an inflatable kayak.) They also run an 11-mile trip on the North Fork of the Shoshone as well as a 12-mile trip on the Clark's Fork of the Yellowstone.

River Runners
1491 Sheridan Ave., Cody, Wyo.
• (307) 527-7238

River Runners operates seven days a week during the summer months from a blue and white building on Cody's main street. The company offers trips on both the North Fork and the Shoshone rivers. Half-day trips cost $45 (includes lunch); 1½-hour trips cost $18 for adults, and three-hour trips cost $24.

INSIDERS' TIP

Combine high elevation with the water's reflection and you've got a prescription for sunburn. Be sure to take extra sunscreen along.

Paddling Schools

Jackson Hole

Rendezvous River Sports/ Jackson Hole Kayak School

1035 W. Broadway, Jackson, Wyo.
• (307) 733-2471

Not only can you get yourself outfitted for whitewater fun here — you can learn what to do with all that gear. Jackson Hole Kayak School offers courses taught by American Canoe Association (ACA) certified instructors. They range from roll classes for non-boaters to private instruction to help you improve upon your current skill level, whatever that may be. You can also go kayak touring in Yellowstone National Park with Jackson Hole Kayak School guides. Tours last from three to five days and can accommodate beginners as well as experienced sea kayakers. All necessary gear can be rented from the shop.

Teton Aquatic Supply/Snake River Kayak and Canoe School

155 W. Gill, Jackson, Wyo.
• (307) 733-3127, (800) 529-2501

What makes this place really cool is the indoor training pool, used by both scuba and paddling schools. The 45,000 gallon pool is 12 feet deep. It's equipped with whirlpool jets to simulate a 4 mph current. The company conducts kayak roll clinics here; more advanced boating classes begin in the training pool and then move out onto the Snake River or a tributary.

The staff offers instruction for a variety of craft: hard-shell kayaks, inflatable kayaks, sea kayaks, canoes, oar and paddle rafts, and dories. Teton Aquatic Supply also conducts three-day guided sea kayak tours on Yellowstone Lake. The company supplies all meals, transportation and gear. Guides are also instructors who can fine-tune your paddling style as well as help you stay safe.

Paddle and Oar Craft Rentals

Grand Teton National Park

Adventure Sports

Dornan's at Moose, Grand Teton National Park, Wyo. • (307) 733-3307

These folks rent stable canoes and kayaks for beginner boaters, anglers and families. These boats are intended for lake floating only, not for the Snake or any other area river. The full-day rate for a canoe is around $30. Adventure Sports is open seven days a week in summer, but hours can vary in spring and fall. In winter the shop is closed.

Grand Teton Lodge Company at Colter Bay Village

U.S. Hwy. 89, Grand Teton Park, Wyo.
• (307) 543-2811

Rent an aluminum canoe from Colter Bay Marina for $8 per hour. Reserve your craft in advance. Colter Bay also rents 9.9-horsepower motorboats.

Signal Mountain Lodge

Teton Park Rd., Grand Teton Park, Wyo.
• (307) 543-2831

Signal Mountain Lodge, perched on the shore of Jackson Lake, rents canoes and oar boats for $8 per hour; fishing skiffs with outboard motors are available as well. Reservations are suggested.

Teton Aquatic Supply/Snake River Kayak and Canoe School

155 W. Gill, Jackson, Wyo.
• (307) 733-3127, (800) 529-2501

Besides operating a paddling school and watersports store, these folks rent canoes, inflatable kayaks, paddle and oar rafts and sea kayaks. Rafts made by Achilles, Sotar and

---

INSIDERS' TIP

Army and Navy Economy Store in Bozeman rents inner tubes for $3 per day. They're popular with locals and rent out fast on hot days. See their entry in this chapter.

Legacy rent for around $50 per day. You can rent a canoe by Sawyer, Dagger or Mohawk by the half-day or longer. The half-day rate is $20. Whitewater kayaks are by Wavesport and Perception.

Adventure Raft Rentals
650 W. Broadway, Jackson, Wyo.
• (307) 733-1418

These folks, conveniently located on your way to the put-in, rent Jet Ski personal watercraft as well as rafts, catarafts, canoes and more. The shop shares a building with Jackson Hole Whitewater, a river company offering trips on Class III Alpine Canyon in the Snake River.

Rent-A-Raft/Jackson Hole Outdoor Center
Lewis Landing, 10925 S. U.S. Hwy. 89, Hoback Junction

Rod Lewis has been in the river business for 26 years. Now from his riverside location he rents Achilles and Hyside rafts ranging from 7.5 to 18.5 feet long. A popular rental is the 11-foot Achilles, which costs $60 for one day. Lewis's staff can rent you a trailer or help you load your rented raft on top of your car. They can also shuttle you up the Hoback (you'll take out on the grassy bank at Lewis's place) or down the Snake. Other services here include inner-tube, sit-on-top and inflatable kayak rentals, kayaking lessons and rental rowing frames for fishing rafts.

Leisure Sports
1075 S. U.S. Hwy. 89, Jackson, Wyo.
• (307) 733-3040

This all-purpose rental shop has rafts and canoes, snowmobiles, trailers, autos and more. In summer rent Avons and Achilles rafts between 12 and 18 feet long. An 18-foot rental costs $90 per day. You can also rent Coleman canoes and inflatable kayaks. If you want to trailer your raft, these folks can rent you one. If your vehicle doesn't have a hitch, they can rent you a car that does.

Eastern Idaho

Idaho Falls, Idaho, Area

Canyon Whitewater Supply
450 S. Yellowstone Hwy., Idaho Falls, Idaho • (208) 522-3932

This shop sells and rents Aire rafts; Prijon, Perception and New Wave kayaks; and Old Town Canoes. A range of rafting and kayaking accessories are kept in stock as well.

Island Park, Idaho

Mack's Inn and Henry's Fork Landing
U.S. Hwy. 20 at Mack's Inn in Island Park, Idaho • (208) 558-7672 Mack's Inn, (208) 558-7272 Henry's Fork Landing

Rent rafts, canoes and skiffs to float placid Big Springs National Water Trail. You'll pay between $25 and $35 for boat, life jackets and a ride up to the put-in. Reservations are a good idea, but are not necessary. Mack's Inn and Henry's Fork Landing are across the Henry's Fork from each other at the junction of the Henry's Fork and U.S. Highway 20. If one can't take you, they'll call across the river to see if the other can.

Southwestern Montana

Northern Lights Trading Company
1716 W. Babcock, Bozeman, Mont.
• (406) 586-2225
Meadow Center, Big Sky, Mont.
• (406) 995-2220

In addition to camping, ice climbing and cross-country skiing gear, Northern Lights rents canoes, kayaks and rafts at both its Bozeman and Big Sky stores. Canoe rentals range from $30 to $40 per day depending on the model; touring kayaks cost $30 per day. You'll pay $75 to $150 per day for a whitewater

---

INSIDERS' TIP

All of our region has 911 service and helicopter-transport capability. In many areas, dialing 911 on your out-of-state cellular phone will still hook you into emergency personnel.

raft. Northern Lights also rents watersports accessories such as paddles, wetsuits, paddle jackets, dry bags and helmets.

Army and Navy Economy Store
539 E. Main, Bozeman, Mont.
• (406) 586-1919, (800) 822-0241

In 1997, Army and Navy rented 13-foot rafts for $40 per day, 14-foot rafts for $50, and 14-foot rafts with a rowing frame for $85. Paddles, life jackets and a foot pump come with the rafts.

Panda Sport Rentals
621 Bridger Dr., Bozeman, Mont.
• (406) 587-6280

Panda rents rafts for $25 to $75 per day depending on the style, and canoes for $25 a day.

Paradise Mercantile
U.S. Hwy. 89, Emigrant, Mont.
• (406) 333-4060

Right next door to the Emigrant General Store, the Mercantile rents Avon six-man rafts for $50 a day or $250 per week. These rafts come with paddles, life jackets and foot pumps. They aren't made for whitewater, but they're great for the flatwater stretches.

Powersports, Sailing and Windsurfing

Yellowstone National Park

Yellowstone Lake

Yellowstone Lake has two boat launches, one at Grant Village near the campground and another that's operated by Amfac at Bridge Bay Marina, (307) 242-3876. Most people, though, seem to opt for either riding with Amfac or renting one of their boats. Each summer Amfac hosts nearly 5,000 anglers on guided lake trips and another 15,000 who tour the lake on one of Amfac's hourlong scenic cruises. These cruises, which cost $7.50 for adults and $3.50 for children ages 2 to 11 in

1997, run five to seven times each day from the first week of June until the last week in September. Amfac's guided fishing trips cost $50 or $65 per hour depending on the size of the boat. Amfac also rents rowboats for $5.50 per hour, and outboards (with a 40-horsepower, electric-start motor) for $25 an hour.

There may have been a windsurfer or two on this lake, but it's a foolhardy pursuit at best in these icy waters. Sailing is more common. Because of the cold waters and unpredictable winds, motorized boaters are generally out sightseeing or fishing.

At Bridge Bay, you'll find 110 dock slips for rent. Rentals start at $9 per night for boats 16 feet and less. The marina sells fuel.

Windsurfing, waterskiing and personal watercraft are discouraged by the Park Service because of the lake's icy waters. It's so cold that even in summer, you could die of hypothermia in 20 minutes. High winds also frequently appear out of nowhere to stir up the waters.

Lewis Lake

Twelve miles from the south entrance, Lewis is the only lake besides Yellowstone that allows motorboats. At the southeast end is a campground and boat launch. At the opposite end is the mouth of the Lewis Channel, which leads from Shoshone Lake. This is a popular brown trout and lake trout fishery with a smattering of brook trout and cutthroat. The lake is 3,000 acres big. Cold waters keep waterskiers off these waters, which means that the motorboats you see on this lake will be full of anglers or sightseers. Occasional windsurfers lift their sails on Lewis Lake's waters, but dry suits are a must.

Grand Teton National Park

Jackson and Jenny Lakes

Jackson Lake has three marinas. All services, including buoy rentals, boat rentals, guided fishing excursions, gasoline and groceries, are available at both Signal Mountain, (307) 543-2831, and Colter Bay, (307) 543-2811. Leek's Marina, (307) 543-2494, offers some services. Jenny Lake has only one marina facility, which offers a ferry service and boat rentals through a company called Teton Boating, (307) 733-2703.

Motors larger than 7.5 horsepower are not allowed on Jenny Lake. For more on both lakes, read their descriptions in the "Rivers and Lakes" section in this chapter. Of the other lakes in Grand Teton Park, only Phelps allows motorized traffic. Only Jackson Lake allows sailboats, waterskiing and jet skis.

Jackson Hole

Lower Slide Lake

Lower Slide Lake formed in 1925 when one side of fractured, unstable Sheep Mountain tumbled into the Gros Ventre River. The natural reservoir is just outside Grand Teton Park. This means you avoid Park restrictions and tag requirements by powerboating here. The single boat ramp is at Atherton Creek (use is free), where you will also find camping, picnicking and restroom facilities. Be careful of the drowned trees still standing in many areas of the lake.

Eastern Idaho

Idaho Falls, Idaho, Area

Ririe Reservoir

Ririe, with water temperatures reaching into the 70s, hosts not only several species of trout, but also warm-water fish like perch and smallmouth bass. Ririe Reservoir is not regular in shape but rather reaches every which way up what were once stream-cut basalt canyons. For you, this means plenty of interesting nooks and crannies to explore and plenty of scenic corners to turn. Ririe consists of only 1,560 acres but seems much larger because from any one point, you can't see most of it.

Paved boat ramps are located at the dam, reached from Meadow Creek Road off Idaho Highway 26, and at Blacktail. Picnicking and camping facilities are available at both sites. Most of the land surrounding the reservoir is public land, so although you won't find other developed sites for recreation, plenty of op-

portunity exists. For more information, contact Idaho Fish and Game, 1515 E. Lincoln Road, Idaho Falls, (208) 525-7290.

Island Park, Idaho

Island Park Reservoir

Of the two large lakes in the area, 8,400-acre Island Park Reservoir is the powerboater's choice. Henry's Lake, draws more anglers; its often-rough, always-cold waters seem to discourage other forms of recreation.) Like Hebgen Lake to the north, Island Park Reservoir is home to both powerboating enthusiasts and anglers. Camping, picnicking and hiking are available along the heavily forested shores. Fishermen catch brook, cutthroat and rainbow trout, as well as coho and kokanee salmon. Boat ramps provide ready access for powerboaters and personal watercraft.

Contact the Island Park Area Chamber of Commerce, P.O. Box 83, Island Park, ID 83429, (208) 558-7755, for more information.

Henry's Lake

This reservoir measures about 4 miles wide by 5 miles long. At its narrowest, it's 2 miles across. Eight boat ramps provide access. Half charge a fee for launch or parking or both. Henry's Lake is as well-known for its sudden winds and high waves as it is for its lunker trout fishing, so keep an eye tipped skyward. Catch trophy cutthroat (about half are wild and half are stocked from nearby hatcheries), a cutthroat/rainbow hybrid called cutt-bow and brook trout.

Henry's Lake State Park offers camping, a boat launch and shower facilities; in summer the entrance gates to the Park often heads a line of trucks with fishing boats in tow and cars filled with would-be campers. Read more about Henry's Lake and Henry's Lake State Park in our Fishing and Hunting chapter and our Camping and RV Parks chapter.

Swan Valley, Idaho

Palisades Reservoir

Sixty miles east of Idaho Falls at the top of Swan Valley is 16,000-acre Palisades Reservoir, created by a dam across the South Fork of the Snake River. The shores of the reservoir are equipped with two paved boat ramps, Calamity and Blowout, and seven unofficial, unpaved access points. Stick to the paved ramps when the water is low or you may end up stuck in the mud. The area also offers seven camping facilities, plus parking and picnic areas and restrooms. U.S. Highway 26 runs along the upper shore of this long reservoir, providing easy access. Much of the lower shoreline is unroaded; access there is primarily by boat. Fishermen pull brown, lake, cutthroat and rainbow trout from these waters. Contact Palisades Ranger District at (208) 523-1412 for more.

Southwestern Montana

Hebgen Lake

About 15 miles long and mostly surrounded by Forest Service land north of West Yellowstone, Hebgen Lake is used for a bit of everything on Hebgen, including water-skiing, windsurfing and sailing. Access is via two Forest Service boat ramps (one at Lonesomehurst and the other at Rainbow campground, both featured in our Camping and RV Parks chapter). Four private resorts also have launch sites they'll let you use for a fee. (The Kirkwood Motel only charges $2.)

Quake Lake
U.S. Hwy. 287, northwest of West Yellowstone

Formed in 1959 when a mountain collapsed and blocked the Madison River after an earthquake, Quake Lake is more of a curiosity than a recreation attraction. You'll find one Forest Service boat ramp here, used mostly by fishing parties. Stumps from drowned trees clutter the cold waters and hair-raising winds howl up the canyon each day beginning just before noon. The lake is on U.S. Highway 287 northwest of West Yellowstone, Mont.

Dailey Lake

This small lake (it's about 150 acres), just a few miles down Old Chico Road from Chico Hot Springs, is a local hot spot for windsurfers and anglers. A road runs along the lake's north and west sides as well as down the length of its east-

ern shore before continuing off onto private property to the southwest. Two campgrounds at Dailey Lake (on the north and east sides of the lake) contain about 30 informal sites. Each has a vault toilet and a boat ramp. Dailey Lake is home to rainbow, German browns and walleye. It is also a popular ice-fishing lake.

Ennis Lake

Known by longtime locals as Meadow Lake (Forest Service mappers renamed it long ago), Ennis Lake was formed in 1905 when Montana Power built a hydroelectric dam on the Madison River at the head of the Bear Trap Canyon. The lake has since been slowly filling with silt, which means the water is warm — just right for water-skiing (in the morning before the wind comes up) and windsurfing (in the windy afternoon). Anglers also haunt the lake looking for rainbow and brown trout. About 3 miles long and 3 miles wide (the braided channels of the Madison River make it look much longer), Ennis Lake is surrounded almost entirely by private property, mostly ranches, and seems to be a management no-man's land.

The Montana Department of Fish, Wildlife and Parks operates one primitive "campground" on the western end of the lake and another one along the river's channels south of the lake. The area has enough room for about 10 sites with a vault toilet and an informal launch site at each. (The channel site, though, is used more as a takeout since the river shore downstream is entirely bordered by private property.)

Near the mouth of the lake, on the north side, the Bureau of Land Management acquired Sandy Beach, which has a vault toilet and informal camping. The Lakeshore Lodge, (406) 682-4424, on the north side of Ennis Lake has a boat ramp and a marina for guests. They also rent small motorboats for fishing. Each spring thousands of trumpeter swans land on Ennis Lake, then spend a few days there before flying on.

The lake is off North Ennis Lake Road east of MacAllister. Take U.S. Highway 287 north out of Ennis, Montana.

Northwestern Wyoming

Buffalo Bill Dam Reservoir

In the early 1980s, *Outside Magazine* included the Buffalo Bill Dam Reservoir on its list of the nation's top-10 windsurfing lakes. No sooner had *Outside* printed its list than the multicolored sails of diehard windsurfers began popping up on the icy waters of this 8-mile-long reservoir tucked into the beautiful North Fork Canyon. Ironically, a three-day event that attracted windsurfers from across the nation brought a quick end to the reservoir's popularity. For the full three days of the event, the wind refused to cooperate. A few diehard locals still windsurf (with their wetsuits), and the wind continues to be capricious. Because of its frigid waters, this lake tends to be used mostly for fishing (including ice fishing). A sailboat also pops up on the lake from time to time.

To find the lake, take U.S. Highway 20 west 8 miles out of Cody, Wyoming.

Outfitters and Boat Rentals

Grand Teton National Park

Signal Mountain Lodge
Teton Park Rd., Grand Teton Park, Wyo.
• (307) 543-2831

Signal Mountain Lodge, perched on the shore of Jackson Lake, offers scenic trips on the Snake below Jackson Lake Dam. The company offers daily guided fishing boats on 425-foot-deep Jackson Lake. Signal Mountain rents fishing skiffs with outboard motors, pontoon boats and deck cruisers that can hold a party of 8 to 10 people. Deck cruisers rent for $50 an hour or $225 for the day. Reservations are suggested. Guest buoys and other services for boaters are available.

Colter Bay Village
U.S. Hwy. 89, Grand Teton Park, Wyo.
• (307) 543-2811

The marina at Colter Bay is home to powerboat and canoe rental facilities, guest buoys and other services for boaters. Lake cruises and fishing trips on massive Jackson Lake originate here. Evening steak-fry cruises are particularly popular.

Teton Boating Company
South Jenny Lake, Grand Teton Park,
Wyo. • (307) 733-2703

This is the only company renting motorized and unmotorized boats on Jenny Lake. Teton Boating also runs a regular ferry service across the clear waters of the lake to the West Side boat dock and back. Climbers and hikers appreciate the shorter trip to the backside of Jenny Lake — West Side boat dock is only a short walk from one of the Park's more popular attractions: Hidden Falls (see our Hiking and Backpacking chapter).

Eastern Idaho

Island Park, Idaho

Sawtelle Sales Service & Rentals
U.S. Hwy. 20 and Sawtelle Rd., Island
Park, Idaho • (208) 558-7818,
(800) 273-1950

Rent a Tigershark personal watercraft from these folks and go play on Island Park Reservoir. These sit-on-top powercraft come in two sizes. The Montego 650 is designed to seat one or two, and the Monte Carlo 770 is a triple rider designed to pull waterskiers or knee boarders. Sit-on-tops are easier to master than stand-on-top jet skis. One-day rates start at $99, not including the cost of rental life jackets (required) and trailer.

Scuba Outfitters

Jackson Hole

Teton Aquatic Supply
155 W. Gill, Jackson, Wyo.
• (307) 733-3127, (800) 529-2501

Diving courses take place year round in the 45,000-gallon indoor training pool. Class sizes range between four and 10. Open-water dives and guided dives are sometimes staged at Freemont Lake in Pinedale, Wyo., with its crystal-clear water and huge underwater rock formations. Visibility at Freemont runs between 50 and 85 feet. Ririe Lake is another option, warmer but with about 20 feet of visibility.

Belmont Springs or Homestead are both warm springs located a couple hours south of Jackson. They're not large enough for satisfying recreational diving, but the warm water makes them perfect for instruction. You can become PADI licensed for $250.

Resources

Bureau of Reclamation
River and Reservoir Line
• (800) 658-5771

This recorded information line supplies water-level information on any river or reservoir in the Upper Snake drainage controlled by a Bureau of Reclamation dam (that's Jackson Lake, Grassy Lake, Palisades Reservoir, the Snake River and more).

Bureau of Land Management Idaho Falls District Office
1405 Hollipark Dr., Idaho Falls, Idaho
• (208) 524-7500

These folks manage the South Fork of the Snake below Palisades Reservoir.

Rendezvous River Sports
1035 W. Broadway, Jackson, Wyo.
• (307) 733-2471

This watersports store and school takes pride in having the latest information on area water, particularly whitewater runs. Staff can tell you about runs scattered throughout Greater Yellowstone, including some that have not yet been described in whitewater books.

Canyon Whitewater Supply
450 S. Yellowstone Hwy., Idaho Falls, Idaho • (208) 522-3932

Dave Gonzalez, owner of this shop, has his finger on the pulse of local river levels. An avid rafter, he knows the best stretches of water around here.

In West Yellowstone, visitors can walk out of their motel rooms, fire up their snowmobiles and head off into the snowy hinterlands on more than 1,000 miles of mostly groomed trails that lead into Yellowstone Park, to Idaho and to Bozeman, Montana.

Winter Sports

Winter lowers the curtain on frenetic summer activity in Yellowstone and Grand Teton parks. One by one, tourist facilities and park gates close. About November the snow begins to fall in earnest until the parks are covered with snow 2 to 8 feet deep.

Just as elk and bison, alerted by age-old signals, begin to head down off the Yellowstone Plateau toward lower less snowy wintering grounds, another call of the wild goes up across the land: "Let the winter sports begin!"

Since 1982, winter use in Yellowstone Park has doubled from 75,000 to about 150,000. Just over one-third of the visitors are snowmobilers. On a winter's day, you might see 1,500 snowmobiles heading from West Yellowstone through the Park's west entrance to spend the day riding the 150 miles of Park roads. A blue haze from the two-stroke snowmachine engines hovers above West Yellowstone streets and the roads into the Park. Yellowstone Park still shuts down each November 1, but it reopens on a limited basis from mid-December until the first week in March. In the heart of the Park, the Old Faithful Snow Lodge is a hub of winter recreation including cross-country skiing, snowmobiling, snowshoeing and snowcoach tours.

Outside the Park, winter recreation has grown just as much. While 1,500 snowmobilers are heading from West Yellowstone into the Park, an equal number are heading onto the 400-plus miles of trails in the Gallatin National Forest. The tiny town of Cooke City, which experiences nine months of winter, recorded nearly 50,000 snowmobilers in 1997. In addition, backcountry skiing has grown so much that Bill Blackford, owner of the Bike Shack, runs two snowmobiles each winter carting skiers into the backcountry so they can ski downhill to their accommodations in Cooke City. Throughout the Greater Yellowstone you'll find snowmobile and cross-country ski trails, often groomed by local clubs.

Snowmobiling is big business here. The Chamber of Commerce in West Yellowstone, Montana, which bills itself as the Snowmobile Capital of the World, spends $80,000 annually to maintain 400 miles of groomed snowmobile trails and another $40,000 to groom the world-class Rendezvous cross-country ski trails adjacent to town. The Park Service grooms another 200 miles in Yellowstone. Once the snow falls, snowmobiles become the primary mode of transportation in and out of West Yellowstone and in the Parks. Visitors can walk out of their motel rooms, fire up their snowmobiles and head off into the snowy hinterlands on more than 1,000 miles of mostly groomed trails that lead into the Park, to Idaho and to Lander, Wyoming.

Avalanches

Increased use of the backcountry by cross-country skiers, snowshoers, snowboarders and snowmobilers has raised concerns about avalanche danger. According to Kim Schlenker of the Southwestern Montana Avalanche Center, headquartered at the Supervisor's Office of the Gallatin National Forest in Bozeman, more people are venturing into avalanche country. Many are unaware that they're in potential danger once they get off the trail.

The Avalanche Center employs one part-time and two full-time experts to monitor avalanche conditions in the Madison and Gallatin national forests, near Cooke City, northern Yellowstone Park and the Lionhead portion of the Gallatin near West Yellowstone. The Center has three hotline numbers folks can call to learn avalanche and weather conditions each morning before heading out. They are (406) 587-6981 in Bozeman, (406) 646-7912 in West Yellowstone and (406) 838-2341 in Cooke City. Advisories are updated each day before 7 AM mid-November through mid-April. Bridger-Teton National

Forest also has an avalanche hotline, (307) 733-2664. Although not specifically an avalanche line, Grand Teton Park also offers recorded daily weather information. Call (307) 739-3611.

Experts say that four out of five avalanches occur during or just after a storm. Sudden temperature changes can also trigger slides, as can heavy winds that deposit unstable snow loads on lee aspects of mountains. Slopes angled between 30 and 45 degrees are the most likely originators of avalanches, although slopes as low as 25 degrees have been known to slide. Angles above 55 degrees are generally too steep to accumulate enough snow to cause an avalanche.

Looking at a snowy slope can't tell you if it's safe, since composition of the snowpack also plays a part in avalanche probability. For example, frigid temperatures can turn the top snow layer to dry crystals called hoar frost. These crystals function much like an ocean of marbles: Snow layers that later accumulate on this unstable foundation can begin to slide.

The best way to avoid an avalanche is to stay at home immediately after a fresh snowfall, get an expert opinion about the current safety of the snowpack in the area you plan to visit, and to stay on established trails.

Weather and Safety

Miles of white snow and blue sky can lull winter recreationists into a false sense of security. Even in the Park, storms can and do blow into Yellowstone Country without warning. For that reason it's best to prepare for emergencies, including an unexpected overnight stay outdoors. Here are a few important safety tips:

• Travel in a group.
• Dress for extreme cold.
• Stay within the capabilities of the weakest person in your group.
• Carry extra food, matches and a first-aid kit.
• Know locations of warming huts, visitor centers and public phones.
• Check weather conditions before starting your trip.

• Practice caution, particularly on the most likely avalanche terrain: slopes between 30 and 45 degrees. Avoid these slopes when avalanche risk is high, such as during or right after heavy snowfall, heavy winds, or rapid temperature changes.
• Don't approach wildlife.
• Use extreme caution when crossing any body of water.
• Drink plenty of water to avoid dehydration.
• Learn as much as you can about winter survival. See our Resources chapter for some books to start with.

Skiing

Mix mountains with snow and you've got a powerful, powderful combination. In all, Greater Yellowstone has eight downhill ski areas, each with its own unique claim to fame. All are expanding like mad.

Jackson Hole

Jackson Hole Mountain Resort
Teton Village, Wyo. • (307) 739-2753

Twelve miles northwest of Jackson on Wyo. Highway 390, Jackson Hole is known for its heart-thumping steep shots, which bomb through cliff bands and down gullies and ridges, and for its 4,139 feet of vertical. Beginners and intermediates will find plenty to do here, too: The resort has nine lifts and one rope tow on two mountains, Rendezvous and Aprés Vous. The altitude at the top of Rendezvous, by far the bigger peak, is 10,450 feet.

Lifts serve 75 runs and a total of 2,500 skiable acres. There's plenty of beginner and intermediate terrain, but the mountain is best known as an experts' playground. You can buy snacks or meals at four locations on the mountain; a full range of services are available at the base, which is called Teton Village. This base has condos, several sporting goods stores that rent ski and snowboard gear, repair shops for skis and snowboards and other shopping opportunities. Teton Village also has motels, restaurants and the Mangy Moose, an award-winning aprés-ski bar (see our Nightlife chapter).

Jackson Hole Ski and Snowboard School offers both instruction and child-watching. Recent mountain improvements include expanded snowmaking capacity (from 80 acres to 110) and the new Bridger Gondola, which transports 2,000 skiers per hour from the base of the mountain to the Headwall. The ride up is comfortable — you're completely enclosed — and fast, about 7 minutes.

One-day rates for winter 1997-98 are $48 for adults. Jackson Hole opens in early December and closes in mid-April.

Snow King Resort
400 E. Snow King Ave., Jackson, Wyo. • (307) 733-5200, (800) 522-5464

This full-service resort is a bit short on vertical and skiable terrain — 1,571 vertical feet and 400 skiable acres served by three chairs and one rope tow. But its location right in Jackson makes it long on convenience. Snow King also offers night skiing, a real treat with the lights of Jackson sparkling below.

Base elevation is 6,237 feet. Most runs are groomed, and 50 percent of groomed runs have snowmaking capacity. Terrain tends to be difficult: 60 percent of the mountain is expert terrain, and only 15 percent is beginner. The mountain generally opens by the end of November and closes in late March. A ski school is on-site.

The resort facility provides other extras, such as an ice-skating rink, a tubing hill, restaurants (including Panorama House overlooking town from the top of Summit Chairlift), a gift shop, an aprés-ski bar and more.

In 1997-98, adult lift tickets cost $28. Night skiing was $14. Discounts are available to resort guests.

Kelly Canyon Ski Resort
400 Market, Ririe Idaho • (208) 538-6261

This locals' ski hill is attractive both for its reasonable lift prices and for its short lift lines. Terrain is mostly beginner and intermediate, consisting largely of stair-stepping runs to the base area. Base amenities include a ski school, cafeteria and ski rental shop. Four lifts and a rope tow serve 740 skiable acres. Elevation at the base is 5,800 feet and at the summit 6,700,

so heavy low elevation snows make for the best skiing at Kelly Canyon. Adult lift tickets for winter 1997-98 cost $25 for a full day. Night skiing, available Tuesday through Saturday from 6 to 10 PM, cost $18.

Northwestern Wyoming

Grand Targhee Ski and Summer Resort
Ski Hill Rd., Alta, Wyo. • (307) 353-2300, (800) 827-4433

Grand Targhee is in the right place — the west side of the Teton Range. Clouds roll in from the Pacific, and 10,200-foot Fred's Mountain scoops the snow out, a powdery blanket laid out fresh, it seems, nearly every morning. Grand Targhee averages 43 feet of cumulative snowfall per season. No snowmaking capacity is necessary. In fact Grand Targhee offers a snow guarantee: If you don't like what you're skiing on, return your lift ticket within one hour of purchase for a "snow check."

This consistent, heavy snowfall means that Targhee gets good snow when nobody else does — you're most likely to encounter lift lines here on the days other ski hills in the region languish in bad snow blahs. Conversely, you'll find Grand Targhee deliciously quiet when good snow hits the other area ski resorts, because it's not as readily accessible as, say, Jackson Hole is to Wyoming residents.

Once primarily a locals' hill where area families and "pin-heads" waved to each other as they cruised along, Grand Targhee's prime powder is increasingly drawing the attention of destination travelers from outside the region. The resort grooms 300 acres of the 1,500 available. Three lifts and one rope tow serve all runs on the mostly intermediate terrain (only 10 percent is beginner and 20 percent expert). A neighboring peak, not served by lifts, is used as a powder preserve for snowcat skiers.

Situated 2,200 feet below Fred's summit is Grand Targhee's pretty little mountain village, with five restaurants, shopping, a spa, a ski service/rentals and a ski school (with childcare facilities). For aprés-ski action, try Trap Bar, where the band is generally great and the burgers better. Accommodations range from motel-style units to condos. Below the village,

15 kilometers of nordic trails loop through meadows and forest; other activities are also available.

In 1997-98, adult lift tickets cost $39; half-day rates are $28. Grand Targhee opens around Thanksgiving and closes in mid-April.

Southwestern Montana

Big Sky Ski and Summer Resort
One Lone Mountain Road, Mont.
• (406) 995-5000, (800) 548-4486

The brainchild of former newscaster Chet Huntley, Big Sky Ski and Summer Resort has grown into a world-class ski area with a list of amenities to amaze even the most jaded skier. Big Sky encompasses 3,500 acres and has 80 miles of named runs on two separate mountains. Of the 75 runs, the longest is 6 miles. The vertical drop is 4,180 feet — the highest in the country — and skiing ranges from groomed runs to knee-deep powder. The average snowfall is more than 400 inches and the average winter daytime temperature is 20 degrees Fahrenheit.

Big Sky also has nearly wait-free lift lines and the capacity to handle 18,000 skiers per hour. A 15-passenger tram takes skiers (and non-skiers) to the summit of 11,166-foot Lone Peak. In addition, three high-speed quads, a gondola, a quad chair, two triple chairs, three double chairs and three surface tows keep skiers moving and dispersed.

Nearby Lone Mountain Guest Ranch offers 65 kilometers of cross-country ski trails along with nordic ski rentals and sales. (For more information, refer to our Resorts and Guest Ranches chapter and the "Cross-country Skiing" section in this chapter.)

Children are not only welcome at Big Sky,

but also expected. Up to two youngsters 10 and younger can ski free with each adult. A single-day lift ticket costs $47, while a half-day costs $40. A standard ski package that includes boots, skis and poles rents for $24. You'll find an international ski school for young and old alike, and a day-care center for kids who don't want to ski.

Off the hill, you'll find a range of accommodations including the 182-room Huntley Lodge, the 94-suite Shoshone Condominium Hotel and six other condominiums in the Big Sky complex (see our Resorts and Guest Ranches chapter). You'll also find some shopping and an array of restaurants and bars in the resort complex as well as in the subdivisions below the ski hill.

Big Sky is open from mid-November until mid-April. A free, scheduled shuttle service stops at various locations in the Meadow and Mountain Village subdivisions, as well as at the Canyon on U.S. Highway 191.

Bridger Bowl Ski Area
15795 Bridger Canyon Rd., Bozeman,
Mont. • (406) 587-2111, (800) 223-9609

This "steep and cheap" ski area ranked seventh among *Snow Country Magazine's* 1996 top-50 ski resorts in North America. Sixteen miles north of Bozeman, Bridger Bowl has 350 inches of annual snowfall, a 2,000-foot vertical drop and six chairlifts with a carrying capacity of 7,300 skiers per hour. The longest run in this 1,200-acre ski area is 2.5 miles. Longtime Bozeman residents like to boast Bridger is where extreme skiing and modern telemark skiing got their best start. Montana State U. students (and dropouts) have long made a habit of climbing into hair-raising chutes for a few seconds of adrenaline rush, and telemark was cool here long before most ski magazines even knew what it was.

rails or at least well-established ski trails in and out of the national parks. We also describe a few of the companies that offer equipment rentals and/or guided ski tours in and around the most popular areas. If you want to get out onto trails or untracked snow but aren't sure you want to do it with skis on your feet, most shops that rent ski gear also rent snowshoes, and most trail systems that allow skiers also welcome snowshoeing. Snowshoes have become lighter and more convenient than they once were, but particularly in deep snow, expect to expend more effort than you will on skis.

Ski Trails

Yellowstone National Park

In the Park

Canyon Ski Trails

This area has three moderate ski trails ranging from 2.5 to 6 miles in the Canyon. A fourth trail on Mount Washburn is more difficult. The only one that is ever machine-set is the portion of the Canyon Rim trail that follows the Rim Road. This area is accessible only by snowmobile or snowcoach.

Northeast Yellowstone Ski Trails

Two easy marked trails and a very difficult one await skiers in this area of the Park where deep snow softens the natural contours. None of them are groomed. Two follow along close to the road. The third, the Pebble Creek Trail, is for very experienced skiers only and is often done as a two-day trip.

Old Faithful Ski Trails

This system of 11 trails is hard to beat for sheer beauty. The combination of geothermal steam and freezing temperatures turns the trees here into lacy winter guardians. And the thermal features are heavenly. Once again, you can't drive to Old Faithful in the winter, which means you'll either have to spend the night or make a very long day of it. If you're planning to stay overnight at Old Faithful, you'll need to reserve a room months ahead of time.

Tower Junction Ski Trails

Several trails begin in the Tower Junction area where a shuttle from the Mammoth Inn makes three regular stops. Tower Falls trail, a 5-mile moderate ski, follows the unplowed Tower Canyon road for about 2.5 miles. A longer trail (5 miles) past Lost Lake offers beautiful scenery and a variety of terrain. The other two trails, Chittenden Loop and Black Plateau Trail, are difficult. All but the Lost Lake Trial are machine-set when weather permits.

Upper Terrace Loop

Early in the day, when the hoarfrost is still on the trees, is the best time to ski this moderate 1.5-mile trail that follows the Upper Terrace Road south of the inn at Mammoth Hot Springs. This trail is groomed. The Upper Terrace Loop is one of six trails in the Mammoth area.

Entrance Communities

Northwest Corner Ski Trails

Four trails lead from U.S. Highway 191 into Yellowstone Park. At Mile Post 18, on the west side of U.S. 191, you'll find the Telemark Meadows. At Mile Post 20, a small parking lot marks the beginning of Bighorn Pass Trail. This trail heads east across a flat, then follows the Gallatin River. Watch for moose, elk, eagles and coyotes.

At Mile Post 22, the popular Fawn Pass Trail takes off from a large parking lot. The trail crosses the Gallatin River then climbs up through woods and meadows. It connects with the Bighorn Pass Trail at 8 kilometers. Specimen Creek Trail follows the creek from Milepost 27. This is another good trail for wildlife viewing. Keep your eyes peeled for standing petrified trees.

Rendezvous Ski Trails

Just ski through the log arch at the edge of the parking lot at the junction of Geyser and Obsidian Streets, and you'll be on your way to the Rendezvous Ski Trails, a 30-kilometer system of groomed trails just south of West Yellowstone. Once you're on your way, you can choose from five different loops depending upon your skill and your mood. The 6-kilometer Rendezvous Loop leads across gen-

Lift tickets cost $29 for a full day and $25 for a half-day. Children 12 and younger ski for $12 a day. Ski rental packages are $15 for adults, $10 for children and $8 for senior citizens. Bridger Bowl also offers a variety of ski lessons and lesson packages for all ages. For a fee, an on-site day-care center will watch your non-skiing children (ages 18 months to 6 years) while you ski. You'll have to call ahead for a reservation, though.

You'll find food and drink at two cafeterias (one of them is the new Deer Park Chalet at midmountain) as well as Jimmy's Bar and Grill.

You won't find accommodations at the ski area, but you will find a well-organized central reservation service that can set you up with area motels, condominiums and guests houses. A few of the condominiums are within a quarter-mile of the ski hill, but there are no ski-in and ski-out accommodations. Bridger Bowl also offers a variety of ski packages that include accommodations.

Bridger Bowl is a nonprofit organization started in 1954 by local skiers who first built a tow and a ski lift. For ski and weather information call 586-2389.

Red Lodge Mountain Resort
101 Ski Run Rd., Red Lodge, Mont.
• (406) 446-2610, (800) 444-8977

Open from mid-November until mid-March, Red Lodge Mountain has a 2,400-foot vertical drop, 60 trails (the longest is 2.5 miles) and seven ski lifts including two high-speed detachable quads. In the heart of the Beartooth Mountains, Red Lodge Mountain's Grizzly Peak juts 9,416 feet into the sky and collects an average of 250 inches of snow each winter. An expansion in 1996 added 12 intermediate and expert runs and two high-speed quads to the ski area's list of amenities. The expansion increased the area's capacity to 10,640 skiers per hour.

What didn't increase (much) was the reasonable lift rates: $32 per day for adults, $26 per day for juniors (ages 13 to 18) and $12 a day for children 12 and younger. Adults and juniors pay $15 to rent a ski package, while children pay $10.

A 10-year master plan includes new base lodges and services, cross-country trails, a year-round restaurant atop Grizzly Peak and

The ride was fast, but the jump at the bottom of the hill provided the thrill.

———

on-site lodging with conference facilities. For now, though, you'll have to stay at one of a dozen local motels or bed and breakfast inns in Red Lodge. Red Lodge Mountain operates on a special use permit from the Custer National Forest.

Northwestern Wyoming

Sleeping Giant Ski Resort
348 Yellowstone Hwy., Wapiti, Wyo.
• (307) 587-4044

This little family-run operation near the east entrance of Yellowstone Park has a T-Bar and a chairlift accessing 17 trails. Generally used only by locals, Sleeping Giant has a lunch counter and a ski school. It also offers ski and snowboard rentals. An all-day ticket for the 1996-97 season cost $18.

Cross-country Skiing

In this magnificent snowscape, you can head out almost anyplace and blaze your own trail, if that's your bag. For your convenience, though, we've compiled a short list of groomed tly rising trails through a pine forest with several short cutoffs. You'll find a warming hut at the Biathlon Range.

Volunteer Loop, 2.3 kilometers, includes several options for lengthening or shortening your ski. The loop traverses rolling hills and offers spectacular views of the Gallatin Range. Two other loops, the Windy Ridge and the Dead Dog loops, offer longer, more challenging trails.

Most of these loops are groomed from early November through April with both diagonal stride tracks and a 12-foot skating lane.

Riverside Ski Trail

Look for the orange trail marker between the snow piles at the intersection of Boundary and Madison Streets on the east edge of West Yellowstone. This trail consists of two loops: the 2.5-kilometer Upriver Loop and the 5.9-kilometer Downriver Loop. This trail generally follows the Madison River and offers exceptional wildlife viewing opportunities.

Grand Teton National Park

Grand Teton Park doesn't groom any of its roughly 40 miles of cross country and snowshoe trails, but it does mark them with flags and provide brochures that describe them. Most of the seven trails are popular, so they're usually well-packed and easy to follow. The trail markers are for days when fresh snow has obliterated the tracks of previous parties. Trails range in difficulty with some routes friendly enough for even the most cautious beginner.

Cross country skiing and snowshoeing is not limited to these trails, several of which are described below, but if you plan to venture away from them, be sure you know which areas are closed to human traffic (mostly river bottoms where wildlife is likely to seek refuge). Also be sure to carry good maps, which can be purchased at sporting goods stores in Jackson or at the Moose visitor center. Learn more about trails and Park regulations by stopping by the Moose visitor center or by calling the Park's dispatch at (307) 739-3300.

Swan Lake-Heron Pond Loop

You're here to view Jackson Lake and the northern peaks of the Teton range decked out in their snowy best. This easy trail winds through level terrain among lodgepole forest, splits to loop the east shore of Heron Pond and the west shore of Swan Lake; the best views are from the edge of Heron Pond. This 3-mile round-trip trail begins at Colter Bay visitor center.

Jenny Lake Trail

Another easy trail with spectacular views, the Jenny Lake loop is long enough to give you a full day's adventure. You begin at the Taggart Lake parking area and ski north along pretty Cottonwood Creek through a series of large meadows and gentle climbs. You'll skirt the base of the Tetons and end at an overlook of Jenny Lake. Turn around and return on the same mostly level trail for a 9-mile trip.

Signal Mountain

This 10-mile round-trip ski requires moderate skill and provides pleasant exercise and lovely panoramic views. Park at the end of the road near Signal Mountain Lodge (it's closed this time of year, but there are bathrooms and pay phones available). Ski south along a snowmobile trail for about a mile until you see the Signal Mountain Road winding up and east. It's a gradual 4-mile climb to the summit. Enjoy eagle's eye views of the ice-choked Snake River on the valley floor and peer up at Mount Moran and other peaks still far above you. Then button up your coat and enjoy the long downhill ride back to your car.

INSIDERS' TIP

Snowmobilers, don't leave well-established, frequently traveled trails unless you carry a repair kit and know how to use it. The least you should have (and know how to replace) are extra spark plugs and a drive belt. You should also carry the clothes and equipment necessary to walk out or spend the night.

Phelps Lake Overlook

This moderate trail begins at a little parking area about 3 miles south of Moose on the Moose-Wilson Road. Its first 1.7 miles runs along a narrow road, gradually ascending to the Death Canyon trailhead. Gradient increases as the trail climbs through lodgepole forest and over open slope to reach the Phelps Canyon Overlook. The Park Service does not recommend continuing past this point because of high avalanche danger. The return trip, all downhill, can be very fast when the trail is packed down; less experienced skiers will feel more comfortable on this trail after a snowfall. The trail is 5 miles round-trip.

Jackson Hole

Jackson, Wyoming

Spring Creek Resort
Spring Gulch Rd., Jackson, Wyo.
• **(307) 733-1004**

Spring Creek Resort is tucked into the hills overlooking the National Elk Refuge. In winter the resort grooms 10 kilometers of skating and diagonal trails with sections suitable for beginner, intermediate and advanced skiers. Your trail pass costs $8. If you don't own your own gear, rental packages cost $9 for a half-day and $12 for a full day. Snowshoes rent for $10 per day; snowshoe enthusiasts get their own separate trails that run along about 5 kilometers of a summer horse trail.

Teton Pines
3450 N. Clubhouse Dr., Jackson, Wyo.
• **(307) 733-1005, (800) 238-2223**

This Arnold Palmer-designed golf course turns into cross-country ski trails in winter, with 14 kilometers of terrain groomed for both skaters and diagonal skiers. Sandwiched between the Tetons and the Snake River, the course offers lovely views. Warm up in the clubhouse after your ski; the lobby area, with its massive fireplace, a bar and fine-dining restaurant, are all available. An all-day trail pass costs less than $10. Ski equipment can be rented at Teton Pines for around $12.

Eastern Idaho

The rolling terrain and plentiful public land that make up much of eastern Idaho create endless opportunities for cross-country skiing. Any summer dirt road is a likely candidate for winter skiing, since it's probably not plowed. Many hiking trails, including trails and back roads in the Kelly Canyon area and around Ririe on the South Fork of the Snake, make interesting challenges for more experienced skiers. Groomed trail systems also exist. A few are described below.

Idaho Falls, Idaho

Local skiers enjoy groomed areas around Tautphaus Park and Community Park. Idaho Falls Parks Department grooms these parks any time enough heavy snow falls to prevent damage to the grass. Skiing at these parks is free. Pinecrest Golf Course is occasionally groomed, although most years there's not enough snow to ensure that the grooming machines won't harm the grass. In years that the course is groomed, a $10 pass allows you to ski here for the season. Call Idaho Falls Parks Department, (208) 529-1480, for more information.

Island Park, Idaho

Harriman State Park
U.S. Hwy. 20, Island Park, Idaho
• **(208) 558-7368**

Fifteen miles of mechanically groomed cross-country ski trails await you at Harriman State Park just south of town. Island Park is a snowmobile mecca. Most popular winter trails

---

INSIDERS' TIP

If you're traveling in Yellowstone country in winter, carry a little digging-out insurance in your trunk. Always pack a shovel and for traction add salt, kitty litter or sand. Salt will actually melt ice if the ambient temperature is greater than about 25 degrees. Kitty litter and sand provide gritty traction at any temperature.

get a lot of snow-machine traffic, but not in Harriman: No snowmobiles are allowed here.

Harriman provides great wildlife viewing in winter. Its open water attracts trumpeter swans and other creatures. One pleasant beginner route called the Ranch Loop takes skiers into the historic Railroad Ranch. The clusters of buildings and corrals here are still part of a working cattle operation in summer. Stop in at the Jones House warming hut to thaw your hands by the fire. Then ski along the north side of Silver Lake, watching for wildlife, before returning to the main trail. Park literature describes seven other loops of varying lengths and levels of difficulty.

A $2 fee allows entrance to the park. Skis can be rented north of the park at Last Chance Texaco, (208) 558-7399.

For information about other cross-country ski opportunities in the Island Park area, call Island Park Ranger District at (208) 558-7301 or the Ashton Ranger District at (208) 652-7442.

Teton Valley

The Big Holes
Targhee National Forest
• (208) 356-3101

The Big Holes are a mountain range on the Targhee National Forest between Rexburg and Teton Basin. The area is home to 240 miles of groomed trails used mostly by snowmobilers, although cross-country skiers and snowshoers are welcome. Plans are in the works to connect this trail system to the roughly 600 miles of snowmobile trails in the Island Park area, possibly in 1999. Right now, Big Holes' trails see around 200 to 300 users per day in winter.

Grand Targhee Ski and Summer Resort
Ski Hill Rd., Alta, Wyo. • (307) 353-2300, (800) 827-4433

Enjoy 15 kilometers of groomed skate and ski track. Beginner, intermediate and advanced loops stretch west and north of the ski village at the base of Fred's Mountain. Trails loop through open meadows and snow-blanketed

forest. If you're staying at the resort, you may use the trails free. Otherwise you'll pay $8 per person for the day. You can rent cross-country ski gear at Targhee for $17; the package includes skis, boots and poles. Lessons are available.

Teton Canyon
Off Ski Hill Rd., Alta, Wyo.

Although not groomed, this side road offers a pleasant downhill grade into an almost endless array of cross-country ski options. Four miles in, you'll find yourself at Teton Canyon Campground. From there, your trails begin to climb toward Table Mountain or Alaska Basin, depending on your choice of routes. For more information, contact the Teton Basin Ranger District at 354-2312.

Southwestern Montana

Bohart Ranch Cross Country Ski Center
16621 Bridger Canyon Rd., Bozeman, Mont. • (406) 586-9070

A hop, skip and a ski from Bridger Bowl Ski Area, the Bohart Ranch offers 30 kilometers of groomed and tracked trails on private and Forest Service lands. This day-use center offers rentals, lessons, snacks and skiing across hill and dale through the forest and across meadows. The Bohart Ranch charges $8 per day.

Lindley Park Trail
Downtown Bozeman, Mont.

This 1.5 miles trail loops around Lindley Park in downtown Bozeman. Day and night, you'll see folks skiing their way around this loop when there's enough snow.

Lone Mountain Ranch
Lone Mountain Rd., Big Sky, Mont.
• (406) 995-4644, (800) 514-4644

Founded in the 1970s as a cross-country haven, Lone Mountain Ranch's ski facilities are known far and wide. In addition to a meticulously groomed 65-kilometer trail system, Lone Mountain Ranch offers guided backcountry ski tours into Yellowstone National Park and the Spanish Peaks Wilderness. For more information about Lone Mountain Ranch, refer to our chapter on Guest Ranches and Resorts.

Red Lodge Nordic Center
Hwy. 78, 2 miles west of Red Lodge, Mont. • (406) 446-9191, cell phone (406) 425-1070

From mid-December until the end of March, you can ski the 15 kilometers of groomed trails at the Red Lodge Nordic Ski Center. It will cost you $6 per day. This day-use area has a warming hut and about 50 pairs of cross-country skis for rent. An adult rental package costs $10 ($8.50 for kids). Snowshoes rent for $10.

Wade Lake Resort
About 8 miles south of U.S. Hwy. 287, Cameron, Mont. • (406) 682-7560

Thirty-five kilometers of groomed trails and five old-fashioned secluded cabins await you at the Wade Lake Resort. Trails follow the shorelines of both Wade and Cliff lakes, two of the lakes in the Hidden Lake chain in the Beaverhead National Forest. One trail leads to a hilltop with a stupendous view. Others offer excellent wildlife and bird-watching opportunities. The trails are groomed by the owners of the Wade Lake Resort where you'll find five cozy cabins tucked into a secluded nook above Wade Lake.

Northwestern Wyoming

Pahaska Trails
Cody folks have to drive a ways to find enough snow for skiing. One of the favorite areas is the Pahaska Trails. About 20 kilometers of groomed trails maintained by the Park County Nordic Ski Association begin at Pahaska Tepee, 3 miles east of Yellowstone Park's east entrance. Two ungroomed backcountry trails, the Cow Creek Trail and the Sunlight Wilderness Trail, lead off the groomed trail. And a regular route through the Park leads to Gardiner, West Yellowstone and the Park loop. For a map and more information, contact Pahaska Tepee at (307) 527-7701, (800) 628-7791.

Ski Rentals

Yellowstone National Park

In the Park

Amfac Resorts and Services
Mammoth, in Yellowstone National Park • (307) 344-7311

Amfac, Yellowstone Park's main concessionaire, rents cross-country skis at Mammoth and Old Faithful. In 1997, the rental rates were $12.50 for a full day and $8 for a half-day. Amfac also offers guided ski tours from Mammoth and Old Faithful to the Grand Canyon, DeLacy Creek near Shoshone Lake and a ski in the Lamar Valley combined with lunch in Cooke City. Amfac also offers shuttles from Mammoth and Old Faithful to and from a few popular ski trails.

Entrance Communities

Bud Lilly's Ski Shop
39 Madison Ave., West Yellowstone, Mont. • (406) 646-7801, (800) 854-9559

In addition to having about 30 pairs of cross-country skis for rent, Bud Lilly's also rents snowshoes. The charge is $15 per day for skis.

Cooke City Bike Shack
U.S. Hwy. 212, Cooke City, Mont. • (406) 838-2412

This place rents cross-country and telemark skis, snowshoes and accessories. Ski rentals range from $12 to $17.50, depending on the type of ski. For $15, owner Bill Blackford will also snowmobile you up to Daisy Pass so you can ski down to town. And for $45 per day, he will act as your guide in the backcountry. Blackford is a member of Professional Ski Instructors of America, works with the Southwestern Montana Avalanche Center and has been skiing the Cooke City area for 15 years.

Free Heel and Wheel
40 Yellowstone Ave., West Yellowstone, Mont. • (406) 646-7744

The Free Heel and Wheel rents a variety of cross-country skis including touring, perfor-

Photo: Randy Hayes/Post Register

It's fun in the sun as two skiers zoom down Chief bowl at Grand Targhee.

mance skate or classic and race skate or classic skis. The rates are $15, $20 and $25, respectively. The shop also rents snowshoes for $15 per day. If you only want to ski for a couple of hours, the Free Heel and Wheel also offers hourly rates. When you're done, you can belly up to the coffee counter and warm up with a hot coffee and a treat from Nancy P's Bakery.

Parks' Fly Shop
U.S. Hwy. 89, Gardiner, Mont.
• (406) 848-7314

Parks pulls out about 20 pairs of cross-country skis for rental each winter. A set of skis in 1997 rented for $9.50 for the day.

Jackson Hole

Skinny Skis
65 W. Deloney, Jackson, Wyo.
• (307) 733-6094

Twenty-three year old Skinny Skis is Jackson's snowshoe and diagonal and skate ski headquarters in winter. Staff tend to be practitioners of the sports for which they sell and rent equipment. Snowshoes rent for $8 per day; cross-country gear costs $12 for a full day. Skate and diagonal gear are both available.

Teton Mountaineering
170 N. Cache, Jackson, Wyo.
• (307) 733-3595, (800) 850-3595

You can rent both your skis and backcountry camping gear here. Skate- and diagonal-ski packages cost $12 for a full day. Telemark and snowshoe gear are available as well.

Eastern Idaho

Idaho Falls, Idaho

Idaho Mountain Trading
Corner of Shoup and B, Idaho Falls, Idaho • (208) 523-6679

Rent alpine, telemark and nordic skis, as well as snowboards. The rental and repair shop has ski mechanics on duty. The shop has been here since 1978. Skate gear rents for $10 per day; diagonal packages cost $8.

Island Park, Idaho

Last Chance Texaco
U.S. Hwy. 20 at Last Chance in Island Park, Idaho • (208) 558-7399

You won't find many places in Island Park that rent ski gear, but this is one. Nordic packages cost $10 per day. Some rental sets are new in 1998. The store also sells ski equipment, both new and used.

Teton Valley

Grand Targhee Ski and Summer Resort
Ski Hill Rd., Alta Wyo. • (307) 353-2300, (800) 827-4433

A complete nordic ski package at Grand Targhee costs around $17 for a full-day rental. Lessons are available for additional charge.

Yöstmark Mountain Equipment
12 E. Little Ave., Driggs, Idaho
• (208) 354-2828

This shop specializes in telemark, cross-country, snowshoe and snowboard equipment for the backcountry. You can rent both touring and skate skis and collect some good advice about where to take them. Nordic packages rent for $14. Telemark packages cost $18.

Southwestern Montana

Bangtail Bicycle and Ski
508 W. Main, Bozeman, Mont.
• (406) 587-4905

Named after the Bangtail Mountains, a hot spot for mountain bikers near Bozeman, this shop rents bikes in the summer and cross-country skis in the winter. A ski package will cost you $7 the first day and $4 for succeeding days. By the way, the Bangtails are a favorite snowmobiling area, but skiers don't go there.

The Round House Ski and Sports Center
1422 W. Main St., Bozeman, Mont.
• (406) 587-1258
15795 Bridger Canyon Rd., Bozeman, Mont. • 587-2838

In town and at the ski hill, the Round House has a complete selection of ski rentals, both for downhill and cross-country. Add snowboards to that list, as well as waxing and reconditioning.

Northern Lights Trading Company
1716 W. Babcock St., Bozeman, Mont.
• (406) 586-2225
Meadow Village, Big Sky, Mont.
• (406) 995-2220

Not only will you find skis to rent here, but you'll find a staff loaded with Insiders' tips on where to go and how to get there. Ski packages range from $10 to $25 per day, with discounts for multi-day rentals. Northern Lights also rents snowshoes for $8 per day.

Grizzly Outfitters
1700 Big Sky Rd., Big Sky, Mont.
• (406) 995-2939

In the summer, Grizzly rents bikes. When the snow flies, though, owner Ken Lancey puts away the bikes and pulls out the skis. Skis here rent from $10 to $25 per day. Lancey has reduced rates for multiple-day rentals.

Ski Tours

Yellowstone Expeditions
511 Gibbon Ave., West Yellowstone, Mont. • (406) 646-9333

For a little more than $100 per day, you can

INSIDERS' TIP

If the windshield wiper fluid in your car isn't blue, it isn't designed for winter use. Methyl alcohol in blue wiper fluids helps detergent evaporate quickly and lowers its freezing temperature, making it less likely your vision will be obscured by ice crystals. Prestone makes an additive called Windshield Melt that you can put in any wiper fluid to lower its freezing temperature by 20 degrees, but the best bet is to buy blue. And don't forget to read the label: Some blue detergents will have lower freezing points than others.

ride a snowcoach to a yurt camp at Canyon, stay for two to eight days, and ski to your heart's content. At camp, you'll find two large communal yurts (the living room and kitchen) surrounded by seven individual yurtlets. One of these will be your home for the stay. Evenings, when you're not skiing the backcountry, you'll be treated to gourmet meals (à la yurt), warm living and sleeping quarters and an on-site sauna and shower. During the day, expect to see lots of wildlife and magnificent scenery.

Teton County/Jackson Parks and Recreation
155 E. Gill, Jackson, Wyo.
• **(307) 739-9025**

These folks offer three kinds of extraordinarily inexpensive cross-country ski outings. On Tuesdays join a one-day ski tour to a different location, usually in Grand Teton or Yellowstone parks. The $6 fee for trips within a 70-mile radius of Jackson covers transportation and guides, but not gear or Park entry fees. For most trips the maximum number is 22; trips typically involve 5 to 6 miles of skiing. Routes vary in degree of difficulty. A couple times per winter, moonlight ski tours are planned. These tours typically involve a 3-mile ski over mostly level terrain at a cost of $6.

In January 1998, Teton County/Jackson Parks and Recreation also offered a three-day cross-country ski trip into Yellowstone Park. For any of these ski tours, reservations and advance payment are required. Detailed itineraries are available, including information that will help you decide if the tour is within your skill level.

Snowmobiles

It's no accident that West Yellowstone is called the Snowmobile Capital of the World. You can walk out of your motel room, hop on your sled and drive more than 1,000 miles across glorious white snow. Almost every motel in town offers "bed and sled" packages that include your motel room and a snowmachine or two (depending on whether you and your partner want to ride together or separately.) Aggressive competition leads

motel owners to throw in such extras as a prime rib dinner, continental breakfast and the Park entrance fee. Since January is the slowest month, you can sometimes find better deals and less traffic during this time. You might even find a last minute opening at the Old Faithful Snow Lodge. (Refer to our Hotels, Motels and Cabins chapter.)

At the edge of town, 400 miles of groomed trails take off into the Gallatin National Forest. Several of these trails top mountain passes and hook up with another 200 miles of groomed trails in Idaho's Targhee Forest. Another 200 miles of trails wind through Yellowstone Park to the east. If you head south into Grand Teton Park you can drive clear to Jackson or to Lander, Wyoming, if that's your pleasure.

In this chapter, we'll highlight some of the more popular trails, then leave the rest up to you. In West Yellowstone, Island Park and other snowmobile meccas you'll find snowmobile trail maps in every store, motel and restaurant. And you'll find plenty of folks willing to help you on your way. In Jackson, you'll find you have to drive or be driven from your motel to the Flagg Ranch or some nearby place where you can then unload your sled and take off into the wild white yonder.

Before you head into the forest or the Parks, it's a good idea to know the rules. For example, both Yellowstone National Park and the Gallatin Forest have 45 mph speed limits. In Yellowstone Park, you must have a valid driver's license to operate a snowmobile. Snowmachine use has increased so dramatically that Park officials liken the experience to highway driving with fast cars and heavy traffic.

While we're at it, here are a few guidelines for avoiding wildlife: If you encounter a bison walking toward you, pull over and let it pass. And if an animal is standing in the road, stop 25 yards away, assess the animal's state of mind, then proceed past cautiously unless the animal is agitated. Remember that pressured animals can suddenly charge you. If you plan to leave well-established frequently traveled trails, carry a repair kit and know how to use it. The least you should have (and know how to replace) are extra spark plugs and a drive belt. You should also carry the clothes and equipment necessary to walk out or spend the night.

Another good wildlife rule to remember is this: If you're close enough that the animal is reacting to you, you're too close.

Snowmobile Trails

Yellowstone National Park

In the Park

Inside Yellowstone Park you'll find nearly 200 miles of groomed trails that follow the Park's roads leading to almost all the major attractions. While most of the 50,000 snowmobilers that go into the Park drive to Old Faithful and back to West Yellowstone, at least half of them take the Lower Loop road through West Thumb, Fishing Bridge, Canyon, Norris and Madison. You'll find six warming huts along the way, and all but one of them is open 24 hours a day. Four of the huts have at least some kind of snack available.

Gasoline is available at Old Faithful, Fishing Bridge, Canyon and Mammoth. In addition, Yellowstone Park Service Stations have drive belts, spark plugs and some accessories for sale at Old Faithful, Canyon and Fishing Bridge.

Off-trail sledding is not permitted in the Park. And the speed limit is 45 miles per hour.

Entrance Communities

West Yellowstone, Montana

Four major trails lead away from West Yellowstone's city limits into Gallatin National Forest. All are joined by loops and most connect to Idaho trails leading to Island Park, Idaho. Each has its own beauty, but probably the most popular is Two Top, a 30-mile loop that will take you to the top of the world where you can see for miles around. It's best to take this ride on a nice day since you'll have a better view. Also, bad weather can roll in fast, making it nearly impossible to find your way. Other trails, such as the Lionhead Loop, offer opportunities for off-trail play, but be aware that you're in avalanche country here.

Cooke City, Montana

Cooke City doesn't have quite the groomed trail system that West Yellowstone has, but there are a few beautiful groomed trails to travel in this country. Check with any local business to find out where they are.

Grand Teton National Park

Riding in the Park is far less popular than on the snowmobile-filled trails of Yellowstone Park to the north. Nevertheless, some trails exist. The most popular is a segment of the groomed Continental Divide Scenic Trail, the CDST, which runs alongside U.S. 287 through the Park. This allows a 26-mile, easy ride from Moran Junction to Flagg Ranch. More challenging riding is possible on Toppings Lake Road and Shadow Mountain Road along the eastern perimeter of the Park. The Teton Park Road, unplowed in winter, also provides snowmobile terrain. From the parking area at Taggart Lake near the Moose visitor center to Signal Mountain on this road is 15 miles.

INSIDERS' TIP

This area saw skiers as early as the 1870s, but their gear looked nothing like today's. Called snowshoes, skeys or skees, early skis were generally homemade and huge — 9 to 15 feet long and at least 4 inches wide. Saturated with wax and oil, each ski weighed at least 10 pounds. Instead of two slim ski poles, early skiers carried one heavy pole as much as 7 feet long. The pole helped the skier steer when sliding downhill as well as assisting the uphill climb. Skiers straddled the pole like a witch rides a broomstick, levering weight onto the trailing butt end to control speed. Some skiers nailed the lid of a can to the bottom of their pole to keep it from sinking too deeply into powdery snow.

Gas is not available inside the Park, but Flagg Ranch just north of Jackson Lake, and Grand Teton KOA 6 miles east of the Moran entrance do provide gas and other services. Pay phones are available at the Moran entrance station, at Signal Mountain Lodge and Flagg Ranch. To learn more, stop by the Moose visitor center for a brochure, ask your snowmobile provider for maps and information, or call Grand Teton Park at (307) 739-3300.

Jackson Hole

Jackson Hole is not the snowmobile mecca West Yellowstone, Montana, or Island Park, Idaho, are, mostly because you can't just jump on your sled and ride out of town. If you're willing to drive between 10 and 70 miles though, extensive trail systems await.

Folks looking for shorter trips close to the town of Jackson often head for Granite Hot Springs; the trail is actually a well-marked 12-mile-long road ending at a commercial hot springs pool (see our Attractions chapter for more on the joys of soaking in Granite Hot Springs). This trip begins east of Hoback Junction on U.S. Highway 191. Folks say that what is in summer a heavily rutted road is faster and more comfortable on a snowmobile than it is in summer in a car. Another popular short trip takes you into the Gros Ventre Mountains along the unplowed Gros Ventre River Road just south of Grand Teton Park. Wildlife such as moose and elk are commonly seen from this trail.

Limited short rides are also possible in Grand Teton Park itself (see above).

Longer, farther away, but still popular are the groomed trail systems of Yellowstone Park; the Continental Divide Snowmobile Trail; the Togwotee Pass area, a popular part of the CDST, and trails south of Jackson Hole adjacent to Grey's River. Both Togwotee Pass and the Grey's River trails provide easy access to powder fields for off-trail play.

The CDST, which runs between Lander, Wyoming and West Yellowstone, Montana, through both Grand Teton and Yellowstone parks, would be a two or three day trip if you tried to ride the whole thing. Most people choose to bite off 20 and 30 mile chunks, which

is easy to do since the trail has many access points. In the Jackson Hole area, access this popular trail at Grand Teton KOA in the Buffalo Fork Valley, from Signal Mountain Lodge in Grand Teton National Park, or at Flagg Ranch just south of Yellowstone Park. You can also jump onto the trail from the Gros Ventre River Road.

People unfamiliar with the area usually choose to be guided rather than striking out on their own, in large part because of the distances involved in getting to trailheads. Look below for providers of guided snowmobile trips in the area, as well as a couple of snowmobile rental companies for those who want to go it alone. Be sure you ask the rental company for recommendations and trail maps. The state of Wyoming produces a fine series of snowmobile trail maps that most area snowmobile providers carry.

Eastern Idaho

Idaho Falls, Idaho, Area
More than 200 miles of marked and groomed trails lace the hills around the dry-land farming community of Bone east of Idaho Falls on the Bone Road. From the perspective of the visiting snowmobiler, Bone consists of the Bone Store, a gas station and a cafe dropped in the middle of windswept miles of hills and plateaus. The rocky hills are cut by narrow canyons and softened by pockets of aspen.

Bonneville County maintains the trails, which are popular with locals. You can get trail maps from the snowmobile rental companies listed below or from the Eastern Idaho Visitor Information Center at 505 Lindsay Boulevard in Idaho Falls, (208) 523-1010.

Island Park, Idaho
Island Park is eastern Idaho's snowmobiling mecca. Its generally high altitude — 6,000 to 10,000 feet — keeps annual precipitation high. Most of this moisture falls as snow in December and January. Snow depths of 6 feet or more are typical throughout the winter.

Island Park maintains more than 400 miles of groomed main trail and 200 irregularly groomed backcountry trails. These trails connect to the even larger maze of trails around

West Yellowstone, Montana, which in turn lead to snowmobiling opportunities within Yellowstone National Park. The local trail maps are so good that people keep them as souvenirs. Trails are so well-marked that if you have basic winter survival and snowmachine repair skills, you'll have little need of a guide.

One popular destination is 8,710-foot-high Two Top Mountain, only about 9 miles from the northern end of Island Park. This trail is suitable for beginners, but experts find plenty of challenge in the off-trail bowls. The combination, plus the view from the top, attracts some 80,000 visitors a winter.

A shorter, easier daytrip takes you out to Upper Mesa Falls near Ashton. This trail is flat and fast, and at the end of your 30-mile trip from northern Island Park, you're rewarded with the sight of water cascading over icicles and mist freezing into sparkles in the air over the 110-foot-high falls.

A pleasant half-day trip for beginners takes you out Big Springs Road to Big Springs, where you can feed the lunker rainbows and marvel at the river of clear, iceless water welling from the ground. Continue on Big Springs Road to loop back to U.S. Highway 20.

Another easy option is the Old Railroad Bed trail, used by nordic skiers in winter and hikers and bikers in summer. Read about this pleasant beginner ride in our Hiking and Backpacking chapter.

Your adventures here are made more pleasant by the fact that every Island Park business you could want to access can be reached by snowmobile. Also, warming huts are available on the Gallatin and Targhee national forests. For information or a trail map, call Sawtelle Sales Service & Rentals at (208) 558-7818.

Teton Valley

The Big Holes

This area offers 240 miles of groomed trails used mostly by snowmobilers, although cross-country skiers and snowshoers are welcome. Located on the Targhee National Forest between Rexburg and Victor, Idaho, the Big Holes trails will someday be connected to the roughly 600 miles of snowmobile trails in the Island Park area, possibly by 1999. Right now the Big Holes trails see around 200 to 300 users per day in winter. Terrain varies from open, rolling valley floor to tree-lined mountain roads. Trails are well-marked. Call (208) 356-3101 for more information.

Southwestern Montana

Big Sky, Montana

Amazingly, you won't find that many groomed snowmobile trails around Big Sky. Most people travel the Buck Creek Ridge Road, which runs east to west south of the Big Sky Ski Area. This trail is suitable for inexperienced snowmobilers and can be reached from U.S. Hwy. 191 to Buck Creek Ridge. Also, you may hear rumors about the Big Sky Trail running north to south from Bozeman to West Yellowstone. You'll hear mostly old-timers talking about this trail since part of it has been closed to snowmobile traffic in order to protect wintering elk. While intriguing and groomed in parts, this trail is strictly for the experienced. A groomed trail runs beside U.S. 191 from the Big Sky entrance south to the Buck Creek Ridge Trail.

Snowmobile Rentals

Yellowstone National Park

In the Park

Amfac Parks and Resorts
Mammoth Hotel Snowmobile Shop
Mammoth Hot Springs • (307) 344-7311
Old Faithful Snow Lodge
Snowmobile Shop
Old Faithful • (307) 344-7311

For $115 per day, ($130 for two) you can rent a snowmobile at either Mammoth or Old Faithful. Clothing rents for $16 per day. Children younger than 11 ride free as a double rider.

Entrance Communities

Backcountry Adventures
224 Electric, West Yellowstone, Mont.
• **(406) 646-9317, (800) 924-7669**

Rent a snowmobile with or without a guide at Backcountry Adventure snowmobile rentals. Jerry Johnson, owner of Backcountry, features a fleet of up-to-date Polaris snowmachines that rent from $79 to $134 per day depending on the model. He also rents clothing for $15 per day. If you're one of the 10 percent that want a guided trip into Yellowstone Park, then Jerry can help you. His guides, knowledgeable about the Park, will take you along for $175 per day.

Cooke City Exxon and Polaris/Ski-Doo
U.S. Hwy. 212, Cooke City, Mont.
• **(406) 838-2244**

If you find yourself in this little berg without a sled, Cooke City Exxon has about 16 rentals that will run you from $110 to $160 per day. A full suit of clothing and gear will cost you $25 for the day.

Travelers' Snowmobile Rentals
Madison Ave. and Electric St., West Yellowstone, Mont. • (406) 646-9561, (800) 548-9551

Owner Glen Loomis has a fleet of 200 mostly Polaris snowmachines. They rented from $79 to $149 in 1997. The faster you want to go the more you'll pay. Loomis also rents snowmobile outfits and has bed and sled packages to go with his sleds.

Yellowstone Adventures
131 Dunraven, West Yellowstone, Mont.
• **(406) 646-7735, (800) 231-5991**

If you're looking for a "bed and sled" package, Yellowstone Adventures specializes in finding just what you want. Besides being a Ski-Doo dealer, Yellowstone Adventures offers clothing and snowmobile rentals. Their sleds rent for $79 to $139. This company has

A skier crosses an open meadow with a sled filled with winter gear in tow.

Photo: Randy Hayes/Post Register

been around longer than any other snowmobile outfit in West Yellowstone.

Yellowstone Arctic/Yamaha
208 Electric, West Yellowstone, Mont.
• **(406) 646-9636, (800) 646-7365**

Mostly associated with three motels in town, the Yellowstone Arctic/Yamaha rents two kinds of snowmachines to walk-ins. They have a fleet of 140 machines in a range of models made by Arctic Cat and Yamaha. A snowmobile will cost you from $94 to $134 for a day. A complete snowmobile outfit rents for $17. They offer a discount for "bed and sled" packages.

Yellowstone Tour and Travel
1211 Yellowstone Ave., West Yellowstone
• **(406) 646-9310, 646-9636 Oct. 1 to April 1, (800) 221-1151**

Affiliated with three motels in town (the West Yellowstone Conference, The Three Bears, and the Big Western Pine)

INSIDERS' TIP

North America has 8 million snowmobilers, and each snowmobiler drives an average of 1,040 miles per year on his snowmachine.

Yellowstone Tour and Travel books guided trips into and out of the Park. For out-of-Park trips onto as many as 1,000 miles of groomed trails on national forest lands, Yellowstone Tour and Travel offers guides for an extra fee. The price of the package depends on the number of people in your party, the kind of sleds you choose, where you're going and where you stay.

Jackson Hole

Flagg Ranch Resort
U.S. Hwy. 89, John D. Rockefeller Jr. Memorial Pky. • (307) 543-2861, (800) 443-2311

Rent a 1998 Polaris 440 snowmachine, a one-piece snowsuit, snowmobile boots, mittens and a helmet for $135. One-day and multiday rentals are available. So are guided tours, but they're not popular, since the well-marked, well-mapped roads of Yellowstone Park make self-guided snowmobiling easy.

The 90-mile trip to Old Faithful Inn and back generally takes a full day. Other visitors needs also available here include lodging, a grocery store and a gas station.

Grand Teton Park KOA
17800 E. U.S. Hwy. 287, Moran Wyo. • (307) 733-1980

Rent snowmobiles just 6 miles from the east entrance to Grand Teton Park. Here you're poised to roll up Togwotee Mountain to the Continental Divide Snowmobile Trail to other groomed terrain on Togwotee Mountain, and to endless powder bowls and meadows. Or head through Grand Teton Park and up into Yellowstone's popular snowmobile trails.

Rentals are available with or without guides. Machines are 1988 Polaris 488s. With no guide, you pay $109 for a single rider. With a guide you pay $150.

Jackson Hole Snowmobile Tours
1000 S. U.S. Hwy. 89, Jackson, Wyo. • (307) 733-6850, (800) 633-1733

Machines are new every year. In 1997-98 they were Polaris Indy Trails. If you want someone else to do the thinking for you, these folks are ready. They'll pick you up in the morning,

outfit you with all the necessary gear, teach you a few snowmobile basics and then guide you to Yellowstone Park, Granite Hot Springs, the Togwotee Pass area or a custom two- to seven-day extended tour. All trips include a hot lunch cooked up by your guides. Trips range between $130 and $150 for the first rider; an additional adult rider costs $75.

Leisure Sports
1075 S. U.S. Hwy. 89, Jackson, Wyo. • (307) 733-3040

These folks rent 13 1997 Arctic Cats, including Jags for $100 per day (these vehicles hold one person) and Panthers for $125 (these hold two). Leisure Sports is located 10 to 70 miles from the trailheads you'll be aiming for; if you don't have a trailer to transport your rented Cats, you can pick up one here. If your vehicle is not four-wheel-drive or you lack a trailer hitch, you can rent the appropriate vehicle as well.

Eagle Rent-A-Car
375 N. Cache, Jackson, Wyo. • (307) 739-9999, (800) 582-2128

This is one of only two companies in the Jackson area that rent snowmobiles for unguided trips. In the winter of 1997-98, the rental fleet consisted of 15 1997 Arctic Cats, ranging from two-seater 440s to performance off-trail 580s. New machines are generally purchased every year. Rates are around $100 per day, with no charge for a rider on two-seat machines. Included in the base rate is your protective clothing and, if you rent two or more machines, your trailer rental.

Togwotee Snowmobile Adventures
650 W. Broadway, Jackson, Wyo. • (307) 733-1418

The owners of the Cowboy Village Resorts in Jackson and on Togwotee Pass also run guided snowmobile tours and snowmobile/accommodations packages. The fleet consists of 130 1998 Polaris 488 Indy Trails and Polaris powder-performance sleds with larger engines, longer tracks and wider paddles. A few sleds are Arctic Cats.

Rides out of Jackson cost $150 per person; the second rider on a sled costs $75. Tours go to Yellowstone Park, the Gros Ventres and along the Greys River south of Jackson Hole. Box lunches or lodge meals are provided.

Eastern Idaho

Idaho Falls, Idaho

American Carriage RV Marine & Ski-Doo
1710 W. Broadway, Idaho Falls, Idaho
• (208) 529-5055

Rent 1997 Ski-Doo sleds for about $90 per day. If you need a trailer, they cost $15 per day.

Rexburg, Idaho

All Season Sports
160 W. Main, Rexburg, Idaho
• (208) 356-9245

Rent newer Arctic Cat and Yamaha snowmobiles from $75 to $125 per day. Trailers rent for around $20 unless you rent two machines, in which case the trailer is free. While you're here, make sure you pick up trail maps for the two most popular area destinations: the Big Holes trail system and the Island Park trails.

Island Park, Idaho

Sawtelle Sales Service & Rentals
U.S. Hwy. 20 and Sawtelle Rd., Island Park, Idaho • (208) 558-7818, (800) 273-1950

These folks rent Arctic Cat snowmobiles in the economy 340 class for $80 per day, but they can also supply a variety of higher-performance machines for a few more bucks. Sawtelle Sales is associated with Sawtelle Mountain Resort, so all services, including guide service, are available. They can arrange accommodations and rental packages.

Teton Valley

Basin Auto Snowmobile Rental
180 N. Main, Driggs, Idaho
• (208) 354-2297

This is the oldest company in the basin offering unguided snowmachine rentals. Rent brand-new Summit 500s by Ski-Doo for $119 per day. You can also rent trailers and snowmobile clothing, arrange a shuttle for your car or a drop-off for you and your sled. Trail maps are available here; so is free information, since the employees are riders themselves. If you're not comfortable without a guide, these folks are also happy to find you one, although they offer no guided trips of their own. Call to find out more about occasional special events such as Poker Runs.

Teton Mountain View Lodge
Idaho Hwy. 33 at Tetonia, Idaho
• (208) 456-2741, (800) 625-2232

You can arrange for guided trips with a snowmobiler in Tetonia, but the well-marked, well-mapped Big Holes trail system starts practically outside the door of this unpretentious newer motel on the edge of Tetonia. Rent 1997 and 1998 machines for between $80 and $125. Free maps of the Big Holes are available.

Southwestern Montana

Gallatin Ridgetop Adventures
U.S. Hwy. 191, 1 mile south of Big Sky, Mont. • (406) 995-3333

Mike Schmidt, owner of Gallatin Ridgetop Adventures, has 30 snowmobiles (Ski-Doos) for rent during the winter. While he doesn't guide snowmobile trips, he does know a lot about all of the trails in the area. Schmidt's snowmachines rent from $89 per day per person to $109 per day depending on the model.

Northwestern Wyoming

Pahaska Tepee
183 Yellowstone Hwy., Wyo.
• (307) 527-7701, (800) 628-7791

Pahaska has a fleet of snowmobiles that rented in 1998 for $80 to $150 depending on the make, model and year of the snowmobile. The shop also rents clothing and gear. Located at the east entrance of Yellowstone Park, Pahaska Tepee offers a variety of snowmobile packages into Yellowstone. Among the packages available are three- and five-day guided and unguided trips, which include overnight stays not only at Pahaska, but also at Old Faithful or West Yellowstone or both.

Snowcoach Tours

Yellowstone National Park

Inside the Park

Amfac Parks and Resorts

Amfac Parks and Resorts offers regularly scheduled snowcoach tours between Old Faithful and South Gate, Mammoth Hot Springs and West Yellowstone. Amfac also has several sightseeing tours that last from three hours to all day. Besides wildlife viewing, snowcoach tours come with an informed guide who can tell you about what you're seeing.

Snowcoach passengers are limited to two pieces of luggage plus cross-country ski equipment. Prices for scheduled shuttles in 1996-97 started at $14. All-day sightseeing tours cost as much as $73 for adults and half that for children 11 and younger.

Entrance Communities

West Yellowstone, Montana

Alpen Guides
555 Yellowstone Ave., West Yellowstone, Mont. • (406) 646-9591

With a fleet of seven snowcoaches, Alpen Guides will take you anyplace you want to go in Yellowstone Park. Alpen offers daily tours from West Yellowstone to Old Faithful. Skiers have the option of being dropped off at Biscuit Basin, then skiing 2.5 miles through the geyser basin to the Old Faithful Lodge. Alpen also has daily tours to Canyon as well as a special wildlife tour that includes a two-night stay in West Yellowstone and a night at the Old Faithful

Snow Lodge. On Wednesdays, Alpen will take you and your skis deep into the Park for a day of cross-country skiing. A daily tour of Old Faithful costs $69 for an adult, while a Grand Canyon Tour costs $79.

Yellowstone Tour and Travel
1211 Yellowstone Ave., West Yellowstone, Mont. • (406) 646-9310, 646-9636 Oct. 1 to April 1, (800) 221-1151

Yellowstone Tour and Travel has a fleet of three snowcoaches that come with guides well-versed in area geology, ecology and biology. They'll take you most anyplace in the Park you want to go. See a previous entry for more information about Yellowstone Tour and Travel.

Jackson Hole

Flagg Ranch Village
U.S. Hwy. 89, John D. Rockefeller Jr. Memorial Pky. • (307) 543-2861, (800) 443-2311

Imagine a giant, glassed-in snowmobile, big enough to seat 10 people. That's a snowcoach. All winter, snowcoaches run between Flagg Ranch Village and Old Faithful about 45 miles away. The daylong trip includes a hot lunch at Old Faithful Inn and interpretive talks from your guide. Children younger than 6 aren't allowed, primarily because they tend not to find the bumpy snowcoaches very comfortable. The price is $95 for adults.

Sleigh Rides

Lone Mountain Ranch
Lone Mountain Rd., Big Sky, Mont. • (406) 995-4644, (800) 646-4644

This renowned cross-country ski center offers weekly sleigh rides over the creek and through the woods to their North Fork cabin where they can feed as many as 55 people a gourmet meal in a rustic setting. They take

---

INSIDERS' TIP

For information about snow conditions at Big Sky Ski and Summer Resort, call (406) 995-5900.

non-guests, but you'll have to make a reservation. Refer to our chapter on Guest Ranches and Resorts for more information.

Ice-skating

Jackson Hole

Snow King Center Ice Rink
100 E. Snow King Ave., Jackson, Wyo.
• (307) 733-5200

This big indoor ice rink operates from August to mid-April. Skate rentals, snacks and warm beverages are available onsite. Adults pay $6 for the regularly scheduled weekday afternoon public skate sessions. A less expensive Saturday session is often available. But call first: The rink hosts many sporting and other events, so ice times can change.

Surrounding Areas

Eastern Idaho

Idaho Falls

Idaho Falls Hockey Shelter
Rollandet and Rogers, Tautphaus Park, Idaho Falls, Idaho • (208) 529-0941

The Tautphaus (say it TOFF-us) Park hockey rink tries to schedule public skate time most days in winter, but they recommend you call and check

before you drive over. This indoor rink is open November through March. Rink admission is $2.75; skate rental is $2.50. Although the rink doesn't have a snack concession, food and drink vending machines are available.

Southwestern Montana

Southside Park
West College Ave. and S. Fifth Ave., Bozeman, Mont.

This rink, open from noon until 10 PM weekdays and 10 AM to 10 PM weekends, offers recreational skating and hockey in an enclosed area.

Beall Park
Villard and Black Sts., Bozeman, Mont.

You'll find recreational skating here most times and broomball on Tuesdays and Thursdays. This rink is open from 10 AM until 10 PM on weekends and noon until 10 PM on weekdays.

Bogert Park
325 S. Church, Bozeman, Mont.

This rink is reserved for hockey after 4 PM. Check the schedule for open-hockey use times.

Skate Palace
2015 Wheat Dr., Bozeman, Mont.
• (406) 586-7770

Hockey and skating are big in Bozeman, and this is one of the town's busiest skating venues. Call to find out free skating hours.

Other Recreation

You've come to a place where recreating is of ultimate importance. Most Greater Yellowstone inhabitants not born on homestead farms or to old ranching families moved here, in large part, to play. Many of us gave up higher incomes and the cultural opportunities of big cities to be here, and we're determined to make the trade a good one.

Look in our closets and basements and you'll find toys, toys and more toys. Even those of us who don't play hard figure we'll get around to it one of these days, maybe next weekend or next summer. And since we're all hooked either on the reality or the idea of playing hard outdoors, most of us are happy to share what we know and try to hook you, too.

So on top of previous chapters' bait — skiing, snowmobiling, whitewater rafting, hiking, hunting and fishing adventures — this chapter takes some parting casts. What follows are a few more of the many recreational opportunities available in Greater Yellowstone: horseback riding, mountain biking, golf and technical climbing. Go ahead, take the bait. We all did.

Horseback Riding

There's something about climbing onto half-ton horse that's irresistible to some and unthinkable for others. If you happen to be one of those folks who dreams about riding the range on horseback, you'll find plenty of outfits glad to take you for a ride. Most offer a variety of options that include one and two hour tours close to the corral, and half- or full-day rides that can carry you quickly into some spectacular mountain country. Some will take you to a mountain lake for a few hours of fishing. Or they'll pack you in for a night or a week. Along the way, most outfitters will teach you things about Yellowstone country that you most likely wouldn't learn any other way.

Throughout Greater Yellowstone you'll see and hear plenty of advertisements for horseback riding. Climbing atop a horse is a wonderful way to travel up and into the backcountry in and out of the Parks. And the area has plenty of topnotch outfitters that can take you fishing or sightseeing for the day or overnight. They'll take you through wide alpine meadows littered with wildflowers, past pristine lakes and sometimes over steep trails that scale high mountain passes. If you're on an overnight trip, chances are you'll sleep in a wall tent and eat food cooked over a campstove.

No matter where you ride in this neck of the woods, it's a cinch you'll climb a mountain on longer rides. Climbing or descending a steep mountain trail can be thrilling or scary. Outfitters select their horses for surefootedness and calm dispositions. Horses are powerful and unpredictable animals, and it's impossible to control all the variables that could cause accidents. Horses can be spooked by rolling rocks, mountain bikes, and sudden movements. They can trip and tumble just like the rest of us. There are plenty of other good outfitters that we haven't listed. Wherever you are, we recommend that you do your own checking. Start by asking the local chamber of commerce if it has had complaints about a particular outfit.

Rates for horseback riding generally run between $15 and $20 per hour for the first hour. Most stables offer a range of rides, from an hour to a day or more. Unguided trips are often possible and tend to be less expensive, but guided rides are more common. Horses and riders can be matched to riders' abilities; make sure the guide knows your ability level. Reservations are a good idea, particularly in summer. In addition to the stables listed below, many dude ranches (see our Resorts and Guest Ranches chapter) offer day rides to non-guests. Few if any stables provide rides in winter. Most stables close down in September or October and open again in June.

Yellowstone National Park

In the Park

Amfac Parks and Resorts
Mammoth, Yellowstone Park
• (307) 344-7311

Amfac, Yellowstone Park's largest concessionaire, leases 150 horses and hires more than 50 wranglers each summer to stock their three stables in the Park. At Mammoth, Roosevelt and Canyon you can rent and ride a horse for one or two hours. Wranglers will lead you and as many as 24 other riders on the trails surrounding the corrals.

Amfac also offers stagecoach rides (they were $5.95 in 1997) and Old West Cookouts on which you can either ride a chuckwagon or horseback. The cost for adults in 1997 was $32 to $41 to attend the cookout on horseback and $28 to ride in the wagon.

Entrance Communities

Parade Rest Guest Ranch
7979 Grayling Creek Rd., West Yellowstone, Mont. • (406) 646-7217, (800) 753-5934

Why ride from a corral next to the highway when you can drive a mere 8 miles north on U.S. Highway 191, then left on U.S. Highway 287 for a mile, to ride at the Parade Rest Guest Ranch? At Parade Rest, you'll find a variety of rides across flower-filled meadows, through timbered forests, below towering mountain peaks and beside beautiful Hebgen Lake. Parade Rest will fix you up with a horse suited to your ability, then take you riding for an hour to six hours, depending on what you want.

Hell's A Roarin' Outfitters
Jardine Rd., Gardiner, Mont.
• (406) 848-7578

In addition to one- or two-hour rides, Warren and Susan Johnson will take you for a half-day or full-day ride in the Absaroka-Beartooth Wilderness. Warren, born and raised in Jardine, knows the area well. He also leads multi-day pack trips, which cost $175 per person per day in 1997.

Beartooth Plateau Outfitters
U.S. Hwy. 212, Main St., Cooke City, Mont. • (406) 838-2328 June through September, (800) 253-8545
HCR 48, Box 1028, Roberts, MT 59070
• (406) 445-2293 October through May

While Beartooth Plateau Outfitters specializes in overnight pack trips into the Park during the summer and hunting in the fall, it is possible — and worth your while — to day-ride into the Park. Occasionally (if you're having a lucky day) you can even walk in and catch a day ride the next day. See our Hunting and Fishing chapter for more information on these outfitters.

Grand Teton National Park

Grand Teton Lodge Company Corrals
Colter Bay and Jackson Lake Lodge, Grand Teton Park • (307) 543-2811

A variety of Park rides begin at these two stables, including breakfast rides, evening campfire rides and rides in horse-drawn wagons.

Scott's Jackson Hole Trail Rides
Teton Village, Wyo. • (307) 733-6992, (307) 739-2753 Teton Village Guest Service Center

Choose from one-hour to all-day rides in Grand Teton Park. This stable is conveniently located near the Moose-Wilson Road entrance to the Park, which sees less traffic than other Park roads.

Jackson Hole

Snow King Stables
400 E. Snow King Ave., Jackson, Wyo.
• (307) 733-5781

Ride an hour or all day out of these stables,

which are located at the edge of Jackson in the Snow King Resort complex. Breakfast and evening steak rides can also be arranged.

A/OK Corral
U.S. Hwy. 89 near Hoback Junction, Wyo.
• (307) 733-6556

Ten minutes south of Jackson enjoy trail rides, cowboy breakfast rides, evening steak dinner rides and covered wagon rides. You can even horsepack into Yellowstone Park with this company; it provides transportation to and from the Park for the 10-hour expedition. Horseback fishing trips are also available.

Surrounding Areas

Eastern Idaho

Idaho Falls, Idaho, Area

Granite Creek Guest Ranch
U.S. Hwy. 26 east of Idaho Falls, Idaho
• (208) 538-7140

This little guest ranch offers guided trail rides and cattle drives; rides accommodate all skill levels. Pony rides for kids cost $10 for a half-hour.

Island Park, Idaho

Harriman State Park
Off U.S. Hwy. 20, south of Island Park, Idaho • (208) 558-7077, (208) 624-7777

Tom Angell of St. Anthony's Halo Ranch brings some of his working ranch horses to Harriman State Park every summer. He and his guides offer a variety of rides ranging from steep, high-altitude trail riding to a gentle loop around game-rich Silver Lake. Dinner rides cost around $35, begin about 5 PM and last until dusk. You'll

stop at Golden Lake for a Dutch-oven feast of spare ribs, scalloped potatoes and hot scones. Reservations are recommended but not required for any ride except the Dutch-oven dinner trip.

Sawtelle Mountain Resort
U.S. Hwy. 20 and Sawtelle Rd., Island Park, Idaho • (208) 558-9366, (800) 574-0404

Sawtelle is right off U.S. Highway 20, so a quick ride is convenient here even if you're just passing through. Guided rides leave hourly throughout the day, with early-morning and late-evening rides available by special request. Chuckwagon dinners can also be arranged if you want to go whole-hog Western.

Teton Valley

Bustle Creek Outfitters
Ski Hill Rd., Alta, Wyo. • (307) 353-2300, (800) 827-4433

Ride for an hour or three days; learn Western or English-style riding. You can even pair your day of trail riding with a chuckwagon cookout. Trips, chuckwagons and lessons are booked with and originate from Grand Targhee Ski and Summer Resort. All rides are guided.

Southwestern Montana

Broken Hart Ranch
73800 Gallatin Rd., Gallatin Gateway, Mont. • (406) 763-4279

During the summer, Lee Hart leads horseback riders on day and multi-day trips in the Spanish Peaks Wilderness and the Gallatin Range. Lee, who has been outfitting since 1969, offers folks customized trips that include daytrips into the backcountry, pack trips and sightseeing trips that take guests horseback to a cluster of private

---

INSIDERS' TIP

The nine-hole Livingston Golf Club may have been the first to be established in what is now called the Greater Yellowstone area. It was created in 1900 and was called the Yellowstone Golf Club. You'll find it along the Yellowstone River on View Vista Drive in Livingston. The phone number is (406) 222-1031, and the greens fee is $14.

backcountry cabins in grizzly country. Hart's rates are among the most reasonable: A daytrip costs $200, which means if there are two of you, you'll each have to pay $100 for the day. If there are three of you, it will cost you each only $75.

Jake's Horses
U.S. Hwy. 191, 3 miles south of Big Sky, Mont. • (406) 995-4630, (800) 352-5956

Jake's Horses, owned by Jake and Katie Grimm, has been around longer than the Big Sky Ski Area. They've been leading guests down the trail on horseback since 1976. Jake's takes about 4,000 people a year for rides ranging from an hourlong tour to all-day and overnight pack trips in the wilderness and Yellowstone Park. He also does dinner rides during the summer and sleigh rides (no dinner) in the winter. If that's not enough, he'll also take you fishing in a high-mountain lake.

Using 50 horses and about seven employees (including wranglers), he runs a second horseback riding operation out of the Cinnamon Lodge south of Jake's on U.S. Highway 191.

A one-hour ride at Jake's will cost you $20, while a full day will cost $95. Hayrides are $12 per person, and dinner rides are $49. Overnight pack trips range from $150 to $375 per person per day, depending on the number in your party and the duration of your trip. (The more people and the longer you stay, the less it is per day.)

Diamond K Outfitters Inc.
Rainbow Ranch Lodge, U.S. Hwy. 191 south of Big Sky, Mont. • (406) 995-4132, (406) 995-4103

Operated by licensed Montana outfitter Chuck Kendall (he's also an elected member of the Montana Wilderness Council and a fifth-generation Montanan), Diamond K Outfitters runs trail rides out of a corral adjacent to the lovely Rainbow Ranch Lodge. (See our Resorts and Guest Ranches chapter for more information on the Rainbow Ranch Lodge.) In addition to two-hour, half-day and daylong rides, Kendall offers dinner rides, riding lessons, fishing trips and overnight pack trips.

Two-hour rides cost $40, and half-day rides are $50 per person. Full-day rides and fishing trips cost $95 per person for a party of three or more or $120 for a party of two. A two hour western horsemanship lesson will cost you $50, while an evening dinner ride costs $65. Kendall is licensed to pack into Yellowstone Park backcountry. He specializes in tailoring his trips to your wants, needs and ability, and takes time for lighthearted education along the way.

Bear Paw Outfitters
136 Deep Creek Rd., Livingston, Mont. • (406) 222-5800, (406) 222-6642

Operated by the Bowers family from their ranch south of Livingston, Bear Paw offers horseback rides ranging from one-hour tours for $20 to overnighters into Yellowstone Park for $200 per day. Bowers also has a deluxe summer tent camp high in the Absaroka mountains. Among the other options he offers are two-hour, half-day and full-day rides. (A day of riding and fishing in Yellowstone will cost you $160.) If you've got a hankering to ride through the Park or pack into Slough Creek, there's no one better to go with. Bowers has his guests meet him at the trailhead. (For information on Bear Paw's fall hunting operation, see our Hunting and Fishing chapter.)

www.insiders.com
See this and many other **Insiders' Guide®** destinations online — in their entirety.
Visit us today!

INSIDERS' TIP

Your bike, boat, boots and broncs can bring foreign weed seeds, tiny snails or whirling disease from one place to another. Before entering National Forest and National Park lands or waters, think ahead and hose off your toys to avoid spreading weeds, disease or other problems in the ecosystem.

Photo: Randy Hayes

Golfers at Teton Pines enjoy a spectacular view of the Tetons.

Northwestern Wyoming

Bill Cody Ranch
2604 Yellowstone Hwy., Cody, Wyo.
• **(307) 587-6271**

Twenty-six miles west of Cody and 26 miles east of Yellowstone Park, the Bill Cody Ranch offers regular ranch rides from two hours to a full day. Owners Jamie and John Parson maintain a herd of 60 horses and use 14 different mountain trails leading into the Shoshone National Forest. All-day rides include lunch. If you plan ahead, you can have dinner at the end of the day in the ranch's old-fashioned dining room.

Gateway Ranch
Yellowstone Hwy., Cody, Wyo.
• **(307) 587-6507, (307) 527-5981**

"Speed" Spiegelberg has been taking folks for rides since 1955. Located halfway between Cody and the Stampede Rodeo Grounds west of town, Spiegelberg employs a wrangler these days to lead trips either into the Canyon below the ranch or up onto the mountain. If you choose to ride for an hour, you'll go downhill; if you ride longer, you'll head up the hill. Spiegelberg charges $15 per hour for rides up to four hours.

Check with him on his rates for longer rides. If you can't reach him at the numbers listed above, try his cell phone at (307) 272-2555 from 6 AM to 5 PM.

Mountain Biking

Mountain biking opportunities abound in Greater Yellowstone, mostly outside Yellowstone and Grand Teton parks. Below are general overviews for some of the better mountain biking areas in the region, as well as information on shops that sell or rent gear.

Rentals generally cost between $15 and $25 for a full day. Hourly or half-day rates are often available. Be sure you ask what comes with your rental; generally you can expect a bike pump and helmet. Some shops throw in a spare tube, maps and even water bottles. Also be sure you are paying for the kind of bike you want. Performance bikes will have different gear ratios and suspension systems than standard bikes. They'll also rent for up to twice as much. If you plan to simply cruise around on level dirt roads, you probably don't need to pay for the whistles and bells.

Bike shops are fine sources of information about area trails; most welcome your call.

They may also provide guided tours or be able to suggest a reputable company that does. Competent bikers probably need little more than directions and a spare inner tube, but beginners or those who've never mountain biked in remote settings may be comforted by the presence of an instructor/guide. Restrictions and weather-related trail obstacles may exist, so be sure to ask locally about your chosen route, even if it's one described below. We've provided you with phone numbers to assist your information gathering.

Yellowstone National Park

While the first bicyclists toured Yellowstone Park in the 1880s, biking on today's Park roads is generally discouraged because many of the roads are barely wide enough for vehicles without adding bicycles to the equation. The updated roads are improved with a few feet of shoulder, but remember that there are lots of oversized recreational vehicles on the road and many drivers are busy looking for wildlife — not bicyclists. These riding obstacles don't discourage some riders, especially Europeans. If you're one of those determined to bike the Park, we recommend you check in with the local experts to learn every possible tip for surviving the highways of Yellowstone.

In the Park

Within Yellowstone Park, mountain biking opportunities are very limited. They include the one-way Fountain Flat Drive, the 3-mile trail into Lone Geyser and a 1-mile trail to the natural bridge at Bridge Bay.

Entrance Communities

The array of biking options in and around West Yellowstone is way too long to list here. We assume if you're a mountain biking mogul you'll bring your own bike and head for the nearest bike shop to find out what's what. For those of you who are more casual, the Rendezvous Ski Trails bordering town are used for biking during the summer months. This 30-kilometer trail system loops over and

around and up hills through timber and across rolling hills for beautiful riding that will pump up your heart.

Local bike shops listed below can supply you with maps outlining a whole series of popular local loop roads and trails. We also recommend that you check with the Hebgen Lake Ranger District, U.S. Highway 191 N., West Yellowstone. The phone number is (406) 646-7369.

Free Heel 'n Wheel
40 Yellowstone Ave., West Yellowstone, Mont. • (406) 646-7744

Owners Kelli Criner and Melissa Buller rent new Trek and Specialized bikes for $4 per hour or $20 per day. Occasionally, you'll find a women's ride out of the shop. These two can tell you where to go depending on your ability.

Yellowstone Bicycles
132 Madison Ave., West Yellowstone, Mont. • (406) 646-7815

Leslie and Gay McBirnie have been selling and renting bicycles in West Yellowstone since 1967. Not only do they have a variety of bikes for rent, including recumbents and tandems, but also packs come free of charge with an extended rental for touring the Park. Rentals here are $3.50 per hour, $12.50 for a half-day and $19.50 per day.

Grand Teton National Park

Like those in cars, bicyclists need a Park pass to enter Grand Teton National Park. Bike passes cost $10. Once inside, you must stay on designated roads and trails. Off-trail riding is not permitted, and the Park offers very little single track for bikers. This means if you're looking for technical riding, you'll fare better on surrounding national forest lands. Grand Teton Park's roads are more bike-friendly than Yellowstone's, mostly because road shoulders are more generous. It helps, too, that drivers seem a tad less likely to be staring out the passenger side window at a bison instead of at you and the road.

One pleasant beginner Park ride is the Antelope Flats loop, a flat 12-mile ride that, unfortunately, runs mostly on narrow, poorly shouldered roads. It takes you past historic Mormon Row, including the famous Moulton barn, which by now you've seen in local postcards and posters. One leg of this ride is on gravel road.

A better (read: wider) road for a flat loop ride is the Jenny Lake loop. This 15-mile ride, all on pavement, leaves the Teton Park Road adjacent to String Lake and loops down toward lovely Jenny Lake. You'll be pedaling almost at the feet of the spectacular Tetons. Remember that those fabulous views also distract the many cars passing you.

A third option, which takes you away from the main Park thoroughfares, is Shadow Mountain, a 7-mile loop ride on gravel road that climbs and loops Shadow Mountain. Good technical mountain bikers should ask about the single-track route that drops off the top of Shadow Mountain, rejoining the main route near the starting area.

For more information, call Grand Teton Park (307) 739-3300, or the folks at Adventure Sports (listed below).

Adventure Sports
Dornan's at Moose, Grand Teton National Park, Wyo. • (307) 733-3307

Mountain bikes by Diamond Back, Cannondale, Giant and Marin are available for rent or sale. Rentals are the current year's models. Bikes are available for half- and full days. Staff can provide area maps and ideas for rides suitable to your skill and fitness levels. They'll also provide shuttle and pickup and dropoff services if you're renting their gear.

Adventure Sports is open seven days a week in summer, but hours can vary in spring and fall. In winter they're closed.

Jackson Hole

Outside Teton Park it's easier to find technical biking. Old logging roads provide miles of two track; hiking trails make for even more

single track. Be aware that any trail open to bikers is typically open to horseback riders as well. If you encounter horses, move off the trail to let them pass. Horses can be made extremely nervous by new and unpredictable things. One popular but strenuous and technical loop is the 18-mile-long Cache Creek ride, which goes up Cache Creek Road, turns single track and includes a steep ascent and matching technical descent. You return to Jackson on Game Creek Road.

Another strenuous, less technical ride is the Old Teton Pass Road. It roughly parallels Wyo. Highway 22's ascent of Teton Pass between Idaho and Wyoming. This 11-mile route is extremely popular with both bikers and hikers, so don't look for solitude here. A good beginner ride is an out-and-back trip of whatever length you like on the Elk Refuge's dirt road, accessed from Broadway in Jackson. Runners and bikers are the main users of this road in summer, although the occasional passing car will kick up some dust.

For more information, call any of the bike and bike rental shops listed below in this section.

Hoback Sports
40 S. Millward, Jackson, Wyo. • (307) 733-5335

Rent Specialized, Trek and Voodoo performance mountain bikes, pick up area trail maps or sign up for a mountain bike tour here. Fat Tire Tours ride directly from the store either to the Elk Refuge or use lift-assist to get up Snow King Mountain. This second, more technical ride descends the backside of Snow King Mountain on a single track trail.

Wilson Backcountry Sports
Fish Creek Center, Wilson, Wyo. • (307) 733-5228

Only 10 minutes from Jackson, you can ride out of this shop at the base of Teton Pass and right onto the trails that loop through the area. Bikes are this year's Gary Fishers. You can also pick up local trail maps and lots of

INSIDERS' TIP

Mountain biking is limited to established roadways in Yellowstone and Grand Teton parks.

free advice here, as well as bike clothing and accessories. Bike repair is available.

Surrounding Areas

Eastern Idaho

Idaho Falls, Idaho, Area

Idaho Falls is flat as Kansas, so it may surprise you to learn that the surrounding area is laced with great mountain biking trails. Our favorites are all two-track roads, some of which see auto traffic, particularly on weekends. They're clustered around Taylor Mountain, Kelly Canyon near the South Fork of the Snake, Tex Creek and the tiny town of Bone. Most of these roads involve pleasant combinations of moderate or extreme climbs up out of canyons and long, mellow plateau or canyon-floor sections. Sometimes roads become deeply rutted by autos that travel them too soon after spring runoff or heavy rains.

For more information on rides in the area, call Idaho Mountain Trading, listed below.

Idaho Mountain Trading
Corner of Shoup and B, Idaho Falls, Idaho • (208) 523-6679
Rent Fisher mountain bikes, both standard and high-end full-suspension models. Bike and in-line skate mechanics are on duty to handle your repair problems as well. The shop has been selling and renting outdoor toys since 1978.

Island Park, Idaho

What in winter is 600 miles of snowmobile trails becomes, in summer, nearly endless opportunity for mountain bikers. Much of what is available here is two-track and fairly level because much of Island Park is a gently rolling plateau. Often you'll find yourself on dirt roads also used by cars. To avoid traffic, bike in early mornings, on weekdays or in the fall.

One place you won't encounter cars is the Old Railroad Bed Trail. Read the description of the 50-plus miles of this gently graded trail in our Hiking and Backpacking chapter. The Old Railroad Bed Trail connects the Warm River in Idaho with West Yellowstone, Mon-

tana. In early summer, downed trees and boggy spots create a bit of hassle for riders, but by midsummer and into fall, riding this trail is like riding on soft sidewalk through lodgepole forest, wildflower meadow, over trestle bridges and even through an old railroad tunnel. If you start at the Black Canyon Loop Road or Big Springs Road, you can ride some 30 miles of almost continuous, mostly gentle downhill track to Warm Springs.

At Harriman State Park south of Island Park, enjoy some 20 miles of trails designated for non-motorized use only. Both steep and level riding are available here. To learn about Harriman's hiking/biking trails, call (208) 558-7368.

For information on other rides in the area, call the Island Park Ranger District at (208) 558-7301, or the Island Park Chamber of Commerce, (208) 558-7755.

Swan Valley, Idaho

The biking terrain around mountain-walled Swan Valley is mostly steep. Both single and double track are available. Plenty of good riding exists on Pine Creek Pass between Teton Valley and Swan Valley. For instance, 5-mile-long gravel Rainey Creek Road travels along a ridge between the pass and the top of the North Fork of Rainey Creek. Here it connects to a maze of technical single-track trails that can drop you down into Swan Valley or past Fourth of July Peak and down into Teton Valley.

Other, shorter two-track roads along Idaho Highway 31 on Pine Creek Pass include the road up Mike Spencer Canyon and one that heads up Fleming Canyon. Some folks like to ride the lower stretches of the Palisades Lakes trail, which originates on the valley floor. Read about this popular trail in our Hiking and Backpacking chapter.

For more information on mountain biking in the Swan Valley area, call the Palisades Ranger District, (208) 523-1412, or Idaho Mountain Trading in Idaho Falls, Idaho at (208) 523-6679.

Teton Valley

Teton Valley is hikers' and bikers' heaven. Lift-assisted technical rides can be had at Grand Targhee Ski and Summer Resort. For the less daring, Grand Targhee has mountain bike trails that wind through the wildflower meadows of Rick's Basin.

Down on the valley floor, loops can be built from the dirt roads that crisscross the valley, taking you through rolling farmland and past recreational cabins. Valley rides offer views of the peaks that ring Teton Basin. Some carry you past scenic Teton River and its wildlife viewing opportunities. In the Big Holes and the Tetons themselves, old logging roads and newer hikers' trails offer challenging, strenuous riding.

For more information, call Grand Targhee Ski and Summer Resort at (208) 353-2300, (800) 827-4433 or one of the businesses listed below.

Peaked Sports
70 E. Little Ave., Driggs, Idaho
• (208) 354-2354, (800) 705-2354

Peaked is the valley's Schwinn headquarters in summer. The shop rents mountain bikes (included are a helmet, an extra tube, a seat pack, a pump, a patch kit, bottle cages and advice about where to go). Peaked closes Sundays in summer. Two-hour, per-day and multiple-day rates are available. You can rent standard or performance Schwinn models.

Teton Teepee Lodge
Ski Hill Rd., Alta, Wyo. • (307) 353-8176, (800) 353-8176

So, you'd like to get off-road and see the west slopes of the Tetons from outside your car windows? How about a mountain bike tour? Teton Teepee Lodge (see our Resorts and Guest Ranches chapter) rents mountain bikes by the hour, half-day and day. They also provide a guide service that includes transportation, bike rental and snacks. They can personalize your tour to your skill level and interests. Bike tours cost about $30 per hour. Teton Teepee Lodge is just inside the Wyoming border near Driggs, Idaho.

Southwestern Montana

Bozeman, Montana

Bozeman is a mountain biking mecca with as many options as there are old logging roads

and trails. Two of the hot spots in the area, though, center around the Bridger Mountains to the north and Hyalite Basin to the south. (See our Watersports chapter for more about Hyalite Reservoir.) In Hyalite, about 15 miles south of Bozeman, there are so many rides that you could take a different one each day for weeks. Some of the more popular trails are loaded with hikers, bikers and horseback riders, while on others you'll barely see another soul.

For specific information about trails, we recommend you stop in at one of the rental shops listed below or the Bozeman Ranger District office at 3710 Fallon, Bozeman, or call (406)587-6920. Reading *Fat Tracks of Bozeman: 39 Great Mountain Bike Rides* by Will Harmon (Falcon Press) is also a good place to start.

Bangtail Bicycle and Ski
508 W. Main, Bozeman, Mont.
• (406) 587-4905

For bike (and ski) sales, rentals and information, Bangtail is a great place to start. During the summer, Bangtail rents Rockhoppers for $15 per day. They don't offer guided rides here, but check at the shop to see about scheduled weekly rides. In 1997, Bangtail organized a regular Monday-night ride. On Wednesdays women rode together, and on Thursdays it was the men's turn. Bangtail sells Trek and Specialized bikes. For information about Bangtail's cross-country ski rentals, see our Winter Sports chapter.

Panda Sports Rental
621 Bridger Dr., Bozeman, Mont.
• (406) 587-6280

This convenience store/gas station rents bikes, river rafts, canoes, skis, and avalanche transceivers. Bikes rent for $15 per day.

Big Sky, Montana

Mountain biking around Big Sky, where the Madison and Gallatin ranges wall in the narrow Gallatin Canyon, is mostly extreme with plenty of old logging roads and trails from which to choose. Trails on Porcupine Creek, in the Beehive Basin and the North Fork Drainage are among local favorites. To get the inside scoop on trails — new ones seem to pop up as soon as someone tries, likes and talks about them — we recommend you talk to someone in a local bike shop or to someone at the Bozeman Ranger District, 3710 Fallon, Bozeman, Montana, (406) 587-6920.

Grizzly Outfitters
1700 Big Sky Rd., Big Sky, Mont.
• (406) 995-2939

Big Sky's only full-service bike shop, Grizzly Outfitters offers 40 bikes for rent. Owner Ken Lancey is also a storehouse of information about mountain biking in the area. A standard mountain-biking package will cost you $9 per hour, $18 for a half-day or $25 for a full day. A high-performance package will cost you more: $15, $25 and $35, respectively.

Grizzly also offers a reduced rate for kid's packages ($6 per hour), as well as Burley bike trailers for (two) tots. One of these will cost you $4 per hour or $10 for the day. Grizzly rents downhill and cross-country skis, too (see our Winter Sports chapter).

Gallatin Alpine Sports
3090 Pine Dr., West Fork Meadows, Big Sky, Mont. • (406) 995-2313

In addition to bike rentals, this loaded-to-the-gills sport shop also rents camping, skiing, and canoeing gear. Bikes — all top of the line — rent from $23 to $30 per day depending on what kind of bike you want to pedal up the mountain. Gallatin Alpine is open year round, seven days a week.

Livingston, Montana

When it comes to biking, Livingston is a little lacking, not because of the terrain, but because access to the mountains is pretty much blocked by private property. Most dedicated riders (there are about a dozen in the area) have to load up their bikes and haul them somewhere, often to the Gallatin Valley, to find a challenging or accessible trail.

Chico Hot Springs
Chico Rd., Pray, Mont. • (406) 333-4933

At the Chico Hot Springs Lodge barn you can rent bicycles for $25 a day or $15 for a half-day. Roads and trails lead away from the Lodge, or you can load up your bike and head for other trails in the area. Shop manager Melissa Taylor knows the area well and can steer you in the right direction.

Saddle Sore Cycles
117 W. Callender St., Livingston, Mont.
• (406) 222-2628

Storrs Bishop sells, repairs, rides and rents mountain bikes ($5 per hour or $25 a day). The more days you keep a bike, the less he charges by the day. Bishop mostly rents to out-of-towners who want to fly in, ride through the Park and over 11,000-foot Beartooth Pass. If you want to know what's up with biking in the area, Saddle Sore Cycles is the place to start.

Northwestern Wyoming

Mountain biking in the Cody area is growing as fast as everywhere else. Among the favorite biking haunts is the McCullough Peak area about 7 miles east of town. Managed by the Bureau of Land Management (BLM), this is both a wild-horse management area and a wilderness-study area. That means mountain bikers must ride the boundary trails and roads, which are intersected by scattered chunks of private property, some of which offer public access and others of which do not. To be sure about where you're going, we suggest you stop in at BLM's Cody Resource Area office at 1002 Blackburn, Cody, Wyoming, or call (307) 587-2216.

Other biking areas include trails on the North Fork of the Shoshone (U.S. Highway 20 west of Cody) and Carter Mountain south of town. For this ride, locals have a friend shuttle them to the top so that they can coast down through the trees, across streams and over meadows.

INSIDERS' TIP

National Forest trails can change dramatically due to weather or lack of maintenance — especially with federal budget cutbacks. To avoid encountering problems, be sure to check with a local national forest ranger district office or visitors center.

Photo: Robert Bower/Post Register

A mountain climber takes a practice climb near the town of Jackson,
Wyoming not far from the Grand Teton Mountain Range.

You'll find a strong women's biking group in Cody, mostly centered around Olde Faithful Bicycles. We recommend you stop in at Olde Faithful Bicycles listed below, the BLM listed earlier in this entry or the Wapiti Ranger District Office, 203 Yellowstone Avenue, Cody, (307) 527-6921, for more information about mountain biking in the Cody area.

Also, to keep up on pedaling in the Cody area, you can subscribe to Olde Faithful's *Chainletter* (see the entry below for more information).

Olde Faithful Bicycles
1362 Sheridan Ave., Cody, Wyo.
• **(307) 527-5110**
Olde Faithful Bicycles rents, sells and fixes bikes of all kinds. Doug and Leslie

Shinaver, owners of this busy biking hub, not only rent mountain bikes, but they also know every good trail or road in the area. The Shinavers publish *Chainletter*, an occasional newsletter full of humor, bike-maintenance tips and information about races and good mountain-biking trails. Behind the store is the brand new Cody BMX Track.

Technical Climbing and Mountaineering

Technical climbing is any rock climbing where ropes and other devices are used to protect climbers or to assist them in their ascent. Devices include bolts drilled into rock, pitons that climbers hammer into rock, or ice axes they carry. Mountaineering is climbing and more: It involves route-finding and other backcountry skills as well as technical rock — and often ice or snow — climbing. Many mountaineering routes take two or more days to complete. Climbing and mountaineering should only be undertaken by individuals in good physical condition, equipped with the right skills, the proper gear and knowledge of the area.

Although interesting cragging areas exist all over Greater Yellowstone, the region is best known for the granite, ice and snow climbs of the Tetons. Many are serious, multi-pitch mountaineering routes. Some are world-class, drawing skilled climbers from all over the planet. The sheer peaks of the Teton range offer so much opportunity for classic climbs that some routes are still waiting to be put up. Several books are available on Teton climbs. The most comprehensive is probably Leigh Ortenburger and Reynold Jackson's *A Climber's Guide to the Teton Range*. It details routes but also describes the climbing history of these famous peaks.

Beginners and less experienced climbers can and do experience the exhilaration of Teton climbing. Smart ones do it with a competent guide. Some folks around here argue that even highly skilled climbers new to the Tetons should hire a guide their first time or two out, especially if they're planning big ascents like the Grand Teton. Either of the well-known climbing schools listed in a following section offer both instruction and guiding services.

Climbing is discouraged in Yellowstone Park because of the loose, crumbling rock throughout the Park. It is outlawed altogether in the Grand Canyon area.

Climbing Schools and Guide Services

Exum Mountain Guides
South Jenny Lake, Grand Teton Park, Wyo. • (307) 733-2297

Basic and intermediate classes are offered daily near Hidden Falls on the back-side of Jenny Lake. Climbers can arrange guided trips up the Grand or any other peak in the Tetons as well, summer or winter, on ice, rock or snow. The company is named after Glenn Exum, who as a teenager in 1931 made a dramatic solo ascent of the Grand Teton along a ridge that now also bears his name.

Jackson Hole Mountain Guides
165 N. Glenwood, Jackson, Wyo.
• (307) 733-4979

These folks offer daily classes on rock, ice and snow climbing. They'll also take individuals or small groups up any route in the Tetons.

Climbing Gyms

Jackson, Wyoming, hosts a fine climbing gym, as does Idaho Falls, Idaho. Climbing gyms provide vertical and overhung walls pegged with rocklike hand and foot holds for climbing practice. They're made safe with ropes attached to chains at the ceiling and, of course, by your friend or instructor, who "belays" from the working end of the rope. Grand Targhee Ski and Summer Resort puts up holds on a lift tower close to the base lodge every summer. Any of the three are fine places to try out a new sport.

Teton Rock Gym, 1116 Maple, Jackson, Wyoming, (307) 733-0707, and Stone Walls, 751 S. Capital, Idaho Falls, Idaho, (208) 528-8610, both offer instruction as well as a place for serious climbers to hone their skills or get a winter workout. Both gyms are described in our Attractions chapter.

For more on Grand Targhee's outdoor climbing wall, call the resort at (307) 353-2300 or (800) 827-4433.

Golf

Golf is not what most people think of when they start packing for a Greater Yellowstone vacation, but that doesn't mean there aren't some pretty good reasons to bring those spikeless shoes. Municipal courses, some pleasantly mature, others relaxed and funky, allow play for prices that may surprise you — some are as reasonable as $10. The region's resort towns are home to award-winning courses (with the higher greens fees you'd expect). Greater Yellowstone courses often make use of the lovely mountain scenery to enhance the beauty of their courses. In winter, many of these courses are laced with cross-country ski trails (see our Wintersports chapter). Below are a few highlights to pique your interest and convince you to toss those shoes in the suitcase.

Jackson Hole

Jackson Hole Golf and Tennis Club
5000 N. Spring Gulch Rd., Jackson, Wyo.
• (307) 733-3111

Like the fine dining and fine art galleries of this little resort valley, Jackson Hole's golf courses are world-class. *Golf Digest* says this one is among the top-10 resort courses in the country. Course designer Robert Trent Jones built water hazards on 11 of 18 holes. Each hole provides fine views of the mountain ranges that ring this valley.

The par 72 course is rated 72.5 with a slope of 126 from the championship tees. It measures 6756 from the white tees. Reserving tee times is recommended. No metal spike shoes are allowed. Greens fees range between $50 and $100, depending on season and time of day.

Teton Pines Resort and Country Club
3450 N. Clubhouse Dr., Jackson, Wyo.
• (208) 733-1733 for tee times

This award-winning course just 6 miles west of Jackson off Teton Village Road was designed by Arnold Palmer and built in 1987. Teton Pines is open to the golfing public in summer and to nordic skiers in winter. The 18-hole par 72 course is rated 74.8 with a slope of 137 from the gold championship tees. It measures 6330 from the white tees.

Please wear spikeless shoes; if you don't have any, a few complimentary pair are available for use. Soft-Spikes™ conversions are also available for a small fee. Greens fees range between $50 and $140 depending on season and day. Lodge guests receive a

discount. Lessons are available for $65 to $80 per hour. Reservations are strongly recommended.

Outlying Areas

Eastern Idaho

Idaho Falls, Idaho

Pinecrest Golf Course
701 E. Elva, Idaho Falls, Idaho
• (406) 529-1485

This municipal course — one of three in Idaho Falls — is a locals' favorite. It's the oldest in the area, with stately old trees that screen players ahead of you from sight. A gentle contour to many of the holes adds challenge. The par 70, 18-hole course totals 6394 yards. No spikes are allowed. Greens fees run around $13.50. Tee times must be arranged one day in advance.

Rexburg, Idaho, Area

Teton Lakes Golf Course
N. Hibbard Hwy., Rexburg, Idaho
• (208) 359-3036

The groundskeepers must work overtime here: The greens are always well-maintained and immaculately cut, and you couldn't find a divot to save your life. The front nine, built in 1978, is open and features trees; each hole in the back nine has water in play. The front nine were built in 1978; the back nine were added in 1984. Each hole in the back nine has water in play. Yardage off the white tees is 5900. The par 71 course is rated 66.6 from the white tees with a slope of 112.

Greens fees are $11.50; plan to make your tee time two days in advance. This is a spikeless course.

Ashton, Idaho, Area

Aspen Acres
4179 E. 1100 N., Ashton, Idaho
• (208) 652-3524

Thirty years ago, Arthur and Velma

The log clubhouse at Pinecrest Golf Course in Idaho Falls, Idaho, was built of logs hauled to town from the Targhee National Forest.

Photo: Monte LaOrange/Post Register

Anderson began to create this anomaly among the potato fields outside Ashton. They retired from full-time ranching, contracted golf fever and built a three-hole course to treat the symptoms. Friends began coming to play, and before they knew it, Arthur and Velma's golf course had taken on a life of its own.

Unlike many courses, Aspen Acres grew organically, following existing contours of the land, shaping itself around the aspen groves. The result is a pleasantly eccentric, relaxed family course that offers lots of chipping practice as well as the opportunity to occasionally view moose and bear from your golf cart. And you have the chance to drive your cart right to your campsite, because Aspen Acres is also a full-hookup RV and campground (see our Camping and RV Parks chapter).

A small pro shop and snack bar are on the premises. Golf carts are available to rent. No tee-time reservations are necessary. The cost for 18 holes of play is $10.

Southwestern Montana

Bozeman, Montana

Bridger Creek
2710 McIlhattan Rd., Bozeman, Mont.
• (406) 586-2333

At the clubhouse you'll find a proshop with cart rentals ($10 for nine holes), space for catered group outings and only pre-made sandwiches and chips for snacks. Greens fees for nine holes range from $12 to $22 depending on how busy the season is. For 18 holes, you'll pay from $14 to $24. Bridger Creek Golf Course is open from about April 1 to November 1.

INSIDERS' TIP

Most of Yellowstone Country is at 6,000 feet or higher. If you live at low altitude and are older, or if you suffer from heart or respiratory difficulties, it's a good idea to consult your doctor before you come here. Even the physically fit and healthy may find themselves unusually short of breath for several days.

Big Sky, Montana

Big Sky Ski and Summer Resort
Mountain Village, Big Sky, Mont.
• **(406) 995-5000, (800) 548-4486**

Big Sky Resort managers have plans for adding 18 more challenging holes to this beautiful golf course designed by Arnold Palmer. While the Big Sky course is so far not a destination golf course, it's hard to beat for pure setting. On the course you're apt to see moose, deer, elk, an occasional bear and a few hardheaded anglers casting their lines into the stream that flows through it. The golf course is a part of the Big Sky Resort complex. The pro shop has a complete line of golf rentals.

Red Lodge, Montana

Red Lodge Mountain Resort Golf Course
828 Upper Continental Drive, Red Lodge, Mont. • **(406) 446-3344**

Tee off from a 40-foot cliff. Down below is the green — an island surrounded by water. Those in the know bring extra balls to the Red Lodge course, not just for the floating green. With two creeks, two irrigation ditches and half a dozen ponds, 13 of the course's 18 holes have some sort of water obstacle lurking nearby. The emphasis here is accuracy, no distance. Built in the mid-1980s, the Red Lodge course was bought in 1995 by the Red Lodge Mountain Resort. You'll find a beautiful clubhouse with an upstairs restaurant that overlooks the golf course and the Beartooth Mountains in the distance. A snack bar and the pro shop are downstairs. Greens fees for nine holes in 1997 were $12 Monday through Thursday, and $14 Friday through Sunday. For an 18-hole round, it cost $14 and $23. The Red Lodge golf course is open from about mid-April to early October.

Northwestern Wyoming

Olive Glenn Golf and Country Club
802 Meadow Ln., Cody, Wyo.
• **(307) 587-5551**

Golf Digest ranks Olive Glenn as the fifth-best golf course in Wyoming. In addition to the 18-hole, par 72 course, Olive Glenn boasts a fully staffed golf shop, club and cart rental, Mulligan's restaurant (lunch and dinner only), tennis courts, a swimming pool and a weight room. Fun for any level golf player, Olive Glenn offers a beautiful view no matter which way you turn. Olive Glenn hosts many Wyoming Golf Association events and in 1997 hosted the Girls' Junior America Cup tournament — the first international golf tournament to be held in Wyoming. The buy-in membership at Olive Glenn costs $2,500, and monthly dues are $105 (per family). Visitors can play by paying a $28 greens fee.

There are still plenty of wide open spaces in Yellowstone country, but the recent buying and building boom, combined with the general accelerated growth since the 1970s, has left enough of a mark on the land to worry newcomers and old-timers alike.

Real Estate

Mountain retreat. Fisherman's Fantasy. Perfect Private Paradise. Magnificent Mountain Estate. Recreational Hideaway.

The list of properties for sale in Greater Yellowstone is as big as the towering mountains and as diverse as the flora and fauna of the valleys below. From 1992 until mid-1996, it seemed as if every piece of property on the market would be snatched up no matter what the price. In some places, ranches and recreational properties sold and resold, and tripled in value during the five-year period. Not since the gold rush and homesteading days has there been such a scramble for land in Yellowstone country.

There are still plenty of wide open spaces in Yellowstone country, but the recent buying and building boom, combined with the general accelerated growth since the 1970s, has left enough of a mark on the land to worry newcomers and old-timers alike.

Until fairly recently, ranchers wouldn't have thought of selling their ranches. But the average age of ranchers in Greater Yellowstone is approaching 60. Tempted by the inflated land prices and tired of enduring the rigors of ranching, the graying ranchers of Yellowstone country have sold or subdivided their ranches 10 by 10.

Cities, counties, conservationists, newcomers and even ranchers have been grappling with ways to manage growth so it doesn't ruin the views, consume the productive farmlands, reduce the wildlife habitat or degrade the water quality of Greater Yellowstone. Already, problems are popping up in developed areas. Twenty years ago, Big Sky Resort was a ranch with important wildlife habitat. Homes and lodges now stand in the middle of prime elk and grizzly bear habitat. Agencies fear, too, that septic and sewage from the community may be degrading the water in the Gallatin River. Yet Big Sky's new comprehensive management plan would allow for 20,000 residents, more than twice as many as the community can currently handle. Throughout Yellowstone country, where once we saw nothing manmade to interrupt the landscape, new homes and roads now mar it.

To protect the wide open spaces and the environment, landowners are beginning either to sell or donate conservation easements. For a hefty sum of money, property owners basically sell forever their right to development or subdivide their property, but they retain ownership of the land and are allowed to continue working it. Throughout Greater Yellowstone, where more than 200,000 acres are protected by easements, land trusts have been set up to buy easements.

Individuals at the land trust offices in Greater Yellowstone can put you in touch

INSIDERS' TIP

The Montana Department of Natural Resources and Conservation has put out a booklet called "Tips on Land and Water Management for Small Farms and Ranches in Montana." Full of helpful hints on such things as weed management, pasture and irrigation management, streams, wetlands and water quality protection, improving wildlife habitat and forest management, this booklet is great for anyone thinking of buying a ranchette in Greater Yellowstone. To get a copy, write: Conservation Districts Bureau, Department of Natural Resources and Conservation, P.O. Box 202301, Helena, MT 59620-2301, or call (406) 444-6667.

with other conservation real estate brokers. Among the land trusts you can contact are: Montana Nature Conservancy, 32 S. Ewing, Helena, Montana 59601, (406) 443-0303; Wyoming Nature Conservancy, 258 W. Main Street, Lander, Wyoming 82520, (307) 332-2971; Teton Valley Land Trust, P.O. Box 247, Driggs, Idaho 83422, (208) 726-3007; and Montana Land Reliance, P.O. Box 355, Helena, Montana 59624, (406) 443-7027.

In this chapter we have provided the names of a few real estate agencies throughout Greater Yellowstone region. Within each area, we generally chose those agencies that have been around the longest. As you will note from our entries, we have also included a few that handle specialized or unique properties.

www.insiders.com

See this and many other **Insiders' Guide®** destinations online — in their entirety.

Visit us today!

Greater Yellowstone Communities

Entrance Communities

West Yellowstone, Montana

If it's a 10-acre parcel with trees and a stream running through it that you want, chances are you won't find it in West Yellowstone. Carved out of a lodgepole pine forest and corralled by National Forest and Park boundaries, West, as it's often called, is a booming tourist town 90 miles south of Bozeman with no place to sprawl. That means land is getting scarce. While West boasts only about 1,000 full-time residents, it has more than 50 motels to accommodate the million-plus tourists that visit the town each year.

The lack of available land, combined with the need for employee housing and the demand for both commercial and recreation property, has driven property prices so high that locals are mostly unable to afford it. A two-bedroom, two-bath, 1,000-square-foot, ranch-style home on Hebgen Lake starts at $120,000.

Gardiner, Montana

Of all the entrance communities to Yellowstone, Gardiner has most retained its small-town, Western atmosphere. You won't find world-class shopping, paved streets or other signs of "dressing up for the tourists" here. You will find big-hearted, hard-working residents who are glad to have retained their easy-going lifestyle.

Once the grand entrance for tourists traveling on the Northern Pacific Railway and now the only year-round entrance to Yellowstone Park, Gardiner ranks third in numbers of visitors entering the Park. Just 5 miles from Mammoth, where permanent Park employees live all year, Gardiner is home to the warehouses of Park concessionaires. Gardiner, which sprang up in the 1880s as a supply town for Ft. Yellowstone soldiers, is still a supply town and bedroom community for those who work in the Park.

Like West Yellowstone, growth in Gardiner is limited by National Forest and National Park boundaries. Available land is even scarcer here than in West Yellowstone. And, despite the fact that a gold mine near Jardine shut down in 1996, homes don't come on the market very often. When they do, they'll cost you plenty. A two-bedroom, one-bath house on a 50-foot by 100-foot lot will cost you around $100,000, while a three-

INSIDERS' TIP

The Corporation for the Northern Rockies prints "Welcome to the West," a guide to private land conservation for people considering the purchase of real estate in the Northern Rockies. To learn more about this publication, write: Corporation for the Northern Rockies, P.O. Box 1448, Livingston, MT 59047, or call (406) 222-0730.

bedroom, two-bath home on the same size lot runs about $155,000. A four-bedroom, three-bath home on a 1-acre lot goes for about $195,000.

Silver Gate and Cooke City, Montana

At 7,600 feet above sea level, winter comes hard and early to Silver Gate and Cooke City, sister entrance communities just outside the northeast entrance of Yellowstone Park. About November 1, depending on the snow depth, the Beartooth Highway is closed for the winter, so the only access to Cooke City is via Yellowstone Park from Gardiner. While Cooke City is gradually becoming a winter recreation destination, it isn't until the snow melts (usually in June) that the streets come alive and the town's population grows from 90 to 300. Then Main Street becomes a moving stream of people and cars. Silver Gate's population grows from a handful to about 100 each summer.

Silver Gate, 3 miles west of Cooke City and a mile from the northeast entrance of Yellowstone Park, was founded in 1932. Silver Gate's founders hoped to create a rustic Western town for tourists and buyers of recreation homes.

Both towns are squeezed into a narrow canyon, and — you may have already guessed — they, too, are bordered by Yellowstone Park and the Absoraka-Beartooth Wilderness in the Gallatin National Forest. While the boundaries may limit growth in the canyon, they make for easy access to the Park and to countless recreation opportunities. You can literally walk out your door and, within minutes, be in the wilderness.

Jackson Hole

Most of Teton County, Wyoming, is owned by the state or federal government. In a valley so pretty and famous that everyone wants to own a piece, that guarantees top-dollar property values. The average three-bedroom house sells for $250,000 to $275,000. A lot in Jackson Hole, if you can find one, will probably command at least $100,000. Larger lots outside of town come dear, too. Start looking for 2½-acre lots at around $150,000.

If those numbers make you reel, consider that figures run higher in desirable locations. Property on the west side of the Snake River (Jackson is on the east) — an area locals call the West Side — is pricier. It's out of the hubbub of Jackson, much of it fleshed in cottonwood trees, and it's close to golf courses, tennis courts, Jackson Hole Mountain Resort and other recreational facilities. Particularly popular, and expensive, is the tiny West Side town of Wilson at the base of Teton Pass.

One proviso about these high numbers: Realtors caution that "average selling prices" can be meaningless in Jackson Hole. There are so many homes sold for more than $1 million — some for as much as $5 million — that averages don't necessarily mean much.

Out toward Hoback Junction, 13 miles south of Jackson, land costs a bit less — not as much less as you might think, but enough that if you could afford a home in Jackson, you can get that home on a small acreage in Hoback.

Once upon a time, folks who worked in Jackson but couldn't afford to buy here purchased their homes in Teton Valley, just over the Idaho border. Many people still live in Teton Valley and commute over Teton Pass, but now they can't afford to buy in that increasingly popular valley, either.

No one knows exactly how many people live in this tourist mecca. Seminomadic locals, part-time recreationists and seasonal employees come and go too fast to be counted reliably. Best guesses usually fall around 6,000 for Jackson and perhaps 15,000 for the whole county. Upwards of 3 million tourists pass through town every summer, most of them in July and August. Residents willing to work in the service sector don't lack for jobs in season. Jackson Hole is largely a second-home market, but local Realtors think their buyers may spend more time in their Hole second homes than folks in other recreational areas.

Eastern Idaho

Idaho Falls, Idaho

Idaho's third-largest town sits in the middle of the Snake River Plain. It's uncompromisingly flat, with rich farmland and mountains like distant mirages on the horizons. It's home to more than 40,000 people.

Property in Idaho Falls is still affordable. Typically a Realtor can show you about 45 homes in the $70,000 price range. Average selling prices in town were about $97,000 last year ($85,000 outside the city limits) and $89,600 the year before. In all of Bonneville County, you could leaf through at least 500 listings for condos, townhouses, homes and residential acreages in a given month. Particularly popular right now are more expensive homes in the area around Sage Lakes Golf Course on East River Road north of town. The town annexed the area and brought city services out to these newer rural homes.

Areas that seem to hold value well include what locals call "the numbered streets," a neighborhood of older (and some historic) residences with mature trees on quiet streets adjacent to downtown. East and south of town, beyond Ammon, you'll find many acreage properties with stable property values. Some of the highest prices are found among the newer homes south of town — $150,000 to more than $1 million.

Rexburg, Idaho

Rexburg offers the charms of a stable, economically thriving small town right out of *Leave it to Beaver*, coupled with the fantastic recreational opportunities of the Greater Yellowstone region. This makes Rexburg, population 14,000, nearly unique in a region where most small towns make their living from tourism, leaving the "real" jobs and industries to cluster in larger communities like Idaho Falls and Bozeman.

Much of the town's charm comes from its strong Mormon influence. If the town seems to you like a place where children walk the streets at night without looking over their shoulders, it is. Mormon communities tend to be strongly family-oriented, and this one is no exception.

Ironically, the other significant factor in the tidy hometown look of Rexburg was a disaster. In 1976, the newly built (and highly flawed) Teton Dam crumbled and released a massive flood that nearly wiped out several towns, including Rexburg. That's why you don't find too many buildings in town more than 20 years old, even though Rexburg is one of the oldest townships in the region.

Local real estate agents say folks are sometimes surprised by what their money doesn't buy in this predominantly rural area. They expect housing to be cheap, but it's not. A smaller three-bedroom, one- or two-bathroom home will sell for $80,000 to $85,000. Sometimes this causes an affordability problem for new home buyers. Nevertheless, this midrange property moves quickly.

Ashton, Idaho

Drive through quiet, unassuming little Ashton, seed potato capital of the world, and you'll get the feeling you're as far from booming tourism and vacation property as it is possible to be. You'll be wrong. Although tourism is mostly of the pass-through kind here, there's plenty of that: Ashton is only a couple dozen miles from Yellowstone Park. The town also claims the only roadless access point to Yellowstone, at a place called Bechler.

What's for sale here in the way of homes is mostly recreational. The first recreational subdivision was constructed in 1970, so Ashton is relatively new as a vacation home area. Most available already-constructed houses are within the town of Ashton; usually you'll have eight or nine from which to choose.

Folks who move here year-round may have difficulty finding employment. Principal employers in the area are the Forest Service and small businesses looking for service personnel. Some residents commute to Rexburg or even Idaho Falls, a 45-minute drive if the pavement is dry. Before buying your dream home here with plans for commuting out of the Ashton area, think "access": In winter, area roads typically close two or three times per season for a day or more.

Lots in the area run from $4,500 to $10,000 per acre, depending on how developed they are and what amenities they offer. For example, Teton views affect the price; so do trees (the more mature trees on a lot, the higher the price). Lots in town are generally very reasonable, running about $1 per square foot.

A final tip: The water table is deep — as far down as 450 feet — in some spots around here. So if you have to sink a well, you may be looking at another $20,000.

Island Park, Idaho

Island Park and its 33-mile-long main street are entirely enclosed by Targhee National Forest. What this means to prospective buyers is that although the area is definitely gathering steam as a vacation home area, it'll be hard for developers to build it to death, since only about 11 percent of the land is in private hands.

Island Park boasts two large lakes — Henry's Lake and Island Park Reservoir — and more than 75 miles of river and stream. This is good since local Realtors say everybody's dream cabin has a creek burbling through it. Of course, you pay for the waterfront. A lot with a view of Henry's Lake might cost you $20,000; that same lot on the lake will go for $100,000.

Although there's a little of everything in the Island Park area, most of what's available (and what's in greatest demand) are best called cabins. They are log or log-sided, rustic and cozy, and, depending on size and accessibility to water, they go for anywhere from $60,000 to $1.5 million. Lots can be had starting at around $8 grand.

Realtors like to say that the Island Park area is just being discovered. Part of the fuel is the bountiful great recreational opportunities, such as fishing and snowmobiling. Another cause of development here is the fact that nearby resort areas like Big Sky and Jackson Hole have priced themselves out of reach for middle-class buyers.

One last word about Island Park and its reasonably priced recreational property: Don't expect it to last. Real estate prices have been climbing at a rate of 10 percent annually for the past few years. Three years ago you could pick up an acre lot for $2,400. Those days are gone.

Swan Valley, Idaho

Most of what's available in this still-undiscovered recreational haven are building lots rather than homes or cabins. If you're willing to purchase land away from the river, you can find property from $2,000 to $10,000 per acre. The prime Swan Valley properties, though, are along the South Fork of the Snake, tucked into the cottonwoods. For one of those, multiply the asking price by 10 — at least. And that's if anything's available.

Much of the rest of the valley is open and treeless. Some of it has winter access problems, since not all valley roads are plowed in winter. The valley can be prone to flooding problems, as it was in the spring of 1997 when the South Fork crept from its banks. The upper part of the valley stayed dryer last year when folks at the lower end, closer to Idaho Falls, were sandbagging.

Right now, especially if your waterfront dream home can be on a parcel with an irrigation canal running through it, property is still plentiful and affordable in Swan Valley. But that is probably changing. This puts little Swan Valley, population 950, in line with a trend seen all over our region: Folks from other regions are beginning to notice what the area has to offer in terms of recreation and quality of life.

Teton Valley, Idaho

Locals call it "the quiet side of the Tetons." Teton Valley (aka Pierre's Hole) is what Jackson Hole could have been: a mountain valley in the midst of recreational heaven, its feet still solidly planted in reality. The valley is surrounded on three sides by mountains. It contains three small agricultural communities, Tetonia, Victor and Driggs, and is increasingly ringed by recreational properties tucked into the wooded foothills and wears a fourth on its cuff, Alta, Wyoming.

More changes are coming. In 1996, valley population was just more than 5,000. Figures commonly touted around here list Teton as the sixth-fastest growing county in the nation. Property used to run through peak-trough cycles, regularly losing and regaining value. Now it rises, plateaus and then rises again.

The most affordable property lies in the lower valley, around Victor and Tetonia (residents of Teton Valley might dispute that Tetonia is in Teton Valley). More expensive recreational property is found on the valley perimeter, particularly to the north, where buyers will find desirable forested areas. Another high-priced area is in Alta, Wyoming, where restrictive zoning in effect since 1979 has left land in larger parcels. These days, new subdivisions in rural Alta can't exceed a ratio of one home per 35 acres.

The dream cabin on dream land — a handhewn, tree-shaded log house of modest size, say 1,000 square feet — doesn't sell for less than $200,000. And that's if you can find it at all. Easier to find are uniform-turned-log homes and frame or manufactured homes on the treeless valley floor. Those start around $160,000 for log. Part of the high cost is explained by the equally high cost of construction up here. Houses must be built to withstand an 80-pounds snow load, high winds and deep-freeze winters.

Southeastern Montana

Bozeman, Montana

This booming hub of Greater Yellowstone has it all. First, there's Montana State University, once a cow college now a university with diversity. Then there's a lively arts community that began at MSU then moved into the community. Next there's Bridger Bowl Ski Area just up the canyon. If that's not enough, about 40 miles to the south is Big Sky Ski and Summer Resort. And 90 miles to south is Yellowstone National Park. In between are millions of acres of public lands and miles of trout-bearing river.

It's easy to see why Bozeman is one of the fastest growing towns in Montana — and why it has some of the highest priced real estate in the state This city (it may seem small to you but to us it seems big and busy — like a city) has 28,000 full-time residents and a diverse economy. MSU also plays a major role in the local economy.

Livingston, Montana

Founded in 1882 as a railroad town for the Northern Pacific Railroad, Livingston was the gateway through which early day tourists passed on their way to Yellowstone National Park. These days Bozeman is the favored northern jumping off point for the Park. And Livingston is a quiet — almost quaint — little town (population 7,500) still unspoiled by development. Residents like the small town life with easy access to recreation and to all that Bozeman has to offer. Compared to Bozeman, you'll see fewer subdivisions and lower prices in town. The biggest local development is the Northern Lights subdivision within the city limits west of town.

Today, with a population of 7,500 and an average countywide income of $22,658, Livingston is the humming hub of the Paradise Valley, where movie stars have quietly bought ranches and driven up property prices. A popular location for Western movies, Livingston was the setting for *A River Runs Through It*, directed and produced by Robert Redford; other scenes were shot on the Yellowstone River and the Gallatin River south of Bozeman. If you look, you can find older residential homes that are reasonably priced. Recreational properties, especially those close to Yellowstone Park or Emigrant, midway between Livingston and the Park, are more dear.

Big Sky, Montana

In 1969, the late NBC newsman Chet Huntley and a group of investors bought what is now known as the Big Sky Ski and Summer Resort. Trailer parks have been outlawed, and that "little cabin in the woods" might sell for $400,000. A studio apartment that used to sell for $35,000 now sells for $70,000. A 20-acre parcel, depending on where it is, runs from $150,000 to $500,000. A 1-acre lot in the Meadow will cost you $150,000, while a quarter-acre lot right on the golf course is may go for $90,000. New homes cost about $150 per square foot to build.

Despite the high prices, Big Sky property continues to be in demand, mostly because the Gallatin Canyon is a recreation mecca. Generally, new development is west of U.S. Highway 191, along the road leading to the Big Sky Ski Area.

Red Lodge, Montana

There is plenty of property for sale in Red Lodge, population 2,300, but if you think you might want to live here year round, you'd better be prepared to like winter and lots of snow. At an elevation of 5,555 feet, Red Lodge averages 150 inches of snowfall per year, with an average of 105 frost-free days. During the winter, the Beartooth Highway — U.S. Highway 212 between Red Lodge and Cooke City, which crawls over a 11,000-foot summit — is buried by snow so deep that even in July, motorists pass snowbanks beside the road. Sixty miles to the north lies Billings, the main supply town for residents, who have one grocery store from which to buy in Red Lodge.

Because of the climate, though, and because of nearby Red Lodge Mountain Ski Area, this town is an up and coming family resort town. In addition to wintersports, Red Lodge is the gateway to the Beartooth Mountains. Real estate prices that have leveled off in other areas appear to be still climbing in Red Lodge. Five years ago, you could buy almost any house in town for $30,000, now these same houses are selling for $80,000. In the past two years, the cost of raw land has doubled.

Northwestern Wyoming

Cody, Wyoming

Don't let the location or the size of this 8,500-person town fool you. Located in the middle of the Big Horn Basin's high desert, Cody is an oasis in the land of cowboys. On Sheridan Ave., Cody's main street, you'll find world class shopping and dining, and a budding collection of art galleries. If that isn't enough, you'll find the town full of energetic, enthusiastic folks who love to show visitors a good time. At the center of their show are two things: the Buffalo Bill Historical Center and the Cody Nite Rodeo which runs from June through August. (See our Attractions chapter.) You'll also find an excellent hospital and schools that aim for quality.

In the summer this hopping little town is busy catering to tourists. Each evening outlaws step out into main street, fire a shot in the air, and start a showdown-shootout on the steps of the Irma Hotel, a grand hotel built by Buffalo Bill Cody in 1902. Buffalo Bill, an army scout and hunter who took the frontier on the road with his Wild West show, was the founder of the town. His dream was for Cody to be a tourist destination with a diverse economy. Today, Cody is just that.

Real Estate Companies

Yellowstone Entrance Communities

All Seasons Realty
303 Canyon, West Yellowstone, Mont.
• (406) 646-7714

Real estate agent Don Stanley just bought this full-service year-round agency; he also owns Yellowstone Realty. The former owner is acting as broker until Stanley completes his training. Otherwise, All Seasons (and Yellowstone Realty) would be a one-man operation. Though new to the field of real estate, Stanley knows West Yellowstone well. He has lived in West 30 years and worked at a variety of jobs including running a cable TV business, working in a lumber mill, driving a tour bus and feeding the bears at Grizzly Discovery Center.

Gardiner Office, Century 21 Payne Realty
Outpost Mall, Gardiner, Mont.
• (406) 848-7904

Associate Broker Karen Hayes, who handles the Gardiner area for Century 21 Payne Realty, has been selling real estate in the area for several years. If you're bent on buying property in Gardiner, it's best to keep in touch with Hayes, since property is snapped up quickly once it goes on the market here.

The Real Estate Agency
15 Madison Ave., West Yellowstone, Mont. • (406) 646-9523

West Yellowstone's oldest established agency, The Real Estate Agency sells all types of property all year round. Owned and operated by John Costello and Robb Klatt, this agency welcomes dreamers and others with questions about real estate in the West Yellowstone area.

Yellowstone Realty
303 Canyon, West Yellowstone, Mont.
• (406) 646-7575

Yellowstone Realty is a full-service agency owned and operated by Don Stanley. For more information about this agency, refer to the previous entry for All Seasons Realty.

Jackson Hole

Century 21 Art Hazen Real Estate
140 N. Cache, Jackson, Wyo.
• (307) 733-4339, (800) 227-3334

Part of the largest real estate organization in the world, these folks can hook you into any place from any other. Agents pride themselves on knowing the Jackson psyche. Agent Bob LaLonde is an example of what this brokerage offers in the way of local understanding: He has been a planning and zoning commissioner, a Wyoming state senator and president of the Jackson Chamber of Commerce. Century 21 doesn't focus as heavily on high-end properties.

Jackson Hole Realty
185 W. Broadway, Jackson, Wyo.
• (307) 733-9009, (888) 733-9009

Founded in the '60s by Paul McCollister, the guy who began development of a ski hill in Teton Village, this brokerage is a Jackson Hole institution. At least 12 of its agents have sold real estate in the valley for more than 15 years, including Greg Prugh and Jackie Montgomery.

Jackson Hole Realty is also the largest real estate agency in Wyoming, with 17 partners, eight offices (including one in Driggs, Idaho) and about 40 agents.

Jackson Hole Realty handles a bit of everything, including commercial properties, condos and lots. Their specialty, though, is high-end second homes, so if you're looking for your castle in the mountains, call these folks.

Prime Properties of Jackson Hole
1230 N. Ida Ln., Wilson, Wyo.
• (800) 800-6455

Broker Bruce Simon moved to Jackson Hole in 1968. He began selling real estate here 10 years later. His brokerage is unique in its Wilson location — most real estate companies base themselves in Jackson or Teton Village. Prime Properties has a niche in subdivision development, although the agency also sells recreational and residential real estate like other valley brokerages.

Photo: Robert Bower/Post Register

This haystack house was built on the south edge of the town of Jackson, Wyoming.

Real Estate of Jackson Hole
110 E. Broadway, Jackson, Wyo.
• **(307) 733-6060, (800) 443-6130**

These folks have a local reputation for selling higher-end properties, but what they pride themselves on is their wide-ranging listings and experience. Listings and branch offices are scattered from Driggs, Idaho, to Alpine, Wyoming. The company has roughly 40 agents, many of them natives to Jackson or other Wyoming areas, whose job is to know those areas and their listings.

Eastern Idaho

American Realty West
76 N. Main, Driggs, Idaho
• **(208) 354-2348**

Locally owned and operated, American Realty West is the oldest and largest brokerage in the Teton Valley. All agents in the office are local property owners. They know the people here, which is an important part of doing business in a small, close-knit community. Broker John McKellar and associate broker Brooke Saindon are the office old-timers. McKellar was already here when the clean air and cleaner lifestyle drew Saindon to Teton Valley in 1978.

Another strength of this brokerage is that it sells property in Teton Valley and Alta, Wyoming. This helps ensure a good working knowledge of any piece of valley property you may want to see.

Century 21 Hathaway-Genta
305 W. Main, Rexburg, Idaho
• **(208) 356-0588**

This brokerage has around 11 agents, several of whom go way back in this area. Nancy White, a Rexburg native, has been with the agency for nearly a decade. Sharon Schindler, born in St. Anthony, 13 miles away, has been selling real estate in the area for 13 years.

Barry Genta, a third-generation local, has 23 years in Rexburg real estate under his belt.

Hathaway-Genta sells 120 to 130 properties a year, which makes it the biggest seller in Rexburg.

Green Tree Realtors
796 Memorial Dr., Idaho Falls, Idaho
• (208) 524-5401, fax 524-5403

This is a unique little brokerage. Co-owners Nila Briggs and Joy Simmons are its only agents. Both have been selling real estate on the Snake River Plain for more than 20 years (Briggs for more than 30). They decided to leave the larger franchise brokerages they worked for 11 years ago because they wanted a small, personal office.

Green Tree specializes in homes, residential acreages and small land parcels. Briggs has been a certified real estate instructor for more than 20 years. She says teaching a few classes a year keeps her current on new property issues.

Harrell Realty
885 Maple, Ashton, Idaho
• (208) 652-7436

Jim Harrell started this company in 1957, and he's still the guy most likely to answer the phone if you call. There's been a brokerage on this spot since the early 1900s. Up until three years ago, Harrell was the only real estate professional with an office in Ashton. Harrell Realty focuses on residential and recreational properties.

Island Park Realty
Valley View at Island Park, Idaho
• (208) 558-7332

Three full-time and three part-time agents staff the oldest real estate agency in town. Broker/owner Lenyce Zenk has been at this agency for 21 years. Like other area brokerages, Island Park Realty specializes in what sells around here: vacation and recreational lots and cabins.

Rainbow Realty
3376 U.S. Hwy. 20, Last Chance in Island Park, Idaho • (208) 558-7116

Seven real estate agents work in this office, whose greatest strength is combined experience in the Island Park area. Because Island Park is primarily a second home market, Rainbow says they spend more time showing homes than trying to hard-sell them: Folks buying their dream cabin know what they want when they see it, apparently.

The Real Estate Office
30 S. Second E., Rexburg, Idaho
• (208) 356-5050

Nine Realtors work out of this office. Dale Walker and Mary Hill are the office old-timers. Mary's been selling real estate in this town since 1976; she's the broker. Dale, an Idaho native now in his early 80s (but still working full-time), specializes in commercial property. Other agents at The Real Estate Office focus mostly on residential property. Mary herself made an impressive 70 transactions in 1997.

Re/Max Homestead Realty
1301 E. 17th St., Suite 1, Idaho Falls, Idaho • (208) 529-5600, (800) 729-5601

Idaho Falls has several franchise brokerages; we've included this one because it tends to attract knowledgeable Realtors. In other brokerages, agents split their commissions in return for paying little or no overhead. At Re/Max agents keep their commissions but pay out of pocket their share of office overhead. This means if you don't know how to sell property, you can't afford to be there — good news for the client.

Fifteen agents work out of this office; all but two have five years or more of local experience. Kevin Murray, who is trying to find us a house right now, grew up around Shelley just south of Idaho Falls. He's been selling real estate in this valley for 10 years. One of his strengths is his high level of professional education: No other real estate person in town has more clusters of letter visibles following his name on Re/Max business card. What this means to you (and to us!) is that Kevin knows his market and his profession.

South Fork Properties
40 Conant Valley Loop, Swan Valley, Idaho • (208) 483-2112, (800) 483-2110

Spence Warner was born and raised in Swan Valley. He inherited his fly-fishing lodge in Conant Valley from his dad. He's probably the only real estate agent who sells nothing but Swan Valley properties; most agents showing Swan Valley property are based in Idaho Falls, 40-odd miles away.

Warner handled more than half of the 50 or so Swan Valley lots and acreages sold from 1994 to 1997. The Warners work with a few farms and businesses, but their bread and butter comes from the sale of recreational property.

Teton Valley Realty
40 N. Main, Driggs, Idaho
• **(208) 354-2439**

Owner Mark Rockefeller has been in business in this valley for 21 years. He's the only valley broker who is also a developer. In addition to selling recreational and residential lots and houses, he creates subdivisions.

His favorite parts of the valley to work in are the wooded foothills at the valley perimeter. There, rolling terrain and habitat requirements make subdividing complicated but rewarding. Rockefeller says he prides himself on being able to divide acreages so that every lot is a great house site. He also has an intimate knowledge of the valley.

Rockefeller takes his housing projects from start to finish, from designing and installing roads to organizing homeowners' associations. He's finished more than a dozen in the area, each consisting of from eight to 44 lots.

Wackerli Realty
255 B, Idaho Falls, Idaho
• **(208) 522-7784, (800) 924-7784**

Both Dick Clayton Sr. and the company he started with his brother 50 years ago are local icons. Wackerli is the oldest brokerage in town; at one point not long ago, Clayton owned much of the property in downtown Idaho Falls.

One of the company's strengths is its diversity. Clayton specializes in commercial property; his son, Dick Clayton Jr., and Dean

Hansen work mostly in ranch and agricultural property. Other Realtors on staff specialize in recreational property in Island Park, Swan Valley and Teton Valley. Wackerli also operates a property management service.

Southwestern Montana

Fay Real Estate Investments for Fly Fishermen
P.O. Box 397, Bozeman, Mont.
• **(406) 586-4001**

Owner Gregory W. Fay, hooked on fly fishing for as long as he can remember, left traditional real estate sales in 1992 to concentrate on sales of land along Montana's rivers and streams to conservation-minded fly fishers, that is, those interested in protecting river corridors from development. Fay handles fly-fishing properties ranging in price from $225,000 to $5 million and works extensively with conservation easements as a means of insuring preservation of the natural landscape. He also offers a buyer brokerage service, researching unlisted properties and those listed by other companies.

Jacobs Western Land Brokerage Inc.
211 W. Main, Bozeman, Mont.
• **(406) 586-8575**

If it's a ranch you're after or a large recreational parcel, the odds are excellent that Ken Jacobs knows the property well. Jacobs came west with Chet Huntley to Big Sky. When Huntley died, Jacobs became a ranch broker in Bozeman in 1971. While he has had as many as 14 ranch brokers working in three states, Jacobs, aiming for retirement, has scaled back to five sales people in Montana.

Bridger Realty
85 W. Kagy Blvd., Bozeman, Mont.
• **(406) 586-7676**

Bridger Realty, in business for more than

15 years, captured more than 30 percent of the total real estate business in Bozeman in 1996. Sixteen full-time salespeople sold more than $80 million worth of property. Bridger Realty specializes in selling mostly in-town residential, commercial, subdivision and lot properties. They also handle some acreages. And they have a relocation specialist on staff.

Century 21 Payne Realty and Housing Inc.
Second and Lewis, Livingston, Mont.
• **(406) 222-6377, (800) 637-7911**

Brokers Bob and Dee Payne have been selling real estate in Livingston for 25 years. A full-service agency, Payne Realty works with 16 licensees selling farm and ranch properties as well as commercial, recreation and residential properties in Livingston and the surrounding area, including the Yellowstone Valley. They are consistently among the leaders in sales in the Livingston area.

Triple Creek Realty
47650 Canyon Rd., Big Sky, Mont.
• **(406) 995-4848, (800) 548-4632**

The oldest established realty company in Big Sky, Triple Creek Realty is first in listings and sales in Big Sky and the Gallatin Canyon. In addition to selling residential, recreational and commercial properties in the Big Sky area, Triple Creek handles vacation condo rentals. With two offices, one in Gallatin Canyon and the other in Mountain Village, Triple Creek is staffed with 10 sales people.

Coldwell Banker/Maverick Realty
125 E. Callender, Livingston, Mont.
• **(406) 222-0304**

Broker owner Michelle Goodwine was born and raised in Livingston and has been with Maverick Realty since 1986. While she sells all kinds of properties, including ranches and businesses, she sells more small acreages and homes than anything else. You'll find seven sales associates, a licensed assistant and a full-time property manager at Maverick Realty.

Blue Grouse Real Estate
3091 Pine Dr., Big Sky, Mont.
• **(406) 995-2318, (800) 799-2919**

Blue Grouse is a small agency operated by husband-wife team Time Cyr and Cathy Gorman. Cyr began coming to Big Sky with

Photo: Susan Short

The exterior of the Original Buffalo Bill Cody House in Cody, Wyoming is decorated with flags and bunting.

his parents when he was a small boy. Now he and Gorman bring friendly, personal service to a market that could easily drive another real estate agent to hurry you through a search or a sale. Blue Grouse handles resort properties because that's mostly all there is in Big Sky.

Northwestern Wyoming

Homestead Realty/ LC/ Better Homes and Gardens
1273 Sheridan Ave., Cody, Wyo.
• **(307) 587-4750**

Founded in 1995 by two Cody natives, Louis Kousoulos and Stan Siggins, Homestead Realty had 13 sales agents in 1997 and is one of the area leaders in sales. Kousoulos began selling real estate in 1985 after retiring from 35 years in the food business. Siggins began his career in real estate in 1990 after retiring from the dude ranch business. This agency has an energetic staff that sells every kind of property.

Western Real Estate
1143 Sheridan Ave., Cody, Wyo.
• **(307) 587-4926**

Owned for 20 years by Jack Peterson, Ed Higbie and Shirley Lehman, Western Real Estate is a full-service agency with nine agents who operate in well-organized teams specializing in farm, ranch and recreational properties as well as building lots, homes and commercial property in and out of town. The agency is staffed mostly by longtime residents of Cody. Peterson is a second-generation native. Western Real Estate, which at one time was the only agency selling recreational property in the area, still sells the lion's share of it.

Real Estate Publications

Montana, Idaho and Wyoming each have publications advertising statewide properties for sale. They are crammed with offerings, and if you're really interested in Yellowstone country property, these publications carry a good representation of the best. Each requires a mailing and handling fee. We'll give you their names and addresses. The rest is up to you.

Idaho Land Magazine, Rocky Mountain Publishing, P.O. Box 6062, Pocatello, ID 83205-6062

The Montana Land Magazine, P.O. Box 30516, Billings, MT 59107 (See the Media Chapter for more information about the *Montana Land Magazine.*)

Discover Wyoming, P.O. Box 70, Powell, WY 82435

**Greater Yellowstone's
larger communities
offer good medical and
emergency facilities and
a long menu of
resources and
opportunities especially
designed for seniors.**

Retirement

For retiring baby boomers, Yellowstone country is a dream come true. It is a land of mountains to climb, streams to fish, places to camp, wildlife to watch and big game to hunt. It's an oasis of clean air, pure water, wide open spaces and myriad natural mysteries.

On the other hand, for older retirees especially, Greater Yellowstone can quickly transform from paradise to nightmare, especially with the advent of winter. Even for those of us who grew up in Greater Yellowstone, the winters can be long, hard and tedious. The rigors of battening your house against arctic weather, stoking the fire, shoveling snow and navigating icy, snow-packed roads can take their toll. Even in the 1990s, the maladies associated with a bad case of cabin fever have driven many a golden ager to the warmer climate of the South, if not forever, then for at least long enough to avoid Jack Frost.

Greater Yellowstone's larger communities also offer good medical and emergency facilities and a long menu of resources and opportunities especially designed for seniors. And you'll find amenities such as public transportation just for seniors and paved streets to make your life easier. In the smaller towns, like Gardiner, Ennis and Irwin, you won't find any senior center at all. Emergency medical care is provided by trained volunteers, side streets are unpaved, the towns pretty much shut down for the winter, and the trip to the nearest hospital is miles away. We know older seniors whose failing health forced them to move elsewhere to be closer to modern medical facilities.

For anyone contemplating retiring in Greater Yellowstone, we recommend researching the facilities in your area of interest. Staffed senior citizen centers in Bozeman, Livingston and Cody are good places to start. The next sections provide descriptions of these centers' programs. For your convenience, we have provided the following clearinghouse numbers where you can get all the information you need before you make your decision: Gallatin County Council on Aging in Bozeman, (406) 586-2421; Cody Council on Aging, (307) 587-6221; and Idaho's Region VII Council on Aging, (800) 632-4813.

Another good resource is *Prime Time News*, published monthly by High Country Independent Press, (406) 388-6762. This publication is chock-full of news, columns and calendars related to older adults in Gallatin County, Montana. Seniors looking for volunteer slots to fill in the community can find them listed in *Prime Time*. Its pages also contain descriptions of upcoming events at the Bozeman, Belgrade, Manhattan and Three Forks senior citizen centers and the monthly menus for each center. *Prime Time News* is published at 220 S. Broadway, Belgrade, MT 59714.

Yellowstone National Park Entrance Communities

West Yellowstone Senior Social Center
P.O. Box 1592, West Yellowstone, MT 57958 • (406) 646-7311

The West Yellowstone Senior Social Center launched its first meal and afternoon activity hour in May of 1997. The center has no building to call home yet, but it meets each Wednesday for a noon meal at the Bear's Den Cinema at 15 Electric Street. Summer residents make up the bulk of the patrons of the meals and field trips. During winter, local seniors who are busy working during the summer look forward to meeting there. This center allows anyone of any age to join. If you happen to be 50 or younger, though, don't expect to vote. The 14-passenger West Yellowstone Foundation/Galavan bus leaves from the Chamber of Commerce parking lot at the corner of Canyon Street and Yellowstone Avenue at 8 AM each Tuesday and Thursday from October until May and each Thursday the rest of the year. It returns about 5 PM. To reserve a seat on the bus, seniors must call the West Yellowstone Police Station at (406) 646-7600.

www.insiders.com

See this and many other **Insiders' Guide®** destinations online — in their entirety.

Visit us today!

are free and run May through September. Every Christmas, Teton County loads up buses with interested seniors for a one-day shopping spree in Idaho Falls' Grand Teton Mall, 80 miles away. Every September, a Parks and Recreation bus takes seniors up to Yellowstone Park for the day to watch Old Faithful blow its top and to check out area gift shops. These programs charge participants an astonishingly affordable $5.

Jackson Hole

Senior Center of Jackson Hole
830 E. Hansen, Jackson, Wyo.
• **(307) 733-7300**

Like other area senior centers, the Senior Center of Jackson Hole serves lunch daily (a $2 donation is requested) to those 60 and older. Reservations are required. The center also provides home care and delivers meals to the homebound. If you want to learn more about these folks and the services they offer, ask for a copy of their fact-packed monthly newsletter. It includes an activities calendar and a menu for that month's lunches.

Teton County Parks and Recreation Department/Recreation Center
155 E. Gill St., Jackson, Wyo.
• **(307) 733-5056**

Teton County Parks and Recreation manages a well-equipped recreation center with an eight-lane lap pool, a therapy pool, a hot tub, a sauna, a gym and a giant water slide. The center offers courses in step aerobics, yoga and low-impact water aerobics. The water aerobics course is a favorite with seniors. Course participants meet three times weekly for one-hour sessions. In 1997, the cost was $36 per month. Another favorite pastime is the Bridge Club, which meets Monday nights at the Recreation Center. Participants' pocket change creates a kitty for the high scorer.

Programs specifically geared to area seniors include the weekly senior walks. Every Friday, Parks and Recreation provides transportation and a guide for a short (3-mile maximum) hike in the Jackson area. Senior hikes

Eastern Idaho

Idaho Falls, Idaho Area

Senior Citizens Community Center Inc.
535 W. 21st St., Idaho Falls, Idaho
• **(208) 522-4357**

This large and active senior center has a membership of 4,500 and a full-time paid staff that keeps the center open 8 AM to 5 PM Monday through Friday. The center sponsors a range of health services from cholesterol and glaucoma checks to a monthly foot clinic. Regular seminars offer information on topics such as investments, fraud and fitness. The center serves lunch Monday through Friday and is the setting for Thursday afternoon dances with a three-piece band and Tuesday morning sing-alongs paired with afternoon bridge games. The center has a large library with over 5,000 titles. You can learn more about these folks from their newsletter or from the community calendar in the local paper. And pay attention to center travel plans: The Senior Citizens Community Center sponsors regular (and affordable) summer trips to places like Lava Hot Springs, Jackson Hole and Yellowstone National Park.

Area VI Agency on Aging
357 Constitution Way, Idaho Falls, Idaho
• **(208) 522-5391, (800) 632-4813**

Emily Hoyt coordinates assistance programs for older people in nine eastern Idaho counties, including Jefferson, Bonneville, Madison, Fremont and Teton. This makes her a

Photo: Robert Bower/Post Register

A member of the Idaho Falls Old Tyme Fiddlers
entertains seniors at the Tautphaus Park.

one-stop resource for anyone who wants to know what is available for older adults in Idaho Falls, Rigby, Rexburg, Ashton, Island Park, Swan Valley and Teton Valley. Services vary by area and availability of funds and volunteers, but most programs are available in Idaho Falls; some operate in other communities as well. Among its programs are those that assist older folks with health and safety problems. The Outreach program provides information on services that benefit older adults.

Homemaker, shopper and chore workers help frailer seniors with difficult household tasks. Respite is a program that provides full-time caregivers of homebound adults occasional breaks from their responsibilities. Legal counsel is available, as is adult day care. Home visits or daily phone calls to seniors living alone and in need of regular human contact can also be arranged. Nearly every community within Area VI offers home-delivered and com-

munal meals, as well as transportation for older people who have no other way to get to doctors or grocery stores. Make sure you call Emily for more information, especially since program availability may change.

Rexburg, Idaho

Madison County Seniors
40 S. Second E., Rexburg, Idaho
• (208) 356-0800

The annual influx of what locals call "sunbirds" — more than 2,000 retirees from the hot-weather states who rent Ricks College's dorm rooms for the summer months — keeps this senior center hopping. Cook Darla Mower has been here, turning out what we're told are exceptional lunches, for many years. These inexpensive meals are served at the center; about 40 lunches are delivered to shut-ins

Tuesday through Saturday. Once a month, the center brings in an area physician to discuss seniors' health issues. Various organizations sponsor tours and activities to area attractions for center seniors during the busy summer months.

Ashton, Idaho

Ashton Seniors
Main St., Ashton, Idaho • (208) 652-3594

Ashton is a small town, and its senior center is small, too. Nevertheless, these folks serve lunches to seniors two days a week. They sponsor a line-dancing class on Tuesday mornings for anyone interested in participating. They quilt on Tuesdays and Wednesdays; in fact, the Ashton Seniors quilting circle has been meeting for at least 10 years. Other services sponsored through the Area VI Agency on Aging may be available from time to time in this area.

Teton Valley

Teton County Senior Citizens
P.O. 466, Driggs ID 83422 • No phone

For seniors 60 and older, dinner is served at Driggs' American Legion Hall on Wednesdays and Thursdays. Thirty to 60 people generally attend. Meals for the 10 to 15 people who can't make it into town are delivered. Another critical service in this rural area is the CART bus, which takes senior citizens to doctors' appointment and the grocery store. It also brings them into town for those Legion Hall dinners. Other services sponsored through the Area VI Agency on Aging may be available from time to time in this area (see our earlier entry on Idaho Falls' Area VI services in this chapter).

Teton Valley Hospital Community Outreach
283 N. First E., Driggs, Idaho
• (208) 354-2383, Ext. 164

Lesley Baer, Community Outreach coordinator at Teton Valley Hospital, says her job is bringing needed services to the community. Some of the services she can help you hook into are the Stretch, Flex and Tone senior fitness classes sponsored by Teton Valley Hospital. Then there's the AARP-sponsored 55 Alive driving class; this two-day course addresses how the changes associated with aging affect driving safety. Community Outreach also assists with transportation for seniors. Baer's newest project, an adopt-a-grandparent program, pairs trained teens and young adults with area seniors for the benefit of both sides of the generation gap.

Southwestern Montana

Bozeman Senior Citizen Center
807 N. Tracy, Bozeman, Mont.
• (406) 586-2421

Since the completion of a new addition — its second in four years — the Bozeman Senior Citizen Center has one of the best senior facilities in Montana. A beehive of activity, the center has 1,600 members who work, play, socialize and dine there. A few hundred more older adults gather in Belgrade, Manhattan and Three Forks under the auspices of the Bozeman Senior Center. In addition to the noon meals served Monday through Friday, the center serves a Sunday dinner once a month. The dining room seats 300, and reservations for meals should be made a day in advance. Meals-on-wheels (about 120 of them each weekday) also roll out of the center's kitchen.

The Bozeman Senior Center also has a well-organized and active travel program. In addition, the center's staff organizes at least one trip per year to Yellowstone Park and an every-other-year tour of Beartooth Highway (see our Attractions chapter). In addition, volunteer seniors organize any number of fundraisers, including dinner shows, style shows, craft shows and dances, in the new dining room which features a roll-out stage and 3,300 square feet of dancing room. The Bozeman Senior Center also has regular health screenings and clinics including those for blood pressure, foot care, health education, nutrition counseling and immunizations.

The center is open 8:30 AM to 3:30 PM Monday through Friday. Membership costs $7.50 per year and is open to anyone 50 years or older.

Galavan, a seniors bus service that transports rural seniors from outlying areas to Bozeman, operates out of the Bozeman Senior Center. Buses are equipped with wheelchair lifts and will often take passengers from their doorsteps to the doctor's office, beauty parlor, grocery store or any place else in Bozeman. In Belgrade, Galavan leaves from the Price Rite Drug Center every Tuesday. For reservations and more information, call (406) 587-2434.

Belgrade Senior Citizen's Friendship Club
92 Cameron Ave., Belgrade, Mont.
• **(406) 388-4711**

Monday, Wednesday, Thursday and Friday, seniors gather here for a noon meal at the cost of a small donation. Affiliated with the Bozeman Senior Center, this center has an annual craft sale and garage sales.

Senior Citizens Center of Park County
206 S. Main, Livingston, Mont.
• **(406) 222-9995**

In the 1960s, Livingston seniors used grant money to buy the fire-damaged Yellowstone Hotel in downtown Livingston. Today, a decade after they paid off the mortgage, the board of this center has 26 apartments that provide low-income housing for seniors. Staffed by several part-time paid employees, the Senior Citizens Center of Park County has 300 members (they've had as many as 600) who pay a $5 membership fee. An in-house thrift store grosses $2,000 to $4,000 per month. Besides serving noon meals Monday through Friday, the center offers card parties, dances, bingo, a pool table, exercise and wellness clinics. The facility prohibits the practice of politics or religion on the premises. It's open Monday through Saturday and publishes a monthly newsletter.

Red Lodge Senior Citizens' Center
207 S. Villard Ave., Red Lodge, Mont.
• **(406) 446-1826**

This volunteer-run center serves three meals a week: soup and sandwiches at noon on Wednesday, a full meal on Thursday at 11:30 AM and a Friday noon meal. The center has 150 members who pay a $5 fee to belong. You'll also find regular card parties, bingo, a blood-pressure clinic and a foot clinic.

Northwestern Wyoming

Cody, Wyoming

Cody Senior Citizens Center
613 16th St., Cody, Wyo.
• **(307) 587-6221**

The hub of senior citizen activity in Cody, the Cody Senior Center claims to have the "best cook in town." While other cooks in town may dispute that boast, it is a known fact that at the Cody Senior Center, you'll find meals just like your grandma used to cook. The meals are served in a dining room that accommodates 200, but usually there are only about 90 diners. A crew of volunteers operates a thriving thrift shop Monday through Saturday from 10 AM until 3 PM. Sales accounted for $23,000 of the center's 1997 budget. The Cody Senior Center has no membership fees.

You'll also find a senior bus service operating out of the center for Cody seniors and the handicapped. Medical and personal services and meals are also offered here. The Cody Senior Citizen Center is open from 8 AM until 4 PM Monday through Friday.

Except for Lake Hospital
in the center of
Yellowstone National
Park, hospitals are in
the outlying areas,
anywhere from 53
to 109 miles from
the Yellowstone
Park boundaries.

Healthcare

Before you enter Yellowstone Country, look at a map and take heed. The Greater Yellowstone area is about the size of Maine, yet towns are few and far between. Towns, separated by long distances, generally lie within the valleys and, with few exceptions, are small rural communities. Many have only clinics to serve the everyday health needs of local residents.

Except for Lake Hospital in the center of Yellowstone National Park, hospitals are in the outlying areas, anywhere from 53 to 109 miles from the Yellowstone Park boundaries. That means life-threatening injuries, serious illnesses or personal health problems such as heart attacks and strokes, may require one or two ambulance transfers to get you to a hospital. If the emergency is extreme, an air ambulance likely will fly you to one of several regional hospitals.

All areas of Greater Yellowstone, including the Parks, have 911 and emergency medical service. Except for the larger towns like Bozeman, Billings and Idaho Falls, emergency medical technicians (EMTs) are volunteers who will leave their jobs, families and beds at a moment's notice to rush to your aid. We hope you won't need emergency medical attention while you're in Greater Yellowstone, but if you do, you'll find fast, efficient help.

Because of the size of Greater Yellowstone, we suggest you call either the clinics or the hospitals listed in your area for information about emergency dental care or doctor referrals.

In the Parks

Two clinics and a hospital in Yellowstone Park and a single clinic in Grand Teton serve the 3 million visitors who pass through the Parks each summer. In Yellowstone Park, between 75 and 100 of the rangers each year have at least emergency medical technician (EMT) status. About 10 of those will be trained medics, and a couple may actually be paramedics. Grand Teton has about as many EMTs, including 16 Park medics.

Steve Sarles, emergency medical services coordinator in Yellowstone, reports that each year the Yellowstone Park Service gets from 700 to 800 emergency calls as a result of illness and injury. (They're evenly split.) Of those calls, about 250 end up needing ambulance services. In Grand Teton, emergency medical services were activated about 232 times in 1996. Of those, the vast majority were a result of motor-vehicle accidents. Once you get to Yellowstone, you'll know why. The roads are narrow, congested and mostly full of potholes and frost heaves. Roadside attractions can quickly become distractions that lead to unhealthy auto interactions. Take your eyes off the road and you're liable to rear-end the last car in what Insiders call a "bear jam."

Since the Yellowstone Park Service changed its bear-management policy, minor injuries from belligerent begging bruins have dropped dramatically. Before, when bears regularly foraged at open dumps and waited by the roadside for tidbits from tourists, minor bear-related injuries were common. Unfortunately, bear sightings have dropped correspondingly. Sarles reports that hospital and clinic staff also treat burns on folks who step off the boardwalks near geysers and hot pools.

www.insiders.com
See this and many other **Insiders' Guide®** destinations online — in their entirety.
Visit us today!

Hospitals

Yellowstone National Park

Lake Hospital
Lake Village, 713 Lake, Yellowstone National Park • (307) 242-7241
Lake Hospital, managed by West Park Hospital in Cody (see subsequent entry), is the only seasonal hospital in the United States. Each May, the doors to this 10-bed hospital open with a new crew of healthcare professionals who offer round-the-clock care to Park visitors. From mid-May until mid-September you can count on finding one doctor at the hospital and another on call. Three — occasionally, four — doctors share the work load. While the staff at this hospital gives quality care, emergency capabilities are limited not only by equipment, but also by the number of individuals on hand to help. A three-patient emergency would tax this hospital to the max, says its manager. Most emergency cases treated here are the result of either an auto accident or altitude-aggravated cardiac problems.

Jackson Hole

St. John's Hospital
625 E. Broadway, Jackson, Wyo.
• (307) 733-3636
This is a hospital with history: It first opened its doors in 1916 in a four-room cabin; three years later, the cabin was expanded to eight rooms. Today's St. John's, only 5 years old, has 102 beds, five trauma rooms and the capacity to deal with everything from plastic surgery to advanced cardiac care to infectious diseases. Some of the top orthopedic surgeons in the nation practice here. Much of the new approach of the hospital focuses on community and outpatient services. A transitional-care unit was built to help prepare patients to go home; the SurgiCenter was remodeled to better handle outpatient surgeries; and rehabilitation programs have been strengthened. St. John's other goal is to save area residents the long drive to Idaho Falls or Salt Lake City. Toward that end, the hospital has grown into a remarkably large and complete facility for such a rural area.

Surrounding Areas

Eastern Idaho

Columbia Eastern Idaho Regional Medical Center
3100 Channing Way, Idaho Falls, Idaho
• (208) 529-6111
This 318-bed facility is the largest hospital in Yellowstone country. The reason? Even though Idaho Falls is home to only about 50,000 people, the hospital's service area includes 200,000 to 300,000. The CEIRMC (say it SIRmac) as it's called, has the only open-heart–surgery program in this area as well as the only bone bank (a bone bank stores donated human bones for transplant into folks who might otherwise lose limbs or use of a joint). These folks have a neurosurgery program and a breast-biopsy machine that saves women from having to have expensive, debilitating surgeries to learn if their breast lumps are benign.

Safety in the Great Outdoors!

CLOTHING - Prepare for a variety of weather conditions by bringing layers. Synthetic, breathable fabrics like polypropylene or polyester fleece are best. Also, be sure to have water repellent clothing for unexpected rain for snow.

HIGH ALTITUDE - If you are unaccustomed to higher altitudes, give your body time to adjust to low oxygen levels. Take a few days to adjust before planning heavy exertion. People with special health problems should consult with a doctor before planning a trip to moderate or high altitude.

MINOR EMERGENCIES - Be prepared for the most common emergencies that occur in the wilderness. Some of these include: Blisters, bruises, scrapes, minor cuts and burns, ankle sprains, bug bites and sunburns

A WELL STOCKED FIRST AIDE KIT SHOULD INCLUDE:
- Sunscreen
- Bug Repellent
- Disinfecting Solution
- Sterile Gauze
- Band aids or tape
- Antibacterial Ointment
- Moleskin
- Ace or Elastic Bandages
- Tylenol or Ibuprofen
- Benadryl
- Any Regularly Prescribed Medications

MAJOR EMERGENCIES - Make sure someone back home knows your itinerary. Talk to local authorities about how to access emergency services.

Eastern Idaho Regional Medical Center

- 24-Hour Emergency Care
- Neonatal Intensive Care
- Air Ambulance Service
- Day Surgery Center
- Surgery Overnight Stay
- Behavioral Health Care
- Home Health Care
- Rehabilitative Care
- Wellness Programs
- Neurology Services
- Open Heart Surgery
- Cardiac Rehabilitation
- Full Laboratory Services
- Sleep Lab Services
- MRI/CT
- Mammography
- Womens' Services
- Health Promotion

"Your Community Hospital"

3100 Channing Way, Idaho Falls, ID 529-6111
http://www.eirmc.org
Clinic at West Yellowstone • 406-646-7668

Because this rural region is so rural — the driving time between an injured or ill person and a hospital can be measured in hours not minutes — the CEIRMC also owns a jazzy helicopter, designed to fly at speeds in excess of 150 mph and at high altitudes, two things most helicopters don't do well. The CEIRMC rescue helicopter is the only one licensed to fly into Yellowstone Park to transport victims of medical emergencies. Affiliated with the ER, Fast Track physician's assistants treat minor emergencies and save you ER waiting time and expense. It's open 10 AM to 10 PM seven days a week. If the Fast Track folks decide your problem is serious, you're already in the emergency room and at the hospital.

Madison Memorial Hospital
450 E. Main, Rexburg, Idaho
• **(208) 356-3691**

If you need medical help in Rexburg, this is where you'll be going. Large for a town of only 20,000 people, this 53-bed hospital is growing even larger. Emergency-room beds will increase from seven to 11. Three surgical suites will be added, along with a new women's center that will house labor and delivery rooms, a postpartum program and other kinds of female surgery. Twenty-four full-time physicians staff the hospital, and the emergency room is staffed by doctors 24 hours a day. The reason Rexburg has such a complete and growing hospital is twofold: This is a college town, and every winter the population swells by about 8,000, or nearly a third. The hospital delivers around 900 babies a year.

Teton Valley Hospital
283 N. First E., Driggs, Idaho
• **(208) 354-2383**

This 13-bed facility just underwent a $3 million renovation/expansion, paid for almost completely by community fund-raising. The little hospital can handle pretty much every-

thing you'd expect from a hospital: surgery, medical imaging, respiratory and physical therapies, lab work and obstetrics. Patient services and community outreach are major focuses. The hospital has a home healthcare program — a nurse comes to a patient's home. The hospital offers a hospice program and a range of classes including prenatal and childbirth, free fitness classes, blood-pressure monitoring and CPR training.

The hospital has a 24-hour acute-care emergency room with a doctor on call.

Southwestern Montana

Beartooth Hospital and Health Center
600 W. 21st St., Red Lodge, Mont.
• **(406) 446-2345**

Owned by the community since 1993, this facility just changed its name in 1997 from Carbon County Memorial Hospital and Nursing Home to the Beartooth Hospital and Health Center. This 22-bed hospital has an attached nursing home and offers 24-hour emergency care. In addition, it offers a range of outpatient surgeries, including knee surgeries, plastic surgery, mastectomies and appendectomies. The facility offers day care and a pharmacy. Other services include obstetrics, cardiac rehabilitation and community health education. Mountain View Medical Center, a private clinic across the street from the hospital, encourages appointments but will accommodate walk-ins.

Bozeman Deaconess Hospital
915 Highland Blvd., Bozeman, Mont.
• **(406) 585-5000**

Bozeman Deaconess Hospital, which opened its doors in 1986, is a full-service hospital with 86 beds. Deaconess offers an inpatient and retail pharmacy, radiology, physical therapy, cancer treatment and cardiopulmonary

---

INSIDERS' TIP

If you plan to spend any part of your visit hiking, fishing or boating in the backcountry, bring a first-aid kit and know how to use its contents. We have effective, well-equipped medical personnel here; but remember, they can't help you until they get to you.

rehabilitation services as well as a full range of surgical services. A third medical office building was added in 1997 to the two that already adjoin Deaconess. The original two clinics are occupied by 49 doctors in 16 different groups. The medical staff is comprised of physicians representing a range of specialties.

Deaconess Billings Clinic
2800 10th Ave. N., Billings, Mont.
• **(406) 657-4000**

Deaconess Hospital and Billings Clinic joined forces in 1993 and are now called Deaconess Billings Clinic. Don't let the name fool you — this is a hospital. It is a 272-bed nonprofit regional clinic, hospital and trauma center recognized nationally for its patient-focused care. Services include emergency, trauma and walk-in care; family practice; internal medicine; obstetrics and gynecology; cardiology; renal dialysis, psychiatric and behavioral health services; orthopedics and sports medicine; neurology; and women's health services. Since opening in 1927, the hospital has evolved from a family-oriented 58-bed hospital to a regional medical center employing more than 1,000 people. Deaconess operates DEACARE/ALS, a fixed-wing air-ambulance service that uses two prop jets.

Livingston Memorial Hospital
504 S. 13th St., Livingston, Mont.
• **(406) 222-3541**

Livingston Memorial Hospital is the closest outlying hospital to the Park. Built in 1955, this nonprofit facility offers a full range of care and is licensed for 45 beds.

Madison Valley Hospital and Madison Valley Clinic
219 N. Main St., Ennis, Mont.
• **(406) 682-4222**

This nine-bed, nonprofit hospital staffs three full-time and two part-time physicians as well as a physician's assistant and a family nurse practitioner. The staff here offers family medicine, gynecological services (but no obstetrics), X-rays, lab testing, cardiology and orthopedics. Madison Valley Hospital provides urgent emergency care 24 hours a day, seven days a week. The clinic attached to the hospital provides general family medicine. The 46-bed Madison County Nursing home is next door to the hospital.

St. Vincent Hospital and Health Care Center
1233 N. 30th St., Billings, Mont.
• **(406) 657-7000**

This regional hospital has 315 beds and offers a range of services including a neonatal intensive-care unit, cancer care, the Sports Medicine Institute, The Women's Center, an emergency helicopter service and Ask-A-Nurse, a 24-hour service that not only provides free healthcare information, but also helps you find a physician.

Northwestern Wyoming

West Park Hospital
707 Sheridan Ave., Cody, Wyo.
• **(307) 527-7501**

West Park Hospital has 24-hour emergency/ambulance services and the latest technology, including MRI and renal dialysis equipment. West Park is well staffed with physicians specializing in family practice, general surgery, gynecology, internal medicine, obstetrics, orthopedic surgery, pediatrics and urology. The hospital is responsible for medical services within Yellowstone National Park, and patients requiring more care than Park facilities can manage are often sent to West Park Hospital

INSIDERS' TIP

Between the strong high-altitude sun and the low humidity, you won't notice yourself sweating — even if you are. Dehydration is no fun, but it easily can be prevented by drinking lots of water — 2 quarts per day is recommended — and keeping your alcohol consumption down. Dehydration is such a common problem around here that if you have a headache after a day outside, water is probably going to fix you faster than aspirin.

by helicopter or ambulance. The Coe Medical Center, attached to the hospital, accommodates up to 22 physicians. The 12-bed inpatient Chemical Dependency Center is one of only four resident facilities in Wyoming. For more information about medical services in Cody, call West Park Hospital Public Relations at the listed number and ask for extension 299.

Healthcare Clinics and Centers

Yellowstone National Park

In the Park

Mammoth Clinic
Mammoth Village, Yellowstone National Park • (307) 344-7965

Visitors to the Mammoth Hot Springs Clinic are apt to find elk grazing on the front lawn. Inside, though, they'll find a friendly doctor and several helpful nurses. The Mammoth Clinic, built in the 1960s, is the only year-round medical facility in Yellowstone National Park. The clinic serves not only Park employees, but also the residents of Gardiner and Cooke City. The clinic has X-ray equipment and an emergency room, but no pharmacy.

Mammoth Clinic is generally open seven days a week between Memorial Day and Labor Day weekends, and Monday through Friday the rest of the year. Check with either the clinic or the Park Service (see our Resources chapter) for specific times, which vary depending on the season.

Old Faithful Clinic
Old Faithful, Yellowstone National Park • (307) 545-7325

Imagine watching Old Faithful erupt while you're waiting for the doctor to see you. You can do just that at the Old Faithful Clinic, where walk-ins are not only welcome, but also expected. The clinic, built in 1996 to replace the old one housed in a dinky little trailer next to the ranger station, has a big picture window facing Old Faithful geyser.

Old Faithful Clinic follows the openings and closings of the Inn and is open from early May until late October. During the spring and fall, the clinic is closed on Mondays and Tuesdays, but you'll find the Mammoth clinic open on those days. Check with the Park Service for hours, which can vary.

Entrance Communities

Clinic at West Yellowstone
236 Yellowstone Ave., West Yellowstone, Mont. • (406) 646-7668

The folks at this cozy little clinic treat everything from sore throats to life-threatening emergencies. It's managed by Columbia Eastern Idaho Regional Medical Center in Idaho Falls (see previous entry) and staffed by a physician's assistant, nurse practitioner and two registered nurses. On the wall near the receptionist's desk, you'll see a photo of a doctor and a Discovery Center veterinarian with an unconscious 9-month-old grizzly bear. The bear, born at the Discovery Center in West Yellowstone with a hip problem, was X-rayed at the clinic in 1996. Elsie, the cow elk — she's stuffed — presides over an outside waiting room.

The staff here operates this clinic year round;

INSIDERS' TIP

West Park Hospital's lobby has an extensive museum-quality display of old-time drugs dispensed by Dr. M.F. Smith, an early-day pharmacist. Included in the display are homeopathic remedies, kidney-ailment cures, pill and suppository molds, Oriental medicines and curatives, and common cough medicines. If you're in Cody and happen to be touring the Buffalo Bill Historical Center, swing into the West Park Hospital right across the street. By the way, West Park Hospital manages the medical services in Yellowstone Park.

Winter snows blanket the Madison River area west of Madison Junction.

nurses have been known to ski to patients' homes for winter house calls. Patients needing acute emergency care are either flown via helicopter to Idaho Falls' Columbia Eastern Idaho Regional Medical Center or taken by ambulance to hospitals in Bozeman, Rexburg or Idaho Falls. The Clinic at West Yellowstone is open year round from 8:30 AM to noon and 1 to 5:30 PM Monday through Friday. It is also open on weekends from 8:30 AM to 2 PM.

Grand Teton National Park

Grand Teton Medical Clinic
Jackson Lake Lodge, Grand Teton Park
• **(307) 543-2514**

At the only clinic in Grand Teton Park, the physician's assistants not only can write you a prescription, but also usually can fill it. This is pretty handy since the nearest pharmacy is an hour's drive away (sorry, they can't fill a prescription they didn't write). They can X-ray that bum ankle and then sell you crutches if necessary. Although no doctors regularly staff the clinic, its physician's assistants can offer most basic care.

Grand Teton Medical Clinic is owned by Emerg+a+Care in nearby Jackson, so these capable folks get on the phone with

Emerg+a+Care's Dr. Blue when they need consultation. The Park's only clinic is open seven days a week from mid-May to mid-October. After hours or off-season, call Park dispatch at (307) 739-3300, or St. John's Hospital in Jackson, (307) 733-3636 (see the previous entry in this chapter). The clinic can bill Medicare, but does not bill regular insurance.

Jackson Hole

Insta Care of Jackson
545 W. Broadway, Jackson, Wyo.
• **(307) 733-7003**

Only a few blocks from town square on one of Jackson's main drags, Insta Care is both convenient and easy to find. Also convenient are the clinic's extended hours and seven-day weeks. No appointments are accepted; just come on in. These folks can do lab work and X-rays on-site, which might save you a trip to St. John's, the town's hospital (see this chapter's entry). Doctors Brent and Ron Gooder are a father/son team.

Jackson Hole Medical Clinic
988 U.S. Hwy. 89 S., Jackson, Wyo.
• **(307) 739-8999**

You're in good hands here, whether your problem is flu or a minor emergency. Dr. Rivers is a board-certified family physician with 22 years of emergency room experience. His clinic is equipped for minor surgery and orthopedic care. He even maintains an on-site pharmacy so he can fill the prescriptions he writes.

The clinic keeps regular hours Monday through Thursday, but Dr. Rivers also makes hotel and house calls by arrangement. Dr. Rivers's staff have been known to locate accommodations for patients' families when a hospital stay was required. Dr. Rivers works a lot with asthma and allergy problems; he also speaks Spanish and a bit of German.

Surrounding Areas

Eastern Idaho

Ashton Family Practice Center
23 S. Eighth St., Ashton, Idaho
• (208) 652-7471

This is Ashton's only medical clinic. It's open during business hours Monday through Friday. The clinic's owner, Dr. Curtis, also runs the Teton Valley Clinic in Driggs (see subsequent entry), 40 miles away. Although a doctor is on-site only one day a week, you'll get competent care here: Rural nurse practitioners and physician's assistants do a lot more than administer aspirin. These folks have an in-house lab, X-ray and EKG equipment and a wealth of experience. Doctors are in constant contact with staff when consultations are necessary. Ashton has no inpatient facilities. For minor maladies that require hospital admission, you can choose to be transported to Idaho Falls, Driggs or Rexburg hospitals.

Family Emergency Centers
East, 1995 E. 17th St., Idaho Falls, Idaho
• (208) 529-5252
West, 250 S. Skyline, Idaho Falls, Idaho
• (208) 525-2600

Unlike many walk-in clinics, you won't be seen by a physician's assistant here. The center's doctors and nurses handle the gamut of minor emergencies and are equipped to do lab work, X-rays and drug screening. They make life easy for travelers because they accept no appointments; just walk in (you can call in advance to see what the wait might be; usually it's short). The 17th Street clinic keeps extended hours seven days a week; Skyline is open six days. Family Emergency Center East was the first freestanding urgent-care clinic of this type in Idaho. It's been doing business since 1980.

Teton Valley Clinic
283 N. First E., Driggs, Idaho
• (208) 354-2302

Driggs' clinic conveniently is in the same building as the local hospital. This means you can have lab tests done or be admitted to the hospital without stepping outside. It also means that if your problem is not a serious emergency, your best bet Monday through Friday during business hours (or, in emergencies, on Saturday mornings) is to call ahead. The clinic does not accept walk-in patients, but the staff almost always can fit you in right away — and they'll save you big bucks over the emergency room.

Two family-practice doctors, one physician's assistant and one nurse practitioner staff the clinic. One of the doctors is always on-site or nearby. This rural clinic also serves folks from Swan Valley and Island Park since these areas have no clinic of their own. Some folks even travel down from West Yellowstone because they like the staff and the care provided here.

Southwestern Montana

Medical Clinic of Big Sky
Mountain Village, Big Sky, Mont.
• (406) 995-2797

Until 1994, folks from West Yellowstone had to drive miles to see a doctor. Now the Medical Clinic of Big Sky, an urgent-care center, has a doctor and a paid emergency medical technician on staff. During the winter, when the clinic also serves injured skiers, staff size increases. The clinic is equipped for general family medicine including X-rays and casting. More extreme emergencies are stabilized, then sent either by ambulance, helicopter or airplane to Bozeman Deaconess Hospital or Saint Vincent Hospital in Billings (see previous entries), depending on the nature of the emergency.

Madison Valley Clinic
219 N. Main St., Ennis, Mont.
• **(406) 682-4223**

See a description of this general family clinic in the previous Madison Valley Hospital listing.

Northwestern Wyoming

Cody Family Practice
225 W. Yellowstone Ave., Cody, Wyo.
• **(307) 527-7561**

This clinic has three physicians on staff and welcomes walk-ins during regular daytime office hours. After hours you'll have to head for the emergency room of West Park Hospital (see previous entry in the "Hospitals" section).

Alternative Healthcare

As is true in other areas across the country, various forms of alternative healthcare are taking root in Greater Yellowstone. In the larger towns like Bozeman, Billings, Idaho Falls and especially Jackson, you will find several individual homeopaths, holistic medicine practitioners, massage therapists (some even do house calls) and certified midwives that offer home births. Even in small towns, where cowboys have pitched too much hay, or have been pitched from one horse too many, chiropractors hang up their shingles. For more information about alternative healthcare, hospice, home healthcare, special health services or veterinarians, we suggest you consult the Yellow Pages.

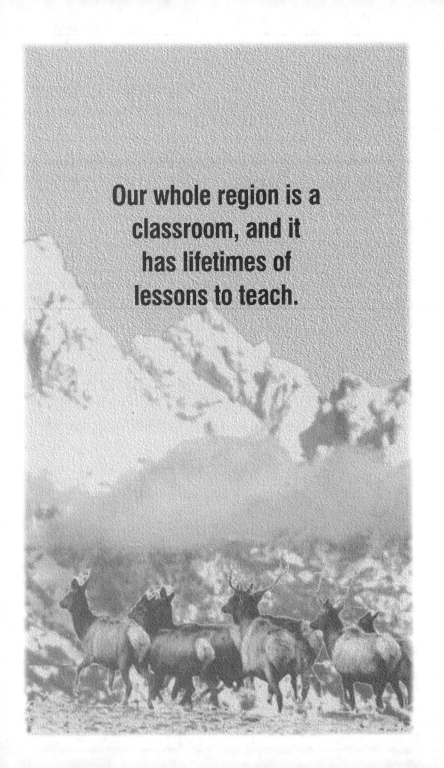

Our whole region is a
classroom, and it
has lifetimes of
lessons to teach.

Education

The unique learning opportunities of Greater Yellowstone go way beyond college. In this chapter we share with you some insights into the region through its unique programs. Ours is a special place, and the opportunities afforded here for learning and growth can be pretty special, too.

So leaf through the educational opportunities listed below. We hope you are tempted to sample one. New understanding is a better souvenir than all the snapshots in the world. But remember that we're not much on formality here: Just because it doesn't look like a classroom or didn't cost anything doesn't mean it can't teach you — if you step inside.

Yellowstone National Park

The Yellowstone Institute
Mammoth, Yellowstone Park
• (307) 344-2294

Formed in 1976 to provide visitors with in-depth, on-the-ground educational experiences, the Yellowstone Institute treats about 850 students each year to an array of multiple-day classes aimed at enrichment, education and, let's face it, entertainment. In 1997, the Yellowstone Institute, the education arm of the nonprofit Yellowstone Association, listed 85 different classes in its catalog. (For more information on the Yellowstone Association, Yellowstone Park's partner in education and research, see our Parks and Forests chapter.) All but a handful of these classes took place between June 1 and September 1.

The classes, based at the Buffalo Ranch, take students into the field to learn about the flora, fauna, geology, ecology, history and mystery of Yellowstone country. Many of the classes offer college credits. A peek at last year's catalog is likely to drive you to spend

your entire summer sampling the institute's menu of offerings. At the very least, you might decide to join the growing group of "regulars" who come each summer from New York to learn a little bit more about the wilds and wherefores of Yellowstone country.

In 1997, the class list included such offerings as "Lakes of Yellowstone by Canoe," "The Bison of Yellowstone," "Family Horsepacking — Doing Things Together," "Mammal Tracking," "Wildflowers of Yellowstone," "Family Days in the Thermal Basins," "Autumn Wildlife Photography," "Fly Fishing in the Fall" and much more. In addition, the institute offers nature-inspired writing, art and photography courses. To teach its courses, the institute uses various modes of transportation including vans, hiking, backpacking, llama packing, horsepacking, canoeing and cross-country skiing. Instructors are mostly from the Northwest and have a wealth of outdoor experience and expertise in their course subjects. Many of them are veteran teachers at the institute.

Facilities at the Buffalo Ranch include sleeping cabins, a historic bunkhouse and a communal kitchen. Situated on the year-round Gardiner-Cooke City Road, the Yellowstone Institute is accessible by road during the winter and is therefore able to offer a few winter courses. If we've tempted you with these field classes, we recommend you write the Institute at P.O. Box 117, Yellowstone Park, WY 82190, and ask for the 1998 catalog. We also suggest you sign up for their classes as soon as possible, since the institute gets a lot of class reservations from "old-timers" who know that some courses fill up fast.

Ranger-naturalist Programs
Yellowstone National Park
• (307) 344-7381

Yellowstone Park employs a battalion of ranger-naturalists each summer who guide walks and give programs tailored to their expertise and interests. *Yellowstone Today*, a publication handed to Park visitors at each entrance, contains a schedule and descriptions of these programs. For an in-depth description of the ranger-naturalist program in Yellowstone, refer to the entry that follows on the Grand Teton Park ranger-naturalists. The two Parks' programs are very similar.

Grand Teton National Park

Ranger-naturalist Programs
Grand Teton Park visitors centers
• **(307) 739-3300**

In 1916 when the National Park Service was established, so were ranger-naturalists. Back then, talking to and educating the public was only part of the job. Now, although all rangers wear the same uniform, their ranks include backcountry rangers, law enforcement rangers, visitor-use assistants (they'll take your money at the Park entrance) and ranger-naturalists. Ranger-naturalists in Grand Teton National Park will help you appreciate the complexity and wonder of the Park — and they do it at no charge.

Three kinds of programs are offered in Grand Teton Park: evening programs, talks and walks. Programs are greater in number and variety in summer — 32 ranger-naturalists work here in summer, and fewer than 10 in winter — but all year, you can bet something good is going on. Evening programs happen in each campground's outdoor amphitheater. They're about 45 minutes long, usually accompanied by slides and music. Presentation topics vary according to the individual ranger's interests and areas of expertise. Learn about fire ecology, birds of prey, wolves, bears and more. Talks are scheduled

at various places and times. Often they provide overview information about the Park.

At Moose, orientation talks often make use of the detailed relief map that dominates the visitors center. Orientation talks like these are given several times a day at both Colter Bay and Moose visitors centers. Hikes vary in length, but usually take no more than a couple hours. They're not physically demanding. For instance, the popular Inspiration Point hike focuses on area geology. It involves a pleasant boat trip across Jenny Lake, followed by a leisurely hike (less than a mile) past Hidden Falls to Inspiration Point, 400 feet above the lake. You walk back down at your own pace after asking the ranger every question you can think of. In 1997, the cost of the boat ride was $4, but the hike itself was free.

Twilight hikes focus on wildlife. It's not uncommon on these hikes to see moose, black bears, red squirrels, pikas and marmots. Wildflower walks meander through sagebrush flats like those around Taggart Lake.

www.insiders.com
See this and many other **Insiders' Guide®** destinations online — in their entirety.
Visit us today!

You learn to identify flowers and see relationships between these lovely plants and the plant and animal communities to which they belong. You'll also learn about edible and medicinal plants. One very popular ranger-led activity occurs only in September and only out of Moose visitors center. A car caravan, limited to 10 vehicles (carpooling is encouraged) leaves the visitors center during the prime evening wildlife viewing hours. You visit three or four locations, learning about the types of wildlife that frequent them. You'll generally see animals, but even if you don't, you'll have learned their addresses.

Another popular fall activity is simply to meet the ranger-naturalist at Oxbow Bend turnout, a rich area for game, particularly moose, and use binoculars or spotting scopes to observe whatever is there to be observed. Fall is

---

INSIDERS' TIP

At motels, hotels and campgrounds in West Yellowstone, look for "Audio Auto Tours," a set of four cassettes produced by Dennis Paterson, a 25-year veteran tour-bus driver in Yellowstone Park. These cassettes, which sell for $6 each, contain colorful details about the nooks and crannies of Yellowstone.

perfect for this activity because the mating season is on, which stirs things up.

In winter, rangers conduct snowshoe hikes out of Moose on old-style wooden snowshoes. The focus of these hikes is winter ecology and plant and animal adaptations to cold weather. Unlike Yellowstone Park which is so popular with snowmobilers, Grand Teton Park tends to be quiet in winter, which makes for pleasant hiking.

In general, there is no limit to participant numbers and reservations are not necessary for ranger-led activities or ranger talks. Exceptions are snowshoe hikes, car caravans and the Inspiration Point hike. Call Park dispatch or stop by any visitors center for a schedule of current ranger-naturalist activities.

Teton Science School
Off Gros Ventre River Rd., Grand Teton Park • (307) 733-4765

Folks in our region are so proud of TSS they could bust. More than 5,000 students ages 8 to 90 attend the school each year. They come from all over the world, but about 80 percent are from the Intermountain West. Courses are taught at the campus, an aspen-ringed former guest ranch at the edge of Grand Teton National Park. Instruction also moves out into Grand Teton and Yellowstone parks and the Bridger-Teton National Forest.

What are these people learning? TSS is a natural science center with a mission: Instructors believe that responsible management of fragile resources like those that make Greater Yellowstone precious is best accomplished by people with an educated, involved appreciation. They also believe that experience teaches. So school programs, teacher-education programs, community outreach and Elderhostel programs all focus on giving you opportunities for hands-on understanding of the natural world.

Students get involved in real research, like the bird banding project that, since 1991, has banded more than 469 birds (51 species) for monitoring. Students also work with the extensive collection of animal specimens collected by noted field biologists Olaus and Adolph Murie and explore the Muries' field journals and sketches. The school is open year-round; opportunities range from residential courses to one-day seminars. Some courses can be taken for college credit. One popular offering has been the four-day "Entomology for Flyfishers," co-taught by an entomologist and a noted fly-tyer and fly-fisherman. The course teaches you how to identify and understand insects important in trout diets. Then you learn imitative patterns and fly-tying tips. Then you go fishing!

You can take advantage of great short courses for birders and wildflower enthusiasts, too. Animal lovers can learn how to identify and interpret the signs animals leave behind, or you can learn more about specific species like coyotes or bears or canoe the Oxbow Bend of the Snake River and learn about the inhabitants of that rich riparian area.

Every year, longer residential programs are available to adults. In 1997, TSS and adult students followed the Lewis and Clark Trail from eastern Montana to the Oregon coast, visiting expedition sites and taking part in scientific and historical explorations based on the journals of Lewis and Clark.

Courses are reasonably priced from $50 for a one-day class.

Great Plains Wildlife Institute
430 Stacy Ln., Jackson, Wyo.
• (307) 733-2623

These folks have three goals: 1) They offer you the chance to do what you see wildlife biologists doing on the Discovery Channel; 2) They want to give you, the visitor, a chance to give back to the wildlife in return for the pleasure you received; and 3) They want to provide local jobs for researchers, paid for by concerned and involved tourists and not by government handouts. For you, the golden opportunity is the chance to work beside field biologists, gathering data that will help wildlife managers better protect sensitive ecosystems. Perhaps you'll help capture and tag study animals; perhaps you'll observe and document raptor behavior; you might help radio-track elk, moose or bats.

Four full-time biologists each manage one project. When you sign up for a daylong safari, you and a maximum of five other guests spend the morning with a staff biologist in the institute's touring vehicle getting oriented and learning about the Park, observing wildlife through institute-provided spotting scopes and binoculars. In the afternoon, you help the researcher gather data. The institute calls it citizen scientry; staff emphasize that although these research projects are real, participating in them requires no expertise, no hardbody stamina. In fact, if you're a family with kids, they'll bring the whole experience down to the kids' level of understanding. (If you don't have kids, you won't be paired with a family that does.)

Daytrips run year round and cost around $140 per person. In winter, the institute provides the snowshoes you'll probably end up on. Longer trips, including the Wolf Weekend Safari in Yellowstone National Park, are also available. Sunrise and sunset outings are available in the busy summer months, but the institute doesn't recommend those: You'll probably see wildlife, but you won't have time to get involved in the research.

Jackson Hole

Snake River Institute
5450 W. Wyo. 22, Wilson, Wyo.
• (307) 733-2214

Since 1988, more than 4,000 people have come to the little town of Wilson at the base of Teton Pass to explore and celebrate Western issues and cultures. The nonprofit arts and humanities institute has hosted classes taught by such writers as Terry Tempest Williams and William Kittredge, historian David McCullough and paleontologist Robert Bakker.

For the past several years, a course called "Creatures in Stone: A Fossil Excavation Adventure for the Family" has received rave reviews from participants. It's a two-day excursion down to Ulrich Quarries in Wyoming. You learn about fossils then hunt for your own; the instructor identifies your finds and helps you prepare them for public display. Another popular course (some folks enroll year after year) is a four-day photographic excursion into Grand Teton and Yellowstone national parks. Part of the popularity of the course is, of course, the intoxicatingly photogenic areas you'll shoot in. But much of the attraction comes from the fact that your three instructors, Ed Riddell, Jon Stuart and John Telford, have been teaching this course together for the last six years. You'll

benefit from their varied approaches and perspective. An offbeat, unconventional offering that draws an eclectic mix of students is called Adventures in Building. What's the adventure? Well, mostly the building material: straw. You and your classmates will, in four days' time, construct an entire straw house.

Class offerings vary from year to year, so the classes described here may or may not be available. You can be sure dozens of surprising, mind-expanding options will. Classes are kept small, fewer than 15 participants usually, so expect them to fill up fast. Snake River Institute generally runs from April to November. A special selection of kids' classes is available in summer only (see our Kidstuff chapter for more). Tuition varies but generally begins at about $50 for a one-day course.

Surrounding Areas

Eastern Idaho

Idaho Falls Area

Idaho State University/University of Idaho at University Place
1776 Science Center Dr., Idaho Falls, Idaho • (208) 535-7800

Question: How do you earn a college degree at home when your town has no university? Answer: With a little help from your friends. Idaho Falls is the largest town in Idaho with no university of its own. So Pocatello's ISU and Moscow-based U of I have combined forces to provide more than 500 academic courses to locals. Nearly 2,500 students per semester, most of them degree-seeking, take general-education courses or obtain bachelor's degrees through this cooperative program.

Eastern Idaho Technical College
1600 Hitt Rd., Idaho Falls, Idaho • (208) 524-3000, (800) 662-0261

The focus here is vocational training. Health occupations, mechanical trades and business are well represented, with the business department attracting nearly 60 percent of stu-

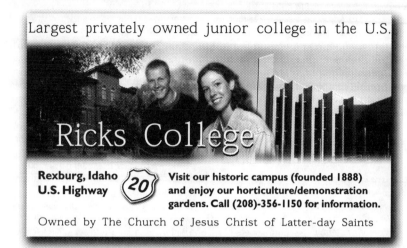

Largest privately owned junior college in the U.S.

Ricks College

Rexburg, Idaho
U.S. Highway 20
Visit our historic campus (founded 1888) and enjoy our horticulture/demonstration gardens. Call (208)-356-1150 for information.

Owned by The Church of Jesus Christ of Latter-day Saints

dent enrollment. Computer training courses are popular: EITC has one of the few Novell-certified computer programs in the West. The full-time population of the college is small, around 450 students.

BYU/Ricks Center
1776 Science Center Dr., Idaho Falls, Idaho • (208) 523-4682

Ricks, a large Mormon Church-owned junior college in Rexburg, provides an important service to degree-seeking students in Idaho Falls. Every semester the school offers a selection of general-education requirements in English, math and science to students in Idaho Falls. The instructors are generally Ricks faculty who drive down to teach these evening courses to students enrolled in degree programs through University of Idaho or Idaho State University who sometimes scramble to meet general-education requirements without having to leave town.

Community Education, Idaho Falls School District #91
601 S. Holmes Ave., Idaho Falls, Idaho • (208) 525-7748

This very active community education program deserves special notice. And it's getting it: 500 to 700 people a semester notice how much fun taking one or more of the program's 80-odd offerings can be. Prices range from $12 to $103 for courses that last from one day to 10 weeks.

Rexburg, Idaho

Ricks College
U.S. Hwy. 20, Rexburg, Idaho • (208) 356-2011

Owned and operated by the Church of Jesus Christ of Latter-day Saints, Ricks is the largest two-year college in the country. Enrollment is held to 7,500 students, about a third of whom are from Idaho. Courses are taught by more than 300 full-time faculty members, nearly all of whom have either master's degrees or doctorates. Ricks also has an active continuing education program. On the main Rexburg campus, short-term, noncredit courses are available, mostly in summer; most focus on the natural or human history of the area. One final thing about Ricks: It adheres to the strictures of the Mormon faith and asks that while you're on campus you do the same. That means no caffeine, tobacco, alcohol, shorts or miniskirts.

Teton Valley

Targhee Institute
Ski Hill Rd., Alta, Wyo. • (208) 353-2233

Learn about Western water issues, outdoor photography, the geology of the Yellowstone region and much, much more. Courses generally run one week at a cost of around $200, which includes meals but not accommodations. Hosted by the Targhee Institute and Boston-based Elderhostel, this is adult education at its most fun. A few classes allow children to attend with an accompanying adult (who must be older than 55 per Elderhostel requirements). Targhee Institute is in the Targhee National Forest at Grand Targhee Ski and Summer Resort. Accommodations are available at the resort itself or down the hill in Teton Valley (see our accommodations chapters).

Southwestern Montana

Off the Beaten Path
27 E. Main Street, Bozeman, Mont.
• **(406) 586-1311, (800) 445-2995**

Working like a finely conducted orchestra, this company's army of staff members creates specially designed vacation experiences intended to give you locals' insights into the culture, history, flora, fauna and science of Greater Yellowstone. The staff, veteran travelers and locals themselves have scoured the region for the very best places, guides, outfitters and accommodations to make the most of your time. In 1998, they will lead five expeditions into the Parks. They include the eight-day "Bears and Wolves of Yellowstone"; "Tracing the Flight of the Nez Perce," a 12-day trek that follows the Nez Perce Trail through Montana and Idaho; and "Winter in Yellowstone Wonderland," an eight-day, cross-country trip that will lead you across pristine ski trails, through thermal basins and to wildlife.

Northern Rockies Natural History
P.O. Box 42, Bozeman, MT 59771
• **(406) 586-1155**

There is no better place in the world to watch wild wolves than Yellowstone National Park. And wildlife biologist Ken Sinay can lead you to them. He can also interpret their behavior while you watch them through binoculars or a spotting scope. Sinay specializes in leading small groups of people (his group size averages three or four) "off the asphalt," then showing and telling them about the mysteries and history of Yellowstone country. Tour the geysers with him and learn astounding facts about what lies beneath the surface of their bubbling, spraying waters. Walk a ways off the road and watch a bear bathing in the river.

Or, if you must, stay in the car, and he or one of his guides will ride along and tell and show you what they know.

If you're inclined to leave your car, he won't have to lead you far for you to see what you never imagined you might see. For example, Sinay offers a daylong river float on the slow waters of the Madison, Gallatin or Jefferson rivers. You will sit in chairs on a 16-foot, flat-bottomed boat, slip into back channels, pull over in eddies and scope out wildlife. Along the way, you might observe muskrats, pelicans, cranes, eagles, river otter playing on the banks, mink, coyotes, osprey catching fish, beaver, and deer.

After eight years in the business, Sinay offers his guests well-rounded insights into the historical, cultural and scientific aspects of the Greater Yellowstone ecosystem. You'll come away from one of his tours with a greater understanding of Yellowstone country and a desire to know more about what's going on in your own backyard. Sinay charges $125 per day per person for his float trips (there's a discount for additional people) and $250 per day for personally guided tours. You need to call ahead to make arrangements for a tour, since Sinay is often booked far ahead of time. He or one of his guides will make plans to meet you.

Yellowstone Ecosystem Studies
13 S. Willson Ave., #9, Bozeman, Mont.
• **(406) 587-7758**

Imagine watching a pack of coyotes trying to pick off and kill a single calf among five cow elk. Or watching while coyotes (or wolves) devour an elk carcass. Or witnessing territorial disputes between wolves and coyotes — both canids. Yellowstone Ecosystem Studies, a nonprofit, nonpolitical research and education organization, leads weeklong "Wild Dog" research trips in Yellowstone Park. If you sign up for one of their trips, you will become a part of the research team. A team of biologists and zoologists will train you to observe canids, gather information and record what you see. After each day in the field, you and your fellow researchers will review and compare field notes. This trip, held each spring, costs $1,300 per person. It includes lodging in Cooke City and three squares a day.

Yellowstone Ecosystem Studies, led by canid biologist Bob Crabtree, shares its research with Yellowstone National Park to track the relationship between coyotes and wolves since they were re-introduced to the Park in 1995. Crabtree has been studying coyotes in Yellowstone since the early 1980s.

Montana State University
120 Hamilton Hall, Bozeman, Mont.
• **(406) 994-0211**

Founded in 1893, Montana State University was the first public institution of higher education in Montana. A land-grant college, it specialized in agriculture and mechanical arts back then. These days, though, the number of colleges at this 12,000-student university, has expanded to eight: Arts and Architecture, Business, Agriculture, Education, Health and Human Development, Engineering, Letters and Science, Nursing and Library.

Many MSU professors use Montana's national forests and parks (Yellowstone Park included) for their outdoor laboratories in the pursuit of such sciences as plant pathology, earth science, biology, sociology and paleontology. Paleontology students are attracted to MSU, where the Museum of the Rockies, an extension of the university, owns the only complete T. Rex collection in the state of Montana. (See our Attractions chapter for more information on the Museum of the Rockies.)

Northwestern Wyoming

Grub Steak Expeditions
P.O. Box 1013, Cody, WY 82414
• **(307) 527-6316**

The landscape of Yellowstone country is beautiful. And Bob Richard, tour guide for Grub Steak Expeditions, brings it to life with historical and other details he learned as a boy from his grandfather and as a ranger in Yellowstone Park. Richard grew up in Cody guiding with his grandfather, who was one of Buffalo Bill Cody's guides. While at his grandfather's knee, he learned to tell a good tale. Now retired, he brings his own and his grandfather's extensive knowledge to tours tailored to suit your needs — art gallery visits, wildlife photography outings and geology expeditions, among others. Reserve your spot well in advance by calling the number above. Richard charges $250 per day.

Northwest College
231 West Sixth St., Powell, Wyo.
• **(307) 754-6111**

Located in Powell, about 70 miles from the east entrance of Yellowstone National Park and about 90 miles south of Billings, Northwest College is a two-year, residential college with about 2,000 students. It has come a long way since it began in 1946 as the first satellite branch of the University of Wyoming, with seven instructors teaching on the second floor of Powell High School. Northwest College offers transfer programs based on traditional arts and sciences and other programs that have strong educational requirements.

The college also operates the Mickelson Field Station in the Absaroka Mountain Range on Dead Indian Hill just off the Chief Joseph Scenic Highway (Wyo. Highway 296). This year-round facility offers a lodge with three buildings containing a total of 12 cabins. Reservations are filled on a first-come, first-served basis and may be made up to two years in advance. The length of stay is usually limited to five nights.

Take the road less traveled

Great books on backcountry adventure driving

Idaho Byways
35 backcountry drives in Idaho's mountains and deserts.
$14.95

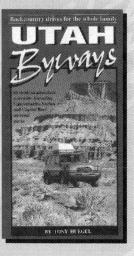

Utah Byways
60 backcountry adventure drives.
$16.95

Also check out the California Byways series

• **California Desert Byways** – 50 drives through some of America's most beautiful desert landscapes. $18.95

• **California Coastal Byways** – 50 drives from Oregon to the San Diego area. $18. 95

• **Sierra Nevada Byways** – 32 drives in California's most famous mountain range. $14.95

Credit card orders accepted

Call (208) 522-1800

Media

Fierce local pride, a thirst for local news and a relative dearth of other media sources make the Yellowstone country newspaper business volatile. Newspaperman Warren Cornwall wrote last April that Fremont County, Idaho, has more newspapers than stoplights: six newspapers, one stoplight.

Already that has changed: Fremont County, population 13,000, home to three small communities and one stoplight, now has only four newspapers. The Ashton paper, one Island Park paper and the St. Anthony paper merged to become one new, countywide publication. This paper and one other, an Island Park publication now loudly proclaiming itself the only local community newspaper, are produced within Fremont County. A third aims at Fremont County, but locals are very aware that it's produced in neighboring Madison County. The fourth is Idaho Falls' big daily paper, the *Post Register*.

This is Fremont County's second ride 'round this particular merry-go-round in the past few decades. Twenty years ago Rexburg's *Standard Journal* swept papers from the same three towns into one countywide publication and infuriated enough county residents to eventually spawn three new newspapers. That's how Fremont County ended up with six newspapers in April 1997: Readers had become tired of having only two, neither of which, they felt, captured the vastly different characters of Fremont County communities.

Every Yellowstone country community wants its own paper. Sometimes every faction within a community wants its own paper. That's how Teton County, Idaho, and Teton County, Wyoming, both ended up with not one but two weekly papers serving their tiny towns. Tough luck for newspapermen, but a windfall of print information sources for residents. For you it's even better, because all those little community newspapers and specialty maga-

zines are a window straight to the collective and competing heart of our region.

Radio and television reception can be iffy in this mountainous country. Most communities are cut off from neighboring towns' radio or television stations by mountains. So local broadcast media choices can be extremely limited. For many Yellowstone country residents, in fact, the only way to get pretty pictures on that glassy-eyed box is a cable or satellite hookup — if it's available where they live. That's why the motels you've looked at advertise cable TV and not just TV. That's also why video rental stores are nearly as ubiquitous as gas stations around here.

What follows is a quick tour through the print and broadcast media of Yellowstone country. Just remember: Things change fast around here — unless, that is, you're looking for us to install more stoplights.

Newspapers and Periodicals

In the Parks

Yellowstone Today
Mammoth, Yellowstone National Park
• **(307) 344-2258**

As you enter Yellowstone National Park, a Park Ranger will give you a copy of *Yellowstone Today*, a 20-or-more-page newspaper that carries enough information about the Park to get you on your way. Except for a five-year interruption from 1980 to 1985, Yellowstone National Park has had some sort of newspaper since 1974. Called the *Yellowstone Explorer* from 1974 to 1979, the Park's quarterly publication became *Yellowstone Today* in 1986, after the Park Service put together a patchwork of funding to resurrect the newspaper. The Park Service hands out about a million copies of *Yellowstone Today* to visitors entering the Park.

The summer issue is the largest of the year with about 20 pages, and it is full of all the information you'll need to get you started in the Park. *Yellowstone Today* includes maps showing locations of lodging, campgrounds, medical services, visitor centers and other facilities in both Yellowstone and Grand Teton parks. The rest of the publication highlights rules, campgrounds and lodging, concessionaire activities, safety, road construction schedules and information about fishing in Yellowstone Park. An eight-page version, the *Yellowstone Guide*, is sent to those requesting an information packet from the Park Service.

www.insiders.com

See this and many other **Insiders' Guide®** destinations online — in their entirety.

Visit us today!

Teewinot
P.O. Drawer 170, Moose, WY 83012
• **(307) 739-3600**

Grand Teton National Park's biannual publication is named for one of the peaks in the Teton Range. Its original purpose was to supply essential safety information to visitors, but you'll also find information about visitor resources, schedules of events, maps and discussions of wildlife and Park issues in this 12-page newspaper. *Teewinot* is produced by Park staff and published by the nonprofit Grand Teton Natural History Association, which also operates bookstores and visitors centers throughout the Park. About 500,000 copies are distributed annually.

Dailies

Post Register
333 Northgate Mile, Idaho Falls, Idaho
• **(208) 522-1800**

Idaho Falls' newspaper is the media anchor for the entire west side of Yellowstone country. It distributes 28,000 copies daily between Pocatello and West Yellowstone, Montana, and between Salmon, Idaho, and Freedom and Afton, Wyoming. The Post Company also owns Idaho 8, KIFI-TV. By Idaho standards, it's a regular pub-

lishing giant, producing recreation and travel guides (including this one!), a small stable of magazines and several weekly newspapers. The *Post Register's* pedigree dates to 1880, when the *Blackfoot Register* was first published by William Wheeler. Since 1925, the paper has been owned by the Brady family, many of whom live in Idaho Falls.

The *Post Register* has won numerous awards recently for coverage of conservation issues such as wolf reintroduction and Snake River management. The *Post Register* converted in 1997 from a six-day afternoon paper to a seven-day morning paper. Its newsstand price is 50¢ on weekdays and $1.50 on Sundays.

Billings Gazette
401 N. Broadway, Billings, Mont.
• **(406) 657-1200**

With a Sunday circulation of 62,000, the *Billings Gazette* is Montana's largest newspaper. The *Gazette* has an incredibly wide circulation. It covers 90,000 square miles from the Canadian border to central Wyoming and from the western Dakotas to Helena, Montana. It supports bureaus in Cody, Wyoming; and Bozeman and Helena, Montana. Each year the *Gazette* publishes 60 special sections including a tab on Yellowstone Park and guides on hunting and fishing.

Bozeman Daily Chronicle
32 S. Rouse Ave., Bozeman, Mont.
• **(406) 587-4491**

The *Bozeman Daily Chronicle*, a morning paper published seven days a week by Big Sky Publishing Company, employs a full time staff writer to cover Yellowstone National Park year around. In addition to covering Yellowstone Park, the *Chronicle* puts out an annual publication called *Explorer*, a guide to outdoor recreation and activities in Yellowstone country. The *Explorer* is jam-packed with nifty ideas for things to do and places to go in Southwestern Montana. In addition to the *Explorer*, the *Chronicle* publishes an annual fishing guide for Southwestern Montana. The *Bozeman Daily Chronicle*, first published in 1911, covers national and regional news, local color and high school and college sports. The *Chronicle* has a daily circulation of 13,500 and a Sunday circulation of 15,000. The daily paper costs 50¢, and the Sunday edition is $1.25.

Livingston Enterprise
401 S. Main, Livingston, Mont.
• **(406) 222-2000**

The *Livingston Enterprise*, published every weekday, has been in continuous publication since the first issue was put out on June 4, 1883, in an office above Frank White's Saloon in the Orschel Building on East Park Street. Since that time, the paper has changed hands several times, switched back and forth from a daily to a weekly and changed location at least four times. Owned by the Anaconda Company from 1919 to 1959, the *Enterprise* was bought by Lee Newspapers then sold to William and Helen Hornby in 1971. The *Enterprise* carries several features each issue and offers diverse news coverage. In the same day, you might read on one page about a presidential visit to Yellowstone Park and on the next page about who went to dinner at whose home in Wilsall. The *Enterprise*, generously supplemented with Associated Press stories, gives good coverage to Yellowstone Park issues and has a circulation of 3,800. The paper costs 50¢.

Semiweekly

Cody Enterprise
1549 Sheridan Ave., Cody, Wyo.
• **(307) 587-2231**

Founded by Buffalo Bill Cody in 1899, the *Cody Enterprise* is the oldest business in Cody. This award-winning newspaper, published every Monday and Wednesday afternoon, reflects the community's general attention to quality. The *Enterprise* sports top quality photos as well as features and general news about Cody and the surrounding area. In addition to lively news reporting, the paper is peppered with local weekly columns like "Quade's Quips," "Tracks Trails and Tidbits" and "Streamside." By the way, the *Enterprise's* 40-foot-by-4-foot blue and yellow sign, installed in 1997, is so spectacular tourists often stop to photograph it. *Cody Enterprise* has a circulation of 6,025; it costs 50¢.

Fremont County Herald Chronicle
P.O. Box 568, St. Anthony, ID 83445
• **(208) 624-4455**

This decade-old consolidation of three Fremont County weeklies is published on Tuesdays and Thursdays by *The Rexburg Standard Journal* in Madison County. Like Rexburg's paper, the *Herald Chronicle* is owned by a local family, the Porters; it shares both a philosophy and some of its pages with the larger Rexburg publication. Both try to provide broader coverage than most weeklies, mixing regional and national news of local interest with strictly local news. Like the Rexburg paper, the *Fremont County Herald Chronicle* is a wire-service paper, unusual for a small weekly. This paper is available by subscription and for 50¢ at countywide newsstands. It has 2,200 subscribers.

Rexburg Standard Journal
P.O. Box 10, Rexburg, Idaho 83440
• **(208) 356-5441**

The roots of this award-winning independent biweekly stretch back a century in the pin-neat farming town of Rexburg. The paper prints 6,500 copies for a community not much more than twice that size. Folks in Rexburg like their paper. Unlike many smaller papers within range of Idaho Falls' big daily, the *Rexburg Standard Journal* provides some regional and national news, although its focus is still the community. This paper costs 50¢ on newsstands throughout Madison County.

Weeklies

Carbon County News
202 S. Hauser, Red Lodge, Mont.
• **(406) 446-2222**

If a picture is worth a thousand words, there's plenty to read between the lines in the *Carbon County News*. Loaded with top-quality interesting photos (even the mug shots are good), you'll swear Editor Shelley Beaumont has a team of photographers scouring the countryside for prize-winning snapshots. The photos and the copy in this weekly, owned by News Montana Inc., mirror the diversity of Red Lodge and the surrounding area. The *Carbon County News*, first published in 1907 as the

Red Lodge Pickett-Journal, has a staff of seven and a circulation of 3,000. It's published on Wednesday and costs 50¢.

The Fremont Current
999 Main, Ashton, Idaho
- **(208) 652-3410**

This weekly, which hits newsstands every Thursday, is a locals' local. It runs no national wire copy. Its writers live and work in Fremont County and stories are about Fremont County. Editor Cathy Koon was born in the county seat of St. Anthony. *The Fremont Current* is also an experiment, a merging of weeklies based in St. Anthony, Ashton and Island Park. Beginning in July 1997, the first six issues were distributed free to every household in Fremont County. Now you can subscribe for $25 per year, or pick up a newsstand copy almost anywhere in the county for 50¢.

Gardiner Community Newsletter
233 Main, Suite A, Gardiner, Mont.
- **(406) 848-7971**

Printed 52 weeks a year for more than 15 years by the Gardiner Chamber of Commerce, the *Gardiner Community Newsletter* hits the streets each Wednesday morning. Printed on both sides of legal-size paper, this free newsletter is for both locals and tourists. It contains brief news about business summer hours and sales as well as reminders to locals about the date, time and location of the next visit by the Schwann's delivery truck. The newsletter also announces the times and dates of meetings and contains a section of classifieds, including rentals, jobs and yard sales. Look for the *Gardiner Community Newsletter* at most Gardiner businesses.

High Country Independent Press
220 S. Broadway, Belgrade, Mont.
- **(406) 388-6762**

The official legal paper of Gallatin County, the *High Country Independent Press* began as the *Belgrade Independent Press* in 1979. After several ownership changes, *High Country* was finally bought in 1987 by Glenn and Devon Sorlie. In 1989, this weekly, which is published every Thursday, switched from a free to a paid-for publication. It quickly grew from a sometimes-12-page paper to its cur-

rent 18 to 24 pages with a circulation of just under 3,000. Covering Belgrade, Big Sky, Bozeman, Manhattan and Three Forks, this paper contains an array of community news. The extensive and detailed Sheriff's Log and Belgrade Police Log make fascinating reading. The newsstand price is 50¢.

Island Park News
PO Box 410, Island Park, ID 83429
- **(208) 558-0267**

This newer weekly prints no wire-service copy: It's for and about the Island Park area. Ironically, though, the paper's Elizabeth Laden says Island Park News has subscribers in all 50 states. Tourists who care about the area come through in the summer, pick up a free newsstand copy and decide they want to keep hearing about Island Park after they go home, she says. The paper prints 10,000 copies in summer and winter but only 2,000 in November and April. This is even more interesting in light of the fact that Island Park has only 250 year-round residents. Island Park News is distributed from Idaho Falls to Billings, Montana, in retail stores and visitors centers.

The Jefferson Star
134 W. Main, Rigby, Idaho
- **(208) 745-8701**

Jefferson County's weekly dates to 1903. It has been owned since 1988 by Terry and Kenneth J. Carr, originally from Texas. Circulation is around 2,000, mostly in Jefferson and Clark counties. *The Jefferson Star* readers often subscribe also to the area's daily, the *Post Register*. This gives the *Star* the freedom to focus on the local news the *Post Register* can't provide. Here's a great trivia tidbit about *The Jefferson Star*: Back when it was called *The Rigby Star*, this tiny paper in a backwater farming area of a backwater state was home to a columnist whose work was syndicated across the country. Vardis Fisher, born in nearby Annis, was an acclaimed novelist (and during his stint as a college professor, the instructor of Pulitzer Prize-winner Wallace Stegner). Fisher's best-known book is *The Mountain Man*. You can pick up a copy of *The Jefferson Star* at area newsstands for 50¢.

Jackson Hole Guide
185 N. Glenwood St., Jackson, Wyo.
• **(307) 733-2430**

Forty-five-year-old *Jackson Hole Guide* is Jackson's oldest newspaper. It publishes a thick weekly edition and a slimmer daily version. The weekly has a circulation of 8,000 and the daily's distribution is 5,000. The paper has subscribers in all 50 states and is available on newsstands from Jackson to Pinedale and from Victor and Driggs to Star Valley. The *Guide* is not Jackson's only paper, though. For years it was seen as a conservative paper, so the *Jackson Hole News* stepped in to tell the liberal story. Those political labels no longer seem accurate, but what is still true is that the competition between two newspapers in such a small market has made both topnotch. Both routinely win national awards. Both are read, sort of interchangeably, by area residents. *Jackson Hole Guide* costs 75¢ on newsstands. The daily edition is free.

Jackson Hole News
1225 Maple Way, Jackson, Wyo.
• **(307) 733-2047**

Jackson's residents tend to be well-educated and very interested in area issues. So it's no surprise that the typical Jackson resident reads two local weekly newspapers. Folks from outside the region subscribe to these papers, too. Headlines about local issues — how grizzlies and bison should be managed or winter recreation conflicts in Yellowstone National Park, for instance — are often compelling to folks outside the region. The *News* is about 28 years old. In 1996 it was named best in its class by the National Newspaper Association, but it started getting attention a long time ago. In the mid-1980s, the University of Missouri singled little *Jackson Hole News* from every other paper in the country for its effective use of photos. The weekly edition of *Jackson Hole News* is available on area newsstands for 50¢. It circulates about 8,000 copies. A slimmer daily edition is free.

Lone Peak Lookout
Meadow Village Center, Big Sky, Mont.
• **(406) 995-4133**

Big Sky is a happening place, and the *Lone Peak Lookout* is just the publication to take you into the nooks and crannies of everyday life in the Canyon. This award-winning independent, privately owned weekly has served Gallatin Canyon and Big Sky since 1982. A free publication, it is jam-packed with articles and columns that represent the spectrum of life in the Canyon. *The Lone Peak* can be found at newsstands almost anyplace in Greater Yellowstone; it's published on Thursdays. It has 700 subscribers nationwide, with a total circulation of between 2,800 and 5,000.

Park County Weekly
306 S. Main, Livingston, Mont.
• **(406) 222-9500**

Sharon Walker first began the *Park County Weekly* on April Fool's Day, 1986, right at the beginning of an economic downswing. Six months later, she put the free publication to rest and moved to Seattle where she started a printing and graphics business. Seven years later, she returned to Livingston and brought her business with her. Three years after that, in 1996, she resurrected the *Park County Weekly* by popular demand. Walker now employs eight people and publishes 7,300 copies each Wednesday. Dubbed "the paper that's read from cover to cover," the *Park County Weekly* is filled with down-home, warmhearted, interesting reading about people, places and events in Park County.

Teton Valley Independent
75 N. Main, Driggs, Idaho
• **(208) 354-3111**

One of two weeklies serving Teton Valley, the *Independent* is larger with a distribution of 4,000 (the other, *Teton Valley News*, has 2,500) in large part because it's mailed free to residents of Teton and Swan valleys. Swan Valley's several hundred residents had no paper of their own before the *Independent* widened its range in June 1997. The *Independent* tries to be a community paper by including a variety of voices and perspectives. Publisher Karl Hanosky promises you'll find the ideas of around a dozen locals every week in the pages of his newspaper. It's distributed on Thursday.

Teton Valley News
80 E. Little Ave., Driggs, Idaho
• **(208) 354-8101**

In 1909, *Teton Valley News* fired up its presses and became Teton Basin's first and only newspaper. It has competition from another weekly now, but the *News* is still the voice of tradition (as well as the traditional voice) of Teton Valley. It prints 2,500 copies. Only 1,600 of the paper's subscribers are valley residents, though, reflecting the wider region's interest in the little mountain valley. In small communities served by two competing papers, each tends to find its niche. The *News* sees itself as the more news-oriented paper. Right now, by coincidence rather than design, this Thursday weekly is produced by an all-woman staff. *Teton Valley News* is available at local newsstands for 50¢.

West Yellowstone News
309 Canyon St., West Yellowstone, Mont.
• **(406) 646-9719**

The *West Yellowstone News*, which bills itself as the "Biggest Little Paper in the West," took a big upswing in 1997. This homey little paper will tell you what's going on in West Yellowstone. It also carries news about Yellowstone Park issues, especially those that relate to the welfare of West Yellowstone. Several columns, including "On the Street," by Editor John Degel, and "Fish Wrapper," by John and Craig of Blue Ribbon Flies, offer insider information on the community in general and fishing in particular. The circulation is 2,500, and it costs 50¢.

Periodicals

Arts Alive!
498 A St., Idaho Falls, Idaho
• **(208) 522-0471**

This 16- to 20-page newsprint magazine is published by the Idaho Falls Arts Council several times a year. You can pick it up free in coffee shops and restaurants from Idaho Falls to Jackson, Wyoming. Expect to find news about local performing and visual arts not just in Idaho Falls but throughout eastern Idaho. Perhaps the most useful item in this little mag is the calendar, which includes not only art shows and festivals, but also community events, rodeos, storytelling festivals and fairs.

Big Sky Journal
101 E. Main, Bozeman, Mont.
• **(406) 586-2712, (800) 417-3314**

A high-gloss, nonpolitical, coffee-table magazine mostly about Montana, *Big Sky Journal* has been published five times a year since 1993. In a single issue, you might find an article on Montana's Hutterites, mountain men, Montana writers or Western photographer Barbara Van Cleve. Somewhere in those pages you'll find a couple of essays on ranching, maybe a photo feature on Yellowstone Park and always some tips on "Eating Around Montana." Special departments in the *Big Sky Journal* include Ranch Life, Western Designs, In Place and Time, Backcountry and The Back Forty. Big Sky Journal also includes reviews of several books relevant to the Rockies. The newsstand price is $5.95; a subscription for five issues is $24.

Caldera
P.O. Box 1540, Jackson, WY 83001
• **(307) 733-2995**

Caldera is a place for "news of the imagination," as one former editor puts it. If that makes you suspect this is not your normal magazine, you're right on target. First, the whole idea behind *Caldera* is to not create a forum for the pet issues of one group of managers and editors. That's why responsibility for the magazine changes hands every issue. Second, all the folks who work on *Caldera* are volunteers. Grants and private donations pay for printing costs. No ads are sold. The 30-odd stores that offer *Caldera* for sale, primarily Albertson's, Valley Bookstore and Hungry Jack's, agree not to profit from magazine sales. *Caldera* is about living in Jackson Hole, about stewardship of the land, about people in relation to place. Material ranges from poetry to personal reflection, sketches to photography and commentary to fiction. The magazine comes out irregularly about once a year. The cover price has been $4.95.

Crone Chronicles: A Journal of Conscious Aging
P.O. Box 81, Kelly, WY 83011
• **(307) 733-5409**

Wisdom is the result of paying attention to your experience, believes editor and co-publisher Ann Kreilkamp, 54. Her 8-year-old quarterly publication is a forum for people to glean from their experience and share what they find. The magazine prints 5,000 copies an issue. Subscriptions are available for $21. The magazine's readers are scattered across the country, as are its contributors of personal reflections, poetry and a smattering of fiction. Issues are themed: Past emphases include war and peace, power and presence, emergence and emergency, soul and money, and journeys. In Jackson, you can pick up a copy for around $7 at the Herb Store, Teton Book Shop and Valley Bookstore.

Intermountain Farm and Ranch
333 Northgate Mile, Idaho Falls, Idaho
• (208) 522-1800

A 6-year-old weekly newsprint magazine with a circulation of 15,000, *Farm and Ranch* is devoted to news farmers can use. It is inserted into *Post Register* deliveries on rural routes. You can also pick it up free on magazine racks from Soda Springs to West Yellowstone. In 1996 The Post Company surveyed *Intermountain Farm and Ranch* readers to learn that 3,400 are full-time farmers, 2,200 are full-time ranchers and 1,700 work part-time or are retired from agricultural jobs.

Intermountain Hunting & Fishing
333 Northgate Mile, Idaho Falls, Idaho
• (208) 522-1800

Eastern Idaho has always been raptly interested in hunting and fishing. Idaho Falls' daily newspaper, the *Post Register*, ran an outdoor page to satisfy readers' desire for hunting and fishing news, but it wasn't quite enough. So three years ago, editor Rob Thornberry launched this newsprint magazine. An avid hunter and fisherman himself, Rob ran four issues the first year, 10 the next and 12 last year. Circulation is approximately 27,000. You can subscribe to *Intermountain Hunting and Fishing* for $15 per year or pay $1.50 at some 100 rack locations throughout eastern Idaho.

Montana Land Magazine
1364 Valley Heights Road, Billings, Mont.
• (406) 259-3534

Known as the real-estate bible of Montana, the *Montana Land Magazine* may be the largest real-estate publication in the country. Gordie Dangerfield, a Billings Realtor, got the idea for the magazine one day as he was driving through Big Sky country dreaming and scheming. Since 1982, when he put out the first 40-page issue, the *Montana Land Maga-*

zine has grown so much that it takes a semi-truck to haul the 125,000 issues distributed in Montana and five other states each summer. Distributed free to the public at 900 locations, this quarterly publication is widely read and has subscribers in several foreign countries.

Montana Free Press Box
Red Lodge, Mont. • (406) 446-2493

When publisher/editor Jim Coates prepared for the first issue of the *Montana Free Press*, he expected it to be an eight-page newsletter. The first issue of this monthly publication, which hit the streets in March 1990, turned out to be 22 pages. The *Montana Free Press*, billed as "the journal of rural Montana," now regularly exceeds 50 pages. Since its early days the *Free Press* has evolved into a vehicle for recording the oral histories of individuals and their communities. Cover stories feature different rural communities throughout Montana and Wyoming. The *Montana Free Press* has a circulation of 10,000. Postal patrons in Carbon and Stillwater counties receive free copies via third class postage.

Northern Rockies Brew Review
333 Northgate Mile, Idaho Falls, Idaho
• (208) 522-1800

Since the West was the birthplace of the microbrew revolution, there's probably room around here for a new publication that discusses all things hoppy and malty. Publisher, editor and homebrewer Dean Miller, who concocts a good porter if he does say so himself, brewed up the first issue of this magazine in early 1996. A Post Company publication, *Brew Review* circulates 25,000 copies biannually. It's good bar reading for casual beer lovers, and in fact that's where it's readily found — in restaurants, bars and brewpubs in Utah, Idaho, Montana and Wyoming. You can also check state tourist information centers. *Northern Rockies Brew Review* is free.

Snake River Echoes
P.O. Box 244, Rexburg, ID 83440
• (208) 356-9101

This biannual publication of the Upper Snake River Valley Historical Society in Rexburg is published out of the same building that contains Rexburg's Teton Flood Museum. Like the museum itself, the magazine is about remembering. Contents include poetry, reminiscence and first-person accounts of events from eastern Idaho's history. Only 750 copies are printed, but they end up in libraries as far away as Seattle, Washington, and Battle Creek, Michigan. You can purchase current and back copies at the museum. Current copies sell for $5.

SnowAction
520 Park Ave., Idaho Falls, Idaho
• **(208) 524-7000**

Smaller than *SnoWest* (see the next listing), this Harris Publishing Company magazine is for snowmobile racers and racing fans. It covers grass and asphalt drags (yes, they really do race on asphalt with specially modified snowmobiles), ovals and hillclimbs and snowcross races. Each issue includes a useful calendar of races nationwide. The magazine is published eight times a year, with five issues saturating the peak racing season, January through March. Subscribers pay $14.95 a year for eight issues of 40 to 60 slick pages full of photos and color. You can't buy this magazine on newsstands, but some snowmobile dealerships handle it. *SnowAction* prints around 22,000 copies per issue.

SnoWest
520 Park Ave., Idaho Falls, Idaho
• **(208) 524-7000**

SnoWest is one of two snowmobile magazines published by family-owned Harris Publishing (the other is *SnowAction*, above) and one of seven recreational and agricultural publications Harris owns. Aimed at recreational riders, this magazine features travel destinations, industry information and consumer reviews of snowmobiles and new products. *SnoWest* focuses on mountain riding.*SnoWest* is published eight times a year at a cover price of around $4. Circulation is 170,000, but subscription is the best way to get hold of this publication.

Tributary
14 S. Willson Ave., Ste. 2, Bozeman, Mont. • **(406) 586-0744**

First published in 1992 by two Montana State University art students bent on covering the arts in Bozeman, *Tributary*, "Montana's Source Beyond the Main Stream," was then called *Happenings*. Now owned by publisher Carter G.

Walker, *Tributary* is a free monthly publication packed with poetry, profiles, essays, fiction and photographs aimed at capturing the evolving community that is the Old and the New West. Outsider, newcomer, Insider and old-timer swap stories and insights across *Tributary's* pages, dancing briefly with the shifting tide of change. An in-depth centerfold events calendar outlines the coming month, and "Harper's Index" at the end of each issue is a reminder of the ludicrous and the outrageous beyond Bozeman. *Tributary*, published the first of each month, can be found in coffee shops and restaurants.

Trout Wrapper
P.O. Box 128, McAllister, MT
• **(406) 682-7995**

One quick look at the cover of the *Trout Wrapper* gives you a clue to the inside content: spoofing with a bit of a bite. Until the fall of 1997, Ron Marr, who bills himself in the masthead as "editor, publisher and janitor," published the *Trout Wrapper* every Wednesday or Thursday from around May to Thanksgiving "except when the snow's too deep, whenever the editor falls apart or he just doesn't feel up to snuff." A well-known columnist whose work runs in numerous Rocky Mountain publications, Marr left the Idaho Falls *Post Register* with enough money to last him four months and a vague idea for a paper. He tries to do as little reliable news as possible and prefers rumors. All of his contributors, like Harley Whiplash, Psycho Bob Quick, and Ransom Jack Reynolds, work for free. While hunting and fishing news is accurate, the rest of the paper, including his sales pitch for subscriptions (Marr uses a photo of his hungry and starving Irish Wolfhound licking a pan on the stove) is off the wall and irreverent. Each issue, the *Trout Wrapper* also features cover photos of readers (some of them celebrities) holding an exposed *Trout Wrapper* in far away places such as the Eiffel Tower or the Leaning Tower of Pisa.

Valley Horse Journal
P.O. Box 665, Wilson, WY 83014
• **(307) 739-1644, (800) 375-4108, Ext. 1234**

This award-winning publication is truly a horse of a different color: Publisher and editor Mary Alice Grossman calls her mag an "equizine." Whatever it is, it's certain you don't have to be a horse lover to love this publication. It's styled more like a literary journal than a vehicle for disseminating equine information. In this area, look at Albertson's, Valley Bookstore or the Teton Bookshop in Jackson, Kellern's Montana Saddlery in Gardiner and Albertson's or Peaches in Idaho Falls. In Teton Valley, try the Knotty Pine or the Phillips 66.

Wyoming Magazine
P.O. Box 10730, Jackson, WY 83002
• (307) 739-4646

Wyoming hasn't had a statewide publication like this for a decade or more, says editor Rich Abendroth. This new quarterly publication (the first issue came out in January/February of 1997) covers events and issues from across the Equality State. You'll enjoy the window into the "real" Wyoming. The calendar is also useful: Every calendar generally includes at least one calendar item for every major town in the state. Subscribe for $19, or pick up an issue for $3.50 at newsstands and bookstores across the state. Circulation is 12,000.

Yellowstone Journal
431 Main, Lander, Wyo. • (307) 332-2323

If you want to keep up on what's happening in Yellowstone country year in and year out, the *Yellowstone Journal*, published in Lander, Wyoming, is the newspaper for you. This lively paper is loaded with color photos, and crammed with interesting stories about people, places and things to do mostly in Yellowstone and Grand Teton parks. The *Yellowstone Journal* features the finer details of the Parks, the things the average person would bypass without ever knowing it. The *Yellowstone Journal* will take you into the world of insects and antelope, into the office of Yellowstone Park Superintendent Mike Finley, through museum exhibits, deep into a geyser, into a wolf den and straight to a hidden waterfall or high mountain lake. Editor/publisher Shelli Johnson and her husband, Jerry, created the *Yellowstone Journal* in 1993 with the tourist in mind. The *Journal*

sells for $1 in Yellowstone and Grand Teton parks as well as at various locations in the entrance and gateway communities to both parks. The paper has subscribers in all 50 states and 12 foreign countries.

Television

Until the 1970s, when cable service brought more channels and better reception to rural television users in Yellowstone country, those beautiful Rocky Mountains translated into poor TV reception for those of us who live in rural towns. For Greater Yellowstone's rural residents, it was cable service provided by small companies that brought the "outside world" — for better or worse — into our living rooms.

Cable Companies

Gateway Cable Company
Gallatin Gateway Inn, Gallatin Gateway, Mont. • (406) 763-4777

This tiny cable company 13 miles southwest of Bozeman has no phone, no fax and only 64 customers who can tune in to 14 channels. Put together in 1987 by the owners of the Gallatin Gateway Inn, an old railroad hotel they had resurrected, Gateway Cable was initially designed only to serve the Inn's guests. Additional customers were added to the system when neighbors of the Inn asked to be hooked up to the service. The phone number listed above rings at the Inn.

High Mountain Communications Inc.
303 Canyon Ave., West Yellowstone, Mont. • (406) 646-7636

When High Mountain Communications brought cable to West Yellowstone residents in 1979, television viewing jumped from one static-riddled channel to 14. Today, High Mountain supplies 314 households and 1,500 motel rooms with cable service providing up

INSIDERS' TIP

For a fishing report, tune into West Yellowstone's 96.5 FM, Yellowstone Country, each summer morning at 8:55.

to 32 channels. High Mountain has to lay temporary cables across the top of the snow during the winter to accommodate new hookups.

North Yellowstone Cable Television
Third and Park, Gardiner, Mont.
• (406) 848-7561

Owned by George Buffington, North Yellowstone Cable Television was the first cable company to service a national Park. In 1983, one year after creating the company, Buffington; his father, Ken Dixon; and a third partner, Dave Lane, ran a cable line from Gardiner to Mammoth to serve Yellowstone Park's permanent employees. Cable service increased their reception from three fuzzy channels to 15 sharp ones. North Yellowstone Cable serves 260 subscribers.

TCI Cablevision of Idaho
1480 Lincoln Rd., Idaho Falls, Idaho
• (208) 523-4567

TCI first brought cable service to eastern Idaho about 20 years ago. The largest cable provider in the area serves from St. Anthony to Idaho Falls and Blackfoot and east to Teton Valley.

TCI Cablevision of Montana Inc.
511 W. Mendenhall, Bozeman, Mont.
• (406) 586-2089

TCI Cablevision of Montana serves the cities of Billings, Bozeman, Livingston and Butte.

TCI Cablevision of Wyoming Inc.
3575 S. Park, Jackson, Wyo.
• (307) 733-6030
2432 Sheridan Ave., Cody, Wyo.
• (307) 587-2219

This company is made up of autonomous offices scattered across the state of Wyoming, each offering service to a relatively small area. The Jackson office serves around 6,000 subscribers in Teton Village, Wilson and Jackson. The Cody office serves mostly viewers within Cody's city limits, with a couple of out-of-town exceptions. Other communities in Jackson Hole, like little Kelly and Hoback Junction, do not have cable service. It's more cost-effective for them to access TV through satellite services.

Galaxy Cablevision
P.O. Box 1007, Sikeston, MO 63801
• (800) 365-6988

Galaxy specializes in bringing cable to rural areas that would otherwise go without. In January 1995, the company hooked up a group of small Wyoming towns, including Pinedale, Dubois, Big Piney and Afton. It also cabled little Ashton, Idaho. Since then about 4,200 Wyoming and Idaho households have subscribed. This national cable company serves 250,000 subscribers, mostly in the South and Midwestern states.

Stations and Network Affiliates

The following major television stations are listed along with their network affiliate:

KJWY Channel 2 (NBC), Jackson, Wyoming

KIDK Channel 3 (CBS and Fox), Idaho Falls, Idaho

KIFI Channel 8 (ABC), Idaho Falls, Idaho

KPVI Channel 6 (NBC), Idaho Falls, Idaho

KISU Channel 10 (PBS), Pocatello, Idaho

KHMT Channel 4 (FOX), Billings, Mont.

KSVI Channel 6 (ABC), Billings, Mont.

KTVQ Channel 2 (CBS), Billings, Mont.

KULR Channel 8 (NBC), Billings, Mont.

KCTZ Channels 7 and 20 (FOX), Bozeman, Mont.

KUSM Channel 9 (PBS), Bozeman, Mont.

KTVM Channels 6 and 42 (NBC), Butte, Mont.

KWYB Channel 8 (ABC), Butte, Mont.

Radio

Depending on where you are, what kind of weather it is and whether it's night or day, you could pick up on any number of stations that broadcast in Yellowstone country. Unless the station has a huge transmitter or a translator to help send its sound waves across the mountains, its signal can fade in and out pretty fast while you're driving along.

There is one notable exception to the rule: Yellowstone Public Radio, which broadcasts from the Joseph S. Sample Studios at Montana State University-Billings. It has the largest geographic coverage of any public radio station in the country. The station, which began as a 10-watt student station, expanded in the late 1970s after getting federal grants. Yellowstone Radio, which can be picked up in the northern part of Yellowstone Park, sends its programs over the air as far north as Cutbank, Montana, east to Glendive and southeast to Thermopolis, Wyoming.

The West Yellowstone Station KWYS 920 AM features fishing reports and tips each morning, and Cody's KODI 1400 AM station carries a community call-in show each morning that not only lets you know what's happening in the area, but also lets you peek into the local culture.

Adult Contemporary

KADQ 94.1 FM, Rexburg, Idaho
KBMJ 95.5 FM, Billings, Montana
KLCE 97.3 FM, Idaho Falls, Idaho
KMXE 99.3 FM, Red Lodge, Montana
KOHZ 103.7 FM, Billings, Montana
KOSZ 105.5 FM, Idaho Falls, Idaho
KTAG 97.9 FM, Cody, Wyoming
KYYA 93.3 FM, Billings, Montana

Christian

KGVW 640 AM, Belgrade, Montana
KULR 730 AM, Billings, Montana

Contemporary

KCTR 102.9 FM, Billings, Montana
KFTZ 103.3 FM, Idaho Falls, Idaho
KGTM 98.1 FM, Idaho Falls, Idaho

Continuous Favorites

KSCY 96.7 FM, Bozeman, Montana

Country

KDWG 970 AM, Billings, Montana
KGHL 790 AM, Billings, Montana
KIDK 96.1 FM, Idaho Falls, Idaho
KIDX 98.5 FM, Billings, Montana
KPOW 1260 AM, Powell, Wyoming
KPRK 1340 AM, Livingston, Montana
KSGT 1340 AM, Jackson, Wyoming
KUPI FM 99.1 FM, Idaho Falls, Idaho

KWYS 920 AM, West Yellowstone, Idaho
KZBQ 93.7 FM, Idaho Falls, Idaho
KZLO 99.9 FM, Bozeman/Livingston, Montana

Full Service

KBOZ 1090 AM, Bozeman, Montana

News/Talk/Sports

KBLG 910 AM, Billings, Montana
KICN 1260 AM, Idaho Falls, Idaho
KIDK 590 AM, Idaho Falls, Idaho
KMMS 1450 AM, Bozeman, Montana
KSEI 930 AM, Idaho Falls, Idaho
KUPI 980 AM, Idaho Falls, Idaho (mornings, easy listening; afternoons, sports talk)

Oldies

KCVI 101.5 FM, Idaho Falls, Idaho
KKBR 97.1 FM, Billings, Montana
KOBB 1230 AM, Bozeman, Montana
KOBB 93.7 FM, Bozeman, Montana
KODI 1400 AM, Cody, Wyoming

Public Radio

KEMC 91.7 FM, Billings, Montana
KGLT 91.9 FM, Bozeman, Montana
KRIC 100.5 FM, Rexburg, Idaho (available at this location in Idaho Falls, Rexburg, Fremont County and Teton County, Idaho; in Dillon, Montana, try 105.5; in Jackson and Afton, Wyoming, look at 104.9; and in Freedom, Wyoming, try 103.9.)

Rock — Album/Alternative/Classic

KLZY 92.5 FM, Powell, Wyoming
KMGI 102.5 FM, Idaho Falls, Idaho
KMMS 95.1 FM, Bozeman, Montana
KMTN 96.9 FM, Jackson, Wyoming
KRKX 94.1 FM, Billings, Montana
KPKX 97.5 FM, Bozeman, Montana
KZJH 95.3 FM, Jackson, Wyoming

Traveler's Information

WBEY 530 AM, Bozeman, Montana

Spanish Language Radio

KRXK 1230 AM, Rexburg, Idaho

The connection between the natural world and religious worship is so strong throughout the Greater Yellowstone region that you'll find several simple chapels here — their doors unlocked.

Worship

In Yellowstone country, where the natural landscape is largely uninterrupted by man-made structures, we only have to walk out our doors or to the edge of town, drive to the mountains or walk into the wilderness to find spiritual inspiration.

Just look at the mountains, capped with snow deeper than the average church and whiter than sun-bleached bones. Like omniscient sentinels, they jut into the blue firmament, so clear that from the valley below you can see the wind whipping the peaks' snow into rooster tails.

Feel the breath-sucking, will-sapping midafternoon heat in a hot, dry, silent sagebrush-strewn draw. Know that this afternoon, this evening, maybe minutes from now, angry storm clouds can gallop over the horizon, dumping damnation and buckets of bale down this same dry draw. We call them gully washers. News folk call them flash floods. Whatever you call them, they are but a flash in the pan of terrifying and terrific natural wonders that daily drive us to dwell on the divine.

All around us, pure, winking water bubbles from its hidden and mysterious source deep within the earth. Rainbows of wildflowers — pink-plumed avens, deep-blue larkspur, lavender lupine, yellow arrow-leaf balsam root, sunny mule ears, cream-colored camas, red Indian paintbrush — follow the melting snow from the valley floor to the highest peaks. Birds call, elk bugle, antelope snort, cougars scream, and the elements rage.

The connection between the natural world and religious worship is so strong throughout the Greater Yellowstone region that you'll find several simple chapels here — their doors unlocked. Father Putka, a regular for 16 years at the Chapel of the Sacred Heart, near Signal Mountain Lodge in Grand Teton, leaves the door unlocked in summer for those who want to stop. Yellowstone country is so beautiful that people are often moved to commune with

their Maker, he says. While some prefer to do so outside, many seek the sanctuary of these chapels. Several of them feature picture windows behind the altars. In each, if the tip of the cross on the altar were a gun sight, it would be perfectly aligned with the very top of a spectacular mountain in the distance. We think these chapels are so charming — and so unique — that we briefly discuss them and their locations at the end of this chapter. If you're near one of them on a Sunday morning, we encourage you to stop and worship with others. Otherwise, feel free to stop at any time.

Ironically, it is not only the beauty of the mountains, but also their impenetrability and unpredictability that has kept us deeply connected as neighbors and communities. Huddled at the feet of the mighty mountains that even now defy modern communication and transportation, our very survival depends on forgiveness and goodwill — and if all else fails, common decency. If a rancher falls ill or is injured, his neighbors finish putting up the hay. If we are injured in a car wreck, or our houses catch fire, our neighbors come as volunteers to help us. If our homes burn to the ground, and we lose everything, we know that tomorrow, food, clothing and temporary shelter will appear at our doorstep. If you are lost in the mountains — like we were while horsepacking as teenagers across the Gravelly Range — search-and-rescue volunteers will find you. In our case, it was a lonely sheepherder who got us back on the trail.

Nurtured by isolation and fertilized by hardship, both economic and physical, these roots are the foundation of community churches. In towns surrounding the Parks, there are plenty of churches from which to choose. And, if the number of churches in a town are any indication, those of us who do attend regular services are particular about the way we worship. For example, Ennis (population 660) has 13 churches. The 8,000 residents of Cody, on the other hand, can choose from 29 churches and chapels, and that doesn't include the Bighorn Basin outside Cody where there are more churches, including 10 Church of Jesus Christ of Latter-day Saints chapels.

Generally, you won't find us particular, though, about what we wear to church. An advertisement by the Presbyterian Church of Jackson sums up the general churchgoing dress code in the Greater Yellowstone: "We don't care what you wear to church. And considering he walked around in a sheet, Jesus probably won't either." You'll also find that some churches, too small to finance a building, assemble on Sundays in public buildings such as schools, motel conference rooms or library basements.

Except in the larger towns, you will find only a menu of Christian denominations. In the larger towns — Bozeman, Billings, Idaho Falls and Jackson — you also might find Unitarian, Jewish, Quaker and Christian Science houses of worship. New Age groups are popping up here and there as well. For more information about churches in your area, we suggest you consult either the Yellow Pages or a local newspaper for listings. For information about worship specifically in Yellowstone and Grand Teton national parks, read on.

A Christian Ministry in the National Parks

Today, thanks to "A Christian Ministry in the National Parks," those who live in, work in and visit Yellowstone and Grand Teton national parks can find interdenominational services at Park amphitheaters, lodges and chapels from Memorial Day until Labor Day. The program — headquartered in Boston, Massa-

chusetts, and recognized by more than 40 denominations — serves 65 national parks, monuments, recreation areas and national forests across the country. In 1997, 55 volunteers provided services in Yellowstone National Park, while about a dozen ministered to those in Grand Teton National Park.

Evolution of Worship

A Christian Ministry in the National Parks, formed in 1953, took root at the Yellowstone National Park Chapel in Mammoth, after Rev. Warren Ost enlisted Princeton theological students to help staff regular church services in 1950, about 85 years after the first missionary entered the Greater Yellowstone area. According to *The Yellowstone National Chapel* by Aubrey Haines, Fr. Francis Xavier Kuppens, a Belgian Jesuit working as a missionary among the Blackfeet Indians, was the first man of the cloth to enter Yellowstone country. Kuppens came to the Yellowstone region in 1865, seven years before it would be set aside as the world's first national Park. Accompanying a band of Blackfeet, he no doubt said Mass someplace within today's Park boundaries.

It wasn't until 1873, though, that William Wesley Van Orsdel, known as "Brother Van," held an official service in Lower Geyser Basin. Brother Van's visit to the Park led to the appointment of Methodist minister George Comfort to serve the Upper Yellowstone Valley. Headquartered in Livingston — then the only gateway to Yellowstone National Park — Comfort held services in a Northern Pacific Railroad box car in the rail yards. By 1886, Methodist circuit riders were traveling up and down the Yellowstone Valley, preaching wherever congregations would assemble — in homes, under trees, perhaps even in saloons.

In 1897, ministers returning from a religious

INSIDERS' TIP

Schedules and locations of worship services in Yellowstone and Grand Teton national parks are posted on bulletin boards outside all visitor centers. Times and locations change according to demand and availability of staff. Be sure to check.

conference in San Francisco toured Yellowstone National Park. One of them, F.T. Proctor of Utica, New York, offered to build a chapel for the soldiers guarding the Park. His offer, though, was rejected as impractical, given the Park management's limited financial resources. About 1900, the Episcopalians arrived on the scene. John F. Pritchard, an Episcopalian minister, settled near Emigrant, about midway down the valley. Serving the settlements up and down the valley, Pritchard would catch the train, ride it to the end of the line in Gardiner, then borrow a saddle horse or a buggy, serving up sermons, baptizing babies, ministering to the sick and burying the fallen wherever he could. Pritchard, also chaplain to the Fort Yellowstone soldiers at Mammoth, held services in the mess hall. By 1909, he had convinced the Secretary of War that money was needed for a chapel at Fort Yellowstone. Before Congress could approve appropriations, though, the commanding officer at Fort Yellowstone was replaced by S.B.M. Young, the same officer who had rejected Proctor's chapel proposal in 1887. Construction of the chapel would be delayed another four years.

Finally, in the spring of 1912, Gagnon and Co. of Billings, Montana, began construction on the Gothic chapel. Native sandstone was quarried from the bluffs overlooking the Gardner River. Douglas firs were felled, cut into timbers for the roof and sliced into boards for the floors and interior walls. Covering the whole was a steeply sloping slate roof.

By 1923, several denominations were using the chapel. Episcopalians as well as the English and Norwegian Lutheran churches had scheduled services. The Congregationalists, Baptists and Catholics used the chapel for sporadic services. All denominations shared the cost of the upkeep of the building. During the summer, services were more regular. In winter, when deep snow and bitter cold made the Park less accessible, services were held less often.

The beginning and the end of World War II brought change to the chapel. No services were held for three years during the war because it had caused a shortage of men in general and preachers in particular. After the war, the stream of visitors to Yellowstone National Park began to grow steadily. Desperate to find a way to provide Sunday worship services for Park employees and visitors, the Park Service formed the Superintendent's Church Committee in 1949. That same year, the committee recruited young men from eastern theological seminaries to help lead worship services. Young Princeton seminarians were the first to respond. The success of their first two years of service led to the formation of A Christian Ministry in the National Parks.

The Latter-day Saints

No mention of the development of organized religion or the settlement of the Greater Yellowstone, can exclude the Church of Jesus Christ of Latter-day Saints (a.k.a. the Mormons). Like the volcanic eruptions and subsequent flows that helped shape the Yellowstone landscape eons ago, a swell of Latter-day Saints seeped into the plains and valleys of the Greater Yellowstone region. Like the rippling aftershocks of an earthquake, they moved from their epicenter: the Holy City, New Jerusalem, Zion in the Valley of the Mountains, Salt Lake City. Now the center of what its chamber of commerce likes to call the Intermountain Empire, Salt Lake City was the gathering place for Latter-day Saints. Whole families — brothers, sisters, aunts, uncles, cousins, in-laws, grandparents — tens of thousands of them, followed the Mormon Trail west to the Great Salt Valley. Bound by an organized framework for command and bolstered by faith, they lost lives and limbs in their zeal to reach Zion. For many, arriving was not the end of the trail, but rather the beginning. As soon as they arrived, some began planting and digging irrigation canals, while others were sent forth to colonize the valleys to the north, south, east and west.

The first church in Jackson Hole was built in 1905 by the Mormons; the first Mormon homesteader in that area was James May, who settled east of Black Butte in 1894. May and those who followed laid out a community with the grid-like orderliness found in Mormon towns in Utah and eastern Idaho in what is now Grand Teton National Park. It came to be known as Mormon Row, both for its "un-Jackson-like" neatness of design and for the religious preference of its inhabitants.

In eastern Idaho, the Mormon influence is still present — and strong. Mormon settlers went there in the late 1860s as hardscrabble farmers. Their forte was cooperation, a requirement in this harsh land where dry farming was a poor bet and irrigation a community project. Even today, meandering canals carry Snake River water across a landscape agriculturally productive in large part because of early Mormon farmers and their canal-building efforts.

Some, like the 100 Mormon families who settled the Bighorn Basin near Cody, Wyoming, came by gubernatorial invitation. In 1900, Wyoming's governor solicited aid from the Utah Saints who colonized the Bighorn Basin. After some investigation, LDS President Snow agreed to send his people, who promptly set to work digging 27 miles of canal still in use today. It took them four years. Shortly after they arrived, the Burlington Northern Railroad paid the Bighorn Saints $80,000 to lay 23 miles of track. The money laid the foundation for the solid LDS community that still thrives today.

Roadside Chapels

Yellowstone National Park Entrance Communities

The Mt. Republic Chapel is just 2 miles from the Northeast Entrance to Yellowstone Park on Mont. Highway 212 between Silver Gate and Cooke City. Built in the 1970s, it serves as a year-round place of worship for local residents. Windows behind the altar frame the towering peak of Mt. Republic. While services are held here each Sunday between Memorial Day and Labor Day (thanks to A Christian Ministry in the National Parks), during the winter locals worship here only once a month when a minister from Gardiner comes to town. Visitors are welcome. Call the church at (406) 838-2397 summer, (406) 838-2359 winter.

Grand Teton National Park

Chapel of the Sacred Heart, a half-mile north of Signal Mountain Lodge in Jackson, (307) 733-2516, is an unassuming brown log structure. Yet people from all over the world come here Saturdays and Sundays, June through August. No, it's not another visitors center — it's a Catholic chapel. Part of the parish of Our Lady of the Mountains Catholic Church, also in Jackson (in fact, that's where the phone number rings), the little chapel was built in 1935. It was designed to serve the Park's visitors, but only later were the surrounding lands made part of Grand Teton Park. Father Putka has been traveling to Chapel of the Sacred Heart for 16 years to conduct the June

Photo: Robert Bower

Winter sleigh rides are a great activity for enjoying the snowy wonderland.

and July services. In winter he teaches political science at the University of Dayton.

The chapel is left unlocked 24 hours a day since the majesty of the mountains moves many to prayer — and not just during scheduled services. Services are offered once on Saturday and twice on Sunday, but you're invited to stop by anytime. Commune a while and then sign the guest book (while you're at it, scan the addresses of other signers; you'll be amazed at how many nations' residents have offered their prayers here). One of the old building's odd quirks: the resident bats. You won't ever know they're there — they're nocturnal, so they spend their days sleeping under the eaves — but the folks who clean up after them wish they would find a new home. Trouble is, neither the Park Service nor the Catholic Church has been able to convince them to leave.

The second of two chapels in Grand Teton National Park, the rustic Chapel of the Transfiguration, on U.S. Highway 89 near Moose, Wyoming, (307) 733-2603, is built of log; its pews, of aspen. The big picture window above the altar frames the granite mass of the Tetons. What better place to meditate upon the beauty of creation? Folks have been coming here to do just that since 1925. The chapel is associated with St. John's Episcopal Church, also in Jackson. The idea for Chapel of the Transfiguration was born one night in 1920 among a group of campers, tired after a long trek to Jackson for worship. The land on which the chapel now sits was donated by a local woman to save others the long ride. From mid-May through September, Holy Eucharist and a morning prayer service are offered here every Sunday. The chapel is available during those months for baptisms and memorial services.

Southwestern Montana

When we first saw The Soldiers Chapel at Big Sky, (406) 995-2777, just west of Mont. Highway 191, we had no choice but to make a quick U-turn. A nondenominational church, this picture-perfect log and native stone chapel was built in 1955 as a memorial to the World War II fallen comrades of the 163rd Infantry. It was built by Col. Nelson Story III, a former member of the 163rd. A huge picture window behind the altar frames 11,000-foot Lone Mountain, home to the ski runs of Big Sky Ski and Summer Resort (see our Winter Sports chapter). Guests are welcome at worship services. The chapel doors are open continuously throughout the summer months for meditation and prayer. Tidy homestyle restrooms with real paper towels (none of those electric blow-driers) sit at the edge of the property.

Meditation Chapel is a tiny frame building situated atop a knoll right next to the only rest area on Mont. Highway 89 between Livingston and Gardiner. This tiny chapel — it has only eight chairs — has a window behind the altar that frames Emigrant Peak. A Bible — it was opened to Genesis when we visited — sits at the front of the chapel. Next to the door, you will find a guest book filled with a wide range of religious writings. Call (406) 587-7911 for more informaiton.

Northwestern Wyoming

The outdoor Wayfarer's Chapel is situated high above Wyo. Highway 14/16/20, about 10 miles from Yellowstone National Park's east entrance. Built in the 1960s as an outreach to travelers, the chapel sports a beautiful stone altar with a semicircle of split-log benches. From mid-June until the end of August, prayer services are held by lay members of the congregation. This chapel is a popular site for weddings. Look for the sign on the north side of the highway. Road construction during summer 1997 tore up the area and forced members of the Christ Episcopal Church to move the chapel's site. There is a dirt parking lot beside the road and a path leading up the hill and through the trees to the chapel. We think this is a rest area worth visiting.

For more information on Wayfarer's Chapel, call the Christ Episcopal Church in Cody, Wyoming, at (307) 587-3849.

Resources

For additional information on communities, area businesses and attractions, try these visitors centers, government offices and chambers of commerce. See our Parks and Forests chapter for information on contacting a Forest Service ranger station. To help you build your Greater Yellowstone library, we've drawn from the best of what's on our own bookshelves, as well as from some of the resources we discovered as we wrote this guide.

Organizations

Regional Information

Yellowstone National Park Entrance Communities

Cooke City Chamber of Commerce — (406) 838-2495; Box 1071, Cooke City, MT 59020

Gardiner Chamber of Commerce — (406) 848-7971; Box 81, Gardiner, MT 59030 (located on U.S. Highway 89)

West Yellowstone Chamber of Commerce — (406) 646-7701; Canyon and Yellowstone Avenue, West Yellowstone, Montana.

Jackson Hole

Jackson Hole Chamber of Commerce — (307) 733-3316; 990 W. Broadway, Jackson, Wyoming.

Wyoming Game and Fish — (307) 733-2321; 360 N. Cache, Jackson, Wyoming.

Eastern Idaho

Eastern Idaho Visitor Information Center — (800) 634-3246; 505 Lindsay Boulevard, Idaho Falls, Idaho. Included in this center are the Chamber of Commerce, (208) 523-1010; Bureau of Land Management, (208) 523-1012; and the Forest Service (208) 523-3278

Ashton Chamber of Commerce — (208) 652-3987 (City Building); 64 N. 10, Ashton, Idaho.

Ashton Visitor Center — (208) 652-7520; 801 N. U.S. Highway 20, Ashton, Idaho.

Bureau of Land Management — (208) 525-7500; 1405 Hollipark Drive, Idaho Falls, Idaho.

Idaho Fish and Game — (208) 525-7290; 1515 Lincoln Road, Idaho Falls, Idaho.

Idaho Sport Fishing Information Line — (800) ASK-FISH

Island Park Chamber of Commerce — (208) 558-7755; P.O. Box 83, Island Park, ID 83429.

Rexburg Chamber of Commerce — (208) 356-5700; 420 W. 4 S., Rexburg, Idaho.

Teton Valley Chamber of Commerce — (208) 354-2500; 10 E. Ashley, Driggs, Idaho.

Southwestern Montana

Big Sky Chamber of Commerce — (406) 995-3000, (800) 943-4111; Box 160100, Big Sky, MT 59716

Bozeman Chamber of Commerce and Visitor Center — (406) 586-5421, (800) 228-4224;1205 E. Main Street, Bozeman, Montana

Ennis Chamber of Commerce — (406) 682-4388; Box 291, Ennis, MT 59729

Livingston Chamber of Commerce and Visitor Center — (406) 222-0850; 212 W. Park, Livingston, Montana

Red Lodge Chamber of Commerce — (406) 446-1718; U.S. Highway 212 north of Red Lodge, Montana

Northwestern Wyoming

Cody Country Chamber of Commerce — (307) 587-2777; 836 Sheridan Avenue, Cody, Wyoming

Other Sources

Greater Yellowstone is home to several groups that can be reached for information about the region's unique features.

Blue Ribbon Coalition — (208) 233-6570; 1540 N. Arthur, Pocatello, Idaho.

Bureau of Reclamation river/reservoir line — (800) 658-5771. This number reaches a recorded message with up-to-date water level information on any river or reservoir in the Upper Snake drainage controlled by a Bureau of Reclamation dam (that's Jackson Lake, Grassy Lake, Palisades Reservoir, the Snake River and others).

Greater Yellowstone Coalition — (208) 522-7927; 1740 E. 17th, Idaho Falls, Idaho; (406) 586-1593; P.O. Box 1874, Bozeman, MT 59771

Henry's Fork Foundation — (208) 652-3567; P.O. Box 852, 604 Main, Ashton, ID 83420. These folks run research and stewardship programs and supply information about the waters of the Henry's Fork drainage.

Rocky Mountain Elk Foundation Visitor Center — (406) 543-4545; 2291 W. Broadway Avenue, Missoula, Montana.

Sportsman's Information Number in Wyoming — (800) 654-1178.

Books

Bartlett, Richard A. *Yellowstone: A Wilderness Besieged*, The University of Arizona Press, Tucson, Arizona, 1989. A history of Yellowstone Park, Bartlett digs into the archives and brings to light the intricate relationships between Yellowstone Park officials, politicians, concessionaires, railroaders and poachers. A teacher of the westward movement and a professor of history at The Florida State University in Tallahassee, Bartlett has written several history books.

Bryan, T. Scott. *The Geysers of Yellowstone*. University Press of Colorado, Niwot, Colorado, 1991. 299 pages. You won't find beautiful photographs in this book, but it's chock-full of fascinating information about Yellowstone's geysers. Bryan, a seasonal ranger-naturalist for the Park for years, has a Master of Science degree from the University of Montana. This is his first book.

Ekey, Robert, and Staff of Billings Gazette. *Yellowstone On Fire!*. The Billings Gazette, Billings, Montana, 1989; 128 pages. Beautiful photos and lively text capture the nightmare of Yellowstone's 1988 fires. For anyone interested in the fires, this book is a must. The photos alone, taken by the *Billings Gazette* staff, tell a compelling story.

Eversman, Sharon and Mary Carr. *Yellowstone Ecology: A Road Guide*. Mountain Press Publishing Company, Missoula, Montana, 1992; 242 pages. Ecology explores connections between living things and their surroundings. This book is organized so that you can read about the unique connections that shape the lives and places you visit as you stand there with that ground under your feet.

Graydon, Don, editor. *Mountaineering: The Freedom of the Hills*, 5th Edition. The Mountaineers, Seattle, Washington, 1992; 447 pages. This book is one of the most comprehensive resources available for backcountry travel, with a long history of offering good advice (the book was first published in 1960). We recommend Freedom of the Hills for anyone interested in serious mountaineering, as well as technical rock, ice and snow climbing. The book also has excellent sections for backpackers and other backcountry travelers on issues such as snowpack and avalanche, route-finding, gear, backcountry cooking and more.

Haines, Aubrey L. *The Yellowstone Story: Volumes One and Two*, University Press of Colorado, Niwot, Colorado, 1996; 385 pages and 543 pages. Retired Yellowstone Park historian Haines researched these books for years. Now they are *the* bible when it comes to Yellowstone Park history. Haines meanders through the subject matter, coloring it with volumes of anecdotes and interesting facts.

Hirschmann, Fred. *Yellowstone*. Graphic Arts Center Publishing Company, Portland, Oregon, 1990; 88 pages. This book is fun to read both for its informative descriptions of Yellowstone Park's most interesting features and for the firsthand accounts Hirschmann pulls from his five years of rangering there. Hirschmann is a nature photographer as well as a writer; his striking images are perfect accompaniment to the information and stories.

Hubbell, Frank and Buck Tilton. *Medicine for the Backcountry*. ICS Books Inc., Merrillville Indiana, 1990; 155 pages. This is an easy-to-read resource to start you thinking about how medical problems and emergencies should be approached in the backcountry, with an emphasis on common sense and planning. No book is a substitute for adequate training, but this is a first step.

Marshall, Mark C. *Yellowstone Trails: A Hiking Guide*. The Yellowstone Association, Yellowstone National Park, Wyoming, 1995; 172 pages. After more than two decades as a Park ranger, Marschall has updated this book several times and is still humble about his knowledge of the Park. The book includes helpful information about caring for the Park and yourself, bear attacks, water treatment and backcountry camping. It also includes topographic maps and detailed descriptions of more than 70 trails ranging from easy to difficult and short to long.

Mathews, Craig and Clayton Molinero. *The Yellowstone Fly-Fishing Guide*. Lyons and Burford, New York, New York, 1997; 164 pages. Mathews and Molinero have more than 30 years of combined fishing time in Yellowstone Park waters. Rather than focusing on just the well-known waters, these two give a streamlined, easy-to-read lowdown on 200 lakes and streams in every nook and cranny of the Park. Besides telling you what kind of fish you'll find, the authors also tell you about wildlife to watch out for, how to get to the site and what insects are hatching and when. Mathews is owner of Blue Ribbon Flies. Molinero has guided in Yellowstone for more than a decade.

Milstein, Michael. *Yellowstone: 125 Year of America's Best Idea*. Billings Gazette, Billings, Montana, 1996; 112 pages. Milstein has been covering Yellowstone issues since 1989 and it shows. This informative, well-written book is packed with interesting anecdotes about Yellowstone. Historic and modern photographs make this book as pleasant to leaf through as to read.

Murie, Olaus. *Animal Tracks, a Peterson Field Guide*. Houghton Mifflin Company, New York, 1982; 375 pages. If you're observant, you'll see the signs that animals leave behind much more frequently than you'll see the animals themselves. Murie's book teaches how understanding can be gained from animal tracks, scat and other signs. We like this book over other tracking books because it's comprehensive, but even more because Olaus Murie was a longtime Jackson Hole resident. Murie was an accomplished naturalist and artist who spent his time watching and learning outdoors, and the book's line drawings, mostly created in the field, are his. The animal behaviors he describes are from firsthand experience.

Ortenburger, Leigh and Reynold Jackson. *A Climber's Guide to the Teton Range*. The Mountaineers, Seattle, Washington, 1996; 415 pages. This book is interesting reading for mountain lovers as well as mountain climbers. The book not only carefully pictures and describes climbing routes in the Teton Range, but it also includes a fascinating climbing history of the Tetons. And there are sections on the geology of the region and each of the region's peaks. Ten years in the writing, this book is the product of two longtime Teton climbers, one a dedicated historian of the area.

Palmer, Tim. *The Snake River: Window to the West*. Island Press, Washington D.C., 1991; 320 pages. If you fall in love with the Snake River or you want to learn more about the water issues that are such beautiful windows onto Western politics — or if you are intrigued with the state of Idaho altogether — this thoroughly researched, well-written book will repay your time.

Reese, Rick. *Greater Yellowstone: The National Park and Adjacent Wildlands*. American and World Geographic Publishing, Helena, Montana, 1991; 103 pages. This beautifully illustrated book takes the reader quickly through Yellowstone's birth, its ecology, its politics and its present threats. A former director of the Yellowstone Institute, Rick Reese is part of Yellowstone's story. Particularly poignant are his tales of how Yellowstone Park is and is not managed as a larger entity and how Yellowstone began to be considered larger and more important than its own boundaries.

Retallic, Ken. *Greater Yellowstone Fly Fisher's Stream Guide*. GBH ink, Idaho Falls, Idaho, 1996; 78 pages. This slim volume covers Greater Yellowstone's fly-fishing hot spots.

Retallic even has suggestions for what kinds of flies to use when in which streams, information you would otherwise only get at the local fly shop.

Righter, Robert W. *Crucible for Conservation: The Struggle for Grand Teton National Park*. Colorado Associated University Press, 1982; 192 pages. Righter argues that Grand Teton's piecemeal construction is a story of conservation success. This book presents a fascinating, if somewhat academic, picture of the complex politics that led to the park's creation. If Western politics intrigues you, you'll find this a worthwhile read.

Russell, Osborne; edited by Aubrey L. Haines. *Journal of a Trapper*. University of Nebraska Press, Lincoln, Nebraska, 1955; 191 pages. Written by 1840s trapper Osborne Russell and edited by Yellowstone expert Aubrey Haines, this book is the historian's main link to the days of trapping in the wilderness. Besides being a general journal of travel and trapping, Russell's account of the years from 1834 to 843 in the Yellowstone Country provide astounding glimpses into his everyday life.

Schreier, Carl. *A Field Guide to Yellowstone's Geysers, Hot Springs and Fumaroles*. Homestead Publishing, Moose, Wyoming, 1992; 122 pages. Like Schreier's *A Field Guide to Wildflowers of the Rocky Mountains* by the same publisher (and also in our library), this book is thorough, stuffed with lovely photos and intelligently organized. If you'd like to understand the lovely geothermal features you stared at in the park, you'll appreciate Schreier's book.

Schwantes, Carlos. *In Mountain Shadows: A History of Idaho*. University of Nebraska Press, Lincoln, Nebraska, 1991. 292 pages. The author is a professor of history at Moscow's University of Idaho. He describes his book as "an extended essay on the character of Idaho." We found it an entertaining and enlightening read about a state whose development has encompassed every major issue of the West, from wars with Native Americans and gold rushes to lumber booms, water wars and outdoor recreation-based tourism.

Stokes, Donald and Lillian. *Stokes Field Guide to Birds*. Little, Brown and Company, New York, 1996; 519 pages. Of all the bird identification guides we've looked at or owned, this one is the most complete. It's organized so non-birders can locate information on their bird by general appearance. Best of all, each species is illustrated with at least two high-quality photographs.

Thompson, Curt. *Floating and Recreation on Montana Rivers*. Curt Thompson, Lakeside, Montana, 1993; 370 pages. Thompson takes the reader down all 81 of Montana's rivers. Along the way, he tells in an organized fashion about floating, fishing and other recreation opportunities. You'll find a simplified map of each river, as well as some entertaining black-and-white photos. Thompson is an avid outdoorsman with degrees in recreation and biology. Thirty years of floating Montana's rivers (and finding no information about them) led Thompson to write this book.

Wilkerson, James. *Medicine for Mountaineering*. The Mountaineers, Seattle, Washington, 1973. More important than gear in your first-aid kit is information, so pack a good wilderness medicine book like this one with your Band Aids and athletic tape.

Wilkinson, Todd. *Greater Yellowstone National Forests*. Falcon Press Publishing Company, Helena, Montana, 1991; 104 pages. Part of the National Forests of America series, this resource provides interesting factoids about area forests, plus attractions, campgrounds, trails, phone numbers and maps.

Whittlesey, Lee H. *Yellowstone Place Names*. Montana Historical Society Press, Helena, Montana, 1988; 178 pages. Written by Yellowstone Park historian Lee Whittlesey, this book is full of interesting anecdotes about how places in the Park got their names. It's also illustrated with some great old photos. Whittlesey began working in the Park in the early 1970s and has held just about every job imaginable along the way.

Index of Advertisers

Index